Starting
and
Managing
the
Small Business

SECOND EDITION

Starting and Managing the SMALL BUSINESS

ARTHUR H. KURILOFF

Formerly of the
University of California, Los Angeles

JOHN M. HEMPHILL, Jr.

Bob Frink Management

McGRAW-HILL BOOK COMPANY

New York St. Louis San Francisco Auckland Bogotá Hamburg
London Madrid Mexico Milan Montreal New Delhi Panama
Paris São Paulo Singapore Sydney Tokyo Toronto

Starting
and
Managing
the
SMALL BUSINESS

1234567890 HALHAL 89210987

ISBN 0-07-035665-3

This book was set in Times Roman by J. M. Post Graphics Corp.
The editors were Kathleen L. Loy and Larry Goldberg;
the designer was Nicholas Krenitsky;
the production supervisor was Denise L. Puryear.
Arcata Graphics/Halliday was printer and binder.

Library of Congress Cataloging-in-Publication Data

Kuriloff, Arthur H.
Starting and managing the small business.

Includes index.
1. New business enterprises. 2. Small business—
Management. 3. New business enterprises—Case studies.
4. Small business—Management—Case studies. I. Hemphill,
John Mearl, II. Title.
HD62.5.K87   1988   658'.022   87-3832
ISBN 0-07-035665-3

About the Authors

ARTHUR H. KURILOFF,   formerly lecturer in the Graduate School of Management, University of California, Los Angeles, brings to his writing an extensive background in small business, line management, and consulting with business organizations. He holds the B.S.M.E. and M.B.A. degrees.

He has started and managed four successful small companies. His experience includes over 20 years in line management. He has served as a senior consultant on the professional staff of Cresap, McCormick and Paget, management consultants, New York. For the past 18 years he has concentrated on the solution of problems in entrepreneurship and starting and managing the small business.

Kuriloff has served as visiting fellow in the Department of Industrial Administration at Yale University, as lecturer in the Graduate School of Administration at the University of California, Irvine, and for ten years as lecturer in the Graduate School of Management, UCLA, where he taught Entrepreneurship and Venture Initiation, and Small Business Management. At UCLA he ran the Small Business Institute.

He has lectured extensively on management subjects for such organizations as the American Management Association and the Industrial Conference Board. He has conducted educational seminars for executives at many universities and colleges.

Kuriloff is the author of *Reality in Management,* McGraw-Hill, 1966, of *Organizational Development for Survival,* AMA, 1972, and coauthor of *Entrepreneurship and Small Business Management,* Wiley, 1979, *How to Start Your Own Business . . . and Succeed,* McGraw-Hill, 1981, and *Starting and Managing the Small Business,* McGraw-Hill, 1983.

JOHN M. HEMPHILL, Ph.D., Vice-President, Marketing, Bob Frink Marketing, Inc., is an authority on entrepreneurship, consumer behavior, and retail trends. He brings unique experience and skills to bear on small business management and forward planning. He has successfully started and managed three consulting and management education enterprises. Dr. Hemphill has consulted with several hundred entrepreneurs, and directed the Small Business Institute at California State University, Los Angeles. He was a member of the White House Conference on Small Business in 1979–1980. He has presented concepts and strategy on small business marketing in dozens of university seminars across the country during the past seven years.

Dr. Hemphill was executive vice-president with J.D. Power and Associates, a small consumer research business specializing in the automotive industry. As such, he was consultant to the Reagan administration on auto policy. Dr. Hemphill was invited on three occasions to present testimony before the Congress about competitiveness in the auto industry and among its dealers. He completed special research assignments for the U.S. Small Business Administration, and for the U.S. Departments of Energy, Commerce, and Transportation.

He currently focuses on sales training, advertising strategy, and customer satisfaction as these apply to retail and small service businesses. In addition to several technical articles and monographs, he is the coauthor of *How to Start Your Own Business . . . and Succeed,* McGraw-Hill, 1981, and *Starting and Managing the Small Business,* McGraw-Hill, 1983.

Contents

PREFACE
xvii

What You Should Bring
to Your Business

SECTION I

1

CHAPTER 1

THE NEED FOR BALANCED BUSINESS EXPERIENCE   3

Topics in This Chapter   3
You Must Know the Business   6
You Must Have Management Skills   7
Developing Your Business Plan: Its Importance   7
Objectives of the Text   8
The Business Plan (or Prospectus)   9
Outline for Developing Your Basic Business Plan (Prospectus)   9
Worksheets   14
Key Terms   14
Worksheet 1: Opinion Survey   15

CHAPTER 2

PERSONAL FACTORS IN STARTING A BUSINESS   16

Topics in This Chapter   16
Objectives of This Chapter   18
The Entrepreneurial Characteristics   20
Reinforcing Achievement Motivation   22
Rewards and Penalties of Owning Your Own Business   26
Personal Factors in Starting a Business—Summary   28
Worksheet 2: Your Personal Assessment   30
Key Terms   34
Study Assignments for Review and Discussion   34

Projects for Students   34
If You Want to Read More   34

CHAPTER 3
FINDING A SOUND IDEA FOR A BUSINESS   36

Topics in This Chapter   36
Objectives of This Chapter   38
Sources of Innovative Ideas   40
Guidelines for Generating Ideas for Product or Service   41
New Approaches for an Established Business   47
Need for Continuing Innovation   48
Innovation in an Existing Business   48
Generating the Unique Idea—Summary   50
Worksheet 3: Your Idea for Your Business   52
Key Terms   53
Study Assignments for Review and Discussion   53
Projects for Students   53
If You Want to Read More   54

Understanding Marketing
for Your Small Business

SECTION II

57

CHAPTER 4
YOUR SMALL BUSINESS AS A MARKETING SYSTEM   59

Topics in This Chapter   59
Objectives of This Chapter   62
Achieving a Customer Orientation   62
What Business Are You Really in?   64
Seizing Opportunities of Change—Summary   71
Worksheet 4: Your Business as a Marketing System   73
Key Terms   75
Study Assignments for Review and Discussion   75
Projects for Students   75
If You Want to Read More   75

CHAPTER 5
ANALYZING YOUR MARKET AND CONSUMER BEHAVIOR   78

Topics in This Chapter   78
Objectives of This Chapter   80
Who Buys?   81
Why Do Consumers Buy?   83

What Do They Buy?	90
How Do They Buy?	94
Where Do They Buy?	96
When Do They Buy?	98
Market Segmentation	99
Pinpointing the Marketing Questions You Must Answer—Summary	110
Worksheet 5: Your Market and Consumer Behavior	111
Key Terms	115
Study Assignments for Review and Discussion	115
Projects for Students	115
If You Want to Read More	116

CHAPTER 6
REACHING YOUR CUSTOMER

REACHING YOUR CUSTOMER	118
Topics in This Chapter	118
Objectives of This Chapter	120
Setting Your Marketing Objectives	121
Your Product or Service Strategy	122
Marketing Strategy	122
Elements of the Selling Transaction	123
Carrying Out Marketing Strategy	124
Your Pricing Strategy	128
Your Distribution Strategy	134
Your Promotional Strategy	137
Reaching Your Customer—Summary	150
Worksheet 6: Reaching Your Customer	153
Key Terms	160
Study Assignments for Review and Discussion	160
Projects for Students	161
If You Want to Read More	161

Retail, Service, and Manufacturing Businesses

SECTION III

165

CHAPTER 7
CONTROLLING YOUR RETAIL OPERATIONS

CONTROLLING YOUR RETAIL OPERATIONS	167
Topics in This Chapter	167
Objectives of This Chapter	169
Selecting a Location	169
Renting or Leasing	173
Identifying Your Customer	174
Purchasing and Inventory Control	176

Elements of Purchasing   176
Elements of Inventory Control   180
Computers in Small Retail Business   185
Advertising and Promoting Your Retail Business   189
Controlling Your Retail Operations—Summary   196
Worksheet 7: Controlling Your Retail Operations   197
Key Terms   202
Study Assignments for Review and Discussion   202
Projects for Students   203
If You Want to Read More   204

CHAPTER 8
MARKETING THE SERVICE BUSINESS   206

Topics in This Chapter   206
Objectives of This Chapter   208
Why Is the Service Business Unique?   209
The Marketing Concept and Buyer Behavior   211
Market Analysis and Marketing Strategy for the Service Business   215
Pricing Your Service   216
Promoting Your Service   220
Distributing Your Service   223
The Marketing of Services Is Different—Summary   225
Worksheet 8: Marketing the Service Business   226
Key Terms   230
Study Assignments for Review and Discussion   230
Projects for Students   230
If You Want to Read More   231

CHAPTER 9
CONTROLLING YOUR MANUFACTURING OPERATIONS   233

Topics in This Chapter   233
Objectives of This Chapter   235
Designing Your Small Plant   236
Overall Plant Layout   238
Working Your Plant More than One Shift?   239
Managing Research and Development   242
Making Purchasing Effective   246
Managing Your Production Variables   249
Key Issues in Manufacturing—Summary   255
Worksheet 9: Controlling Your Manufacturing Operations   257
Key Terms   264
Study Assignments for Review and Discussion   264
Projects for Students   264
If You Want to Read More   265

CHAPTER 10
RAISING MONEY FOR YOUR BUSINESS   271

Topics in This Chapter   271
Objectives of This Chapter   273
Stages of Business Development   273
The Start-Up Stage   274
The Growth Stage   277
The Maturity Stage   281
Cost, Flexibility, and Control—Summary   283
Worksheet 10: Raising Money for Your Business   284
Key Terms   286
Study Assignments for Review and Discussion   286
Projects for Students   286
If You Want to Read More   287

CHAPTER 11
MANAGING YOUR FINANCIAL REQUIREMENTS   289

Topics in This Chapter   289
Objectives of This Chapter   291
Planning Required   292
Your Planning Assumptions and Financial Plans   296
Using Ratio Analysis   319
Key Points in Managing Your Finances—Summary   325
Worksheet 11: Managing Your Financial Requirements   327
Key Terms   329
Study Assignments for Review and Discussion   329
Projects for Students   329
If You Want to Read More   330

CHAPTER 12
MANAGEMENT INFORMATION AND COMPUTERS   332

Topics in This Chapter   332
Formal and Informal Information   334
Guides to Generating Management Information   334
Computers for Small Business   336
What Is an Electronic Computer?   336
Microcomputers and Minicomputers   337
Common Computer Systems—Hardware and Software   339

Data Storage   341
Spreadsheets—Their Importance   342
Word Processing   344
Multifunctionality for Your Business—Summary   346
Worksheet 12: Using a Microcomputer in Your Business   347
Key Terms   349
Study Assignments for Review and Discussion   349
Projects for Students   349
If You Want to Read More   350

Buying a Business Opportunity

SECTION V

353

CHAPTER 13
BUYING A GOING BUSINESS

BUYING A GOING BUSINESS   355

Topics in This Chapter   355
Objectives of This Chapter   357
To Buy or Not to Buy?   358
Steps in Buying a Business   360
Finding the Business to Buy   360
Screening the Offerings in Depth   363
Avoiding Legal Problems   367
Picking a Loser   368
Personal Factors in the Transaction   368
Evaluating and Pricing the Business   370
Closing the Deal   378
Major Points in Buying a Going Business—Summary   379
Worksheet 13: Buying a Going Business   381
Key Terms   385
Study Assignments for Review and Discussion   385
Projects for Students   385
If You Want to Read More   386

CHAPTER 14
IS FRANCHISING THE WAY TO GO?

IS FRANCHISING THE WAY TO GO?   388

Topics in This Chapter   388
Objectives of This Chapter   390
Advantages and Disadvantages of the Franchised Business 390
Recent History of Franchising   391
Types of Franchising Organizations   393
Nature of the Franchise Relationship   394
Evaluating the Franchise Relationship   395
Evaluating the Franchise Agreement   397

Trends in Franchising   407
Pros and Cons in Franchising—Summary   409
Worksheet 14: Franchising   410
Key Terms   413
Study Assignments for Review and Discussion   413
Projects for Students   413
If You Want to Read More   414

CHAPTER 15
DECIDING ON SOME KEY LEGAL MATTERS   416

Topics in This Chapter   416
Objectives of This Chapter   418
Sole Proprietorship   418
Partnership   421
Corporation   426
Expenses of Different Forms of Business Organization   432
Protection of Ideas and Concepts   437
Finding an Attorney and an Accountant   441
Deciding Some Key Legal Issues—Summary   445
Worksheet 15: Deciding on Some Key Legal Matters   447
Key Terms   451
Study Assignments for Review and Discussion   451
Projects for Students   451
If You Want to Read More   452

Some Crucial
Management Functions

SECTION VI

455

CHAPTER 16
MANAGING BUSINESS RISK   457

Topics in This Chapter   457
Objectives of This Chapter   459
Pure Risk Insurance   459
The Risk Manager's Job   460
Risk Transfer   461
Risk Reduction   462
Risk Absorption   462
Selecting an Agent, Broker, or Consultant   463
Types of Coverage   465
Desirable Coverages   469
Measures to Prevent Crime   474

How to Use the Foregoing Information—Summary 478
Worksheet 16: Managing Business Risk 480
Key Terms 482
Study Assignments for Review and Discussion 482
Projects for Students 482
If You Want to Read More 483

CHAPTER 17
MANAGING YOUR PERSONNEL FUNCTION 485

Topics in This Chapter 485
Objectives of This Chapter 487
Developing Sound Personnel Policy 488
Typical Personnel Policies for the Small Company 489
Recruiting the Right People 490
Appraising Performance 498
Training for Work Improvement 499
Training before Performance 499
Management Succession 501
Techniques for Developing Managers 501
Terminating Personnel 503
To Unionize or Not to Unionize: That Is the Question! 506
Key Points in Managing Personnel—Summary 508
Worksheet 17: Managing Your Personnel Function 510
Key Terms 512
Study Assignments for Review and Discussion 512
Projects for Students 512
If You Want to Read More 513

CHAPTER 18
SURVIVING: MANAGING FOR PRODUCTIVITY AND GROWTH 516

Topics in This Chapter 516
Objectives of This Chapter 518
What Is Expected of a Good Manager? 518
Improving Productivity through Teamwork 520
Need to Change Your Entrepreneurial Qualities? 521
The Many Hats a Manager Must Wear 523
Your Basic Concern as a Manager: Productivity 525
A Management System for Improving Productivity 527
Assessing Your Productivity Performance 532
Surviving the Critical First Years—Summary 536
Worksheet 18: Managing for Survival and Growth 537
Key Terms 540
Study Assignments for Review and Discussion 540
Projects for Students 540
If You Want to Read More 541

Cases

SECTION VII

543

Multilube Supply Company	545
A Prospectus for Carla Fashions	549
Buying a Going Business	563
Peak Electronics	571
A Case of Summary Termination	576
Nautilus Engineering Co., Inc.	581

APPENDIXES

589

APPENDIX A: OUTLINE FOR DEVELOPING YOUR BASIC BUSINESS PLAN (PROSPECTUS)	591
APPENDIX B: EXAMPLES OF BASIC PLANNING FOR THE SMALL BUSINESS	595
APPENDIX C: HOW A TYPICAL MESBIC OPERATES	619
APPENDIX D: A SUCCESSFUL PROSPECTUS	622
APPENDIX E: HIRING, FIRING, AND DISCIPLINING EMPLOYEES	640
GLOSSARY	645
INDEX	653

Preface

To the Student

In our years of teaching small business management for students of all ages, in the classroom and in seminars for the general public, we have seen an increasing number of men and women who want to start their own business. They have a keen desire for independence. Working for others, particularly for large companies, does not seem attractive to them.

If you are of this bent, this text is designed to prepare you for the adventure of starting and running your own enterprise. You need not have had preliminary courses in business to use this book effectively. You'll find that we will lead you through the steps required to develop a rigorous plan for starting and running a business. This business plan, sometimes called a prospectus, will act as your major tool in convincing prospective investors to put money into your venture. It will also act as a powerful guide in helping you manage your business once it's started.

We've arranged the text to follow the flow of the business process, moving from personal factors that tend to ensure success, through the founding of the business, to managing for growth and survival. Each chapter carries a worksheet at its end. When you've studied a chapter and filled out the worksheet, you will have created one element of your ultimate business plan. Combining worksheets from the pertinent chapters allows you to build a complete plan. If you want to explore particular subjects in detail, you'll find annotated references at the ends of the chapters.

To the Instructor

This text is undergirded by inputs from two basic sources:

- The experience of over a decade of testing and modifying materials in the classroom and in seminars for the general public.

- Comments and recommendations for improvement from instructors who have used and are familiar with the first edition of *Starting and Managing the Small Business*.

Rationale of Organization

We have designed the text to engage the students with the material. If you select a traditional approach to instruction, students will find the features—small cases, illustrations, problems, figures, examples, and major case material—stimulating and evocative of thought. If you choose to have the students develop a prospectus for individual term projects they originate, they will find the process stimulating and rewarding. We have designed the pedagogy to encourage students to comply with John Dewey's dictum of "trying and undergoing" in the acquisition of competence.

When they are through with the text, students will have achieved extensive knowledge of the steps to take in planning a new business; they will have learned basic principles in management and will have been exposed through the illustrative material to the reality of the ups and downs that the small businessperson experiences.

Section Sequence

For the sake of convenience in organizing material for instructional purposes, the book is divided into eight sections, including the appendixes:

Section I. What You Should Bring to Your Business

Section II. Understanding Marketing for Your Small Business.

Section III. Retail, Service, and Manufacturing Businesses

Section IV. Achieving Proactive Financial Management

Section V. Buying a Business Opportunity

Section VI. Some Crucial Management Functions

Section VII. Cases

Appendixes.

Chapters have been reorganized into six sections of three chapters each. This has permitted a somewhat more logical arrangement of subject matter plus an improved balance among material—and therefore improves the ease of planning student assignments.

Chapter Content

We have designed the chapters to give logical flow of presentation. Chapters follow this pattern:

A chapter-opening page with a list of topics followed by transitional paragraphs that set the stage for what's to come and tie their content to the foregoing material. In appropriate chapters, specific items from the Business Plan outline (shown in its entirety in Appendix A) are listed. Chapters 2 to 18 include a diagram of the business process. A portion of the diagram is shown in **BOLDFACE**, which marks the stage of the business process that pertains to each chapter.

- Objectives of this chapter (what you can expect to learn).

- Illustrative examples (in most chapters), all based in actuality.

- Text of chapter.

- Worksheet for the chapter.

- Key terms, listed with page numbers where they are defined.

- Study assignments for review and discussion.

- Projects for students. These include development of papers on particular subjects, library research, inviting panels of entrepreneurs into class for open discussion, and visiting and interviewing managers in going concerns to find out how they manage various functions in real life.

- Annotated references for those who want to read more.

Unique Chapters

Several chapters present unique contents that broaden the scope of introducing students to venture initiation and small business management:

Chapter 1. "The Need for Balanced Business Experience." Points out that most business failures result from one or more of the following: lack of know-how in the business; ignorance about marketing; deficient financial management. Presents a tested outline for a business plan and explains the intent and importance of each item.

Chapter 2. "Personal Factors in Starting a Business." Outlines major findings about the characteristics of successful entrepreneurs and recommends steps for increasing individual entrepreneurial drive.

Chapter 3. "Finding a Sound Idea for a Business." Presents specific suggestions for ways to generate new and useful ideas for the small business.

Chapter 12. "Management Information and Computers." Focuses on converting raw data into management information; describes the microcomputer and its usefulness; shows how multifunctionality can aid in the management of the small business office.

Chapter 18. "Surviving: Managing for Productivity and Growth." Examines 10 basic rules with which the small business manager should become familiar to manage the business for growth and survival. Treats the problems of funding for growth, planning for achievement, and managing interpersonal relations.

Cases

This section contains six selected cases of actual small business experience. Through study and class discussion of these cases, students will see how the principles and practices covered in the text are used—or misused—to result in success or in failure in real life.

Appendixes

The text offers five appendixes designed to aid the student, as follows:

Appendix A presents the "Outline for Developing Your Basic Business Plan (Prospectus)" as it appears in Chapter 1, but in condensed reference form, without explanations of the intent and importance of each item. Major headings throughout the text carry reference numbers that correspond to particular parts of the outline as given in the appendix. Students can readily see which parts of the text contain material pertinent to specific places in the prospectus.

Appendix B carries three examples of important portions of business plans. These are suggested as models that students can follow in developing their own plans. One plan is for a retail store, one is for a manufacturing operation, and the third is for a service business.

Appendix C outlines the requirements for borrowing money from a Small Business Investment Company (SBIC).

Appendix D contains an actual example of a successful business plan that promoted funding from a small business investment company.

Appendix E treats up-to-date, employee-oriented, legal requirements in hiring, firing, and disciplining employees.

Instructional Modes

Several basic options are available in using this text:

- *Required project.* You may require each student to develop a comprehensive business plan in order to complete the course.

- *Optional project.* Students who are (1) potential entrepreneurs or (2) high achievers can be given the option of completing a business plan project for extra credit. This option is valuable in a class containing a minimum number of present or serious potential entrepreneurs.

- *Mini-assignments.* You may, as another way to use the business plan, assign portions of it to be completed as mini-assignments. This option could be used with students desiring to pursue a specific subject or with small teams wishing to do the same.

- *Discussion topics.* You may use the worksheets at the ends of chapters as the bases for class discussions rather than written assignments.

These options may be varied or combined to suit your requirements. Whatever course you choose offers a sound pedagogical basis for helping students acquire the knowledge and skills needed to found and run a small business successfully.

You'll note that we've adopted two forms of exposition in the text: a first person approach in which we talk informally to the student, and a more formal third person mode in which we treat principles and concepts. The conversational mode makes for ease of comprehension; the more formal diction permits us to bow to academic custom. We and our colleagues have tested this methodology over the past 18 years, in the classroom and in seminars. The response from instructors and students has been uniformly positive. All like it and find it makes for ease of learning.

Supplementary Material

A comprehensive Instructor's Manual prepared as a resource book, includes:

- Lecture outlines and teaching suggestions

- Examination questions and answers

- Comprehensive case analyses, which discuss the cases of Section VII

- Master worksheets for reproduction and handout to students

- Transparency masters of figures and tables in the text for overhead projection as instructional help

Acknowledgments

We are indebted to the following, who gave generously of their time and expertise to review, comment on, and make suggestions to improve the second edition: Gerald L. Cline, patent attorney; Michael M. Kaddatz, chartered property and casualty underwriter; Rudolph Pacht, attorney at law; Jules Pincus, retail merchandising consultant; John R. Rice, president, Associated Southwest Investors, Inc.; Fred E. Winter, certified public accountant.

We are also very grateful to the following professors who gave of their time and advice in preparation of this revision: Skinner E. Anderson, Sonoma State University; Robert Kemp, Drake University; Charles W. Schilling, University of Wisconsin at Platteville; John Todd, University of Arkansas and Leon Winer, Pace University.

We have had the gracious consent of Leonel Gallegos to use his prospectus for a motion picture theater business as an example of a successful business plan in promoting funding for a new small business. We've had valuable help from Sharon McKegney, University of New Mexico, in doing library research, and from Bette Meyerson in typing an impeccable manuscript.

Arthur H. Kuriloff

John M. Hemphill, Jr.

Starting
and
Managing
the
Small Business

What You Should Bring to Your Business

CHAPTER 1
THE NEED FOR BALANCED BUSINESS EXPERIENCE

CHAPTER 2
PERSONAL FACTORS IN STARTING A BUSINESS

CHAPTER 3
FINDING A SOUND IDEA FOR A BUSINESS

The Need for Balanced Business Experience

TOPICS IN THIS CHAPTER

You Must Know the Business
You Must Have Management Skills
Developing Your Business Plan: Its Importance
Objectives of the Text
The Business Plan (or Prospectus)
Outline for Developing Your Basic Business Plan (Prospectus)
Worksheets
Key Terms
Worksheet 1: Opinion Survey

Chapter 1 introduces the basic concepts of this book. It describes the key ideas that furnish the foundation for the structure of the text: the flow of the business process, and the development of the business plan needed to raise capital and manage the fortunes of the company. In conclusion, a questionnaire directs attention to preconceived notions about the characteristics of successful entrepreneurs. Readers are asked to review this questionnaire after studying Chapter 2 to see if they agree with the ideas presented. As a result, perhaps they'll want to revise some of their ideas.

In the early 1980s small business emerged as the nucleus for renewed economic growth in the United States. Many small businesses showed adaptability to change and were very successful during the economic stress of the recession that occurred at that time. This was especially evident in the creation of jobs.

During 1981–1982 small independent firms of less than 100 workers created 2,650,000 jobs while large established industries were losing 1,664,000 jobs. Large, old-line companies, dying during the 1970s and 1980s, primarily from foreign competition, included steel, automobiles, machine tools, and consumer electronics. The decline in these industries reflects structural changes in the makeup of the economy.[1]

These structural changes reflected, in Peter Drucker's terms, "an important new reality: Small new businesses are now the main driving force for economic growth. . . . In entrepreneurship—in creating the different and the new—the United States is way out in front."[2]

The importance of small business in creating jobs through entrepreneurship emerges from the following figures in the presidential report on small business to the Congress in 1984: 7,010,000 jobs created during 1978–1980; 8,413,000 jobs created during 1980–1982. The gain in these figures shows that small firms helped pull the economy out of the recession of the early eighties. Small business generated thousands of new jobs, in many cases absorbing workers who had been cyclically unemployed in conventional heavy industry.

In its April 1986 issue *Inc.* magazine reported how a business developed by entrepreneur Milton J. Kuolt II opened several hundred new jobs in a well-known field. Kuolt started Horizon Air Industries, a regional airline based in Seattle. Starting in the early eighties with three airplanes, intending to serve three cities, Seattle, Yakima, and Pasco, Washington, Horizon under Kuolt's driving energy grew to include the whole Pacific Northwest. Horizon became the fourth largest of the 200 regional airlines in the nation. It now serves more than 20 destinations with a fleet of 30 airplanes—and in 1984 employed 847 personnel. In 1985 the company came out with a second public offering; its prospectus reported an income of $48.7 million in 1984 with a profit of $3.4 million.

In a completely different kind of business, an experienced professional physical therapist showed entrepreneurial drive by setting up a physical therapy rehabilitation center in a small Sunbelt city. John Rhodes prepared for the new business very thoroughly. He solicited future clients by consulting with the local doctors. He would segment his market by limiting his patients only to those referred by physicians. He worked for almost a year in preparing the prospectus for the new business—and accomplished his presentation so thoroughly that, most unusually, he was offered a line of credit of $60,000 by a local bank.

He opened his physical therapy center in the summer of 1984. In 1985 his business grossed a quarter of a million dollars with a 25 percent before-tax profit. At the end of 1985 the business employed five people, with the prospect of adding two more early in 1986.

Although high-tech industry often receives credit for the major part of entre-

---

[1]The State of Small Business, A Report of the President, Government Printing Office, March 1984.
[2]Peter F. Drucker, "Our Entrepreneurial Economy," *Harvard Business Review,* January–February 1984, pp. 59–64.

preneurial activity, in fact it represents less than one-third of this growing sector of industry. The larger part of entrepreneurial activity comes from low-tech enterprises such as health care centers, barber shop chains, and restaurant and fast food chains. The bulk of new business centers in services.

Ecomar Inc. of Santa Barbara, California, has given a new twist to an old business according to a report in *Venture* of April 1986. Robert P. Meek, president of the firm, contracts with the oil companies owning oil drilling rigs in the Santa Barbara channel to clean the platform supports of aquatic life. In return, Ecomar keeps all the mussels that attach themselves to the supports.

The mussels grow in the pristine ocean waters 6 to 12 miles offshore; therefore, they are sweeter and cleaner than those usually found on East Coast ocean floors. Every 3 months six divers scrape the mussels from one of ten rigs in water 40 feet deep and suck them up with a hose. The mussels are machine cleaned on the rig platform, then sorted and bagged. Delivered to shore immediately, the two-ton daily catch is packaged and shipped within an hour to distant customers by air.

Meek sells the mussels to about 100 seafood stores, wholesalers, and restaurants. These customers buy 30,000 pounds of mussels a month at 80 cents a pound, about 20 cents more than East Coast mussels bring.

This business projects a unique combination of service plus product—cleaning the oil drilling rigs of mussels that then become a product.

Meek plans to harvest other seafoods from the ocean. He recently planted 20,000 baby oysters in trays attached to the platform supports. He says, "Wholesalers will buy anything produced."

In the mid-eighties service was a growing area of entrepreneurship, employing over 20 million people. This is more than in all manufacturing in the country. Small business in service industries is expected to grow steadily throughout the rest of the eighties and in the early nineties.

A positive new factor stems from entrepreneurs of a new breed who have entered service businesses. These enterprising persons are better educated and better trained than their predecessors. They show more practiced and systematic skills in managing people, in team building, in planning, in cash flow control, and particularly in innovating unique and profitable ideas in their businesses.

This increase in managerial competence has seemed to make venture capital more readily available than in the past. Investors see many profitable and well-managed new enterprises and have become more willing to risk investing in them. This doesn't mean that venture money is easier to get, but more of it is to be had. No fairy godmother stands by, willing to lend as much money as the entrepreneur needs to start a business or to infuse funds into a going business. Knowledgeable entrepreneurs must be willing to do the homework essential to develop the business plan, or prospectus, required to obtain seed money for starting a business or stimulating its growth once started.

If you want to start your own business, and you have stars in your eyes—good. But make sure they don't blind you, that you know where you're going.

Remember the famous chat Alice had with the Cheshire Cat in *Alice in Wonderland?*

Alice   *"Would you tell me, please, which way I ought to go from here?"*

Cat   *"That depends a good deal on where you want to get to."*

Alice   *"I don't much care where . . . "*

Cat   *"Then it doesn't much matter which way you go."*

Alice   *". . . so long as I get somewhere."*

Cat   *"Oh, you're sure to do that, if you only walk long enough."*

The beginning enterpriser can learn some critical lessons from this brief conversation. Not knowing "where you want to get to" indicates a lack of planning that can be disastrous. And if you haven't thought it through and figured out *how* to get where you want to go, getting "somewhere" may be very costly. You'll get somewhere, to be sure, but it may be a not-too-happy where. You may have to fold up your venture, selling it at a loss at best—or declaring bankruptcy at worse.

Most new businesses fail because their owners don't have balanced business experience.[3] Three basic strengths are required to achieve balanced experience:

1.   Technical competence in the business you have chosen, which means that you should have the know-how to get out the product or render the service in good style.

2.   Marketing competence, which means that you should know how to find your special niche in the market, how to identify your customers, and how to sell enough of what you offer at a price that will return an adequate profit for your efforts.

3.   Financial competence, which means that you should know how to plan for and get the money you'll need to start your business and keep it running without getting into cash troubles.

As a glance at the chapter headings in this book will show you, you'll have to know many other things about starting and running a business, but these three are fundamental. They make the foundation upon which you can build success.

You Must Know the Business

Above all else you should have experience in the business you want to start. It's hard enough to get a business venture going, with a thousand matters to absorb your attention, without trying at the same time to learn how to produce the product or service. If you don't have this essential know-how, you'll be well advised to find a job in that business. Work in it for a year or so. Keep your eyes and ears open. Learn everything you can about the technical and marketing aspects of the product or service. Observe the strong and the weak points in the management of the business. What would you do to improve the way the business is managed? By staying with it, learning about the product or service, and particularly learning the management

---

[3]*The Business Failure Record*, Dun and Bradstreet, Inc., New York. This is a yearly publication prepared by the business economics department of this firm. Year after year it reports lack of balanced managerial experience as a prime cause of the failure of new businesses.

skills, you can acquire the competencies you'll need to start your own company—and you'll be sure to get "somewhere" in good time.

You can use your spare time for the planning you must do to tilt the odds for success in your favor before you set up your own business. And you'll get paid while you learn.

You Must Have Management Skills

This book is designed to help you gain the management skills you'll need before you start your own business and how to manage it once started. We emphasize marketing and financial planning in the beginning, because these have been shown to be essential for success in small business. The text is keyed to helping you develop your fundamental business plan—the carefully drawn road map—that you must have to show you where you want to go and how to get there in the shortest time with the least cost.

The business plan is the basic tool you'll need to raise capital or borrow money. Development of the plan for your business will give you a firm grasp of the requirements you'll have to meet to start and run it. By carefully following the procedures recommended in this text, you'll have such detailed knowledge about your proposed venture that even the most sophisticated investor won't be able to ask you a question you can't answer. You'll show confidence in what you want to do. And by showing knowledge and confidence, you'll assure prospective investors of your ability to carry through your project successfully.

Developing Your Business Plan: Its Importance

In this chapter you'll find an outline for your business plan; it has been tried and tested over the years. Many entrepreneurs have raised money successfully on the basis of plans developed from this outline—and have used the plans to achieve a successful business. The basic theme of your business plan, or prospectus, as it is often called, is shown in Figure 1-1. We'll treat each of the stages of the flow diagram, from "You" to "Profit," in depth.

You will need a business plan, or prospectus, to raise seed money for starting your business and to control and manage it successfully once you've started it. This

FIG. 1-1

Flow diagram of the business process.

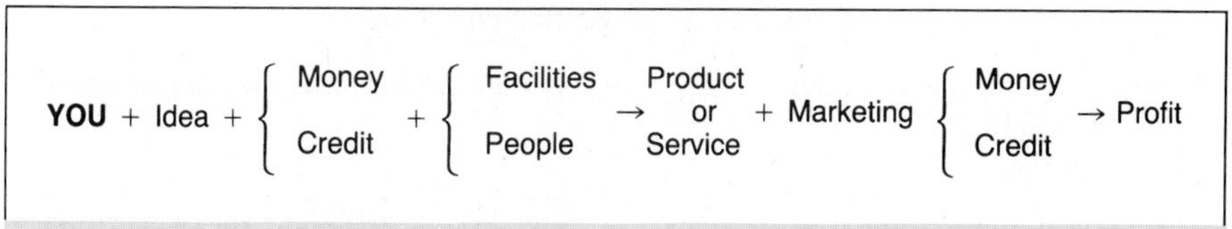

$$\textbf{YOU} + \text{Idea} + \begin{Bmatrix} \text{Money} \\ \text{Credit} \end{Bmatrix} + \begin{Bmatrix} \text{Facilities} & \text{Product} \\ & \rightarrow \text{or} \\ \text{People} & \text{Service} \end{Bmatrix} + \text{Marketing} \begin{Bmatrix} \text{Money} \\ \text{Credit} \end{Bmatrix} \rightarrow \text{Profit}$$

plan demands more than usual concentration on detail to serve you well. Its contents affect many important aspects of your management. So critical are these that you should plan to spend sufficient time to develop an *acceptable* plan. In the experience of many entrepreneurs, to develop an acceptable prospectus for even a comparatively simple business may take 3 to 6 months of concentrated effort; business plans for more complex ventures may take 9 months to a year.

Your business plan assures guides for several purposes:[4]

- The well-prepared plan gives you a powerful tool for convincing prospective investors that you are prepared and capable of doing a good job of starting and managing your venture.

- The business plan also provides leverage to obtain bank loans when you need money for working capital, a problem that sooner or later every business faces.

- When people team together to work up, revise, and rework the prospectus, they commit themselves to making it come true. This is a common psychological phenomenon—the effect of joint labor that binds partners together. Joint planning tends to reduce the trauma of dislocation and separations caused by the demands of running a business. It can often achieve this bond between husbands and wives who must commit themselves to a helping relationship.

- Creating the business plan forces you to evaluate and, from time to time, to reevaluate the basic strategy of the business. You must answer this critical question: "*What business are we really in?*" And you must raise and answer this question periodically as business conditions change. Your answers lead to designing a network of plans for managing the large and small affairs of the business. It is in this way that entrepreneurs create the future of their businesses and keep to a minimum the possibility of failure.[5]

- Sound management practice says that the prospectus should carry an end date. (So should operating plans and policies.) This practice forces modifying of old plans and new forward planning on a regular basis, thereby promoting an efficient and goal-oriented organization.

Objectives of the Text

The text is designed to help you develop your business plan and achieve the management skills you'll need to carry it out. Our major objectives parallel the stages of the flow diagram; we will

- Look at the characteristics of successful entrepreneurs so you can see how well yours match, and what you can do to strengthen them.

- Outline ways of going after capital money and presenting your plan to prospective investors and bankers.

---

[4]See Appendix D for an example of a successful business plan.
[5]George A. Steiner, *Strategic Planning, What Every Manager Must Know*, Free Press, New York, 1979, pp. 37–38.

▨ Describe possibilities in using credit for buying and selling.

▨ Consider desirable ways of acquiring facilities.

▨ Recommend steps in building the organization of people you'll need as you grow.

▨ Look at the requirements of producing your product or service.

▨ Describe the steps you should take to market your product or service successfully.

If you manage these processes well, with a bit of luck you'll be able to convert your product or service into a profit large enough to repay you for all the time, energy, and money you will have put into your venture.

The Business Plan (or Prospectus)

We have keyed the structure of this book to the "Outline for Developing Your Basic Business Plan" (Prospectus) that follows. You'll find reference numbers after almost all major headings throughout this book. These reference numbers identify specific points in the outline. For example, the reference 1.A, 2.A says that the information given under the heading "You Must Know the Business" fits in the outline at point 1.A (description of your proposed business) and at point 2.A (statement of the desirability of your product or service).

Outline for Developing Your Basic Business Plan (Prospectus)[6]

1. Executive summary
   A. Description of your proposed business
      (1) Describe your product or service
      (2) Support with diagrams, illustrations, or pictures (if available)
   B. Summary of your proposed marketing method
      (1) Describe the market segment (or submarket) you're aiming to reach
      (2) Outline the channel you plan to use to reach this market segment (retail, wholesale, distributors, mail order, other)
   C. Summary of your financial estimates
      (1) State the dollars in sales you aim for in each of the first 3 years
      (2) State the estimated profit for each of the first 3 years
      (3) State the estimated starting capital you'll need

Item 1 of the outline, executive summary, is designed to give the prospective investor the highlights of the three basic strengths you and your management team will bring to the business: technical competence needed to produce the product or service; marketing competence required to identify and reach the customer; the financial management competence to control the needs of the business for cash flow and growth. The executive summary affords the hook by which you can catch the serious attention of the sophisticated investor.

---

[6]For quick reference, this outline, without explanations, will be found in Appendix A.

2. Statement of objectives
   A. Statement of the desirability of your product or service
      (1) Describe the advantages your product or service has, its improvements over existing products or services
      (2) State the long-range objectives and the short-range subobjectives of your proposed business
      (3) Describe your qualifications to run the business
      (4) Describe the "character" you want for your business, the image you'd like your customers to see

Item 2, statement of objectives, gives you the opportunity to sell the prospective investor on the unique attractiveness of your product or service. You'll state your ultimate objectives for the growth and quality of your proposed business—and the stages of growth by which you intend to achieve these objectives. And you'll describe **your** qualifications to run the business, showing confidence but not brashness in what you say.

3. Background of proposed business
   A. Brief summary of existing conditions in the business you're intending to enter (the "state of the art")
      (1) *Where* the product or service is now being used
      (2) *How* the product or service is now being used
   B. Detailed explanations of your place in the state of the art
      (1) Describe the projections and trends for the industry or business field
      (2) Describe competition you face (place competitors' advertisements and brochures in the appendix at the end of your prospectus)
      (3) State your intended strategy for meeting competition
      (4) Describe the special qualities of your product or service that make it unique

Item 3, background of proposed business, is the place to discuss the conditions that exist in the business you want to enter. Is it a new kind of business in the early stage of growth? Is it an old business to which you're giving a new twist? Compare your approach with current practice. How do you intend to meet competition? Through superior quality in product or service? Through special advertising or other promotional method? Or through special qualities that make your offering unique?

4. Technical description of product or service
   A. A complete technical description of product or service
      (1) Describe in a technically accurate way how the product works or how the service is used
      (2) Outline tests that have been made and give test data and results
      (3) Outline tests that are to be made and describe the test objectives
      (4) State briefly your concepts for follow-on (next generation) products or services

Item 4, technical description of product or service, is the place to describe your product or service in technical detail, including results of tests made to show the superior performance of your offering or the details of the testing program you plan. This section permits you to show your sophistication in recognizing the need to think ahead and plan for innovative ways to bring out advanced products or services. You'll show the investor that you know that survival of your business demands that you keep ahead of competition.

5. Marketing strategy
   A. A comprehensive description of marketing strategy
       (1) Describe the segment of the market you plan to reach
       (2) Describe in full detail the distribution channel you plan to use to reach your market segment: retailers, jobbers, wholesalers, brokers, door-to-door salespeople, mail orders, party plans, or other means
       (3) Describe the share of the market you expect to capture versus time

Item 5, marketing strategy, gives you the opportunity to show how well you've done your homework in pinpointing the segment of the market that fits your business. Here you'll describe how you propose to reach your customer, whether through direct sales, through a mail campaign, or through some other method.

Describe the share of the market you hope to capture at different time periods. You should be wary of being too optimistic in your figures. Use reasonable time spans: perhaps a quarter or half year, or even a year for the more complicated types of businesses such as industrial firms or consulting firms.

6. Selling tactics
   A. An outline of the activities to be used in selling the product or service
       (1) State the methods you expect to use to promote your product or service: direct calling, telephone sales, advertising, mail orders, radio, television, other
       (2) Include a sample brochure or dummy, advertisements, announcements, or other promotional literature
       (3) Present data supporting your ability to meet your sales goals: actual orders, personally known prospective key accounts, and potential customers
       (4) Explain the margins of safety you've allowed in your sales forecasts

Item 6, selling tactics, is the place to state in detail the tactics you expect to use in reaching your customers and in convincing them to buy your product or service. Support your approach by supplying promotional material such as sample advertisements and announcements, whether in finished or in dummy form. Include copies of actual orders or of key accounts that you believe will buy. Copies of actual orders, of course, are the most convincing evidence of the worth of your product or service.

Do whatever you can to show that a potential market exists for your offering. Explain the margin of safety you've allowed in your sales forecasts. Again, you must be reasonable. Think carefully about what you may be able to achieve by considering the total market in the area you intend to serve. Then estimate how many calls a salesperson can make in a day and calculate how many working days there are in the time period you're using for your estimate, and remember that a salesperson can be successful perhaps only 20 percent of the time. This way of estimating will ensure that your forecast makes sense to the sophisticated investor, and that you are thinking like a responsible businessperson.

7. Plan of operation
   A. Description of the proposed organization
      (1) Show an organization chart describing the needed business functions and relationships
      (2) Describe the key positions and identify the persons to fill them
      (3) Give résumés of the key persons
      (4) List equipment or facilities and the space and location required
      (5) Describe the research and development facilities you'll need
      (6) If manufacturing, outline the kind of production you'll do in-house and what is to be subcontracted

Item 7, plan of operation, calls for you to outline your proposed organization. Your main purpose is to show clearly and positively that you have qualified persons to fill the management jobs in your company. Even if there are only two or three people you intend to start with, show that they have the necessary competencies to fulfill at least the basic management needs in the technical, marketing, and financial functions. This is best done through including their résumés.

This section will also be the place to include the tools, equipment, and space your operations will require, and the research and development facilities you'll need. If you're going to manufacture a product, you'll also need to show what production you propose to do in-house and what you'll subcontract. Be certain to show that you'll work to preserve your cash by subcontracting as much as you can on the outside, assuming that costs are acceptable.

8. Supporting data
   A. Information required to support the major points in the business plan
      (1) Include a set of drawings of the product to be manufactured or a detailed description of the service to be offered
      (2) Show a list of the tooling you'll require for production and estimated costs of the tooling
      (3) List the capital equipment you'll need and its estimated cost
      (4) Provide a layout of your proposed plant, supported by a manufacturing flowchart (include the estimated cost of manufacturing your product)
      (5) Give a packaging and shipping analysis
      (6) List a price schedule for your product or service
      (7) Include your detailed market-survey data
      (8) Supply the following financial data:
         (a) Projected income statement and balance sheet for the first 2 years by the month and for the third year by the quarter
         (b) Cash flow projection for 2 years by the month
         (c) Break-even chart for 2 years, by the year
         (d) Fixed-asset acquisition schedule by the month, showing each item you expect to buy and its cost

Item 8, supporting data, gives the information required to detail the major points in the business plan. Many of these data will support the analysis you'll have used to estimate the capital money that must be invested in the business. The items that should be described in this section are listed in the outline and need not be repeated here. These are not intended to be all-inclusive but are representative of those the sophisticated investor will want to study. Different businesses will need different capital items. You'll have to specify those that you'll need for your business.

You should check to see if it makes better sense to lease some equipment with an option to buy than to invest large sums in buying major items. Again, it's essential that you know the value of preserving cash in a new business.

Other points in this section will pertain to marketing and financial aspects. You'll need to work out and include a price schedule for your product or service. Discounts for quantity and markups in your particular business should be included in your price schedule. Your market-survey data belong in the appendix to your prospectus. Finally, supply the financial plan given under item (8).

9. Conclusions and summary
   A. A statement of proposed approach in starting the new organization
      (1) State the total capital you'll need, the safety factor you've used, and how the capital is to be made up:
          (a) Your share of the starting investment
          (b) How much more you'll need from others and when you'll need the money
          (c) What share of the business you'll give to the investors or lenders for this additional capital
      (2) State how much profit you expect and when you expect to show it
      (3) Tell what percentage of ownership you want for yourself and your partners
      (4) Indicate the total capital you'll need and how it's to be made up
      (5) State your planned schedule for starting your business

Item 9, conclusions and summary, furnishes the summary of key points in starting the business. Here you'll state how much money you'll need to start the business and what safety factor you've used in arriving at this sum. Most beginners underestimate the amount of money they'll need for a new business. Therefore, you should do the best planning you can to arrive at a sum sufficient to start your business. Then add a reasonable safety factor, perhaps 20 to 25 percent, to take care of contingencies and unexpected costs.

Indicate how much profit you expect to make and when you expect your business to show it. The financial projections you've made in your planning will give you the figures.

Tell what portion of ownership you want for yourself and what your partners, if any, are to have. Indicate that you have a legally binding agreement in this regard. Prospective investors will want to be assured that no disputes will arise about ownership or sharing profits.

Indicate how the total capital is to be made up. How much are you and your partners going to put in? Any sophisticated investor will want you and your partners to invest as much as you can in the business. That investor wants your complete commitment to the business, and knows that if you have all you can in it, you'll not walk away when things get rough, as novices have a way of doing in a newly started business. You'll dig in and get matters straightened out, whatever effort it takes.

Investors who put money into a start-up business are not likely to deliver their entire investment at one time. They'll parcel out the funds on a schedule that conforms with your planning. Again you can see the importance of planning in controlling your whole business operation.

You will have to negotiate with prospective investors to reach an agreement on how much of the business you're willing to give up for the money they invest. It's sound practice to use the services of an attorney who is skilled in such matters to represent your interests. The resulting agreements should be spelled out in a legal document that all parties sign.

Finally, present your planned schedule for starting your business. Be aware of possible delays you're likely to meet: overly optimistic delivery dates from suppliers, unexpected trucking strikes, bureaucratic obstacles in licensing, and other kinds of difficulties that must often be overcome. You must be careful, therefore, to allow plenty of lead time in scheduling to avoid the pitfall of unexpected delays.

Worksheets

At the end of each chapter in this book, you'll find a worksheet. Each chapter and worksheet is aimed at helping you understand and write a specific part of the plan for your prospective business. As we've said, major headings in most chapters are keyed by code number and letter to their appropriate place in the outline. Study each chapter carefully. Collect the data required to fill out each worksheet for your business (sources of information are given throughout the text). When you've finished all the worksheets, you'll have the substance of a basic plan for your business. You'll write up and polish this plan, then use it to convince investors and other credit sources to put money in your business.

An outline of the main points in each chapter appears at the front of the chapter; these will aid you in finding points you want to check. A list of suggested readings appears at the end of each chapter; these have been chosen to give you sources of information on subjects that you may want to explore in detail.

Highlights of business plans for retail, service, and manufacturing businesses are located in Appendix B. Appendix D presents an actual business plan, or prospectus, that has been successfully employed in raising money for starting a new business. These are offered as guides to give you direction in preparing your own plan. **You should, of course, work up the data for your own business**; you should **not** rely on the specifics given in these examples. Each business is unique, and you must develop the specific information that fits your business in order to have a sound plan, or prospectus, that will get you where you want to go at the least cost in time and money.

KEY TERMS

At the end of each chapter, you will find a list of key terms. Definitions of the terms can be found within the chapter at the page numbers shown, and further information appears in the glossary and index.

Opinion Survey

Before you begin Chapter 2, please take the time to fill out the Opinion Survey that follows. This survey is designed to help you pinpoint what you now believe about those persons known as entrepreneurs, who are able to start a business and drive it through to success. When you have finished studying Chapter 2, we want you to review your opinions about entrepreneurs. Perhaps some of your ideas as shown in the survey will have changed; perhaps they will have been reinforced. Either way, you'll have set the basis for gaining an understanding of yourself as a potential entrepreneur. And you'll be prepared to take advantage of the suggestions given in Chapter 2 for strengthening your entrepreneurial drive.

OPINION SURVEY

	True	Don't know	False
1. The most noticeable trait of entrepreneurs is their high need for power.			
2. The here-and-now is more important to the entrepreneur than tomorrow.			
3. People who start their own business are gamblers.			
4. Entrepreneurs are inclined to rely on tested and proven ways of solving problems.			
5. When entrepreneurs need advice they rely on their close friends.			
6. Most of the time, entrepreneurs "fly by the seat of their pants."			
7. Entrepreneurs feel very uncomfortable unless they know how they're doing.			
8. Entrepreneurs value money above other kinds of rewards.			
9. Entrepreneurs set impossibly high goals to stimulate themselves to high accomplishment.			
10. Entrepreneurs tend to avoid routine tasks.			
11. The payoff in owning your own business is being your own boss.			

CHAPTER 2

Personal Factors in Starting a Business

TOPICS IN THIS CHAPTER

Objectives of This Chapter
The Entrepreneurial Characteristics
Reinforcing Achievement Motivation
Rewards and Penalties of Owning Your Own Business
Personal Factors in Starting a Business—Summary
Worksheet 2: Your Personal Assessment
Key Terms
Study Assignments for Review and Discussion
Projects for Students
If You Want to Read More

In the first chapter we described key strengths you should have to start your business and to manage it once it is going. We presented an outline for your business plan and told why each section of the plan has its special importance. The plan will help you raise money and will guide you in running your business.

In this chapter we look at *YOU*, the first variable in the flow diagram of the business process as shown in Figure 1-1. We recommended that you check yourself against the personal characteristics of successful entrepreneurs. If you fit, you have things going for you; if you want to strengthen your entrepreneurial drive, we offer some suggestions that will help. In closing the chapter, we tell what many successful entrepreneurs have found to be the rewards and penalties of owning their own businesses; they conclude that the benefits outweigh the costs.

To enjoy the rewards (and to cope with the penalties) of running a successful small business, your behaviors should be founded in solid entrepreneurial values. These are the values that guide entrepreneurial behavior. By studying your reactions to the subjects listed below, and described in detail in this chapter, you'll gain insight into your values—and the behaviors that flow from them:

- Commitment—staying with a task until it's finished

- Moderate risk—not gambling, but choosing a middle course

- Seeing opportunities—and grasping them

- Objectivity—observing reality clearly

- Feedback—analyzing timely performance data to guide activity

- Optimism—showing confidence in novel situations

- Money—seeing it as a resource and not an end in itself

- Proactive management—managing through reality based on forward planning

The flow diagram of the business process identifies significant variables for the acquisition of managerial competence. Each item presents a challenge that may be met successfully through behaving as outlined above. Aptly applied, they can lead to a successful business.

$$\textbf{YOU} + \text{Idea} + \begin{Bmatrix} \text{Money} \\ \text{Credit} \end{Bmatrix} + \begin{Bmatrix} \text{Facilities} & \text{Product} \\ & \rightarrow \text{ or } + \text{ Marketing} \\ \text{People} & \text{Service} \end{Bmatrix} \begin{Bmatrix} \text{Money} \\ \text{Credit} \end{Bmatrix} \rightarrow \text{Profit}$$

Successful entrepreneurs, those who start businesses and make them survive and grow, show special personal characteristics. Not everyone has these qualities. Many studies made by well-qualified researchers have shown what backgrounds entrepreneurs come from and what psychological drives enable them to overcome the problems that a new business usually faces before it becomes profitable.

Objectives of This Chapter

This chapter summarizes major findings from studies about the characteristics of entrepreneurs. You can check your own characteristics against those found in the research. And you can practice strengthening your own entrepreneurial drives by following the suggestions coming from the research. The objectives of this chapter are to:

▪ Define the *need for achievement*

▪ Define the major entrepreneurial characteristics

▪ Describe four ways to strengthen your achievement motivation

▪ Help you to understand the rewards and penalties of owning your own business

---

SAM BRUNELLE

"The third time really was a charm," said Sam Brunelle, "I failed twice before I made this business go."

Sam is the owner of a profitable small business that makes prototype components for electronics manufacturers. Located just off Route 128 outside of Boston, Sam's company has supplied small runs of components for pilot production to middle- and large-sized companies around the country for the past 10 years.

"Yes," said Sam, "I learned the hard way. After I closed up my second shop, I looked back to see what had happened. What had I done wrong?

"It dawned on me that I was playing in a different game as the owner of a business than I had been as a tool-and-die maker. Being a good machinist didn't give me the license to run a business. So I set out to learn all I could before trying again—which I was bound and determined to do."

That Sam had learned what was needed to be a successful entrepreneur is clear. His small business employs 60 people, did almost $2 million in gross sales last year at a profit of 20 percent before taxes—close to $400,000. Sam's bulldog determination, willingness to admit his deficiency, and refusal to give up the idea of becoming his own boss show his entrepreneurial qualities.

What is the key lesson to be learned from the history of Sam Brunelle?

If you want to start and succeed in your own business, you should first of all ask yourself, "Do I have what Sam has—do I have what it takes?" Not everyone does. The personal characteristics of the prospective enterpriser are not found in everyone. Entrepreneurs are special people. They have special strengths upon which to draw for their adventure into business.

The information in this chapter is designed to give you background for looking at your entrepreneurial drive. With this background, you'll be able to fill out the worksheet at the end of this chapter with understanding of its intent.

We know a great deal about the characteristics of successful entrepreneurs, primarily as a result of research done by Harvard's David C. McClelland and his associates over the past 35 years. McClelland's findings suggest that all human beings have psychological needs that may be described in three general classes: the *need for affiliation,* the *need for power,* and the *need for achievement.* We all have some of each of these needs. But in most persons, one is the most powerful and impels them into specific kinds of work or activity. Nurses and social workers, for example, show a high need for affiliation. They want to work closely with others, to be helpful, and to experience the rewards of the helping relationship. Effective salespersons and politicians show a high need for power. They find their reward in manipulating the behavior of others and in controlling the means for making others respond to their sales pitch. The need we're interested in, the one shown by successful small businesspersons, is the need for achievement (often referred to as *n Ach*).[1]

To find out if you have what it takes to be a winner in starting your own business, you should check your characteristics against those found in successful entrepreneurs. Think as honestly as you can about your behavior and activities in the past as you go through the descriptions that follow. Decide whether your characteristics match at least reasonably well those found in successful entrepreneurs. If they do, you have things going for you, and you can strengthen your n Ach as outlined later. If there is a wide gap, you probably have a high need for affiliation or a high need for power and would be better off working for someone else. By choosing this course, you would avoid the possibility of facing a sea of troubles—of losing your money, your time, and your happy frame of mind.

Studying this chapter will enable you to:

- Understand the meaning of need for affiliation, need for power, and need for achievement

- Understand how the need for achievement gives the basis for motivating the enterpriser

- Learn what can be done to reinforce achievement motivation

- Identify many of the major rewards and penalties of owning your own business

---

[1]Other researchers following McClelland have tried to define the characteristics of entrepreneurs. Some have done studies to find out where they come from: their family backgrounds, education, and other personal factors. Others have studied their psychological characteristics. The results of this research add to our knowledge of the enterprising personality. But all the researchers stress the importance of n Ach. For those who want to explore some research other than McClelland's, references will be found in the suggested readings at the end of this chapter.

The Entrepreneurial Characteristics

Prime among the qualities of the high n Ach personality is a commitment to excellence. Successful entrepreneurs value excellence; they demand high performance from themselves and will not be satisfied with less. They aim at accomplishment of worthwhile and challenging tasks. Although they daydream about achievement, they're not content to let it go at dreaming as most people do. Their visions seem to stimulate an inner drive for making their dreams come true. They find a special joy in winning; for them achievement is an end in itself.

Do you have a burning desire to be a winner?

COMMITMENT TO THE TASK

Once committed to a course of action, high n Ach persons become absorbed in it. They do not let go. They cannot forget or forgive themselves for an unfinished project. The burden of failure would bother them too much and too long. Knowing that big achievements do not come easily or quickly, they do not wait for the lucky break. They dig in for the long haul and stay with a project until it is successfully completed.

Do you have this quality of stick-to-itiveness?

CHOOSING MODERATE RISK

Despite a commonly accepted notion, entrepreneurs are not gamblers. They choose moderate risk rather than the wild speculative gamble. Some people prefer the wild risk; some prefer a conservative approach that minimizes their exposure to loss. High n Ach people take a middle course. They want a moderate risk, large enough to be exciting, but with reasonable hope for gain.

Achievement-oriented persons willingly assume responsibility for a project or task they believe they can manage successfully through their own competencies. They know their own skills. Their attitude is therefore one of aggressive realism. Their commitment to a task rests on considered judgment of their ability to influence the outcome successfully.

Do you prefer a middle course when you have studied a risky problem objectively and think you can solve it through your own knowledge and skill?

SEIZING OPPORTUNITIES

Entrepreneurial persons are quick to see and seize opportunities. They show an innovative turn of mind and convert opportunities they observe into active programs for achievement. Because they are intensely realistic, they anticipate and plan carefully how to get where they want to go. They favor logical predictions based upon fact. In realizing an opportunity, they're not overwhelmed by obstacles but, rather, are challenged to figure out ways to get around them. They often come up with innovative ways to overcome obstacles.

Are you alert to opportunities; do you seize them to your advantage?

OBJECTIVITY

High n Ach people are more realistic than others about themselves and the ends they seek. They're utterly unsentimental about undertakings close to their hearts. They're not likely to let personal likes and dislikes stand in their way. When they require assistance, they select experts rather than friends or relatives to help them. They take a businesslike attitude toward their business.

Do you choose the tough, businesslike way to solve problems rather than giving in to personal likes and dislikes in finding help?

NEED FOR FEEDBACK

Entrepreneurs seek immediate feedback on their performance. They want prompt, accurate data on the results they're getting. It doesn't seem to make any difference whether the information they get is good or bad; they are stimulated by it to pour more energy into accomplishing the task.

Do you find it important to know how you are doing when you are working on a project?

OPTIMISM IN NOVEL SITUATIONS

High n Ach persons tend to be optimistic in unfamiliar situations. The odds may not be clear, but the circumstances may be appealing. Entrepreneurial persons may, in such situations, see no reason why they can't win out through their own abilities. They plow ahead, not put off by lack of guidelines, and frequently make more of whatever opportunities there are than more cautious persons who wait for the odds to become better.

As they begin to understand the situation and its elements, high n Ach persons revert to their more usual habits and begin to calculate their chances very closely. Thus they present the paradoxical picture of boldness in the face of the unknown and prudence in the face of the familiar. They move from the ill-defined to the sharply defined and often win out by applying their special knowledge and skills.

Do you welcome tackling and solving an unfamiliar but interesting problem?

ATTITUDE TOWARD MONEY

Persons with high n Ach tend to respect money, but they're not greedy. They don't see money as something to hoard. Rather, they see money as counters in a game. When their operations are profitable, they view the profit as an indicator that they are winning the game.

Profit, or the lack of it, gives entrepreneurs the feedback signal they want. When business is profitable, it tells them that their activities are sound and should be strengthened or enlarged. When profits begin to slide off, it tells them that they'd better identify and solve the problems causing the decline.

Do you see money as an end in itself, or do you see it as a valuable asset that tells you how you are doing?

PROACTIVE MANAGEMENT

Most conventional managers let things happen. Then they race around "putting out brushfires," trying to straighten things out. They practice reactive management. Not so the successful entrepreneur. Although high n Ach persons are careful to keep an eye on the present, they keep a significant part of their thinking directed toward the future. They plan their business worlds the way they would like them to be. They then work hard to bring their plans to actuality. This quality of working out ways to make a desired objective come true is the essence of *proactive* management. Proactive management is the basis for successful management of the small business.

> Do you like to think ahead and plan your future—and then work to make it come true?

Reinforcing Achievement Motivation

In general, people with a high n Ach—those who strive for and become successful in business—are more energetic, more persistent, more realistic, and more action-minded than people with other kinds of motivational patterns. To judge yourself, you must ask the question: How well do I fit the pattern of the high n Ach personality as outlined above? If there's a reasonable fit and you want to strengthen your need for achievement, you may want to adopt the procedures suggested by McClelland and his associates. These are outlined in the following paragraphs.

THINKING LIKE AN ACHIEVER

You can increase your achieving motivation by learning to think like an achiever. Direct your fantasies toward the accomplishment of worthwhile goals. Incorporate standards of excellence in considering what you want to do. Think of newer and better things to do and newer and better ways of doing the things you must do. By paying attention to the act of thinking in this way, you'll stimulate your n Ach.

ADOPTING THE LANGUAGE OF ACHIEVEMENT

You can help to strengthen your achieving motivation by adopting the language of achievement and using it all the time. It's often said that we create our personal worlds by the words we choose to describe them; there appears to be a great deal of truth in this statement. You should try to use positive language to support your positive thinking, without, of course, being brash about it. A strong, continuing effort to think and talk constructively cannot but help you strengthen your n Ach. For example: Instead of saying, "I think, the way we're going, we'll never meet our production goal this quarter," a more positive approach would be, "Let's study the flow of our production; I'm sure we'll find one or two critical spots that are slowing things down. We'll fix them and speed things up—and we'll make our goal."

PLANNING FOR ACHIEVEMENT

Entrepreneurs show a high level of future orientation. You can reinforce your desire to achieve by planning your goals in writing. Set down on paper what you wish to accomplish in the next year, the next month, the next week. Check how you're doing in meeting your stated goals from week to week. In this way you'll be following the course of successful enterprisers. You'll see how effective your activities are; you'll be stimulated to take corrective and more effective actions from the feedback you get; and you'll be enhancing your n Ach.

BEHAVING IN A POSITIVE FASHION

Successful entrepreneurs seize opportunities for improvement and gain by creative positive action. Innovation and creativity underlie a major part of successful enterprising activity. Those who don't think very well of themselves are poorly equipped to take the risky step of venturing into the unknown, which creativity and innovation imply. You should therefore learn to have confidence in yourself, and this can flow only from a positive self-image.

Many psychologists say that we are what we do. To improve your self-image, you should practice new behavior aimed at building your personal effectiveness. For most of us, this is a long, hard road. Recognizing the need for endurance in reaching the goal of an improved self-image, you should dig in for the long haul and practice the new behavioral pattern persistently.

That n Ach may be heightened by these procedures has been shown by McClelland and his associates. McClelland summarizes the results of several n Ach development programs as follows:

The courses have been given: to executives in a large American firm, in several Mexican firms, to underachieving high school boys, and to businessmen in India from Bombay and from a small city—Kakinada in the state of Andhra Pradesh. In every instance save one (the Mexican case), it was possible to demonstrate statistically, some two years later, that men who took the course had done better (had made more money, got promoted faster) than comparable men who did not take the course or who took some other management course.[2]

To sum up the foregoing suggestions, you can reinforce your n Ach by:

- Learning to think like an achiever

- Adopting the language of achievement

- Planning and assessing your level of achievement by timely feedback on your performance

- Behaving in a confident, positive fashion

The foregoing activities can be stimulated by associating with high n Ach people, such as entrepreneurs who own small companies, and by reading (see suggested readings at the end of this chapter). Personal contact with entrepreneurs who have made it and appropriate reading will help to clarify and bring to actuality specific ideas and actions supportive of the development of n Ach.

---

[2]David C. McClelland, "That Urge to Achieve," *Think*, November–December 1966, IBM.

ENTREPRENEURIAL QUALITIES AS POTENTIAL LIABILITIES IN MANAGING

Some of the very qualities it takes to start a new business can cause problems in the operation once it's underway. The behavior patterns of the entrepreneur often include independence, stubbornness (sometimes to the point of bull-headedness), impatience, argumentativeness, and anxiety. These can be intensified by the uncertainties and extraordinary pressures of the early days of the business and can show themselves in alternating periods of elation and depression.

AN ARCHETYPICAL ENTREPRENEURIAL SAGA

If the entrepreneurial company is to grow to a major size, the entrepreneur must adapt to the ways of professional management, or get out. Getting out means selling the company after some growth, or bringing in professional management to take over.

The history of Milton G. Kuolt's adventures in entrepreneurship illustrates the point; one of his exploits was mentioned in the preceding chapter. During the 1960s Kuolt and his family liked to camp out in a 16-foot motor van. But he gradually lost patience with state and federal campgrounds. They proved too crowded, and maintenance was deplorable. Many weren't safe, with boozing, pot smoking, and raucous hooliganism.

Kuolt then conceived an innovative approach to overcome these difficulties. He started what he called Thousand Trails, private campgrounds called preserves, in 1969. These were cleared areas in the forests, equipped with pads for vans, swimming pools, and clubhouses—"modest man's country clubs." Thousand Trails sold life memberships, giving members rights to use any preserves built during their lifetimes.

By 1981, Thousand Trails had 27,600 members who had paid average membership prices up to $5795 for the right to use 19 woodland preserves in five states and British Columbia. By this time the company had more than 900 employees and annual sales of $40 million with profit of $3.3 million.

Kuolt had now become unhappy and uncomfortable with what he considered his outsized company. For two years he said, "I don't like this. I can't get my hand around this anymore." The company had become too big for his taste. He realized that he now needed professional management to take over and run the company along what he thought of as bureaucratic lines. After a year of discussions he brought in a new chief executive and a new chairman of the board. He sold most of his stock and walked out.

As with many entrepreneurs Kuolt found the accomplishment of major growth hollow. He discovered himself disenchanted with a situation in which impulse and intuitive decision making must give way to disciplined planning and routine.

Impelled by his entrepreneurial drives, Kuolt then started Horizon Airlines. Organized in 1981, the airline grew at a prodigious rate, from an initial handful of staff to 847 personnel in 1984. The company was now about the same size as Thousand Trails had been when Kuolt left it. He began to feel the same qualms as he had experienced with Thousand Trails; he was dismayed at the thought of managing an organization that now showed clear signs of needing cost controls, detailed quality maintenance, and management information systems. This company too had grown too large for his taste.

When his associates at Horizon were asked to describe Kuolt's management style, they said, "It is personal and inspirational, tenacious in its goals, yet impulsive in its execution, open and bluntly honest. . . . On occasion it can be intrusive, over-bearing, unpredictable, intimidating, and insulting." These attributes suggest a common problem with entrepreneurial style, decisive in building an organization from scratch—but not conducive to running the organization when it becomes larger and more complex.

In 4 years the company had grown from three airplanes shuttling between Seattle, Yakima, and Pasco, Washington, to more than 30 planes serving more than 20 cities throughout the Northwest. Kuolt, reacting to the realization that the airline now needed a professional hand at the helm, decided to search for a professional executive to take over.

To bring his history up to date, Kuolt has recently bought a major ski resort, Elk Horn Resort at Sun Valley, Idaho. Elk Horn offers vacationers 350 rooms, condominiums, 18 tennis courts, two Olympic-size swimming pools, and a 7100-yard championship golf course. Although the operation had not yet reached break-even early in 1986, Kuolt had invested $10 million in the resort. He expected to take over management of Elk Horn Resort as soon as the key executive position at Horizon was filled. If his history as an entrepreneur affords any criterion, it can be expected that Elk Horn will become profitable soon after Kuolt assumes the key management position.

What does the vignette, "An Archetypical Entrepreneurial Saga," tell us about the entrepreneurial personality? About the kind of management needed to prolong success once the organization has grown to a point at which it no longer holds the entrepreneur's commitment?

The entrepreneur wants desperately to achieve—for the business to succeed. The drive to be achieving and to create a unique enterprise is fueled along the way by the entrepreneur's boundless energy. This quality helps propel the venture forward. But the volatile entrepreneur needs to be cautioned against allowing personal and behavioral assets to become liabilities. There are two ways to deal effectively with this problem.

First, recognize that if carried to the extreme some behavioral tendencies will detract from your ability to run your venture well. This doesn't mean that suddenly you have to become a new person. It does mean that, second, you'll need a thorough understanding of yourself and the willingness to adapt your behavior to the hectic, confused, and emotionally charged environment of your fledgling business.

Entrepreneurs who don't adjust properly typically exhibit negative behavior in these ways:

1. *Reinventing the wheel.* You may automatically reject techniques successfully practiced in other businesses. Convinced that you have a gift of perception and sound intuitive judgment, you may tend to insist on reinventing the wheel and perhaps to use practices that have failed elsewhere.

2. *Overreacting to business problems.* The high-risk environment of the new business and the compulsion to make the business successful often result in entre-

preneurs overreacting to problems. A shipment of goods that doesn't arrive on time, faulty production equipment, a misplaced order, phone calls that aren't returned in a "reasonable" time, the newly hired receptionist who doesn't show up for work, all seem to happen at once. Thus, harried and impatient, you may react impetuously. You may damage future relationships with suppliers, customers, or employees by blowing up. Or your frantic activity to solve an immediate problem may not keep the problem from popping up again.

You must cultivate an even temperament to deal with each problem on its own merits. The tardy supplier won't know the receptionist didn't show up. The equipment supplier won't know that you can't locate an important order. You must approach each problem-solving situation with an eye to resolving it so it stays solved.

Tendencies to overreact result in continual surges of unresolved problems and misdirected activities that center around your special interests and desires.

3. *Dealing ineffectively with employees*. This most serious problem for the newly operating business only partly results from the two weaknesses described above. As your new venture struggles to its feet, all the personnel problems that plague older companies surface quickly. The principal reason we devoted a full chapter to managing personnel (Chapter 17) is this: *Your solutions to personnel problems or your inability to arrive at solutions rapidly become part of your management style*. They become habitual and ingrained and difficult to change later on.

Entrepreneurial qualities conflict to some extent with the objective capability needed to select, hire, train, mediate conflict, and harmonize the purposes of diverse human beings. You're starting your business because of your need to achieve through marketing a new product or service. You didn't get into business for the purpose of working with others. As a result, you're product- and market-oriented, and rightly so. Equipped with entrepreneurial characteristics and with everything at risk in your new venture, you're ill-prepared to deal with people problems. While making your transition from entrepreneur to manager, this will be a difficult but most important area in which you should gain competence.

Rewards and Penalties of Owning Your Own Business

We asked a group of 20 highly successful entrepreneurs from many different kinds of business what they had experienced as the rewards and penalties of owning their own enterprises. After a lively discussion, they came to consensus on the following major points:

- You enjoy the satisfaction of being your own boss, for the most part. You have the power to do things in your own way. If you have foibles—and most entrepreneurs do—you can cater to them in the way you choose to manage. This freedom is exhilarating.

- You can experience the rewards of ownership in tangible and intangible ways. You can secure your own future by putting aside a substantial retirement fund, and you can sell your business when it's profitable to do so. You create jobs for others, and you can help them to grow, which is a satisfying experience.

- You can share your prosperity by paying dividends if you're a corporation or by sharing a percentage of the profits with your partners if you're a partnership.

- You command the respect and deference of others. You will undoubtedly be called upon to serve your community in some way, and you'll get satisfaction out of this public service.

- You have the opportunity to use your skills and develop your potential as you engage in the varied duties of an entrepreneur.

- You experience a sense of achievement. You gain great pleasure from playing the business game and *winning*.

These are some of the more significant rewards attending the creation of a successful business. However, as in most cases in life, it is not possible to achieve benefits without some costs. Following are the more important penalties the successful entrepreneurs agreed upon:

- You are *not* your own boss in some major respects. Your customers, investors, and the various government agencies you must report to are your bosses. Your customers are likely to be finicky and demanding. If you don't continually check their needs and make sure you're satisfying them, you'll suffer a declining business. And meeting more and more legal demands becomes more onerous with time; yet you must pay your taxes and fulfill the requirements of federal, state, and city legislation to stay in business.

- The scope of your operations is limited by your limited resources. You must often abandon a dream for taking on a major project because you don't have sufficient money or other resources. You must therefore content yourself with a scope of operation you can manage—and sometimes this will frustrate you.

- You work long and hard. When you start your own business, you'll find that it's a 10- to 12-hour day and a 7-day week. The business not only will absorb your energies, it will also demand your time. Your social life and your family life will suffer. You should make sure that your wife or husband shares your desire to venture into business with you—and accepts the fact that there'll be many lonely hours without your presence.

- Often you experience failure before you achieve success. Many entrepreneurs fail once, twice, or sometimes three times before they succeed. Failure can be psychologically and financially devastating; working out of the resulting despair takes rebuilding of confidence and rebuilding of your normally positive attitude. Recovery of this kind requires courage and stick-to-itiveness.

- A variety of physical problems often accompany the entrepreneurial act. Many entrepreneurs develop indigestion, backaches, ulcers, insomnia, or nagging headaches. These disabilities come from the stresses of building and running a business. They may be classified as psychosomatic illnesses. You should be aware of their likelihood and be prepared to seek counsel and medical help at the first suspicion of their incidence.

Disrupted family ties often occur in the life of the entrepreneur. Broken family relations often come with the stresses that arise when one spouse goes into a new business without the understanding and acceptance of the other. The resulting behaviors due to pressures of the business lead to quarreling, bitterness, and frequently divorce. Among the twenty entrepreneurs in our respondent group, thirteen had been divorced, and four had been divorced twice. These lamentable figures might have been reduced had the husbands and wives understood the need to work through the possible problems and been willing to cope with the trauma that inevitably comes with a new business.

These, then, are some major pros and cons as seen by enterprisers who have been there. As a prospective entrepreneur, you should weigh them. Those with a high need for achievement will undoubtedly find that the rewards far outweigh the penalties. In this book we suggest ways to achieve the rewards and minimize the penalties by taking the proper steps in starting and running your own business.

Personal Factors in Starting a Business

Summary

This chapter describes the distinctive traits of successful entrepreneurs—those who demonstrate the abilities of seizing opportunities for starting enterprises and driving them through to success. The entrepreneurial characteristics revealed by research include:

- Choosing moderate risk

- Observing and seizing opportunities for improvement and gain

- Dealing objectively with problems

- The need for feedback on performance

- Optimism in novel, attractive situations

- Objective view of money

- Ability to employ proactive management

We've suggested that you can improve your entrepreneurial drive by:

- Thinking like an achiever

- Adopting the language of achievement

- Planning for achievement

- Behaving in a positive fashion

By practicing these recommendations you can, over the long haul, increase your personal—and enterprising—behavior.

Finally, we've reported that many successful entrepreneurs find that, although personal costs attach to being the boss of their own businesses, the benefits outweigh the costs.

WORKSHEET 2

Your Personal Assessment

This worksheet will help you decide where to improve your personal skills in order to strengthen your drive toward achievement. Follow the instructions as honestly as you can. Have your wife or husband, or someone who knows you very well, check your answers. In this way, you will be sure that your answers are sound.

1. STICK-TO-ITIVENESS

Look back on your career. Think carefully about an event in the course of your work that you really like to remember. What was there about the situation that you like to recall? Was there a special challenge? Tough problems that you had to solve? Did you stick to the task in spite of discouraging setbacks? And did you achieve the result you wanted?

On a sheet of paper, write the event you've been recalling. State the major problem or problems and how you solved them. State how you felt while working out the answers and how you felt when you accomplished the task successfully.

Now answer these questions by putting a checkmark on the scale at the point that best tallies with your answer.

Repeat the process for other events of a similar kind.

Every new business faces difficulties that can be overcome only by long, hard effort. If your answers are to the left of 5 on the scale, you should reappraise your attitude and reorient your thinking before trying your own business. If your answers are to the right of 5 on the scale, you more than likely have the stick-to-itiveness to be successful in launching your own business.

2. RISK TAKING

Would you choose to invest at your bank in certificates of deposit at an 8 percent return or in an oil stock at a possible return of 15 percent? Or would you prefer to invest in the stock market, after careful and continued study of trends and projections, with a fairly good chance of making 10 percent through your effort?

Successful entrepreneurs usually choose the middle course in which the possibility for gain is reasonable and the outcome depends to a great extent on the skill and knowledge they can bring to the situation.

Look back on your own approaches to decisions you've made. Describe below a typical decision you made in a matter of some importance to you.

_____

_____

_____

_____

_____

_____

Do you normally choose a middle course in which you can affect the outcome by using your own knowledge and skill?

YES _____. NO _____.

A *yes* answer is a favorable indicator for your future as an enterpriser. A *no* answer doesn't rule you out; it says you'd be wise to change your ways.

3. SEIZING OPPORTUNITIES

Have you ever taken advantage of your company's offer to pay your tuition if you took a course at night school to gain a skill you could use on the job? If you are self-employed, have you ever grasped the chance to make some extra money through recognizing and seizing an opportunity?

List an example from your experience in the space below:

_____

_____

_____

_____

_____

_____

Do you recognize, seize, and convert opportunities to your advantage?

YES _____. NO _____.

The small new business should be founded on a new and exciting idea for product or service. Profitability comes from entrepreneurial innovation, as many economists have pointed out. But innovation can't stop with the first idea. It must be practiced continually to ensure that the firm keeps a competitive edge. Therefore, as a small business owner, you must stay alert always for ways to improve your product or service and to add new products and services to your line.

Alertness is a characteristic that can be acquired with practice. The person wanting to start a business should practice searching for opportunities. Successful search finds its reward in continuing innovation, which is the foundation for profitability.

4. OBJECTIVITY

Think back to a time when you wanted to do something beyond your skill. Perhaps you wanted a cabinet built for your record player or bookshelves installed in your den. Did you choose your good friend, an amateur home craftsperson, to do the job? The work might be passable but certainly not up to that of the skilled cabinet maker—who might charge a fairly sizable fee for the work but whose quality of work you could be certain of.

I'd prefer the skilled craftsperson despite my friendship with the amateur:

YES _____. NO _____.

If you answered *no* above, bring yourself up short! Learn to be objective and unsentimental in choosing people to help you solve your business problems. The successful entrepreneur prefers the expert to the amateur when in need of help, as the research clearly shows, and this objectivity pays off handsomely in running the business.

5. NEED FOR FEEDBACK

Have you ever wanted to know how you were doing on the job? Have you tackled the boss to find out? Do you keep track of the mileage you're getting from your car and see to it that the tires are properly inflated and the engine tuned when the mileage shows signs of falling off? Is it your custom to check on matters of this kind and to make improvement when the signs show the need?

YES _____. NO _____.

A *yes* answer bodes well for your new venture. Enterprisers look to feedback signals from what they do and from what things do for or to them. They want to know how they're doing. They'll do more of the right thing and change course to overcome the effects of having done the wrong thing. A *no* answer suggests that you need to learn how to get and use feedback for improving your performance.

6. OPTIMISM IN NOVEL SITUATIONS

Have you ever tackled a job that you didn't know too much about but decided to take on because it looked exciting and you thought you could do it? For example, have you tried to convert your attic into a playroom, or put together a loom from a do-it-yourself kit?

Although the job proved to be difficult, did you plow ahead, gaining skill as you went, and complete the project?

YES ____. NO ____.

Entrepreneurs sometimes take on projects that interest them even when they are not thoroughly familiar with the details. The novelty may attract them, and they believe they can bring their own special skills to accomplish the job. If you answered *yes* to the question above, you have another indicator of n Ach in your makeup.

7. ATTITUDE TOWARD MONEY

Do you view money as an end in itself, to be accumulated and socked away? Or do you see it as a means for accomplishing goals that you think important?

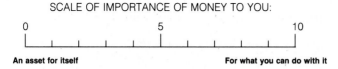

SCALE OF IMPORTANCE OF MONEY TO YOU:

Entrepreneurs tend to see money as a means for doing things they consider worthwhile and also as counters in the business game. They value money but don't revere it. The trick in business is to use it for accomplishment. If your answer on the scale above is less than 5, you'd better start viewing money as a means for doing important things and not as an end in itself.

8. PROACTIVE MANAGEMENT

Are you accustomed to think ahead? Do you set a goal for yourself, such as a new house or a new car? Then do you plan and work consistently to achieve the goal, thinking through your special requirements and setting aside funds for the purchase?

YES ____. NO ____.

To become a successful businessperson, it is important that you learn to plan ahead, yet keep your present circumstances under control. This is the essence of proactive management, and if you said *no* above, you can and should acquire the skill of being proactive. All it takes is practice!

KEY TERMS

entrepreneur 19
need for affiliation 19
need for power 19

need for achievement 19
proactive 22

STUDY ASSIGNMENTS FOR REVIEW AND DISCUSSION

1. Describe the need for affiliation and the need for power. Name several jobs that might require a high level of each of these needs.

2. Describe the need for achievement. What is the relationship between n Ach and the behavior of the entrepreneur?

3. What qualities, such as objectivity and commitment to the task, do entrepreneurs show in their behavior? Identify five more and describe them.

4. What steps can you take to strengthen your enterprising drive?

5. Tell about the rewards and penalties of owning and running your own business.

PROJECTS FOR STUDENTS

1. Two students, working together, interview six small entrepreneur-business owners whose businesses are at least 5 years old. Ask these businesspersons to describe special problems they have had to solve in the first 2 years to make the business survive. Report to the class what the major problems were and how the owners solved them.

2. On the basis of the presentation made in item 1, work in small groups to list those elements of behavior that correspond to the qualities associated with entrepreneurship as outlined in this chapter.

3. Organize a student team to find and bring to class a half a dozen or so entrepreneurs who have been successful in their businesses to act as a discussion panel. Have those entrepreneurs tell about their experiences with the rewards and penalties of being in their own businesses. Ask them: "What would you do differently if you were to do it all over again?" The class can ask questions of the panel.

4. Several students do library research on studies other than McClelland's on the characteristics and origins of entrepreneurs. Report the findings to the class.

IF YOU WANT TO READ MORE

BURCH, John G.: *Entrepreneurship*, John Wiley & Sons, New York, 1986. The first chapter of this book offers an analysis of entrepreneurship: how entrepreneurship may be defined, how economic and general conditions including the culture in a country influence it, and a comprehensive model of entrepreneurship. The second chapter presents a profile of the entrepreneur, including personal characteristics, the sources of psychological stresses on the entrepreneur and how they can be relieved, and the growing importance of *intrepreneurs*—how corporations are developing support for entrepreneurs who are employees of the corporation.

FIERRO, Robert Daniel: *The New American Entrepreneur,* William Morrow & Co., New York, 1982. The author devotes several chapters to description of characteristics of the entrepreneur. He draws on his own experiences and those of others to help future entrepreneurs avoid pitfalls, particularly those resulting from errors of judgment rather than knowledge.

HORNADAY, John A., and John ABOUD: "Characteristics of Successful Entrepreneurs," in Clifford M. Baumback and Joseph R. Mancuso (eds.), *Entrepreneurship and Venture Management,* Prentice-Hall, Inc., Englewood Cliffs, NJ, 1975, pp. 11–21.

McCLELLAND, David C.: *The Achieving Society* (paperback), Irvington, New York, 1976. In this monumental work, McClelland describes the research that went into the development of the concept of the need for achievement and shows how it relates to economic success in business.

McCLELLAND, David C.: *Motivating Economic Achievement,* the Free Press, New York, 1971. This book describes McClelland's activities and research in stimulating economic performance in various countries through helping prospective entrepreneurs strengthen their need for achievement.

MANCUSO, Joseph: *Have You Got What It Takes?,* Prentice-Hall, Inc., Englewood Cliffs, NJ, 1982. The author presents his conclusions about what it takes to start and succeed in small business. He describes, through witty discussions, characteristics of the male and female entrepreneur. He presents personal experiences about every stage in the development of a successful small business. An 84-page appendix lists sources of information and details of importance for entrepreneurs.

SHAPERO, Albert: "The Displaced, Uncomfortable Entrepreneur," *Psychology Today,* November 1975.

SILVER, A. David: *The Entrepreneurial Life,* John Wiley & Sons, New York, 1983. This book centers on persons with what the author terms "heart," enterpreneurs who create small businesses through innovation and thereby introduce change in society. The text aims at helping you decide if you have what it takes to be an entrepreneur. It recommends what you should do to survive the stresses of business and the personal problems that arise when you own your own business.

"Who Are the Entrepreneurs?" *MSU Business Topics,* winter 1974, pp. 5–14.

CHAPTER 3

Finding a Sound Idea for a Business

TOPICS IN THIS CHAPTER

Objectives of This Chapter
Sources of Innovative Ideas
Guidelines for Generating Ideas for Product or Service
New Approaches for an Established Business
Need for Continuing Innovation
Innovation in an Existing Business
Generating the Unique Idea—Summary
Worksheet 3: Your Idea for Your Business
Key Terms
Study Assignments for Review and Discussion
Projects for Students
If You Want to Read More

Now that we've looked at *YOU,* the entrepreneurial characteristics you have or may want to strengthen, we're ready to take the next step in the flow of the business process as shown in Figure 1-1. In Chapter 3, we suggest ways for developing *IDEAS* for your business. We emphasize not only the importance of originating a sound new idea for the new business but also the need to be continually creative in coming up with new ideas in managing the established business. The chapter closes with a discussion of a powerful tool for improving sales in the going business, the product (or service) market matrix.

$$\text{You} + \textbf{IDEA} + \left\{ \begin{array}{l} \text{Money} \\ \text{Credit} \end{array} \right. + \left\{ \begin{array}{l} \text{Facilities} \\ \text{People} \end{array} \right. \begin{array}{c} \text{Product} \\ \rightarrow \quad \text{or} \\ \text{Service} \end{array} + \text{Marketing} \left\{ \begin{array}{l} \text{Money} \\ \text{Credit} \end{array} \right. \rightarrow \text{Profit}$$

The need for creativity in both new and established businesses cannot be overstated. The respected economist Joseph A. Schumpeter stressed the importance of innovation as the criterion that sets enterprise off from other forms of endeavor. He further pointed out that entrepreneurial profit comes specifically from innovation—and that profit inevitably fades away because of competition that always arises.[1] Therefore, an ever-present need exists for the small businessperson to see and seize opportunities for newer and better things to do and newer and better ways of doing older things. And this holds true for *both* new and going businesses.

Nothing is so futile as a "me too" business. To offer a product just like those on the market, or a service with no special features, is to engage in a hard battle for survival. Your new manufacturing business cannot hope to compete head on with a manufacturing firm that is well-established and has special know-how and the loyalty of a satisfied clientele. Nor can the boutique you've bought hope to overcome the business of an established nearby dress shop that boasts a loyal following. To succeed you must develop a *unique and attractive* image.

You must offer a superior product or service to attract and hold enough customers so you can make a reasonable profit. And this means that you need an innovative concept as the basis of your business.

But that's not all. You will need to practice creativity regularly to ensure long-term success, *whether your business is new, or whether you manage one that already exists.*

Objectives of This Chapter

This chapter summarizes approaches to originating ideas for founding a new business, developing new products or services, and making improvements in existing products and services for an established business. It deals with the following subjects:

- Finding sources of creative or innovative ideas

- Examples of different ways of identifying ideas for product or service

- Using new ways for stimulating creativity and innovation in an ongoing business

- Why it is important to practice innovative techniques on a continuing basis

- The product-service market matrix as a tool for expanding existing markets and developing new ones

As professors of small business management, we have always been interested in gaining understanding about how entrepreneurs create new ideas for their business. At one point we met with a group of five highly successful, innovative, small business owners to find out how they went about it.

---

[1]Joseph A. Schumpeter, "The Entrepreneur as Innovator," *Readings in Management,* 2d ed., Ernest Dale, ed., McGraw-Hill, New York, 1970, p. 9.

A summary of the discussion follows:

It seems to us that in developing new ideas for your business, you follow these steps more or less closely:

You're alert to see a need for a new way to improve a product you're making, or to improve a service you're supplying, or to bring out a completely new product to add to your line.

You then define the features or requirements that would ideally satisfy that need. Some of you have found it good practice to write down these requirements so you can check them from time to time as you go ahead.

You then revert for a time to the uncritical imaginative stage of childhood to dream up several approaches that might offer ways to accomplish the results you want. (This is procedure suggested by the respected psychologist Abraham Maslow to help creativity to emerge.)

Then you've found it useful to put aside further thought about the matter for awhile—perhaps 2 or 3 days or more. (Again, this approach is highly recommended by psychologists as a way to achieve a desirable solution. It allows your unconscious to work on the material you have consciously thought about.) The solution comes in a burst of illumination—a flash of insight. You've now reached a solution that seems likely to give you the answers you want.

Now that you have a strategy that may work, you return to the grown-up objectivity typical of the entrepreneur and develop the tactics you need to support that strategy—you work through the details that will bring your improvement, new product, or service to life.

Next you put your answer into practice. You test and modify as required to get as close as you can to the ideal results you specified in the beginning.

What we've outlined here is a procedure that goes from finding a need to filling it. But there's another way to go. That is designing a solution—and then finding a need that it can fill.

For example, one of our enterprising friends saw his wife accidentally spill baby oil on the table as she tilted the bottle to pour oil on a small wad of cotton. Seeing the opportunity for a dispenser to overcome this kind of messiness, our friend developed a product to fill the need. It consisted of a small can, or reservoir, fitted with a plunger pump carrying a cup at the top. Pressing down on the cup with a small ball of cotton pumped a measure of oil into the cotton. This afforded a neat way of dispensing the oil without the danger of splashing.

Our friend perfected the baby-oil dispenser. He had several hundred made up and sold them to local department stores. As time went by, however, and none of the stores reordered, he discovered that although the dispensers had been put on display, neither the prospective customers nor the clerks understood their purpose. None could tell by looking at the product what it was for—that it was intended to help mothers overcome a messy chore. Our friend now had a solution, but not a readily seen problem that it fitted. What to do?

In true entrepreneurial spirit, he searched diligently for another use for his product and found it in medical offices. Doctors and nurses often prepare for a hypodermic injection by cleaning the skin at the point of injection with isopropyl alcohol. Our friend found that his dispenser worked perfectly to pump a measured amount of alcohol into the cotton swab used for this purpose.

He was able to mount a successful marketing program by arrangement with a well-established medical supply house. By agreement, he taught their salespersons to demonstrate the dispenser to doctors. Sales followed immediately and have been consistently good for years.

Sources of Innovative Ideas

Business
Plan
Outline
2.A, 4.A

Before you proceed with the text in this chapter, list as many ways of identifying innovative ideas for your business as you can in 10 minutes. This exercise will prepare you for the creative thinking you'll want to do in Worksheet 3 at the end of the chapter. _____

_____

_____

_____

_____

_____

_____

_____

We have two types of creativity: *external and internal*. External creativity means the introduction of new ideas from the outside; internal creativity means discovering from our own thinking new ways of doing things or new things to do.

EXTERNAL CREATIVITY

You can stimulate your external creativity by systematically exercising your curiosity about new developments, new ideas, new forces in the environment, and events that go on around you. As you do this, you'll build a reservoir of information about many things, including facts, impressions, images and pictures, and a great variety of ideas. You'll find an occasional idea that you can grasp and use immediately. But beyond that you'll build a backlog of ideas upon which you can draw when you're involved in internal creativity.[2]

INTERNAL CREATIVITY

You'll experience sudden flashes of insight when you're engaged in internal creativity. In this kind of effort, your thinking will draw upon the reservoir we've just mentioned.

---

[2]Many examples of innovative ideas for new businesses will be found in the pages of *Venture* and *Inc.* magazines. The November 1985 issue of *Venture,* for example, contains an article presenting 100 ideas for new businesses.

Knowledge is transferable. You'll suddenly see new ways to combine ideas from different fields to get a better answer to a problem or to improve an existing product or service. Sometimes these ideas will pop into your head at unexpected moments. Then the reading and observing you've done will pay off as your unconscious produces the answer you've been seeking. Inventions are sometimes born this way. Edwin Land, of Polaroid fame, is said to have expressed it this way: "Invention is the sudden cessation of ignorance."

Guidelines for Generating Ideas for Product or Service

At a meeting with a group of successful entrepreneurs, our purpose was to find out how they had hit upon the idea for their business. We give here condensed versions of their stories about developing the concept that started them on a successful business venture. We believe you'll find in these episodes guidelines that will trigger your thinking in useful ways for your new business adventure.

Business
Plan
Outline
4.A

HOBBY OR PERSONAL INTEREST

Joan Snelling, of Joan's Apparel: "I'd been wanting my own business for years," said Joan. "My hobby ever since high school has been making my own clothes. And I always thought it would be great to have my own dress shop.

"My opportunity came when my Aunt Sue got married and wanted to move to Chicago with her husband. She had a little dress shop at Cardiff-by-the-Sea, which she suggested I buy. I made the deal to buy her shop for a small down payment and a little each month.

"My aunt's operation had catered to a fairly conservative clientele. But you know Cardiff—lots of teenagers, surfers, young men and young women . . . I decided to change the image of the store, to move it to mod fashions for younger women. This concept took hold, and my store began to do fairly well.

"One day a young woman walked in and showed me a sketch of a very smart dress. She asked me if I could run one up for her, which I thought I could do in the alteration room we had at the back of the store.

"The dress turned out well. Soon I had several requests for similar dresses from friends of the young woman who had asked me to make the first one. Before I knew what was happening, I found myself in the apparel manufacturing business. Volume grew to a point where I decided to give up the retail business and concentrate on manufacturing.

"One thing led to another—and the business grew rapidly. I saw it was getting beyond me; I needed help in managing the business. I talked it out with a management consultant and my husband. They agreed that the future of the business looked bright, bright enough for my husband to quit his engineering job and join me. He took over our manufacturing, and I managed our marketing. Together we worried about and solved the financial problems we experienced with the growth of the business.

"The rest of the story is quite simple. We've just sold the business after twelve years and we're retiring. We are going to take the trip around the world in our own boat that we've always wanted, and that's been in our plans from the very first day we started to work together in the business."

Develop the basic idea for your business from your hobby or special interest!

SECTION I

42

What
You Should
Bring to
Your Business

WHY ISN'T THERE A . . . ?

Ralph Bascom, of Bascom Products, Inc.: "I was trying to clean the bristles of a paintbrush full of old hardened paint one day when I had a sudden thought: 'Why isn't there a disposable paintbrush?' We have so many convenience items that are disposable, everything from diapers to dresses to paper plates—why not a paintbrush that you could use once and throw away when you were through painting?

"I went to work on the idea with a friend. He's in the plastics field, a capable engineer. After several weeks of experimenting we found that we could make an inexpensive practical brush of flexible polyurethane. We could sell a two-inch brush for well under a dollar at retail and still afford the retailer and ourselves a reasonable profit.

"We made a couple hundred of the brushes. Then we got permission from several hardware and paint stores in our area to demonstrate the brushes. We'd set up an easel, keep cans of several kinds of paint handy, and have small pieces of plywood and hardboard to paint on.

"When customers tried the brushes we could see how well they worked for different people, and also test the customers' reaction. The results were promising enough for us to take the next step.

"We had 5000 brushes made. An industrial artist prepared a design from which we had a number of cardboard counter displays made. With these we were able to persuade a dozen hardware and paint stores to display our brushes on their counters.

"In the meantime we had applied for patent protection on the brush, which we eventually got. In the end we sold the patent to a large company and have been happy to receive steady royalties ever since."

Find the answer to the question, "Why isn't there a . . . ?"

SHORTCOMINGS IN EXISTING PRODUCTS OR SERVICES

John Thornley, of Thornley Molded Products: "I'm a technical salesman by background," said John. "For several years I sold electronics components as a manufacturer's representative. In dealing with my customers, I found an extremely desirable niche in the market—at least I thought so, if I could solve the basic problem in filling it.

"In my contacts with many large electronics manufacturing firms, I came to see that they had a real need for short runs of small insulating devices for their new products. They needed insulating bases, encapsulating shells, and molded parts to hold such things as capacitors and resistors. The short runs were needed for pilot production purposes. They'd want 100, 250, or at the most 500 pieces of a specially designed small base, for example, for an electronic component. They didn't want to take the risk of ordering permanent tooling for their new product until they were sure that the design was sound and warranted full production.

"But there was no place they could go to get a small run at an economical price. The usual supplier could manufacture in huge quantities quite cheaply, but this required a major investment in permanent tooling. I saw that if I could figure out a way to make temporary tooling at low cost, I could get many customers for short-run business. This would save my customers much money, as they wouldn't have to machine the item they needed from solid plastic stock.

"It took me almost two years of hard work to figure out how to make the temporary tooling for the short-run needs of my customers very quickly and economically. As a result, I've built my business to the $10 million mark in yearly sales—and it's returning better than $750,000 profit after taxes this year."

Observe and capitalize on the shortcomings in the products and services of others!

EXTRAORDINARY USES FOR ORDINARY THINGS

Lou Rhodes, of the Abbott-Lane Company: "My partner and I started in the specialized wood products business in Oregon before World War II. We learned something about applying baking enamel to pressed wood and metal panels. After processing, these were used as decorative wall paneling.

"One day it occurred to us that fir plywood, which was becoming well known in the west, offered a good possibility as decorative wall paneling if we could sand the surface very smooth and coat it with a glossy enamel. Our objective was to make the surface look like colored plate glass. But try as we would, we couldn't stabilize the grain of the plywood, even with the help of a consulting chemist. And then one day we got the idea! Instead of trying to fool Mother Nature, why not work with her? Instead of trying to stabilize the grain, why not accentuate the grain pattern? You see, every piece of fir plywood has a different pattern from every other piece; each piece is unique. Therefore, by using a finishing method that would make the grain pattern stand out clearly, we could offer a beautiful paneling for walls, store interiors, fixtures, and the like.

"We were able to devise equipment for processing the plywood panels, and with our consulting chemist's help, we developed special finishes for getting the contrast we wanted between hard and soft grain. We then offered the finishes in a variety of colors and called our new plywood product EtchedWood.

"We sold our EtchedWood by the carload to well-rated eastern concerns. Plywood was not very well known east of the Mississippi in those days; so we could command a substantial and profitable price for our product. We believed that it would take competition about eighteen to twenty-four months to begin to hurt us. So we worked at developing another product, which we could have ready to put on the market at the appropriate time."

Find extraordinary uses for ordinary things!

CHANGES IN SOCIAL CUSTOM

Nancy Auburn, president of Auburn Associates, Inc.: "I became involved with the women's movement when I was working for my master's degree in business administration. This interest led me to study intensively in the behavioral sciences. I was particularly excited by the newer findings and techniques that were available for helping people to change their attitudes and behaviors.

"Just before I got my degree, I was invited to participate as a resource person in a workshop aimed at helping women to become assertive—not aggressive, you know, but assertive. That is, the workshop was designed to help the women who attended to express honest feelings directly and comfortably, to be straightforward, and to exercise their personal rights without denying the rights of others and without feeling undue anxiety or guilt.

"I enjoyed the experience immensely. It triggered my thinking about what I wanted to do after I got out of school. I thought, 'This is for me. I can help women improve their lives by helping them to gain new skills in interpersonal relationships, by achieving important behavioral changes. Not only that, I'll use my education and my special training in a way that I believe is vital and socially useful.'

"I found a position with an all-woman consulting firm in this field and spent three years with them. This experience has proved of great worth to me. I learned how to run a management consulting firm, which is really a special kind of business. And while I was learning, I improved my personal skills as a behavioral consultant and change agent. The day arrived when I felt ready to move out on my own.

"I started slowly as an individual consultant. My first break came from a generous gesture from my previous boss, who referred a client to me. Once I got going, I was able to expand my operation as I developed a clientele. I worked for large and small companies, putting on in-house workshops for their employees; I did workshops through university continuing education programs; I put on programs for government agencies, for hospital personnel, and for not-for-profit organizations. Gradually I increased my staff, adding carefully selected women consultants.

"Our firm now has eight full-time women consultants. This year we will gross very close to five hundred thousand dollars. We expect to continue to grow for several years. And we will try hard to add new ideas, new methods and techniques to our services as we grow."

Look for opportunities in social change!

CHANGES IN ENVIRONMENTAL FORCES:
FIRELIGHT CHIMNEY SWEEP

Tom Myers graduated from college in the 1970s. He received a B.A. degree with majors in philosophy and religion—respectable subjects in any language. But Tom had a problem. He found the paying market for philosophy and religion extremely limited.

He had been brought up to believe in the great American Dream: "Go to school, work hard, save your money, marry and raise a family—and success will be yours." This dictum, he saw, was not enough. An adult vocational training center paid him— but not much—to help people learn work and social skills; a filling station paid him to pump gas at a minimum wage; a small-town bar, nonunion, hired him to tend bar—again at minimum wages. He would have to *make* success happen.

In 1978, he found his opportunity. With deregulation of the price of natural gas and electricity, home heating bills soared; increases of 300 to 400 percent were monthly realities for many homeowners in the small town of Taos, New Mexico, where Tom had settled with his wife and family. These homeowners began to see the advantage of inexpensive wood, often free for the cutting—piñon, juniper, pine, and aspen that could be burned efficiently in wood stoves. The homeowners could buy a year's supply of wood with a couple of months' savings on gas or electricity.

But stoves and chimneys need care; they must be cleaned regularly to prevent buildup of creosote, which is flammable and if ignited can cause chimney fires. Many a house has burned as the result of such fires. Tom recognized the opportunity he saw in the change to wood for home heating. He answered an advertisement for a mail-order training program to become a chimney sweep. He learned the skills and invested $2000 in the special tools of the trade and $3500 in a small used truck to carry the tools and get him to the chimneys. He solicited business door-to-door and advertised in the local paper. And slowly but steadily he built a route, cleaning chimneys on a monthly basis.

In 1980, Tom Myers added another service to his chimney sweeping business, cleaning exhaust hoods of restaurant griddles and ranges on a weekly schedule.

By 1987, his business had become a mini-conglomerate. He had added to his chimney sweeping and restaurant hood cleaning businesses a framing shop, which does commercial picture framing for the many art galleries and artists in the Taos area. His alertness in seeing and seizing business opportunities now brings him a respectable five-figure annual income.

His original business, the Firelight Chimney Sweep, took advantage of "reverse technology" by reviving an ancient trade to meet today's need.

NECESSITY, THE MOTHER OF INVENTION

Stan Drexel, president of Drexel Irrigation Products Co.: "I had grown citrus and avocados as an avocation on some seventeen acres in San Diego County for a number of years. It's been customary to irrigate new plantings of citrus or avocados with "spitters." Spitters are small brass fittings screwed onto a cap fitted on a vertical section of pipe that rises about a foot above the ground. The spitter has a small hole in its nozzle end and is designed to emit a fan-shaped spray of water over the area of the tree roots. Water sprays from the nozzle at a rate that permits it to be absorbed by the soil without runoff. When they operate, spitters do a good job.

"However, the water used for irrigating in many southern California areas is hard and often carries small particles of calcium carbonate or even debris that clogs the spitter. You may turn on the main valve to water a new planting of 100 trees only to find that 98 of them are being properly watered but that 2 are getting no water at all because of clogged spitters. This means that you have to walk back to the main valve, perhaps 200 yards away, to turn off the valve, then walk back to the clogged spitter, unscrew it with a wrench, clean out the nozzle with a pipe cleaner or wire, screw the nozzle back on, walk back to the main valve, and turn on the water again. To your dismay, you may then find the same or another spitter clogged. So you repeat the process, but not very graciously. In addition, you must keep an eye on the whole planting until the irrigating chore is finished. By any measure, this is a time-consuming nuisance.

"I thought about the problem. I knew enough about water flowing in pipes to know that there are two kinds of pressure that operate. One is the pressure caused by the flow of the water; the other is static pressure that exists in the pipe when the pipe is closed but has a head of water behind it. When a spitter gets clogged, the pressure of flow changes to a static pressure. Now, I thought, if the orifice in the spitter were made of a flexible material, it might be possible to have it dilate and eject the clogging particle under the static pressure in the piping system.

"I experimented with materials and designs and finally came up with a soft neoprene material that would withstand sunlight without deterioration and would give the necessary flexibility to eject a clogging particle. I had molds made and tested the product in my own orchard.

"This product was the first in a line of irrigating devices. I formed my company a bit later, after the word got around to my neighbors and other orchardists in the area. We've grown quite well since. Next fiscal year we expect to cross the million dollar mark in sales."

Develop new means to solve problems!

TECHNOLOGICAL ADVANCE

Joe Balzano, president of Pacific Coast Faultfinders, Inc.: "My partner, Ed Brock, and I had come out of the electronics engineering test field. Ed's an engineering type—always poking into new ideas, reading about new discoveries in electronics testing procedures, and so on. One day he came to me—we were working for one of the big aerospace companies—and said, 'Joe, look here, here's a new way to check printed electronic circuit boards. You connect the board you want to test to this gadget and make interface connections with a computer. You get a computer printout that tells you exactly what's wrong with the board. It'll say that capacitor C-6 isn't functioning, or you have a bad solder joint at P-11. You can find any fault in a board for just a few cents instead of having a technician spend all kinds of time locating the problem.' "

Joe continued: "Ed's find started us thinking and talking. We'd wanted to start our own business for a long time. We'd talked about it but had never been able to hit on an idea that suited us—until this one came along.

"We decided that this was it. With Ed's engineering and my sales ability, we'd make a strong combination. So we went to work making an arrangement with the New York company that had developed the advanced device that was the heart of the new testing system.

"We had very little money. But we worked out an unusual deal with the people in the east. After they checked us out and found that we were responsible citizens, they agreed to give us title to one of their machines, which sold for over $50,000 at the time. This was a calculated risk on their part, of course. But we were able to go to the bank and borrow $35,000 against the testing machine. And now we were in business.

"Although we went through the usual struggles for a couple of years, things got easier as we built a list of responsible customers; our customer roster today looks like the blue book of the electronics industry.

"Now what we're concerned with is working out new services to offer our customers, as we're expecting to see competitors get into the field before too long."

Turn technological advance to your advantage!

SPINOFF FROM YOUR PRESENT OCCUPATION

Robert Stevenson, partner in Stevenson Associates, manufacturers' representatives: "I'd worked as a purchasing agent for many years, at first in the heavy construction contracting business, in later years in the electronics industry. I'd worked for one firm for ten years. I was the chief of purchasing for a main division of the company. Over the years, I observed what I thought was extremely ruthless treatment of the older employees, particularly the professionals, who were summarily dismissed at the close of a contract or often at the mere whim of top management. I realized one day that I was sixty years old and, because of these circumstances, a likely candidate for getting fired.

"My wife and I talked things over very carefully. We explored my strengths and weaknesses; we talked over all the reasons we could think of for taking on a new business of our own—and those for not leaving the company. Our children were grown, long since on their own; so there was no obligation there. We decided that the risk of going into business was minimal. This seemed quite clear in view of my background, my knowledge of the vendors in the electronics and electromechanical fields, and the wide friendships I had built in the business during the past ten years.

"So we took the step. I've been able to build relationships with several concerns that supply superior products to the electronics and manufacturing companies in our country. I've gone through several different kinds of deals with other representatives and with vendors, and I've screened out the undesirable and the less desirable ones. Now I've reached the point where I have a sound business. I have three associates who work with me and on whose sales I share commission. The company gives me a comfortable income, and I don't worry about getting fired! I have several streams flowing in to make the river, and if one dries up, I can find another. I'm rid of the anxiety I felt when I worked for my old company."

Think about spinoff from your present occupation!

New Approaches for an Established Business

Business Plan Outline 2.A, 3.A, B

We stress the need for uniqueness in your business throughout this book. Uniqueness, however, does not necessarily have to be within the product or the service itself. It can be in some aspect of the marketing effort, in the environment, or in the quality of service offered.

Consider the Baskin-Robbins ice cream stores as an example. There is certainly nothing inherently unique about the product, although its quality is kept very high. Ice cream has been around for a long time. But what is unique about the Baskin-Robbins business is the approach they've taken in creating a special and attractive image.

Early in their history, when the two founding partners were struggling for survival against mammoth ice cream suppliers in southern California, they were advised by a tiny new advertising agency (incidentally spun off by young men from a nationally known advertising firm for which they had worked) to do everything in their power to create an image of fun; to make people want to come in to buy their ice cream because it was good fun to visit a store that was clean and white and decorated with pink and chocolate balloons; and to make it fun, a joyful experience to select from among 31 varieties of ice cream (many of which carried deliberately selected zany names).

The success of this venture needs no elaboration here. In answer to a question from the authors of this book, Irvine Robbins recently said that he expected that the firm would do better than $160 million in gross business for the current year. That is an exemplary record for a company in an old business, started with a few hundred dollars in capital but keyed into the market with a unique image-building approach.

Need for Continuing Innovation

Business
Plan
Outline
2.A, 4.A

The respected economist Joseph A. Schumpeter gave a special twist to the meaning of entrepreneur—an emphasis any person thinking of starting a business should take to heart. He suggested that the true manager is an innovator as well as an administrator. The innovator introduces new ways of doing things and new things to do—and is the originator of all profit. Your profitability, which comes from the introduction of an attractive new product or service, tends to be temporary. It will vanish as competitors come into the market to ride on your coattails after you are seen to be outstandingly successful.

Fortunately there is a lag between your entry into the market with your new idea and the formation of effective competition. This gives you the time you need to prepare improvements, develop additional features, or add new items to your line. As competition arises and eats into your profitability, you can bring out the new features or items and keep ahead in the competitive race.

You must be aware of another factor that emphasizes the need for continual innovative effort in your business. That is the shortening of the life cycle of product or service in recent years. Three decades ago the profitable life of product or service might well have been 10 or 15 years. Today this time span has shrunk to much less—perhaps 3 to 5 years. This shortening of the useful life of product or service comes from the tremendous increase in technical knowledge and available research and from the instantaneous spread of news through modern communication channels. The word gets around in a hurry. Any new idea launched on the market becomes known to potential competitors quickly. The result is a shortening of the time in which marketing countermeasures can be invented and brought to reality.

You must therefore plan for and practice innovative activity continuously to keep your business alive and healthy.

Innovation in an Existing Business

Business
Plan
Outline
5, 6

We've stated the need for continuous innovative effort even after your business has been launched and is well under way. A powerful tool to use in thinking about newer and better things to do and newer and better ways of doing older things is a product (or service) market matrix (Figure 3-1).

Here's the way you can use this matrix. First, think about your existing product or service and the present customers you are serving. This is indicated in the upper left-hand box, labeled 1. Think of all the ways you can increase your business with these customers by upgrading your sales techniques, advertising, merchandising appeal, or image. This kind of thinking can lead to innovative effort that will expand

		MARKET	
		EXISTING	NEW
PRODUCT **OR** **SERVICE**	EXISTING	1. EXISTING PRODUCT/SERVICE, EXISTING MARKET	3. MARKET DIVERSIFICATION
	NEW	2. PRODUCT OR SERVICE DIVERSIFICATION	4. NEW PRODUCT OR SERVICE, NEW MARKET

FIG. 3-1

Product/service market matrix.

the sales of your present product or service. Changing the decor of your store, training your salespeople to be more responsive to customers' requests, packaging your product in colorful and attractive boxes—these are some typical ways in which you may be able to increase your present business.

Second, look at the lower left-hand box in the figure, marked 2. Here we suggest product or service diversification. This means adding new features to your product or new items to your product line or adding improvements or services to those you now furnish. The objective here is to increase your sales to your existing customers.

As an instance, if you were making do-it-yourself kits of small items of furniture for home assembly, you might add a whatnot shelf or a shoe-shine kit or an electric wall clock to your existing line to gain additional sales from your present customers. Firms in the mail-order business constantly add to and change the items they offer to their customers. Experience has shown them that once a customer has bought from them and has been satisfied, that customer is likely to be a steady repeater—if their offerings are refreshed by new additions.

In the case of services, a small firm in the data-processing business added to its original service of preparing amortization schedules for banks, savings and loan companies, and real estate agents the following services, one at a time: truth-in-lending tables, accounts payable, monthly statements, name and address maintenance files, interest tables, and precomputed ledger cards. Starting by adding services for its existing list of customers, the firm was able to expand its business fivefold in 3 years.

Third, examine box 3 in Figure 3-1. The aim illustrated here is to increase the scope of the existing business by adding new customers for the present product or service. For example, the Menda Scientific Products company discovered that the alcohol dispensers they make (originally intended for medical use in preparing a patient's skin for injection) served admirably for cleaning purposes in soldering operations in electronics. By finding this new use for their product, they expanded their market significantly; they added new customers in a field completely different from what they had originally planned.

In a service-oriented business, a young man who operated a small window-cleaning service found that many of his customers had drapes at their windows. In the course of washing windows, he and his crew saw that more often than not these drapes needed cleaning. He made a deal with a reputable cleaning establishment from whom he learned how to estimate cleaning charges, how to take the drapes down, and how to rehang them after they were cleaned. He was able to add a service that augmented his income considerably.

Fourth, look at box 4 in Figure 3-1. This box shows the final combination you may use, new products or services for a new market. This is by far the riskiest of the four combinations in the matrix. But it also offers the best chance for the greatest profit.

If you choose this course, you must build on your strengths and assess the risk in carefully calculated entrepreneurial fashion. You'll want to go through all the steps of product or service feasibility testing and market analysis that you'll find in the following chapters. You'll want to make sure of your planning and key your efforts to your resources. Often the new product can come as a spinoff from existing manufacturing operations.

A small company making electrical measuring instruments found it necessary to manufacture its own precision wire-wound resistors because these were not commercially available to the tolerances they required. They opened a new market by adding precision capacitors to their precision wire-wound resistors. The two items, combined to customer specifications, formed a special product known as an *RC* network. These commanded a high price and opened a new market for the company.

In the service area, the small data-processing firm previously mentioned added a new service that enabled it to open a new market. This was the addition of an addressing and mailing service for firms that did not have their own facilities for this kind of task.

Generating the Unique Idea

Summary

We have stressed the need for innovation in starting your new business and for continuing innovation to run it successfully once you have it started. We have suggested that you use both external and internal creativity in your search for unique ideas, and we have given you the following guidelines to use in generating ideas for product or service:

■ Develop the basic idea for your business from your hobby or special interest

■ Find the answer to the question "Why isn't there a . . . ?"

■ Observe and capitalize on the shortcomings in the products or services of others

■ Find extraordinary uses for ordinary things

■ Look for opportunities in social change

■ Discover opportunities in changing environmental forces

- Develop new means to solve problems

- Turn technological advance to your advantage

- Think about spinoff from your present occupation

Once you've established your business, you'll want to keep improving your product or service to ward off the encroachment of competition. You'll find the product-service matrix a useful tool in working toward this end. The matrix comprises four boxes that show the possibilities for using your resources to increase your sales. These are:

- Existing product or service—existing market, which covers your traditional market

- New product or service—existing market, which suggests selling more items to your present customers

- Existing product or service—new market, which implies diversifying your market by adding new customers

- New products or service—new market, which means developing new products or services and creating a new market through new customers

Of the four possibilities, you'll find the last, new products or new services—new market, the riskiest. At the same time, it is the choice that offers the chance for the greatest profit. You should study each box in the matrix with great care. From this study, you'll be able to plan courses of action that should produce the beneficial results in growth and profit for which you aim.

WORKSHEET 3

Your Idea for Your Business

This worksheet will serve as a memo for you. It gives you a place to record your idea and your thinking about where you can go with it in the future.

Describe your proposed retail, service, or manufacturing business. Why is your offering of product(s) or service(s) unique?

_____

_____

_____

_____

_____

_____

Illustrate your idea, if applicable, by sketch, diagram, illustration, or pictures. Note briefly your thinking about improved versions of your product or service you may want to bring out as "follow-on" improvements or additions.

_____

_____

_____

_____

_____

_____

Although you should start your business with an acceptable product or service, you must be prepared to add improvements, new features, or new products once you are established and have a successful track record. Keep thinking ahead about polishing your image in your market niche. The importance of noting the next steps you see, for adding features or items to your offering, is twofold: It will help you work out a basis for your survival in business, and it will show prospective investors that you understand the need for ensuring the future of your business. You'll show competence—you'll show that you know what you're doing—as a business manager.

This is a good point to start a notebook in which you'll record ideas about your business, product, or service. Paste in ads, pictures, articles, descriptions, and other data pertinent to the development of your product or service.

Also start thinking about a good name for your company—and a logo that will identify it. A logo is a small symbol that identifies a company and its products. A well-known example is the logo of IBM, which consists of the three initials, IBM, in block letters with parallel open stripes across the letters.

external creativity 40
internal creativity 40

product (or service) matrix 48

STUDY ASSIGNMENTS FOR REVIEW AND DISCUSSION

1. Describe what is meant by internal creativity and by external creativity. Explain the difference between them.

2. Review the guidelines for generating ideas for product or service. From your own observations, see how many new businesses you can name that have been formed on the basis of guidelines in this chapter. (*Example:* Health spas for improving physical fitness. These serve to meet a need from a change in social custom that stresses the value of physical fitness.)

3. Name several businesses that have become successful by creating a special attractive image, even though the product they offer is not in itself new. (*Example:* Streamlined hair-styling shops with a standard $8 price. No appointments are accepted; customers simply wait their turn for the first chair open among half a dozen available. The basis for success in these shops rests in employing skillful, fast operators—and a price designed to beat the usual inflated $15 to $30 charge.)

4. Why should small businesspersons concentrate on being continually innovative?

5. Explain the product-service market matrix. Describe the advantages and disadvantages of each of the four approaches offered by the matrix.

PROJECTS FOR STUDENTS

1. One student tells the class, "Think of anything you can do with an ordinary wooden lead pencil. Let your imagination flow." List responses on the blackboard as they are called out. Ask students to discuss the ways they found their answers. (This is an example of an innovative process.)

2. Two or three students bring together in class five or six successful entrepreneurs who started their businesses on a novel idea. Have each entrepreneur describe how the idea occurred to him or her, and how it was developed. Close with a question-and-answer session between students and panel.

3. Two students report to class recent findings on creativity from brain-hemisphere research. Refer to *Use Both Sides of Your Brain* listed in the references at the end of this chapter. Learn the method of diagraming a subject as a fast way of organizing thinking. Lead the class in a blackboard exercise in diagraming a commonly known subject such as "environment." Discuss the method as an aid to innovative thinking.

4. Two students report on the key points made by James L. Adams in his book, *Conceptual Blockbusting—A Guide to Better Ideas,* listed in the references at the end of this chapter.

5. Two students report on the key points in *Synectics,* by William J. J. Gordon, listed in the references at the end of this chapter.

IF YOU WANT TO READ MORE

Below is a sampling of a large number of books that deal with innovation and creativity. You will find references and listings of other publications treating creativity and innovation in them.

ADAMS, James L.: *Conceptual Blockbusting—A Guide to Better Ideas,* W. W. Norton & Co., New York, 1980. This paperback tells of ways to expand your conceptual ability—your ability to gain new ways of looking at problems and problem situations. Much of the book's emphasis is on creativity.

BURCH, John G.: *Entrepreneurship,* John Wiley & Sons, New York, 1986. Chapter 3 of this book offers a number of useful guides for originating and developing ideas for product or service.

BUZAN, Tony: *Use Both Sides of Your Brain,* E. P. Dutton, New York, 1983. This useful and interesting paperback outlines ways to loosen up and free your thinking. It can be helpful in showing you how to produce creative ideas. The language Buzan uses is simple and straightforward.

DE BONO, Edward: *Opportunities,* Associated Business Programmes, London, 1978. The author focuses on opportunity search and outlines a systematic approach. The third section of the book describes thinking methods helpful in originating ideas and finding opportunities for identifying them.

HOLTZ, Herman: *Profit from Your Money-Making Ideas,* AMACOM, New York, 1982. This book details not only how to get money-making ideas but also how to put those ideas to work—that is, how to make money with your ideas. Included are ideas for products, services, and marketing.

KOBERG, Don, and Jim BAGNALL: *The Universal Traveler,* William Kaufman, Inc., Los Altos, CA, 1981. A unique guide to creativity, problem solving, and the process of reaching goals. Presents interesting and useful ways of improving your approaches to innovation and problem solving, based on up-to-date studies in psychology.

MCKIM, Robert: *Experiences in Visual Thinking,* Brooks/Cole, Monterey, CA, 1980. This is a well-designed book with many illustrations, puzzles, experiments, and problems. It will help you to stimulate your visual thinking, which can be the basis for generating many ideas for your business.

MILLER, Murray, and Franz SERDAHELY: *How to Win the Battle against Inflation with a Small Business,* Enterprise Publishing, Inc., Wilmington, DE, 1980. Chapters

1, 2, 15, and 16 outline business opportunities that require a modest investment or a large investment or can be started without costing you a cent.

ROSENAU, Milton D., Jr.: *Innovation,* Lifetime Learning Publications, Belmont, CA, 1982. This book tells how to manage the development of profitable new ideas. The author discusses sources of successful ideas in Chapter 6 and evaluation of ideas in Chapter 7. He stresses the need for continuous innovation in business.

VESPER, Karl H.: *New Venture Strategies,* Prentice-Hall, Inc., Englewood Cliffs, NJ, 1980. This book describes what entrepreneurial work is like and how to perform such work. It draws upon the experience accumulated by hundreds of entrepreneurs. New conceptual schemes for working out entrepreneurial action are introduced.

SECTION II

Understanding Marketing for Your Small Business

CHAPTER 4
YOUR SMALL BUSINESS AS A MARKETING SYSTEM

CHAPTER 5
ANALYZING YOUR MARKET AND CONSUMER
BEHAVIOR

CHAPTER 6
REACHING YOUR CUSTOMER

CHAPTER 4

Your Small Business as a Marketing System

TOPICS IN THIS CHAPTER

Objectives of This Chapter
Achieving a Customer Orientation
What Business Are You Really in?
Seizing Opportunities of Change—Summary
Worksheet 4: Your Business as a Marketing System
Key Terms
Study Assignments for Review and Discussion
Projects for Students
If You Want to Read More

We've followed the plan of the flow diagram of the business process (Figure 1-1) in the first three chapters. In so doing, we've had you look at the state of your experience in business and have presented details of a well-accepted business plan. You will find this plan a powerful tool for guiding you in managing an existing business—and it will set you on the straight road to success in starting a new business. We've examined the psychological patterns of successful entrepreneurs and had you check your personal characteristics against them. And finally we've outlined ways to generate unique ideas upon which you can improve or expand an existing business—or found a new business.

Now we'll address a third major segment in the flow diagram of the business process, the crucial area of *MARKETING*. In this chapter we'll explore the need to develop a customer orientation, to zero in on a clear, sharp definition of your business—and we'll recommend ways you can prosper by anticipating and seizing opportunities offered by change.

Information in this chapter will be found pertinent to these items in the Business Plan:

1.A.   Description of your proposed business

1.B.   Summary of your proposed marketing method

2.A.   Statement of the desirability of your product or service

5.   Your marketing strategy

$$\text{You} + \text{Idea} + \begin{Bmatrix} \text{Money} \\ \text{Credit} \end{Bmatrix} + \begin{Bmatrix} \text{Facilities} \\ \text{People} \end{Bmatrix} \begin{array}{c} \text{Product} \\ \rightarrow \quad \text{or} \\ \text{Service} \end{array} + \textbf{MARKETING} \begin{Bmatrix} \text{Money} \\ \text{Credit} \end{Bmatrix} \rightarrow \text{Profit}$$

We stated early in this book that most small businesses fail because of lack of sales. This seems obvious. However, lack of sales should be seen as a symptom of a failing business, not the cause. A failing business usually results from ineffective management. Dun & Bradstreet, which reports on business failures every year, consistently reports the following major causes of business failure:

- Lack of experience in the line

- Lack of managerial experience

- Unbalanced experience—experience not well rounded in sales, finance, purchasing, and production on the part of the individual in case of a proprietorship, or of two or more partners or officers constituting a management unit

- Incompetence—inability to assume the tasks of management that enable the organization to prosper and endure

Of these four problems, incompetence ranks just above 50 percent of the causes of failure, unbalanced experience as over 20 percent, and the other two taken together at about 20 percent. In viewing these major causes of business failure, it seems clear that they can be overcome by study, training, and experience. Even the inexperienced can achieve entreprenurial competence through commitment to an appropriate educational and training program, as described in Chapter 2.

The beginner would be well advised to start by acquiring competence in the three basic areas of management we stress in this book: competencies in the business selected, in financial management, and in marketing. This chapter concentrates on marketing.

Don't fall into the error of confusing selling with marketing. Making sales is the end result of a carefully planned and effectively carried out marketing strategy. And marketing strategy pulls together all the resources of the business that must be used to perfect a unique idea for product or service and carry it through to profitable sales.

You should therefore picture marketing as a *system* of business activities designed to plan, price, promote, and distribute want-satisfying product or service to existing and potential customers at a profit. This definition emphasizes three critical points:

1. Marketing requires successful relationships and interaction among the business activities that make up the marketing system. Marketing is not a single isolated activity. It is not an assortment of random activities. It *is* a purposeful set of activities, guided by a carefully thought out network of plans, which, in turn, are keyed to a master strategy.

2. Marketing is a managed set of activities. Entrepreneurs must take the responsibility for managing the marketing system of their firms. This includes analyzing, planning, and controlling activities both inside and outside the business.

3. Marketing must be based on a customer orientation. What the customer needs may suggest product or service to fill that need. But only when the need is transformed into a *want* can there be a sale.

As the top executive in your business, you have the responsibility to manage your marketing system. Interestingly enough, your management affects both the inside and the outside of your firm. By doing the right things inside, you can influence your market outside to produce sales. Your customers will see only the outcome of your marketing system. They will see, evaluate, and be influenced to buy your product or service—or not to buy. If they buy, they'll get satisfaction or not get satisfaction from your product or service. It will be your job to develop a marketing system that will convert customer needs into customer wants and sales into customer satisfaction—and profit for you.

Objectives of This Chapter

This chapter aims at introducing marketing as a system of relationships and activities subject to understanding, analysis, and proactive management. If you hold to a customer orientation and manage your marketing system intelligently, your business can prosper. The major objectives of this chapter are to:

- Introduce the concept of marketing as a manageable system

- Explain marketing myopia and its dangers

- Emphasize the importance of viewing your product or service through your customer's eyes

- Define market segmentation and its importance to your business

- Outline the forces of change in the environment and point out how you can find beneficial opportunities in these changing forces

Achieving a Customer Orientation

Business
Plan
Outline
1.B, 5

Your philosophy of business will significantly affect how you plan, launch, and manage your firm. What you value guides the formulation of your philosophy. If you think more highly of the product you have nurtured than of the needs of your potential customers, your business philosophy will be self-centered. You will be looking inward to serve your own needs. This is a dangerous trap you should avoid. Customers don't care about your needs; they care only about their own. You should understand clearly that satisfying the needs of your customers is the only reason for the existence of your company. This is the essence of the *marketing concept*.

The marketing concept should be the foundation of your business. Embedded in this foundation should be two precepts: (1) All planning, policies, and operations of your business should be oriented toward the customer in some way. (2) Your business objective should be to make sales at enough volume—and a high enough price—to produce adequate profit for the time, energy, and money you've put into the business.

AVOIDING MARKETING MYOPIA

As we've indicated, it's dangerous to fall in love with your product or service. If you think your business offers the greatest gadget ever devised to do a certain task—

and that everyone who sees it will buy it—you're in for a severe shock. The buying public couldn't care less about your product or you. They care about what they need. And only by offering them what they need and by converting need into want can you be successful. So don't fall in love with your product or service. Respect it; consider it worthwhile. But be objective enough to change it, modify its performance, or even discard and replace it with something else if it doesn't suit your customers.

In the early days of industrial expansion, it might well have been true that the world would beat a path to the door of the producer of a better mousetrap. Today this isn't true. Consumers can choose from a limitless array of products and services. Entrepreneurs who believe that consumer appeal will be generated by forcing their own perceptions of a desirable product or service on the market are in for bitter disappointment.

Therefore, offer your potential customers a product or service that will fulfill their needs. Don't become the victim of marketing myopia—shortsightedness that can trap you into bankruptcy, as it did John Galley, whose real-life case follows.

JOHN GALLEY

John Galley, a man who wanted to make his mark in the restaurant business, opened a small restaurant in a southern California beach community known for its concentration of high-income residents—movie stars, television producers, business executives, professional persons, writers, and artists. One value high in Mr. Galley's philosophy of business was shown in his statement that he wanted to capture the "carriage trade." He rented space for his restaurant at one end of a dilapidated motel on the landward side of the busy, four-lane divided coastal highway.

Mr. Galley adopted a ship's galley motif for his restaurant (no doubt influenced by his own surname and his closeness to the sea). Items on the menu were named for figures famous in the literature of adventure on the high seas: "Captain Hook's Seafood Platter," "Ishmael's New England Chowder," and the like. Prices were set at a level considerably higher than in competing restaurants along the highway.

Although he'd made elaborate preparation for the grand opening, the response was nowhere near what he had expected. Revenue was low during the first few months, which was not unexpected. But after 10 months, business hadn't improved. Friends suggested that Mr. Galley reduce prices to be in line with his competitors, who catered to the somewhat casual beach-going and local family trade. He was told by knowledgeable businesspersons in the community that his restaurant would never attract the wealthy patron because of its uninviting location and drab external appearance. Customers considered the food good, but not different enough or excellent enough to justify the high prices. They didn't return.

Mr. Galley was so bound by his own outlook that he persisted in trying to attract the well-known and wealthy. His reaction to his business's performance during its first year was, "Well, sales are low, but I offer the best food in town and I'll charge for it. If I can stay with it, the wealthy around here are going to discover me."

His response to advice was, "I'm not going to appeal to families with kids. Why should I? What this town needs is a high-class restaurant."

The business went into its second year with a few marketing changes. Some special dishes were added to the menu and a brightly lighted sign was installed facing the highway. Sales levels remained unprofitable, but Mr. Galley insisted that, "Word'll get around. They'll find my restaurant, you just wait!" Unfortunately, it was John Galley who waited. He waited until he exhausted his savings, until he fell behind in his rent, and until his suppliers withdrew credit. He was forced to close the restaurant after 18 months.

Soon after it closed, the restaurant was reopened under a new name by a seasoned restaurateur. He changed the marketing approach radically with some obvious steps.

He simplified the menu and reduced prices; he offered reasonably priced luncheon specials to the local businesspersons; he featured family-style dinners. In addition to these product changes, he advertised heavily in the local neighborhood papers and carried out a direct-mail advertising campaign in the area. His venture started earning profit after the first 6 months.

What was John Galley's major fault that caused his business to fail?

What steps did his successor take to achieve profitable operation?

What Business Are You Really in?

Defining your business from the customer's point of view is the first step in avoiding marketing myopia. Think about the kinds of customer satisfaction your product or service gives. What kinds of needs are fulfilled by consuming what you have to sell? In short, look at your business through the eyes of your potential customers.

One of the most successful locksmiths in New York City affords an excellent example of how to define a business. This entrepreneur and his two sons sell, install, and maintain security systems for commercial and residential use. When the father was asked recently why, in the midst of dozens of other similar businesses, he is so successful, he replied, "Because I know what I sell—I sell peace of mind." This entrepreneur isn't just selling locks. He's selling products that meet a basic customer need—security, and he defines his business in these terms.

Colonel Sanders's Kentucky Fried Chicken is another example of how to define a business. The things that are sold besides fried chicken—convenience, food at reasonable prices, family atmosphere, and standardized quality—contribute materially to the success of this business.

Answering the question: What business are you in? can pay handsome dividends. A casual answer begs the question and is therefore nonproductive. A proper answer takes hard thought and careful formulation—and can open new vistas for growth of the business.

WHAT BUSINESS SHOULD WE BE IN?

A small midwest manufacturing firm asked for consulting help to reverse losses they were experiencing after several years of profitable sales. This firm made bench-sized environmental test chambers used in engineering laboratories. Miniature electric motors, electronic controls, and similar devices could be run under load within these chambers at controlled temperatures, from -300 to $+1000°F$. Increasing competition had forced the company to lower prices and eventually reduce production.

The consultant met with the five top managers and asked the key questions: *What business are we in?* and *What business should we be in?* The first response was "We make environmental test chambers for our customers." This did not at all satisfy the consultant. It sounded to him as if they had said something like, "We can beans for our customers."

The consultant then asked the group, "What needs are you serving for your customers now?" and "What needs could you satisfy that you are not satisfying now?" The group worked on these questions for three days and after this period of hard thinking came up with the following response: "The one variable we are now working with is ambient air temperature. But we could control other variables: air pressure and humidity."

The engineers in the company thought they could control pressure within the chambers readily enough, but humidity would be harder. Eventually they are able to do both, although the development of humidity control took ingenuity and commitment. With the ability to offer temperature, pressure, and humidity control in its chambers, the company increased its potential national market by an order of magnitude, from 10 million to 100 million dollars per year.

The first trial order it received in the new product line was from a large computer manufacturer for a quarter of a million dollars of humidity-controllable chambers. Thus by properly defining its business in terms of satisfying customer needs, the company opened a vast new market that quickly brought them back to prosperity.

Explain why it is important to answer these two questions:

What business are we in?

What business should we be in?

The first step in developing the marketing system for your business is to answer the question: What business are you really in?

FORCES OF CHANGE

At the right of the diagram in Figure 4-1 is an irregular area called the market. This area may be thought of as the overall market, whether it's a neighborhood, a city, a nation, or a cluster of nations. It's filled with people of all ages, colors, backgrounds, and levels of education. The men and women and boys and girls within it have a wide variety of needs, wants, and expectations. They perceive the world in many different ways, depending on their upbringing, conditioning, and education. They have greatly varied expectations about what a new product or service will do for them. And they are continually exposed to the forces of change that modify their needs, wants, perceptions, and expectations.

Within the market area is a small oval labeled "submarket." This is the segment of the market that you're interested in—it's the specific market you'll want to reach. You will concentrate your effort on the ultimate task of making sales within this *market segment*.

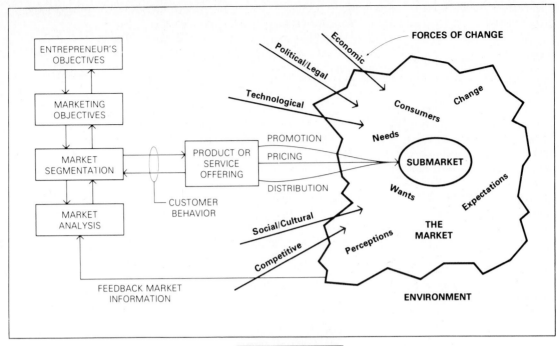

FIG. 4-1

The marketing system of the small business.

The external forces shown along the left side of the diagram produce changes in the market; these forces are beyond your control. Nevertheless, you must try to analyze each for its effect on the behavior of your customers and on the position of your company in your submarket and sometimes in the market.

Economic Forces   Any change in the economy directly affects the amount of money people can spend and the prices they must pay. Inflation and recession have occurred simultaneously in recent times, and the small business failure rate has risen. How does this strange combination of economic forces—*stagflation*—affect consumers? For one thing, they postpone buying some kinds of products and services; for another, they eliminate luxury items from their budget; and they exercise much more care in buying. They look for quality and value in what they buy. Inflation can also speed the buying process. People often decide to buy now in anticipation of higher prices to come.

   Are there opportunities for your small business in a period of stagflation? Perhaps so. Consumers seek value, particularly in products and services, at such a time. They select products that perform well and promise to have a long life and services that offer special rewards. You should be aware that value doesn't necessarily mean low price. *Value* is an illusory term—it's in the mind of the buyer. For example, during 1974, shortly after the Arab oil boycott, luxury car prices declined. The sales of luxury automobiles at lower prices actually increased while sales of medium-priced cars decreased across the board. Purchasers saw increased value in luxury cars at depressed prices, even though these cars burned more gasoline at inflated cost per gallon than the smaller cars.

Value for consumers can lie in personalized, friendly service, trust in the entrepreneur or in the reputation of the business, high quality of the product or service, or status in owning something unique. These are the value considerations you can offer as a businessperson. Your small business, by its inherent characteristics, can readily give personalized service to your customers. In addition, you can build trust and a reputation for excellence by ensuring high quality in what you offer in goods or service.

It's easier for your small business to give these values than it is for the large corporation with its arm's-length, automated, and computerized approach. Consumers are more skeptical and suspicious of large institutions than ever before—even angered by the power they wield. The rising number of product and store boycotts, the increasing size and activity of consumer action groups, and the recent increase in the number of antitrust suits brought by the U.S. Department of Justice attest to the distrust and frustration consumers experience in the marketplace. You can take advantage of this situation by building loyalty among your customers through personalized service and honest value.

Entrepreneurs must keep on top not only of the overall economic picture and its impact on their segment of the market but also of the regional or local economic picture. Regional variation in economic activity and sensitivity to the business cycle make this analysis necessary. You should therefore look to your local bank and business associations for up-to-the-minute information on the state of, and prospects for, the local economic situation.

Political-Legal Forces Shopping behavior can be influenced by political change and by political decisions. Sometimes this happens through economic policy, sometimes, more subtly, through the confidence inspired by apt political leadership. Local governments often make policy and decisions that directly affect the consumer market, especially in real estate and housing. Changes in codes and local ordinances may affect the entrepreneur's business. If your business is subject to these kinds of change, it's wise for you to involve yourself in community affairs. You'll know what's going on and can often influence policy to avoid being hurt.

As an example, the manager of a small canning company in Arizona learned that his city was considering a ban on "convenience containers." This was of immediate concern to him because much of his revenue came from canning soft drinks. He had learned of the proposed action through membership in a citizen's advisory committee in the local government. He was able to block the ban by showing the city council studies indicating that adverse effects on employment and on his industry's antilitter program would follow such a decision. This manager was *proactive*— that is, able to foresee and *avoid* misfortune—because he had timely information from participation in community activities.

As the owner of a small business, you will obviously not be able to cover all bases. You'll have to exercise good judgment in selecting the part you should play in community activities. Whatever you decide to do, you'll get side benefits through such activities. You'll develop new business contacts and gain insights for improving your business.

Technological Change   Many small businesses have benefited from technological change. Technological advance is so widespread and rapid today that it defies cataloging. Any scientific advance may produce an opportunity for your small business. You may be able to devise newer and better ways to do something important to your product or service, or you may find something newer and better to do. As a small example, several kinds of digital readouts are now available. These take the form of displays that show a varying quantity in numerical form: Light-emitting diodes and liquid-crystal displays are two such kinds of readouts. These may be applied to show the temperature, time, or other desired quantity directly in numbers. They replace a dial and needle display. Users therefore don't have to estimate the position of a needle on a dial; the quantity being measured shows directly in numbers. The product becomes more attractive to the consumer through this kind of readout.

Many businesses have been founded on spinoffs from technological innovation. Plastic pipe, for example, can now be substituted for galvanized iron or copper in residential construction. The strength and resilience of this material have led some entrepreneurs to use it as frames for modern furniture. Plastic pipe is easy to work into various shapes, is pleasing to the eye, makes durable and comfortable furniture, and is inexpensive.

Sometimes "reverse technology"—developing something simpler or less sophisticated—opens business opportunities. Hand-driven clothes washers using plastic wringers have been produced and successfully marketed in developing countries. Home wine-making kits are another example of reverse technology.

Government-sponsored research and development have started many new businesses. The Small Business Administration (SBA) maintains an inventory of inventions, improved materials, and new processes coming from research funded by the federal government. This information is public property and can be tapped free of charge by the entrepreneur. Research and development sponsored by NASA, for example, produced a light, compact energy cell for use on the moon rover. This technological advance resulted in a product developed by one entrepreneur for propelling wheelchairs used by paraplegics.

Although technological change brings opportunities in some areas, it produces obsolescence in others. You should keep abreast of "the state of the art," as it can affect your business for better or for worse. If you're aware, you can avoid the impact of obsoleting forces and take advantage of new product or service ideas that flow from this external force for change.

Social and Cultural Change   The small firm can be extremely vulnerable to the forces of social and cultural change. In most cases, the business *responds* to social or cultural change; in very few instances does the business introduce it. You must train yourself to be aware of what is going on in society—the changes that are taking place in life styles, custom, and social or cultural trends. These can have important consequences for your small business. You can identify new products or services to fit a newly growing need, or avoid the pitfall of obsolescence by withdrawing an existing product or service from the market.

A fascinating example of social and cultural change may be seen in the "movement," or counterculture, which has had a large impact on business. The movement cannot be neatly defined but may be clearly seen in the behavioral patterns of a good part of the younger segment of the population. These young people have rejected many traditions and much customary behavior. Their life-style centers around sensory experiences and their preference is for "natural" food. New enterprises catering to the needs of this segment of the population have sprung up and multiplied. Several examples of enterprises that started in a small way are now found everywhere in businesses such as head shops, health food, organic gardening supplies, and water beds. Music and stereo equipment businesses and industries have enjoyed commercial success, as have "natural" cosmetics, mod clothing, and van autos.

We shouldn't make the mistake, however, of tying social and cultural change to any one age group. Men of all ages have shed traditional styles and colors for multicolored, high-fashion clothing. Variety seems to be the key in the newer men's fashions.

We can't speak of social change as permeating American society; we would be wrong to characterize the United States as having one culture. We should recognize that the national market includes several subcultures of differing life-styles.

One significant change seems widespread and growing, and it offers all kinds of opportunity for the entrepreneur. It is the rise of what might be called "experiential" products or services. These are products or services in which the buyer participates and experiences some personal satisfaction, as opposed to the passive involvement in watching baseball games or television programs. Among the experiential products are games, hobby kits, crafts, how-to books, do-it-yourself kits, organic gardening, all kinds of sporting goods, and fix-it and build-it-yourself items.

Alvin Toffler points out in *Future Shock* that "As rising affluence and transience ruthlessly undercut the old urge to possess, consumers begin to collect experiences as consciously and passionately as they collected things."[1]

Toffler identified among the social trends of the seventies the compelling need for people to collect experiences rather than things. In his book, *Megatrends,* John Naisbitt points out that with the growing pervasiveness of high-tech during the eighties, it has become more important than ever for human beings to experience the human touch.[2] Our high-tech information age tends to isolate human beings. Sitting in front of a computer screen does nothing to promote human interaction, nor does working at home by communicating electronically with the office. Such isolation smacks too much of solitary confinement. Human beings seek rapport with others; they must have interaction with others to maintain psychological health.

In Naisbitt's words, "The more high technology around us, the more the need for human touch." We can project that experiential goods and services will grow along with the growth of high-tech. Goods or services of these kinds almost always

---

[1]Alvin Toffler, *Future Shock,* Random House, New York, 1971, p. 200.
[2]John Naisbitt, *Megatrends,* Warner Books, New York, 1982, Chap. 2.

require human companionship to serve the needs for which they're designed. What good is hitting a hole in one on an empty golf course, or scoring 300 in bowling with no companion to share the triumph?

The increasing desire for interesting experiences opens many opportunities for small businesses in such fields as recreation, entertainment, and education. One entrepreneur saw an opportunity in the reactions of the passengers who had been stranded for several days on the *Queen Elizabeth II* when her engines failed in the Caribbean Sea. They said their experience was "exciting," "you can't buy an unexpected fascinating time like that," and "it was a great adventure."

The entrepreneur grasped the opportunity to set up a vacation travel service that offers tours that don't spell out for the client exactly what will happen. Clients choose a tour, within the area of their special interest, such as golf, mountain climbing, flowers, opera, or art. The agency makes all arrangements, including a way of reaching clients' families if necessary. Clients don't know what's going to happen; they're intrigued by the possibilities of the unknown. For example, in an opera tour, the cities rather than the operas may be an unknown; in art, the particular museum may be unknown.

Marketing experiential value is more apparent in the service business than in any other. Airlines have discovered, for example, that an important marketing factor is not the sale of transportation alone but the sale of an experience as well. After all, one airline's planes look like and operate much like another's. Therefore, the airlines now offer carefully designed psychological packages on each major flight. Passengers are given choices in the menu; travel information specialists offer counsel; fashionably dressed flight attendants serve food and drinks; passengers may see color movies and hear stereo music of their choice. Even the decor of the cabins is carefully designed to be attractive.

The Esalen Institute at Big Sur, California, sells human awareness and interpersonal experiences, as does the National Training Laboratories at Bethel, Maine. Even traditional universities have discovered that rather than "retail" facts, concepts, and theories in their extension programs for adults, they can be more successful by offering "intellectual growth," "increased personal awareness," or "expanded human potential."

The desire for experiential products or services can have important implications for your business. Whether you're going into manufacturing, retailing, or service, you can probably benefit from this trend. From landscape consulting to body-awareness classes, from specialized travel agencies to participative home games, from lessons in cross-country skiing to raising ladybird beetles for insect control, consumers seek the unstandardized, the novel, the unique personal experience. You should therefore search for ways to benefit from people's desire to be personally involved in doing something interesting and exciting.

Yet another trend is worth exploration for new business ideas. This trend may be called "use without ownership." What is involved is the renting or leasing of almost anything. Consumers want to rent tools, mobile homes, cars, furniture, appliances, clothing, and even people: secretaries, maids, cooks, gardeners, babysitters, and companions.

Increased mobility of consumers has created needs that are being met by new small businesses. About 20 percent of the population of the United States moves every year. These people represent a special market of large size. They have needs for products or services that are convenient and save time and space. Items moved by singles or young couples have been found usually to include expensive stereo equipment, clothing, and a few cherished belongings. The remaining household items were either discarded or returned to the agency from which they were rented.

One small company in a midwestern city took advantage of the increase in intracity moves made by upwardly mobile young people. This enterprising company developed a moving service to give fast, dependable, low-cost, one-day service. It included an apartment decorating and furnishing service with its business, creatively combining the physical task of moving with serving the settling-in and decorating needs that follow.

Competitive Forces   The foundation of capitalism is open and healthy competition among business firms. Competition requires that the firm continually adjust its marketing strategies and tactics. If your new business is successful and enjoys a monopoly in its market area, you should expect, and be prepared for, other firms to enter and try to copy your success.

The chances for a small firm's survival are greatly improved if the entrepreneur exploits the strengths that launched the new business rather than resorts to cutthroat price competition. Large business offers a lesson for small business; instead of competing through price cutting, large companies compete on the basis of brand image, promotional activities, or store location. Your small business should compete by offering uniqueness, personalized service, and value—building on its special strengths.

The threat of competition highlights the need for two critical competitive tools. First, you should be continually alert for new products or services to offer your customers. Customers, especially repeat customers, have a "what-have-you-done-for-me-lately" attitude. They look for innovation. Your small company can't hope to outadvertise large firms; advertising wars are as disastrous as price wars and should be avoided. Therefore, you must strive to meet competition with new or refined products or services.

Second, you should plan your market segmentation very carefully. You should use a rifle, not a shotgun, approach to marketing in your business. One of the greatest weaknesses of small business is the failure to define the specific submarket it intends to reach. Most small businesses don't take much capital to enter. With barriers to entry low, you must build awareness of your store and product or service quickly; your objective should be to develop customer loyalty before competitors enter your market.

Marketing efforts can be tailored for maximum impact to maintain customer loyalty by defining *target* markets. We'll cover this in the next chapter.

Seizing Opportunities of Change

Summary

As a prospective enterpriser, you should see your marketing effort as a system of organized activities aimed at satisfying your customers' needs. You should understand the critical impact of external forces on the market and on your submarket. These forces pose both opportunities and threats. As a beginner about to start your own business, you should concentrate on identifying the opportunities; later it will be important for you to recognize the threats as well. Your alertness to change of all kinds will allow you to seize and capitalize on emerging trends. You'll avoid the danger of becoming a me-too business by offering unique, attractive goods or services.

Your Business as a Marketing System

1. Develop a marketing description of your business. Answer the question, from the customer's viewpoint: What business am I really in?

_____

_____

_____

_____

_____

_____

_____

_____

_____

_____

2. For each of the forces of change listed below, give at least _one_ example of how current events, apparent trends, or changing conditions could affect your business. Answer the question: How will my business (or my submarket) be affected by changes in each of these factors?

   a. Economic: How could I offset rising prices by giving extra value through specialized service?

   _____

   _____

   _____

   _____

   _____

   b. Political/Legal: What community, civic, or local business group should I join? My choice of group and why I chose it:

   _____

   _____

   _____

   _____

   _____

   _____

   _____

c. What change in the law is likely to affect my business and how do I plan to cope with it?

_____

_____

_____

_____

d. Technological: What is my action plan for keeping on top of advances in my field of business?

_____

_____

_____

_____

e. Social/Cultural: How can I profit by seizing opportunities opened up by change in fashion, custom, or social trends?

_____

_____

_____

_____

f. Competitive: What is my most threatening competition? How do I plan to meet it?

_____

_____

_____

_____

This worksheet is intended merely as a sample of the kind of thinking you must continue to do as long as you're in business. Change of almost any kind offers opportunities for those who can see and grasp them. Alertness to change can open opportunities to you.

KEY TERMS

marketing 61
system 61
marketing myopia 62
market segment 65

stagflation 66
reverse technology 68
experiential products or services 70

STUDY ASSIGNMENTS FOR REVIEW AND DISCUSSION

1. Why is marketing considered a *system?*

2. What is meant by marketing myopia?

3. Describe several classes of forces of change in the environment and how they may be seen to influence consumer behavior.

4. What is meant by "reverse technology," and how could a small business take advantage of it?

5. As a small businessperson, what advantages in marketing might you have over your large competitor?

PROJECTS FOR STUDENTS

1. Write a paragraph telling how you might make sure you have achieved a customer orientation to a product you have developed.

2. Do some library research to find two or three cases in which companies have come to grief because of marketing myopia. (*Example:* Henry Ford, during the last days of the Model T, is supposed to have said that buyers of Ford cars could have any color they wanted—as long as it was black.)

3. Write a paragraph on how periods of inflation coupled with recession affect consumers' purchasing habits.

4. List as many businesses as you can that offer products based on reverse technology. If you can find ads for such products, show them in class.

5. Drawing on your innovative ability, write a brief statement of an experiential product or service.

6. Assume you are going to start a travel agency. Assume your location, class of trade, kind of specialty; business travel, vacation tours, or general travel; decide on other key variables. When you've decided what the issues are, write a statement defining your business.

IF YOU WANT TO READ MORE

ADLER, Lee: "Systems Approach to Marketing," *Harvard Business Review,* May–June 1967, pp. 105–118. This article gives several benefits stemming from the use of the systems concept in marketing. It presents a practical method for problem solving and identifying opportunities.

BREEN, George Edward: *Do-It-Yourself Marketing Research,* McGraw-Hill Book Company, New York, 1982. This book is a practical guide that shows the non-professional how to accomplish marketing research in an unbiased manner. It presents simple procedures to check marketing, sales, and product decisions.

GROSS, Alfred: "Adapting to Competitive Change," *MSU Business Topics,* winter 1970. The author uses as a model a retail firm to illustrate the dos and don'ts of anticipating and reacting to competition.

KOTLER, Philip: *Principles of Marketing,* Prentice-Hall, Inc., Englewood Cliffs, NJ, 1983. Chapter 7, "The Marketing Environment," is an excellent summary of current trends and projections for the future in the demographic, economic, ecological, technological, political, and cultural environments.

KOTLER, Philip, and Keith COX (eds.): *Marketing Management and Strategy,* Prentice-Hall, Inc., Englewood Cliffs, NJ, 1984. This is an excellent presentation of classic marketing problems and strategies. Included are recent articles that open new analytical pathways in marketing. An especially valuable section, "Marketing Management," contains Theodore Levitt's article, "Marketing Myopia."

KURTZ, David L., and Louis E. BOONE: *Marketing,* The Dryden Press, New York, 1984. Chapter 2, "The Environments of Marketing," is one of many excellent sections of this textbook. The authors analyze the impact of competitive, political, legal, economic, technological, and societal environments on marketing strategy.

LEVITT, Theodore: *The Marketing Imagination,* The Free Press, New York, 1983. In the first chapter, the author stresses the often repeated dictum: the imperative requirement of understanding the needs and wants of prospective customers. Management must focus on what goes on in the marketplace rather than what is possible in the factory, according to the author.

MCCARTHY, E. Jerome: *Basic Marketing,* 5th ed., Richard D. Irwin, Homewood, IL, 1984. This book presents an excellent discussion of how government and legislation affect small and large business.

NAISBITT, John: *Megatrends,* Warner Books, Inc., New York, 1982. This book spells out the changing scene in the economy of the United States. On the basis of a dozen years of careful study of 6000 local newspapers by the method of *content analysis,* the Naisbitt Group, a consulting organization, identifies 10 movements in new directions that are changing our society. These represent a surging tide, driving us from an industrial to an information processing economy. Those venturing into business and those managing existing businesses will find this book stimulating and provocative. Study of its contents will surely trigger ideas for new things to do to build or expand a business.

ROBICHEAUX, Robert A., William M. PRIDE, and O. C. FERRELL (eds.): *Marketing—Contemporary Dimensions,* Houghton Mifflin Company, Boston, 1982. The articles in this book were drawn from a wide variety of traditional and nontraditional sources of marketing articles.

SCHEWE, Charles D., and Reuben M. SMITH: *Marketing Concepts and Applications*, McGraw-Hill Book Company, New York, 1983. An introductory textbook on marketing. The book affords a comprehensive treatment of fundamentals in marketing. Basic concepts are illustrated with many examples from real life.

TOFFLER, Alvin: *Future Shock*, Bantam Books, New York, 1971. A thorough description of social change in the United States, this book shows opportunities for small business and gives likely consumer purchasing patterns in the future.

CHAPTER 5

Analyzing Your Market and Consumer Behavior

TOPICS IN THIS CHAPTER

Objectives of This Chapter
Who Buys?
Why Do Consumers Buy?
What Do They Buy?
How Do They Buy?
Where Do They Buy?
When Do They Buy?
Market Segmentation
Pinpointing the Marketing Questions You Must Answer—
Summary
Worksheet 5: Your Market and Consumer Behavior
Key Terms
Study Assignments for Review and Discussion
Projects for Students
If You Want to Read More

The sixth item in the flow diagram of the business process (Figure 1-1) is MAR-KETING. This chapter addresses a special element of this sixth item: getting detailed information about your market and customer behavior. You'll build on the marketing orientation developed in Chapter 4 to pinpoint the specific answers to the questions of: Why will the customer buy your product or service; who'll buy; what, how, where, and when do customers buy? At the close of the chapter you'll find recommendations for sources of information from which you can develop your answers to these questions.

Information in this chapter will be found pertinent to these items in the Business Plan:

1.A.   Description of your proposed business

1.B.   Summary of your proposed marketing method

2.A.   Statement of the desirability of your product or service

3.B.   Detailed explanations of your place in the state of the art

4.A.   Technical description of product or service

5.A.   A comprehensive description of marketing strategy

6.A.   An outline of the activities to be used in selling the product or service

8.A.   Information required to support the major points in the business plan

$$\text{You} + \text{Idea} + \begin{Bmatrix} \text{Money} \\ \text{Credit} \end{Bmatrix} + \begin{Bmatrix} \text{Facilities} \\ \text{People} \end{Bmatrix} \begin{matrix} \text{Product} \\ \rightarrow \quad \text{or} \\ \text{Service} \end{matrix} + \textbf{MARKETING} \begin{Bmatrix} \text{Money} \\ \text{Credit} \end{Bmatrix} \rightarrow \text{Profit}$$

In this chapter we look at those elements of the marketing system shown in heavy lines in Figure 5-1. These include market analysis and segmentation through identification of the unique characteristics of your submarket. We'll suggest ways for you to find out who your customers are and where they are.

Objectives of This Chapter

After studying this chapter you'll be ready to take specific steps, with very little out-of-pocket cost, to analyze your market. From the information you collect you'll develop a detailed profile of the "ideal" consumer in the segment of the market you're trying to reach. You'll be prepared to answer these six basic questions:

- *Who buys?* Who are in your target market? What are their characteristics that would make them buy from you?

- *Why do consumers buy?* Why will they buy your products or services?

- *What do they buy?* Which products or services do they typically choose? What brands do they prefer? How do they allocate their income? And how much discretionary income do they have—that is, income above what is needed for necessities?

FIG. 5-1

The marketing system of the small business.

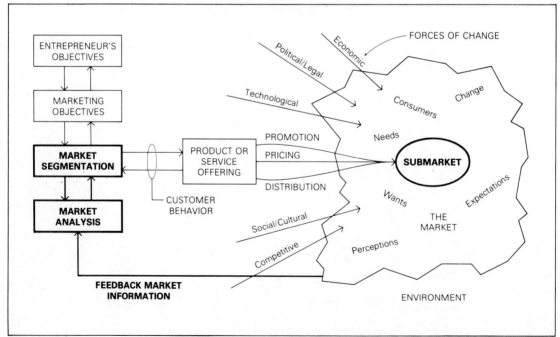

How do they buy? Do they shop around for your kind of product or service, or do they buy when or where it is convenient? Do they prefer to pay cash or use personal credit or a credit card?

Where do they buy? Do your potential customers prefer to buy from retail stores, through mail order, or from door-to-door salespeople? How far will they travel to buy what they want?

When do they buy? Do seasonal influences affect the shopping behavior of your intended customers? How do holidays influence their shopping behavior?

You'll need to know how to answer these key questions thoroughly at minimum cost, where to go to acquire the necessary information, and how to use the information you assemble. This chapter will guide you in accomplishing these tasks. After studying it, you'll be ready to take specific steps, with very little out-of-pocket expense, to analyze your market.

Who Buys?

Business
Plan Outline
1.B, 5.A

Two parties are involved in a simple sale of goods: a seller and a buyer. The sale itself may be thought of as a transaction or exchange. The exchange takes place when the product or service moves from supplier to consumer to satisfy a need in return for payment. Although we are interested in pinpointing who it is that buys, upon analyzing different kinds of transactions we find that the exchange in a sale is not always as simple as a sale between two people.

Many selling transactions involve several people, each playing one or more of six different roles. These roles may be described as follows:

Initiators, persons who get the original idea for buying the product or service

Influencers, persons who sway the buying decision in a direction they prefer

Deciders, those who make the buying decision

Buyers, the ones who actually make the purchase

Consumers, those who use the product or service

Evaluators, those who make judgments about the quality of the goods or services bought

To show these relationships, consider the case in which mother, father, and son are just finishing dinner and mother speaks up, "I got home too late from the dentist's to fix dessert for dinner tonight. Why don't you two hop in the car and bring home something from the market while I tidy up?" (Mother, the initiator.)

Father and son agree to go. In the car, the son says, "Hey, Dad, I noticed that Baskin-Robbins has just come out with this month's new flavor, Plum Nuts. Why don't we get some?" (Son, the influencer.)

Father and son talk it over and agree to try it. (Both are deciders.) At the store, father orders a quart of Plum Nuts ice cream and pays for it. (Father, the buyer.) When they get home, all three share the ice cream. (All consumers.)

"When I saw that you brought home ice cream with that strange name I was sure it would be pretty bad. But it's very good," said mother.

"Yep," said father and son, "it's really first rate." (All three evaluators.)

In many cases one person can play all six roles, as, for example, a small boy selecting, buying, and eating a candy bar. The important idea for our purpose is to understand the need to reach all persons in our segment of the market who can influence the sale in our direction.

DEMOGRAPHIC FACTORS

Demographic variables help you measure the characteristics of consumers: age, sex, ethnic background, family composition, social class, income, and the like. From this information you can build a description of the typical customer you aim to attract. You'll then want to find out how many of these potential customers live in an area you identify as a possible market segment adequate for your business.

Buying habits are shaped to a great extent by family influence, reference groups, and the social class to which that person belongs.

Family Influence   The family presents a potent source of group influence on the individual consumer. When we marry, we become customers for many kinds of household equipment and goods. We buy furniture, a refrigerator, washing machine, vacuum cleaner, and all manner of supplies.

Later in life, when the children have left home to establish their own lives, parents find their needs have changed. They now become consumers of a different class. They get rid of their large houses and buy condominiums or move into a mobile home in Florida. They develop needs for medical assistance, hearing aids, and leisure-time activities.

A shift in the roles of who buys within the family is taking place in today's world. The wife traditionally made most of the household purchases while the husband often was the final authority on major purchases such as a freezer or trash compactor. Today, with both husband and wife likely to be working, either or both may be found shopping in the supermarket.

Reference-Group Influence   Purchasing behavior is often influenced by reference groups. Reference groups provide a standard—a point of reference—in selection of clothing, cigarettes, beer, cars, magazines, and many other items. The individual may or may not belong to the reference group and yet will be influenced by its customs and social values. For example, a high school student attains high status through owning a car. His reference group, the other students with whom he associates, value possession of "wheels." But some cars trigger more status in the group than others: the student who drives his own MG acquires a higher status than one who drives a beat-up 1968 Ford.

Reference-group pressure shows itself strongly in both product and brand within the product line. But it is particularly strong in items that are clearly visible and have somehow acquired the aura of social status.

It is not easy to take advantage of reference-group influence in planning a marketing campaign. Potential customers may be a member of several reference groups: a professional club, a church, a service club, a fraternal organization, and others. However, as a marketer you might on occasion be able to work with a product that is specifically subject to reference-group influence. For example, at the U.S. Grant High School in a western city, the students chose blue and gray as the school colors. A local department store, taking advantage of reference-group influence, was able to sell a few sweaters with vertical blue and gray stripes to several of the student social leaders. Following their example, literally hundreds of students bought similar sweaters.

Social-Class Influence Buying habits are influenced by the social class to which the consumer belongs. Research done by W. Lloyd Warner in the 1940s and by Pierre Martineau in Chicago during the late 1950s showed that both large and small cities exhibit a six-class social structure. Membership in a given class is determined by occupation, source of income (not amount), family background, neighborhood, and education. A description of the members of each class and an estimate of the percentage of population in each is given in Table 5-1.

Social class can be very important in helping you segment your market. You'll want to use different ways and different media in communicating with members of different social classes. If you offer high-priced quality merchandise such as imported Irish sweaters, you might advertise in *The New Yorker* magazine, a journal read mostly by those in the affluent upper middle and higher social classes. You would not place your ads in *True Love Stories*. Nor would you place ads for do-it-yourself products in *The New Yorker,* but you might in *The Country Journal*. In the same way you'd choose the radio station most appropriate for reaching the social class of your target market—the station that broadcasts the kind of programs your consumers prefer.

Why Do Consumers Buy?

Business
Plan Outline
2.A, 3.B, 8.A

Psychological theory holds that human behavior aims at satisfying needs. A widely accepted theory of human behavior along this line was originated by Abraham Maslow.[1] We can gain insight into many parts of our marketing efforts by referring to Maslow's concepts from time to time.

Maslow stated that the human being is a wanting animal whose behavior is directed, consciously or not, at the satisfaction of needs of various kinds. A satisfied need does not motivate behavior; only needs that are not reasonably well satisfied can cause people to try to fulfill them. For example: When we're hungry, we seek food. After we've eaten, the need for food disappears and we turn our energies toward filling another need that has risen. Often we don't realize we're trying to satisfy a need, but the process goes on as long as we draw breath.

---

[1]Abraham H. Maslow, *Motivation and Personality*, Harper & Row, New York, 1954, chap. 5.

TABLE 5-1

The Influence of Social Class on Buying Behavior

Social Class	Behavioral Characteristics	Purchase Behavior	Percentage of Population
Upper upper	Socially prominent, with inherited wealth; elite club membership; children attend private schools and top colleges; social position in society is secure; can deviate from social norms more than other classes—because of security of social position	Spend money as if it were unimportant—but not ostentatiously; conservative clothing; elegance in social parties; possessions reflect British aristocracy— English Tudor homes, large lawns, servants	0.5
Lower upper	People who have "earned" their social position rather than inherited it (nouveaux riches): corporate president, successful entrepreneurs, well-to-do lawyers; socially mobile; college-educated, but not from top school; active people; highly seeking social esteem and prestigious social interactions; children showered with possessions	"Conspicuous consumption" is the rule; products symbolize their success and wealth: swimming pools, yachts, furs, large homes, designer-name clothing	2.5
Upper middle	Motivation centered on career; moderately successful professionals; owners of medium-sized companies, young junior executives on the rise; highly educated class, but usually from state college as opposed to prestige university; "gracious living" is life-style pattern followed; demanding of children; cultivate broad range of interests, from civic to cultural	Purchases reflect quality; want to be seen as fashionable, having a nice home in a nice neighborhood; purchases are conspicuous but not showy; automobile, home, and clothing are symbols of success	12.0
Lower middle	The "typical" American: law-abiding, hard-working, churchgoing; occupations focus on nonmanagerial office workers and blue-collar jobs; these people are continually striving to do a good job; respectability is the key motivation; conformity rather than innovativeness is the rule	Home is central possession: well-painted, respectable area; do-it-yourselfers; buy rather standard home furnishings; rely on magazines and retail literature for home-furnishings information; work hard at their shopping; quite price-sensitive	30.0

TABLE 5-1

(Continued)

CHAPTER 5

85

Analyzing
Your Market
and Consumer
Behavior

Social Class	Behavioral Characteristics	Purchase Behavior	Percentage of Population
Upper lower	"The working class"; routine day-to-day existence; jobs center on manual skills; reluctant to change; children are highly prized; little social contact outside of the home; vacations center on visiting relatives; have little expectation of social movement	Live in declining areas of city, in small houses; purchase behavior is impulsive with new products and brand-loyal with repeat purchases; like national brands	35.0
Lower lower	Unskilled workers and unemployed; characterized as apathetic, fatalistic, and bent on "getting one's kicks" while one can; poorly educated	Impulsive purchasing; often pay too much for products and buy inferior products; do not evaluate quality or search out valuable information	20.0

Source: Reproduced by permission. From Charles D. Schewe and Reuben M. Smith, *Marketing Concepts and Applications,* McGraw-Hill Book Company, New York, 1980, pp. 171–172.

Furthermore, needs can be arranged in sets in accordance with their power to impel behavior. Here they are given in the order Maslow originally listed.[2]

PHYSIOLOGICAL NEEDS

The physiological needs are primary. They include the basic requirements to sustain life: food, water, air, exercise, sex, rest, and sleep are typical.

SAFETY NEEDS

Human beings want to be free from fear, from being deprived of the basic needs given above. They prefer the known over the unknown, the clearly defined over the fuzzy and ill-defined, the familiar over the unfamiliar. These are known as the safety needs.

SOCIAL NEEDS

Social needs define the human being's needs for belongingness and love. These underlie the drives for building teams and working together in all kinds of human effort, work, and play.

[2]Ibid.

ESTEEM NEEDS

This set has two parts: the need for skill and the need for recognition. Mastery demonstrated supports the individual's self-confidence and self-respect. Appreciation expressed for demonstrated skill reinforces the motivating power of the esteem needs.

SELF-ACTUALIZATION NEEDS

This is another term for *self-fulfillment,* which suggests the driving force within human beings that urges them to become what they potentially can be—to bring to actuality latent talents or abilities.

AESTHETIC NEEDS

Before he died, Maslow told of his plan to add *aesthetic needs* to the hierarchy listed above. People want to surround themselves with attractive things—often with beautiful things: paintings, tapestries, sculpture, well-designed furniture, antiques, and artifacts of all kinds. People want to create many of these kinds of things themselves. Aesthetic needs offer the opportunities for qualified entrepreneurs who can set up businesses designed to fulfill them.

INFLUENCE OF ANTICIPATED CONSEQUENCES

The decision to buy or not to buy often comes from what we anticipate will be the consequences of our decision. We almost always automatically evaluate the decision—and we choose the alternative with the highest perceived *net* rewards.

Attached to any particular buying decision, such as having dinner at a restaurant versus eating at home, are several perceived consequences—both positive and negative. The husband's decision making in this case might be viewed as follows:

Positive Consequences	Negative Consequences
▪ I get a special dish that I really like ▪ The atmosphere will be peaceful and relaxing ▪ My wife and I get a night out ▪ I won't have to shop for dinner or help cook ▪ I won't have to clean up later	▪ Driving to get there, a tedious chore ▪ The dinner, expensive ▪ Parking, a nuisance ▪ Baby-sitter expenses

The husband, without formal analysis, decides that the rewards are greater than the negative outcomes. Therefore, he recommends that he and his wife eat out.

If the service at the restaurant has been poor and the dinner mediocre, the husband would probably suggest they eat at home the next time.

This way of facing buying decisions is often known as the *behavioral* approach. It says that the identification and comparison of possible outcomes of behavior determine future behavior. Therefore, in managing your own business, you should try hard to decide what your customers would see as positive and negative outcomes of buying your product or service. Whatever you can do to ensure that your customers perceive a positive outcome in their dealings with you will help to make them repeat customers.

THE FOCUS-GROUP INTERVIEW

The focus-group interview offers a useful tool for finding out why customers might or might not buy a product or service. You can use this method effectively in marketing a new product or service, or in making substantial changes in existing ones. You would gather a group of about ten people representing a cross section of your intended consumer population. Offer the participants refreshments, such as cheese and wine or coffee and sweet rolls, to make them comfortable.

Tell them that you propose to bring out this new widget; demonstrate a working model, or describe the new service in detail. Then ask direct questions in an objective manner about your proposed project. Don't sell; ask in an unbiased way. Ask questions such as: What do you see as advantages in using this widget? What do you see as disadvantages or problems with it? Make notes of the answers, or better still, tape-record the proceedings so you can analyze the responses at your leisure. Then ask: Would you be willing to pay x dollars for this item? If the answer is "too much," then ask: How much would you be willing to pay? By continuing in this way, as you see fit, you can get some idea of a price range that will help you set the selling price.

From the focus-group interview you'll get ideas of what to do to improve the product or service, what features to eliminate, and the approximate price range in which to set the retail price.

You'll want to repeat the focus-group interview with other participants perhaps three or four times. When you've assembled and analyzed all the data from the groups, you'll have solid information about improving the desirability of your offering to your consumers.

The value of the focus-group exercise was shown in the recent case of Elaine Woodworth, who inherited a large collection of antique bric-a-brac and a building in a run-down commercial section of a large city:

ELAINE WOODWORTH, ANTIQUE DEALER

Ms. Woodworth, being knowledgeable about antiques, decided to open her own antique store. She wasn't sure the building was in a location good for her proposed store. The area had numerous small boutiques and restaurants, and a few antique stores—most of them offering furniture and fixtures. Parking spaces were hard to find along the four-lane thoroughfare that bisected the area. Off-street parking was limited to 30 minutes. And the neighborhood was reputed to have a crime problem.

We assisted Ms. Woodworth in her efforts to determine why consumers might or might not shop in her store. First, we asked her to identify what she believed to be the positive and the negative consequences her customers might see. She believed that most of her potential customers were located across town in a high-income, exclusive neighborhood. The wide assortment of bric-a-brac, she believed, would give her an advantage over other antique stores that typically placed these items in small display cases and emphasized other kinds of antiques such as furniture.

Ms. Woodworth planned to charge lower prices than comparable stores because she would not have rent to pay.

We summarized Ms. Woodworth's assessment as follows:

Positive Consequences	Negative Consequences
▪ Wide assortment of bric-a-brac antiques ▪ Lower prices than similar stores in fashionable neighborhoods	▪ Travel time to get to store ▪ Shabby area in which to shop, with reputed danger of being held up or mugged

She concluded from her analysis that her prospects for success appeared to be blank. Her assessment suggested that to attract customers she would have to maintain a high-cost inventory with a wide assortment of items and sell them at a lower price than competitive stores. Furthermore, she'd have to interest consumers enough to drive across town to get to her store. And somehow, reasonable parking would have to be made available, and the negative image of her area would have to be overcome.

We suggested Ms. Woodworth take an additional step with her analysis before deciding whether to sell or rent the building and locate in the high-rent district of her major market. In order to make an informed judgment, data were needed from three different groups: (1) potential customers in the high-income neighborhood, (2) consumers who shopped in the commercial district where her building was located, and (3) proprietors in the immediate area of her building. We recommended the *focus-group interview* as a way she could collect these data herself.

Ms. Woodworth decided to conduct interviews with each of the three groups she identified. She started with potential customers in the high-income area.

She called acquaintances whom she knew were interested in antiques and invited them to a morning coffee at her home. She told her guests that she was planning to start her own business and needed their opinions on some unresolved issues. Twelve people participated in the interview, and she taped the entire session.

Ms. Woodworth told the group about her experience in the antique business; she described the antiques she'd sell and passed around several samples with the price attached to each; she showed them pictures of her building, described in detail the commercial district where it was located, and told them of her remodeling plans. To avoid biasing them, she did *not* tell about her own consumer analysis, and she asked them to be candid with her.

First, she asked each person to list the possible rewards or advantages of shopping in her store as compared with shopping in antique stores in their neighborhood. Second, she instructed each person to list the disadvantages or negative aspects they could see in her proposed business. Third, she asked them to rank items on their lists in order of importance to them. Fourth, she divided the twelve into subgroups of four and asked each subgroup to discuss their findings and to try to reach a combined rank-ordered list of advantages and disadvantages. Fifth, after the small groups had finished, she brought the whole group together and had one member of each subgroup report on that group's discussion.

A lively conversation about the problems followed. Ms. Woodworth reminded the group again to be candid with her. Additional information was volunteered as a result. Ms. Woodworth used probing questions to clarify and expand the discussion. For example, she asked, "What do you mean by that?" "Can you give me an example of what you're saying?" "Why is that the case?"

At the conclusion of the session, she thanked the group and gave the members gifts of antique trivets in appreciation of their help.

She then analyzed the data she had collected. In addition to studying the lists of the rewards and the negative consequences, she listened carefully to the tape recording to pick up anything she might have missed.

Ms. Woodworth was astonished at what she called her "naiveté" in analyzing consumer behavior. For example, the data revealed that there were *two* major market segments for her business—one composed of devoted bric-a-brac antique enthusiasts who would travel almost any distance to shop for rare items, and another that included casual antique buyers who would shop at irregular intervals and at stores convenient to them.

She also discovered that her expertise in antiques was more important to consumers than she'd thought. Other antique stores in the district might also help to attract customers from the high-income area to her store. Some of the group members had expressed some apprehension about shopping in the area because of reports of crime. However, they believed the area had "charm" and was unique because of the numerous old buildings and the concentration of boutique-type stores.

Most participants, she was surprised to learn, believed her proposed prices were too low; they said that the bric-a-brac buff wouldn't pay much attention to price and that the casual consumer wouldn't have enough experience to recognize whether the price was too high or too low.

Ms. Woodworth summarized the findings from the group interview as follows:

Anticipated Consumer Consequences of Shopping at My Store

Positive Consequences	Negative Consequences
▫ Experience and expertise of owner in her specialty of antiques ▫ Access to other types of antique stores in area ▫ Wide assortment of bric-a-brac antiques ▫ Pleasing store environment in which to shop ▫ Status of owning a hard-to-find bric-a-brac antique ▫ Interesting and unique area in which to shop	▫ Travel time to get to the commercial district where store is located ▫ Limited parking in the area ▫ Apprehension of crime in the area

Encouraged by her findings, Ms. Woodworth proceeded to interview consumers shopping in the district. She chose three days she knew to be days of high, moderate, and low business activity. She then conducted ten interviews each day at different locations. Her approach was to introduce herself to shoppers after they had come out of one of the antique stores; she explained that her purpose in the interview was to explore the possibility of opening a specialty store in the area.

Because her interviews had to be limited to a few minutes, her questions were descriptive. For example: Where do you live? Why did you choose this district to shop in? Were you browsing or did you have special items you've been shopping for? How often do you shop here? Would you shop in a store specializing in bric-a-brac antiques? What problems have you encountered in shopping in this area?

Her findings confirmed the idea that there were two market segments represented in the consumer traffic of the district: (1) antique collectors seeking special items who wouldn't be deterred by distance or parking difficulties, and (2) casual shoppers for antiques who drop in to browse and purchase what might catch their eye. Three-fourths of the consumers lived at least 3 miles from the district and shopped there about once a month. The rest were first-time shoppers who had driven through the area previously and had become interested enough to stop and shop. Most of these consumers lived within 1 mile of the district. The parking problem was mentioned often, but reputed crime in the area didn't appear to be a problem with those interviewed.

At this point, Ms. Woodworth began to think that the prospects for her store were looking up because many of the shoppers were already driving some distance to shop in the district, and some were from the high-income neighborhood that interested her. She was further encouraged to find that the district appealed to "drive-through" traffic because of its old-fashioned charm.

Her next step was to interview proprietors in the area. She wanted to see if there were possible solutions to the parking problem in the district, and whether cooperative efforts in promoting it in other ways would be feasible. She found that a store owner's association had been organized recently and that the membership was working with the city's transportation department to expand the local parking facilities. She met several proprietors who were keenly interested in cooperating to improve the image of the district.

Ms. Woodworth opened her antique store in the building she inherited about 8 months after she had finished her consumer interviews. The store is very profitable and continues to specialize in bric-a-brac antiques. Not only is Ms. Woodworth's store successful, but she has also capitalized on her expertise and is now retained by several wealthy buyers to travel around the world in search of rare antiques.

> Describe how Ms. Woodworth identified, analyzed, and resolved the critical factors that came from her study of the potential of the antique business she wanted to enter.

You can use approaches taken by Ms. Woodworth to gain insights into the behavior of consumers. You'll increase your chances for successful marketing efforts by emphasizing the things that potential customers perceive as rewarding and lessening or decreasing the factors they see as negative. Had Ms. Woodworth relied on her own intuition or guesswork, or even her first tentative analysis, she would never have opened her door to business in her own building.

The focus group interview takes a bit of skill to carry through successfully. Entrepreneurs who want to become familiar with this technique would do well to use the services of a competent consultant the first time or two. They should then run a focus group or two under the guidance of the consultant. After this practice they should be able to do as well as Ms. Woodworth.

Never be reluctant to ask good questions of anybody you think can help you. You should always remember that the *marketing concept* stresses consumer orientation every step of the way.

What Do They Buy?

Business
Plan Outline
1.A, 3.B, 4.A, 8.A

When we look at what people buy, we can generalize by including services with products. We usually think of a product as something tangible—we can see it, feel it, weigh it, and so on. Services, although usually intangible, nevertheless may be considered products. When we visit the dentist or consult with an accountant, we're buying a product consisting of knowledge and special competence. Therefore, when we look at what people buy, we'll use the word product to cover both tangibles and intangibles.

What people buy may be divided into two large groups: *consumer products* and *industrial products*. Consumer products are those intended for the ultimate consumer and not for resale or use in producing other goods. Industrial products are those used directly or indirectly in producing other products for resale. Both classes of goods are described in the following sections.

CONSUMER PRODUCTS

Although consumer products may be subdivided in different ways, a widely accepted method depends upon how consumers buy them. On this basis consumer products can be divided into four subgroups: *convenience items, shopping items, specialty items,* and *unsought items*.

Convenience Items Those products that the consumer wants to purchase often, with the least possible effort, are known as *convenience items*. Among convenience products would be gasoline, haircuts, cigarettes, newspapers, magazines, banking services, milk, and eggs. Consumers usually buy convenience products routinely, buying the same brand through habit when their supply gets low. They don't usually seek information about them.

Convenience items are often divided into three categories: *staple items, impulse items,* and *emergency items*.

Staple Items. These are convenience products for which consumers do some planning. Dairy products, milk, cheese, and butter are staple items. Consumers don't usually search for much information about them. But they do *plan* to buy these items when they head for the supermarket. Banking may be considered a staple product in that customers visit their banks routinely. They are likely to do a bit of planning ahead of the visit, but using a bank's services is ordinarily a habitual errand that doesn't demand much planning.

Buyers tend to look for familiar brands when purchasing staples, and they want staples to be readily accessible within the store.

Impulse Items. These items stimulate an unplanned desire to buy because of their exposure to the consumer. Point-of-purchase displays are designed to call customers' attention to items that otherwise would be overlooked. Magazines, gum, candy bars, novelty charms, and ball-point pens are displayed next to the cash register. Shoppers see these items when paying their bills and are stimulated to buy through recognizing a need that a specific item will call to mind. This kind of purchase is called an *impulse purchase*.

Emergency Items. These are items that are bought to take care of some kind of crisis. The customer gets satisfaction by finding what is needed to meet the immediate requirement quickly—when it is needed. A person suffering with an earache or toothache wants the pharmacist to produce a remedy immediately; delayed motorists with a slowly leaking tire want the filling station to repair it immediately before they take off down the highway. Price is of little moment in cases such as these. What is important is that the want be satisfied by the purchase. Posters and various kinds of displays can stimulate sales of emergency products by making consumers aware of products they normally do not plan to buy.

Shopping Products   As the name implies, shopping products are those on which consumers compare prices before deciding what to buy. They will ask their friends, check guides to comparative value such as *Consumer Reports*, study advertisements, and visit several stores to compare prices before deciding which item to buy.

Shopping products are classified in two groups: those that are perceived to be essentially alike (homogeneous products) such as transportation furnished by the different cross-country airlines, and those that are essentially different (heterogeneous products) such as hair-fashioning service or furniture.

Heterogeneous products pose less of a problem in marketing, because products are seen as different, with varied styles, aesthetic qualities, and different price ranges. Homogeneous products test the ingenuity of marketers to impress on consumers the superiority of their product over similar ones—they are forced to great lengths to differentiate the product they promote from their competitors'.

Specialty Products   Items for which there are no acceptable substitutes are known as *specialty products*. Usually the consumer has gone through a careful search to decide on exactly the product for the intended use. Consumers who have made this kind of decision will take unusual pains to find the outlet that handles the item they want. They will search long and hard to find a particular brand of shoe of a particular last and size to fit them. People do not want to accept substitutes for professional services from a doctor they've come to trust or a lawyer who has handled their legal matters successfully. The key point in marketing specialty products is understanding that consumers will take unusual pains to locate a source for what they're after—and they'll go to great lengths to travel to that source to make the purchase.

Unsought Products   Products consumers don't readily realize they need or want are called *unsought products*. Most new products fall into this category. Typical items are personal computers, VCRs, automatic telephone-answering devices, smoke detectors, CB car radios, and cellular phones. Cemetery plots and the services of morticians might well be included in unsought products.

In general, innovative new products fall into the category we've identified with new products—new markets in Chapter 3; this category requires intense marketing effort to produce a successful outcome—but it also offers the possibility for great profit.

A MARKETING MATRIX: MASLOW'S
HIERARCHY—CONSUMER PRODUCTS

One useful tool for pinpointing specific products for specific market segments is the matrix shown in Table 5-2, Maslow's hierarchy of human needs plotted against the

TABLE 5-2

Maslow's Matrix

Maslow's Hierarchy of Human Needs	Consumer Products				
	Convenience Products			Shopping Products	
	Staples	Impulse	Emergency	Specialty	Unsought

Physiological	Bread
	Baby foods
	Soap
	Milk
		Papayas
		Loofahs
		Athletic sox
		Vitamins
			Medications
			Dentistry
			Vitamins
			Suntan lotion
				Exercycles
				Wood stoves
				Pedometers
				Health spas
					Frozen
					  yogurt
					Sleep masks
					Blood-
					  pressure
					  testers

Safety	Bank
	  services
	Safety
	  matches
	Rule books
	Traffic signs
		Flares for car
		First-aid kits
		Dust masks
			First-aid
			  training
			CB car radios
			Parachutes
			Automatic
			  sprinklers
				Smoke
				  alarms
				Home safes
				Playpens
				Bonds, stocks
					Mace
					Electronic
					  locks
					Firesticks

Social	Cigarettes
	Beer
	Haircuts
	Deli foods
		Cosmetics
		Greeting
		  cards
		Party
		  balloons
		Games
			Dating service
			Catering
			  service
				Jewelry
				Stereo
				  equipment
				Dancing
				  lessons
				Recreation
				  equipment
				VCRs
				PCs
					Slot
					  machines
					Social clubs

Egoistic		Trophies Plaques	How-to books	Sports cars Cookbooks Sporting goods	Food processors

Self-actualization	Skills
	  training
	Do-it-
	  yourself
	  books
	Drawing
	  pencils
		Skills training
		Home-study
		  courses
		Specialty
		  magazines
		Self-
		  realization
		  courses
				Musical instruments
				Artists supplies
				Hobby tools
				Training seminars
				  and tapes
				College education
					Solar-energy
					  kits
					Home
					  computers
					Word
					  processors

Aesthetic	Oil colors
	  and paints
	Artist's clay
	Picture
	  framing
	Magnetic
	  tape
		Serigraphs
		Paintings
		Antiques
		Wood
		  carvings
				Paintings
				Fine books
				Recordings
				Interior-decorating
				  services
					Modern
					  sculpture
					Collectibles
					Wind chimes

three basic consumer products and the two basic shopping products. In this matrix we've tried to show how different kinds of products, chosen at random, may come from the human needs as Maslow identified them.

Notice that products sometimes overlap from one column to another; these will show in two columns. This suggests that it's often not possible to draw a sharp line between the basic consumer products. Rather, products may be thought of as on a continuum, merging from one group into another. This need not be of concern, as the matrix can help you develop ideas for consumer products that fit your business; you can use the matrix to guide your thinking.

Some human needs versus some classifications of product do not readily bring to mind specific items; blanks in the matrix indicate this. You should try as an exercise to add products to those given in Table 5-2, and to develop ideas for products that might fit in the blanks.

INDUSTRIAL PRODUCTS

The need for industrial products originates in the demands for consumer goods. In the production process many requirements for industrial goods, products, and services arise. Products can range from tiny screw-machine parts for assembly of cameras to complete plants for the production of petrochemicals.

The marketing of industrial products is quite different from that of convenience and shopping products. Although the end products of industry are subject to consumer demand, along the production chain industry sells to industry. Suppliers must meet buyer specifications. These are usually quite technical and rigorously defined. The marketing process must therefore aim at satisfying technical needs and must be designed carefully to do that.

Those who do industrial buying are professional purchasing agents. They are well versed in the technical requirements of what they buy. And more often than not they collaborate with engineers who've set the specifications in the first place. Advertising for industrial products must therefore be designed to tell what the industrial product can do, with accurate technical data that can be substantiated if need be. It should be aimed at the needs of the user to tell what it can do to improve manufacturing procedure or quality of the user's product. Advertising should be placed in technical journals such as *Machine Design, Iron Age,* or *Product Engineering,* which specialize in the particular business.

The end job of selling the industrial product usually is the task of sales engineers. They must be thoroughly familiar with their products because they must deal not only with knowledgeable professional buyers but also with engineers and technicians. Often they're called upon to help in the design of the product that will use the item they're selling.

How Do They Buy?

Consumers buy for cash or for some form of credit. Little need be said about the cash sale. The customer selects an item, pays the price listed on the sales slip, plus the usual sales tax, and departs. If there is need to complain about the merchandise, the customer returns with merchandise and sales slip and negotiates a settlement. Credit sales take different forms and involve somewhat more complicated procedures.

CREDIT SALES

Credit selling has been found by many small businesses to be a powerful tool in merchandising and a source of profit. The availability of credit can sometimes swing a sale from one store to another or from one source of supply to another. But, as you would expect, the advantages bring with them some disadvantages. If you consider offering credit in your business, you should weigh both before deciding.

Advantages of Credit[3]   The advantages of offering credit:

◻ A friendly personal relationship can be built with credit customers, who become attached to the firm.

◻ Credit customers tend to become more loyal than cash customers who follow the bargains.

◻ Credit customers incline to be more concerned with quality and service than with price.

◻ Use of credit tends to build and maintain goodwill.

◻ Merchandise can be exchanged and adjustments made fairly more easily in credit sales; goods can be sent to credit customers on approval.

◻ Credit account records afford a valuable source of marketing information; this allows the business to:
Develop a mailing list for sales promotion and for market research.
Collect data about sales by department or individual salespersons.
Detect lessening sales to individual customers that might suggest the need to recapture their loyalty.

◻ If credit stimulates sales, the firm's return on investment can increase, provided credit is carefully managed.

Through the careful management of credit, many retailers and suppliers have shown that the demand for their product can be increased—and their profit improved. But, as we've indicated, some disadvantages accompany the advantages.

Disadvantages of Credit   The yearly records of business failures reported by Dun and Bradstreet show poor credit practice is a major cause of business failure.[4] In using credit, you should adopt a rigorous collection policy. Some important disadvantages of using credit are:

◻ Credit customers often take their time in paying their bills. Without firm collection practices, this could lead to difficult cash crises.

◻ The firm's capital can be tied up in goods sold to customers but not yet paid for.

---

[3]After Marquardt, Makens, and Roe, *Retail Management*, The Dryden Press, Hinsdale, IL., 1975, pp. 292–294.
[4]You can obtain a complete index of *Small Business Reporter* publications by writing to Bank of America, Department 3120, P.O. Box 37000, San Francisco, Calif. 94137. A nominal charge is made for each publication you order.

If the businessperson has borrowed the extra money needed to issue credit, interest is added to the cost.

Some losses from bad debts will have to be absorbed by the business.

Some credit customers abuse the privileges of returning goods bought on credit and having goods sent on approval.

Credit increases the cost of doing business through credit checking, additional bookkeeping, billing, and collecting payments.

You can see from the foregoing lists of advantages and disadvantages of offering credit that you must assure yourself of sufficient increased profitability to make the step worthwhile. You should study each disadvantage and find ways to overcome or minimize it. Only when you're sure that the benefits outweigh the costs should you adopt credit selling.

Kinds of Retail Credit   Three kinds of credit are usual in the retail business: *the 30-day open account, the revolving-credit plan,* and *the deferred-payment plan.*

The 30-day open account allows customers to charge goods and pay the full amount within 30 days of the billing date. Interest is usually charged for late payment.

The revolving-credit plan divides the unpaid account balance into equal monthly payments. Customarily, about $1^{1}/_{2}$ percent interest per month is levied on the remaining balance if the account is not paid by the stated due date. Customers are granted credit limits that they can't exceed. So long as they stay below these limits they may charge and make payments as they desire—provided that they make a minimum payment each month.

The deferred-payment plan allows buyers of expensive items to make equal monthly payments, plus a carrying charge. A separate agreement for each sale spells out the monthly payment and carrying charge. An installment contract is one form of deferred-payment plan; here title to the goods remains with the seller until the contract is paid off.

You'll find suggestions for the use of bank credit cards and layaway plans in Chapter 15.

Where Do They Buy?

Where consumers buy depends upon *time utility* and *place utility*. Time utility means that products the consumers want are available *when* they want to buy. Place utility means that products consumers want to buy are available *where* they want to buy. These two variables suggest that many means come into play to give consumers the best combination possible of time and place utility. Thus we see thousands of retail stores across the country, mail-order catalogs, vending machines, door-to-door selling, and telephone canvassing. A quick look at the kinds of goods people buy through different outlets should be helpful in directing your thinking toward that outlet most suitable for your business.

The following chart, based upon the outline of the kinds of goods people buy, gives some typical sales outlets.

Consumer Products	Sales Outlets	CHAPTER 5
Staple products	Markets	97
	Filling stations	
	Hardware stores	Analyzing Your Market and Consumer Behavior
	Drugstores	
	Hairdressers	
Impulse products	Stationers	
	Markets	
	Gift shops	
	Tobacconists	
Emergency products	Pharmacists	
	Dental services	
	Medical rental services	
	Plumbing contractors	
Shopping products	Apparel stores	
	Department stores	
	Appliance dealers	
	Furniture stores	
Specialty products	Model shops	
	Medical offices	
	Antique shops	
	Gourmet food shops	
Unsought products	Outlets for products new on the market	
Industrial products	Manufacturers	
	Wholesalers	
	Specialty machine shops	
	Chemicals suppliers	

This list can be expanded indefinitely. However, you can see that the consumers have varying demands on time and place utility. A person with a bad cold wants to walk into the pharmacist's and get immediate help through buying a given brand of cold-relief pill. A purchasing agent for an aircraft company expects a 6-month lead time in buying landing-gear actuators for a production run of airplanes. Consumers who discover late at night that they're short of orange juice and eggs for next morning's breakfast will hastily visit the local convenience market that stays open until 11:00 p.m. On the other hand, a woman who wants to get a warm winter down coat in a hurry will call a known mail-order firm at a free 800 telephone number, tell what she wants, give her MasterCard credit card number, and ask for delivery by United Parcel's Blue Label service. She'll have her coat within 3 days.

From the foregoing discussion you can see that for convenience items, staples, impulse products, and emergency products, time and place utility are of the greatest importance. If you're to deal in these products, you should make sure that you have what your customers want, handy to get when they want it. If you're to deal in shopping products, place utility is not quite as important as time utility. Your customers will want to shop before they buy; therefore, you must have on hand what they want to compare when they're out to shop. This means keeping up with trends and fashion—and being reasonably near competitors so shoppers can make comparisons readily.

Time utility becomes important when you deal in specialty items, primarily to have these goods on hand when customers want them. Place utility is not so critical here because customers will go great distances to get what they want.

Where you are located is not too critical in marketing industrial products. This is a different marketing game. What is required is a superior product, knowledgeable representatives, and first-rate technical supporting service.

When Do They Buy?

Business
Plan Outline
5.A, 8.A

If you sell at times when customers find it convenient to buy, you can increase the volume of your business. Preferred buying times follow a variety of patterns. Variables include time of day, day of week, month of year, the impact of seasonal variations, and time of life.

TIME OF DAY

Different consumers are able to shop or prefer to shop at different times of day. Teenagers may find it convenient to stop for a snack or school supplies on the way to school. At some schools they're permitted to leave the grounds for lunch. Working adults shop during the lunch hour or after work. Some businesses such as snack shops or restaurants close to theaters or sports arenas may experience rush business before and after shows or events. In families where both mother and father work, shopping may peak evenings or on weekends. And in many resorts, such as Miami Beach or Las Vegas, retailers of products or services may stay open very late at night or even 24 hours a day. In your business you should observe the times of day when you're likely to do a volume of business and arrange your hours accordingly.

DAY OF WEEK

In some businesses the day of the week can be a critical factor in influencing the volume of business. For example, if your retail business is located near a large manufacturing plant that pays its help on Fridays, you would probably be wise to keep late hours on Friday and stay open on weekends.

WEEK OF MONTH AND MONTH OF YEAR

In localities where industry has good-sized payrolls, managerial and supervisory personnel usually get paid twice a month. You may find, if your business is located close to such industry, that these paydays exert a cyclical influence on your business. If so, you'll find it profitable to adjust your schedule to be open for business immediately after these paydays.

Many businesses peak during holiday periods. Trade during the Christmas season expands substantially for many firms—retailers particularly see great increase in volume. As an example, retail bookstores ordinarily take in half to two-thirds of the year's income during the last 2 to 3 months of the year. This suggests that if you're in a business that responds to holidays or holiday seasons, you should be forward-looking enough to build inventory to meet seasonal and holiday trade.

The impact of seasonal and holiday buying usually means long lead times in buying merchandise. Toys for the Christmas season are shown and purchased in March; swimsuits and beachwear are ordered for inventory in December and January for the following vacation season. For single holidays such as the Fourth of July or

Mothers' Day advertising should be prepared and placed in the media at least 2 weeks before the holiday.

TIME OF LIFE

The importance of knowing when people buy allows you, as the proactive manager of your business, to time your purchasing for inventory and to promote your business on a timely basis. In a longer perspective, you may find it valuable in your business to know what people buy during a lifetime. Products that interest people during various stages in their family life cycle are shown in Table 5-3. By studying this table you may be guided to products suitable for the class of consumers you want to serve.

Market Segmentation

We've now looked at the general factors of who buys and why, what, how, where, and when they buy. You must now decide on which segment of the market to concentrate your marketing efforts. *This is one of the most critical decisions you'll make for your new venture.* (In giving assistance to over 150 small businesses experiencing marketing problems, we've found the most frequent root cause of troubles is improper or ineffective market segmentation.)

Market segmentation means the carving up of the mass market into small submarkets. The consumers of each of these markets share unique buying characteristics. Teenagers, for example, only recently have taken on the characteristics of a distinct market segment. As consumers they behave differently from other age groups.

All successful large and small firms practice some form of market segmentation. Your business can't satisfy everyone, nor can you expect all consumers to want your product or service. Use a rifle, not a shotgun, to target your marketing program. Choice of the markets you intend to reach is what will guide all your later marketing plans and actions. The characteristics of your product or service, your pricing approach, your promotional strategy, and how you distribute your product or service should be tailored to the submarket you've selected.

Many small business owners do market analysis by what might inelegantly be called the seat-of-the-pants method. Their approach to marketing consists of guesswork and hunch. Sometimes this works satisfactorily, particularly if the entrepreneur has a solid background in the particular business.

The entrepreneur may, for example, see a possible site for a retail store, observe the pedestrians going by, the quality of cars in the parking lot, the appearance of the neighboring stores—and, without counting numbers or gathering other statistics, conclude that this spot will do. The stored experience in the entrepreneur's mind possibly gets integrated and propels a snap but correct judgment. On other occasions this approach with its lack of accurate information may lead to disaster.

Our objective here is to offer more rational ways to make marketing decisions. We suggest the advantage of using demonstrated successful ways of market analysis and decision making. By following these procedures and techniques you, as a small businessperson, can increase your chances for success in marketing.

Typical Stages in the Family Life Cycle

Age Group	Age	Behavioral Characteristics	Products of Interest
Early childhood	Birth–5	Total dependency on parents; development of bones and muscles and use of locomotion; accident- and illness-prone; ego-centered; naps; accompanies guardian shopping	Baby foods; cribs; clothes; toys; pediatric services; room vaporizers; breakfast cereals; candy; books
Late childhood	6–12	Declining dependency on parents; slower and more uniform growth; vast development of thinking ability; peer competition, conscious of being evaluated by others; attends school	Food; toys; clothes; lessons; medical and dental care; movies; candy; uniforms; comic books
Early adolescence	13–15	Onset of puberty; shifting of reference group from family to peers; concern with personal appearance begins; desire for more independence; transition to adulthood begins	Junk food; comic books and magazines; movies; records; clothing; hobbies; grooming aids
Late adolescence	16–18	Transition to adulthood continues; obtains working papers; obtains driver's license; concern with personal appearance increases; dating; active in sports; less reading for fun	Gasoline; auto parts; typewriters; cameras; jewelry and trinkets; cigarettes; books and magazines
Premarrieds	18–24	Enter labor market on a full-time basis; enter college; interest in personal appearance remains high; increased dating; varying degrees of independence; activity in sports decreases	Auto; clothing; dances; travel; toiletries; quick and easy-to-prepare foods
Marrieds	19–24	First marriage; transition to pair-centered behavior; financially optimistic; interest in personal appearance still high; homemakers; working wives and husbands	Home renting; furniture; major appliances; second auto; food; entertainment; small household items
Young parents	25–34	Transition to family-centered behavior; decline in social interests; companionship with spouse drops; leisure activities centered more at home	Houses; home-repair goods; health and nutrition foods; family games; health-care services
Middle adulthood	35–44	Family size at its peak; children in school; security-conscious; homemaker's time is impinged upon; husband's career advances; picnics; pleasure drives	Durables are replaced; insurance; books; sporting equipment; yard furniture; gifts
Later adulthood	45–54	Children have left home; physical appearance changes; increased interest in appearance; community service; strenuous activity declines; pair-centered	Clothing; vacations; leisure-time services; food; gifts; personal health-care services
Soon to be retired	56–64	Physical appearance continues to decline; interests and activities continue to decline; pair-centered	Gifts; slenderizing treatments; manicures and massages; luxuries
Already retired	65 and over	Physical appearance continues its decline; mental abilities decline in sharpness; home-body behavior; ego-centered behavior	Drugs; dietetic canned foods; laxatives; nursing home care; denture products

Adapted from Fred D. Reynolds and William D. Wells, *Consumer Behavior,* McGraw-Hill Book Company, New York, 1977.

CHAPTER 5

101

Analyzing
Your Market
and Consumer
Behavior

REQUIREMENTS FOR EFFECTIVE SEGMENTATION OF YOUR MARKET

We'll describe several ways you can segment your market. Any method you choose must satisfy these three requirements:

▨ *Market measurements*. You must be able to identify and measure the characteristics and size of the market segment.

▨ *Economic opportunity*. The market segment or segments to which you intend to appeal must be large enough and have enough discretionary income to make it worthwhile; that is, your consumers must have money to spend for whatever they want above their basic living expenses.

▨ *Market access*. The market segment must be "reachable." Can you locate your business or place your products within easy reach of intended customers? Can your promotion program reach and influence consumers in the market segment?

You must answer these questions.

It's not difficult to meet the first two conditions that your market be measurable to some reasonable degree and that it have money to spend. It's in the third requirement that most entrepreneurs experience marketing problems. They fail in some way to gain access to their intended submarket. Consider these two cases:

CASE 1: JOHN MORGAN, THE POOL CLEANER

Mr. Morgan operated a pool-cleaning service. He cleaned residential swimming pools monthly for about 100 customers. He employed two high school students part time; the firm was healthy and growing. He had tinkered with various mechanical pool-cleaning devices over the years and had perfected a model that worked much better than existing products. Excited about the prospects for his invention, he contacted dozens of retailers to see if they would carry his product.

He found that none of the dealers wanted his device, even though it was technically superior and could be sold at lower cost than competitive models. Their reluctance to stock and sell his product was based on two factors. First, each dealer had "exclusive dealing" arrangements with sellers of pool-cleaning devices and accessories—a policy whereby the seller requires dealers to agree to handle only the seller's products. Second, retailers doubted whether Mr. Morgan could produce enough to satisfy demand. They also questioned his ability to furnish adequate warranty protection and service.

Mr. Morgan *couldn't gain distribution access* to a mass consumer market. He then decided to market the device himself to his existing clients. This effort proved successful. Eventually, he sold the patent rights for his invention to a large pool-equipment manufacturer for a substantial sum.

If you were to invent and patent a useful item for the retail trade, such as John Morgan's pool cleaner, what would you do to avoid Morgan's basic error in marketing?

SECTION II

102

Understanding
Marketing
for Your
Small Business

CASE 2: ANTONIO ALVEREZ, THE TORTILLA MANUFACTURER

Mr. Alverez started and operated a small manufacturing plant in a large metropolitan area in the southwest. His plant was located near the center of a community of Mexican-Americans. He made corn and flour tortillas and, along with specialty food products he imported from Mexico, distributed them directly to supermarkets. He had three driver-salespersons who delivered his products by truck. The drivers would stock the shelves and take orders for the next delivery.

Mr. Alverez had been operating his business for about a year when he came to the authors for help. The problem, he said, was that each quarter his income statement showed a loss even though he was meeting his sales objectives.

An examination of his distribution patterns showed that his accounts were widely scattered. With the exception of two stores a stone's throw from his business, all accounts were over 45 miles from his plant. All were located in above-average income areas. Sales volume in each distant account wasn't enough to cover his distribution costs.

A short study showed that Mr. Alverez suffered from three basic problems:

1. Improper segmentation of his market

2. High overhead due to long routes

3. Inadequate access to what limited market existed

Mexican food products in these upper-income areas were considered novelties rather than staple food items. Supermarket managers were allocating only a small amount of shelf space to his products, in hard-to-find locations. When we asked him about this situation, Mr. Alverez said: "But look at the size of these markets! Incomes are much higher there than around here and nobody's selling products like mine there." True enough, but Mr. Alverez was assuming that the mere existence of his products would change the eating habits of his customers to include more Mexican food products. He simply didn't have the resources to reach consumers directly to inform and influence them about his products.

Discuss the basic problems that prevented Mr. Alverez's marketing of tortillas and specialty Mexican foods from being successful.

Following our recommendations, Mr. Alverez phased out his distant accounts within 6 months. He reorganized his distribution to concentrate on supermarkets catering to Mexican-American consumers. As a result, he improved both sides of his profit situation—total sales increased beyond his projections and total costs declined, primarily because of substantially reduced distribution costs. His business is now in good shape financially.

You can see from these cases the importance and the difficulty of gaining access to submarkets. Several suggestions for overcoming this problem will be presented as we explore marketing strategy in the next chapter.

CHAPTER 5

103

Analyzing
Your Market
and Consumer
Behavior

SEGMENTING YOUR MARKET

Most small businesses segment their market on the basis of such demographic variables as age, income, race, or sex, and geographic concentration of consumers with the desired characteristics. Markets are segmented along these lines for three reasons: (1) Demand for most products or services is related to various factors such as age, income, and race. (2) It's relatively easy to measure these characteristics. (3) The data required for measuring are readily available at little or no cost.

Here are the steps you should take to segment your market:

1. Develop a detailed demographic profile of your intended market—average age, income level, racial mix, education level of potential customers, and other factors that describe your target market.

2. Identify where high concentrations of these potential customers with the desired characteristics live.

3. Determine how, where, and when they prefer to buy, the types of stores they usually shop in, their preferences about credit or cash. Also find out about their buying habits. Do they shop and compare price and quality; are their purchases scattered during the year or concentrated during holiday seasons; and to what extent do economic conditions affect their buying?

You may want to consider other factors in segmenting your market. For example, within a particular age or income group wide variations in consumption patterns may be found because of differing life-styles or religious beliefs. And the rate of use or frequency of purchase of various products or services may be different within an age or income group. It may be possible to identify nonusers, light users, and heavy users of products or services in the same category as yours. In short, you may want to combine other factors with demographic and geographical variables to identify your market segment thoroughly.

TABLE 5-4

Typical Data from a Census Tract

The following selected data came from information published by the Bureau of the Census of the U.S. Department of Commerce. Many more kinds of information are furnished, but the information offered here shows the straightforward possibility of selecting important numbers for a market segmentation analysis. These data are for the census tract diagramed, which is in the Washington, D.C., area.

Subject		
Total population	4730	
White	2488	
Negro	2183	
Other races	59	

(continued)

SECTION II

104

Understanding
Marketing
for Your
Small Business

TABLE 5-4

(*Continued*)

Household Relationship

Population in households	4634
Head of household	1802
Head of primary family	1010
Primary individual	792
Spouse of head	739
Child under 18 of head	874
Other relative of head	888
Nonrelative of head	331

Years of School Completed

Persons 25 years old and over	3152
Number of school years completed	19
Elementary: 1 to 4 years	243
5 to 7 years	554
8 years	421
High school: 1 to 3 years	540
4 years	462
College: 1 to 3 years	336
4 years or more	577
Median school years completed	10.9

Family Income

All families	1043
Under $1000	42
$1000 to $1999	48
$2000 to $2999	121
$3000 to $3999	98
$4000 to $4999	102
$5000 to $5999	140
$6000 to $6999	83
$7000 to $7999	82
$8000 to $8999	59
$9000 to $9999	45
$10,000 to $14,999	129
$15,000 to $24,999	75
$25,000 and over	19
Median Income: Families	$5,789

Note: You can see from the income figures that this is a poor neighborhood, with very nearly half the families below the currently accepted poverty level.

You'll find in the experience of the service firm that follows an example of one way to segment a market. Here, because of special knowledge of the area, they were able to use zip codes in pinpointing their market segment. It would have been possible to use census tracts to accomplish the same purpose, but the analysis of census tracts would have been much more time-consuming—and unnecessary in this case. You can see how valuable census-tract information can be, however, by studying Table

5-4 on pages 103 and 104, in which some data have been extracted from a neighborhood census tract in Washington, D.C.

CHAPTER 5

105

Analyzing
Your Market
and Consumer
Behavior

"OVERCOMING FEAR OF WRITING"—A PUBLIC SEMINAR

Pacific Clear Writing Clinics, a private venture based in southern California that aims at teaching adults writing skills, decided to test the market for a unique seminar, "Overcoming Fear of Writing." This seminar is designed as a clinic to help adults who must write for a living, and those who want to write but experience great difficulty in getting started. The clinic is psychologically oriented and teaches techniques for unblocking, for liberating creativity. Developed and presented by Anne I. Grayson, Ph.D., "Overcoming Fear of Writing" is the direct result of her dissatisfaction with traditional approaches to teaching composition—and her intensive research in therapeutic learning.

In deciding how to segment the market, Pacific studied data from a dozen university-sponsored "Overcoming Fear of Writing" seminars they had run. Information collected from about 600 attendees showed that the typical participant was in the 25- to 35-year age group. Women made up nearly two-thirds of the audiences. Participants, by and large, were well-educated and articulate and earned $15,000 to $40,000 per year. From analysis of these data, Pacific decided to try promoting a public seminar through the mail.

The firm took the following steps in mounting the mailing campaign:

1. Found a professional mailing house that could offer advice on the design of a mailing piece, how to use the postal service effectively, and how to prepare and mail the announcements.

2. Set the price for admission to the clinic by checking prices for seminars of various kinds put on by both universities and private firms. A charge of $85 was settled on as a result.

3. Identified by zip code the areas in which people lived who fit the consumer profile desired.

4. Secured mailing lists of people who fit the profile identified in the university seminars.

5. Composed and designed the announcements with the help of qualified graphic artists.

6. Rented a meeting room in a central location.

In fulfilling these requirements, Pacific did the following:

1. Chose Addresses Unlimited as mailing house for the promotion. Agreed to send out a minimum of 5000 mailers. (This is a relatively small number for most mailers, 25,000 being a commonly accepted quantity for mail-order purposes. But because the lists were carefully selected on the basis of the data from the university-sponsored seminars, Pacific believed that 5000 mailers should return 1 percent attendees, or 50 people, which they estimated would be sufficient to ensure at least a small profit.)

SECTION II

106

Understanding
Marketing
for Your
Small Business

2. Decided on and arranged to buy a mailing list of subscribers to *Los Angeles Magazine*, a slick fashionable magazine with wide appeal to younger, affluent people, particularly to women because of its emphasis and ads on current fashions, what's going on in Hollywood, Beverly Hills, TV, and the cinema.

3. Decided on the zip code areas in which likely prospects for the clinic lived. The more affluent residents in the Los Angeles area tend to live toward the west, many near the ocean. This is particularly true of singles and young marrieds who can afford to live near the beaches. Pacific's selection of geographical areas therefore included Westwood, Beverly Hills south, Brentwood, Venice, Pacific Palisades, Malibu, Marina Del Rey, and Santa Monica. Zip code numbers were selected according to the local map as follows: 90025, 90061, 90049, 90291, 90272, 90265, and 90406.

4. Added to the *Los Angeles Magazine* list of 5000 names in the zip code areas selected names of participants in the university-sponsored programs, and a small list of 200 names of professional psychologists who were members of the California Psychological Association resident in the Los Angeles area.

5. Composed and had the mailer designed by Harris & Farber, graphic artists. Arranged to have mailers printed by Pacific Printing. Inserted a small ad in the *Malibu Times,* a weekly throwaway issued in the Malibu area.

6. Reserved a meeting room in a County Parks and Recreation building in Santa Monica.

7. Arranged bulk mailing with the post office.

8. Arranged with the bank to accept bank credit cards in payment for admission to the clinic.

Costs for setting up the clinic were as follows:

Addresses Unlimited, stuffing mailers	$ 455.04
California Psychological Association mailing list	24.96
Harris & Farber, graphic art	689.50
Pacific Printing, printing and envelopes	1023.96
U.S. Post Office, bulk mailing	522.70
Bank, credit card charges	16.49
Malibu Times, ads	36.00
Department of Parks and Recreation, room rent	72.00
Total	$2840.65

The promotional effort produced 49 participants who paid $85 each to attend the clinic. The gross income was therefore $49 \times 85 = \$4165$. Gross profit was $\$4165 - \$2840.65 = \$1324.35$, without considering overhead charges. The response from the mailer was slightly less than 1 percent, confirming the somewhat optimistic prediction made for this first attempt at promoting through the mail. This result suggests that the segmentation of the market was successfully accomplished.

If you had been responsible for promoting this writing clinic, and had adequate funds, what would you have done to increase the size of the audience?

SOURCES OF INFORMATION FOR SEGMENTING
AND UNDERSTANDING YOUR MARKET

CHAPTER 5

107

Analyzing
Your Market
and Consumer
Behavior

Here is a list of some major sources of information:

Daily Newspapers   Each major newspaper conducts ongoing marketing research in the area it serves. Information about this research is usually given free of charge to advertisers or potential advertisers. The newspaper may conduct comprehensive market surveys to determine what people are buying, how frequently they buy certain items, where they do their buying, and the prices they pay. The information is collected for the metropolitan area and, more important, is usually subdivided and related to small geographical areas, called *census tracts.*

The U.S. Bureau of the Census originates and publishes data on these very small population segments known as census tracts—areas with an average of about 4000 individuals who are considered to be fairly homogeneous. This means that census tracts are constructed with the expectation that families within their boundaries will be similar in population characteristics, economic status, and living conditions.

You can do effective market segmentation by using demographic data from census tracts. You can pinpoint submarkets with high potential—those having the most people with the characteristics you want—by using newspaper survey information and census-tract data. You can gain insights from such information on important marketing decisions such as store location, placement of products in existing stores, buyer preferences, and even where to concentrate advertising.

You should keep in mind that census-tract data reveal only demographic information. Market surveys conducted by most larger newspapers, and other institutions we'll mention below, enrich population information with consumer-buying data. The *combination and availability of the two types of information* have great potential for use in your marketing planning.

Newspapers will often supply two additional types of market information: detailed maps that show concentrations of commercial activity—the location of supermarkets and shopping centers, for example—and maps that show average driving time from one place to another within a city; and special market reports for a specific kind of business, like beauty salons or auto parts stores.

Weekly Newspapers   Most large cities have weekly newspapers that cater to small sections of the metropolitan area. Weeklies concentrate on local news and attract local business advertisers. You'll find that the marketing staff of these small newspapers will be one of the best sources for informed opinions on commercial activity and trends in the smaller areas they serve. They'll usually be eager to respond to your questions about their market, because you're a potential advertiser in their newspaper.

Government   The federal government is dedicated to the preservation of a strong, healthy, and profitable small business community. Marketing and management assistance free of charge, financial assistance in some circumstances, and other services have been created by specific legislation. Two federal agencies, the U.S. Department of Commerce (USCD) and the U.S. Small Business Administration (SBA), furnish marketing assistance that will be discussed here. Other services offered by the SBA

SECTION II

108

Understanding
Marketing
for Your
Small Business

will be described in other chapters, as it is the agency created by Congress specifically to help small firms in many ways.

The USCD was established early in this century to develop and promote foreign and domestic commerce. The Bureau of the Census, mentioned earlier, is part of the USCD, but in addition to census data the department publishes a wide variety of information. You should visit one of the 42 field offices, located in major cities, and find out about the services and information they offer. In addition to census data and industry-by-industry sales statistics that you may find helpful, the USCD supplies specific information for small businesses. For example, their publication, *Franchise Company Data,* lists all kinds of franchised operations, firms doing business under those categories, and general information about each firm.

Entrepreneurs often overlook international market opportunities for their business. The USCD (any field office) is the place to go to find out about such potential. Publications on how to get started in world trade, foreign business regulations, international trade statistics, and information on a country-by-country basis are available. A thorough reading of USCD literature will help you decide on your best potential foreign market. Free seminars are also given by each field office on how to set up foreign marketing ventures.

The SBA, established in 1953, also has field offices in every major city and offers two major types of marketing assistance.

First, the SBA publishes hundreds of pamphlets on specific small business subjects, and each local office conducts a free seminar monthly on various aspects of starting your own business. The SBA publications give practical how-to suggestions on several marketing issues faced by the entrepreneur. For example, if you want to explore the opportunities for selling your product by mail order, the SBA's *Selling by Mail Order* is a bibliography that will guide you to books, trade associations, and other sources of detailed information. Most publications of the SBA are free; others are inexpensive. The monthly seminars touch on functional areas of the small business and often include a session on marketing the new business.

Second, you can get direct assistance at no cost through the Service Corps of Retired Executives (SCORE) and the Active Corps of Executives (ACE). The latter group is composed of persons still active in business. Consultative talent may be available through the nearest office of SBA to help you complete your marketing plans.

The SBA will also help you if you see the federal government as a possible market segment. The SBA has the responsibility for making sure that small businesses participate in certain federal government contracts. Meetings and seminars are held to inform entrepreneurs on how to bid for government business.

Banks   The commercial bank you've been using for your personal banking could be an excellent source of local market information. Contact a loan officer who handles small business accounts. Describe your business idea and marketing plans. Ask the loan officer for advice on the areas in which you need information, and find out what kinds of economic data the bank publishes. The loan officer will have insights into local business conditions and activity and may know about other businesses similar to yours.

The Bank of America publishes the *Small Business Reporter,* a series of booklets covering many different kinds of business and treating many subjects that you'll want to know about. Issues of the *Small Business Reporter* come in three categories: business profiles, business operations, and professional management. Business profiles treat fundamental issues in starting small businesses ranging from *Small Job Printing* to *Mobile Home Parks*. Business operations give data on such subjects as *Understanding Financial Statements, How to Buy or Sell a Business,* and *Advertising Small Business.* The professional management booklets deal with subjects such as *Establishing an Accounting Practice* and *Establishing a Veterinary Practice.*

In addition to helping you set your sales forecasts, these publications supply much other information that you'll find useful.

Universities   Many colleges and universities offer courses in small business management. You may want to enroll in one or more of these or use the management library facilities.

Free assistance may be obtained from instructors of small business management courses. Over 400 colleges and universities are members of the Small Business Institute (SBI), which is cosponsored by the SBA. You may want to contact a program coordinator of the SBI in your local college or university to arrange for a student team to counsel and assist you in planning your business.

The university may also have a bureau of business research that offers services for entrepreneurs in the local area. Often these bureaus prepare market and economic studies, and publish reports of interest for small business operators.

Chambers of Commerce   These organizations represent commercial interests in the community. The membership is composed of owners and managers from all kinds of businesses. Regular meetings are held and information about the commercial area is usually published. You should join the local chamber of commerce; it's an excellent way to become acquainted with the business community and to learn from other entrepreneurs.

Trade Associations   There are over 7000 trade associations in the United States. Almost every industry has one. The purpose of the association is to help improve the health of the industry it represents. It does this by furnishing its members detailed industry data, market surveys and forecasts, information on technological breakthroughs, representative sales and cost data, and the like. Moreover, the advertisements in trade journals are an excellent source of information about competitors and their products. Attending trade association meetings and visiting with sales representatives can also be a good way for you to assess competition and gain additional business ideas. So you should join the association of your business. If you're planning to open a bookstore, join the American Booksellers Association; if you're going to open a screw-machine shop, join the National Screw Machine Products Association. Your public or school library will have a directory or encyclopedia of associations that lists all the trade associations and the addresses to write to for membership.

Other Similar Businesses   You can check the current situation by consulting a good source of start-up information—successful entrepreneurs. Entrepreneurs enjoy talking about their experiences in starting their own business. Pick businesses you

CHAPTER 5

109

Analyzing
Your Market
and Consumer
Behavior

SECTION II

110

Understanding
Marketing
for Your
Small Business

won't be in competition with but which are similar to yours, and choose a day when business may not be heavy—perhaps sometime in midweek. Ask the owners about their marketing approach, their successes and failures, who they bank with, and who they use for an attorney or an accountant. Concentrate on asking questions that published literature may not answer.

Pinpointing the Marketing Questions You Must Answer

Summary

In this chapter we've presented the questions you must answer to analyze and segment your market effectively. We've given techniques you can use to gather information, and we've listed sources of assistance. You'll find additional sources of information not mentioned here as you track down references given in many of the publications you'll study.

Concentrate your market research on those sources that are the most helpful to you in planning your business. Market analysis become impossible with too much data. This is known as "planning overkill." We've been selective in our suggestions for collecting information, and you should be also. You'll never be able to eliminate market risk. Your goal in seeking market information is to reduce your chance of being wrong and to increase your chance of being right.

Central to this chapter is the notion that all planning activities of the venture must be based on a consumer orientation. You can avoid the entrepreneurial disease we described in Chapter 4 as marketing myopia by following the suggestions made in this chapter and completing the worksheet that follows.

Your Market and Consumer Behavior

1. Why would customers want to buy your product or service? Ask yourself: What are the advantages or key benefits of my product or service to my customers? What are the disadvantages or negative aspects of my product or service? Be specific. Avoid using generalizations, such as lower price or better quality, without some justification. Be certain to include tangible and intangible benefits the customer would receive from your product or service.

Advantages	Disadvantages

2. After you've completed the preceding assignment, review the steps Ms. Woodworth followed to determine why consumers might or might not buy her products. Change or adapt her procedures to fit your own business. Develop your action plan, outlined below, to collect data on the advantages and disadvantages of your product or service **as perceived by potential customers.**

	Steps or tasks to be completed	**Date task is to be initiated**	**Date task is to be completed**
a.			
b.			
c.			
d.			
e.			
f.			
g.			

3. How are you going to segment your market? What demographic, geographic, or other variables are appropriate for segmenting your market? Be sure to include all the factors that will precisely identify your target market.

4. List the sources you'll check to collect information for segmenting your market. Identify the kind of consumer information you expect to obtain from each source. (You may also want to develop an action plan for completing this assignment, similar to item 2 above.)

a. _____

b. _____

c. _____

d. _____

e. _____

f. _____

g. _____

5. Describe the target market you want for your business. What's the approximate size of the *potential* market for your kind of product or service? What are the demographic characteristics of consumers in your target market? Where are they concentrated geographically? Identify other features of your market segment that will help pinpoint the kinds of customers you want— their life-styles or buying habits, for example. You probably don't have all the information you need to complete this step. Do the best you can with your own knowledge of the market, and finish this exercise once you've acquired all the necessary data.

_____

_____

_____

_____

_____

_____

_____

_____

_____

_____

_____

_____

6. The next chapter concentrates on developing marketing strategy for your business. Marketing strategy depends on how you define your business in relation to the target market you want. Therefore, before plunging into advertising, pricing, and other marketing substrategies, you should compare your response to the first assignment for Chapter 4 (What Business Are You Really In?), with the results from assignment 5 above. Summarize in the space below the definition of your business and the market segment you'll try to reach through marketing strategy.

114

The customer's view of the business I'm really in

The market segment(s) for my business

KEY TERMS

CHAPTER 5

115

Analyzing
Your Market
and Consumer
Behavior

initiators 81
influencers 81
deciders 81
buyers 81
consumers 81
evaluators 81
demographic variables 82
reference group 82
focus-group interview 87
consumer products 91
convenience items 91

staple items 91
shopping products 92
impulse items 91
emergency items 91
specialty products 92
unsought products 92
industrial products 94
market segmentation 99
market measurement 101
economic opportunity 101
market access 101

STUDY ASSIGNMENTS FOR REVIEW AND DISCUSSION

1. Explain what is meant by positive and negative consequences of behavior. In what way are those terms important in marketing?

2. Describe a focus group and its purposes.

3. Name and describe three basic requirements for effectively segmenting your market.

4. Identify at least five sources of information you can use to gather data for analyzing your market.

5. What would you look for in choosing a retail store location in your community?

PROJECTS FOR STUDENTS

1. Starting with the question, "Why do consumers buy?" you must answer five other key questions to understand the specifics of consumer behavior needed to help define your market segment. Name these questions and discuss them.

2. Explain the "behavioral" approach to understanding consumer behavior.

3. Why would you use focus groups in preparing to market a new product or service? List the kinds of answers you'd seek from a focus group.

4. Can you think of other ways than focus groups to get feedback for market analysis and feasibility studies?

5. What three basic requirements must you satisfy for effective segmentation of your market?

6. Describe several sources where you could find data useful in conducting your market analysis and feasibility study.

SECTION II

116

Understanding
Marketing
for Your
Small Business

7. Report to the class on *demographic* and *geographic* segmentation of markets. Give examples of each. (If you want to read about these terms in detail, refer to the books listed in "If You Want to Read More" at the end of this chapter.)

IF YOU WANT TO READ MORE

Your local public or business libraries are among the richest potential sources of information. Journals and periodicals are an excellent source of data on products, industries, and markets. The title of an article can be a good clue to what it is about. Some useful directories of articles in libraries are:

- *Reader's Guide to Periodical Literature*
- *Business Periodicals Index*
- *Applied Science and Technology Index*
- *Wall Street Journal Index*

In addition, most reference libraries keep current and historical material of local civic interest, including newspapers, magazines, and books. Also available are guides to state publications of possible interest.

Bibliography of Publications of Bureaus of Business and Economic Research, Associated University Bureaus of Business and Economic Research, Morgantown, WV, 1957–1975. A useful guide to publications primarily concerned with state and local business information.

DAWSON, John A.: *The Marketing Environment*, St. Martin's Press, New York, 1978. This book presents a clear discussion of marketing, with particular emphasis on geographical characteristics.

GORTON, Keith: *Low-Cost Marketing Research,* John Wiley & Sons, New York, 1983. In seven short chapters will be found desk research sources and methods, field tools, and techniques with evaluations of their strengths and weaknesses for the small firm. Also given are useful diagrams, forms, and checklists.

LEMMON, Wayne A.: *The Owners' and Managers' Market Analysis Workbook for Small to Moderate Retail and Service Establishments*, AMACOM, New York, 1980. Using techniques described in this book, owners or managers of small- to moderate-sized retail and service establishments should be able to perform a basic market analysis to determine the potential profitability of opening a specific business in a specific market location.

Marketing Research Procedures is a leaflet (number 9) published by the Small Business Administration. Reference sources for individual types of businesses are given. Available from any SBA field office.

MCREADY, Gerald B.: *Marketing Tactics Master Guide for Small Business*, Prentice-Hall, Inc., Englewood Cliffs, NJ, 1982. Using a seven-point master plan with emphasis on what the small businessperson can do, this book covers material traditionally presented in more extensive texts. The seven highlighted tactics: (1) researching market opportunities, (2) understanding buyer behavior, (3) offering appropriate products and services, (4) maximizing distribution advantage, (5) pricing goods and services to sell, (6) advertising for results, and (7) building an effective sales organization.

CHAPTER 5

117

Analyzing
Your Market
and Consumer
Behavior

Sales Management and Marketing Magazine can be found in many public libraries and most university libraries. Once each year it publishes its *Survey of Buying Power* issue, which gives figures for every county in the United States and for every city over 10,000 in population. Because the U.S. Census is completely done only once in 10 years, this annual magazine report is particularly valuable for years between census dates. The *Survey of Buying Power* report contains information on total population, households, breakdown of retail sales into divisions for different kinds of business firms, and total purchasing dollars represented in each city and county.

SCHEWE, Charles D., and Reuben M. SMITH: *Marketing Concepts and Applications,* McGraw-Hill Book Company, New York, 1983. A comprehensive text designed as an introduction to marketing. Chapter 5 will be found particularly useful in its treatment of approaches to market segmentation.

SELTZ, David O.: *Handbook of Innovative Marketing Techniques,* Addison-Wesley Publishing Company, Reading, MA, 1981. This book shows how to combine sales and marketing techniques to achieve maximum market penetration for minimum investment.

SHAMA, Avraham: *Marketing in a Slow-Growth Economy: The Impact of Stagflation on Consumer Psychology,* Praeger Publishers, New York, 1980. This book is about forces that Americans have been confronting since the oil shortage of 1973. It tells about the combined impact of inflation, shortages, and recession on life-styles and consumption patterns. The implications are helpful to the small businessperson.

Standard & Poor, *Industrial Surveys.* Can be found in most college libraries. Basic, easy to understand surveys on what's going on in major industries, including sales and market share data. Updated quarterly.

VORZIMER, Louis H.: "Using Census Data to Select a Store Site," *Small Marketers Aid,* no. 154, Small Business Administration, Washington, D.C., 1974. This booklet gives detailed examples and step-by-step procedures for using census and census-tract data for choosing a store location.

Articles on the Focus Group Interview

CALDER, Bobby J.: "Focus Groups and the Nature of Qualitative Marketing Research," *Journal of Marketing Research,* August 1977, pp. 353–364.

FERN, Edward F.: "The Use of Focus Groups for Idea Generation," The Effects of Group Size, Acquaintanceship, and Moderator on Response Quantity and Quality, *Journal of Marketing Research,* February 1982, pp. 1–13.

REYNOLDS, Fred D., and Deborah K. JOHNSON: "Validity of Focus Group Findings," *Journal of Advertising Research,* June 1978, pp. 21–24.

CHAPTER 6

Reaching Your Customer

TOPICS IN THIS CHAPTER

Objectives of This Chapter
Setting Your Marketing Objectives
Your Product or Service Strategy
Marketing Strategy
Elements of the Selling Transaction
Carrying Out Marketing Strategy
Your Pricing Strategy
Your Distribution Strategy
Your Promotional Strategy
Reaching Your Customer—Summary
Worksheet 6: Reaching Your Customer
Key Terms
Study Assignments for Review and Discussion
Projects for Students
If You Want to Read More

Once you've analyzed your market and identified your customer, as outlined in Chapter 5, you not only will know who will buy your product or service but also will have a clear understanding of how, where, and when that customer will buy. Your next efforts will be directed at setting your market objectives. You'll develop several strategies:

▢ Market strategy, which gives the basis for promoting your product or service, and for expanding your market by knowing where your product or service is in its life cycle

■ Pricing strategy, which enables you to set your prices at a level that tells your customer of the value being offered and reflects the image of your business

■ Distribution strategy, which helps you identify the channel that offers the greatest utility for your customers

■ Promotional strategy, which guides you to the most effective ways of promoting your business

Through proper use of these strategies, you'll develop in your market an awareness of your product or service, an interest in it, and a desire to buy it. An easy way to remember these strategies is through the traditionally used key terms: *Product, Price, Place,* and *Promotion* (the 4 Ps).

Information in this chapter will be found pertinent to these items in the Business Plan:

1.B.   Summary of your proposed marketing method

2.A.   Statement of the desirability of your product or service

3.B.   Detailed explanations of your place in the state of the art

5.A.   A comprehensive description of marketing strategy

6.A.   An outline of the activities to be used in selling the product or service

8.A.   Information required to support the major points in the business plan

You + Idea + { Money / Credit } + { Facilities People } → { Product or Service } + **MARKETING** { Money Credit } → Profit

SECTION II

120

Understanding
Marketing
for Your
Small Business

This chapter concludes the discussion of the marketing system for the small business. When you've set marketing objectives and decided on specific strategies for achieving them, the marketing plan for your new business will be complete. It will specify how you expect to reach your target markets. The tools available for reaching these markets are your product or service and your pricing, promotion, and distribution strategies (Figure 6-1). The actual sales you make will depend on the effectiveness of these marketing strategies.

We'll make several suggestions to aid you in completing the marketing plan for your business. The worksheet at the end of this chapter will guide you in this effort.

Objectives of This Chapter

After studying this chapter you will be able to:

- Set major marketing objectives for your business

- Understand the product or service life cycle and your need to identify the point where your business is in it

- Use the product-service life cycle as a management tool to anticipate and adjust to market change

- Develop a sound pricing strategy for your product or service

FIG. 6-1

The Marketing System of the Small Business

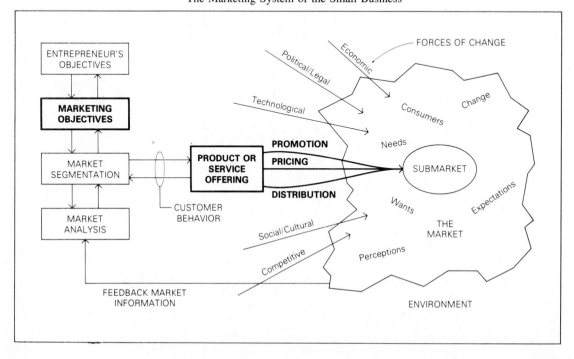

- Determine the appropriate distribution strategy for your business

- Plan promotional strategy for your business, including advertising and using an advertising agency

- See how to benefit from personal selling, publicity, and sales promotion

Setting Your Marketing Objectives

After you have analyzed your market and decided on which market segments to concentrate, you're in a position to develop realistic, but challenging, marketing objectives. An objective identifies an intended result to be accomplished within a specific time, usually 1 year. Your marketing objectives will answer the question: "What results do I expect to achieve in my target markets through my marketing efforts?" Your product or service, promotion, pricing, and distribution strategies must be keyed to achieving one or more marketing objectives. In this sense what you actually do in these areas is programmed by your objectives.

A clearly written set of marketing objectives and well-thought-out action plans for achieving them serve as the bases for measuring your firm's market performance. Marketing objectives give you a yardstick for assessing your efforts in the marketplace.

The specific objectives you'll set depend on the kind of business you're in and the market opportunities you've identified. But certain categories of objectives appear to apply to most businesses. A few examples follow:

Category of Objectives	Examples
1. Sales	Achieve $8000 in sales from customers located within walking distance from my store within the next 6 months
2. Market penetration	By the end of the current year, complete the mailing of 6000 brochures describing my business to potential consumers who have not shopped in my store
3. Market share	Increase my share of the market over local competition by 5 percent during the next year
4. Growth	Increase sales during the second 6 months of operation by 10 percent over the preceding 6 months
5. Diversification	Add three new products appealing to professional women within 9 months after opening my shop
6. Profit	Achieve after-tax profit by the end of the first year of operation that exceeds my present take-home salary by at least 5 percent

At a minimum, you should set objectives in these six categories. Additional objectives, for example, in the areas of developing a favorable business image and establishing good community relations, will no doubt be needed.

A concise written statement of marketing objectives gives you a road map for your marketing actions. Objectives aren't inflexible, but they should be formal enough to guide you in setting plans and evaluating how well your venture is doing.

Your Product or Service Strategy

Business
Plan
Outline
1.B, 3.B, 5.A

We've stressed the need to define your business and what you sell from the customer's point of view. If the customer sees your product as a need satisfier furnishing intangible psychological benefits, you should package and display the product accordingly. If technical qualities of the product or service are most important to consumers, this should determine the features to emphasize in performance, in design, and in warranty. Again, try to view what you sell as the customer views it and adapt your marketing strategy with this in mind.

Marketing Strategy

Business
Plan
Outline
5.A

Strategy for marketing product or service can be based on *market aggregation* or *market differentiation*. Although market aggregation is adopted primarily by large companies, once in a while a small company with adequate resources may employ it.

MARKET AGGREGATION

Market aggregation (sometimes called *undifferentiated marketing or product differentiation*) involves standard items with mass appeal. Products include items such as candy bars, cigarettes, razor blades, gum, coffee, beer, and soap. The mass market is not divided into subunits or segments. Consumers see very little difference among competing products. One beer is pretty much like another no matter how hard the TV sell for a given brand; and one soap is just as effective in cleaning as another if *Consumers Union* can be believed. Enough potential customers of reasonably similar characteristics exist in the mass market to be the target of mass merchandising. Mass merchandisers believe that most customers are flexible enough to accept a product that is not precisely what they want but close enough to do the job.

Basic advantages of market-aggregation strategy lie in the lower unit cost of production and marketing. The company gains greatly in manufacturing through economy of scale; it buys materials in huge quantities at economical prices. It produces one, or a limited line, of products on production lines—with minimal changes—thereby keeping manufacturing costs low. And in advertising it gains the advantage of minimum cost through a large-scale advertising campaign.

A basic disadvantage of market aggregation comes through its inability to meet the needs of some consumers. Because it can't meet the needs of a portion of the market population, the company leaves itself open to competition. For example, many service stations are now equipped to wash cars automatically. The customary price for an automatic car wash is $1.50 or $2.00—a service obviously aimed at a broad market. Yet many personalized car washes exist, often on the same lot, for customers who prefer to have a more careful job done, particularly in interior housekeeping, although the cost may be $10 or more.

Obviously, the market-aggregation approach doesn't fit most small businesses. Marketing for the mass market takes large investments that the small business can't begin to afford. The small businessperson must seek another route.

MARKET SEGMENTATION

That route lies in *market segmentation*. Market segmentation means dividing a large market into small sections in which the population contains a large percentage of people of similar characteristics. As a small businessperson, you'd use demographic information to estimate the potential of your market. For example, suppose you were in a metropolitan area in the retail business, specializing in high-quality toys for children. You might concentrate on miniature electric trains or radio-controlled model airplanes and cars—items upon which fond parents could spend $100 or more per purchase as a present for their sons or daughters. The demographic data you'd want would aim primarily at parents and grandparents. Children and grandchildren would range from 6 years of age to the teens. You'd want to find a trading area in which there were many executives and managers between 25 and 40 years of age—and 50 and 65 years of age. These would be fathers, mothers, and grandparents, of children in the appropriate ages for your market. Both groups should be affluent enough to be able to buy high-priced toys. Where would you locate your store?

You'd probably try to find a location in a mid-city shopping district within a cluster of high-rise office buildings housing headquarters of large firms. The executives and managers who work in these offices would see your show windows at least when going to and coming from lunch—and you would be appealing to the consumers you wanted.

Elements of the Selling Transaction

Once you've analyzed your demographic data and have arrived at the profile of the consumers you're aiming at, you should give some thought to elements of the selling transaction that customers see. These include such items as packaging, service, and warranties.

PACKAGING

The containers that products come in serve several functions. These deserve careful consideration, for if they are well done they can enhance the appeal of the product. If you package a product, you should study these items:

- Shape and color. Packaging has today developed into an art form. Choosing the right shape of package and the color can significantly influence the sale. For example, bright yellow and orange tones attract attention; according to a major publisher, these colors improve the sales of paperback books. Certainly, boxes containing powdered soaps are offered in these colors.

- Shapes of containers should be chosen for ease of handling, and even more important, for ease of fit and display on retail shelves. Shelf space in retail stores is limited; marketers fight for space and particularly for space at eye level.

- The container you choose should give maximum protection to the product. Delicate goods can be placed within a form-fitting molded polystyrene insert. Small products, such as picture hooks, combs, or shoelaces, can be sealed in transparent plastic on a display card. Be sure that the consumer can see what is inside the

SECTION II

124

Understanding
Marketing
for Your
Small Business

package, even if it takes a drawing or picture on the outside. Also make sure that the consumer understands how the product is to be used; this may require a sketch on the outside of the package showing it in use.

Packaging should be approached with care, because the package can often make the difference between success and failure. Your package should project the attractive kind of image you'd like your customers to see.

SERVICES AND WARRANTIES

You can improve the image of your business by increasing customer satisfaction through services you offer with your product. Services are activities intended to give benefits or satisfactions to the customer. They are included in the sale with the aim of improving the value of the product to the buyer. Examples are many: free home delivery, free installation, no-charge wheel balancing with the purchase of new tires, free service of a new typewriter in the first year of use, special extension of credit such as no payment required for 90 days after purchase, or reduced rate for prepayment of a year's monthly housecleaning. If your business is such that you can take advantage of attractive services in connection with a sale, by all means grasp this opportunity to seal your relationship with your customers.

A warranty assures buyers of your product that it will perform up to their reasonable expectations. It is essentially a guarantee that the product is free from defects and will serve the purpose for which it is intended. Warranties are usually tied to relatively complex expensive products. A warranty often states a time period in which defective parts will be replaced and the product serviced at no cost, or minimal cost, to the purchaser—or the purchase price will be refunded. Should it be desirable that your product be warranteed, it would be good practice to have your attorney approve the language. You should promise enough to make your customer feel good about the merit of your offering, without overpromising that might raise problems in a difficult circumstance.

Carrying Out Marketing Strategy

Business
Plan
Outline
1.B, 5.A, 6.A

Carrying out your marketing strategy deserves the very best planning you can develop. You will set *strategic objectives* in the areas of major importance as described earlier in this chapter. Under each objective you'll devise subobjectives, which when completed will ensure your reaching each objective you seek. And, of overriding importance, you'll work out *action plans* to achieve each subobjective. This system of planning is described in detail in Chapter 18. You'll find guides for writing action plans in Chapter 18, and you'll see examples that you can use as models in Figure 18-2.

The product or service "life cycle" is a helpful guide to use in preparing your marketing plan. Any product or service moves through identifiable and predictable stages from the time it's first conceived and introduced to the market. Four distinct stages in the life cycle of a product or service can be identified as in Figure 6-2; introduction-growth, maturity, saturation, and decline.

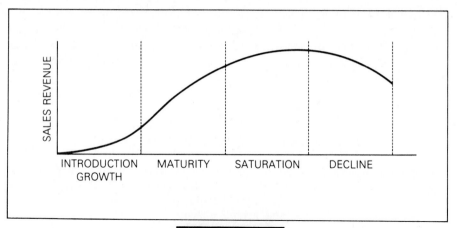

FIG. 6-2

Product or Service Life Cycle

Introduction-growth stage. If a product or service is introduced and catches on, it may enter a period of rapid growth lasting several months or even years. Many firms may enter the industry during this period of expanding demand. Sales volume grows at an increasing rate, and profits for firms in the industry rise sharply. Competition also increases, but the entry of rival firms with their additional promotion efforts may actually enlarge the market.

Maturity stage. Eventually the level of market acceptance and sales volume reaches a peak. Sales revenue may continue to rise somewhat, but the rate of increase falls off, resulting in a decline in rate of profit. This is a stage of intense competition. Expenses for promotion become heavy, price cutting may occur, and consumers are pressured to be "brand loyal." Firms that cannot keep pace drop out of the market or are acquired by others. Large firms begin to dominate the industry.

Saturation stage. At this stage the consumers who can or will use the product or service are already buying—the market is saturated. Sales volume and profit in the industry begin to fall. Marginal firms have left the market, and the number of competitors stabilizes. The firm's promotion strategies concentrate on taking customers away from others rather than on enlarging the market.

Decline stage. Demand for the product or service falls at an increasing rate at the end of the cycle. Promotion is curtailed and becomes highly selective, and prices are cut to stimulate sales. More and more rivals drop out of the market. New products or services are developed to take the place of those that are now obsolescent.

The total length of the life cycle and the length of each of the stages vary considerably. A new clothing fashion may have a life span of one calendar year with an introduction-growth stage of 2 months. But the automobile has been in the maturity

SECTION II

126

Understanding
Marketing
for Your
Small Business

stage for at least 50 years. In any case your firm's market environments—economic, technological, social, and competitive—are constantly changing. When markets change, product or service strategy must change with them. Customers' acceptance of your product or service also changes. Therefore, you'll find it necessary to adjust your marketing strategy to the change.

A REAL-LIFE CASE: THE PRODUCT LIFE CYCLE

A small electronics company developed the digital voltmeter and put it on the market a few years ago. This instrument measures voltage in electric circuits with far greater precision than previous instruments and offers the added advantage of showing the voltage being measured in a large, lighted, easy-to-read, digital display.

The gross income from sales for 10 years following the introduction of the product on the market follows the curve shown in Figure 6-3, virtually a textbook model. The graph presents a typical life cycle for an innovative product accepted in the marketplace. The introductory period brought a modest increase in sales each of the first 3 years. The product then began to show increasing profitability. The next 2½ years, the maturity stage, brought rapidly increasing sales and marked improvement in profitability. But it also saw the entry and buildup of competition. Major competition came from a company started by two engineers who had spun off the originating firm. Other competitors followed, entering the market at the start of the saturation stage. Income for the original company peaked in the seventh year—and then fell off sharply because of decreasing sales and reduced prices. Production of the instrument was no longer profitable at the tenth year. Seeing its profit decline in the eighth year, the company began, somewhat too late, an intensive campaign to develop other products to restore its former profitable performance.

EXTENDING THE PRODUCT-SERVICE LIFE CYCLE

It's often possible to extend the product life cycle if actions are taken early in the maturity stage. Such products as Scotch Tape, Jell-O, Arm & Hammer Baking Soda, and nylon have all been given extended commercial lives through marketing efforts designed to find new uses for them.

We all know the spin-offs from Scotch Tape and Jell-O. The new uses for nylon are perhaps not so well known. It was originally used by the military during World War II in the production of parachutes, thread, and rope. The product then revolutionized the women's hosiery industry and has since been used in producing sweaters, tires, carpets, and ball bearings, to name only a few.

Arm & Hammer Baking Soda had been marketed for 125 years when a decision to emphasize a new use revitalized it as a consumer product. Baking soda was promoted as a deodorant for refrigerators. Six months after promotion began, an estimated 70 percent of the nation's refrigerators contained a box of Arm & Hammer Baking Soda. More recently, this baking soda has been promoted as a "natural" deodorant and toothpaste.

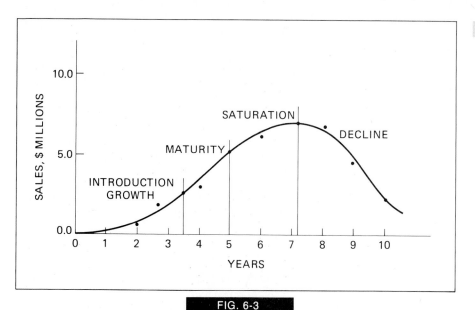

FIG. 6-3

A Real Life Product-Life Cycle

THE PRODUCT-SERVICE LIFE CYCLE AS A PROACTIVE MANAGEMENT TOOL

You can use the product-service life cycle as a tool to evaluate the timeliness of your business. What stage of the life cycle are your competitors in within the area you've selected for selling your product or service? A telephone-answering service may be in the saturation stage in one geographical area and in the introductory-growth stage in another. If you conclude that in a particular location your business would be entering during the late introductory or maturity stage, you should be extremely cautious. It's best to be first—not a me-too business.

The product-service life cycle should also be used to anticipate market changes. Knowledge of the natural progression of each stage in the life cycle of your product or service will help you plan your marketing strategy to cope with market changes as they occur. If you know that the saturation stage is approaching, you'll also know that your primary concern should be to extend the cycle by finding new product uses or otherwise modifying your product or service to meet the changing market conditions.

Study of the concept of product-service life cycle reinforces several recommendations we've made in this book, such as the need to be proactive in planning your business and to continually innovate in what you offer consumers. One of the best ways to keep your present customers and attract additional ones in later stages of the life cycle is to offer unique features, to develop and present a new twist to keep customers loyal and satisfied. You'll find this works much better than increasing your outlay for promotion or cutting prices to meet competition. The suggestions we made in Chapter 3 for developing new business ideas aren't limited to the start-up of your venture; they can be used continually after your business is operating. You'll find the product or service market matrix (Chapter 3) particularly useful for this purpose.

Your Pricing Strategy

Price is a measure of what the customer must exchange in order to obtain goods or services. But price is also an indicator of *value* to the customer. Value, like beauty, is in the eye (or mind) of the beholder. Thus, we return again to the premise that all marketing decisions, in this case pricing, should be based on your customers' perceptions of what you offer and the value they perceive in it. Your prices should reflect what potential customers believe to be the value of your product or service.

PRICE CONVEYS IMAGE

The prices you charge are part of your business image. Price tags say many things. Price on a tag tells the potential buyer something about the quality of the item: It can indicate extra value for the customer if two figures appear, the higher one marked out; or it can suggest that the very high price is insignificant compared with the status conferred on the buyer. The following case illustrates this point.

**MARTIN FURNITURE: THE LIVING-ROOM SUITE
THAT WOULD NOT SELL**

Jim and Roger Martin are brothers. They owned one of two furniture stores in a small midwestern town. A three-piece living-room suite had been sitting on their showroom floor for 14 months but had not sold at the marked price of $399.95.

The furniture was upholstered in imitation black leather with small silver stars printed on the material and silver piping around the edges. Jim Martin described the suite as being "in the modern tradition."

The brothers pondered the best way to sell the suite. They finally concluded that rather than put the furniture on sale they would raise the price substantially, because, as Jim put it, "this was a one-of-a-kind design." They priced the three-piece set at $799.95 and placed it just inside the store's entry.

The set sold the following week. Jim described the transaction as a "payday sale." "Payday customers come in on Saturdays when they have just been paid and have ready cash. They're usually with their families, and they're usually impulse buyers. I don't know what happens, but I don't even have to give them my sales pitch."

What is your opinion of the ethics involved in raising the price of this living room set from $399.95 to $799.95?

It's difficult to determine exactly what role the higher price actually played in making the sale for the Martins, but it's safe to say that with little information and inability to compare quality, consumers often use price as a yardstick of value. In the case of the living-room set, perhaps the price conveyed the idea of quality or status or uniqueness to the buyer. Jim Martin told the authors that he was certain that's what had happened.

The ethics of this particular case may be questioned. But the importance of price reflecting what customers believe to be the value of your offering cannot be overstated.

COMMON MISTAKES IN PRICING

Two errors in setting prices for their goods or services commonly trap unwary entrepreneurs. The first we call the "I-can-do-it-cheaper" mistake. Rarely can the small business manage to charge less than a larger enterprise. There are several logical reasons why this is so. Production costs per unit will be higher for the small business because of relatively small output. The small enterprise usually can't take advantage of large-volume discounts on purchased supplies. In a small service business, overhead expenses may be the same over a wide range of output or sales, resulting in higher costs per unit of sales in the first years of operation.

Chances are that if small business can enter an industry and sell "cheaper," others can do it also. With low barriers to entry, this can mean either that competition will be fierce and will focus on price or that the industry is in a late stage of the product life cycle—the saturation or even the decline stage. Neither situation is attractive; and neither holds much promise for the success of the entrepreneur.

The other pricing mistake we call "timid undercharging." It often occurs in firms offering services performed personally by the entrepreneur, who believes lower prices compensate for lack of experience and furnish a security blanket for gaining market acceptance. Low prices are set during the early months of operation with the idea that they can be raised as more and more customers are attracted.

This policy more often than not proves to be a fatal mistake, because it is always easier to lower prices than to raise them. The reason has to do with *image*. During the start-up phase, new businesses usually have to rely heavily on a core group of loyal repeat customers—attracted by the business image—and fringe customers—attracted by word-of-mouth advertising from the core group. The entrepreneur faces the prospect of losing both groups by raising prices. Higher prices change the image of your business in the eyes of your customers. Remember, *price communicates image*. Not only must your customers pay more for what they get when you raise your prices, but also they are likely to be confused about what kind of a business you really are.

If, on the other hand, the entrepreneur continues to undercharge timidly, the message the customer receives is: I can't do this as well as the competitor down the street; so I'll charge less. But the image of the entrepreneur and the image of the business are one and the same. It's a second-best image that's difficult, if not impossible, to overcome.

If you really can't do as well as others in the business, our advice is for you to work for someone else until you've mastered the skills required to perform your service expertly. Then charge for it accordingly.

MARKETING APPROACHES TO PRICING

The prices you charge obviously must cover all costs of producing the product or providing the service. The financial consequences in pricing are covered in Chapter

SECTION II

130

Understanding
Marketing
for Your
Small Business

10. What we've been discussing here are some of the marketing implications of pricing. Three basic marketing approaches are possible:

- A high-price strategy, often called "skimming-the-cream" pricing. This approach sets prices of the product or service well above costs of production.

- A low-price strategy, sometimes referred to as "market-penetration" pricing. This strategy calls for setting prices just above production costs in the attempt to achieve a high volume of sales rapidly.

- A meet-the-competition strategy, known as "me-too" pricing. This approach is intended to match prices charged by other similar businesses.

The approach you select depends, of course, on the kind of business you want to create. Skimming-the-cream pricing reinforces the uniqueness of your business. The high prices take advantage of any status connotations your product or service may have. Skimming-the-cream pricing is *not* price maximization. At no time do we advocate price maximization. What we do suggest is that your goal should be to set prices that will help you to achieve *maximum sales and profits*. If General Motors wanted to maximize the *price* of a Cadillac, it would produce and sell just one per month or one per year. Instead, GM charges a price well above production costs, consistent with the image of high quality and status the Cadillac conveys to its market.

As we've said before, it's easier to lower prices than to raise them. Many companies regularly use the skimming strategy for new products and gradually reduce price after the product is introduced at a high price. Early adopters, consumers who enjoy being the first to buy the newest, buy the product and tell others about it. Almost all early adopters have high income and are relatively insensitive to price.

As word spreads about the new product, the price is reduced so others can afford to buy it. Products that have been sold through this strategy are numerous: hand-held electronic calculators, microwave ovens, electric toothbrushes, and digital-display watches to name just a few. This pricing strategy enables the company to recover its initial investment costs quickly, to meet competitors' attempts to copy its success, and to reach more segments of the market. Sales and profit are kept high early in the product's life cycle.

Market-penetration pricing is usually used for products that become fads; they progress through the life cycle rapidly. Hula-hoops and Superballs are good examples. The products are unique. The objective is to gain quick access to the market, to obtain shelf space in dealers' stores, and to achieve a high level of sales within a short time. Penetration pricing affords the entrepreneur the most profitable way to sell easily copied products that appeal to a large market.

Meet-the-competition pricing is a strategy we do not recommend. If your new business can't charge more for its product or service than its competitors, it's a me-too business. The only conceivable reason to be in it in the first place would be if you were using the product or service as a holding action, giving the customers more value for their money than your competitors, while you were developing a truly unique product or service. We can't emphasize too often or too much that "I can do it cheaper" is not a good reason to start a new business.

PRICING STRATEGY

A critical step in your marketing endeavor requires that you set an effective strategy for pricing your product or service. We have discussed the virtue of skimming-the-cream pricing for unique products and services. We consider here factors that influence pricing essentially at the retail level. These tend to be heavily influenced by the psychology of the consumer. Your objective here should be to adjust selling prices to make them attractive to the consumer—and to lead to increased sales.

Psychological Pricing   Customers respond to prices in accordance with their perceptions, which are influenced by custom in some cases and by some kind of inner response in others. An odd price of $8.37 for a muffler or $293.43 for a microwave oven may find possible buyers psychologically uncomfortable. Many items, such as $2.57 for a pound of sweet butter or $0.99 for a loaf of bread, on the other hand, appear quite acceptable. The attempt psychologically in "odd" pricing is to make the price seem lower.

However, this approach to pricing can be used to bring out the relationship of price to quality. An antiperspirant priced at $0.67 will usually not appeal nearly as much to the consumer as the same one costing $2.48. The higher price induces the idea of higher quality; the lower price suggests inferior quality.

Odd-Even Pricing   Many retailers believe the psychology of ending selling prices in odd numbers improves sales. They will therefore set selling prices to end in 1, 3, 5, 7, or 9—and often just below some round number. For example, the price for an item may be set at $9.99, which marketers believe seems lower to customers than $10.00 even. Presumably this difference of 1 cent gives the illusion that the price fits in a range of $0.01 to $9.99 rather than in the higher range of $10.00 to $19.99. Although studies aimed at determining the validity of this way of setting prices have not proved statistically valid, this usage has become customary. It's interesting to note that so-called quality merchandisers do not use odd prices. For example, Brooks Brothers, a highly regarded quality apparel merchandiser, uses round-numbered prices: $15 for a tie, $275 for a suit, $90 for a sweater.

Flexible Pricing   In general, one-price policy typifies retailing. Variable, or flexible, pricing will usually be found in industrial marketing. However, certain retailing operations do engage in flexible pricing. The same products may be bought from some dealers in home appliances for different prices. The usual reason for this lies in the bargaining power of knowledgeable customers who are willing to dicker.

You'll observe that an advantage may come from the flexible price approach; it may permit swinging a sale that otherwise might not have been made. However, there are disadvantages: Customers who have paid higher prices may become disaffected with the store; competitors may retaliate in their pricing; the dealer may run into trouble with the Robinson-Patman Act, federal legislation that prohibits price discrimination not based on difference in cost.

Price Lining   Price lining, used widely in retailing, is the practice of offering merchandise at a limited number of prices. A men's clothing store might carry three

SECTION II

132

Understanding
Marketing
for Your
Small Business

lines of suits: one at $175, one at $250, and a luxury line at $375. Customers judge the relative quality by the difference in pricing of the "lines." They would expect the $375 suit to be of superior cut, material, and fineness of workmanship. The three price levels tell the customer that the lower price line is for the economy-minded, the middle line aims at those who want medium quality, and the high-priced suits are for those who want superior quality, perhaps with the spice of prestige.

Price lining, in theory, permits you as a merchandiser to serve different market segments through different prices. You may find it hard to determine how many market segments you should deal with. But with experience through feedback from your business you'll be able in time to segment your markets accurately. You must set your pricing levels sufficiently far apart so your customers can see the differences in the merchandise lines. But be careful not to price the lines so far apart as to serve no clear market segment.

Some manufacturers and wholesalers also practice price lining. Household appliances, for instance, are often marketed in two or three price lines: stripped-down economy models, standard models, and deluxe high-priced models replete with gadgetry.

Whatever the retail business, price lining simplifies buying for inventory and makes it easier for consumers to distinguish among the products offered.

Promotional Pricing   Promotional pricing, usually done at the retail level, occurs when some goods are priced very low to attract customers in the hope that they will buy other things at regular prices. Promotional pricing of this kind involves the use of *loss leaders*—items on which very low prices are set, often below cost. Food markets are notorious for practicing promotional pricing of this kind, usually by offering low prices on standard items such as coffee, butter, or some cuts of meat.

If you adopt a loss-leader practice, be careful to note that some states have unfair trade legislation that you should not violate. Furthermore, if you practice loss-leader pricing on a particular product for a long time, you may train your customers to accept that price as customary.

Discounts   In rounding out this section on pricing, we consider the practice of discounting. Discounts are allowances that reduce the list price on the basis that the customer performs some marketing service of value to the seller. A sample discount schedule is shown in Table 6-1. We'll look at five forms of discount: cash, quantity, trade, promotional, and seasonal.

TABLE 6-1

Sample Discount Schedule

Units of Product Bought	Price and Discount
1	List price
2 to 10	List price less 10 percent
10 to 25	List price less 15 percent
Over 25	List price less 20 percent

Cash discounts are reductions in price given customers for prompt payment of bills. Two conditions governing the discount are given on the bill: the amount of the reduction and the time within which the bill must be paid to get the reduction. For example, 2/10,n/30 says that the buyer may reduce the bill by 2 percent by paying within 10 days of the date of invoice; but if the bill is not paid within the 10 days, the entire amount is due within 30 days of the date of invoice.

Both buyer and seller profit by taking the discount for prompt payment. Most companies ordinarily take advantage of cash discounts. The total of discounts taken during a year can be very large even though the amount of each discount may be small. The seller gains through improved cash flow, which is money that can be used in many ways in the business. Discounts when accepted also reduce the risk to the seller of contending with the problems of collection and bad debts.

Quantity discounts are reductions in price to encourage buyers to order larger quantities than normal or to buy from one source rather than to buy smaller quantities from several vendors. Again, both buyer and seller gain. The buyer gets a reduction in price; the seller reduces selling expenses and may shift part of the burden of storing, shipping, and financing to the buyer. Quantity discounts may be one of two kinds, *noncumulative* or *cumulative*.

Cumulative quantity discounts are reductions dependent upon the sum of purchases over a stated period of time. For example, a buyer of a minimum of $50,000 of goods in a 1-year period might be granted a 6 percent refund on the total. A buyer of over $100,000 during the year might be allowed 12 percent. Discounts of this kind are intended to lock the customer in to one source of supply.

Trade discounts, also called *functional discounts*, are compensation to members in the distribution channel for performing some marketing function for the manufacturer. Trade discounts are based on the retail price to the consumer; they specify the discounts that retailer and intermediate can take from the manufacturer's price. For example, a lumber products manufacturer may set the retail price of goods and specify a discount relationship of 40-15 percentages. This means that the retailer takes 40 percent off the sales price to the consumer, and the distributor keeps 15 percent for immediate handling, storing, and delivering of the manufactured goods to the retailer.

Trade discounts offer the manufacturer some advantages. They give some control over the retail price. The manufacturer can coerce wholesalers and retailers to sell the product at a desired price—a price that ensures profitability by adjusting the trade discounts. In some cases the manufacturer may want to enlist high-quality high-cost wholesalers or distributors. High trade discounts can be a powerful tool for accomplishing such a relationship.

Promotional discounts come into play when manufacturers want to pay intermediates such as wholesalers for special effort in carrying out promotional activities. Manufacturers who seek a national market must rely on local distributors for help in promoting through advertising because the total job is too

SECTION II

134

Understanding
Marketing
for Your
Small Business

complex for them to take on alone. They parcel out authority for this task of reaching the local level to the many intermediaries around the country. The intermediaries are compensated by a promotional discount in the price they pay for goods or by a direct cash payment. Sometimes payment takes the form of promotional materials prepared and supplied by the manufacturer.

■ *Seasonal discounts*: Many products suffer highly seasonal demand. Skis are not in great demand during the heat of summer, nor are tennis rackets in the snows of winter. Manufacturers give *seasonal discounts* to those who buy in the off seasons. They attempt in this way to smooth out their production operations, reduce their costs, keep labor steadily employed, and shift some of the cost of storing the product to those in the distribution channel.

From the foregoing descriptions of discounts, you can see that the practice offers alert managers opportunities to improve the outflow of goods from inventory and to help control problems of cash flow. If your business puts you in a position in the channel of distribution, from manufacturer to retailer, be sure to take advantage of these opportunities.

Your Distribution Strategy

Business
Plan
Outline
1.B, 5.A

A channel of distribution consists of firms that facilitate the flow of goods from the producer to the ultimate user. It may be viewed as a series of links in a chain, with each link being a business performing specialized functions that add utility to the product or service.

The best distribution strategy for your business depends on which channel affords the greatest utility for your potential customers. Utility defines the degree to which the product or service satisfies the customer.

Your customers can use your product only if it's in their possession at the right time. And if they are to purchase your product, it must be in a place convenient to them. Therefore, the channel of distribution you select must offer two kinds of utility:

■ Time utility. Your product is available *when* the consumer wants to buy.

■ Place utility. Your product is available *where* the consumer wants to buy.

The importance of these forms of utility is obvious. Owning a stock of coffee located in Brazil certainly has drawbacks. And what value to you would tire chains be at the factory during a snowstorm or electric fans in a warehouse during a heat wave?

You may be able to produce the products that consumers are demanding, but no transaction takes place unless you and the buyer can get together. You must match your ability to supply or sell products with the specific time- and place-utility demands of your target markets. The best channel for vacuum cleaners may be direct from manufacturer to consumer through a house-to-house national sales force of 7000. The best channel for frozen pies may be from food processor to agent to merchant wholesaler to supermarket to consumer.

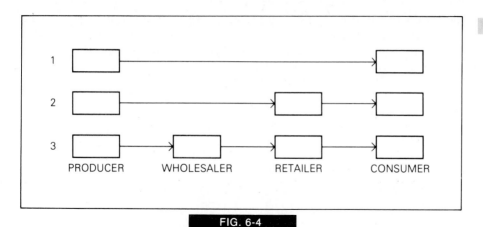

1	PRODUCER		CONSUMER
2	PRODUCER	RETAILER	CONSUMER
3	PRODUCER	WHOLESALER	RETAILER	CONSUMER

FIG. 6-4

Typical Channels of Distribution

Figure 6-4 illustrates the traditional channels of distribution for consumer goods.

Of three channels shown in the diagram the third, manufacturer or wholesaler to retailer to consumer, is that most often used by small producers. The small company with a limited line of products usually needs the financial and promotional resources and the market access of large wholesalers to reach the hundreds of retailers who will eventually stock its products. The wholesaler's large sales force is responsible for reaching the market with the manufacturer's output. This channel of distribution carries the lowest distribution costs to the small manufacturer. But it has the disadvantage that the manufacturer loses control of marketing because title to the product passes to the wholesaler.

The first channel shown in Figure 6-4, producer to consumer, gives the producer complete control of marketing and sales. It's also the most costly method of distribution. This means that you may have to make a trade-off between cost and control in choosing your distribution channel. Such a trade-off is illustrated in the following case.

THE CASE OF R & H PANELING COMPANY

Jim Ross was a remodeling contractor in the Pacific northwest. He found that increasingly his jobs involved paneling the walls of basements, family rooms, and dens. Local sources of finished hardwood panels were few. These materials were expensive and availability was unpredictable. It became more and more difficult to keep up with orders for jobs.

Ross's partner, Tolly Hansen, was a graduate engineer. Hansen suggested they try making their own engraved panels of enameled tempered hardboard in streamlined patterns. Ross liked the idea, and Hansen built an oven for baking enamel on the raw panels. Ross arranged with a local wholesaler to supply them with 100 sheets of hardboard at a time. Hansen designed and built special tooling for engraving the desired patterns.

Ross and Hansen now thought they could benefit by easing out of the remodeling

SECTION II

136

Understanding
Marketing
for Your
Small Business

business and concentrating on manufacturing their prefinished wall panels. They sold their finished wallboard to a wholesaler who in turn sold to retail outlets.

After a few months of following this distribution strategy, they found they were just breaking even. Finished wall panels were selling at retail for about 50 cents per square food. After retail and wholesaler discounts were subtracted from the selling price, Ross and Hansen were collecting just enough to cover their overhead, material, and processing costs. The trade-off between cost and control of distribution wasn't working to their advantage.

Hansen suggested they try another approach. They would produce, sell, and go back to installing the wall panels themselves; they would employ what is called vertical integration. They'd market "home beautification," remodeling with custom wall panels, directly to consumers. In this way they'd bypass wholesalers and retailers (the third channel of distribution shown in Figure 6-4).

This time the trade-off between cost and control distribution worked in their favor. In spite of increased operating expenses—they had to advertise and maintain a sales force to sell door to door directly to homeowners—they were successful. "We had complete control. We sold the concept of customer design, supervised installation, and guaranteed completion dates." The success of the channel of distribution Ross and Hansen chose was in great measure attributable to the superior time and place utility afforded their customers.

R & H Wall Paneling Company expanded rapidly with the use of this distribution strategy. Additional salespeople were hired, and new products were developed, such as etched-grain fir plywood paneling. After 3 years of profitable operations, they started to establish franchises across the country. Ross and Hansen furnished materials to order and trained franchises to sell and install their products. After 10 years of operating R & H Wall Paneling Company with success, both men were able to retire.

What is meant by vertical integration? Discuss its advantages and disadvantages.

Manufacturers increasingly use more than one marketing channel for similar products. In the case of Ross and Hansen, they continued to manufacture and sell directly to customers in their local area and with their franchise operations developed another channel of distribution. They became sole-source suppliers of wall panels for their franchisees.

Another example of more than one distribution channel is the case of the sale of soap products. These products are distributed through traditional grocery wholesalers to food stores to consumers and at the same time through a second channel: directly from manufacturers to large retail chains and motels. Manufacturers serve different target markets through different distribution channels.

The channel of distribution you choose depends on the kind of business you enter and customer preferences in shopping for products like yours. Tupperware and Avon cosmetics are firms whose marketing moves directly from producer to consumer. Almost all service businesses use this approach. If your business enterprise is a retail store, you're more than likely to be at the end of the distribution line. In this case the distribution channel decision is out of your hands. Your concern would be for the best possible location for your store. But no matter what the nature of your business, you'll have to consider several things in making decisions about distribution:

■ *Your consumer*. Results from your completed assignments about consumers at the end of Chapters 4 and 5 on marketing should give you some insights about the best channel of distribution for your business. In general, the geographic location and the needs of your potential consumer market will influence your choice.

■ *Your product*. The kind of channel, its length, and the functions to be performed within the channel are influenced strongly by the nature of the product you'll move through it: the weight and bulk of the product, its unit value, its technical characteristics, the amount of service it requires, its perishability, and the degree to which it's standardized or custom-made.

Perishable products, such as fruit or fresh produce, typically move through short channels directly to the retailer or consumer. Complex or highly technical products, such as computer equipment, are also sold directly from manufacturer to buyer. A general rule is that the more standardized the product and the lower the unit value, the longer the channel will be. Convenience goods and industrial supplies with low unit prices are usually marketed through longer channels. Installations and more expensive industrial and consumer goods are marketed through shorter, more direct channels.

■ *Your competition*. Which channels your competitors use is an important factor for you to consider. You'll have to decide whether you should use a similar channel or an entirely different one. Similar channels should probably be used for most target markets because of established patterns of customer shopping behavior. Occasionally, however, a unique channel approach is called for.

One entrepreneur we know owes her success to her unique distribution strategy. Her product is a small cake. It comes in six "natural" flavors such as lemon and pumpkin. She bakes the cakes in the morning and carries them from her car in a large basket to sell in beauty salons during the afternoon.

Your distribution strategy should be carefully designed to ensure the greatest utility for intended customers. Your products become accessible within your target markets through the channels of distribution you choose. You should make your decisions about your channels simultaneously with other marketing decisions, particularly those concerned with market segmentation, pricing, and promotion.

Your Promotional Strategy

Successful marketing of your small business calls for more than developing a good product or service, pricing it correctly, and making it easily available to your customers. An effective program of promotion is also essential for every business that wants more than "walk-in" sales.

Two serious deficiencies are often apparent in promotional activities of small

SECTION II

138

Understanding
Marketing
for Your
Small Business

businesses. Many entrepreneurs waste promotional dollars on consumers who aren't potential customers, and promotion is often viewed by entrepreneurs as a one-shot deal—a way to boost sales in slow periods. Promotion should be a deliberately planned and continuing program of communication tailored to the market segment you want to reach. It's probably the most flexible marketing tool you'll have, and you should use it to gain a competitive edge for your business. At the end of this chapter we'll ask you to develop a detailed promotional campaign including schedules to use during your first year of business operation.

Promotion is a special form of communication intended to influence target consumers; it may take any of the following forms: advertising, personal selling, publicity, or sales promotion.

As you read through the discussion of each of these elements, keep in mind that effective promotional strategy communicates continually to the *target* market. It develops awareness of, interest in, and desire for your product or service.

ADVERTISING

Advertising is intended to get your message to a large number of potential customers at the same time. It presents the ideas, goods, or services of an identified sponsor. It is paid for by your business. Advertising includes

- Direct mail

- Store sign

- Radio and television

- Magazine and newspaper

- Outdoor sign, poster, and skywriting

- Novelties such as calendars, blotters, and pencils

Advertising bolsters your personal selling efforts with nonpersonal forms of communication. A McGraw-Hill study called *The Mathematics of Selling* uses an advertisement that illustrates this relationship. The ad shows a salesperson facing an industrial buyer. The buyer's thoughts (shown in a balloon) are

I don't know who you are.

I don't know your company.

I don't know your company's product.

I don't know what your company stands for.

I don't know your company's customers.

I don't know your company's record.

I don't know your company's reputation.

Now—what was it you wanted to sell me?

Personal selling, as the ad suggests, can't always handle the whole selling job. Mass selling through advertising can do much of the spadework for you so that your personal follow-up can be concentrated on answers to specific questions and on closing the sale. Your goal in advertising is to increase the likelihood that the customer will buy your product or service.

You'll need to make three basic decisions to achieve your advertising goals. They are

1. How much should I spend?—Budget strategy

2. What media should I use?—Media strategy

3. What should I say, and how should I say it?—Copy strategy

Budget Strategy There is no pat answer to how much you should spend on advertising. What you spend will depend on your promotional objectives, your target customers, the characteristics of your product or service, and the type of business you're in. Several methods for deciding on a budget are used successfully by small businesses. A typical 1-month advertising budget is shown in Figure 6-5.

FIG. 6-5

Typical One-Month Advertising Budget

JUNE — *Advertising Budget* — **WINSTON HARDWARE**

SUNDAY	MONDAY	TUESDAY	WEDNESDAY	THURSDAY	FRIDAY	SATURDAY
Advertising budget for June: 10% of Sales = $725.00, Co-op funds = 140.00, Reserve fund = 50.00, Total = $915.00		**1** RADIO: 3 30-sec. spots. Flag Sale Cost – $60	**2** NEWSPAPER: 100 lines. Flag Sale Cost – $70 ($50 from reserve)	**3** RADIO: 3 30-sec. spots. Flag Sale Cost – $60 open Tonight	**4** NEWSPAPER: 100 lines. Housewares for Brides Cost – $70 open Tonight	**5**
6	**7**	**8** RADIO: 3 30-sec. spots. Flag Sale Cost – $60	**9**	**10** RADIO: 3 30-sec. spots. Flag Sale Cost – $60 open Tonight	**11** NEWSPAPER: 200 lines. Workbench for Father's Day. Cost – $140 ($70 from co-op) open Tonight	**12**
13	**14** FLAG DAY	**15** DIRECT MAIL: To all charge account customers, sprinkler systems Cost – $45	**16**	**17**	**18** NEWSPAPER: 200 lines. Hand tools for Father's Day. Cost – $140 ($70 from co-op) open Tonight	**19**
20 FATHER'S DAY	**21** FIRST DAY OF SUMMER	**22**	**23** NEWSPAPER: 100 lines. Camping Equipment Cost – $70	**24** Open Tonight	**25** NEWSPAPER: 100 lines. Camping and Picnic Equipment. Cost – $70 open Tonight	**26**
27	**28**	**29**	**30** NEWSPAPER: 100 lines. 4th of July needs. Cost – $70	Advertising expenditures as of 6/30: $3,425.00. Balance of general ad budget: $4,000.00. Balance of reserve ad budget: $700.00		

SECTION II

140

Understanding
Marketing
for Your
Small Business

The *percentage-of-sales* method is probably the most frequently used. A percentage of projected sales revenue to be devoted to advertising is predetermined. Suppose you learn from your trade association that firms similar to yours allocate 5 percent of revenue to advertising. You'd estimate the amount of your sales for your first year of operation to determine what your advertising expenditures should be.

The *fixed-dollar-per-unit* method uses an absolute dollar amount in the advertising budget for each unit of product sold or produced. You'd have to estimate how much it would take to sell each unit and then set your advertising budget for the year. A boutique owner who plans to sell 500 dresses might estimate a cost of $1 to sell each dress. The advertising budget for the year would be $500. The fixed-dollar-per-unit method, like the percentage-of-sales method, represents "formula thinking"; it ignores the goal that advertising must achieve—to bring sales.

Matching competition can be viewed as a defensive way to develop your advertising budget. The method of simply spending as much as your competitors assumes that your advertising strategy should be similar to theirs. It also assumes that your competitors know the "right" amount to spend. And it's almost impossible to find out how much your competition is actually spending in any case. This is not a method we recommend.

The *affordable method* isn't really a method at all. It simply answers the question: How much am I willing to spend on advertising? Entrepreneurs who use this procedure as a basis for deciding on an advertising budget don't truly understand the function of advertising. Of course, there are practical limits to how much you can spend; the flaw in the how-much-can-I-afford approach is the self-fulfilling prophecy. Advertising leads to sales; the amount you spend on it should be keyed in some way to the amount of sales you want. Suppose an entrepreneur is willing to spend only a small amount on advertising during the first year of operation. At the end of the year, meager sales and disappointing profits—the result of the inadequate advertising program—might lead to even less money being budgeted during the second year. This method of developing an advertising budget could result in the ultimate failure of the business.

As a practical matter the amount you decide to spend on advertising should be related to planned sales targets and the objectives for your advertising program. This means you should carefully assess your firm's need for advertising and set specific objectives before you make your budget. The advertising objectives must be based on your sound understanding of the target audience and identification of the results the advertising must produce. At this point you can determine the costs of reaching your objectives. In this way you have a budget that results from what you want to achieve rather than having your achievement limited by what the budget will permit.

Media Strategy Several forms of communication are available to aid you in meeting your advertising objectives. They offer enough flexibility for you to reach any specific target market by using a particular medium or a combination of media. The suitability of any medium for your advertising strategy depends upon the following four factors:

1. *Your target market.* When you begin to advertise, use the media that your customers pay attention to (see Table 6-2). You'll then have some assurance that your message will be heard, read, or seen by these target customers. Most

TABLE 6-2
Advertising Media Comparison Chart

Medium	Market Coverage	Type of Audience	Sample Time/Space Costs	Particular Suitability	Major Advantage	Major Disadvantage
Daily newspaper	Single community or entire metro area; zoned editions sometimes available	General; tends more toward men, older age group, slightly higher income and education	Per agate line, weekday; open rate: Circulation: 8,700: $ 0.20 19,600: $ 0.35 46,200: $ 0.60 203,800: $ 1.60	All general retailers	Wide circulation	Nonselective audience
Weekly newspaper	Single community usually; sometimes a metro area	General; usually residents of a smaller community	Per agate line; open rate: Circulation: 3,000: $ 0.35 8,900: $ 0.50 17,100: $ 0.75	Retailers who service a strictly local market	Local identification	Limited readership
Shopper	Most households in a single community; chain shoppers can cover a metro area	Consumer households	Per agate line; open rate: Circulation: 10,000: $ 0.20 147,000: $ 2.00 300,000: $ 3.20	Neighborhood retailers and service businesses	Consumer orientation	A giveaway and not always read
Telephone directories	Geographic area or occupational field served by the directory	Active shoppers for goods or services	Yellow pages, per half column; per month: Population: 14,000–18,000: $ 15.00 110,000–135,000: $ 35.00 700,000–950,000: $ 100.00	Services, retailers of brand-name items, highly specialized retailers	Users are in the market for goods or services	Limited to active shoppers

(continued)

TABLE 6-2

(Continued)

Medium	Market Coverage	Type of Audience	Sample Time/Space Costs	Particular Suitability	Major Advantage	Major Disadvantage
Direct mail	Controlled by the advertiser	Controlled by the advertiser through use of demographic lists	Production and mailing cost of an 8½-by-11-inch 2-color brochure; 4-page, 2-color letter; order card and reply envelope; label addressed; third class mail; $0.33 each in quantities of 50,000	New and expanding businesses; those using coupon returns or catalogs	Personalized approach to an audience of good prospects	High CPM
Radio	Definable market area surrounding the station's location	Selected audiences provided by stations with distinct programming formats	Per 60-second morning drive-time spot; one time: Population: 400,000: $ 35.00 1,100,000: $ 90.00 3,500,000: $ 150.00 13,000,000: $ 300.00	Businesses catering to identifiable groups; teens, commuters, housewives	Market selectivity, wide market coverage	Must be bought consistently to be of value
Television	Definable market area surrounding the station's location	Varies with the time of day; tends toward younger age group, less print-oriented	Per 30-second daytime spot; one time; nonpreemptible status: Population: 400,000: $ 100.00 1,100,000: $ 300.00 3,500,000: $ 500.00 13,000,000: $ 600.00	Sellers of products or services with wide appeal	Dramatic impact, wide market coverage	High cost of time and production

Medium	Coverage	Audience	Cost	Typical users	Advantages	Disadvantages
Transit	Urban or metro community served by transit system; may be limited to a few transit routes	Transit riders, especially wage earners and shoppers; pedestrians	Inside 11-by-28-inch cards; per month: 50 buses: $ 125.00 400 buses: $1,000.00 Outside 21-by-88-inch posters; per month: 25 buses: $1,850.00 100 buses: $7,400.00	Businesses along transit routes, especially those appealing to wage earners	Repetition and length of exposure	Limited audience
Outdoor	Entire metro area or single neighborhood	General; especially auto drivers	Per 12-by-25-foot poster; 100 GRP* per month: Population: 21,800: $ 125.00 386,000: $ 135.00 628,900: $ 150.00	Amusements, tourist businesses, brand-name retailers	Dominant size, frequency of exposure	Clutter of many signs reduces effectiveness of each one
Local magazine	Entire metro area or region; zoned editions sometimes available	General; tends toward better educated, more affluent	Per one-sixth page, black and white; open rate: Circulation: 25,000: $ 310.00 80,000: $ 520.00	Restaurants, entertainments, specialty shops, mail-order businesses	Delivery of a loyal, special-interest audience	Limited audience

*Several boards must be purchased for these GRPs.

Source: Reprinted with permission from Bank of America, NT&SA, "Advertising Small Business," *Small Business Reporter*, vol. 15, no. 2, copyright 1976, 1978, 1981.

Note: In outdoor advertising, gross rating points (GRP) measure the number of panels needed to deliver in one day the desired percent of exposure opportunities, 100 percent being that which would reach the entire population desired in a specified market.

SECTION II

144

Understanding
Marketing
for Your
Small Business

of the major media use marketing research to develop profiles of the people who buy their publications or live in their broadcasting area. Although they can't tell you exactly who reads each page or sees or hears each show, their data can give you guidelines appropriate to your market segment.

2. *Cost.* One measure that isn't subjective is cost. Two important dimensions of media cost are absolute cost and relative cost. Absolute cost is the actual dollar outlay for running an ad. For example, a message carried by a number of newspapers takes considerably fewer dollars than a message transmitted by television. Relative cost is the relationship between the actual cost and the number of consumers the message reaches. A common measure is the cost per thousand consumers reached. For example, suppose you want to compare the relative cost of a full-page ad in two different magazines. You'd obtain the following information from each:

	Ajax Magazine	Tabloid Magazine
Circulation	30,000	25,000
Percent of readers that appear to be potential customers— persons within a particular age group in a certain kind of occupation, for example	30%	50%
Potential customers reached with your ad	9,000	12,500
Cost of ad	$2,000	$2,500
Cost of ad per potential customer reached	$\dfrac{\$2,000}{9,000} = 22.2$ cents	$\dfrac{\$2,500}{12,500} = 20$ cents

This analysis shows that even though *Ajax* has a larger circulation and the absolute cost of running an ad is less, you'd prefer *Tabloid* because it has a lower cost per *potential customer reached*. See Table 6-3 for more information.

3. *The right media.* Some media will be better than others for the message you want to convey about your product or service. For example, for women's cosmetics, radio is limited because it carries only sound, whereas print media can show color pictures. You will also have to consider the message itself—its length, its degree of complexity, its need for repetition, and other factors—to determine which media can best handle what you want to communicate.

4. *Availability of media.* The local situation may determine the number and kind of media you use. A retailer in a small town wouldn't have as many options as a retailer in a large city. Whether your market is large or small, the medium you choose may not be available at the time and place you desire; the radio station you select may be sold out of advertising time.

Copy Strategy   This is the development of the actual advertising message—the idea or information you want to convey translated into effective words and symbols for your target market. Copy strategy involves formulating what is to be said, and

TABLE 6-3

Advertising as Practiced by Selected Small Businesses

Type of Business	Averge Ad Budget, % of Sales	Favorite Media	Other Media	Special Considerations	Promotional Opportunities
Apparel stores	2.5–3.0	Weekly or suburban newspapers; direct mail	Radio; yellow pages; exterior signs	Cooperative advertising available from manufacturers	Fashion shows for community organizations or charities
Auto supply stores	0.5–2.0	Local newspapers; yellow pages	Point-of-purchase displays; exterior signs	Cooperative advertising available from manufacturers	For specialty stores, direct mail is a popular medium
Bars and cocktail lounges	1.0–2.0	Yellow pages; local newspapers (entertainment section)	Tourist publications; radio; specialties; exterior signs	Manufacturers do all product advertising	Unusual drinks at "happy hour" rates; hosting postevent parties
Bookstores	1.5–1.7	Newspapers; shoppers; yellow pages; local magazines	Radio; exterior signs	Cooperative advertising available from publisher	Autograph parties
Coin-op laundries	0.6–2.0	Yellow pages; handbills distributed in area; local newspapers	Direct mail; exterior signs		Coupons in newspaper ads for "free trial"
General job printing	0.4–1.0	Yellow pages; trade journals	Local newspapers; direct mail; exterior signs		Samples of work can be used as promotional tools

(continued)

TABLE 6-3

(Continued)

Type of Business	Averge Ad Budget, % of Sales	Favorite Media	Other Media	Special Considerations	Promotional Opportunities
Gift stores	1.5–2.5	Weekly newspapers; yellow pages	Radio; direct mail; consumer magazines; exterior signs		Open houses; in-store demonstrations of products such as cookware
Hairgrooming/beauty salons	2.5–3.0	Yellow pages	Newspapers; name credits for styles in feature articles; exterior signs	Word-of-mouth advertising is very important to a salon's success	Styling for community fashion shows; conducting free beauty clinics and demonstrations
Health-food stores	1.1–2.8	Local newspapers; shoppers; college newspapers	Direct mail; point-of-purchase displays; exterior signs		Educational displays and services
Restaurants	0.8–3.0	Newspapers; radio; yellow pages; transit; outdoor	Local entertainment guides or tourist publications; theater programs; TV for chain or franchise restaurants; exterior signs	Word-of-mouth advertising is relied upon heavily by independently owned restaurants	"Free" advertising in critics' columns; specialties; birthday cakes or parties for customers

Figures compiled by *Small Business Reporter* in California.
Source: Reprinted with permission from Bank of America, NT&SA, "Advertising Small Business," *Small Business Reporter*, vol. 15, no. 2, copyright 1976, 1978, 1981.

how it's to be said, what form it will take, what its style and design will be. Rather than attempt to master the professional skills of copy design you'd be wise to rely on specialists—graphic artists and public relations people—for your copy strategy.

HOW TO USE AN ADVERTISING AGENCY

Depending on the advertising needs for your new business, you may want to use an advertising agency. If you do, you should interview two or three agencies to get a line on their services. The case at the end of this section describes how a small agency assisted in developing one of the most successful franchise operations in the world.

Advertising agencies specialize in designing and carrying out tailored advertising programs for their customers. The larger full-service agencies offer these kinds of services:

- Creativity: They can develop unique ideas for promoting your business, product, or service.

- Media selection and use: Agencies analyze and evaluate media to fit your advertising plan, and will schedule and place the ads for you.

- Technical production: They will apply specialized skills in such areas as preparing illustrations, photoengraving, artwork, and setting copy into type.

- Marketing research: The agency's research staff can advise you on the potential market for your product or service and on possible sources of distribution.

- Other functions: Many agencies also furnish such services as developing sales promotion and public relations programs.

You can readily see that the advertising agency can be an organizational extension of your business in performing several marketing services. Small, boutique-type ad agencies are growing in number, some of these specialize in helping small business clients. These agencies have limited services but would be more likely than large agencies to want you as a client.

You'll have to pay for the services of the ad agency. The most common method of compensation is the commission plan. Agencies generally get most of their revenue from selling advertising space and time. You, the customer, pay the list price to the medium in which the ad is placed by the agency. The medium then returns a commission to the agency for placing the ad. Thus, it's the medium—newspaper, magazine, radio, or television—that provides a good share of the agency's income.

In some cases agencies simply charge a flat fee for services to the client; in other cases the "cost-plus-percent" fee is used. The agency charges the cost of the advertisements placed plus a given percentage of that cost for other services performed. Fees or commissions can be negotiated; you should shop for the best value for the services you need.

Advertising makes your business known to the consumer. The advertising agency can furnish expert talent to make your message effective and get it to your intended customers. The potential value of establishing a working relationship with an agency is dramatically illustrated by a business that is now known to millions.

SECTION II

148

Understanding
Marketing
for Your
Small Business

BASKIN-ROBBINS 31 ICE CREAM STORES

Burton Baskin and Irvine Robbins returned to the United States after a stint on a supply ship in the Navy during World War II. They had discovered that of all things they delivered among the South Sea Islands, the troops in the South Pacific enjoyed ice cream the most. They decided to start their own ice cream business after the war to take advantage of the universal acceptance of this favorite confection.

Their first customers, as Irvine Robbins tells the story, were two or three small stores that sold their ice cream to retail customers. Soon after they got these outlets, a representative of a very large dairy product firm tried to persuade these stores to give up the partners' ice cream and take on their brand. The dairy products firm made attractive promises to the small store owners: new freezer cabinets, counter displays, and widespread newspaper advertising to stimulate the sale of their ice cream. The representative said, "Why do you want to deal with a peanut firm, when you can have our massive support?"

Baskin and Robbins were shaken when they learned of the attempt to take their business away from them. What to do to counteract the attack by the large competitor? The partners saw that if they lost these first outlets for their ice cream they would be out of business.

They talked through a strategy to improve their position with their retailers. "Let's put an ad in the *Los Angeles Times*—as big a one as we can afford. That'll show our retailers that we have substance and they can count on our being here permanently to supply their needs."

Checking their bank account, they found that they could manage $500 to buy an ad.

Then came the next question: How do you prepare an ad? Neither knew. So they decided in true entrepreneurial fashion to locate expert help. They found a small, new ad agency formed by two young, competent partners who had spun off a major national firm to form their own, called the Carson-Roberts agency after themselves.

When Baskin and Robbins told these two young men of their predicament, the two decided to take a chance on going along with the young entrepreneurs despite their obviously precarious financial condition. Perhaps they could grow a client relationship that would be sound and profitable for the long haul—if they could help Baskin and Robbins out of their crisis.

After they heard the Baskin-Robbins story, they said to the ice cream makers, "We're inclined to think that putting an ad in the paper is not the best way for you to spend your money. The ad will appear once and that's it. You won't get any mileage out of your investment. Let us think about your problem for a day or two. Then we'll make our recommendation to you."

At the next meeting, the two advertising men said, "Here's what we suggest you do with your $500. Your customers should get the image of fun when they see your company name. We recommend that you develop this image by using a white background with pink and chocolate colored balloons on it everywhere you can. Paint your little ice cream delivery truck white with pink and chocolate balloons on it. Change your stationery to carry the same colored balloons. And paint the inside of your retailers' stores white with pink and chocolate balloons on the walls. That'll carry out the theme you should have—fun to go into these clean stores, select a flavor, and eat a high-quality ice cream.

"Oh, yes, one important point—you should have lots of flavors your customers can choose from. That'll make it a game for your customers to enjoy—selecting a flavor."

"O.K.," said Baskin, "that's a great idea—31 flavors."

How did he arrive at that number? There happened to be 31 days in that particular month. As you know, the image of Baskin-Robbins is tied to 31 flavors and pink and chocolate colored balloons on a white background. Variety and fun have evolved a chain of hundreds of Baskin-Robbins stores with a gross business approaching $2 hundred million a year.

What lessons can the entrepreneur learn about the advantages of using an advertising agency from this Baskin-Robbins story?

The Baskin-Robbins turning point toward success came from that first meeting with the small advertising agency. The relationship has held firm over the years. The outstanding marketing success of Baskin-Robbins 31 Flavors Ice Cream Stores is directly attributable to the advice they got from their advertising agency.

PERSONAL SELLING, PUBLICITY, AND SALES PROMOTION

These three forms of promotion, personal selling, publicity, and sales promotion, along with advertising should be part of your overall consumer communication strategy. An advertisement can't make a sale by itself. In any promotion program it is the salesperson who must finally make the sale. Free publicity about your business can give you market exposure that will create consumer interest in your business. And sales promotion can result in temporary stimulation of demand for what you sell.

Personal Selling Personal communication with customers is vital to the survival of most businesses. It can be used for several purposes: creating awareness of your product, developing preference for your product, arousing interest, negotiating terms of sale, closing a sale, and furnishing reinforcement to the customer after the sale.

It's essential that you recognize the distinction between personal selling and all the other marketing tools: Face-to-face selling probably furnishes the only opportunity you'll have for two-way communication with customers. It's an interactive relationship between you and your customers; it involves learning and observing the characteristics and needs of buyers.

The modern approach to selling is not to *sell* the customers, but rather to *help them buy*. This is accomplished by presenting both the advantages and disadvantages of your product or service and showing how it will satisfy their needs. The result is satisfied customers and the establishment of long-term buying relationships. Instead of viewing personal selling as just moving products, your direct sales communication with customers should involve personal attention and interest in their buying needs.

Publicity Another name for publicity is free advertising. When your company or its product comes to the attention of the public simply by being newsworthy, it gets publicity. You pay nothing for the media exposure you receive. Most local daily newspapers will print stories about a new store or business opening in their area. Publicity releases describing your business should be sent to editors for possible

SECTION II

150

Understanding
Marketing
for Your
Small Business

inclusion in their papers. In addition, new information about your product or information describing your unique service may gain the interest of editors. Every new business serving local customers should take advantage of any publicity it can get. You might, for instance, have an advertising agency or professional copy writer prepare written materials and photographs to be sent to local media just prior to your grand opening. Then as you add new products or services or perhaps perform special community service, publicity can become a regular component of your promotion strategy.

Sales Promotion   This is a catchall term for promotion tools such as free samples, contests, coupons, discount offerings, and trading stamps. It also covers specialty advertising like giving away calendars, matchbooks, ashtrays, and key rings with your firm's name on them.

You might use sales promotion for a variety of reasons: a temporary promotion when you open your business, giving away a bonus item with the purchase of your product (called a premium in the trade), or a coupon offering a discount to stimulate sales during low seasonal buying periods to attract new customers or to induce present customers to buy more. However, the coupon really represents a temporary price reduction and may be inconsistent with the image of your business. Furthermore, the price-off sales promotion is suitable only for products that customers buy frequently. A caution applies to the use of sampling, contests, and trading stamps. In the long run these can involve much more expense than they're worth. Most small businesses should limit sales promotion to specialty advertising and occasional use of premiums.

Reaching Your Customer

Summary

Setting challenging but realistic marketing objectives will guide you in designing effective marketing strategies. Your marketing objectives are crucial to planning, since they help to assure that your efforts and expenditures are directed toward reaching a predetermined target.

Marketing strategies spell out how you intend to achieve your objectives and reach your market segments by pricing, promoting, and distributing your product or service. The effectiveness of these strategies will be reflected in sales. They will determine the number of new and repeat customers you attract and the degree of product awareness your business achieves. The acid test for assessing how consumer-oriented you are will be seen in the results of your marketing strategies.

Your product or service strategy should consider the life-cycle concept, which identifies four stages marked by a changing set of problems and opportunities. In the introduction-growth stage initial sales expand slowly for a time, then rise rapidly as the availability of the product or service becomes known and word-of-mouth advertising spreads. Competition enters as the market success becomes clear. To stay on the offensive, the firm that introduced the new product or service must improve it, add new features or new products, enter new market segments and distribution channels.

The maturity, saturation, and decline stages follow. Sales growth slows down and profits stabilize. Innovation is required to renew market acceptance and sales. Major modification of the product or service is usually needed. Finding new uses for the existing product or service also should be explored.

The product or service life cycle offers a useful framework for identifying the major marketing features of each stage and suggesting marketing strategies to consider in each. It can also be used to evaluate the timeliness of your business in a particular market segment.

Your pricing strategy has two major dimensions. First, the price you set conveys image and suggests the level of quality to the consumer. This is the marketing side of pricing. Second, price has financial implications, since the total dollars your business takes in results from price times the number of units (quantity) sold. This chapter concentrated on the marketing dimension.

Entrepreneurs often make the mistake of believing they can produce and price their product or service more cheaply than others in the business. Another common error they make is consciously to undercharge for a product or service with the hope that low price will help them gain entry into the market. These can be serious mistakes that once made are hard to correct.

If feasible, you should adopt a strategy of "skimming-the-cream" pricing. A high price capitalizes on the uniqueness of your business, conveys a high-quality image, and reinforces any status symbol that owning your product or using your service may have. If the price you set seems too high after some experience with it, it's easier to lower price than to raise it. Your strategy may then call for gradually reducing your first high price to attract the more price-sensitive customers or to meet competitors who enter the market stimulated by your success with your high-price strategy.

You can adopt ways of pricing that will stimulate sales; these apply largely at the retail level. Techniques include psychological, odd-even, flexible, and promotional pricing. You can use price lining, offering a group of items at a limited number of prices, which permits you to serve different market segments. In concluding the discussion on pricing, we suggested the utility of trade, promotional, and seasonal discounts in promoting business.

Distribution strategy varies from direct selling to using one, two, three, or more intermediaries to reach consumers. The best channel of distribution is the one that offers the greatest utility to your potential customers. Distribution here matches your ability to produce and supply products with your customer's needs for time and place utility. The special characteristics of your potential customers, product, and competition have to be carefully evaluated to develop the right distribution decisions.

Your promotional strategy represents your attempt to stimulate sales by conducting persuasive communications with potential buyers. The instruments of promotion are advertising, personal selling, publicity, and sales promotion. Together they may be the most flexible marketing tools you'll have.

Be careful not to waste promotion on consumers who aren't potential customers. Just as important, don't view promotion as gimmickry or as a one-shot deal to boost sales temporarily. Promotion should be a deliberately planned, carefully scheduled, continuing communication program aimed at the market segments you want to reach. And your budget for promotion should be determined by your promotional objectives and the sales results you desire.

SECTION II

152

Understanding
Marketing
for Your
Small Business

Use professionals in designing your promotional campaign. Graphic artists will help in preparing effective, eye-catching symbols or other unique identification for your business, product, or service. An advertising agency can advise you on the best media to use and your copy strategy.

Your marketing strategy will be an ongoing challenge. The tools you use, the skill and creativity with which you coordinate and employ them, and the consumers' response determine whether your business thrives or fades in the market.

Reaching Your Customer

1. Develop concise written statements of your marketing objectives. For each area write at least one objective to be accomplished within one year after opening your doors for business. (Note: You might want to jump ahead to Chapter 18 and read the section on managing by objectives. There you'll find the criteria your written statements should satisfy.)

   a. Sales: _____

   _____

   _____

   b. Profit: _____

   _____

   _____

   c. Product or Service Strategy: _____

   _____

   _____

   d. Pricing Strategy: _____

   _____

   _____

   e. Distribution Strategy: _____

   _____

   _____

   f. Promotional Strategy: _____

   _____

   _____

2. Evaluate carefully your intended market, competition, available products or services, and apparent trends in each, then answer this question:
   At what stage of the product or service life cycle will your business be entering the market? Then specify the evidence for your conclusion.

   a. The stage at which I'm entering the market is: _____

   _____

   _____

   _____

   _____

   _____

   _____

b. The trends that I've observed as evidence for my conclusion are: ____

_____

_____

_____

_____

_____

3. If you've concluded that your business is entering the market at the beginning or during the introduction/growth stage, develop and describe your marketing plans to deal with the problems and challenges each subsequent stage will bring. Here you should play the "what-if" game. It works like this: Suppose, as we hope, your venture is truly new and unique in your market and your sales grow rapidly. What if all of a sudden a competitor copies your success and opens up a business across the street offering the same products or services? What could you do to stay on the offensive? Remember, the variables *you* control are your product or service, your pricing strategy, your distribution strategy, and your promotion strategy. Describe briefly the kinds of adjustments or modifications you would consider in each area of strategy.

a. Product or Service: _____

_____

_____

b. Pricing Strategy: _____

_____

_____

c. Distribution Strategy: _____

_____

_____

d. Promotional Strategy: _____

_____

_____

4. If you've concluded that your business is entering the market at some later stage in the life cycle, justify clearly why you believe you can succeed. Do so by describing how your marketing strategies will set your business apart from the rest of the pack.

a. Product or Service: _____

_____

_____

b. Pricing Strategy: _____

_____

_____

_____

c. Distribution Strategy: _____
_____
_____

d. Promotional Strategy _____
_____
_____

5. a. What will be your basic pricing approach? Will you be skimming the cream, using a market-penetration approach, or a meet-the-competition strategy?

My pricing strategy can best be characterized as _____
_____

b. What price(s) will you charge? What evidence do you have consumers will buy from you at the price you set?

The price I'll set (or range of prices) will be $_____ for my product or service. I have the following evidence that indicates consumers will buy from me at this price: _____
_____
_____
_____
_____

6. What is the relationship between the price you will charge and the image of the business you will be trying to create? Is your price compatible; will it enhance the image of the business? Why? (Before you attempt to answer this, review your responses to assignment 6 in Chapter 5.)

The price(s) I'll charge are compatible with the image of my business because: _____
_____
_____
_____
_____

7. a. Describe the distribution strategy for your business. Will you go directly to consumers or will you use intermediaries?
_____
_____
_____
_____

b. Justify your distribution strategy in terms of the time and place utility it will offer potential customers.

My distribution strategy will assure that my product is availabe *when* the consumer wants to buy because: _____

_____

_____

_____

My distribution strategy will assure that my product is available *where* the consumer wants to buy because: _____

_____

_____

_____

8. a. Which method will you use to determine your budget for advertising?
_____

   b. Apply the method you choose to estimate how much you plan to spend for advertising during the first year of operation.

   The method I'll use to determine my advertising budget is: _____

_____

   I estimate my first year advertising budget to be $ _____

9. Listed below are media for advertising. Check the ones you plan to use and beside each one briefly describe its advantages as you see them in reaching potential customers.

	Plan to Use	Advantages
Direct Mail	_____	_____
Store Sign	_____	_____
Radio	_____	_____
Television	_____	_____
Magazines	_____	_____
Newspapers	_____	_____
Billboards	_____	_____
Handbills	_____	_____
Novelties	_____	_____
Others (specify)	_____	_____

10. Prepare a list of specific questions you will ask an expert in advertising for small business to answer (an ad agency, very likely). For instance, if you've checked direct mail and believe it to be most effective in reaching potential customers, you might want to know about cost per potential customer reached, brochure design and production, obtaining good mailing lists, what to expect in sales per 1000 pieces mailed, and many more items.

My questions about the media and their use are:

_____

_____

_____

_____

_____

_____

_____

_____

_____

_____

_____

11. Have you had experience in personal selling?

Yes _____, No _____.

a. If yes, describe it briefly, list your strengths and weaknesses in face-to-face selling situations, and describe what you will do to overcome your weaknesses: _____

_____

_____

_____

_____

_____

_____

b. If no, describe how you will acquire personal selling skills and overcome any perceived weaknesses: _____

_____

_____

_____

_____

_____

_____

_____

_____

_____

12. When and how will you seek publicity for your business? What media will you contact and what will you say to them that will be interesting enough to print or broadcast? In the space below, write two paragraphs about your business that you'd like to see in your local newspaper. (You might study the business section of a local newspaper and evaluate the articles about new businesses before you attempt this exercise.)

Here's what I'd like to read in the newspaper about my new business: ___

_____

_____

_____

_____

_____

_____

_____

_____

_____

_____

13. What forms of sales promotion fit your kind of business? How do you plan to use them and what results do you expect? _____

_____

_____

_____

_____

_____

14. The best way to coordinate and integrate your promotional strategy is to lay out an action plan for the year ahead that identifies for each month the promotion tasks to be accomplished. This will be your Master Promotion Calendar.

Procedures to follow in completing your Master Promotion Calendar.

a. You will need a large sheet of paper for this—brown or white wrapping paper perhaps. Along the bottom, you should note key dates such as holidays or other heavy buying periods. Under advertising on the left, list the specific media you will use during the year. Then, opposite each form of advertising you plan to use, show target dates for completion. For the other forms of promotion, personal selling, publicity, and sales promotion, you may want to make notes for yourself about the kinds of activities or events that will take place, and their target dates for completion. The general format for your calendar might look like this:

Advertising	Jan	Feb	Mar	Apr	May	Jun	Jul	Aug	Sep	Oct	Nov	Dec
1. Radio												
2. Newspaper												
3. Direct Mail												
4. Other												
Personal Selling												
Publicity												
Sales Promotion												

Then make brief notes on what will be done and when it will occur. For example, let's say you're going to conduct a direct mail campaign right after your business starts to announce your opening and to describe what your business offers. This will require designing the brochure and mailing brochures. The direct mail portion of the Master Promotion Calendar might look like this:

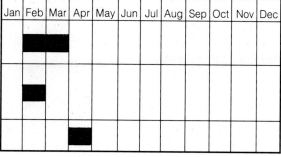

1. Direct Mail	Jan	Feb	Mar	Apr	May	Jun	Jul	Aug	Sep	Oct	Nov	Dec
a. Develop and design brochure with graphic artist		■	■									
b. Locate and select firm specializing in direct mailing and buy mailing lists		■										
c. Print brochures and get mailing out				■								

SECTION II

160

Understanding
Marketing
for Your
Small Business

KEY TERMS

objectives 121
market aggregation 122
undifferentiated marketing 122
product differentiation 122
market segmentation 123
warranty 124
introduction-growth stage 125
maturity stage 125
saturation stage 125
decline stage 125
product life cycle 126
skimming-the-cream price 130
market-penetration price 130
me-too pricing 130
price lining 131

quantity discounts 133
trade discounts 133
functional discounts 133
promotional discounts 133
seasonal discounts 134
channel of distribution 134
promotion 137
percentage-of-sales 140
fixed-dollar-per-unit 140
matching competition 140
affordable method 140
personal selling 149
publicity 149
sales promotion 150

STUDY ASSIGNMENTS FOR REVIEW AND DISCUSSION

1. Describe several different kinds of marketing objectives. Write two sample statements of marketing objectives.

2. What is meant by the product or service life cycle?

3. Name and define the four stages in the life cycle of a product or service.

4. What could you do as the owner of a small business to extend the life cycle of the product your company makes? Assume the product is a special long-handled tool to remove weeds from the garden.

5. Explain the statement: Price conveys image.

6. Why should the small company avoid "penetration" pricing?

7. Describe three different channels of distribution for reaching the customer.

8. Name the budget strategy you'd choose for advertising your product or service.

9. How would you select one from among several magazines in which to advertise?

10. What advantages could you get from personal selling as the owner of a small business?

11. What could you do to get publicity (free advertising) for your small business?

12. What kinds of activities could you engage in to use sales-promotion devices in your small business?

PROJECTS FOR STUDENTS

1. Three or four students invite the owners of three different kinds of business to participate in a panel discussion for the class. Businesses represented should be retail, manufacturing of technical products, and service. Students should be prepared to ask pertinent questions about the approaches the owners use to plan and carry out their marketing efforts: objectives, how they plan to extend their product or service life cycle, budgeting for advertising, and other subjects covered in this chapter.

2. Suppose you were manufacturing canvas tote bags for shopping, carrying books, or similar uses. Using the product-service market matrix given in Chapter 3, what specific things can you visualize doing to increase your business?

3. Identify at least three businesses that use the following channels to reach their customers: door-to-door selling; manufacturer to retailer to customer; manufacturer to wholesaler to retailer to customer; mail order (direct to customer). Give the advantages and disadvantages of each of these channels of distribution.

4. Ask a key member (partner perhaps) of a small advertising agency to speak to the class on how the small business owner can best use the services of an advertising agency. (Two students might well take on the assignment of locating and inviting the speaker to class.)

IF YOU WANT TO READ MORE

"The Advertising Agency—What It Is and What it Does for Advertising," *Advertising Age*, November 21, 1973, pp. 34–42. This article presents the services advertising agencies perform in a clear and detailed fashion. Topics covered range from media planning to package design, and the expert advice agencies can often give on pricing, distribution, and marketing research.

ANTHONY, Michael: *Handbook of Small Business Advertising*, Addison-Wesley Publishing Company, Reading, MA, 1981. This book details advertising strategies geared specifically to the small business.

BIANNEN, William H.: *Practical Marketing for Your Small Retail Business*, Prentice-Hall, Inc., Englewood Cliffs, NJ, 1981. This is a marketing text for small retailers of consumer goods and services. It adapts the consumer-oriented marketing concept to the needs of small retailers.

BIANNEN, William H.: *Advertising and Sales Promotion: Cost Effective Techniques for Your Small Business*, Prentice-Hall, Inc., Englewood Cliffs, NJ, 1983. This book describes in a practical way good advertising and sales promotion practices. It shows how strategy and tactics can be planned to produce effective ideas for advertising and promotion in any small business.

SECTION II

162

Understanding
Marketing
for Your
Small Business

BLAKE, Gary, and Robert W. BLY: *How to Promote Your Own Business*, NAL/Plume, New York, 1983. This paperback tells how to get the advertising job done. It covers topics such as budgeting of promotions; when to hire a professional consultant; copyrighting; graphics; media advertising; trade shows; direct mail; and how to measure the results of your efforts.

BRANNEN, William: *Successful Marketing for Your Small Business*, Prentice-Hall, Inc., Englewood Cliffs, NJ, 1978. This book is for anyone interested in small business marketing. The basic theme is that the marketing-management concept that has proved so successful for big business can and should be adapted to small business.

BURSTINER, Irving: *The Small Business Handbook*, Prentice-Hall, Inc., Englewood Cliffs, NJ, 1979. Chapters 11 to 15 address a wide variety of subjects ranging from marketing, the management of prices, and promotion management to marketing research.

COOK, Harvey R.: *Profitable Advertising Techniques for Small Business*, Reston Publishing Co., Reston, VA, 1981. This remarkable little book shows you how to analyze the market you have chosen to serve. It will show you how to select the best, most cost-effective medium (from television to direct mail) to reach your market. In addition it will show you how to pick an ad agency if you feel you need professional help.

DEAN, Sandra Linville: *How to Advertise*, Enterprise Publications, New York, 1980. This is essentially a planning guide for retail advertising. The author explains in a clear, unadorned text exactly how to define your target audience, how to buy local media to get your message across, and how to budget for and plan a campaign.

KURTZ, David L., and Louis E. BOONE: *Marketing*, The Dryden Press, New York, 1984, pp. 267–291. This is a chapter on product strategy from an excellent basic marketing textbook. It presents an overview of the elements to consider in formulating product strategy including the product or service life cycle, how the consumer adoption process works for new products or services, ways to classify products in terms of consumer shopping behavior, and the implications of this for strategy.

LEVINSON, Jay Conrad: *Guerrilla Marketing*, Houghton-Mifflin, New York, 1984. The author stresses the importance for the small business of maintaining a carefully developed marketing plan to ensure success. He analyzes advertising media and shows the advantages and disadvantages of newspaper ads and practices such as trade shows and the use of free samples.

LEVITT, Theodore: "Exploit the Product Life Cycle," *Harvard Business Review*, November-December 1965, pp. 81–94. This article is a classic. It is straightforward and presents specific suggestions for staying on the offensive in each stage of the life cycle. Although published in 1965, the advice the author offers for entrepreneurs applies just as much to today's changing business world.

SCHEWE, Charles D., and Reuben M. SMITH: *Marketing Concepts and Applications*, McGraw-Hill Book Company, New York, 1983. A first-rate basic text on marketing. Clearly written, it offers excellent supporting material on promotion, pricing, and distribution with which this chapter is concerned.

SHAPIRO, Benson P.: "The Psychology of Pricing," *Harvard Business Review*, July-August 1968, pp. 14–25. This is another classic article. It summarizes studies showing how consumers perceive price in relation to product quality and how they make purchase decisions on the basis of price.

SIEGEL, Gonnie McClung: *How to Advertise and Promote Your Small Business*, John Wiley & Sons, New York, 1978. This volume offers a concise commonsense guide for the small firm in small- and medium-sized communities. It provides helpful guidelines and hints for creative thinking in marketing.

SECTION III

Retail, Service, and Manufacturing Businesses

CHAPTER 7
CONTROLLING YOUR RETAIL OPERATIONS

CHAPTER 8
MARKETING THE SERVICE BUSINESS

CHAPTER 9
CONTROLLING YOUR MANUFACTURING OPERATIONS

Controlling Your Retail Operations

TOPICS IN THIS CHAPTER

Objectives of This Chapter
Selecting a Location
Renting or Leasing
Identifying Your Customer
Purchasing and Inventory Control
Elements of Purchasing
Elements of Inventory Control
Computers in Small Retail Business
Advertising and Promoting Your Retail Business
Controlling Your Retail Operations—Summary
Worksheet 7: Controlling Your Retail Operations
Key Terms
Study Assignments for Review and Discussion
Projects for Students
If You Want to Read More

This chapter will be found a bit different from the majority in the book in that it deals with a specific kind of business—retailing. So many entrepreneurs start in retailing, selling merchandise directly to the consumer, that we believe it important to point up the special characteristics of this business and to highlight the important aspects required to manage it successfully. This chapter offers closure

SECTION III

168

Retail,
Service, and
Manufacturing
Businesses

by showing how the basic principles of the foregoing chapters are employed in a whole business operation.

Information in this chapter will be found pertinent to these items in the business plan:

1.A.   Description of your proposed business

1.B.   Summary of your proposed marketing method

2.A.   Statement of the desirability of your product or service

3.B.   Detailed explanations of your place in the state of the art

5.A.   A comprehensive description of your marketing strategy

6.A.   An outline of the activities to be used in selling the product or service

7.A.   Description of the proposed organization

8.A.   Information required to support the major points in the business plan

$$\text{You} + \text{Idea} + \begin{Bmatrix} \text{Money} \\ \text{Credit} \end{Bmatrix} + \begin{Bmatrix} \text{Facilities} \\ \text{People} \end{Bmatrix} \rightarrow \begin{array}{c} \text{Product} \\ \text{or} \\ \text{Service} \end{array} + \textbf{MARKETING} \begin{Bmatrix} \text{Money} \\ \text{Credit} \end{Bmatrix} \rightarrow \text{Profit}$$

Of about 1.8 million retail stores currently operating in the United States, over 1.1 million employ three or fewer people. The U.S. Bureau of the Census consistently reports that 55 percent of all disposable income is spent in retail stores. This confirms our experience that many entrepreneurs want to go into retailing. We've therefore prepared this chapter to describe the special features that make retailing somewhat different from other kinds of business. The key principles that fit any business will be found in other chapters of this book; we'll refer to them from time to time without repeating them in detail. But we'll concentrate here on those elements that make retailing different.

Retailing is buying goods from suppliers and selling them directly to the consumer for personal use, not for resale. However, many service businesses that offer special skills to consumers, other businesses, or government or nonprofit agencies have characteristics in common with retailing as we ordinarily view it. Some of these firms sell products or merchandise in addition to performing skilled labor: barber shops may sell hair tonic, shoe repair shops may sell shoe trees, shoelaces, and shoe polish. Even if the small service firm doesn't handle products, it has to contend with many of the issues faced by the small retail firm. We'll therefore use the term *retail* in this chapter to include service operations.

Objectives of This Chapter

After studying this chapter, you'll understand the critical factors that make for success in retailing, and how you can apply the concepts you'll learn here to control your retail operations. You'll understand how to:

- Select a location for your retail store

- Purchase and control inventory

- Organize records for management control of operations and expenses

- Adopt a credit policy

- Advertise and promote your business

Selecting a Location

Business
Plan
Outline
1.B, 5.A, 7.A

Once you've decided who your customers are, you can begin to plan where you should locate your store. In no other business is location so important as for the typical retail store. The old adage holds, "If you want to catch fish, you should cast your net where the fish are." You'll want to make a careful study of all the possibilities.

Several possibilities exist for locating a retail store. The small community, town, or village; the city—downtown, neighborhood, or secondary business district; and the large shopping center are all possibilities. You should study the special qualities of each before deciding on a location.

SECTION III

170

Retail,
Service, and
Manufacturing
Businesses

THE SMALL COMMUNITY

The small town or village can support a cluster of retail shops offering household goods, food, and a variety of services if conditions are suitable. Suitability can be estimated from the demographics of the trading area served by the retail establishments. The Department of Commerce of New York State finds that a center of 10 stores will draw from the population within a 3-mile circle. Your analysis of the marketing potential in such an area will show you the desirability of setting up shop within that central cluster of retail stores.

Unusual problems need to be recognized. If the town is economically dependent on one major industry, a decline of that industry could be disastrous for a retail operation. Some small towns are known as bedroom communities; many of the town's residents commute to jobs in a nearby city. Invariably they will do their shopping for major items in the city, which offers a greater variety of choice, or they will drive to a shopping center 10 to 30 miles away to buy major items, such as clothes, furniture, refrigerators, or health-care services.

THE CITY: DOWNTOWN, NEIGHBORHOOD, OR SECONDARY BUSINESS DISTRICT

Some retail businesses do well in the central business district of the city; some are better off in a well-chosen neighborhood. Men's clothing stores specializing in high-quality, conservative business suits and haberdashery prosper in an area in which office buildings house corporate headquarters and professional offices; so do specialty eating places that serve fast, high-quality breakfasts and lunches. Other kinds of retail business, including service businesses such as hairdressers, children's play-schools, shoemakers, and independent markets, do better in outlying neighborhoods.

The first thing you must decide, if you want to locate in the city, is what category your business fits. Once you decide whether it should be in a downtown or secondary business district, or in a neighborhood within the city, you can perform a careful analysis that should tell you where to locate.

Downtown   What kinds of businesses might you expect to find in the central business district of the city? Large department stores, hotels, theaters, and major restaurants locate in the heart of the city. Large department stores through their massive advertising and promotional efforts draw heavy patronage from women. Small specialty shops devoted to men's and women's wear cluster around the large department stores. Central business districts also attract other kinds of specialty shops: high-fashion women's boutiques, luxury jewelry shops, shoe stores, lingerie shops, and the like. You'll also find specific kinds of high-volume stores such as chain drugstores, variety stores, and fast food establishments at strategic locations within the district.

The basic attraction for small business ventures in the central business district lies in the concentration of potential customers—the large number of people who work and shop there regularly. You can guess then that the advantage of hordes of potential customers in the center of the city must be paid for in high rent, high overhead, and high costs of advertising.

The magnet that attracts consumers to the city, according to many consumer surveys, results from four advantages:

- The many kinds of business clustered there

- The wide selection of goods

- Prices that tend to be lower than in other shopping locations in independently owned stores

- The possibility of accomplishing several errands in one trip

Some disadvantages accompany the advantages, but the advantages clearly outweigh them. Consumers believe major disadvantages of the city business district are:

- Difficulty in parking

- Heavy traffic

- A crowded area, which makes it a burden to get around on foot

- Lack of accommodations for child care

Locations within the central business district differ in desirability. One side of a main street may be favored over the other; for whatever reason, pedestrians may throng one side and seem to avoid the other side of a main street. Side streets may not offer advantages for walk-in business but may be perfectly adequate for businesses that promote customers by mail, by yellow page advertising, or by telephone. Musical instrument repair shops, custom tailors, and art galleries would fit these side-street locations.

Sometimes retail stores do a thriving business in the evening. Being close to places of entertainment can make late-hour operation profitable. A snack shop, candy shop, or ice cream parlor near a large theater often does a handsome business before and after the show.

In locating your retail store in the central business district, you should pinpoint a spot appropriate to your business at the lowest cost and with easy customer accessibility and parking.

The Secondary Business District Secondary business districts tend to form concentric rings around the downtown core, or central business district. Don't overlook these secondary districts when you explore city locations. You'll see two types of secondary districts: One is the expansion of an older downtown section—in which the population has changed or is changing. Inspect this district for deterioration. The other is the newer development that accompanies population growth. Make sure the district that captures your interest shows signs of vitality and growth. Such a district may have both the advantages and disadvantages of the central business district. Nevertheless, this secondary business district might prove to be exactly right for your business, and less costly.

The Neighborhood The neighborhood shopping district is centered in a predominantly residential area. Most of its customers come from within an easy walking distance. The businesses offer convenience goods or personal services: groceries,

SECTION III

172

Retail,
Service, and
Manufacturing
Businesses

shoe repairs, tool rentals, dry cleaners, delicatessens, hairdressers, book sales and rentals, and TV repairs.

Popularity of the neighborhood location has been slowly declining in favor of the new shopping centers and malls since World War II. However, a new version of the "strip" center is coming back. When you look at the possibilities of a neighborhood location, be sure to study the trend in the area. Much will depend on the geographical area of your search. More densely populated residential communities in older sections of the United States seem to offer more chance for successful site location than the newer developments in the west, for example. Neighborhood stores in Mt. Aery, a Philadelphia suburb, do well; but there would be small chance for a neighborhood store in Escondido, California, a rapidly growing community 30 minutes by car from San Diego.

The crucial decision of where to locate your retail store must come from a careful assessment of the characteristics of the trading area.

SHOPPING CENTERS

Three kinds of shopping centers offer sites for the more experienced and managerially sophisticated entrepreneur. These are the neighborhood shopping center, the community shopping center, and the regional shopping center. Each does business in a successively larger trading area; each operates at a higher overhead; and each has the opportunity for making more profit, given knowledgeable management.

The Neighborhood Shopping Center   The neighborhood shopping center presents a convenience facility for goods and services. Its focal point is usually a supermarket, typically surrounded by a drugstore, dry cleaner, hardware store, hairdresser, hi-fi store, and similar retail establishments. The supermarket and the drugstore tend to generate shopping traffic; they are therefore strategically placed to cause shoppers to walk by—and thus patronize—the other stores in the shopping center.

The typical neighborhood shopping center houses 4 to 15 stores on a plot of 4 to 10 acres. It serves a trading area containing 10,000 to 40,000 persons. Driving time from home to shopping center ranges from 5 to 20 minutes. Ordinarily no important competition exists within 1 or 2 miles of the center.

The neighborhood shopping center affords the least expensive location for the small retail store. This location seems suitable for the small retailer whose yearly gross business (in the context of our economic times) seldom exceeds $150,000.

The Community Shopping Center   The community shopping center presents a much larger and more diversified picture than the neighborhood center. It usually houses 12 to 50 stores and serves a population of 40,000 to 150,000. Driving time from home to shopping center can range from a few minutes to $1/2$ hour. Generous parking space makes it easy for customers to park. The community center offers great variety that, because several stores usually carry similar goods, allows the customer to compare quality and price. A small department store, or the branch of a large one, ordinarily occupies a center position. Small clothing and specialty shops located alongside the department store, take advantage of the traffic it generates. Small retailers and service businesses radiate from the central core.

The community shopping center represents a middle position in operating and overhead costs between neighborhood and regional shopping centers.

The Regional Shopping Center   The regional shopping center occupies an open-air facility or, more recently, an enclosed shopping mall. The regional center offers shopping of great variety for populations up to several hundred thousand. The trading area often covers 200 to 300 square miles, with driving times ranging from a few minutes to an hour. The regional shopping center makes available acres of parking space, and in some cases guards who direct and control parking traffic and customer safety.

Shoppers in a regional center expect to find stores that duplicate those in the downtown central area: major department stores, well-known chain stores, and a multitude of specialty and convenience retail operations and service facilities. The stores number between 50 and 100. One or more major department stores in a regional center attract large numbers of customers, and the department stores attract a flow of buyers to the smaller stores. Customers are readily able to do comparison shopping. Special features designed to draw customers to the regional centers include theaters, medical and dental clinics, banks, child-care centers, and branch post offices.

Many of the newer regional centers occupy enclosed, air-conditioned malls. Customers can shop at their ease no matter how bad the weather outside. They can buy everything from shoes to a wedding dress under one roof and have lunch or afternoon tea, or even dinner, in one of several clean, well-managed restaurants. Modern shopping malls are attractive, pleasant places to go; shoppers find themselves able to take care of all their buying needs in one excursion.

WHICH CENTER?

If you are a newcomer to the retail business, you can see from the foregoing descriptions of the three basic shopping centers that you would be well advised to steer clear of locating in a regional shopping center. Costs are too high for the novice; it's unlikely that, as a beginner, you could develop the high volume needed quickly enough to ensure success. You'd be much safer to gain experience in a neighborhood center where costs are much less and the competition is less likely to be overwhelming. We suggest that you can tip the odds in your favor by observing the precautions that we've stated, and those that follow.

Renting or Leasing

Business
Plan
Outline
5.A, 7.A

The rent you can afford to pay depends upon your volume of business, overhead expense, and profit margin. The very best locations demand the highest rent. For example, rents for clothing stores in prime locations in shopping malls run 5 to 10 percent of gross sales per month. On the other hand, locations for lumber and building materials operations, which do not require prime locations, may run as low as 1 to 3 percent of sales. When you try to gauge the rent you should pay, you should check with neighboring stores to find what they pay. In the end your rent will be fixed by the terms of the lease you negotiate with the landlord.

SECTION III

174

Retail,
Service, and
Manufacturing
Businesses

Rent may be paid in one of two ways, by a fixed amount per month or by the sum of a base amount plus a percent of gross sales per month above a minimum volume.

LEASING

Negotiating a leasing contract can be quite complex. If you were to lease a location in a shopping mall, you'd be likely to find the contract running from 40 to 60 pages. Obviously such complexity suggests the need for expert help. Even a lease for a less expensive location involves items in which you would want to be protected. Use the help of a competent attorney in negotiating the terms of the lease. Have your insurance agent also examine the lease before signing it because of provisions it may contain for responsibility for damages to the building. And if you are borrowing money from a bank or other lending institution, the loan officer will want to see the terms of your lease to ensure that you're protected from possible liability.

The provisions of the lease spell out liabilities and obligations of the landlord and tenant.

The lease should deal with minimum standards in provision of heat, cooling, water, and electrical and gas services—and the allocation of their costs. It should treat such items as who is responsible, and to what extent, for interior and exterior repairs—for painting, remodeling, rewiring, or other so-called leasehold improvements. Who is to furnish insurance for what? How about storage space? And how is security for the lease to be handled? These should be fully discussed and handled to the landlord's and your satisfaction. And undoubtedly there will be other items to consider in your specific case.

You should reserve the right to sublet the premises in the event of failure of the business or your desire to close it—and you should have an option to renew. The new business will probably not want a lease covering more than a few years, perhaps 3 to 5. The option to renew, even at a higher figure, will give you protection against having to relocate. If your business is successful, you can afford the increased rent. If you want larger quarters, your ability to sublet will allow you to move without suffering financial damage.

Sometimes a landlord will insist on a cancellation clause in the lease. In this event, your attorney should include safeguards to protect your interest. These might stipulate that you be given adequate notice so that you can find another location, or that you be compensated for renovation or improvement of the premises.

Frequently a provision of the lease will restrict the kind of business operation. The landlord may be forced to limit the lines of merchandise you want to sell because of protection against competition given previously to other tenants. Or you may be forced to keep specified hours in line with those maintained by other tenants. Many department stores in a shopping mall, for instance, keep open nights and on weekends.

The best lease is that which anticipates contingencies and gives equitable resolutions to protect the interests of both parties.

Identifying Your Customer

Once you've decided on the kind of center you want for your store, you'll want to find out if there are enough potential customers to warrant establishing there. To find out, you'll do a traffic study of the trading area.

You'll look at several critical variables: the number of pedestrians who pass by at different times of the day, on different days of the week, at different seasons, under different weather conditions. You'll record the number of women, of men, of teenagers, and you'll try to judge how many might be buyers. Observation of how they're dressed—the kind and quality of clothing they wear—will help you judge their power to buy the merchandise you will offer.

You'll note how people get to your proposed location. Do they come on foot, by auto, bus, or, as in some cities, by subway? Is there adequate parking for cars? Are there traffic regulations or unusual or difficult street conditions that would discourage potential customers from trying to reach your store? Extensive street repairs, new paving, digging up the pavement and installing a new sewer line can disrupt traffic for weeks—and can bankrupt a retail operation dependent on pedestrian or auto traffic. Are crowds released from nearby sports arenas, theaters, or schools at times that might either help or hinder your business? Weigh these factors because, properly gathered and interpreted, they will give you a sound basis for comparing the value of different sites.

Interviews with passersby can be used to add to the data collected by other means. Refer to Chapter 5 for suggestions on conducting interviews of this kind. The questions you ask must be carefully prepared to prevent influencing the answers and to avoid embarrassing the respondents in any way. You'll find guidelines on how to prepare questionnaires in the suggested readings at the end of this chapter.

If you are planning to locate in a shopping center with a large parking lot, you can take advantage of license-plate analysis. Unobtrusively observe the cars of customers coming from particular stores. Note the kind of cars they drive and their license-plate numbers. By checking with the appropriate motor vehicle department, you can, in most states, get the addresses of the owners. If you do this during peak business hours for several days, you can define the trading area in which your potential customers reside. Place dots for their addresses on a large-scale map and you'll develop a clear picture of the trading area.

THE SELLING RELATIONSHIP

The selling transaction in the small business offers great opportunity for profiting through harmonious relationships with customers. Salespersons can build a loyal clientele by being alert and listening carefully to what customers say. Knowing the tastes of a good credit customer, for example, a saleswoman in an apparel boutique can phone that customer and suggest that she might like a gown or two from a new shipment just in—and would she like to have two or three sent out on approval.

Similarly, the proprietor of Barbara's Bookstore in Chicago made it a point to chat with repeat customers. She made notes of the books they bought. When a new book in a category they had bought came in, she would phone them and suggest that they might enjoy the new book. She made many sales this way.

Salespersons should be careful of how they approach the prospective customer. The kind of product the customer wants should determine the relationship. Ordinary courtesy between clerk and customer might be sufficient in a five-and-ten-cent store. But it would take far more than that to close a sale on a big ticket item, perhaps a shopping item such as a mattress and bedding. Frances Torbert, formerly management training director for R.H. Macy Co., the famous New York department store, reports that she once wanted to find out why one salesman in the bedding department made

SECTION III

176

Retail,
Service, and
Manufacturing
Businesses

far more sales than any of the others. Posing as a housewife wanting to buy a mattress and bedding she approached a different salesman from time to time. She found the only significant difference between the top man and the others was that *he talked much less*. He was clever enough to make a low-key brief sales pitch and to answer questions, allowing customers to make up their minds without high-pressuring them. He knew that the customers had done comparison shopping. Often the sensitivity to refrain from talking creates rapport between salesperson and customer.

Purchasing and Inventory Control

Your success in retailing will depend upon offering your customers what they want, when they want it, in the quantity they need, at acceptable prices. To do this effectively, you'll need to do a superior job of managing the cycle of buying and inventory control. These two functions influence each other; they are inseparable. You must learn to keep track of movement of merchandise from receiving room to your customer.

BUYING

An old maxim in retailing says that "goods well-bought are half-sold." You must develop good buying sense—knowledge of what to buy, when, and at what price to be successful. To ensure that your customers can buy what they want in the right quantities, you'll depend on a practical purchasing policy and a controlled inventory. All starts with buying.

You'll want to keep track of your fast-selling merchandise—and those items that move slowly. Fast-moving items can drain your inventory, so you'll require assured sources of supply from which you can order quality and quantity quickly at the right price. And you'll want to know when to take steps to rid your inventory of slow movers. You'll need to keep abreast of the state of the market: what's new in products, materials, processes, or merchandise. The suppliers' sales representatives you deal with are valuable sources of information and can help you decide what to do in these matters. Be careful therefore to develop friendly relations with the sales "reps" who call on you, because they can help you manage your inventory.

Inventory Defined   The meaning of inventory can vary from industry to industry; it may even vary within the same industry. It may mean raw material, work in process, finished goods or supplies, or all of these taken together. We confine the definition in this chapter to the stock of merchandise you offer for sale in the normal course of business. We do not include raw materials in the storeroom, or supplies such as stationery, wrapping materials, or gasoline for the delivery truck. In retailing for purposes of management of purchasing and control of inventory, *inventory means merchandise for sale*.

Elements of Purchasing

Management of the cycle of purchasing and inventory control depends upon nine elements that are common to all businesses, whether large or small manufacturing, wholesaling, retailing, or service enterprises. Using the term purchasing in an all-inclusive sense, these elements are:

1. Determining the demand for a specific item

2. Determining the supply (or inventory) on hand

3. Identifying the kind, brand, and quantity needed

4. Selecting a supplier (sometimes called vendor)

5. Settling the terms of purchase

6. Placing the order

7. Receiving and inspecting the goods

8. Placing the goods in stock

9. Checking the sales trend of the article

As you can see, item 9 leads back to item 1, and movement through the cycle depends upon how a given article of merchandise is selling. These steps are often telescoped, or divided into substeps, in any given business. But all these steps contribute to intelligent buying. Good buying in turn makes for more sales—and more profit.

Managing each step in the cycle will help you achieve the goal of smooth flow of profitable merchandise from your suppliers to your customers—at minimum cost and with reasonable freedom from shortages or oversupply. You can see that several of the steps are as much a part of inventory control as they are of purchasing.

The basic principle in managing inventory may be stated this way: You must have available in any given period enough merchandise to cover expected sales and still have some left in your ending inventory with which to start business in the next period.

BUYING PLANS

Buying plans enable you to add inventory to replace what you've sold during the period *and* to add what's needed to meet expected (planned) sales during the next period.

Open-to-Buy Estimate The amount you allocate for buying inventory comes from your open-to-buy estimate, which is a form of budget planning. You would plan for a specific period, often 3 months. To figure open-to-buy you'll need the following data, all *based on retail prices:*

▪ Planned inventory level

▪ Anticipated sales

▪ Markdown planned (markdown means reduction in price intended to move goods that do not sell readily)

SECTION III

178

Retail,
Service, and
Manufacturing
Businesses

To arrive at the open-to-buy figure for the period:

Add the planned inventory, the planned sales, and the planned markdown. Subtract from this sum the sum of inventory on hand and stock on order. The result will be the open-to-buy figure.

Example

$ 50,000 planned ending inventory	$45,000 inventory on hand
70,000 planned sales	34,000 stock on order
5,000 planned markdown	$79,000
$125,000	

$125,000 − $79,000 = $46,000 open-to-buy

You will usually incur freight charges for shipment of the goods. A freight allowance of 5 percent should cover usual shipments. The open-to-buy figure should therefore be reduced by this amount:

$$\$46,000 - (0.05 \times 46,000) = \underline{\$43,700}$$

To find the actual cash outlay for the open-to-buy, reduce this figure by the standard markup for your goods, say 40 percent:

$$0.60 \times \$43,700 = \underline{\$26,220} \text{ cash outlay required}$$

GUIDELINES FOR BUYING

You can achieve sound management of inventory by following these control practices; they come from the experience of many successful retailers:

1. Purchase frequently to avoid out-of-stock situations, to assure fresh stock, and to achieve maximum stock turnover.

2. In a falling market, buy reduced quantities. This practice avoids the losses of lower selling prices, stock shrinkage, markdowns, and capital tied up in inventory.

3. In a rising market, do not be tempted to overbuy or speculate. But *do* buy in suitable quantities to protect your competitive position.

4. Buy the right merchandise. Old stock that is not salable cannot be sold by clever sales pitches, brilliant advertising, or smart displays. Only when the goods are "right" can these kinds of sales aids promote success.

5. Know your merchandise and your market. Whether you sell staples or specialty merchandise, study your trading community carefully. You must know what your customers need and want. Do not gamble by guessing; guessing has led to innumerable losses in the retail business. Sound purchasing plans can come only from knowing what you can sell, how much, and at what prices. (Refer to Chapters 4, 5, and 6 for background material here.)

6. Keep adequate sales and inventory records. Avoid what too many merchants do—rely on their memories and actually guess about the most important facts affecting their businesses. Keep accurate records so you can buy the right quantity of the right brands, styles, materials, sizes, colors, and price lines.

SAMPLE BUYING PLAN

After the dollar plans by month have been developed for your sales and inventory, the next step is to develop a unit plan to actually use when you start your purchasing activities with your vendors. Even though you are ultimately spending dollars, you have also to think in terms of buying units of merchandise when working with the suppliers.

In order to develop a logical and precise unit buying plan you should follow a specific sequence in order to arrive at the final plan.

Step 1—general merchandise content. In your initial business planning, you should already have determined what type of merchandise you will be selling, your customer demographics, and the income level and price ranges that you want to feature. This information is essential before you start your specific planning.

Step 2—classification or category breakdown. Whether you will be selling furniture, appliances, hardware, clothing, or just one product like shoes, you'll first need a classification breakdown. Proper classification is crucial not only for purposes of a buying plan, but also for tracking sales results whether you use a computerized or manual method. For the purposes of example, we'll take a men's apparel store:

Men's suits

Men's sport coats

Men's tailored slacks

Men's topcoats and outerware

Men's sweaters and knit shirts

Men's casual slacks and jeans

Men's sport shirts

Men's furnishings and accessories

Because the emphasis of this particular store is on the clothing side, we are using only one broad furnishing and accessories category even though it includes dress shirts, ties, socks, underwear, and leather goods.

Step 3—assortment and SKU plan. Once you have established your classification plan, you'll want to make a further breakdown in order to have a workable plan to use when you go into the market to buy. The extent of this breakdown will depend on your planned sales and inventory. For example, if the total annual

SECTION III

180

Retail,
Service, and
Manufacturing
Businesses

sales plan is $500,000 and your average inventory is $150,000 at retail, your assortment breakdown will be more limited than that of a store planned for $2,000,000 sales and an average inventory of $600,000.

An assortment and stock keeping unit plan (SKU) is merely a dissection of each of your planned classifications into styles or models, sizes, colors, and any other factors that identify your product precisely when you are buying or analyzing sales results.

As an example of an assortment and SKU breakdown, we'll use the men's suit classification:

5 retail price ranges: $150-$175-$200-$250-$300

3 styles: 2 button—3 button—double breasted

3 fabrics: all wool—wool/synthetic—all synthetic

5 colors: gray, blue, brown, navy, beige

24 sizes: 36–44 short, 38–46 regular, 40–48 long

Step 4—The purchase plan. Now that you have determined a workable unit assortment by classification, you are ready to make a budget buying plan by dollars and units. From your previously planned *dollar* inventory and open-to-buy plan you will now match your unit assortment plan with those dollars.

Let's say you'll be going into the market to purchase for a 3-month delivery period. Table 7-1 is an example of how you would arrive at a unit purchase plan from your original dollar plan.

Step 5—going to market and summary. You now have a detailed "spreadsheet" buying plan by units and dollars; you can plan your actual visit to your vendors. This plan should tell whom you are going to see and how many vendors you propose to use. In addition to the normal process of selecting all the components we've discussed, you should also be prepared to discuss and negotiate advertising allowances, freight and shipping terms, markdown allowances, extended payment terms, and other aids and assistance your vendors have available. In many instances, if you don't ask for these pluses, they won't be offered.

A certain amount of flexibility and deviation from your original plan should be expected because of market changes, but close adherence to your dollar plan would be prudent.

Elements of Inventory Control

Since inventory represents capital tied up but not earning, you should control your inventory to ensure a balanced stock on hand. Achieving a balanced stock means adding goods at the right time in correct quantities, sizes, and colors to serve the needs of your customers—and therefore to produce profit for you. In short, sound inventory control will guide you in knowing what to buy when—and in economical quantities.

TABLE 7-1

Men's Suit Unit Plan

	Delivered in		
	Month 1	Month 2	Month 3
Planned *dollar* retail purchases	$100,000	$150,000	$120,000
Planned *unit* retail purchases	502	754	603
1. Price ranges			
20% (of $) at 150 retail each	133	200	160
20% (of $) at 175 retail each	114	171	137
25% (of $) at 200 retail each	125	188	150
20% (of $) at 250 retail each	80	120	96
15% (of $) at 300 retail each	50	75	60
100% of $ all prices	502	754	603
2. Styles*			
40% (of units) 2 button	201	302	241
50% (of units) 3 button	251	377	302
10% (of units) double breasted	50	75	60
3. Fabrics*			
50% (of units) all wool	251	377	302
35% (of units) wool/synthetic	175	264	211
15% (of units) all synthetic	75	113	90
4. Colors*			
30% (of units) gray	151	226	181
20% (of units) blue	100	151	121
25% (of units) brown	126	189	151
10% (of units) navy	50	75	60
15% (of units) beige	75	113	90
5. Sizes*			
20% (of units) shorts 36–44	100	151	120
50% (of units) regular 38–46	251	377	302
30% (of units) long 40–48	151	226	181

*Please note that we do not show that you would have to spread these totals within your five price changes in a balanced manner.

This kind of management will help you to detect slow-moving items early; perhaps these goods are priced too high, or the customers just don't like them. You'll be extremely careful not to overbuy fast movers; in buying large quantities, you run the risk of obsolescence. What you will try to do is to steer a middle course between buying such small quantities as to lose quantity discounts or such large quantities as to tie up too much money.

You should use every management effort to control inventory at a middle level, recognizing that profit comes from "turnover" of the money invested in your inventory.

STOCK TURNOVER

Stock turnover measures the number of times you sell your average inventory and replace it during a given period—a month, a quarter, or a year; it is often called the

SECTION III

182

Retail,
Service, and
Manufacturing
Businesses

stock-to-sales ratio. It is figured by dividing the sales for the year by the average monthly inventory. For example, consider a women's clothing store:

Monthly Inventory

Jan.	$ 18,000
Feb.	21,000
Mar.	24,000
Apr.	21,000
May	24,000
June	25,000
July	22,000
Aug.	24,000
Sept.	19,000
Oct.	20,000
Nov.	25,000
Dec.	23,000
Jan.	20,000
Total	$286,000 (13 months)

$$\frac{\$286,000}{13} = \$22,000 \text{ average inventory per month}$$

Sales for year = $84,000

$$\text{Stock turnover} = \frac{84,000}{22,000}$$

$$= \underline{3.8} \text{ times}$$

Typical annual turnover ratios in apparel shops as reported by the Bank of America:

▓ Men's clothing: 2 to 2.5

▓ Men's sportswear: 3 to 4

▓ Children's clothing: 2.5 to 3.5

▓ Women's dresses and sportswear: 6 to 8

▓ Women's coats and lingerie: 2.5 to 4

From the range of turnover ratios in this table you can see the wide variation possible within a general retail classification. Knowing the turnover ratio you can expect in your specialty can help you steer a clear course not only in your control but also in your financial planning. You'll find sources for these kinds of data in the publications of the trade associations in your kind of business.

By careful control of your turnover you can reduce your investment in inventory, reduce depreciation of stock to a minimum, and decrease the storage space for goods. Here are some suggestions for achieving a good turnover ratio:

1. Try always to have balanced stocks. You must recognize that your inventory is composed of several categories of merchandise:

▓ Basic stock, the items of each style, size, color, or other characteristics that the average customer expects to find in your store at all times.

▓ Hot items, items that are extremely popular and in great demand for a short time.

▓ Fringe assortments, items that add to your store's image and goodwill.

Promotional items, items in enough quantity to meet promotional and special sale events, above the requirements of your basic stock.

2. Order the right quantities, colors, sizes, and styles. Control of ordering can be most intelligently managed through a sales forecast (see Chapter 11 for information on the development of sales forecasts) made on the basis of answers to the following questions:

How many units of each kind were sold during the last year in the period you are now forecasting?

How does this year's business compare with last year's?

What seasonal variations must you consider?

What external forces of change must you take into account, for example, do-it-yourself trends or the increasing impact of experiential sports or games? (See Chapter 4 for guides in analyzing forces of change.)

What trends are now apparent in your business?

3. Time the deliveries of your stock orders so your merchandise is available in the right quantities when needed. The following suggestions should help:

You should know how many days or weeks of sales your order must cover. The money you can allocate for buying for inventory, negotiations on terms with your vendors, the costs of transportation of goods, of taking stock counts, and of processing and storing the merchandise within the store—all influence the timing of your purchases. As you can see, all these can be managed most effectively by the planning you do in inventory control.

OVERSTOCKS AND MARKDOWNS

When your inventory has more merchandise of a particular kind than you can sell in your planned selling period, you have an overstock. No matter how carefully you buy, once in a while this condition will occur. You'll likely find it difficult to take the prompt action you should to overcome this condition; it's much easier to succumb to this trap than to avoid it.

But you can't afford to carry merchandise over to the next selling season, for these reasons:

Your investment in the merchandise is locked in and your turnover suffers.

If the goods you sell are subject to change in style, fashion, or utility, their value to your customers may decrease substantially.

The merchandise may become shopworn and lose its eye appeal.

The money tied up in frozen merchandise reduces the amount you can spend for new, attractive stock.

SECTION III

184

Retail,
Service, and
Manufacturing
Businesses

The moment you detect an overstock during the selling season you should take steps to get rid of the slow-selling items. Advertise the items, display them prominently, talk them up—and if necessary mark down the price. An old saw in merchandising says "the first loss is the best loss." Use a markdown as early as you can during the prime selling season; a small early reduction nearly always prevents a large loss later. This action will help to preserve your gain in the long run by improving your turnover and protecting your profits.

Markdowns are used not only to move slow-selling items but also to get rid of soiled, damaged, discontinued, or broken lots of merchandise; to meet competition; and to adjust prices for special promotions. Markdowns are often milestones of managerial misjudgment; they result from errors that usually can be avoided. The most common errors that result in excess inventory are:

Buying merchandise that doesn't meet the demands of your customers

Buying too many sizes, colors, or styles of items that don't meet the demand of your local market

Buying at the wrong time, either too late or too early in the season

Failing to promote merchanise promptly

Failing to mark down items soon enough to ensure selling them at minimum loss

You can see from this list of common errors the importance of keeping alert to the forces of change in the marketplace—to adjust your management activities on a timely basis to avoid committing these errors. In essence, your actions should result in smooth and effective control of the goods in and out of inventory.

TOOLS FOR INVENTORY CONTROL

Fortunately, tools for inventory control are readily at hand and simple to use. An adequate inventory-control system tells you what's in stock and what's been sold. The basic system should give you two kinds of control: dollar, or classification, control and unit control.

Dollar control keeps track of how general categories of merchandise have been selling. With this information you can decide how to spend money on future purchases. Unit control, sometimes known as perpetual unit control, divides the broad classifications and identifies the quantity of each specific item in stock by size, color, style, or combinations of these. This control also records the specific items sold.

The least costly method of merchandise management is to print unit and classification control information on price tags that are removed as each item is sold. These data are then organized in a systematic manner—kept in files, binders, or card boxes. By following this procedure, you can review the flow of goods in and out of inventory and gain the feedback you'll want to keep ongoing control of your investment in merchandise. The newer trend, even for smaller retailers, is to use computerized sales registers for both dollar and unit inventory control.

INVENTORY VALUATION

To determine your profit for any given period, month, or year, you must know the value of your inventory at the end of that period. You can find the dollar amounts of your purchases, sales, and expenses from your records as shown in Chapter 11. To place a value on your inventory for the period, however, you'll have to exercise managerial judgment.

In your retail operation, the goods you sell are the goods you buy; you don't change them as manufacturers do by processing raw materials. Therefore, you'll probably adopt the customary way retailers value goods—on the basis of their retail price. This is commonly known as the retail method of inventory valuation. If you want to find the cost of the goods in inventory, you merely find the percentage markup in dollars and apply the markup to the retail price by subtracting it from that price. For example, an item bought for $100 and sold for $150 would show a 50 percent increase over cost. In the retail method, the percent increase would be $33^1/_3$ percent (50/150). Therefore, to value an item for inventory, merely deduct the markup at retail.

In summary, the retail method allows you to compare plans, sales, purchases, stocks, markdowns, turnover, and discounts for different periods—and with minimum difficulty. Adequate records and good management of inventory will keep you on the road to profitable operation.

Computers in Small Retail Business

Business
Plan
Outline
7.A

We have consistently recommended that the entrepreneur avoid doing bookkeeping but rather concentrate energy on the important functions of managing the business for survival and growth. But much of managing depends upon collecting and using accurate data on a timely basis. With the incredible development of the electronic data-processing industry it is now possible for the small business to acquire management data rapidly and accurately, thus giving the executives up-to-the-minute information on which to base decisions (and also saving time in accounting and bookkeeping functions).

HANDLING MAJOR FUNCTIONS

Two of the major management problems in the retail business are inventory control and, if your business has grown and offers credit to customers, accounts receivable. An automated approach to both these functions can prove enormously helpful.

Inventory Control and Sales Analysis   Inventory control by automation starts with the classification of goods into workable breakdowns as described previously in this chapter. As each purchase is rung up on the cash register, the register records, on computer-readable tape, the purchase, the classification, cash or charge, and markdowns, and other data as may be coded in.

The computer output then feeds back by classification, beginning and ending inventory figures for that time period, turnover, and open-to-buy figure (that is, the amount left in the purchasing budget).

After you've received several weekly or monthly reports, you'll begin to see where your business is making—and losing—money. You'll then be able to do a better job of buying and selling.

Accounts Receivable   An automated approach to keeping track of accounts receivable in the credit side of the business includes, as basic, customer statements, aged

SECTION III

186

Retail,
Service, and
Manufacturing
Businesses

trial balance (a review of overdue accounts by customer, amount, and period of delinquency), sales analyses, and salesperson productivity report. Many small retailers do not take advantage of the finance charges they could make on delinquent charge accounts because of the difficulty and time-consuming effort to make the calculations. With an automated accounts receivable system the calculations are done by computer and the retailer improves the return on credit business.

Professional Consulting Help   When you reach the stage of employing a computer or data-processing service, you would be well advised to look to an expert for help. The field is so complex for the novice and it is moving so fast that you should get advice from a knowledgeable consultant in the field. With help of this kind, you'll be able to develop a tailor-made system for your business—it will give you the data you want without swamping you in extraneous detail.

PRICING AND INVENTORY CONTROL

Pricing affords an important regulatory element in inventory control. You can vary the rate of flow of goods in and out of inventory by raising or lowering price. You should consider the first price and those you adjust afterward as experimental; you'll change price to get the speed of flow of goods you want.

The first price set at retail is used to determine the initial markup. It's the difference between the delivered cost of an item and the original selling price. You'll set this price on the basis of policy from your experience—and you'll know from this experience that this price is very likely to be tentative because retail merchandise almost always depreciates from the moment you put it in stock.

When merchandise doesn't sell rapidly, you'll lower the price judiciously until it does. You'd be careful under this condition not to mark the price down too much—or too often. Otherwise your customers may develop a poor impression of your business. Not only that, you may train them to buy only during sales.

Keep accurate records of markdowns on items of merchandise. Analysis of these records will help you to pinpoint the items you should buy in the future and reduce the size of future markdowns.

Pricing Terms   Customary pricing terms used in retailing include the following:

- *Maintained markup*. After the price is reduced through markdowns until the item moves the way you want it to, the difference between the original cost and the reduced selling price is known as the *maintained markup*.

- *Gross markdown*. The original reduction in the retail price is sometimes called the *gross markdown*.

- *Cancellation of markdown*. If gross markdown is later canceled and the original price restored, this change is known as *cancellation of markdown*.

- *Net markdown figure*. The final amount of markdown (widely called a price reduction) is expressed as a percentage of net sales. With this figure you can estimate ahead of time the markdown percentage to use in the new season. You'd do this to allow for price reductions in the initial markup until you reach the maintained markup. This would permit you to control your gross margins or gross profits.

- *Keystone*. This term applied originally to clothing retailing; clothing retailers generally "keystone," or double wholesale costs, to set the sales price. This is equal to 100 percent markup on cost, or 50 percent margin on selling price.

Pricing   Skillful pricing of your merchandise is one of the most important functions in operating a sound and profitable retail business. After you have determined your total operating costs of doing business you'll be ready to plan what you will have to add to the cost of your merchandise to set profitable selling prices.

Other factors that will affect your pricing decisions are merchandise shipping costs, price reductions (markdowns) from the original prices, inventory shrinkage, alteration or workroom costs, and earned discounts.

Here is an example of the basis for determining your general policy of pricing for an apparel store:

Operating costs	30 percent
Shipping costs	5
Markdown costs	10
Shrinkage costs	2
Alteration costs	3
Total costs	50 percent
Earned discounts	6
Net costs	44 percent

Now that we have a minimum net cost percent we can target a markon goal for pricing merchandise. Let us assume that we want a 6 percent net profit on sales as a goal. We'll then want an average initial markon of 50 percent, markon being the amount *added* to the cost to arrive at the original selling price.

Here is an illustration of pricing:

Cost of item	$50 each
Desired markon percent ...	50 percent (known as keystone)
Retail price of item	$100

Other factors that may affect your pricing decisions will be how your competition is pricing identical or similar merchandise, and what your vendors are suggesting based on the market position of their goods. Flexibility is a key in pricing in order to stay competitive.

Proper management of inventory requires you to keep accurate records. And appropriate control of flow of merchandise through inventory will improve your profitability. But other kinds of record keeping are necessary if you are to manage your business proactively. These have to do with financial management and are dictated by your needs for managing money and taxes.

SECTION III

188

Retail,
Service, and
Manufacturing
Businesses

KEEPING RECORDS

Your suppliers, your bank, the Internal Revenue Service, and state and local agencies will require you to keep and submit accurate financial statements and returns. As stated in Chapter 11, several of the financial plans you should do yourself; these are for guiding your activities in managing your business. But most of the record keeping should be turned over to others. Don't waste your time doing bookkeeping. Hire a person to do clerical work that is essentially historical. This would include such tasks as preparing inventory records, daily sales and expense records, purchasing records, and statements for your bank.

You should be able to understand these records and analyze them for planning purposes. But you shouldn't waste time putting numbers in books. Your time will be better spent in managing your business, improving your marketing, monitoring your cash flow, and increasing your profitability.

FINANCIAL STATEMENTS AND RECORDS

Of the financial projections and statements given in Chapter 11 you should have prepared at least the following:

- A list of assumptions that give the bases for your development of the various projections

- Balance sheets at key times during the year

- Sales projections for the quarter and year ahead by the month

- Cash flow analyses for the year ahead by the month

- Income statements for the year ahead by the month

- Income statement for the year

- Break-even analyses by the month or quarter

- Ratio analyses, perhaps the following: current ratio, acid-test ratio, net profit to net sales ratio

Once you have become thoroughly familiar with these estimates and have learned how to make them readily, you can turn over their preparation to your accountant. You'll then be able to influence and monitor your accountant's work intelligently— and you'll be free of the burden of writing numbers on paper. You can leave the preparation of bank statements, government forms, and income tax returns to your accountant, subject to your inspection, of course.

Daily Records   You will need some daily records in your retail business. The most important are those that record your cash balance, your sales, and your purchases. Your cash records will show not only how much your cash balance is every day but also the amount of ready cash you need to handle a typical day's sales and purchases. Your sales records will show the kinds of merchandise in most or least demand— and also which salespersons are being most effective. Your purchase records will give you data on your expenses for merchandise, equipment, supplies, and overhead—all knowledge you'll need in developing your cash flow analyses and other projections.

Credit Management   Most seasoned retailers offer this advice to the beginning retail merchant: "Don't open a charge account for anyone—not even your best friend or your brother-in-law." For the small merchant, store accounts create more headaches than sales. The small operator can't afford to tie up large sums of money in credit accounts. Managing credit involves running credit checks, sending out monthly bills, monitoring slow payers, and collecting delinquent accounts. These activities take time and money—and can do nothing but build overhead.

You can avoid these troublesome tasks by honoring major credit cards such as Visa or Mastercard. By paying a small percentage of charged sales, you'll receive immediate payment for these sales, and you'll avoid credit checking, billing, record keeping, and the trouble of collecting your money.

If you decide to adopt a "layaway" plan, you should observe some cautions. Use a formal system of controlling layaways. Exercise a firm time limit on these transactions, say 30 to 60 days, and require a minimum deposit of 15 to 25 percent on the purchase. Call your customers as the end of the hold period approaches to remind them of unclaimed items. You can prevent excessive layaways by following these suggestions. Otherwise, customers may put items in layaway without much thought—and later decide they don't want them.

Advertising and Promoting Your Retail Business

Business
Plan
Outline
2.A, 3.B, 6.A, 8.A

Before studying this section on advertising your business, we suggest you review the concepts and procedures given in Chapters 4, 5, and 6 on marketing. We'll restate here some essential questions you must answer from your special point of view as a retailer:

- How would I describe my potential customers accurately?

- How many do I estimate to be in my trading area?

- Can they reach my store easily?

- Do they prefer to buy for cash or on some form of credit?

- Do they want their goods delivered?

- Where do they buy my kind of merchandise now?

- Can I offer features they're not now getting? If so, what are they and how can I supply them?

- How can I convince them to deal with me?

The material and suggestions in previous chapters will guide you toward answers to the foregoing questions. The retail business, however, demands some special attention to the last question; you'll have to develop persuasive advertising as a major tool for convincing potential customers to deal with you.

SECTION III

190

Retail,
Service, and
Manufacturing
Businesses

CHARACTERISTICS OF PERSUASIVE ADVERTISING

Advertising, to be persuasive, as the experience of successful retailers shows, must be brief—to the point, specific—telling your story precisely and directly, using simple, clear language.

And advertising must be honest. People resent being fooled or having their intelligence underestimated. To build a large group of repeat customers, you must tell a straight story—the facts on the tabletop. The Farmers Market in Los Angeles started during the worst days of the Great Depression as an open field where farmers rented space for their pickups and brought their farm-fresh produce for sale to the public.

Over the years the Farmers Market has become a multimillion dollar institution—a specialized shopping mall with a great variety of retail stores, restaurants, and services. They have developed their own unique approach to advertising, which appears as a daily column in the *Los Angeles Times*.

Here is what a key executive of the Farmers Market says about their advertising in a letter to the senior author of this book:

> We do appreciate your recognition of our truth-in-advertising, it is a tenet we believe in. It has always been the policy of the column to keep light-hearted in general and "newsy" in specific about the shops and the merchandise they sell. In regard to product offers and sales, we promote them in the column. We admonish substandard or less-than-quality merchandise and would not promote it intentionally in our column. It is too valuable a tool to all our tenants for us to use it in any other way.

See Figure 7-1 for typical ads run by the Farmers Market before Christmas.

Another kind of ad, from the *White Flower Farm* in Connecticut, aims at a sophisticated market. It is shown in Figure 7-2. This ad, which appeared in *The New Yorker,* avoids mentioning price (a procedure not recommended for most ads). It is a classic example of a well-written piece designed for a specified affluent market. Appearance and tone are calculated to draw the attention of consumers who have the space and the serious desire to do a high-class job of gardening.

In addition to being specific in your advertising, you should always mention price. The price should be given for a particular item. This allows the customer to make a clear judgment of how your price compares with that of competition. If your item compares favorably and your price is right, the quality of your advertising should swing the sale your way.

ADVERTISING MEDIA

Media suitable for advertising the small retail business include newspapers, radio, television, mail, display cards, door-to-door, window displays, and store layout. Whatever medium you choose for your advertising, you should consider these points in developing your copy:

- Timeliness. Time your advertising to fit the seasonal calendar: holidays, local events, opening of the fishing season, and similar occasions. Advertising for Easter, Father's Day, Thanksgiving, and other holidays should begin 2 weeks

FARMERS MARKET

YOU'VE heard about those folks who try harder than the other guys. Well, that's the way it is here at

FARMERS MARKET, 3rd & Fairfax. For instance . . .

★

A RECENT visitor from Phoenix, Federal Judge Mary Schroeder, was sampling the Market fare along with Judge Robert Kelleher, an old friend of Farmers Market. Judge Shroeder was involved with plans for a dinner to benefit the Phoenix Art Museum, and she remarked wistfully that it would be nice to find fresh raspberries for the dinner.

★

SO A CALL went out to Bisbano's Citrus about fresh raspberries. Could they be had? Could they be shipped overnight to Phoenix in time for the benefit affair? Could they get there without all being squished? They could, they were, and they did . . . and everyone said the dinner was the berries.

★

OF COURSE, shipping fruit packs is nothing new for our harder-working fruit and produce stalls, especially near this holiday season. Fmrs. Mkt. fruit gift packs are famous, and they should be, being made up of the best and biggest fruits available. As we reported a while back, there are no restrictions on these fruit gift packs, which can be shipped to every state. But the squeeze is on now to get those gifts shipped in time for the holidays. Better place your order soon. December 15th is about the last-ditch date to guarantee Christmas delivery. One thing you can be sure of . . . our produce people will work a little longer and later to make both giver and giftee happy with something special from

FARMERS MARKET, 3rd & Fairfax.

FARMERS MARKET

NOW THAT December is here, **FARMERS MARKET**, 3rd & Fairfax, has more things going for the holiday shopper than an economist has explanations. You'll find over 160 shops and stalls and kitchens, plus acres of parking on all sides.

★

SELMA PALMA at the Sweden Shop always has surprises for her customers, and this gift season is no exception. Like the small, important animals created by Royal Copenhagen and Bing & Grondahl—a seagull, hare, chicken, duck and sheep are new additions.

★

SWEDEN SHOP also has special edition bells and plates, lovely Norwegian pewter pieces, the new crop of hand-knit Norwegian sweaters (you'll look great even if you can't ski), and some traditional Christmas linens from Norway and Sweden, homespun and hand-blocked. And for something different and special in jewelry, see the Bing & Grondahl porcelain pendants, earrings and other pieces.

★

WORD from Eli Tweer at the Fmrs. Mkt. Post Office is that December 5 (this Saturday) is the latest you should wait to ship Christmas parcels, with December 10th the date to get all your cards out to be sure of delivery before Christmas.

★

FMRS. MKT. NEWSTAND by Gate 15 and Pearson's Alley in the stores section have just received long awaited copies of the special December Collector's Edition of Architectural Digest, with its 18-page full color spread on the "Private White House Apartments of President and Mrs. Ronald Reagan." Get your copy at **FARMERS MARKET**, 3rd & Fairfax.

FIG. 7-1

Typical light-hearted newsy ads for Farmers Market and tenant shops.

in advance of the actual date of the holiday. On the day after such events your advertising is dead; it should be replaced immediately.

- Buying habits. Know the buying habits of your customers. Let your ads state that you're open Friday and Saturday nights to accommodate those whose working hours make it difficult for them to come in at other times.

This Nursery Guarantees to Make You a Better Gardener

Pyrethrum

Pacific Coast Hybrid Delphinium

Bergenia cordifolia

The commitment in our headline is neither hubris nor public relations blather. It is true, and these are the facts.

— Full-color catalogues describe 1,200 items and include proper names (with pronunciation), hardiness ratings, and detailed cultural information for every plant offered.

— Plants are grown by us to stringent standards, then graded, stored, and shipped using traditional English techniques which are superb. We guarantee every plant to be true to variety, of blooming size, and in prime condition.

— Every plant is accompanied by planting instructions and a pre-printed garden label.

— A full-time staff horticulturist is available to answer questions by phone or mail at no charge. He will also assist in locating unusual plants which we don't offer.

— Our nursery store in Litchfield offers 10 acres of display gardens and 25 acres of growing blocks which are open to the public. The staff are trained horticulturists who can intelligently assist you in your selections.

— A plantsman of 50 years experience is available by appointment to assist you in the design of borders.

That is our complete sales pitch. Superb plants backed up with service to match. If you find it persuasive, the first step is a subscription to our catalogues, known collectively as *The Garden Book*. The fee is $5 which includes all of the above plus a $5 credit good on any purchase. It is difficult to imagine a more rewarding purchase.

Sincerely,
Amos Pettingill

White Flower Farm
P l a n t s m e n

Litchfield 9031, Connecticut 06759-0050

Variety. Spice your advertising by offering novelty from time to time. If you're in the hardware business, offer a set of metric wrenches; if you sell housewares, suggest the desirability of a new gadget for unscrewing jar caps. Educate your customers to look for the new and unusual in your merchandise.

Although offering a special appeal through novelty once in a while is good practice, your cardinal rule should be to stock what people want when they want it.

You'll use advertising as a tool to move inventory, to help regulate the outflow and inflow of merchandise. Purchasing is therefore tied closely to advertising. Again: "Goods well-bought are half-sold."

Pointers for Newspaper Ads   Metropolitan newspapers often serve wide areas; these will have special sections designed to cover given areas of the city or outside counties. You may find one of these special sections just right as an ad medium. Neighborhood weeklies or throwaway papers as *Shopping Guide* or *PennySaver* can often meet your advertising needs. These will cost considerably less than the metropolitan paper.

Whatever kind of paper you choose for your advertising, be sure to find the proper timing for your business. For example, food stores usually advertise on Thursdays and Fridays; real estate ads do best on Sunday, as do higher-quality stores.

Repetition builds customers; a series of small ads at regular intervals works better than a larger "one-shot" ad. And many newspapers will assist you in developing ad layouts and copy at no cost.

TV and Radio Advertising   As you might expect, television advertising would probably be too costly for your small business. However, you might be able to take advantage of special rates for short spots on local telecasts.

Local radio may be quite within your budget; spots on local radio programs afford a relatively inexpensive way to reach specific audiences. Radio stations design their programs to reach special audiences: country and western, middle-of-the-road standard music; classic, all news, and talk shows. You can select the appropriate station for your retail operations from the typical customer profile you've developed in your marketing studies. Over 400 million radio sets in the United States receive programs from almost 8000 radio stations. You therefore have a wide selection of stations and programming from which to choose for your purpose.

Television and radio combined seem to offer the best combination for effective advertising. Preparing program presentations for either demands intimate knowledge of the techniques of the trades—not a job for amateurs. Many radio and TV stations offer their advertisers help in writing and producing ads. They frequently allow free use of their facilities; take advantage of it. Otherwise you should get help through an advertising agency. (See Chapter 6 for recommendations on how to use an advertising agency.)

Radio and TV spots repeated frequently produce the best results. Plan scheduling for spots carefully, as recommended in Chapter 6. Test the effectiveness of your campaign through at least a 13-week program. Work with your ad agency to make adjustments that will improve the power of your program to attract customers.

In scheduling, choose the right time periods for your spots. The best time period for children's programs is 4:00 to 5:30 p.m.; for adult news and sports, 5:30 to 7:00

SECTION III

194

Retail,
Service, and
Manufacturing
Businesses

p.m.; for adults going to and from work, 7:00 to 9:00 a.m. and 4:00 to 6:00 p.m.; but these times may be different for a particular market segment.

Advertising by Mail   Advertising by mail offers a direct way to reach qualified customers, if the mailing list has been carefully compiled. You have the opportunity to use a rifle instead of a shotgun in aiming at your target. You can do this by keeping a record of customers, what they buy and their names and addresses. Sales slips, properly filled out, can provide the data for building such a mailing list. You can also turn to direct-mail companies that can supply specialized mailing lists.

Make your mail advertising productive by inserting enclosures with bills if you sell on credit. Introduce new products or services; often the manufacturer or distributor will supply circulars for this purpose. Tell your customers about sales in advance of the date given the public—your customers will welcome the chance to select their purchases before the general public learns of the sale. Use inexpensive bulk mailing rates to send out circulars and return order forms.

Transit Advertising   In cities or communities served by buses, taxis, subways, or other public transportation, display cards offer an effective way to advertise. You may find it possible to use display cards in vehicles that serve your particular neighborhood or trading area.

This medium offers several advantages: wide coverage, low unit cost per potential customer, deep penetration, and frequent repetition, and it allows the use of graphic displays in color. Furthermore, it is a continuous form of advertising, reaching potential customers day and night, every day of the month.

Messages may be changed each month at nominal cost. New cards may be prepared by the silk-screen process, which is widely available and quite inexpensive even in small quantities.

Door-to-Door Advertising   You may find it profitable on occasion to use throwaways such as handbills, circulars, or business cards. A flier announcing a sale may be especially useful. Adopt this method with care. Avoid placing throwaways where they would litter or annoy possible customers. Don't put them in mailboxes, and above all, avoid distributing them in communities where local ordinances forbid this practice.

Directories   Your retail business will undoubtedly find the yellow pages of the telephone directory a profitable place to advertise. The directory listing can stand you in very good stead because the readers have already made up their minds to buy and are just deciding which business to buy from. Telephone directories also have longer life than most other media. Issued annually, their life often extends well beyond the year of issue.

In-Store Advertising   Experienced retailers say that half the sales they make, at least in the first instance, are made by their window displays. Merchants go to great trouble—and pay high rent—to locate on a busy street and on the busiest side. Why? So many people can see their window displays and be attracted into their store.

Your store window projects the image of your business and your character as the person in charge. You'll want to put up a good front and make a good impression with the merchandise you offer. Your show window is the most valuable selling space in your store; it deserves careful study, planning, and work.

The following guides have been found to pay off in developing window displays:

- The name of your store should appear prominently on the window or in the display.

- Keep the glass and display itself spotlessly clean.

- Change displays often. The same people pass by every day; let them experience variety to stimulate interest in your offerings.

- Tie in with seasons, holidays, local events, and national advertising campaigns of suppliers. Take advantage of help from suppliers and manufacturers. Allow at least 2 weeks' advance announcement time in promoting sales for special events.

- Your show window should present a simple, harmonious appearance. Focus on a central theme, on one main idea at a time.

Be sure to keep a record of displays in company with your advertising calendar (see Chapter 6). Record how long the displays were kept, known results in sales, and both favorable and unfavorable comments. You may be able to repeat a display once in a while, using display materials and showcards, if these are carefully wrapped and stored.

STORE LAYOUT

Store layout combines advertising and promotion. The arrangement of the inside of your store gives you the opportunity to display *and* promote merchandise. You can show items in and on showcases, on counters, aisle tables, floor stands, ledges, and niches. Don't clutter the floor space, but look for opportunities to display goods— so long as you use good taste. Be sure that your store is well lighted and well ventilated. Stimulate your business by making your store comfortable and convenient for your customers.

Keep staples out of the main flow of traffic. People use these items all the time, and will seek them when they are in the market to buy. Use free-standing and point-of-purchase displays along the main traffic paths in your store. Let your customers see an array of items close up to tempt them to buy. Free-standing displays take the form of self-contained shelving or hooks to hold merchandise on a pedestal; the display can be placed at the intersection of aisles or any desired spot where traffic is heavy. A well-known example of a free-standing display is the l'Eggs stand offering women's hose, which may be seen in many different kinds of stores, including supermarkets. The point-of-purchase display can often be seen as small fiberboard, tent-shaped constructions showing a drawing or picture of the item in use, with several of the actual articles clipped alongside.

Point-of-purchase displays are particularly suited to small items, new products, and items being specially promoted. Supermarkets sell candy bars, gum, and small

SECTION III

196

Retail,
Service, and
Manufacturing
Businesses

magazines this way. Placed near the cash register or checkout counter, point-of-purchase displays advertise and promote self-selling, profit-making opportunities.

Controlling Your Retail Operations

Summary

In this chapter we've emphasized the importance of selecting a suitable location for your retail business. We've outlined the advantages and disadvantages of the three basic locations and the variations that can exist within them. If you're a beginner with limited means, we've recommended that you start in a shopping center of moderate rental cost, but with sufficient marketing potential to permit your business to be profitable. And we've suggested ways for you to estimate the quality and number of possible customers.

We've given some guidelines for you to follow when you negotiate a lease for the store you've decided upon. You should try to anticipate contingencies so that you and the landlord agree upon whose responsibility it is to repair a leaky roof and whose to paint the interior. The best lease affords fair solutions for both.

We have dwelt at length upon the importance of your controlling your inventory by monitoring sales—the outflow of merchandise—and purchasing through an open-to-buy procedure—the inflow of merchandise—to meet the requirements of anticipated sales. And you'll want to know how to value your inventory when it comes time to figure your profit. You'll also want to control your inventory through knowledge of turnover and to know how to maintain a balanced stock of goods. These are covered in this chapter, as are a number of tools for inventory control.

You should prepare certain key financial statements yourself in the beginning. Later on you can turn these over to your accountant for preparation under your guidance. Daily records of sales, cash balance, and purchasing can be designated to a bookkeeper or some other person; you should examine these regularly to gain knowledge of trends in your business. A computerized approach can be very helpful here (and will be discussed in Chapter 12) and can include control of credit selling if you should decide at some time to go that way.

As a retailer, you should be aware of the methods used by successful stores to advertise and promote their business. Observe what your competitors do—and what retailers in other lines do. Make notes of their attractive window displays, their store layout, advertising, customer relations, and anything that you see that tends to make their operation effective. Clip and save ads that strike you as especially attractive. Search continually for newer and better ways to advertise and promote your business.

Above all, talk with people. Talk with your employees. Never stop surveying your customers. Find out what they like about the way you do business—and where they see opportunities for improvement. Accept the idea that neighborhoods change and that buying habits change. Learn why a customer drifts away—and you'll take corrective measures. Keep continually alert to change—and adjust and modify your advertising and promotional efforts to keep your business profitable.

Controlling Your Retail Operations

This worksheet gives you a checklist for assuring that you've covered the important factors in setting up and managing your retail business. Be sure to refer to many of the basic concepts and principles treated in various chapters of this book; you'll find them referred to in this chapter. Care in preparing this worksheet will allow you to take advantage of the experience of many successful retailers in many kinds of business.

Check the statements that follow to show you understand them and fill in the lines where they're appropriate for your business. Answer this question for each choice you make: *Why did you make this choice?*

SELECTING A LOCATION

I recognize these possibilities for locating my retail business:

■ The small community, town, or village _____

■ The city—downtown, neighborhood, or secondary business district _____

_____

■ The large shopping center _____

I've check-marked the location I've decided upon.

ADVANTAGES AND DISADVANTAGES

The site I've chosen has the following advantages and disadvantages:

Advantages: _____

_____

_____

_____

_____

Disadvantages: _____

_____

_____

_____

_____

IDENTIFYING YOUR CUSTOMER

I've counted the number of pedestrians who walk by the site at different times of the day and on different days of the week—and under a variety of weather conditions.

Here's what I've found:

| | | Number of Pedestrians | | | | (Date: _____) | |
| | | | | | | (Weather: _____) | |
	M	TU	W	TH	F	S	SU
Women	____	____	____	____	____	____	____
Men	____	____	____	____	____	____	____
Teenagers (B or G)	____	____	____	____	____	____	____

Make a table like this for the different times of the day that would be important for your business: morning, noon, evening, or night. Record data on a similar chart for bad weather, and for different seasons if possible. Repeat your observations until you're satisfied that your information is reliable.

Transportation. I've observed how people get to the site. The majority arrive by private car _____; bus _____; on foot _____; by subway _____.

I've found the parking area adequate for the business _____. There are no traffic regulations or difficult street conditions that would make it hard for people to reach the store _____.

Are there any other factors in the site you're considering that would help or hinder your business? Note them: _____

_____

_____

_____

Interviews. I've interviewed _____ (number) of passersby. A copy of my interview schedule is attached. My analysis of the results confirms _____ (or denies _____) my opinion of the potential business at this site.

License-Plate Analysis. I've done a license-plate analysis of the cars in the parking lot in the shopping center located at _____.
From this effort, I've defined my trading area and have plotted it on the attached map.

RENTING OR LEASING

I have arranged to negotiate a lease on a store at _____.
I've worked through the requirements I want from the landlord with my attorney, _____. We're going to try for concessions in the matters of: term (_____ years with option to renew); minimum requirements for heating, air conditioning, water, gas, and electricity. We'll be responsible for interior repairs; the landlord will be responsible for exterior repairs and maintenance of the property. We'll also want the right to sublet should circumstances demand.

Other items my attorney will negotiate: _____

_____

_____

_____

PURCHASING AND INVENTORY CONTROL

I recognize that purchasing and inventory control are interrelated. I've set up a simple system of record keeping to keep track of my fast-selling items—and to learn which are slower-moving _____.

BUYING

I've collected information on sources of supply that I can count on—and I've begun to establish cordial relations with their key people, including salespersons. _____I'll talk with salespeople on a continuing basis in order to keep abreast of trends in the market. _____ I know that inventory means merchandise for sale, and I'll do all within my power to think about inventory as outflow and inflow of merchandise.

Buying Plans. I have studied the planning needed to arrive at open-to-buy estimates and will use this method in my business. _____

STOCK TURNOVER

I understand the importance of stock turnover and will figure my turnover on a regular basis, by the _____ (month, quarter, or year).

INVENTORY CONTROL

I have arranged to adopt classification and unit control of my merchandise _____. Here's a brief description of how I will know what has been sold and what should be done to add goods to inventory. _____

_____

_____

INVENTORY VALUATION

I understand that I must place a dollar value on inventory at the end of any period for which I want to find my profit. To do this in the retail method, I'll subtract the markup from the retail selling price of the goods in inventory.

USE OF COMPUTERS

When my business has grown to a point at which the use of automated data processing looks promising for many of my management functions, I'll seek a reputable consultant to help me select the system most appropriate for my business. _____

KEEPING RECORDS

I am committed to doing the following planning myself: _____

_____

_____

_____

_____

I have hired the following to do my bookkeeping and record keeping: ____
_____. These data include the following: _____

_____

_____

CREDIT MANAGEMENT

I will not involve the business in credit management until I've grown large enough and prosperous enough to warrant it. _____ At the beginning I'll accept VISA and MASTERCARD credit only. _____

ADVERTISING AND PROMOTION

I have studied Chapters 4, 5, and 6 on marketing and promotion and have answered the questions on page 175. I have listed my answers here:

- I describe my potential customers this way:

_____

_____

_____

- My estimate of the number of potential customers in my trading area: ____
- Are there any unusual traffic or other conditions that would make it hard for customers to reach my store? If there are, what could I do to improve conditions? _____

_____

_____

_____

- Do my potential customers prefer to buy for cash or on credit? _____

_____

- Do they want their goods delivered? If so, how can I arrange for delivery?

_____

_____

_____

- Where do they buy my kind of merchandise now? _____

_____

- Can I offer features they are not now getting? If so, what are they and how can I supply them? _____

_____

_____

PERSUASIVE ADVERTISING

I understand the need for competent help in developing advertising and promotion campaigns that will persuade people to trade with me. I have chosen

the following advertising firm or consultant to work with me: _____
_____

ADVERTISING MEDIA
I have studied the possibilities of advertising in the various media: newspapers, radio, TV, mail, display cards, and door-to-door. Of these, I've chosen the following as fitting my present needs and budget: _____
_____
_____

WINDOW DISPLAYS
I have thought about my window displays and have studied those of successful competitors. To start with, I plan to key my window displays to these themes:
_____
_____
_____

STORE LAYOUT
I have done the same here: thought through how my store is to be laid out and how to use fixtures, free-standing displays, and point-of-purchase displays to best advantage. I've attached a sketch of the floor plan, done to scale, to this page. _____

PERSONAL INVOLVEMENT
I'm keeping a scrapbook in which I paste ads I think are effective. These include competitors' and ads for other kinds of business. I'm also including notes on attractive window displays, special features of store layouts, and how successful competitors handle customer relations. I recognize the need to be always on the alert for newer and better ways to promote my business. _____

SECTION III

202

Retail,
Service, and
Manufacturing
Businesses

KEY TERMS

trading area 170
open-to-buy 177
markdown 177
stock turnover 181
stock-to-sales ratio 182
vendor 183
classification control 184
unit control 184

initial markup 186
maintained markup 186
gross markdown 186
cancellation of markdown 186
net markdown figure 186
keystone 187
point-of-purchase display 195

STUDY ASSIGNMENTS FOR REVIEW AND DISCUSSION

1. Describe what is meant by retailing. How is it different from manufacturing?

2. What features do the retail and service businesses have in common?

3. Describe the three basic locations for a retail store.

4. Describe three possible kinds of locations within a city.

5. What are the advantages and disadvantages of the three basic locations? Of the three kinds of locations within the city?

6. Define what is meant by trading area.

7. What measures could you take to identify your typical potential customers at a location you've selected for your store? How could you estimate the number of potential customers you might draw into your store? How could you define your trading area?

8. List six or more features you'd want in a lease for your store.

9. Explain why purchasing and control of inventory are linked.

10. Name the nine elements in managing the cycle of purchasing and inventory control.

11. Explain "open-to-buy" and how to figure it.

12. Define "stock turnover" and explain how it's calculated.

13. Define "markdown" and its purpose.

14. Describe "dollar" control and "unit" control of merchandise.

15. Describe the customary way of placing a value on inventory in retailing.

16. For what functions might you use a small computer effectively in your retail business?

17. Name at least six financial statements and records you should prepare to help you manage your retail business.

18. Describe the characteristics of persuasive advertising.

19. Name three cardinal factors you should base your advertising on, no matter what advertising medium you use—newspapers, radio, TV, mail, display cards, or other media.

20. Explain the importance of window displays. What features should be employed to make an attractive window display?

21. What features make for an effective store layout?

22. Describe what your attitude and behavior toward the business should be, as the owner of your retail business.

PROJECTS FOR STUDENTS

1. Obtain a standard lease form from a stationery store. Study it. Observe whether or not it favors one or the other party to the lease. If it does, whom does it favor, landlord or lessee? Write a short paper listing the changes you'd want in the lease if you were going to lease a store in a small community shopping center.

2. Prepare a small newspaper ad for a fictitious retail store of your choice, perhaps apparel, sporting goods, greeting cards, hairdressers, or whatever appeals to you. Check it to see if it follows the recommendations given in this chapter.

3. Write a brief paper on the importance of financial planning in the small retail business. List the projections and statements you'd include for your own small business and state why you'd want each.

4. Observe half a dozen window displays in retail stores the next time you go shopping. Write a short paper: Describe the one that appealed to you the most and tell why you liked it. Describe the one you found least appealing and tell why.

5. Observe point-of-purchase displays the next time you're in a retail store or stores. Describe three different kinds and the products they promoted.

6. Observe the store layouts of three retail stores. What features impressed you as promoting business? What features would you have improved if you were the boss?

7. Assume you are studying the potential of a location for a sporting-goods store in an existing regional shopping mall in or near your community.
   You plan to interview shoppers who now buy at many of the shops in the mall. Prepare a schedule of questions you'd ask in the interviews.

8. Three or four students acquire literature from six or more companies making small computers suitable for small business. Add information from companies making word processors having computer capabilities that small business can use. Prepare and present a summary report of your findings to the class.

SECTION III

204

Retail,
Service, and
Manufacturing
Businesses

9. Two students invite a cooperative lawyer to donate an hour of time to talking about leases to the class.

IF YOU WANT TO READ MORE

Although many references are available on retailing, we've chosen the few that follow as containing good coverage of the essential aspects of managing this kind of business.

BRANNEN, William H.: *Practical Marketing for Your Small Retail Business,* Prentice-Hall, Inc., Englewood Cliffs, NJ, 1981. As the title implies, this book affords a complete guide to marketing techniques tailored toward the owner of a small retail establishment.

BRIEF, Arthur P., ed.: *Market Analysis Workbook: Managing Human Resources in Retail Organizations,* Lexington Books, Lexington, MA, 1984. Four broad areas of research are covered in this collection of eight articles. These are: (1) the effectiveness of goal-setting programs as means of boosting employee performance, (2) performance appraisal, (3) ways to manage stress, and (4) techniques for improving employee productivity.

BURSTINER, Irving: *Run Your Own Store,* Prentice-Hall, Inc., Englewood Cliffs, NJ, 1981. This is a practical "how-to" book filled with the nuts and bolts of running a store and designed for the millions who dream of someday managing a successful business of their own. It's an easy-to-follow operations manual that offers the useful facts you need to succeed in independent store retailing.

CLARK, Leta W.: *How to Open Your Own Shop or Gallery,* St. Martin's Press, New York, 1980. This down-to-earth book is about shops and shopkeeping. It covers many relevant topics including research, record keeping, taxes, merchandise, display, advertising, and publicity.

FREGLY, Bert: *How to Be Self-Employed,* ETC Publications, Palm Springs, CA, 1977. This book approaches business and management from a practical standpoint. It outlines how to develop solutions to the dozens of business problems that arise each day. Part III, "The Independent Retailer," contains 15 chapters that should be particularly helpful to potential retail-store owners.

MARQUARDT, Raymond, A., James C. MAKENS, and Robert G. ROE: *Retail Management,* The Dryden Press, Hinsdale, IL, 1983. This is a basic text on the principles of retailing. It takes into account some of the more recent concepts from a variety of disciplines: marketing, finance, economics, statistics, and the behavioral sciences. The language is straightforward and easy to understand. It is a good reference for those who want to explore a particular subject in somewhat more detail than space permits in this chapter.

PERRY, Phillip M.: *Retailer's Complete Guide to Bigger Sales—Lower Costs—Higher Profits,* Institute for Business Planning, Inc., Englewood Cliffs, NJ, 1982. This easy-to-read, how-to guide includes a section called "How to Design Your Store for Profit."

SCHEWE, Charles D., and Reuben M. SMITH: *Marketing Concepts and Applications,* 2d ed., McGraw-Hill Book Company, New York, 1983. Chapter 4 in this text treats methods and techniques for doing market research. You'll find an excellent discussion on designing and using questionnaires for gathering market information, pp. 106–112.

State of New York, Department of Commerce, *Your Business,* Albany, NY. This booklet carries the subtitle, "A Handbook of Management Aids for the New York Businessman." Its purpose is to help new and existing small businesspersons in New York State to understand and cope with many of the management problems they face in starting and running their own business. The booklet was developed with the aid of experienced businesspersons, trade groups, and organizations affiliated with small business. Published from time to time, it is available only to residents of New York State.

Marketing the Service Business

TOPICS IN THIS CHAPTER

Objectives of This Chapter
Why Is the Service Business Unique?
The Marketing Concept and Buyer Behavior
Market Analysis and Marketing Strategy for the Service
Business
Pricing Your Service
Promoting Your Service
Distributing Your Service
The Marketing of Services Is Different—Summary
Worksheet 8: Marketing the Service Business
Key Terms
Study Assignments for Review and Discussion
Projects for Students
If You Want to Read More

This chapter, which concludes the basic ideas indicated by item 6, *MARKETING*, in the flow diagram of the business process (Figure 1-1), concentrates on the marketing of services. Services have some unique characteristics that make them different from products; services can't be seen, weighed, smelled, touched, or otherwise observed through the senses before the customer buys, as with products. Although many of the features of marketing described in the foregoing chapters apply to the marketing of services, the differences are highly significant. If you enter the service field, you should understand them clearly before you attempt to mount a marketing program.

Information in this chapter will be found pertinent to these items in the Business Plan:

1.B. Summary of your proposed marketing method

2.A. Statement of the desirability of your service

3. Background of proposed business

4.A. A complete technical description of the service

5.A. A comprehensive description of marketing strategy

6.A. An outline of the activities to be used in selling the product or service

7.A. Description of the proposed organization

8.A. Information required to support the major points in the business plan

$$\text{You} + \text{Idea} + \begin{cases} \text{Money} \\ \text{Credit} \end{cases} + \begin{cases} \text{Facilities} \\ \text{People} \end{cases} \begin{matrix} \text{Product} \\ \rightarrow \quad \text{or} \quad + \textbf{MARKETING} \\ \text{Service} \end{matrix} \begin{cases} \text{Money} \\ \text{Credit} \end{cases} \rightarrow \text{Profit}$$

SECTION III

208

Retail,
Service, and
Manufacturing
Businesses

The growing importance of services in the economy of the United States was emphasized in *The State of Small Business, A Report of the President,* in 1984. *Services* includes two different sorts of jobs: the first, traditional services such as retailers, transportation, utilities, restaurants, and beauty salons—in which the number of jobs in the country is likely to remain relatively constant; the second, the *information sector,* which includes teachers, clerks, accountants, lawyers, insurance brokers, computer programmers, and persons who process information or move it about. Daniel Bell, the eminent Harvard sociologist, has studied the rapid growth of the information sector. He estimates that the number of information workers in the United States has risen from 17 percent of the Labor force in 1950 to about 65 percent in the mid-1980s.[1] This growth seems likely to continue in the foreseeable future.

The business that deals in products sells tangibles; the service business sells intangibles, which cannot be touched, weighed, or smelled. Marketing services therefore poses more problems and more challenges than marketing products.

Services are often sold as part of the marketing of some physical product. Marketing the service that goes with the product requires special attention.

In market analysis, the market segmentation, pricing, promotion, and distribution, as well as the procedures of planning for the marketing of services, are essentially the same as for products. The major differences lie in the distinctive characteristics of services and the resulting close relationship between seller and buyer.

Objectives of This Chapter

This chapter tells about marketing services and marketing the special services accompanying the sale of a product. After studying this chapter, you will be able to understand

- The unique qualities that differentiate the service business from the product business

- The intangibility of services

- The close relationship of sellers to buyers of service compared with buyers of products

- What perishability of services means in managing the service business

- The importance of delivering a standardized service

- Why consumers buy services

- Why consumers don't buy services

- Important factors in market analysis and marketing strategy for the service business

- The improving environment for the service business

---

[1] Max Gelden, "The New Job Frontier," *World Press Review,* December 1984, pp. 25–27.

- How to price your service
- Promoting your service through advertising and personal selling
- Variables to consider in locating your service firm

Business
Plan
Outline
1.B, 2.A, 3, 4.A

Why is the Service Business Unique?

A service is an intangible product performing tasks that satisfy consumer needs in chosen market segments. When you market a service, your customer comes away empty-handed from the resulting sale. A product can be seen and handled; a service cannot. A product is *produced;* a service is *performed.* As a result, successful marketing of services takes more than conventional marketing methods.

If your business is services, you'll find several features important beyond those required in marketing products. These key features follow.

SERVICES ARE INTANGIBLE

Your customer can't hear, see, smell, taste, or touch your service. This places a heavy burden on your promotion strategy. When physical goods are marketed, the product itself can communicate value to the consumer. Not so with services—your sales effort must concentrate on the benefits your customer will get from the service rather than on the service itself.

Because of difficulty in demonstrating, displaying, or illustrating an intangible product, consumers are often unable to evaluate the quality of a service before buying. As a result, the reputation and image of the service business become paramount in buying decisions.

BUYERS AND SELLERS OF SERVICES ARE INTERDEPENDENT

This means that the seller performs the service for the buyer, and the buyer frequently plays a major role in the production and marketing of the service.

There is no transfer of ownership in the sale of a service; buyers are usually dependent on the seller *during* the consumption or use of the purchased service. In contrast, after purchasing such items as clothing, food, appliances, or books, the buyer is not dependent on the seller.

As the seller you are often dependent on the buyer in the creation and marketing of your service. This implies that the adequacy of the service depends on the ability of your customers to communicate their specific needs and your skill in perceiving and satisfying these needs. Unlike a product, the quality of a service depends partly on the experience, knowledge, and ability of the consumer to communicate and the opportunities the entrepreneur creates for buyers to tell about their needs.

To summarize, there is a dependency relationship—a personal or professional relationship—between buyer and seller during the creation and consumption of a service. This dependency does not exist to the same extent when products are produced, sold, and consumed. The marketing implication is that the value of the service to your customer quite often depends on the quality of the personal relationship between the buyer and you.

SECTION III

210

Retail,
Service, and
Manufacturing
Businesses

THE SERVICE AND THE SELLER ARE OFTEN INSEPARABLE

In only a few businesses can the service performed be separated from the creator-seller. A broker, an insurance salesperson, a travel agent, for instance, may represent and sell the service actually being offered but performed by another person or institution. In most cases, however, the service cannot be separated from the person of the seller. This follows from the dependency relationship described above and the characteristics of services being performed by activity, which is quite different from the service, or value, offered by a product. Services are created and marketed at the same time. For example, a barber creates a haircut service and dispenses it simultaneously.

Inseparability of seller and service has two important marketing implications. First, it means that in your service business direct personal selling is the only channel of distribution possible. Second, since your customers are buying "you" as much as the service you sell, your capacity for supplying the service limits the scale of operation of your business.

SERVICES ARE PERISHABLE

The service business doesn't have inventory problems; it has *capacity* problems. One person can repair just so many appliances in a given time. A beautician can give only a limited number of facials per day. Services cannot be stored and sold according to fluctuations in demand. The usefulness of the service to the consumer is usually short-lived. It cannot be created ahead of time and sold when demand reaches a peak.

From a marketing standpoint the perishability of services means that your strategy will have to address the problem of fluctuating demand. You may find it necessary to discover new uses for idle facilities and ways to stimulate demand during the off season.

IT IS DIFFICULT TO STANDARDIZE SERVICE QUALITY

Human beings perform services, and performance is therefore subject to human frailty. The performance of a service is usually "person-intensive"; this characteristic can result in variations in quality of the seller's performance. As instances, customers can experience differences in quality of service performed by an auto mechanic, a psychiatrist, an airline, or an advertising agency. Unless consistent, high-quality performance can be maintained, the entrepreneur in a service business cannot build customer confidence. Positive word-of-mouth advertising is vital to the success of the service business. You must exert every effort, therefore, to keep the performance of your service consistently at a high level.

The marketing of services poses differences from the marketing of physical goods. With few exceptions, services cannot be purchased and resold. Service charges are often expressed in terms of time required, rate, fee, honorarium, or premium rather than as a price in dollars. Moreover, rather than being called customers, service buyers are known as clients, patients, participants, or spectators. Finally, the consumer experiences no pride of ownership in a service. The customer must be satisfied with symbolic value or the functional benefits of an intangible product. In short, the service "product" is different from a product "product," and the reasons for buying a service are different from those for buying a product.

The Marketing Concept and Buyer Behavior

Business
Plan
Outline
5.A, 6.A

The marketing concept in a service business is vital for success. Intangibility, buyer-seller interdependence, perishability, and nonstandardization all add up to mean that customer orientation is even more important for the service firm than for product marketers. Consider that the buyer almost always has the option of doing it himself or herself. On the service supplier's side, most sellers think of themselves as creators, producers, professionals, or specialists—not "marketers" of a service. They take pride in performance—their ability to repair an automobile, give advice on landscaping, fly an airplane, or diagnose an illness. We stress that you must be an expert in the service you're planning to sell.

There is a special problem facing your small service business: Consumers often believe they can do it themselves; so they have to be convinced they will be better off by letting you do it for them. Although sellers must have a high degree of professional competence and pride, they have to bend and shape their service and performance to the specific needs of the customer.

Inflexibility in serving customer needs can be disastrous, as illustrated by an entrepreneur who operated (we use the past tense because he's no longer in business) a small contracting business. He was a superior plumber, which even his competitors acknowledged. He had worked for his father and had taken over the business when his father retired. His attitude toward customers was shown by comments such as "I don't have customers, I deal with contracts." "I'm so good at this people will always come to me." "I know what's best for them." The result of this attitude was that he was usually late in completing work ("I'm the best, they'll wait for me," he would say). He seldom took the time to explain his work or answer questions. The number of jobs he was asked to bid on dwindled as word got around that he was cold and indifferent toward his customers and took his own sweet time in finishing contracted work. He failed to take advantage of a change in the local building codes, which now allowed the use of plastic (polyvinyl chloride, or PVC) pipe in residential construction. Potential customers increasingly found they could do many plumbing jobs themselves, because PVC pipe is easy to work with compared with steel or copper pipe. His reaction was: "Let 'em, they'll find out in the long run they would have been better off with a professional like me." He didn't recognize he had marketing problems; he went bankrupt waiting for the long run to arrive. Entrepreneurs of this sort are expert at solving technical problems, but their businesses fail because they refuse to adopt the marketing concept.

WHY CONSUMERS BUY SERVICES

As we indicated in Chapter 5, consumer behavior depends on the actual or anticipated consequences—both positive and negative—of buying. The same principle applies to buying services. Yet there are some notable differences in consumers' motives and predispositions as they evaluate the results of obtaining certain services. These differences stem from the special characteristics of services and the close relationship between buyer and seller. Our approach to these differences is to view them as *opportunities* for successfully marketing the service business.

SECTION III

212

Retail,
Service, and
Manufacturing
Businesses

The consumer's desire for personal attention is often the dominant need satisfied by a service. By appealing to the consumer's need for personal attention, you as the provider of service offer a form of satisfaction the seller of products cannot easily match. This is clearly an advantage for your small service business. You're in a unique position to cultivate the consumer's personal feelings and loyalty toward your service.

The insurance industry is an example of a service business that has lost some of this advantage. Several of the larger companies have introduced mass selling of conveniently packaged insurance policies with lower prices (premiums). This has resulted in a decline in the role of the insurance agent and loss of personal contact with the customer. There are strong indications that consumers dislike the lack of personal attention, because sales have not increased as anticipated.

Consumers are more likely to weigh subjective impressions of the service business and its seller when contemplating the purchase of a service. With physical products, the consumer can use appearance and objective performance data to compare similar products. Not so with intangible services. Consumers cannot inspect or sample your service before purchasing. So they turn to their next-best source: the comments of friends, coworkers, and neighbors who have experienced your service.

A subtle but extremely valuable *promotional* advantage for service marketers exists because of the key role of personal influence in the selection of services. Upon successful completion of the service—particularly if your customer sees significant value from your personal attention—you can benefit from the referral form of promotion. This offers one of the easiest, least costly, and most effective tools in marketing. You simply ask the satisfied customer to recommend your service to friends who could benefit from it. You may ask your customer personally to contact a prospective customer. After this contact has been made, you follow up with a sales call. In addition to being straightforward, personal, and inexpensive, this way of promoting improves your chances of reaching *potential* customers for your services. In contrast to product marketers, it is the personal involvement of buyer and seller in the service transaction that makes the referral form of promotion a natural and effective tool for you to use.

Sometimes the service business is based upon nothing more than the marketing of a good idea that fulfills an "unrecognized" need. The most important raw material for the service business is usually a novel idea.

Many an entrepreneur finds opportunity in what can be called an unrecognized need—a need that exists but has not been brought to light. Such needs are often uncovered in the service field. The following news item from the *Los Angeles Times* tells about a unique business originated by an alert entrepreneur.

RENT A KVETCH

Everyone has complaints: a fountain pen that leaks in airplane flights, a battery that expires the day after the warranty does, or a disputed dentist's bill. Many people either dismiss the matter or fire off an enraged letter that ends up in a company's "nut file."

B. L. Ochman, president of a New York public relations firm bearing her name, has been so successful over the years in resolving complaints for friends and on her own behalf that she's formed a new company, Rent A Kvetch, that will do the complaining for you for a fee.

For $25 and up, depending on the complexity of the complaint, Ochman will compose and mail letters outlining the nature of your complaint and explaining how you want it resolved. Ochman says she's gotten satisfaction from a New York telephone company, a pen company, a parcel-forwarding firm, and her landlord.

Keys to being a successful kvetch (yiddish for complainer) she says, are: (1) Documentation. Have all your facts in the complaint letter. (2) Go straight to the top. The complaint will filter down to the appropriate person with the president's or chairman's initials on your letter. (3) Don't get emotional. You can be ignored as a nut. (4) Be persistent. Most companies would rather settle than hassle with a good complainer.

Identify a successful small service business based on an unrecognized need.

The world has become more complex, and the hassles and frustrations in contending with day-to-day problems have increased; in defense consumers seek self-expression, personal growth, and involvement in creative endeavors. The result has been a heightened consumer awareness of the tyranny of time. Time-saving services afford the opportunity for consumers to redirect their activities into more satisfying channels.

Remember that consumers have the alternative of doing services for themselves. However, they often perform tasks that a service firm could do better or faster. And the need for the service often goes *unrecognized* by potential buyers until the service becomes available. This is why the reaction of the consumer to a new service business is frequently, "Why didn't I think of that?"

Here is an excellent example of a new service firm that is marketing an idea to satisfy a hitherto unrecognized need. Each household must perform accounting and bookkeeping functions: bills must be paid, bank deposits made, tax records kept up to date, and checking accounts balanced. This is usually done by husband or wife and often takes several hours each month. The higher the income of the household, the more complicated the bookkeeping chore. If both wife and husband work, the paperwork becomes even more of a burden. Two women in southern California recently formed a service firm that deals with this problem. Their idea is simple and effective.

Their firm offers two basic services that relieve the drudgery and frustration of household cash management. They come to the home and, after taking an inventory of all financial transactions of the family, set up an efficient record keeping system. They classify expenses by type: personal, home improvement, cash, or credit. They schedule payments to minimize interest charges and checking-account fees. They prepare ledgers for recording expenses for income tax purposes. In short, they design a complete accounting system for the home similar to that used by small businesses.

SECTION III

214

Retail,
Service, and
Manufacturing
Businesses

The service their firm provides takes care of all the financial transactions of the household for a monthly fee. It works like this: On a predetermined day each month, one partner visits the home. While there, she prepares the necessary checks for signature, records the transactions, balances the checkbook, brings all the ledger accounts up to date, and summarizes the family's financial standing. She even prepares envelopes and mails the checks.

Both women had worked as clerks in an accounting firm. Before striking out on their own, they tested their idea by working evenings—moonlighting—with a few selected acquaintances as clients. The response encouraged them to expand. Within 3 months they had enough referrals from their first clients to devote full time to their new business.

Consumers will want more of a good service than the entrepreneur can supply. This is a "when-it-rains-it-pours" problem unique to the service business. A product manufacturer can satisfy additional demand by adding extra shifts or installing a new production line. But the *capacity* problem for services is not so easily solved because consumers usually buy the *time* of the entrepreneur. (We hope you do run into the capacity problem, for this would be a sure sign that your service fills a real need.)

We have three specific suggestions for anticipating and dealing with the capacity barrier. First, become expert in the management of your own time. There are several excellent how-to books on the subject, some of which are listed at the end of this chapter. Short courses or seminars are offered through university extension programs. Second, we strongly recommend that you carefully schedule service work and take on new clients selectively in order to prevent becoming overcommitted. You should avoid the temptation to accept too many clients during the first few months of operation. You must not rush. You must do a good job with these clients, since so much of your future business will depend on favorable word-of-mouth advertising. Third, in early stages of operation you should begin selecting and training a staff of personnel who will be as proficient and reliable as you are in performing the service you offer.

WHY CONSUMERS DON'T BUY

A service buyer's dissatisfaction with one element of the service may lead to dissatisfaction with the entire service. There is a tendency for customers to remember any negative aspect of a service and to allow this to overshadow the positive satisfaction they've received. For example, an entrepreneur whose accounting practice was growing rapidly suddenly found that his volume of business was tapering off. He finally found the cause when a client complained about the telephone-answering device he had installed. He asked other clients about this and they confirmed that, although pleased with his work, they were put off by the mechanical, impersonal response and as a result hesitated to call him. Many people are blocked by the need to talk to a tape.

Again we see the crucial importance of regular personal attention. Because consumers don't have something tangible in hand to remind them of the value they received for their money, they will often recall and be guided in their relationship by their most recent personal experience with the seller.

Market Analysis and Marketing Strategy for the Service Business

Business
Plan
Outline
3, 4.A, 5.A, 6.A

The procedures involved in market analysis and strategy are basically the same whether the firm is selling a product or a service. The service entrepreneur should understand population characteristics as they affect the market for the service. And it is essential that customer buying motives be understood. The guidelines in Chapter 5 for analyzing consumer behavior are just as effective for services as they are for products. The service marketer must also analyze shopping behavior and should answer the *who, when,* and *how* questions by following procedures and consulting the sources of information we've suggested. The following pinpoints some special considerations in analyzing the market for your service and developing your marketing strategy.

SOCIAL, ECONOMIC, AND COMPETITIVE CHANGE

The environment for small service firms has changed radically during the recent past, presenting both opportunities and threats for the new service business. As the economy has matured, spending for all kinds of services has soared. Personal spending on services is predicted to surpass total expenditures for durable and nondurable goods within the next few years. Rising discretionary income means that consumers can buy more than basic household and personal necessities. Put another way, increased buying power results in less individual self-sufficiency and more desire for services. Thus, more demand for travel, health, beauty, culture, and education. Services have replaced durable goods as status symbols in many instances. The reaction against materialism has clearly benefited the service sector. It would appear that acquiring experiences rather than acquiring goods fits the current consumer movement toward self-fulfillment. In such areas as education and travel, services more than products enable consumers to reach their personal growth goals.

Other societal trends such as more women in the labor force mean greater markets for services—for example, in child care, dry cleaning, and transportation. The shorter workweek results in more leisure time and the demand for recreation and entertainment. To "do your own thing" usually requires the purchase of services in some form.

As opportunities for service firms have increased, however, competition has become fierce for consumers' discretionary dollars. Inevitably, direct competition between products and services has grown. Recognizing the shift in consumer preferences, manufacturers are adding more conveniences or services to their products. Drip-dry permanent-press clothing competes with the conventional laundry service. Improved household appliances that reduce the need for domestic service help, and custom television programming that competes with other forms of entertainment afford other examples. Perhaps the most significant threat of product competition for services comes from the manufacturers of do-it-yourself products.

Competition also comes from the growing number of other service firms. The barriers to entry into the service field are usually low. As one cynic put it, "With a little knowledge and a great brochure, you have a new service venture." This condition exists because almost anyone can offer some sort of service. The implication is that competitive service businesses may multiply rapidly. The importance of attracting and retaining a core group of loyal, satisfied customers becomes crucial in this intensely competitive world.

Pricing Your Service

The word *price* is seldom attached to services. Instead, other terms such as *fee* or *premium* are used to describe charges for services rendered. Regardless of terminology, the basic approach to pricing applies: Price measures value perceived by customers. To be more precise, since what your customer gets is often intangible or subjective in nature, your price reflects the quality, degree of specialization, and value of your performance to the buyer. With the exception of services regulated by government, there is more opportunity for creativity and imagination in pricing services than in other marketing areas. Since the consumer can usually either postpone the purchase of a service or perform the service personally, setting your price is one of the most important decisions you'll make.

In Chapter 6 we stressed the advantages of a high-price versus a low-price strategy. The same arguments apply generally to pricing a service. However, there are some additional factors that can make the high-price approach even more favorable. Instead of lower prices and price reductions having a positive effect on sales, the reverse is often true—especially for the human-intensive service. In most cases, buyers of a specialized service are reluctant to display sensitivity to your price because they perceive a professional-layperson relationship. Furthermore, the price of your service signals to the buyer the quality of your skill and competence. And to complicate matters, the price you set affects the value your customers perceive.

To see how this works, consider the difficulty encountered by Ruth Blackstone, an independent child psychologist. She started her own business after serving for 6 years as a counselor in a local high school. Her marketing approach had two related parts. First, she felt that the effectiveness of her service would be improved if she could observe and deal with behavioral problems in the home—an environment familiar and nonthreatening to the clients and the place where most parent-child interaction takes place. Second, she could charge lower fees than most psychologists because she could operate from her home and avoid office rent and associated overhead expenses. She expected that lower prices would allow middle- and even low-income families to benefit from her in-home service. It turned out that her first assumption was right but that her second was dead wrong.

She set hourly fees at about half the prevailing rate of other independent psychologists. Her first clients were parents and children she had dealt with at the high school. Although she had no problem attracting clients, she found that parents weren't following the recommendations she made. They didn't seem to listen actively or to acknowledge her observations of behavioral problems. "For a long time, I thought the problem was with me," she said. "And I did a lot of soul searching to see if my kind of therapy had something to do with it." Finally, she visited an old friend who had been her major professor during graduate school. She summarized their conversation this way, "He listened patiently to my story, and then he said: 'Your advice to clients is worth just as much as they have to pay to get it.' Then it dawned on me that my clients weren't listening to me because my consultation cost them so little."

It wasn't easy for her to raise her fee, since she knew that persons referred to her by former clients would know what she had charged. The solution was to start all over again. Eventually she was able to attract new clients through short courses she taught at the local university and speeches she made on child development at civic and professional meetings.

Ms. Blackstone learned a difficult lesson: The more the buyer is involved in performance and quality of the service, the more crucial the role of price in affecting the perceived value of the service. This is true in almost any professional service; it increases in importance as the degree of specialization increases. Customers are more willing to listen to advice if they have given up something of value to obtain it. To sum up, your clients' perception of your power to solve their problems may be enhanced by charging high prices for your service.

There are other considerations in pricing your service. For example, your pricing decision can be affected by whether your service will be purchased routinely (haircuts), contractually (small construction jobs), or occasionally (travel, recreation, or repairs). A trade or professional association is often the price setter within an industry. Local barber unions often set the price of haircuts; dry-cleaning associations set the price of cleaning trousers; professional associations influence the fees of doctors, dentists, accountants, and architects.

ESTIMATING YOUR PRICING

Although few generalizations are possible in pricing a service, we can sum up by reemphasizing that the value given by the seller and the value received by the buyer can be related to the time required to perform a particular service and the duration that the results of service performed are experienced by the buyer. As you can see, estimating value and attaching a price to it can be a much more complex task for the invisible service than for the tangible product.

Services cover a very wide range. It doesn't matter whether the service you offer is relatively simple such as carpet cleaning or relatively sophisticated such as management consulting. You'll want to set your prices at a profitable level—and you'll want to know how they compare with competitors' prices.

For some services you can do comparison shopping in the fashion of large retailers. They send experienced "comparison shoppers" into the stores of competitors. These professionals pose as prospective customers and find out what various lines of merchandise are retailing at. You may do the same by phoning competitors with questions about prices—or you may have a friend inquire for you. You can check advertised prices quoted by competitors in ads in the yellow pages or local newspapers. If you belong to a trade association, you can get valuable information about what members charge. These are some of the ways you can gain information that will tell where you stand in pricing.

Whatever the service you offer, you can gain an idea of the kind of financial approach that should serve your purpose by starting with an estimate of how much money you want to take in for a given period, say a year. Then you can figure your costs and your income on the basis of serving a reasonable number of customers during the year. From these estimates you can set your fees—and position them against the rates in the marketplace. If you're outside a reasonable range, you would rework your figures until you're satisfied that they fit the market and give you the

SECTION III

218

Retail,
Service, and
Manufacturing
Businesses

return you want. Two examples of estimating prices follow: one is for a fairly sophisticated business, management consulting; the other is for a simpler service, chimney sweeping.

Management Consulting Service   Joe Horchak, a newcomer to management consulting, wanted to estimate the total cash inflow needed per year to provide $1800 per month net income. He proceeded on the basis of these assumptions:

- As a newcomer he would charge toward the lower end of the current consulting-fee range, which scaled from $300 to $2000 a day.

- He did not need a fancy office because he called on his clients; they did not come to his office. His office was in his home, where he had a desk, file cabinet, and typewriter.

- He would employ a competent secretary because the reports that he prepared as a final product for his clients had to be carefully organized and immaculately typed.

- He would use an answering service for off-hour calls; he knew that many clients did not like the impersonality of an electronic answering machine.

After several trials he came up with the following estimate, which satisfied the conditions he had decided upon.

Joe Horchak's Cash-Inflow Requirement
as an Individual Management Consultant

Expenses per Month

Electricity, gas	$ 45
Telephone	100
Stationery and supplies	25
Mail	35
Automobile expense, insurance	175
Travel expense, not chargeable to clients	125
Telephone-answering service	35
Promotional material, printing brochures	50
Entertainment	100
Secretary	950
Miscellaneous expenses	150
Personal net income	1,800
Estimated income taxes	825
Monthly total	$ 4,415
Estimated income required for the year .... 12 ×	4,415
	$52,980

This would require 118 consulting days per year at $450 per day, or about $2^1/_2$ days per week, on a 50-week yearly basis.

FRED RENQUIST, CHIMNEY SWEEP

Fred Renquist decided to start his own business as a chimney sweep. He had put aside $15,000 in savings; he invested $8500 in chimney-cleaning equipment and supplies, and a small pickup truck for the business. After carefully studying his market and the expenses he would incur, he made a rough estimate of the gross business he would have to do to bring home $1200 clear per month during the heating season. He revised his estimate several times before he was satisfied that his figures were reasonable.

He proceeded on the basis of the following assumptions:

- The heating season in the midwest area where he lived was about 7 months long, from September to April.

- He wanted a net income after taxes of $1200 per month.

- He did not need an office for his business; therefore, he would work out of his house.

- He would put aside $185 a month in a fund to replace equipment and truck in time.

- He would not expect to attain a $1200 per month income during the first year. He would bend his efforts toward promoting and establishing the business during this time. With what money he could earn in the first year, augmented by his savings, he should be able to manage.

In his spare time during the first year he would try to build up other sources of income, such as cleaning grille hoods and exhaust ducts in restaurants.

The estimate he was satisfied with looked like this:

Cash-Inflow Requirement for Fred Renquist, Chimney Sweep

Expenses per Month

Income	$1200
Resale items	100
Sweeping supplies and equipment	55
Advertising	58
Pickup truck expense	90
Insurance	75
Telephone	80
Taxes and miscellaneous	125
Fund for replacement of equipment	185
Monthly total	$1995

Renquist had found that the average chimney-sweeping job brings in $45. At this figure, the number of jobs per month to gross $1995 would be

$$\frac{1995}{45} = 44$$

At 2 jobs per day, Renquist decided that he could readily accomplish his goal in 22 days of work each month for the 7-month period. He believed this estimate to be conservative—and he would have time during the 7 months to work on expanding his business.

Promoting Your Service

In this chapter we have emphasized the differences between promoting products and promoting services. It is easier to sell something that can be handled, tasted, smelled, or demonstrated than it is to sell the benefits of an intangible service. (The principles and procedures are about the same, and the suggestions in Chapter 6 will generally apply for promoting your service. However, you should check to see whether your trade or profession has legal or ethical restrictions on specific promotional methods.) We'll concentrate here on the somewhat different forms of promotion and the alternatives you have in developing your strategy for promoting your service.

Although you may decide to let your service performance speak for itself, communicating with potential customers through advertising, publicity, or personal selling is usually necessary for the new service business. The purpose of promotion for services is the same as for products: to develop awareness of, interest in, and desire for your service. But for services, your strategy should be geared to promoting three key features of your business:

Availability	Consumers in your target market must know where and when you are available and how to reach you
Image or reputation	Consumers must become acquainted with your capabilities—the quality of performance of your service
Use benefits	Intended customers must understand how the results of your service will benefit them

Each form of promotion, advertising, publicity, and personal selling can be used to communicate these three features.

Regardless of the forms of promotion you use, you should stress a consistent theme in advertising, personal selling, and publicity messages. For example, if your methods or techniques of service performance are unique, they could serve as a unifying theme for promotion. Or if you have key personnel who have established reputations in the service you offer, you could highlight this in promotional messages. You can use a third approach after your new service firm gets going: stressing the benefits already gained by satisfied customers.

ADVERTISING

Your service business will probably attract mostly local customers. Therefore, media that reach just the local market are the ones to use. The yellow pages of the telephone directory, direct mail, and newspapers are examples (see Figure 8-1). Note that with any of these you can display your firm's identifying symbol as well as where, when, and how to find you. Broadcast media are not as effective because of the temporary nature of the message. If your services are to be purchased only on an "as needed" basis by customers, awareness of your availability is vital. The purpose of the message is to keep your trade name or business location exposed to potential customers so that when your service is needed, they'll remember you.

FIG. 8-1

A variety of service ads.

SECTION III

222

Retail,
Service, and
Manufacturing
Businesses

Special attention should be given to developing an identifying symbol for your service business. Large service firms like the airlines have spent thousands of dollars developing unique corporate identification. A clever symbol is effective in reminding consumers of the availability of your service and makes it easy to remember. Your symbol becomes part of the image your business projects to consumers; it differentiates your service from other businesses offering similar service. The symbol is to some extent a substitute for having a physical product to display. We've found that it is well worth the investment to have a professional graphic artist develop such a symbol for use on your store sign, stationery, and business cards.

Whenever possible, show the benefits of your service. Use in-store displays showing consumers enjoying or benefiting from your service. An example would be the posters and brochures used by travel agencies. Also, tell of benefits through testimonials of personal satisfaction, often called "the verbal-proof story," or by before-and-after comparisons.

Be sure to relate your message to shopping behavior. For example, if your service will be purchased routinely and repeatedly, stress dependability. Note that banks often feature trust and confidence in their advertising messages. It is even possible for some service businesses to change shopping behavior of consumers by promoting the "preventive" value of their service. Any service business that deals in repairs could well use this approach.

Advertising messages for services are particularly difficult to create because they must appeal to the buyer's imagination. Think of it this way: In a marketing society that emphasizes the acquisition of things, the service advertiser must create a message that appeals to the buying of experiences, achieving a better future, or avoiding inconvenience. For these reasons, we suggest consulting a professional advertising agency in preparing your message.

PERSONAL SELLING

As in advertising products, it is easier for a salesperson to extoll the virtues of a product than it is for the supplier of a service to promote something the consumer cannot see. The buyer faces greater risk in purchasing services than in purchasing products. Not only is a service usually completed before its quality can be judged, but also the defective service cannot be returned for refund or substitute. The only recourse unsatisfied customers have in most cases is to try another supplier the next time or do the work themselves.

The personal selling job should concentrate on reducing the prepurchase uncertainty consumers usually experience. To relieve this uncertainty, you might stress (1) your unique methods or techniques in performing your service, (2) the skill and competence of your employees, and (3) significant benefits your firm's customers are already receiving. The task is not easy, because to sell your service *you must sell yourself*—without appearing to brag or boast. Therefore, personal selling often requires you to take a more indirect and subtle approach.

Your goal is to obtain the maximum amount of *exposure* in your target market. A professionally acceptable practice is to make business contacts through presenting speeches to local clubs, participating in trade or professional associations, making contributions to charitable causes, sponsoring public events, serving in community or civic groups, writing professional articles, or appearing at conferences that suit your business purpose.

After you've established your reputation, the most effective selling tool will be word-of-mouth advertising. How effective this will be, of course, depends on your performance record. But you should always remember that the manner in which the buyer-seller relationship is conducted is a form of personal selling. All client contacts by you or anyone working for you should be viewed as a way to promote new business.

PUBLICITY

A way to get free advertising is through publicity releases to local newspapers. These should be written to create a favorable impression of your organization and its employees. This is the principal form of promotion for many service firms, since consumers tend to accept the authenticity of news stories more readily than that of paid advertisements. You'll find that most service business "news" articles in your local newspaper are originated as publicity releases by the firm itself. The opening of your business, the addition of a new employee, or the offering of a new service would all qualify for favorable and free publicity.

SALES PROMOTION

Sales-promotion techniques have very limited application to the small service business. Tools that may be effective are carefully designed specialty advertising: calendars with your business name displayed on them or premiums giving the customer a bonus item with the purchase of your service. If you use specialty advertising, be sure to choose an approach that projects a professional image of your business.

Distributing Your Service

The distribution strategy for your service boils down to decisions on business location and service delivery. With very few exceptions, there are no channel alternatives as there are for products, since you'll be dealing directly with consumers. However, the concepts of offering time and place utility (discussed in Chapter 6) are important—in most cases more important for services than for tangible goods. Your location and delivery strategy are particularly crucial for success because consumers can perform many services themselves and because demand may be irregular.

Business
Plan
Outline
1.B, 5.A, 7.A

OPTIMUM LOCATION FOR YOUR SERVICE FIRM

The optimum location for your service firm depends upon the type of service you'll provide. We'll approach the distribution strategy in two ways: We'll examine consumer buying patterns and implications for the location of your business; then we'll present specific suggestions for site analysis.

Services purchased by consumers can be classified according to three basic kinds of shopping behavior.

Convenience Services Convenience services are those the consumer knows a great deal about. They are purchased with a minimum of time and effort. Being willing

SECTION III

224

Retail,
Service, and
Manufacturing
Businesses

to accept any of several substitutes, the consumer buys the service from the most accessible person or firm. In this case the consumer works to complete the purchase as easily and quickly as possible. Almost any relatively inexpensive service that is purchased frequently would fit here; a dry-cleaning business would be typical. Convenient and visible location is essential for this type of service.

Shopping Services   These services are those for which the consumer wants to compare quality and price before buying. Here the consumer lacks specific knowledge about the service and believes that taking the time to compare costs and benefits will be worthwhile. Location is important but to a lesser degree, since the consumer will expend some effort to seek out alternative service firms.

Specialty Services   These services are those that the consumer has complete knowledge of but insists on buying from only one supplier. The consumer does not compare substitutes; the only problem is in finding the right supplier. Consequently, a low-rent and inconvenient location may be sought out, since the consumer is willing to make a special effort to find it.

These classifications are not rigid, since (1) different target markets and even consumers within the same target market may have different buying patterns, and (2) as income, life-styles, and demographic characteristics of a target market change over time, service-buying behavior may change. As a practical matter, you should view this scheme of classification as covering a range to which the potential customer responds. Consumer behavior in spending time and effort to do business with you depends on the kind of service you sell and how well the consumer knows what you offer.

ANALYZING A LOCATION

There is no easy solution to the location problem. The selection you make will probably involve a trade-off between the high-cost, convenient location and the low-cost, inconvenient location. In making your choice, consider location cost along with promotional cost. In the long run you may incur considerable advertising expense if you don't have a business site easy for your customers to find.

Once you've narrowed down the possible locations for your service business to a few, your task is to conduct a specific site analysis. The factors to consider for the service business are similar to those for the business that sells products.

- *Land and buildings.* For vacant land, the adequacy of site and size. For land with improvements, the suitability of building placement and design, frontage, access, and exposure

- *Zoning and use restrictions.* Conformity of type of business with local commercial land-use controls

- *Supporting services.* Availability of fire and police protection, liquid and solid waste disposal, and street lighting. Suitability and quality of streets, alleys, and parking

- *Cost and carrying charges.* Availability of financing, lease and improvement provisions, taxes, maintenance, and fees

You'll want to assess these and other features for each site. For physical aspects, such as land and building, you may need to consult an architect or engineer. You'll require the help of an accountant or attorney in evaluating legal and financial aspects of the property you choose.

The Marketing of Services Is Different

Summary

Your marketing approach will have to stress the unique features of your intangible services—a harder job than to sell the advantages of tangible products. The special characteristics of intangibility, buyer-seller interdependence, service-seller inseparability, perishability, and difficulty in standardizing service quality have important implications for your pricing, promotional, and distribution strategies.

Intangibility means that your promotion will have to be creatively designed and executed. Buyer-seller interdependence limits your distribution strategy to making choices about business location. And the size of your operation will be limited because customers will be purchasing you and your time instead of a product that could be produced in large quantities. Durability of your service will result in idle time and the need to stimulate demand during slow periods. Finally, the difficulty in standardizing your quality of performance for customers places a special burden on you to be consistent in satisfying each customer.

Most purchases of a service can easily be postponed, or in many instances, consumers can perform the service themselves. The consumer cannot evaluate service quality before purchase and therefore relies heavily on the opinions of others who have been your customers. This means you must be technically proficient at performing your service, flexible in meeting specific customer requirements, and skilled in establishing and maintaining good interpersonal relationships. Your competence in dealing with people will be as crucial for your success as your professional abilities in the service you actually perform.

The opportunities for the success of the small service business are increasing. They will continue to grow as long as a trend away from consumer self-sufficiency continues. You're on the right track if your service results in added convenience for consumers, enables them to experience personal growth, or improves the quality of their everyday lives.

WORKSHEET 8

Marketing the Service Business

Special note: Your completed assignments for Chapter 6 will apply to some of the exercises here, but you may want to review them after studying this chapter.

1. Answer the question(s) following each special characteristic of service.
   a. Intangibility: What will you stress as benefits to your customers?

   _____

   _____

   _____

   _____

   _____

   b. Buyer–Seller Interdependence: What kinds of things can you do to help potential buyers communicate their specific needs so you can adapt your service offering accordingly?

   _____

   _____

   _____

   _____

   _____

   c. Inseparability of Service from Seller: What are your weaknesses and strengths in managing your own time? What will you do to expand the time available for performing your service for customers?

   _____

   _____

   _____

   _____

   _____

   d. Perishability: What actions will you take to boost sales during slow periods?

   _____

   _____

   _____

   _____

   _____

   _____

   _____

e. Difficulty in Standardizing Service Quality: What standards will you set in performing your service? How will you assure that your performance is consistently of high quality?

_____

_____

_____

_____

2. After you render your service, what actions will you take to follow up and make sure your customer is truly satisfied and helps to promote business for you?

_____

_____

_____

_____

_____

_____

_____

_____

3. What feature could you incorporate into your service or its promotion that would appeal to potential customers on the basis of saving them time?

_____

_____

_____

_____

_____

_____

_____

4. On what social, economic, or other trends are you basing the need for your service business? Describe them.

_____

_____

_____

_____

_____

_____

_____

5. Here are some statements about your service. If you believe them to be true and you answer *yes* to any of them, then a higher rather than a lower price is probably the way to go.

Yes	No	
____	____	1. There will be no readily available substitute for my service to consumers. (Or, to get my kind of service, consumers cannot easily shift to less expensive alternatives.)
____	____	2. Consumers interested in my service cannot easily make price and quality comparisons. (Or, consumers will not shop around or bargain for a lower price.)
____	____	3. Demand for my service will be of a crisis nature. (Or, consumers will not be able to postpone their purchase.)
____	____	4. Unlike the purchase of staple food items and necessities like clothing and shelter, my service fulfills higher-ordered human needs. (Or, consumers will not be price-sensitive to my service because it appeals to their need for status, esteem, or intellectual or emotional growth.)

6. What price will you charge for your service? How does it compare with prices for similar services? How does your price fit the market image you will try to establish? We've stated that your clients' perceptions of your power to solve their problems may be enhanced by charging high prices for your service.

_____

_____

_____

_____

_____

_____

_____

_____

_____

_____

_____

_____

_____

_____

_____

_____

7. In the spaces below summarize how you plan to use the various forms of promotion to communicate availability, reputation, and use benefits.
   a. I'll let consumers in my target market know where and when I'm available and how to reach me by: _____

   _____

   _____

   _____

   _____

   b. I'll promote my capabilities and reputation by: _____

   _____

   _____

   _____

   _____

   c. I'll let consumers know how the results of my service will benefit them by:

   _____

   _____

   _____

   _____

   _____

8. If you've made a decision on the location of your service business, describe the factors that you considered and the advantages and disadvantages of your location. Be sure to state whether you've made a trade-off between the high-cost, convenient location and the low-cost, inconvenient location and your justification for your decision.

   _____

   _____

   _____

   _____

   _____

9. If you haven't decided on an area in which to locate your service business, what specific factors will you consider? Also, point out how the shopping behavior for your kind of service will influence your decision.

   _____

   _____

   _____

   _____

   _____

SECTION III

230

Retail,
Service, and
Manufacturing
Businesses

KEY TERMS

tangibles 208
intangibles 209
"unrecognized" need 212

discretionary income 215
publicity 223
site analysis 224

STUDY ASSIGNMENTS FOR REVIEW AND DISCUSSION

1. Explain why the service business is different from the product business.

2. On the basis of these differences, in what ways should marketing for services and products be handled differently?

3. Tell why consumers buy services.

4. What factor might cause a consumer not to buy a service?

5. What forces of change currently tend to widen the overall market for services?

6. Describe the reasons for setting a relatively high price for your service.

7. How could you best promote your service?

8. For the particular service you would choose, what factors would you study to locate your service business?

PROJECTS FOR STUDENTS

1. Search the yellow pages of your local phone book and prepare a list of a dozen different kinds of service business. See if their characteristics fit the descriptions given under the major heading in this chapter: "Why Is the Service Business Unique?"

2. Perform a search of the financial sections of newspapers, check financial magazines, and see if you can locate a description of a service business that fills an "unrecognized" need. Bring the information to class for discussion.

3. The class should be divided into small groups of five or six students. Each group should appoint a recorder. The assignment: Each group should come up with ideas for a service business based on "reverse technology," going back in time to simpler ways of doing things, or thinking ahead to advanced ways of doing things. Allow 20 minutes for this procedure. The class should then reassemble. The recorders then are to report to the class the ideas generated by the groups. Finish with an open discussion of how we generate ideas for new ways to do things.

4. What elements would you look for in finding a location for the following services: a travel agency, an advertising agency, a shoe-repair shop, an art gallery, a sporting-goods shop?

IF YOU WANT TO READ MORE

CHAPTER 8

231

Marketing
the Service
Business

BERRY, Ronald L.: "Service Marketing Is Different," *Business*, May–June 1980, pp. 24–29.

BOOMS, Bernard H., and Mary J. BITNER: "Marketing Services by Managing the Environment," *The Cornell HBA Quarterly*, May 1982, pp. 35–39.

BURSTINER, Irving: *The Small Business Handbook*, Prentice-Hall, Inc., Englewood Cliffs, NJ, 1979. Chapter 22, "Improving Results in Your Service Business," outlines the 10 keys to repeat sales in a service business; it also touches on making the most of your facilities and increasing sales volume through promotion.

CZEPICE, John A., et al., eds.: *The Service Encounter*, Lexington Books, Lexington, MA, 1985. This book presents the papers given at a symposium titled "The Service Encounter," which was cosponsored by the Institute of Retail Management and the Marketing Science Institute. Throughout the articles the authors stress that the quality of the service encounter is an essential ingredient in the quality of service perceived and experienced by the customer.

DONNELLY, James H., Jr.: "Marketing Intermediaries in Channels of Distribution for Services," *Journal of Marketing*, January 1976, pp. 55–57; KURTZ, David L., H. Robert DODGE, and Jay E. KLOMPMAKER: *Professional Selling*, Business Publications, Dallas, 1982; BOONE, Louis E., and David L. KURTZ, *Marketing*, The Dryden Press, Hinsdale, IL, 1984, pp. 625–646. The first reference is a practical book dealing with many aspects of personal selling. The second is a chapter of a basic marketing book that covers most of the personal selling methods. Both are excellent for entrepreneurs with little direct sales experience.

FELDMAN, Sidney P., and Merline C. SPENCER: "The Effect of Personal Influence in the Selection of Consumer Service," in Peter D. Bennett (ed.), *Marketing and Economic Development*, American Marketing Association, Chicago, 1967, pp. 440–452. This material explores purchase behavior as a cause of differences between products and services. Discussion focuses on the nature of purchasing decisions as they relate to proper timing and selection of a source for a service.

HAYNES, Marion E.: *Practical Time Management*, Penn Well Publishing Co., Tulsa, OK, 1985. This study guide will help you analyze your time management problems. It offers principles and techniques to help you master your use of time.

JOHNSON, Eugene M.: "The Selling of Services," in Victor P. Buell (ed.), *Handbook of Modern Marketing*, McGraw-Hill Book Company, New York, 1970, pp. 12–110 to 12–120. As suggested by the title in which this work appears, this is a how-to coverage of service marketing. It includes suggestions on advertising, sales promotion, publicity, and personal selling.

JOSEPH, William: *Professional Service Management*, McGraw-Hill Book Company, New York, 1983. This book aims at helping the manager or owner who must deal with the practical problems of the service operation: how to satisfy the customer;

SECTION III

232

Retail,
Service, and
Manufacturing
Businesses

how to make profit; how to run the business. Chapters 9 and 10 treat the marketing aspect of the service business.

LEMMON, Wayne A.: *Market Analysis Workbook for Small to Moderate Retail and Service Establishments,* AMACOM, New York, 1980. Using the techniques described in this book, owners and managers of small- to moderate-sized retail and service establishments should be able to perform basic market analysis. The potential profitability of a specific new business in a specific market location can be estimated from this analysis.

MCCAY, James T.: *The Management of Time,* Prentice-Hall, Inc., Englewood Cliffs, NJ, 1959. This book draws on the field of general semantics in a unique way to present a number of practical ways for becoming more effective in the use of time.

NAISBITT, John: *Megatrends,* Warner Books, New York, 1982. In the first chapter, titled "From an Industrial Society to an Information Society," the author points out that a capsule history of the United States might be contained in these three words: farmer, laborer, clerk. Although the great majority of jobs have gone through these stages since the turn of the century, the current trend shows that the so-called clerical jobs are moving rapidly toward professionalism. Here the job focuses on the creation, processing, and distribution of information.

RATHMELL, John M.: *Marketing in the Service Sector,* Winthrop Publishers, Cambridge, MA, 1974. This is quite possibly the best book available that deals exclusively with marketing the service business. It contains an in-depth, thorough, and practical treatment of the various facets of marketing services. Numerous case examples are given, too.

STIFF, Ronald: "The Changing Role of Professional Service Marketing," in Kenneth L. Bernhardt (ed.), *Marketing: 1776–1976 and Beyond,* Educators' Proceedings, American Marketing Association, Chicago, August 1976, pp. 283–286. This is a concise survey of trends in marketing professional services. It describes the increasing emphasis on promotion, market segmentation, and consumer orientation.

UHL, Kenneth P., and Gregory D. UPAH: "Service Marketing: Why and How It's Different," in Jagdish W. Sheth (ed.), *Research in Marketing,* JAI Press, Greenwich, CT, 1983, pp. 231–256.

WEBBER, Ross A.: *Time and Management,* Moffet Publishing, Nutley, NJ, 1982. This reference covers the typical reasons why managers waste time. It recommends several ways to overcome the factors that cause time to be wasted. The author's point of view is particularly suited to the entrepreneur, as it emphasizes the need to lessen the overloading of the present with time-consuming activities and shows how to carve out some time to plan for and make the future less time-haunted.

CHAPTER 9

Controlling Your Manufacturing Operations

TOPICS IN THIS CHAPTER

Objectives of This Chapter
Designing Your Small Plant
Overall Plant Layout
Working Your Plant More than One Shift?
Managing Research and Development
Making Purchasing Effective
Managing Your Production Variables
Key Issues in Manufacturing—Summary
Worksheet 9: Controlling Your Manufacturing Operations
Key Terms
Study Assignments for Review and Discussion
Projects for Students
If You Want to Read More

You will find that manufacturing is somewhat more complicated than many other kinds of business, such as retailing or service. When you alter the physical state of materials by machining or fabricating, you are usually faced with a number of choices: How are particular operations to be performed? This is true not only in how to make things but also in how to put them together.

We have designed this chapter to help you find the most direct and eco-

SECTION III

234

Retail,
Service, and
Manufacturing
Businesses

nomical ways to convert your funds through effective procurement and manufacturing to profitable operation.

Information in this chapter will be found pertinent to these items in the Business Plan:

4.A. A complete technical description of product or service

7.A. Description of the proposed organization

8.A. Information required to support the major points in the business plan

You + Idea + $\left\{\begin{array}{l}\text{Money} \\ \text{Credit}\end{array}\right.$ + $\left\{\begin{array}{l}\textbf{FACILITIES} \\ \textbf{PEOPLE}\end{array}\right.$ $\begin{array}{c}\textbf{PRODUCT} \\ \rightarrow \text{ or } + \text{ Marketing} \\ \text{Service}\end{array}$ $\left\{\begin{array}{l}\text{Money} \\ \text{Credit}\end{array}\right.$ $\rightarrow$ Profit

If you plan to go into manufacturing, you'll be dealing with issues that are quite different from those in other kinds of business. These issues will be more complex in many cases, and there are likely to be more of them. As a beginning manufacturer, you must plan in such a way as to make every dollar you put into the business pay off. To do this, you'll have to set sound policies in managing production and operations.

Policies are guides to action; sound policies beget sound action. You'll want sound policies for gaining control of assets and operations. These will include policies for buying, leasing, or building a plant; buying or leasing equipment; making or buying parts, components, or subassemblies; designing your product line; managing inventory; and controlling production and costs of all kinds.

Like most entrepreneurs starting a venture, you probably have limited funds. Your very first policy should therefore say that you'll husband your money in every way that makes sense. Rather than put a large amount of money into a huge purchase of raw stock at a bargain price, you'd buy less at a higher price in order to preserve your cash. Rather than invest a large sum in a high-speed screw machine, you'd arrange to buy it on terms—again to conserve your available cash. These are a small sample of the kinds of decisions you'll be faced with early in the game.

You'll want to adjust your policies as your company grows and prospers. Then you can take advantage of bargains and the desirable features of new and expensive equipment. You'll be able to capitalize on your company's strengths and build to overcome its weaknesses. You'll adjust your policies, expanding their scope to achieve broader objectives, as your business gains in resources.

Objectives of This Chapter

This chapter covers a variety of subjects of particular importance in developing and manufacturing a product. One of our main purposes is to point out the variety of functions and activities that go into manufacturing and to show how they are interrelated. Careful thinking, planning, and management will ensure control in these activities—and will help materially to produce profitability. By studying this chapter you will learn:

- Important features in locating and designing your small manufacturing plant

- How to make your plant arrangement work efficiently through proper layout of the production process

- The advantages and disadvantages of working your plant more than one shift

- About learning curves, changing trends in working hours, and managing seasonal variations in production

- Key points in managing research and development

- What to look for in designing for production

- How to make the purchasing function effective

- What to observe in managing and controlling your inventory

SECTION III

236

Retail,
Service, and
Manufacturing
Businesses

Business
Plan
Outline
7.A, 8.A

■ Important points in managing your production variables: scheduling, production cost, and scrap and waste

■ About value engineering and how to make it work for you

Designing Your Small Plant

Whether you plan to build, buy, or lease a plant, you should follow three guidelines in making your decisions. These have to do with plant location, community features, and plant layout. If you lease or buy, you may not be able to meet the guidelines in full. Whichever way you go, you'll find some of the items suggested here to be mandatory and others to be desirable. You'll want to meet those that are musts in full; you should try to meet the others to the greatest possible extent.

LOCATION

When you choose the location for your plant, look for ease of access to your market and to the raw materials you'll need. If your product uses large quantities of lumber, these materials will come from the mill or distributor by rail or truck. You'll want easy access by railroad siding or road. Your plant should have a loading dock at the right height to unload and load boxcar or truck readily. If your product is light and easy to handle, you may need only the simplest facility. Electrical measuring instruments, for example, can be boxed in small cartons and carried to airport or post office by pickup.

Watch Zoning Restrictions Choose your plant site with careful attention to zoning restrictions. Zoning ordinances in today's world require attention to the ecological impact of your operations. Many communities don't want plants that spew out noxious fumes or emit smoke, noise, dust, or waste products. Special areas are usually set aside for heavy industry. Whatever your current requirements, you should choose your site with both present and future requirements in mind. If you think that the characteristics of your business will change in time, you should locate your plant in an area where zoning restrictions won't prevent you from making the change. Planning for the future may save you disruption of your business when you want to change.

Make Sure of Your Labor Supply The kind of labor you'll need in your manufacturing operation will depend on the kind of work to be done. You should make very sure that you can draw on a labor market adequate to meet your needs. Local agencies can usually give you information about labor in your community. Your product may not require highly skilled people. If so, your problem is lessened. You may need only semiskilled people whom you can train without too much effort.

HOWARD PRODUCTS COMPANY

This was the case with the Howard Products Company, which made small components used by the electrical manufacturing industry. This company, owned by a sole proprietor, Jack Howard, hired an assembly force composed mainly of women to do the assembly of tiny parts. His plant was located in an isolated backwater area near a large metropolitan city. Public transportation wasn't available, and it was difficult for many of his people to get to work. Even those who had cars found the drive to work tedious. Howard was faced with a high turnover in the labor force. Despite this problem, his company had prospered in the 7 years of its existence, and he wanted to move to a more attractive location.

After several months of searching, Howard found a beautiful small town nestled in the hills not far from the sea. The town offered several advantages for his small plant: A new industrial park on the outskirts gave him the chance to buy 10 acres at a reasonable price. His operations didn't emit fumes, noise, or dust and therefore conformed with local ordinances. The town was a haven for older people who were semiretired and would welcome part-time employment. And a nearby college with a school of business afforded the opportunity to hire and train supervisors and potential managers.

Howard had a competent architect design his plant. He developed a 4-day work-week that permitted his work force a great deal of flexibility in setting their personal working schedules. As he hired the older personnel in the new plant, he put them through a carefully worked out training program staffed by experienced people he had moved from his old plant.

Howard followed the guidelines we give here in building his new plant. It has turned out to be a model of a good place for people to work. It's clean, attractive, and efficient. His company has developed a stable and productive workforce.

What precautions did Howard take to ensure satisfactory conditions for excellence in operations of his new plant?

MAKE SURE ABOUT UTILITIES: POWER, GAS, AND WATER SUPPLIES

When you select your plant site, make sure that the supplies of power, gas, and water are adequate for your intended operation. Work out your needs for these requirements ahead of time. If you plan to use a significant amount of electricity, be certain that it's available in the right quantity, voltage, and phase. Be sure that your supply of electric power can meet the growth you expect. Be certain also about gas and water supplies. If you need large quantities of water in your process, be sure that you can get approval to dump the outflow into the sewer system.

Watch Those Taxes   Find out what your tax burden will be in the location you select. Some communities offer special tax relief for new plants moving in—at least for a given period. If this is your situation, be certain that the tax benefit doesn't override the more important items we've listed above. You'll find that local taxes will run about 2 to 5 percent of the estimated true value of your real estate and property. This would be a rather small portion of your total investment; nevertheless, be careful to check the tax-assessment policy and rates in the community you choose.

DESIGN FEATURES

Use expert architectural help in designing your plant or in remodeling an existing plant. Through this kind of help, you can arrive at a design that permits expansion

SECTION III

238

Retail,
Service, and
Manufacturing
Businesses

for future growth *and* meets your current needs at minimum cost. You'll be able to select from the many modern construction methods one that gives this kind of flexibility. Methods available include modular construction, shell structures, geodesic domes, independent steel frame, or independent long-span concrete frame construction.

You'd do well to be influenced by the needs for good citizenship in planning your new plant. Measures should be incorporated for the abatement of possible public nuisances such as noise, smoke, fumes, or other pollutants. Often the capital investment for abatement may be more than recovered through an improvement in efficiency or the reclamation of waste products. For example, if you use a heat-treating furnace in your operations, you'll find that a furnace that burns clean uses its fuel efficiently; the amount of fuel used will be less and will cost less than if your furnace emits smoke.

Build a Good-Looking Plant   Be certain that the design of your buildings and grounds meets aesthetic requirements. Your buildings should be kept in good repair and the grounds around them carefully landscaped and well tended. You'll make your plant a pleasant workplace for your personnel by taking care of the appearance of your buildings and grounds. Pleasant, well-kept, tidy surroundings will help to keep the morale and productivity of your workforce high. Your investment in appearance will help you establish good relations with your community as well.

Overall Plant Layout

Your physical plant is the tool you use to combine the input of people, material, and money to make the product you sell. It should be so designed as to give a smooth and therefore efficient flow of process. Anything that interferes with the flow of process costs money, and that lowers the profitability of your whole manufacturing operation. Use the greatest care in designing the plant layout to make the flow of the manufacturing process as smooth as you can make it. However you do it, be certain that working conditions are safe and comfortable.

MAKE YOUR LAYOUT WORK FOR YOU

You can arrive at a straightforward efficient flow of your production process by observing certain precautions in designing the layout of your plant. These include provisions for storing, handling, and moving material and work in process.

The layout can be visualized through a scale drawing showing the arrangement of facilities and equipment within the plant. It may also take the form of a scale model displaying the physical arrangement in miniature. In either case, the objective is to arrive at a layout that allows material and work in process to be moved easily over the shortest possible distances while permitting the manufacturing process to be carried out smoothly, step by step.

You should seek ways to move material with minimum handling over the shortest route. Moving material and work in process costs money; therefore, anything you can do to eliminate a stage in handling or to shorten the distance that material must be moved will save you money. You can try different arrangements by changing the layout until you arrive at the most efficient location of facilities and equipment.

BUILD IN FLEXIBILITY OF DESIGN

You can be sure that you'll want or need to change your product design or add new products to your line as your business grows. You should therefore incorporate in your basic plant design features making it easy to adjust your plant to new production requirements. The features you can build in for ready adaptability include clear floor space without posts or columns; high enough roof and sturdy enough supporting structure to accommodate overhead handling equipment such as traveling hoists for moving material or for installing tall equipment or machinery; under-floor ducts or overhead conduits for carrying high-voltage electric lines; movable mounts for ease in relocation of production equipment; and floors strong enough to take highly concentrated loads. You'll find that some of these features will add some expense to construction costs. But forethought in these matters will allow you to save much more money later when you need these facilities.

MAKE YOUR PLANT MAINTENANCE EASY

Great care should be taken in choosing your building materials. Some are easier to maintain than others. By careful selection of materials, you can lower the long-range costs of maintenance. No building materials are free from maintenance, but some are more suitable for a given purpose than others. Natural concrete walls may not need paint, but they may need to be steam-cleaned on occasion to get rid of soot and dirt. Tile or stainless steel panels are easier to keep clean in washrooms than other materials. Whatever you select, you should consider the cost over the long term when you choose building materials. Savings over time may be worth a somewhat higher first cost.

SELECT ADEQUATE MACHINE CAPACITY

When you select a machine to do a job, you'll find it wise to choose one with somewhat more capacity than you think you need. A machine that can handle larger jobs or more work can easily take care of the first job for which you bought it. But it can do more and will be on hand when you want to move to more demanding jobs. The larger capacity machine will require less maintenance than the smaller, and it will be there when you want it. The extra capacity will cost a little more, but it will pay off the extra cost many times over in the long run. It will especially pay off if you're careful to make provision for regular maintenance of it and of all your production machinery and equipment.

Working Your Plant More than One Shift?

It seems clear that you can turn out more work in your small plant if you work your facilities more than one shift per day. Under some conditions you may find this profitable. However, you should weigh the disadvantages as well as the advantages before adding shifts to your operations. If you adopt a three-shift operation, you'd be using your equipment *intensively;* in a single-shift operation you'd be using your equipment *extensively.*

You'd probably reduce your overhead costs per unit of production by going to a three-shift operation. This would hold for certain items of expense such as taxes,

SECTION III

240

Retail,
Service, and
Manufacturing
Businesses

building depreciation, interest on investment, and obsolescence of machinery. You might also be able to take advantage of lower rates for electricity during night operation.

Unfortunately, other costs usually offset these gains. Cost of labor is higher for second and third shifts. Saturday and Sunday work commands even higher labor rates than off-normal shift rates. Labor on other than first shift tends to be somewhat less productive, thus increasing unit labor costs.

Maintenance of machinery and equipment is easier on one-shift, 5-day operation. Repairs and adjustments may be done without interfering with production.

The experience of many small plant executives shows that, all in all, it is generally more desirable to have a larger plant that can produce what's normally needed in a standard workday and workweek.

Many plants use part of their facilities intensively and part extensively. If you have one or two very expensive special-purpose machines, you may find it profitable to work them more than one shift per day. You'd then work the rest of the plant during normal hours.

CHANGING TRENDS IN WORKING HOURS

You may find advantage in going to a 4-day workweek in all or part of your manufacturing operations. The 4-day workweek was first adopted by small manufacturing firms in the late 1960s. Since then all kinds of organizations have gone this route: retail trade, hospitals, banks, trucking firms, wholesalers, and a variety of service firms. But small manufacturing concerns still seem to be at the forefront of this movement.

If you were to adopt the 4-day workweek, you'd want to study the requirements of your business for labor and production very carefully before you introduced the new schedule. Some companies place the total workforce on 4 days, including men and women employees. Others exclude employees who must serve customers, such as clerks and salespersons. Each firm must plan the move to the 4-day workweek on the basis of its special needs.

You'd also want to adjust wage rates so neither your firm nor your employees experience inequities. Some firms reduce the standard 40 hours to 35, 37, or some similar figure. Hourly rates are reduced a bit to minimize the effect of higher overtime rates. In this way the worker's take-home pay is the same as it was before the change.

Surprisingly, companies that have adopted the 4-day workweek have experienced few disadvantages. It takes a while for people to adjust to the new schedule, and customers must be educated to the new business hours. But once a business is running smoothly on the 4-day schedule, few problems seem to arise. The advantages that come with the 4-day workweek are primarily person-related. Most people like to have a 3-day weekend. The plant on the short workweek can often attract a superior workforce of qualified personnel for this reason. Managers find the long weekend a positive feature in that it allows them sufficient time to regenerate their energy for the next week. And you, as the owner of the business, may find the quiet time the long weekend permits extremely beneficial in doing your thinking ahead and planning for the future of your business.

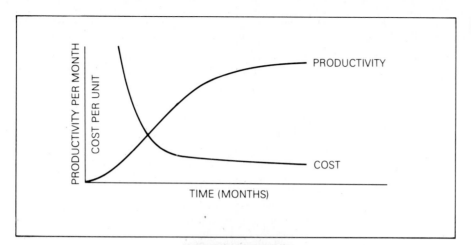

FIG. 9-1

Typical learning curve.

LEARNING FROM LEARNING CURVES

When we approach a strange new task, we tend to be slow and relatively inefficient. As we experiment with ways to perform the task, we correct our errors and inadequate ways of doing things and we become more efficient. We use less time to do the job and we do it better. This is particularly true in production.

You'll find that as your personnel acquire skill through experience in a new production task productivity will go up and costs will come down. The curves of Figure 9-1 show the typical relationship between productivity and costs of production as learning takes place.

The reduction in time and cost stems from a variety of factors. You can find ways to speed up the learning and cost-reduction process by studying the implications of these factors: better planning by management as they learn the elements of the production task; increased skill by workers; improved tooling, jigs, and fixtures; specially developed production equipment; and reduced scrap. You'll be able to predict quite accurately the unit cost when you rerun a product. One guide you can use comes from the aircraft and electronics industries: Every time your production quantity doubles you can expect that your direct labor cost will decrease to 60 to 80 percent of its former level.

You'll predict your costs with increasing accuracy as you collect data. It's an important procedure to keep careful records of cost and production. If you develop your own learning curves as you go, you'll soon have a sound basis for predicting the costs of new runs and of runs of new products.

MANAGE SEASONAL CHANGE

The business of some manufacturing plants is highly seasonal. Sporting goods like skis and tennis rackets have up and down manufacturing requirements during the year. Toy manufacturing and apparel manufacturing have their ups and downs. If your business has seasonal characteristics, you'll face the critical problem of man-

SECTION III

242

Retail,
Service, and
Manufacturing
Businesses

aging your cyclical manufacturing demands. In all likelihood you won't want to hire and fire personnel at the demands of the season. You couldn't build an effective workforce for the long haul if you did. Seasonal demands can be handled in ways that have been found helpful by manufacturing firms faced with cyclical production. Here are some suggestions for handling peak loads:

- Do some building to inventory. The extent to which you can follow this course will depend upon the strength of your financial position, of course. You won't want to tie up too much cash in stockpiling inventory. However, you can often finance building inventory through a relatively short-term bank loan.

- Use special marketing efforts to stimulate sales in off-season periods. You might mount an export sales effort, develop a new market for your existing product, or offer special discounts for off-season orders.

- Increase the number of shop hours during peak manufacturing periods and decrease them in off periods. You'll have to be skillful in doing this to make sure that your personnel go along with you in this procedure. You may be able to hire a supplementary group of retired or semiretired people to work during peak-load periods; these people often prefer to work part time; therefore, their desires would fit your needs.

- Keep a small, steady workforce and farm out work during heavy production periods. Bring the work back into your plant when you come to slack periods.

You can use any of these approaches singly or in combination to take care of the ups and downs of your production requirements. Whatever course you take should be taken on the basis of sound proactive planning.

Managing Research and Development

Business
Plan
Outline
4.A, 7.A

If you're dependent on research and development (R&D) in your business, you probably will have to work on a limited budget, as is the case with most small new firms. This means that you'll seek ways through your own ingenuity and that of your personnel to solve your R&D problems.

You can turn to the services of many small firms that specialize in a variety of technical fields to bolster your own efforts. Some companies offer services such as electroplating, precision grinding, chemical milling, dynamic balancing of rotating parts, and tool and die fabrication.

Knowing that you can add outside special services to your own, you should concentrate on building an R&D facility suited to your special requirements. If, for example, you're entering the electromechanical manufacturing field with the intent to supply other manufacturers with small precision components, you'll want a model shop equipped with three or four basic precision machine tools, perhaps a lathe, grinder, drill press, and milling machine. You might require a small sheet-metal shear and welding equipment also. You'd want some simple tools to handle the electrical fabrication and testing: soldering tools, small printed-circuit equipment, and electrical measuring instruments: an oscilloscope, voltmeters, and ohmmeters.

The model shop shouldn't be used for production. You should view it as a highly specialized tool designed to support your efforts at creating newer and more attractive products or improvements in products you're making.

The model shop should be seen as an arm of the marketing function. It's the tool you'll use to bring innovative ideas to actuality—a highly important aspect of your practice of proactive management. If you should fall into the trap of using your model shop for production, tempting as this may be on occasion, you'll have set a precedent that can do nothing but harm to the future of your business. The focus of your attention would be drawn away from the main purpose of the model shop, which is to develop the products upon which the very future of your firm depends. The model shop develops the products, or the improved features, you'll badly want to take up the slack caused by obsolescence or competitive forces. Model-shop myopia can be as disastrous inside your firm as marketing myopia is outside your firm. Don't trade the future for the sake of a bit more profit today.

It follows that your model-shop operation should be keyed to the marketing function. When a new idea for a product or feature comes up within your plant, you should test it for commercial worth from the outside in, which means that you should use the marketing techniques given in previous chapters to find out how well the idea may be received in your segment of the market.

When you consider an idea for a new product, you should make certain that it fits your capabilities. You might well take on the development of a new type of

FIG. 9-2

Sample progress and control chart for a development program (Gantt chart).

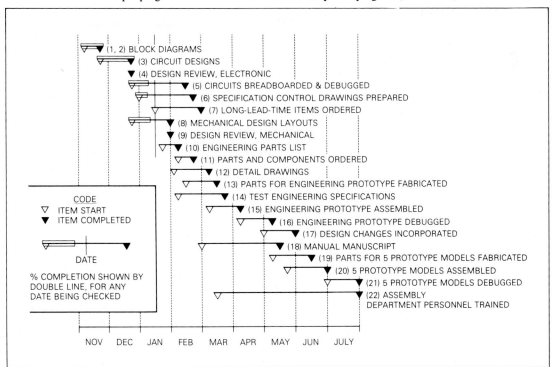

SECTION III

244

Retail,
Service, and
Manufacturing
Businesses

digital electric switch. But you'd be in a bad way if you attempted to develop a turboprop aircraft engine. The characteristics and scope of the development job should fit the resources you have available or can readily manage.

The R&D function takes just as careful management as the financial affairs of your firm. Your project leader, or you yourself if you assume the job, works with people, money, materials, and time to achieve the objective of the development program. You can set your plans on the basis of three criteria: a product that meets the specifications that have come from your marketing study, completed on time in accordance with the schedule you've laid down in your planning, and within the financial budget your planning calls for. You may choose any of several simple techniques for controlling the development project: Gantt charting, Program Evaluation and Review Technique (PERT), Critical Path Method (CPM), or the equivalent.

An example of a Gantt chart actually used by a small company of 250 people is shown in Figure 9-2. This kind of charting should fit most development tasks you may want to do in your small company. If you take on a more complex program, you'll probably find PERT or CPM suited to your planning purpose.[1,2] You'll find information on these approaches to planning in the references at the end of this chapter.

DEVELOPMENT PROGRAM FOR AN ELECTRONIC MEASURING INSTRUMENT

The first thing the project manager of this development program did was to list the important tasks in the total program. The end point of each task is considered a *state point*.

Development Program and State Points

1. Start of development project, receipt of marketing specifications

2. Conceptual development complete; basic block diagrams established; inputs and outputs, with tolerances, established

3. Circuit design for each block complete

4. Design review, electronic

5. Circuits breadboarded and debugged

---

[1]Bittel and Ramsey, *Handbook of Professional Management*, McGraw-Hill, New York, 1985, pp. 597–604. These pages present a section called "Network Planning Methods." This section discusses the usefulness of the *critical path method* (CPM) and the *program evaluation and review technique* (PERT) for managing and controlling a variety of projects. These are typical network planning methods; these plus others are described in detail. Examples show how they are developed and used in scheduling and controlling projects.

[2]Koontz, O'Donnel, and Weihrich, *Management*, McGraw-Hill, New York, 1985, pp. 775–782. In these pages, under the heading of "Time-Event Network Analyses," is given a description of the transition from Gantt charting to a network of state points that become elements of PERT charting. A PERT chart is illustrated on p. 778. The discussion of network planning concludes with a summary of its strengths and weaknesses.

6. Specification-control drawings prepared

7. Long-lead-time items ordered

8. Mechanical design layout finished

9. Design review, mechanical

10. Engineering parts list compiled

11. Components and parts for five prototype models ordered

12. Detail drawings completed

13. Machined parts for engineering prototype fabricated

14. Test engineering specifications prepared

15. Engineering prototype assembled

16. Engineering prototype debugged

17. Design changes incorporated

18. Service manual prepared

19. Machined parts for five prototype models fabricated

20. Five prototype models assembled

21. Five prototype models debugged

22. Instrument assembly personnel trained

Whatever technique you use to plan and control the progress of the development job, you should make sure that it's planned carefully and thoroughly. That's the only way to exert the kind of managerial control that will ensure a project well done, on time, and within the funds you've allocated.

DESIGNING FOR PRODUCTION

Parts and components may be fabricated and assembled in a manufactured product in many ways. Some ways take expensive production equipment but require little hand labor. Some take much labor but need little production equipment. What's important to the small manufacturer is to choose a design that will allow the item to be made at a cost compatible with the resources available—and sufficiently low so that the product can be sold at a profit. The original design, down to its smallest details, controls these possibilities.

Don't overlook the importance of tailoring the design of your product to your resources in equipment and skilled labor. Study the trade-offs in costs of large capital investment in production machinery versus the ongoing costs of labor to do the same job. As a simple example, you can join two sheets of metal in many different ways. You might choose spot welding as against riveting or seam bending as against sheet-metal screws. Or you might adopt fastening with a special adhesive. You'd want to make careful estimates of relative costs once you've decided that the fastening method

SECTION III

246

Retail,
Service, and
Manufacturing
Businesses

is suitable for the purpose intended. And you'd want to estimate for different production quantities. From these analyses you could single out the best way to do the job, taking into account the funds you could make available for fixed-asset capital investment in production equipment as against the cash flow requirements you'd take on in performing the task manually.

You'd be very careful also to keep in mind the end use of the product in laying out the basic design. Performance to the specifications identified by your marketing study will help to ensure the acceptance of your product by your intended customer. Your product must do what you claim it can do. And you *must* be able to manufacture it economically with your resources.

Making Purchasing Effective

The small manufacturing entrepreneur very quickly discovers the critical importance of the purchasing function. Purchasing isn't merely a matter of buying. It proves to be a linking element between the major functions of the company that make the product and the distribution channel that serves the customer's needs. Purchasing contributes to and is involved in every aspect of company operations: production, sales, engineering, distribution, marketing, and other functions, in greater or lesser degree.

Anything that's done at any place in your company affects several other functions. In the R&D process, for example, engineering will depend upon purchasing to find suppliers for hard-to-get components. In distribution, purchasing will be asked to locate a dependable source for cartons with inserts designed to protect your product during shipping. And, of course, keeping production supplied with the right parts at the right time at the right price is a major purchasing requirement.

Purchasing personnel can do their job best when they know the sales you expect within the foreseeable future. This suggests that purchasing personnel should be involved in the production planning schedule on a continuing basis. A good way to do this is to have regular planning meetings involving people from sales, production, engineering, and any other part of the firm you think necessary. When they know the status of current sales and what sales can be expected, purchasing can schedule with due regard to lead times, quantities, costs, and availability of the necessary components, parts, and service.

You should insist that purchasing personnel keep abreast of what's going on with your vendors. They should know immediately of any change in price, delivery, quality, or availability of goods and services. You can often take advantage of a profitable opportunity by building close relationships with your vendors. Your purchasing people can ask for, and get delivery of, items you need in a tight market. Friendly relationships with your vendors may allow you to stretch your credit in a time of stress. Be careful not to overdo this practice, but once in a while you may find it a good way to overcome a tight cash flow position.

You'd be well advised to have purchasing work closely with receiving inspection. Indeed, you may find it a good idea to attach receiving inspection to purchasing. Purchasing can then keep on top of the quality of the items they buy. If there's any problem, purchasing can let the vendor know and get it solved immediately. This approach gives purchasing the power to enforce the delivery of parts and components that meet the specifications to which they were bought.

WATCH YOUR COSTS OF ORDERING AND INVENTORY

You should watch your costs of ordering and inventory. The major costs, which you should identify and control, include placing orders, receiving and inspecting material, and handling and stocking inventory. Study each step and make certain that there's no wasted motion in the process. In ordering and record keeping adopt the simplest kind of paperwork. A purchasing form with three or four copies should take care of your needs in ordering, receiving and inspection, payment, and record keeping.

Keep careful control of inventory to avoid tying up more money than you need to. Costs you should watch are those for investing in, handling, stocking, and insuring inventory. You'll be concerned with a variety of purchased items, the methods of assembly of your products, the shelf life of perishable materials such as paints or chemicals, and perhaps the seasonal characteristics of your sales. When you view the problem this way, you can see the importance of teamwork among marketing, sales, engineering, and production in planning for production. The part purchasing must play is to keep sufficient materials of the kind required on hand without building up too much inventory.

Manage Your Inventory   You can take straightforward steps to manage your inventory. Just as in managing your financial affairs, the first planning that enters into control of inventory is to schedule sales. A good way to do this is to key your planning to three categories of orders: those in hand, those likely to come in during the next standard period—say 1 month, and those that may possibly come in in the following 2 months. You can set a reasonable schedule for production for perhaps 3 months ahead with this information. The purchasing effort can then be weighted to buy at full scale for the certain orders and to use some care in buying for future requirements.

You'll want to control your inventory to ensure that materials, components, work in process, and finished goods don't become obsolete on the shelves. The profitability of your business depends to a great extent on the immediate usefulness and worth of your inventory. The surest way to guard your inventory against decay is to exercise ongoing control of the status of the items that make it up.

Control Your Small Parts and Components   The *two-bin* method is a practical device you can use to make sure you do not run out of small parts and components used regularly in production. Storage bins for these items are divided by a loose panel of plywood between a reserve stock on the bottom of the bin and a supply stock on top. Quantities in each section of the bin are set by your manufacturing requirements. When the top stock is used up, the part or component is reordered. Sufficient quantity is kept in the bottom section of the bin to give enough lead time for delivery so no stockout occurs. Reserve stocks of very small items like washers, screws, or rivets may be placed in bags or boxes rather than stored beneath a partition.

Control Mixed Inventory by the ABC Method   The ABC method gives you a practical way to control inventory if your company requires a variety of items ranging

SECTION III

248

Retail,
Service, and
Manufacturing
Businesses

from inexpensive to costly and from small and easily handled to large and heavy. In this method, parts, components, and supplies to be purchased are classified in three groups: A, B, and C.

You assign items to the A category if they fit the following description:

- High cost

- Expensive to handle, if the part is delicate or bulky

- Likelihood of spoilage or rapid obsolescence

- Long lead time, which can disrupt production schedule or increase the chance of stock outage

- Irregular use of part, so that it must be watched carefully to make sure it is on hand when needed

B and C parts take less attention than A parts. You can control them with an automatic system like that of the two-bin method. You may give responsibility for keeping stock up to production requirements to a clerk for B and C parts. You should give responsibility for A parts to a supervisor.

You identify B parts on the basis of such variables as cost per unit, lead time, annual usage, size, weight, and rate of spoilage or obsolescence. You can use the following list as a guide for identifying B parts:

- Moderate cost per unit

- Intermediate lead time—3 to 4 weeks as against 10 to 12 weeks for A parts

- Moderate quantities compared with C units

- Moderate size and weight (can be lifted readily by one person)

- Not likely to spoil or become obsolete within a reasonable period—3 to 4 months

- Seasonal usage

C parts are generally small, inexpensive, and used continually. You'd classify items such as washers, small fasteners, rivets, nuts, and bolts as C items.

The classification of parts in A, B, and C groups takes judgment. With experience and some practice the procedure becomes relatively simple and routine and can prove well worth the time by keeping your company free from delivery delays caused by stock outages.

GRAPHING INVENTORY

You'll find that one helpful device in controlling inventory is to keep an up-to-date graph of the total inventory. The surest way to get a reliable picture of the status of inventory is to make a physical count and evaluation on a regular basis, say every fourth week. We suggest 4 weeks rather than a monthly count. The 4-week period gives you an equal caliper of time in your measurement. Your profit will ordinarily depend on the last day or two of shipments in the period. By using a 4-week time span, you'll avoid the irregularity (except for one period in the year) of unequal numbers of days in the months.

Your graph of the value of inventory will show a fairly regular ebb and flow; it will go up and down during the year. You'll be able to see irregularities at a glance. You can then take steps to correct unwanted variances by applying corrective measures to the causes.

One way you can add a measure of control over the amount of money tied up in inventory of materials is to work with your purchasing personnel to set maximum and minimum figures for the total of money represented by inventory to meet the existing and near-future production requirements. You should include a small cushion on the high side. You can then increase these values gradually as your business grows. You'll help your purchasing people understand how their efforts contribute to the orderly management of cash flow and to the profitability of the firm by involving them in this planning process. This effort will gain their commitment to practicing good husbandry in their purchasing activities.

Managing Your Production Variables

The objective of successful management of production is to produce a sound product as efficiently as possible. This implies careful control of costs at every point in the manufacturing process, from scheduling for production to minimizing waste.

It's the customer who sets production goals. Every aspect of the manufacturing operation is governed by the need to fill the orders of the customer. Therefore, planning for production starts with the sales forecast.

A good way for you to schedule production is to classify your orders in groups, as we've suggested previously: those actually in hand, and those that you expect within the next 1-, 2-, and 3-month periods. Set percentages according to the best estimates you and your salespersons can make about the possibilities of orders being realized: 90 percent for those that seem quite sure and 50 percent for those that seem fairly likely to materialize. You may then work out schedules for production for the next quarter by comparing expected deliveries and sales orders with shipping dates. You'll want to use your experience and judgment to smooth the figures for sales. As you work with your salespersons, you'll find out who's optimistic and who's pessimistic in estimating future sales. You'll then be able to adjust the information accordingly. Through this suggested procedure, production and purchasing will have guidelines for their operations.

Plan to do your production scheduling on a rolling schedule. Involve those people who have key responsibilities in the firm in planning and scheduling sessions on a regular basis. Representatives from marketing and sales, production, purchasing, and engineering might form a typical planning team. A proved way to schedule these planning meetings is to start with weekly meetings. As the team gains experience and skill, the time between meetings can be stretched. You'll probably find that a 4-week period will serve the company very well after a year or so of experience with the procedure.

The advantage of the team approach to planning for production is that it gets everybody involved. You and your key people communicate with each other. The

SECTION III

250

Retail,
Service, and
Manufacturing
Businesses

chances are improved for clear understanding of what's required to do a first-rate job of meeting your customers' delivery needs. You gain efficiency in your plant and improved morale among your people.

SCHEDULE YOUR PRODUCTION

Production volume and the rate of production govern the tempo of the manufacturing operation. Both are influenced by variables such as required delivery dates; availability of raw materials, parts, components, and services; lead times for procurement; and seasonal ups and downs in the business. Production scheduling is therefore affected not only by the customers' delivery requirements but also by the cooperativeness of your suppliers in delivering materials and services as needed. Lead times are critical in meeting production schedules.

As the chief executive officer your problem is to make sure that you have first-rate working relationships with your suppliers and that you have a trim inventory. You can take two actions to keep a balance between the outflow of materials and services built into the products going to your customers and the inflow of raw materials and services from your suppliers: Develop, and have your people develop, warm relationships with your suppliers, and adopt the rolling planning procedure we've described. When you build a favored relationship, friendly but not too close, with specific suppliers, you incline them to deliver materials as you need them. This can be very important in times of shortage or if you must have special quality in the materials. Proactive planning and scheduling will support sound husbandry in managing the flow of materials in your manufacturing process.

CONTROL YOUR PRODUCT COST

As the owner of a small manufacturing business, you'll seek a high level of productivity together with efficiency. In most small manufacturing companies labor costs are a large part of the cost of making the product. Anything you can do to increase productivity will help your company make profit.

But you won't be able to tell if your operations are gaining in productivity unless you keep regular records. You'll get the feedback you need to see how well your management effort is doing from these records. With these data you'll be able to plan and apply corrective steps for overcoming problems and you'll be able to increase effort that's paying off.

You should know the cost of every part and component that goes into your product. To do this you must have up-to-date information. You'll want to examine the time that each operation takes, for you'll find that time threads through all operations in your manufacturing process. Whatever you can do to shorten the time required for an operation will pay off in increased profit. You can judge the advantage of a capital investment in a more efficient production machine by comparing the new against the old in a time and cost framework.

And, of course, in a similar way, anything that reduces the scrap in an operation contributes to profitability.

Manufacturing costs can be divided roughly into *fixed* and *variable* categories. You can think of fixed costs as being spread uniformly through the year. These include expenses such as rent, insurance, indirect labor, telephone, advertising, and miscellaneous small supplies. These tend not to vary significantly throughout the year. However, variable costs change with the volume of production. By and large, these include the cost of direct labor and material. To these you'd want to add the costs of electricity, gas, or water if used in the manufacturing process.

You'll want to control your variable costs carefully, as they contribute in large measure to the cost of the manufacturing operation.

CONTROL YOUR SCRAP AND WASTE

Three variables influence the amount of scrap and waste in your manufacturing process: (1) the complexity of your product, (2) the suitability and condition of your production equipment, and (3) the skill and experience of your workforce. You should study these variables closely to see how you might make improvements in each.

Complexity of Your Product　As the product gets more complex it becomes more difficult to produce and the amount of scrap is likely to increase. To hold the concentricity of a precision-ground gear to 0.0002 inch is an exceedingly demanding task. It is many times more difficult than to hold the tolerance to 0.005 inch, which is a close tolerance in itself. The skill in craftsmanship to produce the tighter tolerance would necessarily be much higher to assure getting the fine job done right. We would expect to see more scrap in the fine job than in the relatively rough one.

Rougher work takes less skill, of course, and we would see less waste of material. For example, to make scrapbooks with plywood covers and leather string bindings doesn't take highly skilled workmanship. Tolerance here would be about plus or minus 1/8 inch in sawing the covers from a sheet of plywood. Scrap could be limited by getting the maximum numbers of covers from a sheet of plywood.

To minimize scrap in your product, you should design in such a way as to use the material to best advantage and keep tolerances as wide as possible without impairing the performance or appearance of the final product.

Suitability and Condition of Your Production Equipment　You should be certain that any production equipment you use has sufficient capacity to handle the job and that it's maintained at peak efficiency. It makes sense for you to buy equipment that's somewhat oversized for the first task you intend to use it on. The cost will be a bit higher, but the extra capacity is more than likely to pay off the day you want to tackle a task that's just a little bigger than the ones you've been doing. A sheet-metal shear able to cut an 8-foot panel can't handle a 9-foot size, but a 10-foot shear can do it with ease. The extra cost of the larger piece of equipment is certain to pay off as your company grows and you find it desirable to take on bigger jobs.

We need hardly call your attention to the importance of proper maintenance of your production equipment and tools. Machines should be kept clean and well lubricated. Parts that wear should be replaced before the wear impairs the performance of the equipment. Cutting tools should be kept sharp at all times and lathes and milling machines supplied with the right cutting fluid for the task in hand. Proper maintenance will improve the profitability of your production effort.

Skill and Experience of Your Workers　You can cut scrap and waste in production by hiring workers with the skill and experience to do the job properly. The more

SECTION III

252

Retail,
Service, and
Manufacturing
Businesses

complex the job, the higher the level of skill required. You can improve your chances for hiring the kind of craftspeople you need for the work by screening applicants for jobs in accordance with sound hiring practice. You'll find some suggestions on how to go about this task in Chapter 17.

It may be that your production process involves proprietary procedures or special equipment you've developed yourself. You may find it necessary in this case to train people to do this work.

Performance at all levels in your company follows from skill and mastery of the job that's to be done. But people don't gain skill without training. As a proactive manager, you have the opportunity to see that your people get the training and practice to help them acquire skill and mastery. You can see to it that training takes place in production, which is a good place to start. Training at this level could start you on a systematic program of training your personnel throughout your firm as it grows.

Skill and mastery of the task not only cut scrap and waste but also give the trained person the chance to grow with the company. Many a top manager learns the business from the ground up—starting on the workbench and, by acquiring skill and mastery through training, moves up as the company grows.

Salvage Your Waste Materials   Scrap and waste materials can often be salvaged or sold for recycling. For example, if your screw-machine operation is large enough to make it worthwhile, you can centrifuge cutting fluid and reuse it. Or if you fabricate steel pipe for overhead fire-control sprinkler systems, you can make pipe nipples from left-over short ends and you can find other concerns that can use the short lengths left from your fabrication process. Whatever your business you'll usually be able to find profitable ways to make use of scrap materials that otherwise might be dumped beyond retrieval.

PUT VALUE ENGINEERING TO WORK

You'll undoubtedly find, as do most entrepreneurs entering a manufacturing business, that your need to get your product into production and on the market prevents you from making an elaborate search for the most economical design. Your effort will be aimed at making a satisfactory product at a reasonable cost. But once you're rolling, you should search for less costly ways to get equivalent value. Better still, you can often seek and find better performance at lower cost. You can do this through value engineering, sometimes called value analysis.

Value engineering may be described as a creative study of every material, part, or process used in a product with the objective of achieving comparable, or better, performance at less cost. You can use value engineering to study your material selection, fabrication methods, and manufacturing processes. In applying value engineering you must take two broad steps:

- Discover through creative thinking promising ways for cutting the designed-in, production, or purchase cost of each item, part, component, or assembly of your product.

- Decide through study and evaluation of alternatives on the changes you want to make in the design, production process, or selection of material, to maintain or improve performance at a reduction in cost.

You'll need comprehensive sources of information to do a good job of value engineering. Your engineering and purchasing personnel should work together to find materials, processes, and components that will do an equal or better job at less cost. They'll search through data sheets, catalogs, test records, and cost records to specify cases in which improvement may be made. You'll apply design and production experience, drawing on the background of your people in manufacturing, fabrication, shop practice, and materials handling. You and your people should look at every step of the production process, every bit of material, and every design feature to see how costs may be lowered while performance is maintained or improved.

Above all, you'll find that value engineering can best be done in a climate that supports innovation and creativity. The idea is to freewheel in looking for ideas and concepts without criticizing them in the beginning. You'll avoid squashing your people by scoffing at what might seem like an outlandish suggestion. Only after you've gathered a number of ideas on one subject should they be subjected to careful checking and analysis. Then your effort becomes critical but constructive. It's important that you support a climate in your firm that makes it easy for your people to speak out with new ideas. This will be helpful not only in value engineering but also in many other areas—from marketing to inventory control.

As an instance of how value engineering made practical and reduced the cost of an operation in processing decorative wall panels, a small company found it difficult to control the application of enamel in straight grooves cut the length of 4- by 8-foot panels. An expensive semiautomatic device that was supposed to roll paint into the grooves at a uniform rate proved erratic. Paint overflowed the grooves in some places and didn't fill them in others. Hand labor had to be used to clean up overflows and to fill in misses—an exasperating and time-consuming procedure. Workers were asked for ideas and suggestions, as were all key personnel. One workman finally hit upon a simple, inexpensive solution. He found that the grooves could be painted neatly by allowing the enamel to flow from a 10-cent oil can while the can was drawn by hand along a groove. Although this is a simple example of solving a small problem, many instances in any manufacturing operation offer opportunities for improvement and cost reduction. The following section lists some questions you can use to guide your procedure in value engineering.

Test for Values We suggest that you check the answers to the following questions to judge whether it's worthwhile to do a value-engineering job:

Does it really add value?

Is the benefit worth the cost?

Do we need all the features in the present design?

Can we find something better for the purpose?

Can we make a usable part by a method that costs less?

Can we find a standard part to replace one we make specially?

Is our tooling right for the quantities we make?

Can we find another dependable supplier who can furnish the part for less?

SECTION III

254

Retail,
Service, and
Manufacturing
Businesses

■ Are our competitors buying it for less?

■ Are our costs for labor, material, and overhead in line with those in our industry?

You can decide by asking and answering these questions, and others of a similar nature that will occur to you, whether it's worthwhile to tackle a value analysis for any given purpose.

WHAT ABOUT QUALITY CONTROL?

The product you send to market must do what it's supposed to do. If it doesn't perform to specifications, you'd put your business in jeopardy. To ensure quality and performance in your product, you must start with a sound concept, a sound design, and a thorough testing program.

Most firms use quality-control procedures to make sure that the product being manufactured is well made and meets specifications. Quality control usually requires careful inspection of components, parts, subassemblies, and final assemblies to make certain that they meet the details of design and performance specifications. In a sense, this approach is like a policing action—it's after the fact.

The small manufacturer can seldom afford the necessary staff for quality control. You may find this situation a blessing in disguise. For you can avoid the necessity for inspection, with the exception of final performance testing, by practicing proactive management in a special way. You can see to it that your people are properly trained to do a good job every step of the way. You'll agree that it makes sense to do a good job every step of the way. You'll agree that it makes sense to do a high-class job at each step. When your people have skill and master each task in the manufacturing process, they'll build quality into your product at every step. The need for you to have a quality-control function will vanish (or certainly be reduced to a minimum).

As your company grows, you may want to add a *quality-assurance* function. Personnel in quality assurance would act primarily as coaches and trainers. You'd give them the authority to check the performance of products taken at random from final stores. If they found defects in craft or performance, they would help the person who did the job improve in skill by coaching and teaching, using the defective item as a takeoff point.

TAKE ADVANTAGE OF GROUP ASSEMBLY METHODS

We know from much study of assembly-line methods that people on the line tend to get bored and depressed. The result is often poor morale and slovenly workmanship. Boredom can take strange directions: More than one high-priced auto has come off the line with a pop bottle or a banana skin entombed in its tailfin. As a small manufacturer, you have the opportunity to take advantage of what may be called a group-participative method of putting things together. Where you think you can use this group method of assembly, you'd do well to try it. In so doing you may underwrite improvement in productivity and in morale.

The trick is to let the members of your firm experience job enrichment. Give them the chance to learn more and to acquire more skills by letting them do a whole job. Let them assemble a whole piece of equipment or at least a complete subassembly so they can see the fruits of their labor. People working in small groups can communicate, be friendly, and fulfill some of their needs as human beings. That this way of doing things pays off becomes more and more certain as evidence from industry grows. Some companies are now building even automobiles this way.

Some products or parts, of course, may not lend themselves to production through group methods. You can be guided by giving routine operations that can be best performed by automation to machines—and by giving relatively complex problems that are better handled by human beings to your workforce.

Key Issues in Manufacturing

Summary

We pointed out the need for your small manufacturing business to be managed by sound policies. Because policies guide the actions you take in every aspect of your operation, you'll find it of overriding importance to set your basic policies carefully and clearly before you take action. The first policy you should set states that you'll conserve your funds with care, making every dollar pay off.

Whether you buy, build, or lease a plant for your purpose, you'll want to take into account the features of the location: zoning restrictions; availability of labor; electric power, gas, and water supplies; and local taxes. If you build a plant, use materials that are easy to maintain. Make sure the design is flexible to provide for growth and that it's aesthetically pleasing.

The overall plant layout should support the smoothest and most efficient flow of material and process possible. The layout should permit the shortest possible paths for moving material and the most direct routing through the steps in the manufacturing process.

We discussed the possibilities of working your plant effectively by operating more than one shift. The evidence from many plants that have used this approach suggests that you'd do better to install enough capacity to handle your normal work loads on a one-shift basis. The exception here would be the desirability of working very expensive special equipment on a two- or three-shift schedule.

We also suggested that you may want to consider the 4-day workweek as a way of encouraging the hiring of a stable workforce, and of allowing your managers to have more time to relax and rest before tackling the management chores of the week ahead. If you adopt the 4-day workweek, be sure to study the procedures you'll need to change and ways for acquainting your customers with your new schedule.

As you take on new production tasks you'll find that your workforce will acquire the new skills needed on a learning curve. The cost of production will come down gradually as learning takes hold. One rule of thumb you'll find applicable to production says that every time you double your production quantity your direct labor cost will decrease to 60 to 80 percent of its former amount.

If your business is seasonal, you can take care of peak loads by building to inventory; stimulating sales through special campaigns in the off season; increasing working hours during peak periods and decreasing them during slack periods; or keeping a small, steady workforce and farming out work during peak periods. You can use any or all of the tactics singly or in combination.

SECTION III

256

Retail,
Service, and
Manufacturing
Businesses

You'll want to build up your own model shop if you're doing research and development. Your shop should be capable of handling your unique needs. Many of the more conventional requirements such as electroplating, dynamic balancing, and casting can be done for you by outside sources. You should *never* permit your model shop to be used for production; you should think of it as a highly specialized tool to be used only for innovative model-building purposes. And whatever you do in developing a new product, be sure it fits your resources. The scope and kind of project should fit your equipment, know-how, and pocketbook. The development project should be carefully planned and managed. Techniques such as PERT, CPM, and Gantt charting are appropriate tools for controlling the progress of the development project. Be careful to design your new product so it can be manufactured readily and economically. And above all it must perform as you claim it will.

Your purchasing function links together many other functions in your company. Its relationship with production is crucial—but so is its contribution to several other functions: engineering, marketing, sales, receiving inspection, and the control of inventory. Require your purchasing people to build good relationships with reliable suppliers. You'll then be able to count on getting materials in a tight market and receiving special consideration when you need credit.

We've recommended some techniques you can use to manage your inventory. These are the two-bin method for controlling inventory of small parts and the ABC method of controlling a wide variety of items from inexpensive to costly and from small to large. Keeping a graph of the value of inventory allows you to see deviations from normal and to take steps to make corrections when such variances occur.

We've also recommended a way to go about planning for production by classifying orders into those in hand, those you're 90 percent sure to get in a short time, and those that seem 50 percent certain. From these figures you can work out a schedule for production for some time ahead. You can arrive at a reasonable estimate of your production and purchasing requirements by adjusting the figures on a continuing basis. Planning for production should be done by teamwork among purchasing, marketing, sales, and engineering people, as a typical team.

Controlling Your Manufacturing Operations

This worksheet presents a checklist for helping you make sure you've taken care of the major items involved in controlling your manufacturing operations. Some of these items may not apply to your particular business. What may be important in other operations may not be in yours. Each business is different. You may find therefore that you can skip some of the items listed here. However, be certain to do a careful job of gathering the information you'll need to complete those you do find important in your business. *State your reasons for the choices you make.*

FEATURES OF YOUR MANUFACTURING PLANT

This section of the worksheet lists the features you should check in locating, building, or leasing your plant. Place checkmarks at the points appropriate to your answers.

Location
The raw materials for my product are:
- Heavy, bulky, or otherwise hard to handle _____.
- Moderately heavy (up to 50 pounds) and can be handled by one person

    _____.

- Light and small, little problem to handle _____.
- I will need a railroad siding _____; access by truck _____; normal street or highway access _____. If I plan to ship by air, the nearest airport is at _____,_____ miles from my proposed plant site.

Zoning Restriction
- I've checked the local ordinances for zoning restrictions _____; I've found there are no restrictions against foreseeable changes in the kind of business I'm planning _____.

Labor Supply
- I've checked the local labor market and find there are enough skilled people available for my purpose _____. Enough unskilled people are also available to serve the needs of my business _____.

Utilities

- My operations require electric power of this kind: _____ phase, _____volts, _____kilowatts maximum load. I've been assured of adequate service to meet these requirements _____.
- My requirements for gas are: _____thousand cubic feet per month. This is available to my proposed plant _____.
- The manufacturing process in my business takes _____gallons of water per hour. This quantity of water is available _____. I can dump the outflow into the sewer system _____. If not, I can recycle the water _____, or drill a return well to pump it back into the ground _____.

Taxes

- I've checked the local tax assessment that my plant may have to carry _____. I'm certain I can live with these taxes _____.

FEATURES OF ARCHITECTURAL DESIGN

- I've selected a competent architect to help me plan the new plant (or remodel an existing plant). We've agreed on floor plan, method of construction, maintenance, appearance, parking, and the general landscaping around the plant _____.

Plant Layout

- An analysis of the production process has given me a plant layout that I'm satisfied with: I'm reasonably sure that I've taken proper care of storing, handling, and moving material in efficient and economical ways _____.

Flexibility of Design

- I've studied the needs I may have for flexibility in the plant: clear floor areas without columns, high and strong roof structure to carry heavy movable loads, conduits for electric power lines, movable mounts for production machinery, and floor construction adequate to support heavy concentrated loads _____.

Easy Maintenance

- My architect and I have chosen materials that look well and are easy to keep clean _____.

Adequate Machine Capacity

- I've chosen production machines with somewhat more power and capacity than my first production needs require, understanding that this is a conservative and wise approach to ensure my ability to meet more demanding production requirements in the future _____.

WORKING MORE THAN ONE SHIFT

- The results of my study of my production needs show that I would gain some financial advantage by operating my plant more than one shift _____.

  If so, I've decided on the following shift schedule: _____

  _____

- If it appears desirable to work certain production machines more than one shift, here's what I plan to do: _____

  _____

  _____

USING THE LEARNING CURVE

- I've studied the learning curve given in this chapter and I'll apply the concept to my cost of production _____.
- I'll keep records of my production costs and will use the learning curve data to adjust my costs on successive runs of the same product _____.
- I'll also use these figures to help me estimate costs for the production of new products _____.

MANAGING SEASONAL CHANGE

- My business is subject to wide seasonal variation in sales _____. If so, I'm adopting the following ways of handling peak demands, as suggested in this chapter: _____

  _____

  _____

  _____

MANAGING RESEARCH AND DEVELOPMENT

- My approach to building my R and D facility is as follows: _____

_____

_____

_____

_____

_____

_____

_____

_____

_____

_____

_____

_____

_____

- I understand the need for carefully controlling development costs _____.
  I plan to use Gantt charting (or equivalent) to help control these costs
  _____.

Designing for Production

- The design of my product has been carefully worked out to make sure that I can build it with the facilities I'll have, with the skills of the people who'll work for me, and within the funds I can assign to the job. I'll try to test the product sufficiently to know that it will do for the customer what I claim it will _____.

MAKING PURCHASING EFFECTIVE

- I understand the importance of building teamwork among my purchasing, marketing, sales, engineering, and production people _____.
- I'll see to it that they all work together in projecting production requirements to meet sales for the near and farther out future _____.
- My purchasing people will understand the desirability of building friendly relations with selected suppliers, so our needs will be taken care of at all times _____.
- I'll see to it that purchasing works closely with receiving inspection to ensure our getting the quality we need in our purchased supplies _____.

Costs of Ordering and Inventory

- I'll study the costs in placing orders with suppliers, receiving and inspecting material, and handling and stocking inventory _____.
- I'll eliminate waste motion and excess cost in these steps _____.
- I'll also study my costs for investing in inventory, for handling, stocking, and insuring the materials that make up my inventory _____.

Controlling Mixed Inventory

- The two-bin method of controlling small components makes good sense for some of my inventory; we'll use it _____.
- I've studied the ABC method of inventory control for mixed inventory and find it fits our requirements; therefore, we'll adopt it _____.

Graphing Inventory
▪ I understand the benefit in keeping a running graph of the value of total inventory: raw materials, work in process, and finished stores _____.
▪ I'll keep this graph up to date on a regular 4-week or monthly basis _____.

MANAGING PRODUCTION VARIABLES

▪ We'll use teamwork to plan and schedule our production _____.
▪ The planning team will be composed of representatives from sales, purchasing, production, engineering, and _____.
▪ We'll meet on a weekly, biweekly, monthly, or _____ schedule.
▪ We'll follow the idea suggested in this chapter for assigning probabilities to expected sales on the following basis: _____

_____

_____

_____

_____

_____

_____

_____

_____

_____

_____

Controlling Product Cost
▪ I understand the need for knowing the cost of parts, components, and labor in producing my product and I'll keep accurate records of these costs _____.
▪ I'll compile the fixed and variable costs in my business _____.
▪ I'll concentrate on getting these costs as low as I reasonably can, with the knowledge that the variable costs are the ones most likely to require the most careful attention _____.

Controlling Scrap and Waste
▪ I'll take steps to widen the tolerances in my product as much as possible without impairing its performance _____.
▪ The design is such that we'll make the most efficient use of raw materials, taking into account standard sizes of these materials _____.
▪ The production machinery we plan to use is of adequate size and performance capacity to handle the assigned operations efficiently _____.
▪ I'll make sure production machines are kept clean and well lubricated, and that cutting tools are kept sharp _____.

▪ My workforce will have the skill necessary to do the quality of work required in our production process _____.

▪ I'll hire people who have the kinds of skill necessary to do the work _____.

Salvaging Waste Materials

▪ I've studied ways to recover some money from waste materials and scrap produced in our manufacturing process _____.

▪ Here's what I'm going to do: _____

_____

_____

_____

_____

_____

_____

_____

Using Value Engineering

▪ I've studied the section in this chapter on value engineering _____.

▪ I'm going to put these concepts to work in the following ways: _____

_____

_____

_____

_____

_____

Quality Control

▪ I've thought about the difference between quality control and quality assurance as described in this chapter _____.

▪ I've decided we can avoid the need for quality control by training our people to do a first-rate job in each step of the process of production _____.

▪ Quality assurance as a training and coaching function makes good sense for my production operation _____; I'm going to adopt the idea as soon as practicable _____.

▪ I do want a quality inspection function and am going to arrange for it _____.

Group Assembly Methods

▪ My product lends itself well to group assembly methods _____; I'm going to put this approach into practice _____.

OTHER ITEMS

Your business may need items not included in the foregoing. Here's some space to make notes about them:

_____

_____

_____

_____

_____

_____

_____

_____

_____

_____

_____

_____

_____

_____

_____

_____

_____

_____

_____

_____

_____

_____

_____

_____

_____

_____

_____

_____

_____

_____

_____

_____

SECTION III

264

Retail,
Service, and
Manufacturing
Businesses

KEY TERMS

policies 235
ordinances 236
intensively 239

extensively 239
inequities 240
stockout 247

STUDY ASSIGNMENTS FOR REVIEW AND DISCUSSION

1. Describe three features you should look for if you were selecting a location for a new small manufacturing plant.

2. In building a new plant, what features would you include in the design?

3. What would you do to ensure the most effective plant layout for manufacturing by progressive assembly?

4. Identify the advantages and disadvantages of working your manufacturing plant more than one shift per day. Under what conditions would you work part of your plant more than one shift?

5. How would you develop a learning curve for the production of a given product? How could you take advantage of learning curves to manage the production of successive runs of the same product?

6. Suppose your manufacturing business was subject to varying seasonal demand. What alternatives would be available to you to meet the needs of changing demand during the year?

7. How should a model shop for research and development be used in the overall management of the business?

8. What variables should you bear in mind in designing a product for production?

9. Name some of the steps you could take to make your purchasing function effective.

10. What actions could you take to improve your management of the variables of production, such as scheduling, cost of product, scrap and waste, kind and condition of production equipment, and skill of your workforce?

11. Describe value engineering. What are some of the ways you could test to estimate the worth of a particular study (or analysis) you might think of doing?

PROJECTS FOR STUDENTS

1. Assuming you were to make a small, lightweight, expensive product, what features would you look for in selecting a site for your small manufacturing plant?

2. How would you judge the suitability of the labor market in the location you've chosen?

3. What design features would you consider desirable in building a new plant?

4. Describe the advantages and disadvantages of working a manufacturing plant more than one shift per day.

5. What is meant by learning curves and how can management use them in predicting manufacturing costs?

6. Discuss the use of Gantt charting to control an R&D project.

7. What steps could you take to increase the effectiveness of the purchasing function in your plant?

8. How might you go about developing a reasonable production schedule for 3 months ahead?

9. What steps would you take to control scrap and waste in producing your product?

10. Describe what is meant by value engineering.

11. How might you go about minimizing the need for quality control in your manufacturing operations?

12. What advantages, under proper conditions, might result from a group-participative method of assembly? Describe these conditions.

IF YOU WANT TO READ MORE

It's impossible to do more than suggest a few representative examples of the many books in the field of operations and production management. These cover every aspect you can think of, and more, about manufacturing. Every book in the following list has references in it. You can find out in detail about any subject by looking it up in specific references.

BUFFA, Elwood S.: *Modern Production Operations Management,* John Wiley & Sons, Inc., New York, 1980. The level of this text is quite sophisticated compared with others we've listed. For those who want to investigate some of the more technically advanced ways of dealing with operations in manufacturing, the material presented will be found informative.

BAKER, Richard C., and Rick Stephan HAYES: *Accounting for Small Manufacturers,* John Wiley & Sons, New York, 1980. The author's text addresses ways to aid the owner-manager of the small manufacturing business to improve managing financial affairs. A useful inclusion is a copy of the Small Business Administration's "Business Plan for Small Manufacturers."

CRINKLEY, Robert A.: *Your Manufacturing Company,* McGraw-Hill, New York, 1982. This book aims to provide everything needed to organize and manage the day-

SECTION III

266

Retail,
Service, and
Manufacturing
Businesses

to-day operations of a small manufacturing company. It offers real-world functional business systems that can be readily put into practice.

DORFF, Ralph L.: *Marketing for the Small Manufacturer,* Prentice-Hall, Inc., Englewood Cliffs, NJ, 1983. This book addresses many of the unique problems the small manufacturer faces in marketing. It affords manageable answers to complex questions. Well-structured answers may be found by going directly to the page with the needed data.

ELBING, Alvar O., Herman GADON, and John R. M. GORDON: "Flexible Working Hours; It's About Time," *Harvard Business Review,* January-February 1974. The authors describe the benefits of flexible working hours and some of the problems of changing over from the standard workweek. Among the more significant benefits are less absenteeism and happier employees.

LEWIS, C. D.: *Operations Management in Practice,* Philip Allan Publishers, Southampton, Great Britain, 1981. The aim of this book is to bridge the gap between the nontechnical orientation of the manager and intelligent layman, and the lengthy specialized texts on production and operations management. The majority of the chapters are supplemented with illustrative case studies from practicing managers.

MOORE, Franklin G.: *Production Operations Management,* 8th ed., Richard D. Irwin, Inc., Homewood, IL, 1980. This book, highly regarded as a text in the field, is full of useful information about many aspects of the management of production. You will find, for example, a thorough treatment of the problems of locating a manufacturing plant.

MORRISON, Robert S.: *Handbook for Manufacturing Entrepreneurs,* 2d ed., Western Reserve Press, Cleveland, OH, 1974. The author of this book has had many years of business experience in manufacturing. At the time of writing this book he was the chief executive officer of a moderate-sized company. The text is directly and plainly written, covering many subjects of interest to the small manufacturer. Section IV, titled "Manufacturing," gives 100 pages of useful information about many facets of the manufacturing operation, from packaging and shipping to quality control and inspection.

Small Business Administration Publications. The SBA publishes many leaflets on all kinds of subjects of interest to small business owners. Many among them treat the manufacturing business. Some are free and others cost a small amount. Check with your nearest SBA office to get up-to-date lists of titles.

TERSINE, Richard J.: *Production/Operations Management,* Roth Holland, New York, 1980. This book builds on the substantial contributions made by the numerous texts that have preceded it to give broad and contemporary coverage of production and operations management. The approach is analytical, offering an understanding of the nature, significance, and problems of operating systems. While a knowledge of statistics would be helpful, the only mathematical prerequisite is some proficiency in algebra.

WILSON, Frank C.: *Production Planning and Control Handbook,* Prentice-Hall, Inc., Englewood Cliffs, NJ, 1980. The procedures detailed in this work can be applied both to small businesses using manual reporting and to more complex businesses using on-line data processing. The techniques offered can assist managers in improving performance in the areas of sales forecasting, production planning, physical distribution, and inventory control.

SECTION IV

Achieving Proactive Financial Management

CHAPTER 10
RAISING MONEY FOR YOUR BUSINESS

CHAPTER 11
MANAGING YOUR FINANCIAL REQUIREMENTS

CHAPTER 12
MANAGEMENT INFORMATION AND COMPUTERS

Raising Money for Your Business

TOPICS IN THIS CHAPTER

Objectives of This Chapter
Stages of Business Development
The Start-Up Stage
The Growth Stage
The Maturity Stage
Cost, Flexibility, and Control—Summary
Worksheet 10: Raising Money for Your Business
Key Terms
Study Assignments for Review and Discussion
Projects for Students
If You Want to Read More

Small businesses often fail from lack of adequate capital. You should have a sound estimate early in the game of how much money you'll need and where it will come from. There is no fairy godmother out there willing to lend you all the money you want when you think you need it. You will probably have to do what most entrepreneurs do to gather enough money to start your business: borrow from several sources to add to your own contribution of starting capital. By completing the exercises in the worksheet at the end of this chapter, you'll have a good idea of what funds and amounts you will need for fixed assets and working

SECTION IV

272

Achieving
Proactive
Financial
Management

capital and when you'll need these monies. This chapter will help you determine where these funds will come from.

Information in this chapter will be found pertinent to these items in the Business Plan:

1.C.   Summary of your financial estimates

2.A.   Statement of the desirability of your product or service

4.A.   A complete technical description of product or service

5.A.   A comprehensive description of marketing strategy

8.A.   Information required to support the major points in the business plan

9.A.   A statement of proposed approach in starting the new organization

$$\text{You} + \text{Idea} + \left\{ \begin{array}{l} \textbf{MONEY} \\ \textbf{CREDIT} \end{array} \right. + \left\{ \begin{array}{l} \text{Facilities} \\ \text{People} \end{array} \right. \begin{array}{c} \text{Product} \\ \rightarrow \quad \text{or} \quad + \text{Marketing} \\ \text{Service} \end{array} \left\{ \begin{array}{l} \text{Money} \\ \text{Credit} \end{array} \right. \rightarrow \text{Profit}$$

Your ability to raise the required funds is an extremely important factor in determining the type and size of business you can enter. Keep in mind that there is no one best method of financing and that financing methods vary over time as a result of legal, legislative, and economic changes. More importantly, the way you finance your business will depend upon the stage of development of your enterprise.

Objectives of This Chapter

After studying this chapter, which deals with the three typical stages of business development, you'll have gained knowledge about:

- The start-up stage, which needs seed money before the doors can be opened for business

- The growth stage, in which the business is expanding and financing becomes possible through several sources

- The maturity stage, in which the firm needs a substantial input of capital to support continuing (and usually fast) growth

- Sources of funding for the new, and the growing, business

Stages of Business Development

There are three typical stages of business development, each requiring different financing approaches. We've organized this chapter around these different stages. We'll discuss start-up financing, but it's also important for you to understand how business financing requirements usually change during the growth of the business. This will help you do the right things early so that financing your business later will be easier.

STANHOPE CARPET CLEANING

Joe Stanhope runs a small carpet cleaning business in a town east of Los Angeles. The business had been stuttering along for five years producing just a bare living for Joe and his family. And suddenly Joe had had it; it dawned on him that for the time and effort he was putting in he really was getting nowhere. He began to look for ways to make significant improvements in the productivity and profitability of the business in order to make it worthwhile.

In a flyer put out by a nearby community college he learned of a small business seminar to be presented by two professors, an expert in marketing and a specialist in small business management. Joe thought that if he could come up with even one good idea for the $65 fee it would be worth the time and money; so he registered and attended the seminar.

Some months after the seminar Stanhope met one of the professors at a chamber of commerce meeting.

"Professor," he said, "Your seminar was great. I'm sure glad I attended. The

SECTION IV

274

Achieving
Proactive
Financial
Management

discussion about the need to plan and to work with your own banker was particularly helpful. I'd never had a close relationship with my banker. But about three months ago I wanted a loan of five thousand dollars to put into my business. I planned to expand the shop and hire another person—and I wanted to do a better and, of course, more expensive job of advertising. I reread your notes and followed your recommendations: I gave him balance sheets, cash flow projections for two years, projected sales—and the other plans you taught us. My banker was flabbergasted when he saw the financial projections I had prepared. He said, 'I've never seen a small business plan as good as this one.'

"You know what? I got the money just like that." Stanhope snapped his fingers. "I'm sure glad I took the time to do a little studying; my business has already picked up twenty-five percent—and it's growing steadily."

What preparations should you make before approaching a banker for a loan?

The generalizations we'll make about financing the business during each stage of development will not apply in every case. For example, there are a few instances in which an entrepreneur with an exceptional business idea and a carefully prepared business plan has marched into a commercial bank and obtained a sizable start-up loan on the basis of his or her signature. These cases are rare. They usually occur when the entrepreneur has contracts in hand and has a proved financial and business track record. But even when this has happened, in almost every instance the entrepreneur has had to contribute a sizable proportion of the needed seed money.

In addition to needing money for investment in your business, you'll need money for personal expenses. Few new businesses produce enough revenue in the first year to 18 months to pay the owner a salary. As a rule of thumb, you should have enough money set aside to support yourself and your family for about 18 months. Funds for personal support should be above and beyond those needed for the business.

The Start-Up Stage

The first stage we'll call the start-up stage—the period when the entrepreneur needs seed money for rent, supplies, inventory, equipment, wages, advertising, licenses and fees, and other expenses associated with starting the business.

PERSONAL RESOURCES

You, and your business partners if you have them, will be the major source of cash during the start-up stage. Besides savings you've accumulated, other personal resources might include borrowings backed by secured collateral, such as stocks or bonds, loans against the cash value of existing life insurance policies, or borrowing against the equity you've built up in your home. Most small service firms, boutiques, manufacturers, and other types of businesses start in this way: Funds come from personal resources and personal borrowings of the entrepreneur.

Knowledgeable investors will not put money into a new business unless they have concrete evidence that the entrepreneur has personally made a sizable financial commitment in the business. They know from experience that if the venture turns sour it will be easier for you to back out if you don't have your own money at stake. Thus, to obtain sufficient financing, you will have to invest a substantial portion of your personal worth in your venture.

Investors, whether financial institutions, venture capital firms, or individuals, invest in people as well as in companies, products, or ideas. Your money talks when you show your personal commitment to the venture by putting up your own resources. And investors will not usually listen to you unless you do.

WEALTHY INVESTORS

Numerous studies have shown that when the entrepreneur's cash contributions are not enough to finance start-up business operations, outside funding usually comes from wealthy individuals. As a general rule, try to put in at least 50 percent of needed seed money yourself. There are two reasons for this: (1) individual sophisticated investors probably won't be interested unless you've contributed about this proportion, and (2) contributions by individuals will often take the form of equity or ownership interest in your business. When *you* put up more than 50 percent of the total capital, your independence in controlling the business becomes greater and your share of the profit becomes more substantial.

When wealthy individuals supply start-up money for new ventures, it's usually in the form of equity capital. It's not easy to locate wealthy investors, but there are persons called *finders* who specialize in matching entrepreneurs searching for seed money with private individuals interested in new investment opportunities. Commercial loan bank officers, stockbrokers, lawyers, and others involved in financial matters can sometimes refer you to a good finder. A finder may be able to steer you to individuals specifically interested in your type of business.

FRIENDS AND RELATIVES

Seed money from friends or relatives is common in start-up operations, even though borrowing from friends or relatives is generally frowned upon by experienced businesspeople. It's dangerous to mix social or family relationships with business. Friends and relatives can, and often do, interfere with business policy and operational matters.

REPAYMENT TERMS

It will probably be best if you can arrange a loan with favorable repayment terms instead of giving up ownership interest in your business in exchange for seed money. The agreement should be clearly understood, with specific written arrangements for retiring the loan, provisions for early repayment, and procedures if the loan becomes delinquent.

APOLLO SOLAR CORPORATION

Stanley Kuchak, a structural engineer, became intrigued by the idea of adapting solar energy to residential needs. He invented a clever way of assembling solar rooms from

SECTION IV

276

Achieving
Proactive
Financial
Management

aluminum structure frames covered by transparent plastic sheets. His design permitted modular fabrication and assembly, thus enabling do-it-yourselfers to assemble a solar room to the size needed for the south side of their houses. These rooms could serve as sun rooms or greenhouses in winter and could be ventilated for use as porches or playrooms in summer.

Kuchak started in business in 1975 as a sole proprietor to make and sell his solar rooms as prepackaged do-it-yourself kits. He invested his personal savings, approximately $25,000, in the business, and a wealthy uncle lent him another $25,000.

Kuchak struggled with the business for a couple of years, just breaking even. In the third year business began to pick up. Kuchak realized that to meet increasing sales more effectively he had to improve his home-made manufacturing tooling, his purchasing, and his promotion of the product. After careful planning, he estimated that the firm would require an infusion of $200,000 in new capital to accomplish his plans. This amount added to Kuchak's original investment of $25,000 and the $25,000 put up by the uncle would see the firm capitalized at $250,000.

Kuchak discussed his ideas with his uncle, who studied the planning carefully. As a result of their conferences they decided on the following program: They would form a Subchapter S corporation. The uncle would get three friends to contribute $25,000 each, becoming shareholders with him. Thus, they would have four shareholders, each holding a $25,000 block of shares in the company. Kuchak would be permitted to acquire an interest equal to the total of that of the others from the earnings of the company as the company became profitable.

In the beginning, Kuchak would be paid a reasonable salary, and the losses expected for the first couple of years would help the four shareholders reduce their income taxes. When the firm, known as Apollo Solar Corporation, became profitable it would be converted to a standard corporation.

To raise the balance of funds required by this plan, the firm went to the SBA and negotiated a guaranteed bank loan for $125,000. The four sophisticated investors cosigned the note with the bank.

On the basis of the improved financial resources of the company, Kuchak was able to convince his mill supplier to give him substantial discounts on the special shapes he needed in aluminum extrusions because he could now afford to order large quantities per mill run.

The financial package was a combination of personal savings of the entrepreneur, money borrowed from a relative, investments by sophisticated wealthy persons, and an SBA guaranteed loan. **Financial packages that combine money from several sources to start a business are not uncommon.**

The firm showed substantial improvement in profitability in 1982 and the founders looked forward to converting to a standard corporate form within two years.

Name several possible sources that you might use in putting together a package of funding to stimulate growth of your small business.

If you must seek outside sources for funding, be careful not to accept more than you need. It may be comfortable to have a capital cushion, but the cost will be either dilution of your ownership and control position or early burdening of your cash flow with excessive loan repayment charges. The financial performance of your business becomes more impressive to future investors if it has been achieved with a small rather than a large amount of seed money. And this will make it easier for you to obtain the additional funding you'll need as your business grows.

The Growth Stage

The second, or growth, stage is the period when you'll need additional financing for business expansion—the hiring of full-time sales personnel, building new production facilities, purchasing new equipment, investing in new production machinery, or investing in new product development. By this time the business will have developed its product or service, successfully marketed what the business offers, and generated respectable sales revenue.

Several alternatives now exist for acquiring growth-enabling funds. Your suppliers may be persuaded to finance inventory and equipment; commercial banks, the Small Business Administration, venture capital groups, and others become interested at this stage of development.

SUPPLIERS

Your firm's suppliers can give financial assistance. Most important are suppliers of inventory. Wholesalers who want a retailer's business will often offer attractive terms for paying invoices, and manufacturers will do the same for a desirable wholesaler. For example, if you can buy a $100,000 inventory that will sell within 1 month for $50,000 as the down payment, with the balance due in 30 days, your wholesalers will have supplied you with $50,000 worth of capital for 30 days.

Another form of trade credit is the discount offered when inventory is sold to a retailer. For example, a discount often used is the 2/10, net 30. This means that the retailer gets a 2 percent discount off the total due if payment is made within 10 days; if not, the full amount of the invoice is due in 30 days.

Trade credit is a way you can either postpone payment until your inventory itself is returning cash, or realize savings on your accounts payable through taking discounts by paying for inventory immediately. Planning for use of trade credit is essential. Its effective use is the principal reason large businesses buy products for less money than small firms. Do not depend too much on trade credit from one supplier. If you run into difficulty in paying on time, you may find your source of supply cut off when you most need it to fill your customers' orders.

You can often finance capital equipment and plant facilities like shelves, display cases, counters, and delivery trucks through your suppliers. It's usually easier to obtain financing on these items than it is to get a loan for ordinary working capital because the equipment itself secures the loan. Suppliers will often give favorable terms to sell their equipment, even to new companies. A modest down payment of 10 to 20 percent with the balance spread over 2 to 3 years is not unusual.

COMMERCIAL BANKS

Banks supply debt financing; they don't want an ownership (or equity) interest in your venture. They will lend money for working capital or for purchasing fixed assets when they have clear evidence that your firm's cash flow can meet principal and

SECTION IV

278

Achieving
Proactive
Financial
Management

interest payments. They'll want to know how and when their money will be repaid, and they'll usually want some form of collateral to secure their loan.

As we've stressed earlier, you should select a bank and establish good relations long before your need for financing growth arises. The sooner you do so, the sooner you'll learn what types of loans and how much credit will be available to you.

Select your bank on the basis of your business and financial needs. Compare services offered and get to know key officers you'll be dealing with. At some early point in the growth of your business, assess their willingness to lend you money. Show them your business plan and keep them informed of financial developments. Invite them to see your business in operation during the start-up phase. After you've selected a bank, do all your business banking and personal banking there; don't split your accounts among banks. By following these suggestions, you'll improve your chances of getting money when you need it.

Here are some of the types of financing a bank supplies:

- Short-term commercial loans: These are the most common kinds of loans to small businesses. The loans are for short periods, 30 to 180 days; they are usually made to cover seasonal or other temporary needs for personnel or inventory. Repayment is usually made in one lump sum, which includes interest.

- Longer-term loans: With longer repayment terms of up to 5 years, these loans have a regular repayment schedule, usually monthly, including interest to date plus payment against principal. These loans are for such purposes as buying fixed assets, equipment, or other items for business expansion.

- Accounts receivable financing: Banks will often lend money on your accounts receivable if they are pledged as collateral. You must pay the bank if the accounts pledged are not paid on time. You would still own the receivables and would yourself go after your customer for collection. This type of financing is frequently used by small retail and service businesses for purchasing additional operating inventory or operating supplies.

- Other types of financing: Commercial banks will lend money for building construction or improvement and for buying land. The loan is usually long-term and is always secured by the asset for which the loan was made.

- Bank credit cards offer another form of financing. By accepting them for payment from customers, the business affords credit to customers without having to assume any credit risk, record keeping of receivables, or financing of the sale. It costs the entrepreneur 3 to 6 percent of the sale price to use this service—a small fee for the service rendered.

THE SMALL BUSINESS ADMINISTRATION (SBA)

The information and management assistance offered by the SBA has been described previously. The SBA is also a source of financing. It is prohibited by law from granting financial assistance unless the entrepreneur is unable to obtain funds from the private sector on reasonable terms. It does not compete with the banking industry; instead the SBA works with private capital suppliers to assure availability of funds to potentially profitable small businesses. Business loan proceeds can be used for working capital, purchase of inventory, equipment and supplies, or for building construction and expansion.

These are the major SBA loan programs at present:

1. Before the first Reagan administration, the SBA was able to lend money directly to qualified small business, provided adequate collateral was available. Since 1981, funding has been severely curtailed. Although limited, the agency may on occasion make a direct loan to applicants unable to secure private financing or an SBA-guaranteed or participation loan.

2. Loans made by private lenders, usually banks, and guaranteed by the SBA. By law, the SBA can guarantee a portion of a loan made by a bank or other private lender. The SBA's guarantee cannot exceed $500,000.

In addition to its basic loan programs, the SBA offers loans for low-income and other disadvantaged persons, loans to help small firms owned by handicapped persons and nonprofit sheltered workshops employing the handicapped, loans to small firms engaged in manufacturing, selling, installing, servicing, or developing specific energy conservation measures, loans to development companies for projects aiding small businesses in urban or rural communities, loans and revolving lines of credit for export purposes, and guaranteed loans for qualified employee stock ownership trusts.

Loans made directly by the SBA have a maximum of $150,000. When neither private financing nor a loan guarantee is available, the SBA may provide loan funds on an "immediate participation" basis with a bank. The bank disburses part of the loan, at market interest rates, and the balance of the loan is disbursed directly by the SBA, at a lower interest rate. The SBA's share of an immediate participation loan may not exceed $150,000. (These administrative limits are subject to change.)

The SBA credit policy at present, during times of tight federal budgets, is to omit loans to applicants of weaker credit and emphasize loans to strengthen existing borrowers; also to make term loans available to stronger operating business enterprises. Applicants should show the following strengths in requests for financial assistance:

Strong credit history record when applying for a new business, including a large equity in cash invested in the business

Strong collateral as security for the loan

Extensive experience on the part of management within the specific industry

The business should be needed in the community and should provide an essential service.

3. Special loan programs: These include displaced business loans for small businesses that have suffered economic loss due to federally financed construction such as urban renewal or highway projects. In addition there are several disaster-related loan programs. A little-known form of assistance is the lease guarantee program. The SBA will guarantee the rental payment for the small firm to the

SECTION IV

280

Achieving
Proactive
Financial
Management

landowner or building owners, allowing the entrepreneur to compete with larger firms for commercial space.

It is outside the scope of this book to describe all the SBA's assistance programs. *New legislation constantly creates new loan programs and changes existing programs.* Your best approach will be to visit your local field office of the SBA, study the literature, and discuss the programs with their financial and management assistance officers.

SMALL BUSINESS INVESTMENT COMPANIES (SBICs)

These privately owned companies are licensed and regulated by the SBA and were created to supply equity capital, long-term loan funds, and management assistance to small business. They exist in most states and are ready to help firms that show attractive potential. The excellent financial record of SBICs reflects the success of the small firms they have helped. The SBA or your bank can assist you in contacting an SBIC.

MINORITY ENTERPRISE SMALL BUSINESS INVESTMENT COMPANIES (MESBICs)

Federally established and licensed, the Minority Enterprise Small Business Investment Companies (MESBICs) serve small businesses completely owned by members of minority groups of economically or socially disadvantaged citizens. MESBICs are restricted by federal regulations to grant loans only to firms that don't exceed the size requirements given by the SBA: assets of $9 million, net worth $4 million, and net profit after taxes $450,000. MESBICs may also contribute to equity funding from their own resources.[1]

BUSINESS DEVELOPMENT CORPORATIONS (BDCs)

These organizations exist in every state and supply financing similar to SBICs. They are privately owned and their capital base is made up of funds from private sources. Private businesses and individuals form these corporations to promote local commercial growth by attracting new and different types of business. They will often grant long-term business loans to small firms that have been turned down by banks, and on occasion they will buy stock in a promising new venture.

VENTURE CAPITAL FIRMS

These are firms specializing in supplying equity capital for businesses with high growth potential. The venture capital firm looks for unique, exciting, fast-growing companies in an expanding field.

Venture capitalists become interested in the small business when it has demonstrated (1) market acceptance for its products by sizable sales generated over a period of time, (2) its potential for rapid growth, and (3) competence in managing

---

[1]See Appendix D, "A Successful Business Plan," for an example.

other people's money. This source of capital will want large returns for supplying equity financing. It would not be unusual for venture capital firms to expect ten to twenty times their initial investment within 5 years. Although venture capitalists would have an ownership interest, they do not want management control of the business unless things go wrong. Instead, they look for a well-balanced and experienced management team with technical, marketing, and financial competence.

Don't waste your time (and credibility) by seeking financing from a venture capital firm before you've met the requirements we've just described. Several sources of information about them are given at the end of this chapter. Learn about them and what they can do for you before you approach a venture capital firm for an infusion of capital.

SUMMARY: DEBT VERSUS EQUITY FINANCING

We have outlined several sources of funds for financing the growth stage of your business. Some, such as banks, supply loans to small businesses. These debts must be repaid out of current earnings. Others, such as venture capital firms, offer mostly equity financing. Funds of this kind represent ownership interest in the business for which a handsome financial return is expected.

Some equity financing during the growth stage is usually required. There are several reasons for this. First, growth requires cash—cash to pay for increased facilities, new personnel, research, and promotion efforts. Meeting fixed repayment schedules for loans can place an undesirable strain on your cash flow at a time when you'll want to conserve cash for expansion. Second, loans are extremely difficult to obtain for such intangible purposes as new product development and market research. Loans are usually made to help a firm acquire tangible assets like equipment or inventory. Third, you'll multiply the risk of business failure by not having the protection of long-term equity and the resulting financial strength required to borrow money on favorable terms when you need it.

Permanent equity financing is something to plan for. It involves strategic decisions and technical knowledge of the capital market. This is another area where professionals, such as your accountant or attorney, can help.

The Maturity Stage

During this stage the enterprise tends to outgrow its ability to finance further expansion with cash generated from its own internal operations and the external sources described previously. At this point the business will want to move into new markets, construct new plants or distribution outlets, and purchase more equipment. Sizable sums of money for marketing may be needed to meet increased competition. Large sums of equity money are usually sought from such sources as public sale of stock or merger. We will examine these sources only briefly, since financing at maturity is a highly complex and technical subject beyond the purpose of this book.

Public sale of stock is a viable alternative for raising capital when the business has a well-established track record. The public equity offering sometimes has the dual purpose of raising additional funds for the company and enabling original

Business
Plan
Outline
2.A, 4.A, 5.A

SECTION IV

282

Achieving
Proactive
Financial
Management

investors to realize a financial gain by selling a portion of their shares. The expenses involved in "going public" are significant. There are legal and auditing expenses as well as the cost of good placement services—the reputable investment banking firm that agrees to underwrite or sell the stock offering. Often these costs can amount to 20 percent or more of the total proceeds of the stock sale. The company will have to devote a lot of its efforts to maintain good relations with its stockholders and the Securities and Exchange Commission. There will be strict disclosure and reporting requirements. And if the company doesn't perform well with its equity capital, additional public financing will be out of the question.

On the other hand, sale of public stock can net the company more debt-free funds than, say, venture capital firms can supply. Going public will often produce a higher stock price than selling stock to a single buyer.

Finally, although managerial efforts may be diverted to reporting requirements and public investor relations, working with private investors, banks, and venture capital firms also takes time.

Expanding markets, new technology, and need to diversify often mean that large infusions of cash will be needed beyond the company's own resources and credit available from financial institutions. A public offering of stock permits the owners to retain control of their company while reaping the benefits of an increasingly valuable equity position if growth continues. But it should be noted that buyers of stock in a public offering look primarily at the potential for capital gain rather than dividends. This means that for the stock offering to be attractive, the company's growth record must far exceed the industry average.

In addition, going public alters the character of the company and changes the way the entrepreneur is accustomed to operate. Profit margins, market share, and other information may have to be disclosed, which could affect the firm's competitive position. Stockholders, analysts, auditors, and brokers will also want access to information and will feel they have a right to question a variety of decisions and actions management has made. The effect is that the closely held company accustomed to a low-profile and free-wheeling operation now becomes accountable to many outsiders.

Another way to raise funds for continued expansion of the business is through merger with a larger company. Although this may be the answer for financing, small businesses often do not consider this alternative until they've tried without success to find another way. At the maturity stage merger should be viewed as one tool available to meet the company's goals—a means to conquer new markets or develop existing ones fully, expand production, or increase productivity.

A merger is a transaction in which the seller is the small business and the buyer is the larger acquiring business. From the seller's viewpoint, there can be personal and business reasons for considering a merger. The seller's original investment will be more valuable and marketable if the acquired company is healthy and growing. And the buyer will have to give up enough cash, perhaps combined with stock in the larger company, to compensate the owners of the small business for their success. The benefit to the acquired business is that by merging it achieves a better position to grow. There may be advantages in marketing, production, and management by combining the talent, assets, and financial strengths of the companies.

Cost, Flexibility, and Control

CHAPTER 10

283

Raising Money
for Your
Business

Summary

There are several sources of funds for the small business with a good record. But in the start-up phase, your personal funds and borrowings will almost always be the major form of capital. There is ordinarily no substitute for putting your financial assets on the line in starting your own business.

Trade credit is an excellent way to finance inventory; if you use discounts wisely, it can be very economical. New equipment may be financed on an installment basis or by leasing from the supplier.

Establishing and maintaining good relationships with your bank will assure ready access to short-term funds and even term loans up to 5 years. These will usually have to be secured by existing business assets. Your need for bank loans should be anticipated well in advance. You should assess bank services and select the bank to deal with before opening your doors for business.

Continued growth of your business will require you to consider long-term financing. Loans from the SBA, SBICs, MESBICs, and SBDCs are available.[2] Equity financing may become necessary with growth to prevent burdening the cash flow of the business with fixed repayment expenses. SBICs, BDCs, and venture capital firms can supply this form of funding, but they'll want a well-balanced management team guiding a rapidly growing business and selling unique products or services.

The cost of obtaining capital must be weighed against the benefits. Loans must be repaid—interest and principal—out of business earnings. But they will not affect your ownership interest in the business, unless things go wrong. Nor will they impair your flexibility in making decisions that affect your business operations.

One of the most difficult strategic decisions you'll have to make concerns long-term financing. This usually boils down to whether or not you want your company to grow. If you do, you'll probably have to sacrifice some of your ownership and control in the business. And your entrepreneurial flexibility may be diminished. You'll have to reexamine the reasons you went into business for yourself in the first place. It may be possible to stay small and remain profitable. If your firm grows too large to suit you, it may be better to sell out and start another business. This will very likely be your course if your dominant need is for achievement through entrepreneurship. As you'll see in the next chapters, surviving business growth will require you to develop skills beyond those it takes to be an entrepreneur.

---

[2]A pamphlet titled "Venture Capital, Where to Find It" may be had through the National Association of Small Business Investment Companies, 1156 15th St. NW, Suite 1101, Washington, DC, 20005. This directory lists by states over 350 SBICs and MESBICs representing over 90 percent of these investment agencies in the United States. The introduction tells which SBICs or MESBICs you should approach and answers questions about presenting your case. All entries are coded to show the preferred limits for loans or investments, the investment policy, and the industry preferences of each SBIC or MESBIC.

WORKSHEET 10

Raising Money for Your Business

1. (a) Of the total start-up capital your business needs, what percentage will you be contributing? ____% Refer to items 8 and 9 in your business plan for required financial data.

   (b) What personal assets will you use to come up with the amount needed? List them and indicate how much each will supply:

Item	Amount
a. _____	$ _____
b. _____	_____
c. _____	_____
d. _____	_____
e. _____	_____
f. _____	_____

2. Are there other investors who will supply seed money for your venture? List them below along with how much you expect them to contribute and the terms (debt or equity position) on which you are willing to let them come into the business.

Investor	Amount Expected	Terms
a. _____	_____	_____
b. _____	_____	_____
c. _____	_____	_____
d. _____	_____	_____
e. _____	_____	_____

3. What are the sources you'll seek for capital to finance business expansion? What will you use the money for? Rank sources in order of importance as you see them for your kind of business, and describe the purpose of money they'll supply.

Sources	Purpose of Funds
a. _____	_____
b. _____	_____
c. _____	_____

d. _____ _____

e. _____ _____

f. _____ _____

4. How much have you set aside for maintaining yourself and family for the next year and a half it usually takes to get the business rolling—in addition to the funds you need to start the business? $_____. List your family budget for $1\frac{1}{2}$ years here:

SECTION IV

286

Achieving
Proactive
Financial
Management

KEY TERMS

seed money 274
start-up stage 274
equity capital 275
finder 275

growth stage 277
venture capital 280
maturity stage 281

STUDY ASSIGNMENTS FOR REVIEW AND DISCUSSION

1. Name the more common sources of money for starting a business.

2. What cautions should you observe when getting funding for your new business from sophisticated investors? From relatives or friends?

3. How could you take advantage of trade credit in the growth stage of your company? What cautions should you take here?

4. What can your bank do to help you in your business needs for money? What can't they do?

5. Get and read the latest pamphlet on the role of the Small Business Administration in helping small businesspersons borrow money.

6. What do venture capital firms look for when considering investing in a small business?

7. Describe the conditions that exist in the maturity stage of the growing small company. Name some of the changes that occur in the characteristics of management of the company that has gone public.

8. Can you see advantages that might benefit the owner of the small company that merges with a large company?

PROJECTS FOR STUDENTS

1. Name the three typical stages of business development and state why the business requires funding at each stage.

2. As the owner of a rapidly growing business, how could you use supplier credit as a substitute for capital? What precautions should you use in this situation?

3. Under what circumstances would you expect to go to the bank to borrow money for your business?

4. What services might you expect to get from your bank for your business, aside from loans?

5. Two students invite a lending officer from a local bank to address the class on, "What banks can and can't do for you as a small business owner."

6. Two students interview the loan officer at the local SBA office. Find out what the up-to-date regulations are in the way the SBA can help small businesses obtain loans.

7. Two students do library research on what conditions should exist in the maturity stage of the small, rapidly growing company to encourage the company to go public. Report your findings to the class.

IF YOU WANT TO READ MORE

ADAMS, Sam: "What a Venture Capitalist Looks For," *MBA*, June/July 1973, vol. 7, no. 6, pp. 6–9. As the title suggests, this article gives specific suggestions for entrepreneurs who are looking for venture capital.

"Borrowing Money from Your Bank," *Small Business Administration Publication* 1.10/2:2, Annual No. 2, No. 33, and "What Kind of Money Do You Need?" *Small Business Administration Publication* 1.10/2:11, Annual No. 11, No. 150. These two SBA publications tell you how to determine the kind of money you'll need and about conventional sources that supply it. Bank borrowing is discussed: what banks want in the way of collateral and for what purposes banks will lend money to you.

"Financing Small Business," *Small Business Reporter*, Bank of America. This is another pamphlet in the *Small Business Reporter* series published by the Bank of America. It describes sources of capital and credit for the small business and the risk and cost associated with each. Especially useful is its discussion of developing good relations with your bank and bank services.

GOLDSTEIN, Arnold, S.: *Starting on a Shoestring*, John Wiley & Sons, New York, 1984. This book addresses those entrepreneurs who have the ambition and survival skills to become successful in their own business, but are short on cash. Key topics include selecting a business and borrowing money. Especially noteworthy are case studies telling how five entrepreneurs went about solving these problems.

KRAVITT, Gregory I., et al.: *How to Raise Capital*, Dow Jones–Irwin, Homewood, IL, 1984. The objectives of this book are to help the entrepreneur raise and preserve capital. Presented in questionnaire form, the text is designed to elicit information specifically required by the prospective investor.

MARTIN, Thomas J.: *Financing the Growing Business*, Holt, Rinehart and Winston, New York, 1980. This book brings order out of the chaos of finding capital. Subjects touched on range from financing sources, the various and alternate terms and conditions for such financings, loan agreement, valuation, the use of intermediaries, and the determination of equity percentage give-up.

PRATT, Stanley E.: *Guide to Venture Capital Sources*, 7th ed., Capital Publishing Corp., 10 S. La Salle St., Chicago, 1983. This is a financial encyclopedia for the entrepreneur. The initial chapters in the *Guide to Venture Capital Sources* not only present some basic information on raising venture capital but also discuss the pros and cons of going public. There's a directory section that lists venture capital firms,

SECTION IV

288

Achieving
Proactive
Financial
Management

their officers, who to contact, and descriptive information on the areas of investment and investment limits they prefer.

RUBIN, Richard, and Philip GOLDBERG: *The Small Business Guide to Borrowing Money,* McGraw-Hill, New York, 1980. This book is for both newcomers to business and seasoned entrepreneurs. It will help any businessperson avoid the pitfalls of borrowing and obtain the fastest and best financing. Topics discussed include determining financial need, where to go for money, how to present your case, how to negotiate, and what to look for in a loan agreement.

SILVER, A. David: *Up Front Financing: The Entrepreneur's Guide,* John Wiley & Sons, New York, 1982. This book aims to clear up the mystery of raising capital to launch, expand, or acquire a small business. Various methods are outlined, discussed, and compared. Written at a somewhat difficult level, this book offers a helpful guide to answering questions that investors most often ask.

STEVENS, Mark: *Leveraged Finance: How to Raise and Invest Cash,* Prentice-Hall, Inc., Englewood Cliffs, NJ, 1982. This book helps a potential entrepreneur learn how to use the power of leveraging to magnify the value of the money personally raised many times over. You will also learn to use the language of leveraging and how to design a balance sheet that helps raise cash.

Managing Your Financial Requirements

TOPICS IN THIS CHAPTER

Objectives of This Chapter
Planning Required
Your Planning Assumptions and Financial Plans
Using Ratio Analysis
Key Points in Managing Your Finances—Summary
Worksheet 11: Managing Your Financial Requirements
Key Terms
Study Assignments for Review and Discussion
Projects for Students
If You Want to Read More

In this chapter we come back to the financial aspects of business indicated in the flow diagram of the business process as *MONEY* and *CREDIT* (Figure 1-1). The importance of these terms is shown by their occurrence on both sides of the flow diagram. Not only are they variables in the equation of business, but also they lead directly to the end term of *PROFIT*. The quality of your management of your business will be shown by black ink on your income statement, period by period. You should look at profit as a critical feedback signal telling you how well you are managing: the more the profit, the better your management. This

SECTION IV

290

Achieving
Proactive
Financial
Management

chapter is designed to give you powerful tools to help you manage your financial requirements for profitable operation of your business.

Information in this chapter will be found pertinent to these points in the Business Plan:

1.C. Summary of your financial estimates

2.A. Statement of the desirability of your product or service

3.B. Detailed explanations of your place in the state of the art

6.A. An outline of the activities to be used in selling the product or service

8.A. Information required to support the major points in the business plan

You + Idea + $\left\{\begin{array}{l}\textbf{MONEY} \\ \textbf{CREDIT}\end{array}\right.$ + $\left\{\begin{array}{l}\text{Facilities} \\ \text{People}\end{array}\right.$ $\begin{array}{c}\text{Product} \\ \rightarrow \quad \text{or} \\ \text{Service}\end{array}$ + Marketing $\left\{\begin{array}{l}\textbf{MONEY} \\ \textbf{CREDIT}\end{array}\right.$ $\rightarrow$ **PROFIT**

Competence in financial management is a fundamental strength you must have to run your business successfully. To become a proactive financial manager, *you must do the basic planning yourself*. That's the only way you can get a solid grasp on managing the financing your business will need to survive.

Planning for finances will tell you how much money you'll need and when you'll need it. With these data at your fingertips, you'll prepare for the investments or loans required well ahead of time—and improve your chances for getting the money. Prospective investors, lenders, or bankers will gain confidence in your ability to repay your loans because they'll quickly see that you know what you're talking about.

You'll require three kinds of money: capital for permanent investment in your business; liquid cash, or working capital, for operating your business; and personal money for your family and yourself.

You'll estimate the capital investment you need for fixed assets by totaling the sums for such items as machinery and equipment, cost of freight and installation, storage bins, store fixtures, decoration, office equipment, and sales or use tax. And you'll want to add a reasonable safety factor to the total.

You'll project the liquid cash, or working capital, your business will require to pay for inventory or raw material or stock and for labor and current expenses each month.

And finally, you'll prepare a budget for living expenses for your family. It's a hard fact of life that most new businesses don't return enough in the first year or two to pay the owner a salary. You'd be on solid ground to figure living expenses enough to take care of your family's needs for at least a year and a half ahead. You'll want this money above and beyond that required for the business itself.

Objectives of This Chapter

This chapter is designed to give you enough background in financial planning so you'll be able to control the financial affairs of your company in a proactive management fashion. After becoming familiar with the material given in this chapter, you should be able to:

- Understand the advantages of formal planning for managing the flow of money in your company

- Project the long-term and short-term needs for financing—and develop the necessary plans for meeting these needs

- Collect the data you'll need to make reasonable assumptions upon which to base your financial planning

- Prepare the following specific financial plans for your business: balance sheets, sales forecasts, cash-flow analyses, income statements, and break-even analyses

- Understand and use ratio analyses to see how your business is performing

Planning Required

In general you'll find that your funding needs will fall into two categories: long-term and short-term. The long-term funds will be used for capital investment in setting up your business; the short-term funds will be used for taking care of cash deficiencies that occur from time to time in any business, and to cover seasonal bulges, as in businesses that must build a large inventory for the Christmas trade. If your business prospers and grows very rapidly, you'll develop a need for major outside investment in your company. Most businesses don't generate enough profit to furnish the capital to support significant expansion. You'll find a discussion of sources of funding in Chapter 10.

PLANNING FOR LONG-TERM FINANCING

Each business has unique requirements for capital investment. It isn't possible therefore to give detailed information on what items make up the list of purchases required to open the doors of a business. You'll find it necessary to draw on your own data for this purpose. With technical competence in your business, you'll know the items needed to turn out the product or render the service. You'll draw on your knowledge to compile a list of the equipment and fixtures necessary to open your business. By referring to the planning examples given in Appendix B, you'll pick up some hints about the kinds of items you may have to consider in figuring your capital budget.

PLANNING FOR SHORT-TERM FINANCING

Once you have a capital budget that covers your initial long-term investment in the business, you'll want to prepare your short-term operating plans. These are crucial in controlling your operating affairs day by day, month by month, and year by year. These plans, which are in essence budgets, include projections about sales, expenses, balance sheets, income statements, and break-even analyses. You'll also want to learn how to use financial ratios in your financial planning.

PERSIST IN YOUR PLANNING

The characteristics of the planning required for you to know what your financial needs will be just simply will not allow you to do it in one pass. You'll find that your projected results will vary when you change your assumptions. You'll want to develop a feeling that your planning is somewhere near what the actuality is likely to be. To accomplish this, you'll have to make several estimates: optimistic, pessimistic, and what you think reasonable.

Your first plans, even after you've made repeated trials, will still not be what will happen, unless you're very lucky. But that doesn't matter. What does matter is that you've now become a proficient planner; it's in your blood. You now see what a powerful tool it is for controlling your financial affairs—indeed, your whole business. And what you'll do after you open your business is to substitute the real figures for the estimates, month by month. Each month you'll run out your projections and plans for 1 and 2 years ahead, by the month. You'll have a rolling set of plans that will allow you to see very clearly what your financial requirements are likely to be, a long way ahead. Then you'll be able to prepare for those needs in adequate time to be assured of success in meeting them. And the feedback you'll get from the whole planning process will enable you to correct deviations from the course you want and to do more of whatever is producing success.

RECOMMENDED PLANNING FOR PROACTIVE MANAGEMENT

We recommend the following plans as key tools that will help you manage your financial requirements proactively:

- *Balance sheet.* Simply defined, a statement of the assets of a business (what the business owns) and the claims against them (what the business owes), including the claims of its owners; both are given for a specific date.

- *Forecasted monthly sales.* A projection of sales expected, month by month, for a given period—often 1 or 2 years ahead.

- *Cash-flow analysis.* A statement of what has happened or what is expected to happen (or a combination of both) to the cash position of the business, month by month.

- *Monthly income statement.* A statement that shows revenue less expense, and therefore the net profit for the month.

- *Yearly income statements.* A statement that collects the gross income for the year and subtracts the total of expenses for the year.

- *Break-even analysis.* In its simplest form, a chart or formula that gives the estimated sales volume per period at which the company neither makes nor loses money (breaks even).

The development of these tools is illustrated in exhibits in this chapter through planning from a real-life prospectus, Waterbeds East—A Retail Store. Other examples of planning for financial control will be found interspersed among those for Waterbeds East.

WATERBEDS EAST—A RETAIL STORE[1]

The Store Concept This proposal aims at the establishment of a retail store specializing in waterbeds and related furniture and accessories. The store is to be located in South Portland, Maine, in the Maine Mall, the major shopping center for the Portland area; this would enhance the credibility of the product and the company and ensure maximum exposure to shoppers.

The store will be well appointed to project a substantial image as a quality furniture store and will carry a wide selection of waterbeds—from the modest to the luxurious. It will display a variety of frame designs, arranged in a homelike setting, with accom-

---

[1]Prepared by Douglas Markley.

SECTION IV

294

Achieving
Proactive
Financial
Management

panying furniture. Bedspreads, sheets, and other accessory items will be stocked, as well as a line of contemporary "beanbag" and foam-filled chairs and lounges. Waterbeds with frames, ranging in price from $75 to $500, will be on hand for cash-and-carry sales. A more complete selection will be available to order.

The new Portland store will complement an existing retail outlet in Brunswick, Maine, 30 miles up the coast, and will use the same name: Waterbeds East. The Brunswick store includes a facility for manufacturing waterbed frames and accompanying furniture. It will supply these items to the Portland store.

The Brunswick store will oversee the operations of the Portland store and will coordinate and combine purchases and advertising. Significant economies of scale are envisioned, particularly in advertising and, to a lesser extent, in purchasing and production. With the opening of the Portland store, television advertising, which is expected to increase traffic and sales dramatically, should become feasible. More promotion and sales should result from present radio schedules, because the same stations serve both areas.

Indications from the small Brunswick store have been quite favorable. On the basis of sales in Brunswick, estimates show that the proposed new store should gross about $200,000 per year within 3 years. It should net approximately $35,000 per year on an initial investment of less than $10,000.

The Product Waterbeds are available in twin, full, queen, and king sizes; the king and queen sizes are by far the most popular. They come in a great variety of styles, from colonial to contemporary, with rich furniture-quality wood finishes or upholstered in fur or synthetic leather. Some have elaborate bookcase headboards or canopies. Matching high and low chests and night tables are usually available.

The Industry The waterbed is a product that has high consumer recognition but that so far has been severely undermarketed. This is especially true in Maine. Its introduction in the seventies was followed by sudden "fad" production and distribution of inferior products by inexperienced people drawing on inadequate knowledge and research. These shortcomings were compounded by insufficient knowledge on the part of the users, who often installed and used the beds improperly. The fad image and a great body of misconceptions about waterbeds have endured, especially in Maine and similar locations where no penetrating marketing of modern waterbed systems has taken place.

Today the industry has begun to coalesce. A trade magazine has been widely distributed for nearly 9 years. Manufacturing and retailing associations have begun to discuss common problems and to establish standards and goals. An industry advertising group now addresses that critical area. Retail outlets are benefiting from this activity. They are also becoming more sophisticated marketers as more well-qualified managers enter the industry.

The Owner The owner holds bachelor of science and bachelor of business administration degrees granted by the University of Wisconsin and an M.B.A. from UCLA. He spent 6 years in the Navy as an officer and a pilot of multiengine patrol aircraft. While stationed in Maine during his naval service, he conceived and opened the Brunswick waterbed store.

Market Analysis People are curious about waterbeds. Product recognition is generally high, but marketing experience in Maine has shown that potential buyers require extensive consumer education. This education should include a thorough description of the waterbed system, an explanation of its safety, and a clear demonstration of its construction.

The Portland location offers a superb opportunity for staking a claim to the under-developed waterbed market. The ambience of the Maine Mall is ideal for attracting browsers and for increasing the general level of familiarization with the product. The proposed location on the main concourse of the mall should attract a high volume of traffic. In short, a high-visibility, high-traffic location that prominently displays attractive modern waterbed systems, that employs a competent staff, and that advertises adequately will draw well and will cultivate a substantial market unhindered by significant competitive drain.

Brunswick experience has shown that a substantial low-end market exists, with sales averaging in the $200 to $300 range. This market will not necessarily predominate in Portland, because the more elaborate and complete store should encourage higher-priced sales. Nevertheless, considerable demand exists for less expensive bedding. And the least expensive waterbeds are of better quality and of significantly lower price than inexpensive conventional beds. The store will be prepared to handle both elaborate and modest systems, as well as individual components such as mattresses and heaters.

This broad-based approach is consistent with data from sales in Brunswick, which indicate that waterbed customers are difficult to categorize beyond their being predominantly in the 18 to 35 age group. No correlation could be established with respect to sex, race, marital status, employment, education, or income.

Selling Selling strategy is based on three interdependent aims: attracting customers to the store, projecting an image of professionalism and competence, and educating the customer about the product.

Every effort will be made to induce people to visit the store. Although the novelty of the waterbeds will draw many shoppers in for a quick look, the experience of the Brunswick store shows that radio advertising will draw customers from all over the southern part of the state, and even from out of state. Television advertising will also be used to increase store traffic.

Good salesmanship will be a major goal; it will focus on educating the customer to the advantages of the waterbed, to understand and accept the facts about the product. The sales technique will focus on a helpful and informative posture aimed at earning the confidence of the customer—an essential prerequisite to doing business successfully in Maine. Emphasis will be on the safety and comfort of flotation sleeping, and on the integrity of the company and its product. Experience shows that if browsers leave the store feeling goodwill and carrying literature about waterbeds, sales will follow.

Contrary to popular belief, waterbed customers are not easily categorized but, instead, are quite diverse, and no pat profile can be established. Consequently, it is not productive to direct advertising at a narrow segment of the market; this may alienate more potential customers than it attracts. In particular, a focus on the youth culture will be avoided, as this stereotype is considered counterproductive.

Advertising is recognized as an essential element in the development of the business. It will not present a financial problem to the new Portland store because there will be no additional cost at first. Present advertising for the Brunswick store will simply be amended to include Portland. Once sales volume is sufficient to permit television advertising (planned for the fourth month of operation), Portland will be able to assume its share of this expense.

SECTION IV

296

Achieving
Proactive
Financial
Management

Plan of Operation The owner will act as manager of the store. Initially, one sales-person will be hired; this person will be trained at the Brunswick store prior to the opening of the new location. Because of limited warehousing space and for simplicity in managing it, the Portland store will operate as a satellite of the Brunswick store. Brunswick will do all purchasing, warehousing, and manufacturing and will supply the Portland store as required. Accounts of the two stores will be kept separate, but goods will be transferred at cost. Portland will maintain only a minimum inventory, mostly in display stock, and will incur no advertising or administrative expense initially, simplifying management of the cash flow.

Experience at the Brunswick site has been quite favorable despite its small size and its relatively poor location. With the excellent mall location near the population center of Portland, with the goodwill already attached to the store name, it is expected that Portland sales should double those of the Brunswick store within 3 months of opening, and triple within a year. Because of the simplicity of the operation and the help of the Brunswick store, the Portland venture should show a profit from the first month of operation.

Planning for Waterbeds East, based on assumptions coming from this background, is incorporated throughout this chapter.

Your Planning Assumptions and Financial Plans

To start your financial planning for your new business, you'll have to make some assumptions. Some will be easy to make, as you'll have the information at hand. Others will take some crystal-ball gazing. But don't despair; in most situations there is a wealth of information to be had. The trick is to know where to look for it. We'll point you in the right direction—give you a number of sources that you can check to find the data upon which to base your planning.

YOUR INITIAL CAPITAL INVESTMENT

The first planning you'll want to do is to estimate how much money you'll need for permanent investment in your business. As we've said, each business is unique. Therefore, you'll have to list all the items you must have to produce the goods or service you intend to sell. For a sheet-metal shop, for instance, you might require shears, sheet-metal brakes, welding equipment, workbenches, and a variety of other equipment depending upon your particular specialty. You'd also want an assortment of hand tools. You'd need adequate space for shop and office and at least minimum office equipment: desks, file cabinets, typewriters, and miscellaneous items for long-time use. Lumping costs for equipment and permanent tooling together will allow you to prepare a capital budget figure. If you buy a building, the cost of the building and the cost of modification would be a major item in your capital budget.

If you were starting a retail store, perhaps a bookstore, the capital budget for fixed assets would be quite different. It would include such items as display cases, counters, shelves, and office equipment. Your largest single initial investment wouldn't

TABLE 11-1

CHAPTER 11

297

Managing
Your Financial
Requirements

Capital Required and Miscellaneous Data—Waterbeds East

Cost of fixtures	
Carpet—90 yards at $10 per yard	$ 900
Partitions and interior finishing	N/C
Sales counter	100
Cash register	300
Sign	600
Total cost of fixtures	$1900

(Straight-line depreciation over 36 months
52.78 per month × 6 months = 316.67)

Purchase of delivery van (used)	$4000

(Straight-line depreciation over 36 months
111.11 per month × 6 months = 666.67)

Initial inventory	
5 display beds at $200	$1000
Accompanying furniture	500
Bedspreads	400
Sheets	300
Beanbag chairs	300
Accessories	100
Mattresses	200
Heaters	200
Total initial inventory	$3000

Store rental fee
Dimensions—15 feet wide × 60 feet deep
900 square feet at $7.50 per square foot per year =
$6750 per year = $598.75 per month

be in capital items like these; it would be in a beginning inventory of books. This would be an operating expense and would take working capital as contrasted with fixed-asset capital.

Once you have the estimated figure for capital equipment, you should add to it a reasonable safety margin. This might be 10 percent in today's inflationary economy. If you plan to renovate or remodel a building for your purpose, we recommend a higher cushion to protect yourself against rises in the costs of building materials and construction labor.

The estimate of capital needed for the Portland store of Waterbeds East is given in Table 11-1.

YOUR DETAILED PLANNING ASSUMPTIONS AND PLANS

With the starting capital set for both fixed assets and operating expenses, you'll now want to establish the basic assumptions for your first try at financial planning. The following are customary items that appear in the assumptions, although your business may need an addition or two because of its special characteristics.

DATE OF STARTING BUSINESS

This date sets the schedule for all the rest of your plans. It can also mark the beginning of your fiscal year, which determines when you pay income taxes. You must, how-

SECTION IV

298

Achieving
Proactive
Financial
Management

ever, observe the legal requirements for setting your fiscal year. As a sole proprietor you must use the same tax year in which you report your personal income. In a partnership you must use the same tax year as the principal partners unless you get a special authorization. If you have a choice, you may want to choose a fiscal year that gives you the advantage of paying taxes when seasonal sales produce a large amount of cash.

BALANCE SHEET

The balance sheet is a statement that shows what your company owns, and what it owes. What it owns are termed assets. What it owes, which includes debts of various kinds plus the money invested that represents ownership, are called liabilities, or sometimes "liabilities and equity." (In a sense, the company "owes" the investors the money they put in to form the capital.) The balance sheet shows the financial condition of the company at a specific time. It's like a snapshot picturing the financial condition of the company at that moment. A balance sheet prepared for the opening day of business affords a base from which changes in the financial health of the company may be judged.

You'll want to prepare a balance sheet for the opening day of your business. You'll then want to check the health of your operations regularly to see how you're doing; you'll do this through monthly, quarterly, and yearly balance sheets. By comparing current figures against previous ones, you can see whether your business is losing or gaining in net worth.

One way of pinpointing how you're doing is to see how much increase or decrease in each asset and liability there has been in dollars and percentage from the figures in a previous balance sheet. The percent figure will give you another way to see clearly the trend of improvement or worsening of performance. You can use both dollars and percentages as feedback to show you where you're doing well and where you should put more effort to make improvement. The balance sheet also gives you some critical figures you need to do ratio analysis on your business. A ratio is a comparison of one item with another. These will give you additional feedback signals on the status of your business. You'll find a detailed explanation of ratio analysis later in this chapter.

Continuing with our examples of projections, **the opening day's balance sheet for Waterbeds East is shown in Table 11-2;** the opening date is July 1, 1987.

For the sake of illustration we have included here a balance sheet for the XYZ

TABLE 11-2

Balance Sheet—Waterbeds East—July 1, 1987

Assets		Liabilities and Equity	
Cash	$ 500	Bank loan	$6400
Inventory	3000	Proprietor's	
Fixtures	1900	capital	3000
Truck	4000	Total	$9400
Total	$9400		

TABLE 11-3

CHAPTER 11

299

Managing
Your Financial
Requirements

XYZ Boutique Children's and Infants' Wear—Balance Sheet—December 31, 19XX

Assets

Current Assets			
Cash on hand		$ 345.40	
Cash in bank		4,136.74	
Inventory, merchandise		26,179.20	
Accounts receivable		1,757.32	
			$32,418.66
Fixed Assets			
Prepaid expenses		$ 1,500.00	
Fixtures and furniture,			
original cost	$ 7,500.00		
Less reserve for			
depreciation	1,000.00		
		$ 6,500.00	
			8,000.00
Total Assets			$40,418.66

Liabilities

Current Liabilities			
Accounts payable		$ 3,275.36	
Note payable to bank		1,750.00	
Provision for income taxes			
		1,500.00	
Total liabilities			$ 6,525.36
Capital or Net Worth			
Capital, Jan. 1, 19XX		$28,010.72	
Profit after taxes, Jan. 1-		5,882.58	
Dec. 31, 19XX			
			33,893.30
Total Liabilities and Capital			$40,418.66

Boutique, which shows how current and fixed assets and liabilities may be displayed for improved clarity.

Let's look at the items that comprise the balance sheet for the XYZ Boutique, given in Table 11-3. The owner of this retail store has prepared a balance sheet for the close of business, December 31, 19XX.

Assets are listed as current assets and fixed assets. Current assets are those that are either in cash on hand, which includes currency, checks, bank drafts, and money orders, or items that would ordinarily be turned into cash through sales during the coming year. Inventory, merchandise, gives the worth at cost of the merchandise on hand at the time the balance sheet is prepared. Accounts receivable show how much credit customers owe the business.

Fixed assets are those items used in carrying on the business but not expected to be sold or used up during the year. These can include land, building, fixtures and furniture, delivery trucks, and machinery. In the case of the XYZ Boutique, the

SECTION IV

300

Achieving
Proactive
Financial
Management

owner leases the premises and pays rent. Prepaid expenses include items paid in advance, for example, rent and insurance. Since fixtures and equipment deteriorate with use, the balance sheet shows the original cost of these items minus depreciation, a deduction allowed by law.

Many other assets may be added from time to time, but they are of minor importance in most small businesses. Stocks of office supplies, prepaid interest on loans, and prepaid services might be among these.

Liabilities can also be divided into "current" and "fixed." Merchandise that has to be paid for during the coming year, bank loans, and promissory notes are included among current liabilities. A long-term loan such as that secured by a mortgage is classified as a fixed loan. The XYZ Boutique has no fixed liabilities at this time; therefore, none is shown. The items shown under current liabilities are quite self-explanatory. A point of interest is the setting aside of a reserve to pay income taxes in the coming year.

The capital or net worth statement simply adds the worth of the company from last year's balance sheet to the net profit after taxes for this year. This new sum tells the owner what the capital, or net worth, of the company is now, after this year's operation.

As your business moves along from month to month and year to year, your balance sheet will give you a wealth of information. It will tell you whether your business is growing in worth. It will show you if your business is stagnating or declining. It will tell you the soundness of your financial position.

Small businesspersons always face the danger of eating into their capital. If they take out funds to cover living expenses from time to time, they don't know whether they have earned that money. A comparison of capital figures in the balance sheets for a few years will show any tendency to dissipate the company's capital.

Finally, the sum of assets will show you what progress you've been making. This figure represents the total amount of resources under your control. Even though such resources are partly offset by liabilities, they give a good measure of your economic strength.

You'll be required by law to pay quarterly your estimated income taxes for the current year. It's wise to build a running reserve for this purpose. Putting aside earnings to meet these quarterly payments makes good management sense.

SALES FORECAST

A critical item in your financial planning is the sales forecast. The ability of your business to generate sales in sufficient volume at the proper price level determines whether your business can survive and grow. Because all other financial variables in your business depend upon sales, you must exert great care to do as good a job as you can of forecasting them.

You may say, "But I've never been in this business before. How can I possibly guess how my sales are going to come in?" The answer is *you must*. You must do the very best guessing you can, because all other plans hinge on sales. And don't despair. Many sources of information are open to you, and most cost nothing or very little. We'll identify some of them here.

You'll find it wise to forecast sales by the month for 2 years and possibly 3 years ahead. It's a good idea to try three approaches: optimistic, high estimate;

pessimistic, low estimate; and realistic, somewhere in the middle, your best estimate of what may actually happen in sales. You'll recall that we stated early the importance of knowing something about the specific business before starting your own and that if you had no experience you'd better work for a company in that business for a year or two before starting your own. With this background you'd have some feeling for

FIG. 11-1

Pattern of monthly retail sales.

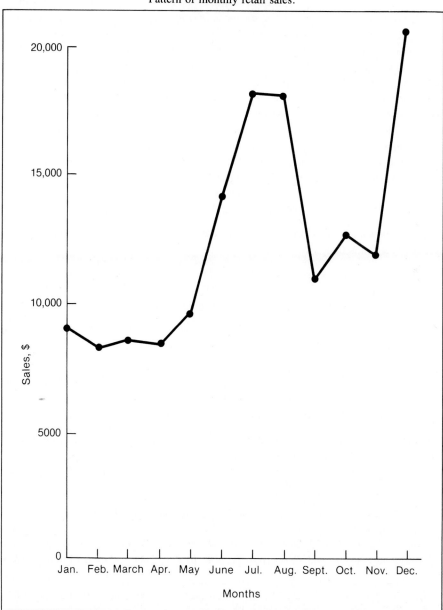

SECTION IV

302

Achieving
Proactive
Financial
Management

such things as the seasonality of the business and the daily, weekly, monthly, and quarterly pattern of sales.

Understanding the cyclical characteristics of sales volume can be critical to running a business successfully—and most businesses do have ups and downs as a function of time. For example, you can see from the graph of Figure 11-1 that the bookstore represented experiences two major peaks of sales during the year. The first, in July and August, comes with the influx of summer vacationers. The second, in December, results from the buildup of Christmas trade. From this information the owner knows when to start building inventory for the two peak business periods.

If your own knowledge of the business of your choice is not sufficient to allow you to define its cyclical characteristics, you can get pertinent information from the appropriate trade association or other sources given in this chapter.

In addition to this kind of data, with experience you'd know something about costs and profitability of the business. And knowing about how many dollars annually you'd like to take out of the business, you could work backward and see how many dollars in sales you'd need to produce that income.

We gave some sources of information for segmenting and understanding your market in Chapter 5. You'll find these sources also useful in gathering data for financial planning. Therefore, we'll list them briefly here and add to them some other sources in which you can find basic financial information.

- Data from your own experience in the business.

- Daily newspapers. Although not a prime source of financial information, you may get leads that will help you gain such data.

- The Small Business Administration (SBA). You should check with the closest office of the SBA to see what pertinent publications are to be had and what other help they can give you in gathering the financial information you're after.

- Banks. Your banker can probably put you in touch with successful entrepreneurs in businesses similar to yours; you can talk with them about financial and other matters.

- The Bank of America's *Small Business Reporter,* which is an excellent publication that gives financial information on specific businesses. You should check their list for titles to see if there are any you can use.[2]

- Chambers of commerce or business development departments in your community. It would be good practice for you to see what help these organizations can give you.

- Universities and colleges. The professors of management or finance in schools of business can sometimes be helpful in your quest for information. They often seek live projects for their students. The best way to get help here is to make sure you know exactly what you want to ask, identify the professor, phone and make an appointment. You may be able to get a team of two or three bright

---

[2]The *Small Business Reporter* is available from Small Business Reporter, Bank of America NT&SA, Dept. 3120, P.O. Box 37,000, San Francisco, CA 94120.

students to compile the information you need and to help you with your financial planning.

■ Trade associations. The association in your industry can furnish all kinds of important financial data that you'll find basic to your needs. Don't overlook this very important source.[3] You'll be able to get figures for companies of different size on such matters as sales, expenses, capital requirements, profit percentages, and many other basic inputs you'll need for your financial planning.

■ Other similar businesses. As we've said, successful owners who have built their business from scratch can give you a wealth of information of all kinds. Take advantage of their hard-earned store of financial wisdom. Draw on it as well as on their marketing and other knowledge.

■ Financial data from Dun and Bradstreet reports.[4] This organization publishes several kinds of reports that give useful information. One report that you may find helpful is *Key Business Ratios*. This gives figures in each of several business ratios, ranging from current assets to current debts, to funded debts to net working capital. Three figures are given in each case: the median, the upper, and the lower quartiles. The ratios represent the experience of many companies in a given business and cover what may be considered good, average, and not-so-good performance. The companies surveyed tend to be rather large "small" companies, usually over $100,000 in net worth. Nevertheless, the ratios will give you some feeling for good management practice. The businesses reported upon include retailing, wholesaling, manufacturing, and construction.

■ If you're planning to enter a retail business, you'll find The National Cash Register Company publication, *Expenses in Retail Business,* particularly useful.[5] This booklet gives operating percentages that will help you set the level of sales for your forecasting. It contains much other valuable information about expenses in retail business. The booklet can serve as a guide not only for sales forecasting but also for many other aspects of financial planning. Retail businesses covered range from appliance dealers to women's apparel and specialty stores.

■ Don't overlook libraries! A recent report published by a Louisiana university says that only 3 percent of a large number of small businesspersons interviewed ever set foot in a library. Yet the public library and business school libraries are great reservoirs of information. Many libraries, particularly in metropolitan areas, have research librarians who would be pleased to help you dig out specific data. In the library you can find all kinds of reference books on business and the

---

[3]You can find out about the trade association in your business in *National Trade & Professional Associations of the United States and Canada,* Columbia Books, Inc., Publishers, Room 601, 734 15th St. N.W., Washington, DC 20005. This directory is published in an updated version every January.

Another source of information about trade associations is the *Encyclopedia of Associations,* a three-volume set, published by the Gale Research Company, Detroit, MI; vol. 1, National Organizations of the United States; vol. 2, Geographic and Executive Index; vol. 3, New Associations and Projects. Volume 2, arranged geographically, includes association names, addresses, phone numbers, and executives' names.

[4]A list of Dun & Bradstreet publications may be obtained from the Business Economics Department, Dun & Bradstreet, Inc., 99 Church Street, New York, NY 10017.

[5]This publication may be obtained from the Marketing Services Department, The National Cash Register Company, Dayton, OH 45409.

SECTION IV

304

Achieving
Proactive
Financial
Management

financial reports of many small publicly held corporations. These can furnish you with operating ratios, data about sales, and much other important information.

The foregoing are some, but by no means all, of the sources of basic information available to you. Most of them are free; some can be had for a small fee. By pursuing these sources and the references given in most of them, you can track down what you'll need to know to do your sales forecasting and other kinds of financial planning. And you can do this yourself. Indeed, that's the best way, for then you'll become an expert in your own business.

The forecasted monthly sales for Waterbeds East are shown in Table 11-4.

CASH FLOW ANALYSIS

Cash moves in and out of your business as your customers pay their bills and as you pay for goods, services, and labor. You'll be vitally concerned with what is called cash flow. Although cash flow is sometimes defined in somewhat different ways by accountants, here we define cash flow as the difference between what you take in and what you spend. It's usually figured by the month. If your business pays out more than it takes in, you'll find yourself short of cash.

If, however, you know several weeks or months ahead that you're going to need money to avert a cash crisis, you can take the steps to have the money on hand when you need it. You know, if you suddenly find on a Friday afternoon that you'll need $10,000 next week to keep your business going—pay your labor and cover some critical bills—your chances of raising the money on time are pretty slim. If you knew that you'd need $10,000 of working money 2 or 3 months ahead of time, ordinarily you'd be able to arrange for a loan without too much trouble. The tool you'll use to anticipate your cash needs is cash flow analysis. This is one of the most important management techniques you can learn.

Cash flow analysis not only tells you about shortages of funds that are likely to develop, but it also tells you when you are likely to have surpluses of cash. Knowing this, you can plan for ways to invest the surplus in improving your business.

TABLE 11-4

Forecasted Monthly Sales—Waterbeds East

	1987	1988	1989
Jan		$ 8,000	$ 10,000
Feb		10,000	12,000
Mar		15,000	18,000
Apr		12,000	15,000
May		15,000	18,000
Jun		14,000	16,000
Jul	$ 5,000	14,000	16,000
Aug	6,000	15,000	18,000
Sep	10,000	18,000	20,000
Oct	12,000	15,000	18,000
Nov	12,000	15,000	18,000
Dec	12,000	15,000	18,000
Total	$57,000	$166,000	$197,000

Your cash flow analysis is a proactive management plan that forecasts the amount of dollars you'll have on hand at the end of each month. You'll develop your cash flow by projecting your income each month and subtracting from it what you must spend to keep your business going. The first cash flow chart you make will necessarily be based upon many figures that will be estimates. Some, like your rent, you'll know exactly. Others, like sales for each month ahead, will be estimates or forecasts. You'll do the best you can in making these forecasts, relying on the sources of information we've outlined previously and those you will add yourself. Next to the estimated figures for each month you'll leave a blank column for the actual numbers. After you start your business, you'll replace the estimated numbers with actual numbers from the month's records. And you'll rework your projections for cash flow (and the other financial projections we cover in this chapter) for a full 2 years ahead by the month and the third year ahead by the quarter. In this way you'll gain a sharp insight into the financial requirements of your business. You'll know if you'll require cash and how much, month by month. You'll be able to anticipate your needs for loans well ahead of time, and you'll be in a favorable position to get the money to meet your needs.

Cash flow analysis is simply a statement of income from which expenditures are subtracted for each month. In Table 11-4, the owner of Waterbeds East, having had experience with sales trends during the year from records at the Brunswick store, made educated guesses about what was likely to happen to sales in the new Portland store.

If it is necessary to project monthly sales without the help of experience, you must turn to one or more of the sources of information given in this chapter. Many avenues for getting data are available to you—and new ones will open up as you involve yourself in the search. As instances of different approaches, consider the following:

In the mail-order business, it is possible to buy tested lists of potential customers from successful mail-order houses such as Brookstone of Peterborough, New Hampshire, or specialty magazines such as the *Country Journal* of Vermont. If you enter the mail-order business, you can expect a return of roughly 1 percent of your total mailing, provided you mail a sufficient number of flyers. An accepted standard in the business is 25,000 mailers per minimum mailing in order to get a 1 percent or larger return. You could therefore guess at the buildup of sales by planning one mailing per quarter and being conservative in setting sales for the first year. Perhaps you'd start with $1/2$ percent return from the first mailing, increasing gradually to 1 percent at the end of the fourth mailing. Each quarter you would readjust your estimates for the following four periods on the basis of the actual returns you experienced.

In the retail-bookstore business, it is customary for the average store to do one-half to two-thirds of the year's business during the months of November and December. You can get a great amount of useful information that would allow you to make an intelligent guess of sales during the year from the American Booksellers Association. This organization publishes basic data from bookstores around the country on a continuing schedule. From this information alone you'd

SECTION IV

306

Achieving
Proactive
Financial
Management

find it possible to project your first year's sales by the month. Again, you'd substitute actual sales figures at the end of each month and redo your projections for a year or more ahead.

Another way to estimate the first year's sales is by commonsense judgment. For example, suppose you wanted to sell a new article through drugstores. You plan to do this through salespeople who will call directly on the store owners. You can afford to hire three salespersons. How much business can you expect them to do? Questions you should ask yourself might be the following:

How many calls can the average salesperson make in a day? Perhaps eight on the average.

How many calls per week? Five times 8 equals 40 calls.

How often can a call produce a sale? Perhaps 10 percent of the time, therefore, four successes per week per salesperson. Or twelve sales per week for three salespersons.

How many sales for the year? Fifty times 12, or 600 sales for the year.

How to translate this into the first year's forecast? Assume a slow start with one salesperson; then add one more and another at 2-month intervals. Estimate the total dollars per sale and extend the figures out over the months.

Then, of course, you'd follow the recommended procedure of modifying your projections at the end of each month on the basis of the actual sales made during that month. Gradually your projections would improve in accuracy. After a few months, you'd have your sales projections well in hand.

To take a final example, in a technical manufacturing operation, where you would have a sales force in various regions of the country, your procedure might be quite different. Here you might bring in your sales representatives from all over the country for an annual meeting. You'd get from each person an estimate of sales for each quarter of the coming year. You would then apply percentage correction factors, depending upon your knowledge of the optimism or pessimism of each representative. Putting the whole together, you'd arrive at a reasonably sound estimate of upcoming business. Again, you'd modify the projections periodically on the basis of actual sales figures.

With the forecasted monthly sales made, the cash flow analysis can now be prepared. **The cash flow analysis for Waterbeds East for the first 6 months of business will be found in Table 11-5.**

The first group of items from 1 to 6 shows the money spent in purchases:

Line 1 repeats the projected sales from July through December; these figures come from the projected sales of Table 11-4.

The cost of goods sold is 50 percent of the retail price. Line 2 therefore shows figures at 50 percent of line 1.

Line 3 indicates that the proprietor desires an ending inventory for the month of $3500. But because $2500 has moved out of inventory through sales, the total goods available during the month is the sum of lines 2 and 3, $6000, which is shown on line 4.

TABLE 11-5

CHAPTER 11

307

Cash Flow Analysis for 1987—Waterbeds East

	Jul	Aug	Sep	Oct	Nov	Dec
1. Sales (cash)	$5,000	$6,000	$10,000	$12,000	$12,000	$12,000
2. Cost of sales	2,500	3,000	5,000	6,000	6,000	6,000
3. Ending inventory	3,500	3,500	3,500	4,000	4,000	4,000
4. Goods available	6,000	6,500	8,500	10,000	10,000	10,000
5. Beginning inventory	3,000	3,500	3,500	3,500	4,000	4,000
6. Purchases	3,000	3,000	5,000	6,500	6,000	6,000
7. Salary—proprietor	0	0	0	1,000	1,000	1,000
8. Salary—salespersons	500	600	1,000	1,200	1,200	1,200
9. Rent	600	600	600	600	600	600
10. Advertising	0	0	0	500	500	500
11. Supplies	100	20	20	30	30	30
12. Telephone	35	20	20	25	25	25
13. Utilities	25	25	25	25	25	25
14. Insurance	60	60	60	60	60	60
15. Truck operation	80	80	80	100	100	100
16. Taxes and misc.	100	100	100	100	100	100
17. Expenses	1,500	1,505	1,905	3,640	3,640	3,640
18. Beginning cash	500	936	1,367	3,408	3,724	4,055
19. Cash receipts	5,000	6,000	10,000	12,000	12,000	12,000
20. Cash available	5,500	7,036	11,567	15,708	16,124	16,555
21. Purchases	3,000	3,000	5,000	6,500	6,000	6,000
22. Expenses	1,500	1,505	1,905	3,640	3,640	3,640
23. Interest	64	64	54	44	29	9
24. Loan amortization	0	1,000	1,000	1,500	2,000	900
25. Loan balance	6,400	5,400	4,400	2,900	900	0
26 Cash balance	936	1,367	3,408	3,724	4,055	5,506

Notes:
1. All sales are cash (or credit card).
2. Purchases will all be from the Brunswick store. Normally there will be an immediate cash exchange, but, of course, this will be as flexible as necessary.
3. Cash-on-hand figures are higher than required to show the comfortable margin allowed.
4. Loan will be arranged as balance due in 6 months. Schedule allows for probable prepayment.

The beginning inventory for the opening month was $3000, which comes from the balance sheet of Table 11-2. Therefore, to start the next month at the desired inventory level of $3500 requires purchases of $3000, the difference between lines 4 and 5. (Note that the owner here has great flexibility in being able to buy inventory at will from the Brunswick store, with almost instant delivery. In most businesses, with appreciable lead times for delivery of inventory, some kind of operating rule must govern purchases for inventory to ensure that the firm doesn't run out of stock.)

Line 6 shows the cost of purchases for inventory from Brunswick at cost.

The next group of figures, from line 7 through line 16, shows the expenses of doing business. These are self-explanatory. Note that the owner plans to draw no salary for the first 3 months. The total of expenses is shown on line 17.

SECTION IV

308

Achieving
Proactive
Financial
Management

The third group of figures sums up the cash position of the firm at the end of the month:

- Line 18 gives the amount of cash available at the opening of business. This figure comes from the opening balance sheet of Table 11-2.

- Line 19 indicates the cash taken from sales during the month.

- Line 20 gives the sum of the figures of lines 18 and 19, which is the cash available to the business at the end of the month.

- Lines 21, 22, and 23 show the purchases and expenses for the month, plus the interest paid on the original bank loan of $6400, which comes from the opening balance sheet of Table 11-2.

- Line 24 gives the amount of money repaid to the bank to reduce the principal of the loan—0 in July but $1000 in August, building up toward the end of the 6-month period.

- Line 25 shows the remaining balance of principal on the bank loan, which is paid off by December.

- Line 26 displays the amount of cash left at the end of the month, and therefore the funds available with which to start the next month.

The notes at the bottom of Table 11-5 are worth inspection, for they spell out the assumptions that underlie the derivation of critical figures in the cash flow analysis. All sales are for cash; therefore, no credit payments are shown on the cash income projections. The flexibility in handling inventory replenishment is shown in the second note, which spells out the relationship with the Brunswick operation. The proprietor has arbitrarily increased the cash available, line 20, by adding a safety margin of $100 in August and increasing this margin by $100 each succeeding month. This money will come out of personal funds and presumably will be withdrawn by the owner as conditions permit. The last item assumes that the business will prosper according to the plans given and will be able to repay the bank loan within the first 6-month period.

We recommend that you set up your cash flow analysis in a table as shown in Figure 11-2. Here, for the sake of illustration we've adopted a well-accepted tabular form in which actual monthly results are entered in columns alongside forecasted figures. The forecasted results for February are modified to reflect judgment based on the actual results for January. In the same way, actuals for February are used to modify the projections for March. In each case the numbers should be projected for a year or more ahead, and should be adjusted each month for that period on the basis of actual experience.

MONTHLY INCOME STATEMENT

You'll want to know month by month how much you are making or how much you've gone in the hole. To do this, you'll prepare an income statement each month. This statement is made by subtracting the cost of goods sold and the operating, selling, and administrative expenses for the month from the gross sales made during

FIG. 11-2

CHAPTER 11

309

Managing
Your Financial
Requirements

Cash-Flow Analysis for 3 Months Ending March 31

	January		February		March	
	Forecast	Actual	Forecast	Actual	Forecast	Actual
Forecasted receipts						
Cash sales	8,000	7,812	10,000	11,600	15,000	16,210
Credit sales	—	—	—	—	—	—
(1) Total cash in	8,000	7,812	10,000	11,600	15,000	16,210
Forecasted cash payments						
Cost of goods sold	4,000	3,906	5,000	5,800	7,500	8,105
Purchases of goods needed	4,500	4,500	5,500	6,000	7,000	8,000
Salaries proprietor	1,500	1,500	1,500	1,500	1,500	1,500
Salaries, other	800	800	1,000	1,200	1,500	1,400
Payroll and other taxes	300	270	300	350	400	377
Rent	700	700	700	700	700	700
Utilities	30	36	42	48	45	47
Telephone	30	42	47	56	65	72
Supplies	`30	21	39	23	25	38
Advertising	700	650	700	700	700	700
Bank borrowing	0	0	0	0	0	0
Interest	0	0	0	0	0	0
Repayment of loan	0	0	0	0	0	0
Insurance	60	60	60	60	60	60
Truck operation	80	91	120	111	135	155
Miscellaneous						
(2) Total paid out	8,730	8,670	10,008	10,748	12,130	13,049
(3) Net cash increase (or decrease): Difference between (1) and (2)	(730)	(858)	(8)	852	2,870	3,161
Beginning cash on hand	5,506*	5,506	4,648	4,648	5,500	5,500
Add (or subtract) item 3	(730)	(858)	(8)	852	2,870	3,161
= cash on hand at end of month	4,476	4,648	4,640	5,500	8,370	8,661

*From last year-end balance sheet.

the month. This procedure follows the general statement that revenue less expense equals net income.

A useful management tool for guiding planning can be made by comparing income statements for current against previous years, month by month. You can do this best by placing your data in parallel columns as shown in Figure 11-3.

SECTION IV

310

Achieving
Proactive
Financial
Management

FIG. 11-3

Yearly Income Statements Compared

	Jan 1988	Jan 1987	Increase or (Decrease) $; %	Percent of Total 1988	Percent of Total 1987
Sales	15,600	13,700	1,900; 13.9	100.0	100.0
Less cost of sales	8,736	8,080	656; 8.1	56.0	59.0
Gross margin	6,864	5,620	1,244; 22.1	44.0	41.0
Less operating expenses:					
Cash payments*	2,262	2,130	132; 6.2	14.5	15.5
Administrative	1,200	1,000	200; 20.0	7.7	7.3
Interest	270	—	—	1.7	—
Depreciation	75	75	0	.5	.6
•					
•					
•					
•					
•					
•					
Miscellaneous	90	110		.6	.8
Total expenses	3,897	3,315	582; 17.6	25.0	24.2
Before-tax profit	2,967	2,305	662; 28.7	19.0	16.8

*For labor, materials, supplies, and services.

The increases or decreases in percentages of the various items will give you clues about trends in sales, costs, and expenses. You'll then be able to adjust your planning to improve the efficiency of your operations; you'll know exactly where to concentrate your efforts.

YEARLY INCOME STATEMENT

The yearly income statement collects the gross income for the year and subtracts from it the cost of sales, the total of expenditures in the various categories, and the incidental taxes paid.

The income statements for Waterbeds East for the first 6 months of operation are shown in Table 11-6. Here from the gross profit margin are subtracted the operating expense, interest paid the bank, and depreciation of truck and fixtures for each month, month by month. The net profit before taxes shows at the bottom of each month's column. The owner therefore has a running picture of net profit (or loss) by the month.

The resulting net profit (or loss) is combined with the proprietor's capital at the start of the year to show increase (or decrease) in the value of ownership at the end of the year. The yearly income statement for Waterbeds East (1987) is shown in Table 11-7.

TABLE 11-6

Income Statements for 1987—Waterbeds East

	Jul	Aug	Sep	Oct	Nov	Dec	Total
Sales	$5,000	$6,000	$10,000	$12,000	$12,000	$12,000	$57,000
Cost of sales	2,500	3,000	5,000	6,000	6,000	6,000	28,500
Gross margin	2,500	3,000	5,000	6,000	6,000	6,000	28,500
Operating expense	1,500	1,505	1,905	3,640	3,640	3,640	15,830
Interest expense	64	64	54	44	29	9	264
Depreciation (truck and fixtures)	164	164	164	164	164	164	984
Total deduction	1,728	1,733	2,123	3,848	3,833	3,813	17,078
Net profit	772	1,267	2,877	2,152	2,167	2,187	11,422

TABLE 11-7

Yearly Income Statement, 1987—Waterbeds East

Sales		$57,000
Cost of sales		28,500
		28,500
Salaries	$ 8,700	
Rent	3,600	
Advertising	1,500	
Supplies	230	
Telephone	150	
Utilities	150	
Insurance	360	
Interest expense	264	
Truck operation	540	
Taxes and miscellaneous	600	
Depreciation	984	
Total expenses	$17,078	17,078
Net profit		11,422
Proprietor's capital, beginning		3,000
Net profit 1987		11,422
Proprietor's capital, ending		$14,422

TABLE 11-8

Balance Sheet, Waterbeds East—December 31, 1987

Assets			Liabilities and Equity	
Cash		$ 5,506	Proprietor's capital	$ 3,000
Inventory		4,000	Add net profit	
Fixtures	$1,900		1988	11,422
Depreciation	317	1,583	Total	$14,422
Truck	4,000			
Depreciation	667	3,333		
Total		$14,422		

SECTION IV

312

Achieving
Proactive
Financial
Management

TABLE 11-9

Cash Flow Analysis for 1988—Waterbeds East

	Jan	Feb	Mar	Apr	May
1. Sales (cash)	$ 8,000	$10,000	$15,000	$12,000	$15,000
2. Cost of sales	4,000	5,000	7,500	6,000	7,500
3. Ending inventory	4,500	5,000	4,500	6,500	6,500
4. Goods available	8,500	10,000	12,000	12,500	14,000
5. Beginning inventory	4,000	4,500	5,000	4,500	6,500
6. Purchases	4,500	5,500	7,000	8,000	7,500
7. Salary—proprietor	1,500	1,500	1,500	1,500	1,500
8. Salary—salespersons	800	1,000	1,500	1,200	1,500
9. Rent	700	700	700	700	700
10. Advertising	700	700	700	700	700
11. Supplies	30	30	30	30	30
12. Telephone	30	30	30	30	30
13. Utilities	30	30	30	30	30
14. Insurance	60	60	60	60	60
15. Truck operation	80	100	150	120	150
16. Taxes and miscellaneous	300	300	300	300	300
17. Expenses	4,230	4,450	5,000	4,670	5,000
18. Beginning cash	5,506	4,776	4,826	7,826	7,156
19. Cash receipts	8,000	10,000	15,000	12,000	15,000
20. Cash available	13,506	14,776	19,826	19,826	22,156
21. Purchases	4,500	5,500	7,000	8,000	7,500
22. Expenses	4,230	4,450	5,000	4,670	5,000
23. Interest	0	0	0	0	0
24. Loan amortization	0	0	0	0	0
25. Loan balance	0	0	0	0	0
26. Cash balance	4,776	4,826	7,826	7,156	9,656

When you prepare a yearly income statement, you'll have a greatly condensed financial summary of the complex of activities and events that have taken place in your business, just as you've been able to do with month-by-month income statements. By comparing percentages of the different items, you can see trends that will allow you to take proactive management steps for improvement. Figure 11-3 shows how this can be done.

TABLE 11-10

Income Statements for 1988—Waterbeds East

	Jan	Feb	Mar	Apr	May	Jun
Sales	$8,000	$10,000	$15,000	$12,000	$15,000	$14,000
Cost of sales	4,000	5,000	7,500	6,000	7,500	7,000
Gross margin	4,000	5,000	7,500	6,000	7,500	7,000
Operating expenses	4,230	4,450	5,000	4,670	5,000	4,890
Depreciation (truck and fixtures)	164	164	164	164	164	164
Total deductions	4,394	4,614	5,164	4,834	5,164	5,054
Net profit	(394)	386	2,336	1,166	2,336	1,946

TABLE 11-9

(Continued)

Jun	Jul	Aug	Sep	Oct	Nov	Dec
$14,000	$14,000	$15,000	$18,000	$15,000	$15,000	$15,000
7,000	7,000	7,500	9,000	7,500	7,500	7,500
6,500	6,500	7,000	7,500	7,500	7,500	6,500
13,500	13,500	14,500	16,500	15,000	15,000	14,000
6,500	6,500	6,500	7,000	7,500	7,500	7,500
7,000	7,000	8,000	9,500	7,500	7,500	6,500
1,500	1,500	1,500	1,500	1,500	1,500	1,500
1,400	1,400	1,500	1,800	1,500	1,500	1,500
700	700	700	700	700	700	700
700	700	700	700	700	700	700
30	35	35	35	35	35	35
30	35	35	35	35	35	35
30	30	30	30	30	30	30
60	60	60	60	60	60	60
140	140	150	150	150	150	150
300	300	300	300	300	300	300
4,890	4,900	5,010	5,310	5,010	5,010	5,010
9,656	11,766	13,866	15,856	19,046	21,536	24,026
14,000	14,000	15,000	18,000	15,000	15,000	15,000
23,656	25,766	28,866	33,856	34,046	36,536	39,026
7,000	7,000	8,000	9,500	7,500	7,500	6,500
4,890	4,900	5,010	5,310	5,010	5,010	5,010
0	0	0	0	0	0	0
0	0	0	0	0	0	0
0	0	0	0	0	0	0
11,766	13,866	15,856	19,046	21,536	24,026	27,516

The remaining exhibits for Waterbeds East carry out these projections through 1988: Table 11-8 (page 311), the balance sheet for the end of business 1987, which shows a substantial increase in ownership value; Table 11-9, cash flow analysis for 1988; Table 11-10, monthly income statements for 1988; Table 11-11, yearly income statement for 1988; and Table 11-12, balance sheet for the close of business at the end of 1988.

TABLE 11-10

(Continued)

Jul	Aug	Sep	Oct	Nov	Dec	Total
$14,000	$15,000	$18,000	$15,000	$15,000	$15,000	$166,000
7,000	7,500	9,000	7,500	7,500	7,500	83,000
7,000	7,500	9,000	7,500	7,500	7,500	83,000
4,900	5,010	5,310	5,010	5,010	5,010	58,490
164	164	164	164	164	164	1,968
5,064	5,174	5,474	5,174	5,174	5,174	60,458
1,936	2,326	3,526	2,326	2,326	2,326	22,542

SECTION IV

314

Achieving
Proactive
Financial
Management

TABLE 11-11

Yearly Income Statement, 1988—Waterbeds East

Sales		$166,000
Cost of sales		83,000
Gross margin		83,000
Salaries	$34,600	
Rent	8,400	
Advertising	8,400	
Supplies	390	
Telephone	390	
Utilities	360	
Insurance	720	
Truck operation	1,630	
Taxes and miscellaneous	3,600	
Depreciation	1,968	
Total expenses	$60,458	60,458
Net profit		22,542
Proprietor's capital 1987, beginning		3,000
Net profit 1987		11,422
Net profit 1988		22,542
Proprietor's capital, ending		$36,964

TABLE 11-12

Balance Sheet, Waterbeds East—December 31, 1988

Assets			Liabilities and Equity	
Cash		$27,516		
Inventory		6,500	Proprietor's capital	$36,964
Fixtures and truck	5,900			
Depreciation	2,952 =	2,948		
Total		$36,964		

BREAK-EVEN ANALYSIS

All firms experience both direct and variable costs in doing business. Break-even analysis affords a method of finding out how much business a firm must do just to come out even during a given period. The method is straightforward in a routine manufacturing operation, which we'll use in our example; we can assume that the following table shows typical fixed and variable costs.

Fixed and Variable Costs

Fixed Costs	Variable Costs
Rent	Production labor
Executive salaries	Materials
Engineering salaries	Sales commissions
Office staff salaries	
General office expense	

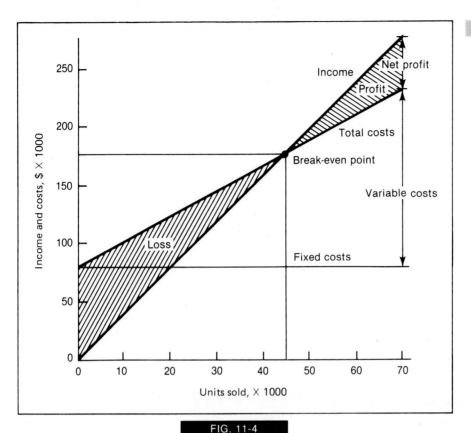

250

200

Income and costs, $ × 1000

150

100

50

0

FIG. 11-4

Break-even chart.

From these items a break-even chart can be developed in its simplest form as shown in Figure 11-4. Draw an *X-Y* graph, labeling the vertical axis with a dollar scale and the horizontal axis with a units scale, as shown. Project a line from the *X-Y* axis at 45 degrees to the horizontal. Draw a horizontal line at the sum of the fixed costs parallel to the *X* axis. Find the dollars of cost for any known reasonable quantity of units sold. Plot the point for that quantity on the chart and draw a line from the intersection of the fixed-cost line and the *Y* axis through that point. The point where the total-costs line passes through the 45-degree line establishes the break-even point.

The break-even point may be found arithmetically if desired, as follows:

Given:

P = sales price per unit

Q = quantity produced and sold

F = fixed costs

V = variable costs per unit

SECTION IV

316

Achieving
Proactive
Financial
Management

It follows that:

$$P \times Q = F + V \times Q$$
$$P \times Q - V \times Q = F$$
$$Q = \frac{F}{P - V} \text{ at break-even } Q$$

To answer the question: How many units (Q) must be sold at $4 with labor and material at a variable cost of $2.20 per unit and a total fixed cost for the period of $80,000?

$$Q = \frac{80,000}{4.00 - 2.20}$$
$$= 44,444 \text{ units}$$

Break-even point based on dollar sales:

$$\text{Break-even point} = \frac{\text{total fixed costs}}{1 - \text{total variable costs/total sales volume}}$$
$$= \frac{FC}{1 - VC/S}$$

Using the values in the previous example, find the sales volume at the break-even point at any sales level, say 27,500 units sold:

$$FC = \$80,000$$
$$VC = 27,500 \times \$2.20 = \$60,500$$
$$S = 27,500 \times \$4.00 = \$110,000$$
$$BE = \text{break-even point}$$
$$BE = \frac{FC}{1 - VC/S}$$
$$= \frac{80,000}{1 - 65,000/110,000}$$
$$= \frac{80,000}{0.45}$$
$$= 177,777, \text{ or } \$178,000 \text{ (rounded)}$$

You should know what sales volume you'll need in a given period of time to break even, the point at which there's no profit and no loss. As we've pointed out, a straightforward way to find out is through the construction of a break-even chart. This chart will show you graphically how many dollars in sales you must have during the period to break even.

The break-even chart shown in Figure 11-5 was prepared from data furnished

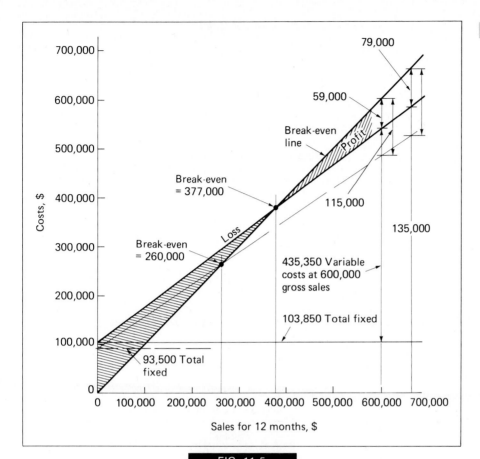

FIG. 11-5

Break-even chart—one year—for Any Company Insulation Contractors.

by an actual company, known here as Any Company Insulation Contractors. We'll see how this elementary chart can importantly serve management purposes. Production, sales, and administrative expenses, plus material, direct labor, and direct job costs are totaled for 12 months. These are divided into variable (V) and fixed (F) costs, and are all the expenses for company operation at a gross income of $600,000, as shown on the income statement (profit and loss statement). These data shown in Table 11-13, following the procedure of the foregoing example, resulted in the break-even chart presented in Figure 11-5.

The break-even point occurs at $377,000 for the year. The total fixed costs at this point are $103,850, and the variable costs are $273,150. A critical management question arises: What would happen to gross business and profit if the company could lower its fixed costs by 10 percent without affecting its variable rate? Fixed costs would then drop to $93,500 and the break-even point would fall to $260,000; this would increase profit to $115,000, almost doubling it. And if sales could simultaneously be moved up to $700,000 for the year, profit would increase to $135,000. In this fashion the break-even chart offers guidance to management. It could alert

SECTION IV

318

Achieving
Proactive
Financial
Management

TABLE 11-13

Break-Even Analysis,
Any Company Insulation Contractors

Assumptions:
- Business gross: $600,000 for the year
- Sales breakdown: 35% new construction batt insulation,
  65% blown-in insulation for existing residences

Income (Profit and Loss) Statement

Sales for 12 months			$600,000	
Material used	$294,000	49%		
Direct labor (1)	90,000	15%		
Direct job costs (2)	18,000	3%		
Total cost of sales			$402,000	67%
Gross profit			198,000	33%
Expenses			139,200	23.2%
Net before taxes			$58,800	9.8%

Notes:
1. Includes direct labor, payroll taxes, and benefits.
2. Includes truck and machine operation, repair expenses, and job supplies:
   - Truck operation   2.0%
   - Truck and machine repairs   0.8%
   - Supplies and tools (staples,
     guns, hoses, tarps, etc.)   0.2%

Expenses (12 Months)

	Fixed (*F*)	Variable (*V*)	%
Production expenses:			
Warehouse labor	$ 6,000	—	1
Equipment rental (50%–50%)	600	$600	0.2
Rent—building	13,200	—	2.2
Machine and truck depreciation	6,600	—	1.1
Supervisory labor	19,800	—	3.3
Misc. production, maintenance, and small errands	1,200	—	0.2
	$47,400	$600	8%
Sales expenses:			
Salary (owner-boss: 50% draw +50% "commission")	$21,000	$21,000	7%
Telephone (75% *F* + 25% *V*)	2,250	750	0.5
Auto lease and operating (pickup) (40% *F* + 60% *V*)	1,600	2,600	0.7
Advertising	3,000	—	0.5
Entertainment	—	600	0.1
Bad debts	—	3,000	0.5
Misc. supplies (for sales use: estimating forms, mail, etc.)	—	4,200	0.7
	$27,850	$32,150	10%
Administrative expenses:			
Salaries (office manager)	$12,000	—	2
Payroll taxes, Workmen's Comp. and benefits (boss + office personnel)	2,400	—	0.4

TABLE 11-13

CHAPTER 11

319

Managing
Your Financial
Requirements

(Continued)

	Fixed (F)	Variable (V)	%
General and vehicle insurance (liability, trucks, autos)	12,000	—	2
Printing and office supplies (job sheets, invoices, etc., 50% F +50% V)	600	600	0.2
Postage	600	—	0.1
Taxes and licenses (for various towns)	1,800	—	0.3
Utilities	600	—	0.1
Misc. incidentals	600	—	0.1
	$28,600	$600	5.2%

Total Expenses (12 Months)

			Fixed (F)	Variable (V)
Production			$ 47,400	$ 600
Sales			27,850	32,150
Administrative			28,600	600
		Total	$103,850	$ 33,350
Material	(49%)			294,000
Direct labor	(15%)			90,000
Direct job costs	(3%)			18,000
			Total	$435,350

you to planning and activities that would help you improve your business. Your break-even chart will give you valuable information in planning in many areas: in budgeting; in pricing; in controlling expenses; and in setting sales policies, among other things.

Another example of a break-even chart is given in Appendix B; it's been prepared for a retail bookstore and should prove informative as a model in any retail business.

Using Ratio Analysis

Another type of analysis that will help you guide the financial affairs of your company is *ratio analysis*. A ratio is simply a comparison of one item with another, from the balance sheet or operating income statement. By checking your current ratios against previous ratios on a regular basis, you can see how you're doing; these data permit you to improve the quality of your management decisions—and therefore the performance of your company. You'll also want to check the ratios from your operations against those customary in your kind of business. This will tell you if you're doing better or worse than the average firm in the business you're in. You'll find information on the ratios typical to your business in the publications listed earlier, such as those of Dun and Bradstreet, of the National Cash Register Company, and of the various trade associations.

SECTION IV

320

Achieving
Proactive
Financial
Management

CURRENT RATIO

An important financial ratio is the current ratio. It is given by

$$\frac{\text{Current assets}}{\text{Current liabilities}}$$

This will tell you how healthy your financial condition is. For example, if current assets = \$12,600 and current liabilities = \$5950, the current ratio would be 12,600/5950 = 2.12. In figuring this ratio, you should omit any prepaid expenses from current assets. Current assets are those you could turn into cash if the need arose; therefore, it is good practice to omit prepaid expenses from this calculation.

The figures you use to calculate the current ratio also tell you how much working capital you have available. In this example, the difference between \$12,600 and \$5950 is \$6650, which is the *working capital*. This shows the ability of the business to pay for current operations after taking care of its current bills.

The customarily acceptable current ratio for most businesses is at least 2:1. This means that your business should keep current assets at twice the figure of current liabilities. The 2:1 ratio shows a reasonable safety margin. If your business had some slow-moving merchandise in stock, these would be considered assets. But you'd have trouble getting rid of them at a good price in case you wanted to raise money quickly. You can see from this the importance of having a safety cushion in this ratio.

Some businesses may do with a ratio smaller than 2:1; such might be the case in a conservative business dealing in nonperishable goods in a stable market. A higher ratio than 2 should be maintained when the current debt must be paid off quickly or on demand. You should find out what is customary in your business and try to keep your current ratio at least at that level.

ACID-TEST RATIO

A refinement of the current ratio is the *acid-test ratio*. It is similar to the current ratio but shows the comparison between the quick assets and the current liabilities. Quick assets are limited to those that can be readily turned into cash; these include such items as cash, collectible receivables, and securities that can be sold immediately.

You find the acid-test ratio by dividing your quick assets by your current liabilities. Suppose your company has quick assets of \$8400 and current liabilities of \$7600, your acid-test ratio would be

$$\frac{\text{Quick assets}}{\text{Current liabilities}} = \frac{\$8400}{\$7600} = 1.13$$

A business is customarily considered in good shape when this ratio is at least 1. This means that the company of the example could raise enough money on short notice to pay off its existing liabilities. The 1.13 ratio is a sign of financial health.

PROPRIETORSHIP RATIO

The relationship of the owner's investment in the company and the total assets being used in the business is the *proprietorship ratio*. It's simply the owner's investment divided by total assets.

Suppose the balance sheet of your company at the end of a fiscal year shows total assets to be $25,490 and the proprietor's capital on the liabilities side shows $15,590. Your proprietorship ratio would then be

$$\text{Proprietorship ratio} = \frac{\text{your investment}}{\text{total assets}} = \frac{\$15,590}{\$25,490}$$

$$= 0.61, \text{ or } 61 \text{ percent}$$

This figure would show you that you are well above the 50 percent level considered to be a conservative minimum in any business.

RATIO OF NET PROFIT TO NET SALES

One of the more significant ratios is the *ratio of net profit to net sales*. It shows the number of cents profit for every dollar of sales. The most informative way for the small businessperson to view net profit is to see this figure as the one remaining after taxes, and net sales as sales for which money has been collected and is due for product or service delivered. There are other ways of setting these figures for other purposes. But looking at them as we've said is a clear, hard-headed managerial way that gives the percentage that is the real measure of the efficiency of a business.

Let's say for illustrative purposes that your company has had profit of $129,300 after taxes for the fiscal year and that your net sales have been $1,645,000; your ratio of net profit to net sales would be

$$\frac{\$129,300}{\$1,645,000} = 0.0786, \text{ or } 7.9 \text{ percent}$$

You should study the variation in this percentage on a regular basis. By comparing statements for past periods, you'll be able to put your finger on items that have caused deviations from the performance you'd like. Searching examination of the items in the comparative operating statements such as that shown in Figure 11-3 can give you the clues you need to reduce costs and increase efficiency. Or you may find it imperative to raise prices. However, you should increase prices cautiously, recognizing that raising prices too much can seriously cut your sales. You may find that what you need to do is to increase your volume of sales. Reference to your break-even analysis will help you decide how much money to put into increased advertising, promotion, and sales efforts to move your operation higher into the profit area.

COLLECTION-PERIOD RATIO

This ratio shows how long the money from sales is tied up in credit. It gives a measure of efficiency in the use of funds invested in accounts receivable. Obviously,

SECTION IV

322

Achieving
Proactive
Financial
Management

the more quickly money comes in from credit sales, the more efficient is the use of funds. As the owner, you will try to reduce to a minimum the time for collection of credit accounts. The collection period ratio is usually measured by the average number of days required for collection (the number of days' sales "on the books" as of the date of the balance sheet). This number gives you a combined test figure of the quality of your accounts receivable and the effectiveness of your credit policy.

As an example of how the collection period is figured, assume a children's and infants' wear retail store to show net sales for the year of $112,000 and the existing accounts receivable from credit sales to total $11,700. The accounts receivable turnover would measure

$$\frac{\$11,700}{\$112,000} = 10.4 \text{ percent}$$

Assuming 360 days in the year, as analysts commonly do, the store's accounts receivable equal 10.4 percent of 360, or 37.4 days. For a retail business of the kind indicated, this would suggest a well-managed credit policy. For the figures to be most useful, the owner should know the usual terms of sale for the firm and for the trade. A rule of thumb in the retail business says that a collection period should be considered too long if it is 10 to 15 days longer than those stated in selling terms. It will be up to you as the owner to know what the customary percentages and ratios are for your kind of business, so that you can judge the effectiveness of your credit policy.

COLLECTING YOUR MONEY

Jonathan (Joe) Small, the president of a small automatic sprinkler contracting firm, told the management specialist he was consulting, "We're slow collecting our accounts; somehow we've got to improve our cash flow."

"What's your average time from date of invoice to receipt of your money?" asked the consultant.

"I'd guess it runs about two-and-a-half months or more."

"I'd think that would really hurt," said the consultant. "You should be averaging under 60 days. Perhaps we'd better look into some of the things you can do to improve your collections."

"There aren't any secrets about collecting money. Some contractors do a good job of collecting and some not so good."

"Then what makes the difference?" asked Joe.

"It seems quite clear to me that the difference is one of attitude. The firms that do a good job in collecting their money are keen about it. They figure it's critical to their business, like doing a first class job of contracting—and they pay careful attention to it."

"What do they do specifically?" asked Joe.

"I'll bet you know everything they do. The important thing is that they go about it systematically—and conscientiously. Perhaps you should be doing some of the things they do.

"In the first place they're extremely careful about getting up-to-date, accurate credit information on their customers before signing the job. They check with their credit agency. They ask their banker, with whom they maintain close relations, to check with their customer's bank. You know, bankers talk with each other, and they tell each other things they very often won't tell anyone else. Not only that, when you make your banker privy to your affairs, you improve your own image. Your banker's bound to be interested in helping you because that help can strengthen your position as a more valuable customer. I'd recommend that you work closely with your banker, if you're not already doing so.

"Some simple mechanical operations are helpful, too. Check your contract carefully to make sure you haven't overlooked anything in preparing your invoice, an elementary precaution that many small firms, and sometimes big ones, overlook. Supply your customer with the number of copies of the invoice requested, in the right format, to avoid delay in getting your money. And use professionally printed invoice forms. They're formal, look authoritative, and they identify your company."

"You certainly have a point there," said Small. "We use a fairly good looking standard form—but we'll change that. We do tend to leave too many loopholes and I'll make certain they are properly prepared. What else do you suggest?"

"The next points are procedural, and they reflect the kind of attitude I mentioned. You should follow up on your invoice; insist on being paid. This will mean you'll need to establish a procedure for collecting: use a letter, a telephone call, a telegram—it's surprising how effective a telegram can be—and finally, you may need to get your attorney on the job. Use all these steps in logical sequence. Follow up on each and don't make idle threats.

"To ensure that collections are handled effectively, centralize the billing and the responsibility for collections. One person in your office should have total responsibility for these functions."

"Do you think I can trust someone to handle this for me?"

"Of course you can; people respond to trust in their ability to accomplish tough tasks, and given authority with responsibility will more often than not come through."

"OK, I'll give it a whirl."

"In another area, train your salespersons to make accurate estimates. Too often they tend to be more than a bit wild in setting prices. And you can train them, coach them, to help collect delinquent accounts. Their help in this area assures their success as salespeople.

"Put the terms of payment in your proposal. Spell them out. This step reduces the chance for later disagreement and delay in collecting your money. Remember, the day the contract is signed, the customer starts to use your money. Make it easier for yourself to get it back."

"OK, that sounds good. We'll try it. We have another problem, one that many businesses don't have. We're subject to retainers. Is there anything we can do about that?" asked the president.

"A couple of contractors I work with talked about this problem. As subcontractors they're subject to having a portion of their payment, usually 10 percent, held by the major contractor for a period of time after their work is completed. They say that they are sometimes able to do something about negotiating the retainer downward as they conclude their installation. Perhaps you should try that. And another thing, when you act as a subcontractor acquaint your banker with the peculiar nature of the retainer. He can help you in your financing when he knows this part of your business."

"You've given me a good deal to think about," said the president. "One more thing I'd like to know is how can I tell accurately how I'm doing with my collections?"

"Some firms I work with use a simple formula to tell them that," replied the con-

SECTION IV

324

Achieving
Proactive
Financial
Management

sultant. "They multiply their average accounts receivable for the last three month-ends by 90 and divide that number by their billings for the last 3 months. That gives them the average number of calendar days their bills are outstanding. If it's under 60 days, they're doing well; if it's between 60 and 70, only fair; if it's over 70 they figure they've got a bad cash flow problem."

"Good," said the president. "We'll go to work on it. We should be able to correct the problem if we follow your suggestions."

"Check with me in seven or eight weeks," said the consultant. "If you're down to 60 days on your collections, you can buy me a drink."

"If we're down to 60 days, I'll add the best dinner in town to that drink," replied the president.

Describe the recommendations the consultant made to improve the collection of bills outstanding.

Explain the reasons behind each recommendation.

STOCK TO SALES RATIO

This ratio is often called inventory turnover or net sales to inventory ratio. A hypothetical average inventory turnover figure allows you, the owner of a business, to compare your company's performance with that of others in the business, or those customary in the industry.

To find the inventory turnover figure, simply divide the average inventory into the net sales for the period chosen. For example, using the data given in the preceding example, divide $112,000 (net sales for the year) by the average inventory for the year (found by adding the previous year-end balance-sheet inventory of $21,500 to the current year-end figure of $26,200 and dividing by 2), as follows:

$$\frac{21,500 + 26,200}{2} = 23,850$$

Then

$$\frac{112,000}{23,850} = 4.7 \text{ times inventory turnover}$$

This is a quite respectable figure for the children's and infants' wear business. This ratio affords the owner a way of making comparisons from one period to another, and for checking against customary performance in the industry. It is not an indicator of physical turnover, which may be found only by counting the physical items in the inventory and comparing the figures with actual sales of the various physical items.

EXPLORE THE USE OF RATIO ANALYSIS

A number of other ratios that you may want to use for specific purposes are those derived primarily from figures on the balance sheet and from items on the income statement. Because these are intended for rather special purposes, we prefer not to include them in this text. Instead, we give you several pertinent references at the end of this chapter in which you will find excellent information on how to prepare and use many different kinds of ratios.

Key Points in Managing Your Finances

Summary

You'll need three kinds of money to start your business: capital-asset investment, working capital, and personal money. Therefore, you should plan for both long- and short-term financing. Capital assets take long-term money; working capital and personal financing may be thought of as short-term. In all cases you should do the planning yourself. This will give you the knowledge and skill you'll need to guide the financial affairs of your company.

Before you start your business, your planning will necessarily be based on assumptions. In this chapter and in the chapters on marketing, we've given a number of sources of information you can draw upon to start with. As you do business, you'll be able to replace the figures you've assumed with actual figures. We recommend that you redo your financial planning every month, projecting from the actual figures into the future. You'll gain both speed and accuracy of predictions as you do this planning each month.

We suggest that you prepare the following plans each month: a balance sheet to see what the financial picture looks like; a sales forecast 24 months ahead by the month and perhaps a forecast for the third year by the quarter; a cash flow analysis in the same time frame as the sales forecast; an income statement, projected at least 12 months ahead; and a break-even analysis from time to time, to see how much you need to sell by the month just to break even.

You should learn to use ratio analysis as a check on different aspects of your financial condition. Of the many variations of ratio analysis we suggest the following as of key significance for your management purposes:

- Current ratio, which is your current assets divided by your current liabilities. Most businesses are considered to be financially healthy when this ratio is 2 or a bit above.

- Acid-test ratio, which is a refinement of the current ratio. You find the acid-test ratio by dividing your quick assets by your current liabilities. Quick assets are those you can turn into cash immediately: collectible receivables, securities, and cash itself. Your acid-test ratio should be at least 1, which would show that you could pay your existing debts quickly in case of need.

- Proprietorship ratio, which is your total investment divided by the total assets of your company. This number should be at least 50 percent to show a healthy ownership position.

- Net profit to net sales. This ratio is obtained by dividing your after-tax profits by the net sales for your fiscal year.

SECTION IV

326

Achieving
Proactive
Financial
Management

■ Collection-period ratio, which shows how long money from credit sales takes to become cash inflow. This figure will give you understanding of how effectively your credit policy works.

■ Stock to sales ratio (inventory turnover). This ratio allows you to compare the performance of your company with that of others in the business or industry.

To practice the best kind of proactive management, you should compare your figures in these various indicators on a regular basis, month by month and year by year. This practice will alert you to potential difficulty so you can take corrective steps quickly. It will also show what you're doing well—and what you should be doing more of, and better.

Managing Your Financial Requirements

This worksheet is a bit different from the others in that you'll want to take advantage of standard accounting sheets with vertical columns to prepare your financial plans. These are available at any stationery store. We'd recommend that you buy a dozen five-column sheets and a dozen thirteen-column sheets to work on. You'll find these standard forms a great convenience in tabulating your figures.

1. Prepare a budget for your living expenses for eighteen months ahead. Stationery stores usually carry printed forms that you'll find easy to use for this purpose. This is a good point to involve your spouse and family. You'll want their support and commitment to your venture. By preparing the family budget as a team, you'll improve the chances for a healthy climate of cooperation in the affairs of the new business.

2. Prepare a list of equipment, machinery, fixtures, or other equipment you'll need for your business. Find and assign costs to the items and add these figures to find your required fixed asset capital investment. Be sure to add a reasonable safety factor to the total. Don't forget to consider the possibilities of leasing or renting equipment to conserve cash.

3. Prepare your short-term operating plans. Here you'll want to follow the text of this chapter. You'll also want to check your planning by referring to the examples in Appendix B. Beginning with setting the date for starting your business, include the following plans:

   - Balance sheet for the day you start your business.

   - Sales forecast for two years ahead, by the month. You may find it good practice to try forecasting the third year by the quarter.

   - Cash flow analysis for two years ahead by the month, possibly the third year by quarters.

   - Income statement for two years ahead by the month, possibly the third year by quarters.

   - Break-even analysis for the first year. (You'll very likely want to find your break-even point by the month, four-week period, or week once your business is rolling.)

   - You may want to compare your estimated figures against those considered appropriate for your business through ratio analysis. Check these ratios by quarters, for example:

Current ratio	Collection-period ratio
Acid-test ratio	
Proprietorship ratio	Stock to sales ratio
Ratio of net profit to net sales	(inventory turnover)

As a concluding reminder, be sure to repeat your planning on the basis of three approaches: optimistic, pessimistic, and at a moderate middle level. Later, as you use real figures from your business to replace your estimated figures, your planning will show reality. You'll be able to practice proactive management effectively.

KEY TERMS

CHAPTER 11

329

Managing
Your Financial
Requirements

budget 291
assets 291
balance sheet 293, 298
break-even 293
liabilities 298

equity 298
cash flow 304
depreciation 310
ratio analysis 319

STUDY ASSIGNMENTS FOR REVIEW AND DISCUSSION

1. Describe the three kinds of money you should have to start a new business.

2. Describe five basic plans you'll want to develop for managing the financial affairs of your company.

3. Does cash flow analysis tell you how much profit you are making? Explain.

4. What sources of data can you use to make your sales forecasts before you open your doors for business?

5. What is the main purpose of break-even analysis?

6. How is a simple break-even analysis prepared?

7. What is meant by ratio analysis?

8. Define the following ratios and describe their use in managing your business: current ratio, acid-test ratio, proprietorship ratio, net profit to net sales ratio, collection-period ratio, stock to sales ratio.

PROJECTS FOR STUDENTS

The following assignments may be done by individual students or teams of students working in twos or threes.

1. Interview a loan officer at the local office of the Small Business Administration. Find out what common errors or deficiencies occur in the applications for loans made by entrepreneurs. Report your findings to the class.

2. Interview three owners of small businesses to find out what kind of planning they do for controlling their finances. Report your findings to the class.

3. Do a library search and study of at least six ratios used in business planning and analysis, other than those given in this chapter. Make a presentation to the class explaining these ratios and how they are used. (A particularly good reference for this purpose is Richard Sanzo, *Ratio Analysis for Small Business*, Small Business Administration.)

SECTION IV

330

Achieving
Proactive
Financial
Management

4. Refer to Spencer A. Tucker, *The Break-Even System* referred to at the end of this chapter, or other texts. Present to the class several different applications of break-even analysis for special management purposes.

IF YOU WANT TO READ MORE

GUMPERT, David E.: *Growing Concerns,* John Wiley & Sons, New York, 1984. This book consists of 36 articles that have appeared in the *Harvard Business Review.* These address the management problems of smaller companies. Part three contains six articles on effective financial management; two significant pieces are "A Small Business Is Not a Little Big Business" and "Performance Measures for Small Businesses."

LASSER, J. K.: *How to Run a Small Business,* 5th ed., McGraw-Hill Book Company, New York, 1982. A clearly written handbook on small business management, the text gives examples of the use of financial data for controlling business operations. In addition, the book contains many practical suggestions about managing a small business.

LIPAY, Raymond J.: *Accounting Services for Your Small Business,* John Wiley & Sons, New York, 1983. This author stresses the need for small businesspersons to know the basics of accounting practice. He includes chapters on accounting services furnished by accountants, selecting an accountant, and measuring company performance.

NICKERSON, Clarence B.: *Accounting Handbook for Non-Accountants,* Van Nostrand Reinhold, New York, 1979. A comprehensive text aimed at helping managers understand and use accounting concepts and terms. The presentation is at a relatively high level but offers basic concepts in clear, comprehensible language.

OSGOOD, William R.: *Basics of Successful Business Planning,* AMACOM, New York, 1982. The primary purpose of this text is to establish a methodology and framework for planning geared toward businesses that have the potential of developing into successful medium-sized operations. Areas dealt with include forecasting, break-even and ratio analyses, pro forma income statements, balance sheets, and cash flow projections.

PICKLE, Hal B., and Royce L. ABRAHAMSON: *Small Business Management,* 3d ed., John Wiley & Sons, New York, 1984. This text presents a simple explanation of financial record keeping and cash control. It is aimed at the beginner in small business.

RAUSCH, Edward N.: *Financial Keys to Small Business Profitability,* AMACOM, New York, 1982. This book offers a variety of financial management tools and techniques. The author points out that financial management activities contribute greatly to all business decisions, not just financial decisions. Break-even analysis is discussed in detail in Chapter 5.

SANZO, Richard: *Ratio Analysis for Small Business.* Small Business Administration, Washington, DC, 1977. This booklet offers a straightforward, simple explanation of business ratios and how they work. It also contains examples, information on evaluating and interpreting ratios, and sources of data on ratios for various industries.

SLATER, Jeffrey: *Rx for Small Business Success,* Prentice-Hall, Inc., Englewood Cliffs, NJ, 1981. A comprehensive text on accounting, planning, and record keeping for the small businessperson. Emphasis is on interpreting financial reports, budgeting, business ratios, break-even analysis, and bookkeeping procedures.

STEINHOFF, Dan: *Small Business Management Fundamentals,* 4th ed., McGraw-Hill Book Company, New York, 1986. This is a fundamental text that tells about financial planning and forecasting for the small business. It is an excellent basic book for the beginner. The text focuses to a considerable extent on the small retail firm.

TUCKER, Spencer A.: *The Break-Even System,* Prentice-Hall, Inc., Englewood Cliffs, NJ, 1963. This reference tells about break-even analysis in detail. You will discover here the many variations of break-even analysis and how to use them for all kinds of proactive management purposes. The text has numerous illustrative examples, which make it easy to see how break-even analyses apply in practice.

CHAPTER 12

Management Information and Computers[1]

TOPICS IN THIS CHAPTER

Formal and Informal Information
Guides to Generating Management Information
Computers for Small Business
What Is an Electronic Computer?
Microcomputers and Minicomputers
Common Computer Systems—Hardware and Software
Data Storage
Spreadsheets—Their Importance
Word Processing
Multifunctionality for Your Business—Summary
Worksheet 12: Using a Microcomputer in Your Business
Key Terms
Study Assignments for Review and Discussion
Projects for Students
If You Want to Read More

[1]Code numbers referring to the Outline for Developing Your Basic Business Plan (Appendix A) are not used in this chapter, which aims at giving you background on management information and small computer systems.

The rapidly growing influence of the electronic age is nowhere more evident than in the management of the small firm. Today even the office of the smallest company gains efficiency through the application of technical sophistication. The day is past when a competent secretary could manage with one telephone, an error-correcting typewriter, and an office copier. The secretary has now been replaced by a well-trained specialist in the operation of electronic computer systems. These enable the business to gain the advantage of multifunctionality— the ability to do many tasks rapidly and easily, tasks that formerly took several employees.

This chapter presents a brief survey of typical electronic office equipment now available to collect, store, and convert data to useful management information—and to process information and words for more effective analysis and decision making in the tasks of managing the business.

The electronic computer industry is moving so fast that it's impossible to predict what breakthroughs may lie ahead. The small business chief executive should keep up with advances in the field through pertinent magazines and journals such as *Byte, PC World,* and *The Journal of Financial Software and Hardware.*

$$\text{You} + \text{Idea} + \begin{cases} \text{Money} \\ \text{Credit} \end{cases} + \begin{cases} \textbf{FACILITIES} \\ \text{People} \end{cases} \begin{matrix} \text{Product} \\ \rightarrow \quad \text{or} \quad + \text{Marketing} \\ \text{Service} \end{matrix} \begin{cases} \text{Money} \\ \text{Credit} \end{cases} \rightarrow \text{Profit}$$

SECTION IV

334

Achieving
Proactive
Financial
Management

We have consistently stressed throughout this book that careful planning undergirds success in managing the business. But as the chief executive of your own business you cannot plan in a vacuum. You must have accurate and timely information upon which to base your planning. Information can be derived only from reliable data.

Data consist of raw facts: gross sales by the month, payroll costs per week, inventory level of material by the week, and similar quantities fundamental to assessing what goes on in the business. For prediction, guidance, and control of managerial actions, the raw data must be analyzed and presented in a way useful for making management decisions. For example, gross sales per month may show peak and low periods during the year. If this were true in your business, you would plan intensive advertising and special sales to bolster your business during the slack periods. Or you may find that your inventory level is too high for your level of output during slack seasons of the year. You would then cut inventory during those periods. Your management activities can be intelligently designed only after the raw data have been converted to information.

The information that you receive as the chief executive of your company not only must be reasonably accurate but also must get to you early enough so you can act to take advantage of opportunity or to correct what's going on before some undesirable costly event occurs. Accounting data ordinarily are very accurate, but often too late for proactive management use. You, in the key management spot, need up-to-the-minute information with reasonable accuracy, say plus or minus 5 percent in most cases. This usually allows management decisions to be formed and activated effectively. By observing this need for timeliness, you can ensure that information gets to the right people at the right time.

Formal and Informal Information

You and your managers will receive both *formal* and *informal* information. Formal information includes many items mandatory to running the technical and administrative aspects of your business. These include such considerations as accounting procedures, budgets, legal requirements, credit information, and management control and decision-making activities of many kinds. Formalized information such as this leads to carefully worked out procedures that can be developed or manipulated by either manual or computerized operations, or by a combination.

Informal information includes opinions, gossip, hunches, rules of thumb, unwritten customs ("that's the way things are done around here"), dress codes, and the like. These are not subject to formal documentation but can help the boss steer a sound psychological course. Information of this kind can be particularly helpful in guiding the planning that goes into improving organizational effectiveness, as in the dialogues between chief executive and managers in a management by objectives system (see Chapter 18).

Guides to Generating Management Information

One way to identify the needs for specific management information comes from defining the major and detailed parts of the organization, and then studying the transactions that must take place between them for the company to operate and prosper.

The company may be considered as comprising three major systems: the *technical,* the *administrative,* and the *social.* The technical system produces and distributes product or service; the administrative system regulates and controls affairs within the company; the social system represents human beings working together to achieve the objectives of the company.

- The technical system depends for superior performance on competence in specific areas: research and development, purchasing, production, marketing, and accounting—as needed to get out the product or produce the service.

- The administrative system focuses on policy and procedure, on developing and installing compensation and reward programs, on financial and accounting procedures, and on other matters needed to regulate and control internal nontechnical processes.

- The social system involves the relationships and interactions of people throughout the organization. Here the need is to detect opportunities for improving knowledge and skills—and morale and commitment—of the members of the company: the objective is to increase the effectiveness and efficiency of the whole company.

These three major systems afford an overall map of the entire company. A detailed analysis of transactions that take place within the company can then be made by use of a matrix in which the elements of the company can be related to one another.

For example, assume the small company of which you are the chief executive comprises four levels of organization: These can be categorized as the *individual,* the *group* of which that individual is part, the *department,* and finally the total *organization,* or company. Information must pass between these various segments as shown in Figure 12-1.

This matrix offers a tool for examining the transactions across the various interfaces. As the key executive you must always be attentive to the communications that take place across the organization-environment interface. You'll want to collect data and convert to information such things as consumer requirements, demographic factors, legislative requirements, and economic changes.

Information from this source can affect many of the other interfaces in your company. The organization, for example, may respond to information that a competitor has just brought out a product that is somewhat improved over one of your major items. You'll now instruct your production department to make significant improvements in your product. In turn, production will pass necessary information to your design group. The group will transmit the information to a key individual or two across the group-individual interface; they will be authorized to design the improvements.

You can check the impact of your decision in the company by asking if the resulting activities need technical help or administrative help or need to be handled directly with individuals. You can then take desirable action where needed to ensure that the improvements are carried out.

SECTION IV

336

Achieving
Proactive
Financial
Management

	Organization	Department	Group	Individual
Environment	✓	✓	✓	✓
Organization		✓	✓	✓
Department		✓	✓	✓
Group			✓	✓
Individual				✓

Source: Kuriloff, Arthur H., *Organizational Development for Survival*, New York: American Management Association, Inc., 1972, P. 36.

FIG. 12-1

Transactional matrix.

Computers for Small Business

In today's world of exploding electronic technology, even the smallest company can improve the management of its affairs through manipulation of data and information by *multifunctionality*. Multifunctionality simply means that every office device can now do much more than it did in the past. The electronic typewriter of today becomes an application tool for many chores other than straight typing. It may be used to produce several dozen identical letters, a balance sheet, or a sales report. It may be further equipped with more advanced features: memory capabilities, calculation abilities, or a routine for checking spelling.

Moving up in sophistication, the new typewriter may become a "printer." It may now be capable of producing images as well as words, including graphs and charts even in color. It may employ a variety of type sizes and characters—and print material that formerly would have had to go to a typesetter or graphic artist.

The electronic typewriter plus an up-to-date telephone system and office copier may offer enough increase in communication efficiency to be all that the small business may need. However, multifunctionality may now be had in a small computer system at reasonable cost. As the owner of a small business, it would be well for you to study the possibilities of a microcomputer system for enhancing your performance of proactive management.

What Is an Electronic Computer?

You, or your secretary, need not be an electronics engineer to use the small computer (microcomputer) in managing your business. It's like operating a microwave oven, a programmable dishwasher, or a TV set; what you need to know is what you want the machine to do and how to push the right buttons to make it do it. If you're not used to computer terms, don't be put off by strange lingo such as *software, mainframe, floppy disk,* or *peripherals.* As you delve into how a computer can help you manage your business, you'll become familiar with these terms. You'll discover that those in the computer business are fond of making up acronyms, that is, condensations made by combining parts of words into a short version. Examples are *modem* (*mod*ulator/*dem*odulator), *pixel* (*pi*ctures *el*ement), and *crom* (*c*ontrol *r*ead-*o*nly *m*emory). You'll also find anthropomorphism in many terms associated with computers, terms that ascribe human qualities to the machine: *user-friendly, intelligent* and *nonintelligent* terminals, and *leader.*

Your small computer system can produce as if by magic at the touch of a finger a sales forecast, a payroll complete with all necessary deductions for taxes and insurance, manufacturing costs for all products in a line, or a myriad of other management information. Information of these kinds would usually take days to produce and check if done by hand. But the rapid computer must be prepared and instructed to perform its magic.

The "teaching" of the computer may be understood by analogy to the human being. Human behavior follows from conditioning, previous training, and experience; that is, the *mind* shapes behavior. The computer similarly must have a "mind" to shape its behavior. "Programs" give the computer a mind. Programs instruct it with detailed information that causes it to perform specific tasks.

But it takes human "programmers" to create minds for computers. Because computers have no imagination and cannot reason (at least at this time), programmers must implant in the computers reservoirs of experiences (called *software*) that will shape their activities. These take the form of instructions, called *programs,* that guide computers.

If you select a computer for your small business, a key variable would be the complexity of the tasks you would want the computer to perform. A simple program can function on a small computer with limited capabilities, but a larger computer would be needed to do more complex tasks. The size of the computer and its ability to handle more difficult functions would, of course, influence its price (see Figure 12-2). The more complicated your needs for management information and decision making, the more sophisticated your computer system must be—and the more expensive (see Figure 12-3). A very simple business, perhaps a hamburger stand, might be well managed with pencilled notes on the back of an envelope. But a more sophisticated one-person business such as management consulting would find a small computer invaluable. With an appropriate program to keep track of time spent on assignments, costs, schedules, and billing clients, it would greatly improve the consultant's personal efficiency.

Microcomputers and Minicomputers

Microcomputers and minicomputers are two categories of computers of different processing power. Microcomputers are usually seen in a single small desktop unit. These usually contain the basic components of a computer system: a display screen, a keyboard, and disk storage for retaining data and information. Most are used for

SECTION IV

338

Achieving
Proactive
Financial
Management

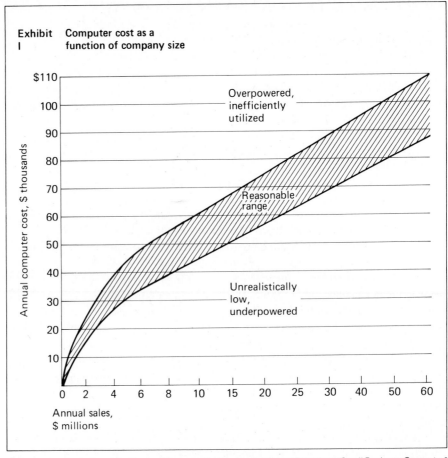

Exhibit   Computer cost as a
I   function of company size

Reprinted by permission of the *Harvard Business Review*. Exhibit I from "Selecting a Small Business Computer" by Myron S. Karasik (January/February 1984). Copyright ©1984 by the President and Fellows of Harvard College; all rights reserved.

FIG. 12-2

Computer cost as a function of company size.

single-task purposes, although many can process as many as five tasks at the same time. These now range in price from less than $1000 to about $2000.

Minicomputers derive increased processing power from more complex circuitry. They can perform several data-processing activities simultaneously. A number of users can operate at the same time through terminals at different stations. The less expensive systems can accommodate about 12 persons, the more expensive up to about 50. Minicomputers range in price from about $20,000 to over $50,000.

A minicomputer system would be well adapted, for example, to serving several management needs in a business with complicated requirements. An auto parts and accessory store might be representative. The needs here might include inventory control at the command of data from the cash register with automatic reordering of parts as the stocks became low, automatic billing of credit customers, mailing lists

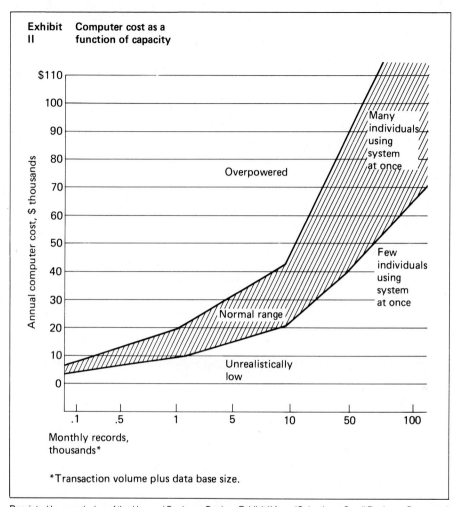

Exhibit   Computer cost as a
II   function of capacity

FIG. 12-3

Computer cost as a function of capacity.

of customers, cash flow projections, accounting procedures, payroll records, and accounts payable.

Common Computer Systems—Hardware and Software

The common computer system contains *hardware* and *software*. Hardware refers to the computer and its related equipment known as *peripherals*. These consist of such items as:

SECTION IV

340

Achieving
Proactive
Financial
Management

▦ Computer, the central machine in the hardware. It is often called the central processing unit (CPU), or *mainframe*. The term mainframe generally refers to large computers.

▦ Cathode ray tube (CRT), the television-like screen upon which the computer displays data, information, and graphics.

▦ Keyboard, a typewriter-like keyboard through which the operator communicates with the computer.

▦ Printer, a device that prints out the displayed information on paper.

▦ Memory, a magnetic disk accessory that stores information beyond the capacity of the computer's built-in memory device.

▦ Special printer that operates on instructions from the computer.

▦ Magnetic-tape auxiliary storage device that acts as a reservoir for information the computer will not use very often.

▦ In many small business computers, the CRT, keyboard, disk storage device, and computer are combined in one unitized desktop machine.

The diagram in Figure 12-4 illustrates the relationship of basic components in the computer system and the concept of input and output. In this example, time-card

FIG. 12-4

Typical microcomputer system.

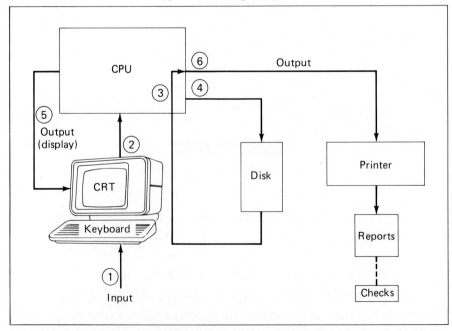

information will be processed to produce payroll reports and paychecks. A payroll program performs all the calculations and manipulates the information to produce the output as follows:

1. Information from time cards is input from the keyboard.

2. The time-card information is transmitted to the computer (CPU).

3. The payroll program manipulates the time-card input and combines it with information in the program that defines job cost analysis and computes payroll taxes.

4. The computed payroll information is stored on disk.

5. A display is output to the CRT so the operator can examine the information before the reports and checks are printed.

6. Output, in the form of payroll reports and paychecks, is sent to the printer.

Computer *software* includes written or printed data such as programs, routines, and symbolic languages essential to the operation of computers. Documents containing information on the operation and maintenance of computers are also included in the definition of software.

As the owner–chief executive of your own small business, it is not necessary for you to be expert in the selection of programs and other software that become the mind of your computer system. What should be important to you is that whatever software fits your specific management purposes should be *user-friendly*. This term implies software that is easy to understand and to use.

Unless you are thoroughly conversant with the computer field, you'd be wise to hire a well-experienced and reputable consultant to help you decide on both computer system hardware and software. It's not a game for amateurs.

Data Storage

The microcomputer usually adopted for small-business purposes has limited built-in storage capacity. Data that the computer's memory can't accommodate or preserve for future reference can be transferred to a magnetic disk storage device. Several kinds of storage accessories suit this purpose:

Floppy disks, flexible plastic disks coated with magnetic material. These are sometimes called diskettes; they are most widely used for small-business computers storage. Floppy disks come enclosed in a permanent plastic wrapper; the wrapper has a small opening through which a *head,* a small electric sensor, *reads* data from or *writes* data on the magnetic surface of the disk as it spins at high speed.

The computer should have two *disk drives,* so that one can easily make copies from the other. This ensures that one stored copy of every disk prevents loss of important business data should the original floppy disk be accidentally erased or lost.

SECTION IV

342

Achieving
Proactive
Financial
Management

Hard disks offer the expanded storage capacity needed by the minicomputer. Hard disks are made of magnetic material and are spun at high speed under heads that read or write data. Several hard disks may be stacked vertically in some designs of drives. Here multiple heads read from or write on the disks at the same time. Microcomputers, which sometimes come with hard disk storage, use floppy disks for extra storage. Minicomputers use magnetic-tape storage, as floppy disks would be too time-consuming to be practical. Magnetic-tape devices may come as reel-to-reel drives or in cassettes similar to standard audiocassettes. Tapes can be driven at high speeds to keep up with the hard disk drives, which record at much higher rates than floppy disks. Tape-recording speeds can be as fast as 125 inches per second.

Spreadsheets—Their Importance

The *spreadsheet* has come to be considered the major tool for decision making in small-business computer usage. Originally aimed at developing information for decisions in financial matters, spreadsheets are now used for many purposes: for salary records, manufacturing costs, marketing analyses, administrative data, and a host of other data critical to management decision making. The spreadsheet has become a widely accepted tool for data storage and analysis. It can be adapted to practically any area of a business—and in any decision making requirement.

WHAT IS A SPREADSHEET?

A spreadsheet presents a rectangular grid of horizontal rows and vertical columns affording boxes for entering data. A typical spreadsheet is shown in Figure 12-5. Practically any subject may be treated in a structured way by placing data in rows and columns. The operator can manipulate and use the information and can store and retrieve it at will.

The computer creates an electronic spreadsheet similar to that done by hand on accounting paper. The CPU screen display usually does not show vertical and horizontal separation lines, however, but simply shows the data in rows and columns. Even the simplest computer can present 255 horizontal rows and 52 vertical columns; others can show many times more. The spreadsheet matrix is formed by software called a *template*.

The data on the screen can be moved about at will. The screen therefore acts like a movable window that can display any desired portion of the spreadsheet. It is possible to view two (or more, depending on the capability of the computer system) spreadsheets at a time.

If you're able to view two spreadsheets simultaneously, you can answer important management questions. You can find, for instance, what gross profit you might expect if you raise sales by 15 percent in the next 12 months. Or you can compare two successive years' budgets on the top screen and then project an increased budget for next year on the bottom screen.

The microcomputer system offers a flexible command structure. With such flexibility built into your computer system you can insert or delete data, copy, format, organize arrangement of data, store, print, move about the spreadsheet at will, or

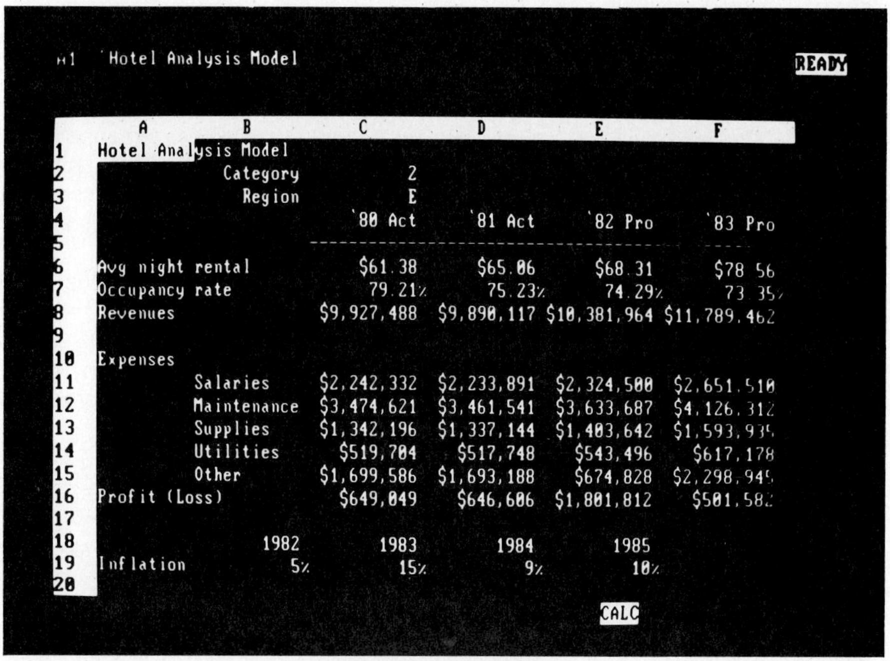

H1   Hotel Analysis Model   READY

```
          A         B            C          D          E          F
 1  Hotel Analysis Model
 2              Category         2
 3              Region          E
 4                            '80 Act    '81 Act    '82 Pro    '83 Pro
 5                           ------------------------------------------
 6  Avg night rental          $61.38     $65.06     $68.31     $78.56
 7  Occupancy rate            79.21%     75.23%     74.29%     73.35%
 8  Revenues               $9,927,488 $9,890,117 $10,381,964 $11,789,462
 9
10  Expenses
11              Salaries    $2,242,332 $2,233,891 $2,324,500 $2,651,510
12              Maintenance $3,474,621 $3,461,541 $3,633,687 $4,126,312
13              Supplies    $1,342,196 $1,337,144 $1,403,642 $1,593,935
14              Utilities    $519,704   $517,748   $543,496   $617,178
15              Other       $1,699,586 $1,693,188   $674,828 $2,298,945
16  Profit (Loss)            $649,049   $646,606 $1,801,812   $501,582
17
18              1982         1983        1984      1985
19  Inflation     5%          15%          9%       10%
20
                                                   CALC
```

© Lotus Development Corporation 1985. Used with permission.

FIG. 12-5

A typical spreadsheet.

produce graphic displays of information derived from various data. The spreadsheet, in short, has become an overall tool for storage and analysis of data for almost any kind of management need in the small business.

As we have seen in Chapter 3, advancing technology often spins off new business. Here's a small business in which two experts consult with businesses that have got into confusion in using spreadsheets.

A BUSINESS BUILT ON SPREADSHEET SUPPORT[2]

Jeffrey Freedman and Jacqueline Treese, a pair of highly successful consultants in Berkeley, California, have based their business largely on supporting clients with template construction and organization. Both Freedman and Treese have extensive background in accounting as well as in spreadsheet use. They say they are typically called in when the proliferation of spreadsheet models in a business has gotten completely out of control. Their method is to sift through all the existing models and then start their clients on a new course by organizing the elements of those models

[2]Reproduced by permission from *The Journal of Financial Software and Hardware*, May/June 1985.

SECTION IV

344

Achieving
Proactive
Financial
Management

into a master model which holds the data, plus command files to extract portions of those data for different uses.

For Freedman and Treese, the generic template marketplace is too limited. Their clients have usually exhausted these resources, they say, and their task is to create templates specifically tailored to a given client's needs. They stress the importance of logical construction of templates, so that the data can go in as they are gathered. Treese says that the input operation should look as if done by hand. "You shouldn't try to fit input to the intended form of the output; just put the data in naturally and let the computer do the organization. That's what it's for," she advises.

Freedman notes that documentation is essential in any case where there are multiple users: "You come into a place and find that the people who created most of the templates they're using are gone, and there's no record for anything. Just seeing one of these situations is strong motivation for always providing hard copy documentation and extensive error trapping so the system can be used without problems after you finish," he says.

Their experience with templates has given Freedman and Treese the know-how to train others in spreadsheet use. They have become almost as much involved in training as in the consulting part of their business, since both are convinced of the value of proper training. Their approach stresses correct spreadsheet design even at the basic level, including such seemingly obvious points as stating the purpose and components of the model at the very beginning. Both feel that today's spreadsheets present users with so much power that it becomes easy to forget these simple points. Yet, it is this disciplined approach to spreadsheet power that makes them most useful. Treese sums it up: "Design it right once for maximum use."

Identify the critical steps that the consultants recommend be taken in designing a template for a specific business.

Word Processing

The written word still prevails as the way most information gets transmitted in the business organization. Word processing, the technology for managing words, offers the oldest and best-established technology for managing the written word. Word-processing technology can vary from a simpler form in the computerized electronic typewriter to a sophisticated form in the full computer system. Your decision on what equipment to adopt will depend on the needs in your business for volume and sophistication of documents of various kinds. Years of development have made word processing user-friendly *and* powerful.

Many features essential to computerized word processing are now available. These include:

- Setting and changing format.

- Features such as automatic underlining, centering, boldface, superscript, subscript, insertion and deletion of text, pagination, tabs and indenting, column manipulation, global search and replace, block moving, and copying.

Document handling features: automatic page numbering, headers and footers, copying, moving, and renaming and deleting entire documents.

PRINTING THE DOCUMENT

The final stage in word processing comes in printing the document. The quality of the printing your business requires plays a large part in the price you'll have to pay for your system. Prices range from inexpensive for dot matrix printers through medium expensive for letter-quality impact printers, to quite expensive for laser printers.

Dot matrix printers, which form letters from small dots, offer two modes of operation: draft quality and improved quality. Improved, or better quality, results from the print head passing over each line twice. The print becomes about twice as dark as in the draft quality, but usually only approaches letter quality. Draft or near letter quality may be acceptable for your business.

Impact printers produce the next improvement in quality. They give quality of type like that of a good typewriter; printing comes from the impact of a print wheel, either flat or cup-shaped like the familiar "golf ball" printing device.

The most expensive and highest-quality word-processing printer now available is the laser printer. This device has revolutionized the application of graphics to management needs for information. Although it can be used as a conventional printer, its usefulness to your small company would be based on the applications you require: the need to develop formal presentations in color, with bar charts, pie charts, layouts, and the like; the volume of reports or other documents you're planning to make; the length of time documents should be held in storage and "accessed" (the frequency with which they will need to be withdrawn from storage).

You can see from the above that the needs appropriate to your business will determine how much you should invest to achieve the flexibility and quality of printer you should have.

LEASING OR BUYING COMPUTER SERVICE

When your small business has reached a point at which electronic data processing by computer looks promising, there are alternatives open to you. You can buy a microcomputer system; you can use a service center that will do your work for a fee; or you can lease input and output terminals that allow you to hook into a large central computer, for which you will pay by the time used.

Many banks now offer computer services to their customers. Services include a wide range, such as accounts receivable, accounts payable, inventory control, and payroll management.

The scope of equipment and services open to you is very wide. If you'd rather not invest in a microcomputer system, you may have the work done at a service organization. If your gross volume is over $150,000 annually, you can well afford to spend the $1/2$ percent it would cost to have data collecting and analyzing done by

SECTION IV

346

Achieving
Proactive
Financial
Management

a service bureau. This course would avoid the need to train a person in your office to run a computer. However, at some point in the growth of your business it makes sense to own an in-house computer.

Multifunctionality for Your Business

Summary

Before you can decide on an electronic computer for your business, you must set clear requirements for what you want the computer to do. One effective way to establish these requirements is through the use of a transactional matrix. The matrix maps the various interfaces inside and outside your organization across which communications must take place. These include relationships that you and your personnel must manage: such items as promotion and advertising, production schedules, billing, payroll, accounts receivable and payable, and a multitude of other matters. From study of these requirements you can define what you'd want a computer to do.

Whatever computer system you decide on should have the advantages of multifunctionality, including word processing and various features you may find desirable in your business. Features might incorporate proper quality of printing, spelling checker, color presentations of graphs, modem, ability to operate several terminals, and others.

When you've arrived at a fairly good set of requirements for the computer system you want, you should employ the services of a reputable consultant to review your requirements. That expert should then help you select the right microcomputer system and the hardware and software, and train your people to run the system.

Using a Microcomputer in Your Business

This worksheet will guide you in setting the specifications for a microcomputer suited to your small business. The steps given here will help you identify activities that would be well served by multifunctionality.

1. Prepare an organization chart for your business (see Chapter 15 for examples). Sketch your chart here:

2. Refer to the transactional matrix on page 336; compile a list of all the important transactions critical to the operation of your company. Record them here; attach an additional sheet if required.

   _____
   _____
   _____
   _____
   _____
   _____

3. From the foregoing list, record those items that you think a microcomputer might help you manage effectively.

   _____
   _____
   _____

4. From the advertising and promotional literature available to you, select a microcomputer that you think would meet your specifications. _____

   _____

348

5. Record here any items you think you might want to add in the future; these would enhance the multifunctionality of your microcomputer system:

_____

_____

_____

_____

6. Additional notes:

KEY TERMS

CHAPTER 12

349

Management
Information
and Computers

transactional matrix 335
multifunctionality 336
user-friendly 337
intelligent terminal 337
nonintelligent terminal 337
leader 337
program 337
software 339
hardware 339
peripherals 339

mainframe 340
memory 340
floppy disk 341
head 341
hard disk 342
spreadsheet 342
template 342
dot matrix printer 345
impact printer 345
laser printer 345

STUDY ASSIGNMENTS FOR REVIEW AND DISCUSSION

1. Why is it mandatory to determine the management information needs of a small business before deciding on the use of a computer system?

2. Describe the transactional matrix. How can it be used for the purpose of defining the management information needs of the small business?

3. What is meant by multifunctionality? What is its importance in the management of the small business?

4. Describe the elements of a microcomputer system. How is the microcomputer different from the minicomputer?

5. What is the function of software in the computer system?

6. Describe the spreadsheet and some typical functions it can serve in the small business.

7. Describe word processing and name some of the functions that may be associated with it.

PROJECTS FOR STUDENTS

This exercise should be performed by students working in teams of two or three:

1. Locate a small business that uses a microcomputer. Ask the owner how the decision was made to install one. Then ask the following questions:

   Did the owner employ a consultant to select a computer? To train personnel to operate it?

   How was the management information needed for selecting a microcomputer determined?

   How was software selected?

SECTION IV

350

Achieving
Proactive
Financial
Management

■ Who operates the computer and how were they trained?

■ What difficulties were encountered and how were they overcome in putting the computer into operation?

■ What purposes is the computer now serving? Does the owner intend to add functions, and what would they be?

■ Has there been any effort to find out if the computer saves money; if so how much per year? Or is the estimate merely a seat-of-the-pants guess?

The student teams should report their findings to the class.

2. All students should collect advertising brochures from several manufacturers of microcomputers and word-processing equipment, and perhaps sophisticated electronic typewriters. List the features they offer. Bring the brochures to class and make one composite list on the blackboard.

IF YOU WANT TO READ MORE

BRADLEY, Charles W.: *Manager's Guide to Small Computers,* Holt, Rinehart and Winston, New York, 1984. This book aims to help the small business owner faced with the perplexing problem of buying a first computer. It discusses the need to make decisions on hardware and software based on sound business principles rather than technical features. The author suggests the use of a request for proposal (RFP) and gives a sample in Chapter 12.

CALMUS, Laurence: *The Business Guide to Small Computers,* McGraw-Hill Book Company, New York, 1984. This text offers an extremely thorough, easy-to-understand guide to selecting a small business computer. The author stresses the importance of detailed planning that precedes the successful implementation of a computer system. Appendixes include helpful measurements and a list of questions to ask before choosing a computer.

COHEN, Jules A., and Catherine Scott McKINSEY,: *How to Microcomputerize Your Business,* Prentice-Hall, Inc., Englewood Cliffs, NJ, 1983. This book, designed primarily as a working guide, may be used as a workbook. It offers specific techniques to find your company's information needs, assess your data-processing capabilities, and select the equipment or services to suit your purposes.

DOLOGITE, D. G.: *Using Small Business Computers,* Prentice-Hall, Inc., Englewood Cliffs, NJ, 1984. The main focus of this book is on applications of small computers; applications are considered computer programs that perform user tasks. Included are step-by-step tutorials offering hands-on experience with electronic spreadsheets, word processing, and database management.

FALK, Howard: *Handbook of Computer Applications for the Small and Medium-sized Business,* Chilton & Co., Huntington Beach, CA, 1983. The author describes in lay terms the workings of a generalized computer system. Without dwelling on technicalities, the text covers the hardware and software selection process. Case histories of business applications are given, ranging from anesthesiology to welding fabrication, which should reassure the small business owner of the feasibility of computer application for the small business.

GARETZ, Mark: *Bits, Bytes and Buzzwords: Understanding Small Business Computers,* New American Library, New York, 1983. A serviceable guide to small business computers, divided into four sections: the makeup of a basic computer system, the peripherals, the software and hardware, and how to buy a computer. A section is given over to buzz words and their definitions. The book avoids overly technical language and even offers some mild humor.

HILLIARD, Brooks R.: *Buying a Computer for Your Growing Business,* Dow Jones–Irwin, Homewood, IL, 1984. This book aims to help the first-time business computer buyer cut through the often misleading sales pitches and tactics to find the right computer. The text covers the many traps in the computer buying process; it discusses computer basics, shopping techniques, negotiating strategies, and system implementation.

HOCKNEY, Donald: *Personal Computers for the Successful Small Business,* Macmillan, New York, 1984. The author outlines a logical, step-by-step procedure for purchasing a computer system that would satisfy the needs of your business. Given throughout the book are guidelines on what features to look for. Also included are extended appendixes reviewing popular and proven personal computers, portable computers, and multiuser systems.

KOLVE, Carolee Nance: *How to Buy (and Survive) Your First Computer,* McGraw-Hill Book Company, New York, 1983. Geared specifically to business computer acquisitions, this book makes easy reading for the mini- or microcomputer consumer. Complete with horror stories and how they could have been avoided, this handbook makes good use of charts and checklists to clarify your needs and expectations. The author emphasizes software compatibility and stresses the need for caution in dealing with "customized" software.

McNICHOLS, Charles W., and Thomas D. CLARK: *Microcomputer-Based Information and Decision Support Systems for Small Business,* Reston Publishing Co., Englewood Cliffs, NJ, 1983. This book offers the concepts needed to decide whether a microcomputer system would be useful in a small business. The text tells which system's components make most sense if the decision is made to automate, and how to implement such a system.

McNITT, Jim: *The Art of Computer Management,* Simon and Schuster, New York, 1984. The author describes the personal computer as the catalyst for the renaissance of small business. The book aims at introducing the basic concepts of personal computing as they apply to three fundamental managerial challenges: office productivity, decision making, and financial controls.

SANDERS, Bruce D.: *Computer Confidence,* Springer-Verlag, New York, 1984. The author is a psychologist who has conducted seminars throughout the United States about the material in this book. He examines what works well and what doesn't in setting up and using computer systems, allowing you to judge the human factors involved before investing time and money in a computer system.

SECTION IV

352

Achieving
Proactive
Financial
Management

SMITH, Brian R.: *The Small Computer in Small Business,* Stephen Greene Press, Brattleboro, VT, 1981. This small book contains a large amount of practical information for the small businessperson who desires to buy a computer. The text gives detailed guidelines for deciding whether buying a computer is justified for a given application. Checklists of pros and cons are included to help the user evaluate and select both hardware and software.

WILCOX, Russell E.: *Computer and Microcomputer Systems for Small Business,* Oryx Press, Phoenix, AZ, 1984. On the basis of his own experiences as a small business owner, the author stresses the importance of business owners learning fundamental things about computers and how to select and install them. The book deals primarily with microcomputer and small minicomputer installations. The text takes a systems approach to their design, installation, and operation.

SECTION V

Buying a Business Opportunity

CHAPTER 13

BUYING A GOING BUSINESS

CHAPTER 14

IS FRANCHISING THE WAY TO GO?

CHAPTER 15

DECIDING ON SOME KEY LEGAL MATTERS

Buying a Going Business[1]

TOPICS IN THIS CHAPTER

Objectives of This Chapter
To Buy or Not to Buy?
Steps in Buying a Business
Finding the Business to Buy
Screening the Offerings in Depth
Avoiding Legal Problems
Picking a Loser
Personal Factors in the Transaction
Evaluating and Pricing the Business
Closing the Deal
Major Points in Buying a Going Business—Summary
Worksheet 13: Buying a Going Business
Key Terms
Study Assignments for Review and Discussion
Projects for Students
If You Want to Read More

Until this point to a large extent our focus has been on starting a business from scratch. But other ways exist to get into business. One way that often presents advantages to the entrepreneur, particularly those with some experience, is to

---

[1]Code numbers referring to the Outline for Developing Your Basic Business Plan (Appendix A) are not used in this chapter. The worksheet in this chapter will guide you through the planning required to assess the desirability of buying an ongoing business. When you have finished Worksheet 13, check the items in Appendix A, point by point, to make sure you haven't omitted any important considerations.

buy a going business. This chapter calls to your attention important factors you should consider in deciding whether or not to buy an existing business.

$$\text{You} + \text{Idea} + \begin{cases} \text{Money} \\ \text{Credit} \end{cases} + \begin{cases} \textbf{FACILITIES} \\ \textbf{PEOPLE} \end{cases} \begin{matrix} \textbf{PRODUCT} \\ \textbf{OR} \\ \textbf{SERVICE} \end{matrix} \rightarrow + \text{Marketing} \begin{cases} \text{Money} \\ \text{Credit} \end{cases} \rightarrow \text{Profit}$$

If you are thinking of buying an established business, you'll want to consider both the benefits it will bring and the problems that inevitably will come with it. Most important, you'll need to be certain the problems are outweighed by benefits that will enable you to make the move a profitable venture.

Objectives of This Chapter

This chapter presents key points for guiding your decisions in buying a going business. The objectives given here focus on major considerations you should weigh in:

- Deciding whether to consider buying a going business

- Finding the business to buy

- Taking steps, from early search to detailed analysis, in screening the company's potential worth

- Studying the possibilities of a "loser" you might turn into a success

- Evaluating the personal factors both you and the seller may be injecting into the deal

---

DAVE ROMNEY, AUTO WRECKER

"Some of my friends said I'd paid ten thousand dollars too much when I bought my auto wrecking business in White Plains," said Dave Romney, newly retired and enjoying life in the Florida sun. "The owner was a middle-aged bachelor who'd been spending more and more time sailing on the Hudson in the three years before I bought. He'd let the business run down; one of his employees managed it in his absence—and it was just barely squeezing out a living for him.

"But I saw opportunity there. I felt I could turn the business around fast. After all, I'd had years of experience in auto wrecking and used parts sales. I could see two major ways to increase profits. One was to concentrate on late model cars by building good relations with insurance companies—offer prime prices for wrecked cars they covered. The other was to get the word around that parts for late model cars were available at my place. I called on the local repair people and put ads in the town papers.

"Well, I was right. The business made good money. Not long ago I sold it—and here I am, my wife and I, quite comfortable as retired senior citizens."

What led Romney to believe he could turn the business around?

What two steps did he take to increase profits?

What Dave Romney had done was to build a run-down business to prosperity through the skills he had achieved in his past experience. If you have the background and can see ways to improve the earning power of the business, you may be able to do what Dave Romney did. In most cases, however, you'd avoid the dying business.

Either way requires detailed study to dig out the facts you need to make up your mind to buy or not to buy.

To Buy or Not to Buy?

Your investigation of going businesses will reveal both advantages and disadvantages in buying. Before you decide to buy, you should make sure that the advantages clearly outweigh the disadvantages, because *one major disadvantage can easily overbalance any number of advantages*.

ADVANTAGES IN BUYING

Significant advantages in buying a going business can be as follows:

- *Reduced risk*. Buying a business that is already successful is less risky than starting one from scratch. The firm has a proved market segment with an established clientele. Management has established sound relations with bankers, suppliers, and customers. If location is important, the business shows by its record that the location is satisfactory. A usable inventory will probably be on hand. And acquiring some experienced and expert employees with the purchase of the business is not uncommon. All these advantages tend to reduce the risks encountered in starting a new business.

- *Profits sooner*. The successful going business will return a profit much faster than the new business. As the buyer, you would not have to struggle through the problems of building a business from the start. You'll recall that most new businesses don't bring in enough money during the first year or so to pay the owner a reasonable salary, if any at all. The going concern can pay you a salary right from the start if you make the transition to ownership smoothly.

- *Planning easier*. Financial and market planning are much easier for the going concern than for the new business venture. Historical records afford a much firmer basis for projecting financial and marketing data than the information gathered in planning for a new venture. Knowing the strengths and weaknesses of the existing company, you'd be able to build on the strengths and overcome the weaknesses. Using the market-product/service matrix described in Chapter 3, for example, you could plan improved or new products or services for further penetration of existing markets, or expansion into new ones. And reference to Chapter 6 will help you to identify the point of the existing product or service in its life cycle, so you can judge when to launch the new product or service.

- *One financial transaction*. The new business venture usually takes more than one financial transaction before it becomes capitalized, well-launched, and stabilized. Buying the going concern, however, can ordinarily be accomplished in one transaction. Once through this you can focus on marketing and delivering the product or service; your energies are concentrated, and you can manage more effectively to achieve the profit you're after.

Nevertheless, where you find advantages, you are more than likely to find disadvantages also.

DISADVANTAGES IN BUYING

Major disadvantages that may occur in buying a going business can be:

- *Inheriting ill-will.* As the buyer, you may inherit ill-will. The product or service may have been allowed to deteriorate, alienating customers. Or the attitude of sales personnel toward customers may have destroyed a good image. In taking over ownership, ill-will can get you off on the wrong foot.

- *Inheriting incompetents.* It is possible to acquire incompetent personnel with the purchase of the going business. Indeed, one reason for owners wanting to sell may be their inability to acquire or hold competent help. This can be a serious flaw in the business. You should check it carefully.

- *Bad precedents.* Some bad precedents in policies, procedures, or customs may be inherited with the business. These could be in external relationships, such as selling to poor credit risks or long delays in paying company bills. Or bad conditions could exist in internal operations, such as not having a consistent and well-understood salary review program for employees, or having unsafe working conditions.

- *Antiquated facilities.* The buildings and equipment may need modernization. Nothing is so frustrating as trying to fit a manufacturing line into chopped-up floor space or turning out accurate screw-machine parts in quantity on an old-fashioned, slow machine. Make sure that the facilities are up to date and adequate for your purpose.

- *Obsolescent inventory.* The inventory of merchandise, raw stock, or supplies may be obsolescent. The usability of inventory is often extremely difficult to determine, yet you should conscientiously make the effort. The seller may be carrying inventory on the books at original value when in fact it may be essentially worthless. If you are not aware of this, you might pay good money for worthless stock.

- *Uncooperative landlord.* In buying a business in leased premises, you may inherit an uncooperative landlord. On occasion, this can be not only exasperating but also frustrating. If you wind up with a landlord who won't make major repairs to plumbing in the plant or repair a leaky roof, you may have to spend precious time in argument, or in legal procedures, which take *both* time and money to get a satisfactory solution.

- *Overpaying.* A major disadvantage in buying can come from overpaying for the business. If you should overpay significantly, you'll find that your profits will be limited. It will take a long time to recover from this hidden loss. You'll need to plan proactively to increase the profitability of the business.

You can see from this list of possible disadvantages in buying a business that you must be sure not to take on any more problems than you have to. What is needed is your careful, systematic study and analysis of the proposed purchase. This doesn't mean that uncovering one or two disadvantages should prevent you from buying the business; if you see your way clear to overcoming a couple of minor disadvantages with effort you can comfortably manage, then you might use them as bargaining points to arrive at a reduced price for the business.

Steps in Buying a Business

You'll go through several phases in assessing and buying a business. The list given here suggests a logical set of steps to follow. These are not necessarily in sequence. You may have to back up a bit on occasion to pick up some details that occur to you as a result of your findings as you go. But this list will give you an overall guide to help you on your way.

LOOK AT YOURSELF

If this is your first venture into business, examine your own entrepreneurial characteristics. Reread Chapter 2 and check your answers to the questions raised in Worksheet 2. Assuming that you're satisfied with your entrepreneurial qualities, you should then answer the next question, about the business.

LOOK AT YOUR BUSINESS EXPERIENCE

What business do you know and like? Recall that we've recommended that you should be technically competent to produce the product or the service. Such competence keeps you clear of the pitfall of trying to learn the business while managing it. It goes without saying that you should really like the business. You'll spend so much time at it that it would be disastrous not to enjoy what you're doing.

Finding the Business to Buy

When you search for a business to buy, you'll find that it takes time and energy. You must be prepared to be patient and to spend some money in the effort. You'll use several sources of information in your search: newspaper and trade journal ads, business brokers, bankers, lawyers, accountants, and people in the business.

ADVERTISEMENTS

Newspapers carry business opportunities advertising. Ads in this category tend to be sketchy, telling little of importance about the business. Here are two examples drawn from a leading metropolitan paper:

LANDSCAPING CO., set up for $1 million operation per year. Undercapitalized. Good business opport. Owner, 919/624-4911.

PAINT SALES (exper. a must) to invest in small but profitable paint mfg. co. Owner to retire. P.O. Box 701, Elk Grove, N.Y., 40905.

As you can see, ads like these don't offer much information. All they do is give you some general idea of what the business is. They say, "Here's a door labeled landscaping or paint sales. Open it and find out, if you're clever enough, what this business really is and what opportunity it offers."

In one case you're to phone the owner; presumably you could arrange an appointment to explore details. In the other case the owner is hiding behind a box number. On inquiry, you may find yourself dealing with a business broker—not the owner. If it turns out to be the owner, you may ask why he or she should choose to hide behind a box number.

Box numbers are used for a variety of reasons. They can conceal the broker behind the number (prospective buyers usually think they can get a better deal directly from the owner). Public advertising of a business for sale can have bad effects on the business. Key employees may decide to leave. Creditors may get edgy, particularly if the firm's credit is shaky. Customers may search for new suppliers if they are uneasy about a firm that's for sale.

Many approaches are used to advertise businesses for sale and to reply to ads. In some cases all parties are frank and open. In others, they are secretive. Both approaches have worked in practice. However, in the overall picture, everyone saves time (and therefore money) by laying the cards on the table. Owners pinpoint the requirements for prospective buyers when they are specific about the business: what kind of business, cash requirements, price, and other important points. Searchers can shorten the search by being frank about what they're looking for, and how much they can pay.

Although frankness may put you on a few sucker lists when you search for a business to buy, it can give you clear advantage not only with owners but also with brokers. Brokers will see that you mean business and are not merely shopping. Knowing what you want, they'll try to find what you're looking for. Their income comes from a percentage on the sales they make—and they don't want to waste time and effort in making a living. One of their most annoying tasks is to rid themselves of prospects who are just shopping—who have no intention of buying.

BUSINESS BROKERS

Your search for a business to buy will inevitably lead you to the business broker. Business brokers work like real estate brokers. They are paid by percentage commission on the sales they arrange. Commissions, regulated by the state, can amount to 10 percent of the sale price.

Business brokerages tend to be small, often one-person operations. In smaller towns and rural areas business listings will often be part of the typical combined real estate and insurance office. In metropolitan areas, brokerage firms may be larger and will often specialize in one kind of business, such as electronics manufacturing or bars and restaurants. Brokers who specialize develop a keen feeling for pricing the business they deal in. For example, one broker who deals in liquor stores, bars, and restaurants, states that these properties are valued at five times their net profit, regardless of the worth of the fixtures, equipment, and furniture. This is one way to judge the worth of a business; for the entrepreneurially minded seeker a better way—setting the price on the future earning power of the business—will be discussed later.

The business brokerage is a service business. It requires little capital to enter. This accounts to a considerable extent for one-person brokerages. Some of these may be seedy operations working from a rented desk in a run-down office building. On the other hand, you'll find well-managed operations that can be of real service to you. You'll want to use several brokers in your search because their small size usually limits the selection of businesses available to them.

GETTING LEADS THROUGH OTHER SOURCES

Don't overlook your ability to get leads through your personal connections. Your banker can be helpful in identifying businesses that can be bought. Through their own experience bankers can direct you to reputable brokerage firms. Your attorney and accountant come across prospective opportunities in their work with their clients. They know when a business client wants to retire and sell or when a business must be sold to settle an estate. Another source of information about a particular business is someone who is familiar with the industry you want to enter. You can usually find such a person by asking among your friends. Suppliers to the business also may prove to be good sources of information. They know what's going on in the industry and can often tip you off to a firm that might be for sale.

POINTERS IN PERSONAL OBSERVATION AND SEARCH

When you have set out in earnest to search for a firm to buy, you'll find it helpful to focus your activities by deciding what business or businesses you will consider, what limitations you'll put on where you want to locate, and what major reasons owners have for selling.

You'll discover that only by the rarest kind of good luck will you be able to locate the business you want in the area where you want to live. This suggests the need for flexibility in your thinking. You'll probably have to compromise to get the best of the available choices. And it may take a long time to find an acceptable compromise. Trying to find the right kind of business in the right place and understanding why people want to sell underlines the need for flexibility and patience. Meeting your needs and those of the seller will take care and study. The effort will be time-consuming. But the payoff can be productive—and profitable.

PRELIMINARY SEARCH

Preliminary search is the next step. The ideal search would locate potential purchases in a business you know and like—and in places where you'd be willing to live.

STAGES OF SCREENING

If things look good at this point, you'd go through the following three stages of screening before you'd consider closing the deal.

First Stage: Rough Screen   Following the preliminary search, you'd use a rough screen to narrow the number of possibilities. Your aim would be to eliminate all but one or two likely businesses for more careful study.

Second Stage: Medium Screen In this step you'd assess the strengths and weaknesses of these concerns. You should concentrate primarily on the three basic requirements we've dealt with in this text. How do the businesses you are considering shape up in technical, marketing, and financial management qualifications?

Third Stage: Fine Screen Once you've satisfied yourself on the performance of a company in the foregoing respects, you would conduct a fine screening. At this time, you'd make a carefully detailed analysis of the financial and management history of the company. And you'd prepare your own projections of *what you could expect the business to do for you after you buy it*. You should take into account the seller's biases, and your personal desires. Your ultimate goal would be to arrive at an acceptable price for the business.

CLOSING THE DEAL

In the final step, you'd close the deal. At this time you should get the help of your attorney and your accountant to take care of the many details of legal and tax issues. They will protect your interests in buying the business.

Screening the Offerings in Depth

The foregoing three levels of screening should be done whether you are looking for a retail, manufacturing, service, or other kind of firm. And as you might expect, you'll go into greater detail as you conduct these levels of investigation.

PRELIMINARY SCREENING

In your first-stage investigation, you'll visit and inspect the premises and operation and interview the seller. In interviewing, the trick is to get the owner to talk—to listen *actively* to what you hear. In a productive interview the interviewee is encouraged to do 90 percent of the talking. Listen for discrepancies and distortions; let the owner talk, but when you want to check a point, guide the conversation by a well-chosen question. The owner will try to make a positive (and usually glowing) sales pitch. This need not bother you because you'll search for hard data that will allow you to form your own opinion in the checking you'll do later. Your task will be to remember the main points and to try to verify them.

SOME SUGGESTIONS FOR PRELIMINARY SCREENING QUESTIONS

Here are some suggested questions you might use in talking with the owner during preliminary screening. They are keyed to the three basic areas we've addressed in this book.

About the Business

▪ Tell me a little about yourself, your background and experience.

▪ How did you happen to get into this business?

Do you own the business yourself, or are you a partnership or corporation? If a partnership, how many partners and who are they? If a corporation, how many shareholders: Who owns controlling interest and how much? How much stock has been authorized and how much has been issued?

About Financial Aspects

May I see your income statements for the past 3 years—and your income tax returns for the past 5 years?

May I see a tab run on the value of your existing inventory?

What value would you put on your fixtures and equipment or machinery?

About how much does your payroll run per month?

About Marketing

Tell me about your product or service. What would you say are its special features or advantages?

Show me how you've promoted and advertised your business.

Tell me about your competition. Who are your toughest competitors?

General Information

How many people do you have working for you? Who are your most valuable people? How long have they been with you?

Tell me why you want to sell the business. (*Note:* Do not ask questions that can be answered by a *yes* or *no*. Only occasionally do you want a yes or no answer; your main purpose is to get information, and by asking open-ended questions you'll encourage the owner to talk. The foregoing questions are guides. Other points will come to you as you ask these. Follow–up questions will then suggest themselves, and you should ask them.)

Observe the Premises   Are things neat and tidy? If a retail store, is the interior attractive? Would you like to walk into the store as a prospective customer? If a manufacturing operation, is the shop well laid out? Does the flow of the manufacturing process follow the recommendations made in Chapter 9? How efficiently is inventory managed? If a service organization, how are client contacts made, and how are jobs scheduled? Do procedures ensure adequate attention to the needs of customers? You should raise and answer questions like these in your preliminary survey of the business.

Financial Data   Before you leave, make a first check of financial data. Ask to see a current balance sheet: What assets does the business own and what liabilities does it owe? Look at income statements for the last 2 or 3 years, and the current one too.

Does the income show a seasonal pattern? Or is it steady by the month? Check several years of income tax statements, the last 5 years if the company has been in business that long. And by all means, get copies of these items to take along with you for further study.

SECOND-STAGE SCREENING

Your purpose in the second-stage screening will be to eliminate unpromising prospects. Several considerations will help you to narrow your choices.

The Facilities   Are they adequate to serve the needs of the business, at least to start with? If so, you can plan to add equipment, tools, or other facilities as you see the necessity or desirability.

Estimated Financial Strength   Another check you should make is to compare financial ratios of the company against those of others in the same business. See the section, "Using Ratio Analysis," in Chapter 11 for suggestions on how to use ratio analysis. Ratios that differ widely from those customary would raise red flags pointing to the need for careful investigation of underlying causes; comparative financial data afford the chance to verify the internal financial strength of the firm you're considering.

Character of the Investment   If you're assessing a small corporation, it is important that you know who owns the stock. Your investment would be essentially nonmarketable should a small group of shareholders own more than half the stock.

Capital Requirements   You'll want to estimate the capital you'll require to keep yourself out of trouble in taking on the business. You should judge the potential of the business for growth—and your assessment of the capital you'll need should include an allotment to support such growth.

Qualifications of Personnel   Do you believe the personnel you may be acquiring with the business have the potential to grow with the business if you buy it? Are they reliable? Would you feel comfortable for the long haul in working with them? Can you trust them without question? If so, you'll acquire an asset of great worth. If not, you should face the issue of staffing the business with help you can rely on.

The Marketing Program   Look carefully at the program the company has been following. Check the market segment the business has been serving. Does it seem right for the business? Can you see ways to expand the market? Check back on the product-service market matrix given in Chapter 3 and the product or service life cycle given in Chapter 6 to see the possibilities in the existing market and in developing new markets. Read through the discussions on marketing, Chapters 4 through 6, to pick up important points to check. This review will prepare you to examine the marketing questions you'll want to study thoroughly, not only in this second stage of your investigation, but also in the third stage.

Some Special Questions   These final questions should be answered to the best of your ability at this second stage of investigation: (1) What exactly would you be buying? Would it be physical assets such as plant and machinery, a fully equipped retail store, patents that have real value, goodwill in an existing clientele of repeat customers, an exclusive franchise in an established chain of fast-food outlets, or other assets? (2) If you can trust the accuracy of the financial records you've got, would the business be a profitable investment at the asking price? If not, what is your best estimate of a proper price?

Finally, in view of your answers to these questions, would you be better off by starting a new venture than by buying the existing business?

If your answers to these questions suggest the advisability of more detailed investigation, you'd be ready to do a final study of your possible purchase.

FINAL SCREENING

Although you may approach the final screening of the business from any of many points of view, we suggest that an effective start can be made by analyzing the market that the business serves. We recommend that you follow the procedures given in Chapters 4 through 6, which cover market feasibility analysis in sequence and in detail. When you review the subjects presented in these chapters, you'll prepare yourself to answer the questions they raise. You'll find numerous hints and suggestions about points you'll want to check to satisfy yourself in deciding about present marketing effectiveness and the potential for making significant improvements in the marketing effort.

If you're examining the possibilities of buying a service business, read Chapter 8 for pointers. Pay particular attention to the unique aspects of the service business—its intangibility, the need to maintain a consistently high level of performance, the special requirements in advertising and promotion, and the importance of setting the right price for the service. In Chapter 8 you'll find guidelines that will help you assess the effectiveness of the existing business in meeting these needs. And you are very likely to see ways to make improvements should you buy the business.

LOOKING AT INTANGIBLE ASSETS AND LIABILITIES

The intangible assets of the company, particularly in the service business, may be the most important part of the package you'd be buying. Some typical questions you'll want to answer are these:

- What kind of image does the existing business project, quite favorable or unfavorable? What kind of reputation does the company have with its suppliers, customers, and banker?

- Are there negative things about the product or service you'd have to overcome?

- Is the business dependent upon special skills or personal relations the present owner shows with customers? If so, could you acquire them upon buying the business?

If any of these factors are adverse, you should think hard about what you would have to do to overcome them. Changing the image or reputation of a company may be quite possible if you can apply the elements of proactive management we've stressed throughout this book. If the task looks overwhelming after due study, you'd probably be better off starting a new business.

EVALUATING PHYSICAL ASSETS

Any business you are contemplating buying will have some kind of equipment that you'll want to evaluate. Appraise what's offered cautiously. Whether it's in a small manufacturing plant, a retail store, or a service facility, examine the equipment to find out if it's in good shape, modern, and really suitable for the function intended.

▨ Can you see ways to improve productivity or profitability by adding modern equipment or changing procedure or process?

▨ How much would the machinery or equipment bring as used merchandise?

Appraisal of this kind will give you a realistic value of the physical assets and put you in a sound position to negotiate for the business.

SOURCES OF EVALUATION

If you have need for information upon which to evaluate the physical assets of the business, you can turn to sources such as the following for help.

▨ Land and buildings. Professional real estate appraisers offer their services for a fee. These are people certified by the state as qualified to estimate realistically the value of land and property. To locate them, check with your bank, the local real estate association, and the chamber of commerce, and search the classified ads in local newspapers. These same sources can help you judge the fairness of the rental or leasing terms of property you may want to occupy. In this case, do not overlook talking with neighboring store or property renters to see what they pay.

▨ Equipment or machinery. Metropolitan areas have businesses that deal in secondhand equipment and machinery. You can estimate the value of these items in the business you're studying by spending a bit of time with these secondhand dealers. You can often get the kind of data you want by consulting the trade association in the business you're interested in. If you have access to a metropolitan area, you can attend auctions of equipment or machinery from defunct stores or machine shops and get a clear idea of what the items you're evaluating are worth.

Avoiding Legal Problems

Be sure to check legal issues that can be critical in buying a business. The following questions will suggest points to be investigated in your assessment of the business you're thinking of buying:

▨ Does the business have any encumbrances against it or the property such as mortgages, legal judgments, liens, zoning restrictions, environmental requirements, or condemnation proceedings?

What is the status of patents, trademarks, service marks, copyrights, and logos owned by the company?

Does the company have clear title to land and buildings? What are the terms and conditions of existing leases on buildings, machinery and equipment, trucks or automobiles?

Are there any restrictions on free access to alleys, driveways, or streets? Is there adequate parking space?

How can you deal with ongoing contracts to buy or sell goods?

Will you experience any problems in getting city, state, or federal licenses to do business? This can be an especially critical issue in food, drug, and liquor businesses.

Can you ensure that all outstanding debts, accounts payable, notes payable, or other outstanding obligations are shown on the books?

These are typical subjects for investigation. You'll become aware of other significant items you'll want to look into when you study the worksheet at the ends of the chapters in this book. Your lawyer and your accountant can give you the expert help you'll need to check the legal issues involved in buying the ongoing business you're considering. Be sure to draw on their help.

Picking a Loser

For some persons it makes good sense to pick a loser. If you can find a company in which you can clearly identify opportunities the present management can't see, and you are certain of your ground, you may find it profitable to buy. Once more we must point out the importance of technical competence. You must know the business well enough to see how to move it toward the achievement you want.

Your study of possibilities for turning the business around can start with the concepts of the market-product/service matrix of Chapter 3. This will help you see how the existing market may be expanded or how you may gain new market segments.

In considering the possibilities, you would be wise to think as if you were starting a new company. Go through the stages of market analysis and financial projections we've given in this book. When you have arrived at what is essentially a prospectus for a new business, on the basis of data gathered from the existing business, you'll have a sound background upon which to form your *buy* or *reject* decision.

Personal Factors in the Transaction

When looking for a business to buy, you, the buyer, and the seller too, bring personal factors to the transaction. When you have some understanding of these factors and their implications, you're in a better position to negotiate and have the deal meet your expectations.

PERSONAL FACTORS THE SELLER INJECTS

The seller will probably have legitimate and, more than likely, hidden reasons for selling. Your problem is to do the best you can to uncover and understand both. Some of the reasons the owner wants to sell can be these:

- The owner may want to retire because of ill health or old age, and therefore to convert the business into cash.

- The owner does not have the desire to learn to be a professional manager, as the growth of the company demands, and prefers to cash out and start another business.

- The owner has been unable for financial or for personal reasons to arrange for adequate management succession.

- The company has grown so fast it needs an infusion of capital, which the owner can't find.

- The company is experiencing a diminishing market and the owner doesn't know how to cope with it.

- The technology of the business is changing rapidly and the owner is unable to adapt to its complexity, which may require the acquisition of new skills or a massive capital investment.

- The owner fears that the product or service is obsolescent and can't be improved or replaced.

- Fear about the financial future of the business and the family may trigger the owner's desire to sell. The owner may be poor in cash but rich in the resources of the company—and sees converting the assets to cash as the way out.

PERSONAL FACTORS THE BUYER INJECTS

Just as the seller has personal reasons for wanting to sell, so you, the buyer, will have your own special factors that will influence the deal. You'll want to compare the prospective return on your investment against other forms of investment. Does the return compare favorably with those available from stocks, bonds, rental property, or Treasury bills? Would you be able to draw a reasonable salary for actively managing the company, perhaps including some perquisites, or fringe benefits, such as a company car, season tickets to sports events or theater, boat, or the like? If the foregoing seem to be favorable, you might be willing to pay a little more for the company than you would under other circumstances.

Or perhaps your own special desires would lead you to offer a somewhat higher price than you would otherwise. You may understand the business and like it. You may want to live in the area where the business is located. You may have any of a number of other personal requirements that would cause you to offer a substantial price for the business. Only you can judge the impact of such personal factors on the price you're willing to pay.

Evaluating and Pricing the Business

SECTION V

370

Buying a
Business
Opportunity

If you're not thoroughly experienced in the business you're considering buying, you should get the help of an expert broker or consultant in valuing the business. This person would be a member of your "buying team," which might well include an accountant, lawyer, facility appraiser, and banker. You could draw upon their advice as needed during your study and analysis of the various aspects of the business previously described.

You may set the price for buying a business in three different ways, depending on your point of view or the circumstances in which the business exists. The business can have any of these three values: its *liquidation value,* its *market price,* or its value as an *investment* capable of producing profit.

LIQUIDATION VALUE

The liquidation value (sometimes called the doomsday value) is the lowest. It is computed from a pessimistic estimate of what the tangible assets would bring at a forced sale. These assets include accounts receivable reduced to a reasonably safe value, machinery and equipment figured at secondhand prices, and inventory estimated at distressed prices for quick sale. The total would represent the value in case of bankruptcy.

MARKET PRICE

The market price for a going business reflects the rule-of-thumb estimate of the business broker. Although this estimate can be helpful, it is important to know that exceptions to the rule abound. Some hardheaded business brokers' ways of judging the price for typical small businesses, as quoted by Thomas P. Murphy, follow.[2]

Franchised Business   Where a contract is signed for protected territory, set the price at the amount of 1 year's net profit plus the inventory at cost.

Bakery and Pastry Business   A 6-day operation with $1000 weekly gross sales is worth $10,000; $1500 weekly gross is worth $15,000 to $17,000; and a bakery or pastry shop with $2000 weekly gross is worth $25,000 to $30,000.

Manufacturing Concern with Product Involved   Pay the appraised value of machinery plus the actual cost of raw materials, packing materials, and finished goods; also add to the price from $1/2$ to 1 year's net profit.

Restaurant   Pay replacement value of equipment plus food inventory at cost, plus one-half annual net profit.

---

[2]Thomas P. Murphy, *A Business of Your Own,* McGraw-Hill Book Company, New York, 1956, pp. 184–185. In these pages the rules of thumb for market pricing some small businesses are quoted from the experience of a well-qualified New York business broker. Although this book was published in the mid-fifties, the concepts and ratios quoted are still useful; inflation has raised the dollar amounts but has not changed the relationships.

Service Business   *Example:* Dry-cleaning pickup store (not plant or unit). Pay $3500 for every $100 per week of net income to $250. Pay $5000 for every $100 weekly net over $250.

Soft Goods and Ladies' Ready-to-Wear   Pay 25 to 50 percent of cost of fixtures plus inventory at 50 to 100 percent depending on salability, styles, and brand names. Very little goodwill is usually paid in this classification.

These rules of thumb are just that—rough estimates. Nevertheless, they can be helpful in estimating a fair price for the business you want to buy. Note that these approaches don't allow for goodwill. The underlying assumption is that the business for sale is in a bad way financially. Although this approach may give you some idea of the price for a business, it will not meet your personal needs for buying for profit.

Another approach to estimating the range of fair market price for a business is given in Table 13-1. In this guide, net income is considered earnings before interest expense and income taxes but includes the salary, if any, of the seller.

When shares are bought in a corporation, the quantities given in columns 3, 4, and 5 are usually included in the net book values as shown in corporation statements. Therefore, only the information given in column 2 should be used. The multiplier would be applied to the adjusted net income. For example, assume the book value for a large manufacturing firm is $100,000. Column 2 shows the multiplier as $1\frac{1}{2}$ to 3 times net. If the net income is $50,000, using the lower multiplier of $1\frac{1}{2}$ gives a value of $1\frac{1}{2}$ times $50,000, or $75,000. Adding $75,000 to the book value of $100,000 results in a sales price of $175,000. If the multiplier at the high end had been used, the sales price would be three times $50,000 plus $100,000, or $250,000. The range of sales price in this case would be from $175,000 to $250,000.

The information in all the columns, 2 through 5, would be used in buying the assets of a small company.

You should be aware that these data give a rule-of-thumb way of estimating selling-price ranges. The actual price will be set by your negotiation with the seller, as we have recommended throughout this chapter.

BUYING FOR PROFIT

You will note that the liquidation and rule-of-thumb methods rely on appraisal of the physical assets. We recommend a third way, which seems to fit the entrepreneur much better. That is to set the price on the basis of the business's power to make profit. You should figure profit after deducting a reasonable salary for your efforts in running the business. The profits of the business should be at least equal to or better than what you could earn by investing an amount equal to the purchase price in securities, mortgages, or other worthy investments.

The next two steps outline the procedure for arriving at a price for the business. This price is based on the future earning power of the business.

Step 1. Assess the company's power to earn.

Step 2. Capitalize these earnings at a rate in keeping with the risks involved in the business. (Capitalization means the sum total of the owner's investment and the borrowed capital invested in the business. Sometimes it is defined as the owner's equity plus the long-term debt of the business.)

TABLE 13-1

A Guide to the Evaluation of Small Business (Under 2 Million in Gross Sales)

1 Type of Business	2 Guide to Price Multiplier	3 Inventory	4 Fixtures and Equipment	5 Hard Assets: Cash, Accounts Receivable, Real Estate, etc.	Check the Following, and *Use Common Sense*
Full-service car wash	1 year's gross income	Add	Include	Add	Labor and utility bills may verify income
Coin-operated business	1/2 to 1 year's gross income	Add	Include	Add	Utility bills and supplies verify income
Liquor stores	3 to 5 × 1 month's gross + license	Add	Include	Add	Check sales tax receipts
Beer bars	3 × 1 month's gross	Add	Include	Add	Verify cases and barrels bought
Cocktail lounge	3 to 4 × 1 month's gross + license	Add	Include	Add	Verify cases of liquor, beer, and wine bought
Fast foods	1 year's net income	Add	Include	Add	Personally count people at different times and register receipts
Full-service restaurants	1 to 1 1/2 year's net + license	Add	Include	Add	Verify food and liquor bought
Small retail	1 year's net	Add	Include	Add	Check sales tax receipts. Have professional company take inventory
Large retail or chain	1 to 2 × net	Add	Add	Add	Check sales tax receipts. Have professional company take inventory
Small manufacturing	1 to 1 3/8 × net	Add	Include	Add	Check if line is too limited
Large manufacturing, over 1 million gross	1 1/2 to 3 × net	Add	Include	Add	Is line too large? Check for outdated inventory
Small distributor	1 to 2 × net	Add	Include	Add	Same as small manufacturing
Large distributor, over 1 million	1 1/2 to 3 × net	Add	Add	Add	Same as large manufacturing
Service business	1 to 2 × net	Include	Include	Add	Check contracts if any
Phone-answering service	3 to 4 × net	Include	Include	Add	Is there a rapid turnover of employees?
Insurance	1 1/2 to 3 × net	Include	Include	Add	Is bonus included in gross? Is company rated?
C.P.A., M.D.s, etc., professionals	1 1/2 to 2 × net	Add	Add	Add	How long will seller stay with you?
Auto and appliance repair	1 year's net	Add	Add	Add	Are customers happy, and how many repeats?
Bookkeeping service	1/2 year's gross	Include	Add	Add	Will seller stay on for 1 year?
Beauty and barber shops	25 to 50% of 1 year's gross	Add	Add	Add	Check turnover of help
Employment agency	1/2 of 1 year's gross	Include	Include	Add	Any contracts with large companies and repeats?

TABLE 13-1

(Continued)

1 Type of Business	2 Guide to Price Multiplier	3 Inventory	4 Fixtures and Equipment	5 Hard Assets: Cash, Accounts Receivable, Real Estate, etc.	Check the Following, and *Use Common Sense*
Florist shop	$1/4$ to $1/2$ year's gross	Add	Add	Add	How many repeats and how many commercial accounts?
Newspaper	1 year's gross	Add	Add	Add	50% of lineage should be paid advertising
Publishing company	$1 1/2$ to $2 \times$ year's net	Add	Add	Add	Industrial better than retail book type
Pet shop	$1/2$ year's net	Add	Add	Add	Pet supplies are important for profit
Print shop	$1/2$ to 1 year's net	Add	Add	Add	Check equipment if modern, and are clients industrial?
Real estate office	$1/2$ of 1 year's gross commission	Include	Include	Add	How long have salespeople been there?
Travel agency	$1/2$ of 1 year's gross commission	Include, if any	Include	Add	How long have salespeople been there?

Source: Reproduced by permission of Lester L. Lynch, president, American Acquisitions, Inc., Encino, CA.

To estimate the future earnings of the business, you should analyze the earnings of the business from income statements for at least the past 5 years. Make adjustments for nonrecurring items that you would not expect to encounter in the future. These could include such expenses as the purchase of a patent or the purchase of a special machine tool. Deduct unusually large bad debts, inventory write-offs for obsolete merchandise or supplies, and excessive salaries. Estimate the reduction in earnings from the impact of raising low salaries that would have to be increased to hire good help. Take note of the accounting procedure used; it can have a direct effect on reported earnings. For example, one company may charge off the whole cost of tools, jigs, dies, or fixtures in the year bought; another may amortize these costs over several years, thereby increasing earnings.

Two methods for estimating bad-debt losses are commonly used. One is based on a percentage of sales, the other on percentages of accounts receivable. In the first method, if you've had experience in the business, you'd apply a percentage to the sales figures for a given period, perhaps a year. This percentage would come from your knowledge. For example, in the retail book business credit losses are usually very small, the national average being one-tenth of 1 percent. However, department stores may run as high as 6 percent.

Under the second method, accounts due are grouped by age. A very small percentage of expected loss would be assigned to those accounts 1 month or less old, a somewhat higher percent to those 2 months in arrears, and so on. The percentage used for each group must come from judgment backed by experience. If you are familiar with the characteristics of the particular business, you could use this method. By and large, the assignment of a straight percent for the yearly gross sales, as in the first method, would be the most appropriate for your purpose. If you have doubts about the percentage the owner might supply, you should rely on your banker, accountant, or trade association to supply this figure.

Gauging the worth of inventory can be treacherous. Coming in as an outsider you don't have the intimate knowledge of the worth of the merchandise, stock, components, raw materials, or work in process that the owner has. The owner is in a position to gloss over the true current worth of the inventory and to give you a blown-up value. If your knowledge of the business is up to date and you can get an accurate count of inventory, you'd be able to estimate the true worth of the inventory quite accurately. If you have any doubts, your best bet would be to hire a qualified consultant to do this for you. You can find expert help in many cities—from retail merchandising consultants to industrial engineers who can perform this service for you.

As the buyer, you should adjust for nonrecurring items and varying accounting practices to judge what future earnings might be *under your management*. The return on your investment (ROI) must come from future earnings.

You can start, as we've indicated, on the basis of adjusted historical earnings. But you should project for 5 years ahead, figuring as the business *would be run under your management*. The following is a case in point:

GAUSS ELECTROMECHANICAL, INC.

Gauss ElectroMechanical, Inc., is a small, closely held family corporation. The company is noted for the accurately controllable temperature chambers it manufactures for experimental scientific purposes. Adolph Gauss is the president and chief executive officer. When asked about his experiences in buying the company, he came up with some pertinent and valuable comments for those thinking of buying a going concern.

"I was extremely cautious in buying this company. I tried to follow all the advice you professors put in your books. I went down the checklists and checked everything I could think of. Here are some key data I put together to arrive at an estimated price for the business.

"First," Gauss said, "I put together the sales and profit picture for the 5 years before I took over. It looked like this:

Year	Annual Gross Sales	Net After Taxes	Net Profit, %
1980	$1,199,600	$63,578	5.3
1979	1,069,600	60,967	5.7
1978	930,552	45,597	4.9
1977	809,580	45,336	5.6
1976	655,760	34,099	5.2

"As you can see, it shows a reasonably consistent growth and profit picture for these 5 years. I felt that with my experience in business, and with some expert help, I could capture a good part of the special market we serve.

"As the next steps toward setting the price for buying the business, I did an intensive market study; I studied the plant and production facilities; I looked at the level of the work in process—and the inventory of raw stock and components.

"And then I thought about what I wanted from the deal. I concluded that I wanted a return on my investment—an ROI—at least comparable with what I could get in a substantial investment in solid bonds or money market funds, for instance, at the current rate of about 15 percent.

"Finally, here's how I priced the business. I thought I could improve the profitability of the business through my management; therefore, I could make my estimate on the basis of the most recent numbers, those of 1980."

Here Gauss handed over another sheet of paper:

Estimated Price for the Business
(all figures rounded)

3 times net profit after taxes, 3 × 63,578	$190,000
Accounts receivable	85,000
Fixtures and production equipment	30,000
Inventory of work in process, raw stock and	
components	55,000
Real estate: building plus land	75,000
Estimated price	$435,000

"And $435,000 is what I negotiated to pay."

Note that the method Mr. Gauss used for calculating the selling price is that given in Table 13-1 for a manufacturing concern doing over $1 million gross annual business. A 7-step procedure, a variation of this approach, will be found in Table 13-2.

You can follow the recommendations we've given in this book for the needed proactive management planning in the critical financial variables. These should include at least the following:

Identification and analysis of the market segment or segments suitable for the business

The assumptions upon which you base your financial estimates

Balance sheets

Cash-flow projections

Income statements

TABLE 13-2

Suggested Price Formula

	Business A	Business B
Step 1: Determine the adjusted tangible net worth of the business (the total value of all current and long-term assets less liabilities)		
1. Adjusted value of tangible net worth (assets less liabilities)	$50,000	$50,000
2. Earning power—at 10%*—of an amount equal to the adjusted tangible net worth if invested in a comparable-risk business, security, etc.	5,000	5,000
3. Reasonable salary for owner-operator in the business	12,000	12,000
4. Net earnings of the business over recent years—this means net profit before subtracting owner's salary	20,000	15,500
5. Extra earning power of the business (line 4 minus lines 2 and 3)	3,000	−1,500
6. Value of intangibles using 3-year profit figure for moderately well-established firm (3 times	9,000	None
7. Final price (lines 1 and 6)	$59,000	$50,000 (or less)

Step 1: Determine the adjusted tangible net worth of the business (the total value of all current and long-term assets less liabilities)

Step 2: Estimate how much the buyer could earn annually with an amount equal to the value of the tangible net worth invested elsewhere

Step 3: Add to this a salary normal for an owner-operator of the business. This combined figure provides a reasonable estimate of the income the buyer can earn elsewhere with the investment and effort involved in working in the business

Step 4: Determine the average annual net earnings of the business (net profit before subtracting owner's salary) over the past few years. This is before income taxes, to make it comparable with earnings from other sources or by individuals in different tax brackets. (The tax implications of alternate investments should be carefully considered.) The trend of earnings is a key factor. Have they been rising steadily, falling steadily, remaining constant, or fluctuating widely? The earnings figure should be adjusted to reflect these trends

Step 5: Subtract the total of earning power (2) and reasonable salary (3) from this average net earnings figure (4). This gives the extra earning power of the business

Step 6: Use this extra, or excess, earning figure to estimate the value of the intangibles. This is done by multiplying the extra earnings by what is termed the "years of profit" figure. This "years of profit" multiplier pivots on these points. How unique are the intangibles offered by the firm? How long would it take to set up a similar business and bring it to this stage of development? What expenses and risks would be involved? What is the price of goodwill in similar firms? Will the seller be signing a noncompetitive agreement? If the business is well-established, a factor of 5 or more might be used, especially if the firm has a valuable name, patent, or location. A multiplier of 3 might be reasonable for a moderately seasoned firm. A younger, but profitable, firm might merely have a 1-year profit figure

Step 7: Final price = adjusted tangible net worth + value of intangibles (extra earnings × years of profit)

In business A, the seller gets a substantial value for intangibles (goodwill) because the business is moderately well established and earning more than the buyer could earn elsewhere with similar risks and effort. Within 3 years the buyer should have recovered the amount paid for goodwill in this example

TABLE 13-2

(Continued)

CHAPTER 13

377

Buying a
Going Business

In business B, the seller gets no value for goodwill because the business, even though it may have existed for a considerable time, is not earning as much as the buyer could through outside investment and effort. In fact, the buyer may feel that even an investment of $50,000—the current appraised value of net assets—is still too much because it cannot earn a sufficient return on investment

*This is just an arbitrary figure, used for illustration. A reasonable figure depends on the stability and relative risks of the business and the investment picture generally. The rate should be similar to that which could be earned elsewhere with the same approximate risk.
Source: Reprinted with permission from Bank of America, NT&SA, "How to Buy or Sell a Business," *Small Business Reporter,* copyright, 1969.

From these statements you can capitalize the business's earning power. The higher the risk of generating projected earnings, the lower should be the capitalization rate. In a business considered to be high-risk, the return customarily expected ranges from 15 to 20 percent; in a business of moderate risk, 5 to 10 percent. Here's an example of how this might work, a comparison of two companies, each earning $50,000 per year on a current basis:

Company A	Company B
Small specialty paint manufacturer	Small pest control company
Established 10 years	Established 3 years
Steady growth for last 7 years	Growing slowly, but not firmly established
Highly favorable prospects for future	Highly competitive industry
Might be capitalized at 20 times earnings, or $1,000,000	Buyer would need a high ROI, perhaps 20%; might be capitalized at 5 times earnings, or $250,000

In this example, the lower-risk paint manufacturer would be worth four times more than the higher-risk pest control company would seem to be. The results of analyses such as these reflect what might be called internal variables of the business. Before beginning negotiations to buy it, you would be wise to weigh external factors in modifying the rate of capitalization.

External Factors in Setting the Capitalization Rate After you've found the capitalization rate as described in the foregoing section, you should check the impact of external forces on the business. You may find factors here that would cause you to modify your first estimate of capitalization rate. In Chapter 4 we outlined several environmental forces that could cause sudden change in a business: economic, political or legal, technological, social or cultural, and competitive. What effect could any of these forces have on the business you're thinking of buying? Refer to Appendix A, Outline for Developing Your Basic Business Plan, particularly item 3, Background of Proposed Business, for clues to details on the possible effects on the business of changes in the above forces. It might be disastrous, for example, to buy a business specializing in the manufacture of a proprietary herbicide if the Food and Drug Administration has plans to prohibit that product from being marketed. Similarly, it would be a grave error to buy a retail nursery without knowing that it was in the path of a proposed freeway. Changes in any of these external forces can have serious effects on the proposed business.

SELLING—PRICE FORMULAS

We have indicated previously some rules of thumb for setting the price for several kinds of retail businesses. In most businesses there are no such guidelines. What is needed, as we have said, is a way of arriving at a proper price on the basis of the present earning power and the potential for profit in the future *under your management*. The Bank of America suggests a useful formula, which is given in Table 13-2.

One stumbling block that often poses a problem in using a formula such as this is goodwill. Goodwill, the value of intangibles, is defined by the U.S. Treasury Department as "the value attached to a business over and above the value of the physical property." The assumption behind the concept of goodwill is that the firm has developed a clientele of repeat customers, who are a valuable, although intangible, asset.

As the buyer, you should deal with the question of goodwill with reasonable skepticism. The past effort of the owner in building effective customer relations will undoubtedly be seen in a high figure for goodwill. However, the future earning power of the business should be the key variable in estimating the worth, if any, of the goodwill. Table 13-2 gives two examples of how to treat the evaluation of goodwill, one showing it at substantial worth, the other at no worth.

Closing the Deal

Assuming that you've done the analysis and have considered your personal requirements and the other key points made in this chapter, you're ready to close the deal. Don't work alone in this final step. Legal requirements and tax implications tend to be much too complicated for the nonexpert; you'll want expert counsel in these matters.

You should consider the impact of taxes on the method of payment. Some ways are available for reducing the tax load—effecting savings—in choosing the method of payment. For example, if you make a smaller down payment and incur interest on the balance, you may deduct the interest in figuring income taxes. Or you can reduce the purchase price and take on the previous owner as a salaried employee or consultant. Here, too, the expense would be deductible. With a noncompeting agreement with the seller for a definite period of time, a value may be set on the agreement and payment for it may be deducted over the life of the agreement.

As we've said, consult your attorney and accountant in closing the deal. Follow your entrepreneurial inclinations—get the best counsel you can to ensure that your interests are well served in this final phase of buying the business.

Major Points in Buying a Going Business

Summary

Buying a going business has both advantages and disadvantages. The trick is to ensure that the advantages can make for a profitable outcome. To evaluate the potential of the going business, your investigation should follow essentially the same pattern you'd use if you were starting a new business.

Study of the pertinent chapters and the appendixes in this text will allow you to arrive at key ideas, methods, and techniques to:

■ Raise important questions you may not otherwise hit upon

■ See how to analyze significant factors in the operations of the business

■ Make the necessary projections in marketing and financial planning to estimate future earnings of the business

You'll find that the potential earning power of the business is very likely to be the pivotal factor in your decision to buy—and in your decision about the price you'd be willing to pay.

You'll protect your interests by going through several steps in studying a business to buy. After you're sure of your own qualifications to run the business you're attracted to, you'll screen the deal in more and more detail as you gather information and numbers. When you're reasonably sure that physical, financial, and marketing data look sound, you'll check to clear away any existing legal problems.

Some entrepreneurs can do well by picking a loser—if they have the necessary experience in the particular business and can see how to make it a winner. If this description fits you, you may find it advantageous to buy a run-down business and turn it around through your special skill.

Remember that both you and the owner bring personal factors to the deal. Your task is to uncover the owner's hidden reasons for selling. You must then see how to overcome any problems posed by these reasons. If you're sure you can solve them and you feel good about the prospects of the business, you'll choose to close the deal.

We've pointed out several avenues for finding the business to buy. Among these are ads in newspapers and trade journals; services of business brokers; contacts with bankers, lawyers, and accountants; talks with owners and managers in similar businesses, and those who supply the business with goods and services.

When you've selected a business to buy, you'll need to evaluate and price it.

We've suggested that a business can be valued in three ways: (1) at its liquidation value, (2) at its market price, or (3) at its value as an investment. We recommended the third way, buying for earning power. We've outlined several ways of estimating the price for the business, including recognized selling-price formulas. Unless the deal is unique in its prospect for profit, the entrepreneur would be well advised to buy a going business on the basis of its potential to earn a profit appropriate to the investment.

In closing the deal, you should work with the professionals on your buying team as you need them, with particular help from your accountant and attorney.

Buying a Going Business

You'll find that the text of this chapter carries the questions you should answer in each of the sections listed below. We've allowed space under each heading for your answers to the questions given under that heading within the chapter.

TO BUY OR NOT TO BUY

I've studied the first sections of this chapter and have decided that buying a going business is right for me.

▪ I've searched and identified a business I might want to buy.

Name of company _____

Individual proprietorship _____ Partnership _____ Corporation _____.

Principals _____

_____

Address _____

Phone _____

ADVANTAGES IN BUYING

▪ Here are the advantages I see in buying:

_____

_____

_____

_____

_____

DISADVANTAGES IN BUYING

▪ Here are the disadvantages I see in buying:

_____

_____

_____

_____

_____

PRELIMINARY SCREENING

■ In this first stage of investigation, I've visited the premises, interviewed the seller, and observed the operation of the business. Here's some background data on the business:

_____

_____

_____

_____

_____

SECOND-STAGE SCREENING

■ What needs to be done to the facilities to fit them for the business as I project it under my ownership:

_____

_____

_____

_____

_____

■ I've made a preliminary check of the financial condition of the company. I have copies of the following: current balance sheet __; income statements for the past __years; income tax statements for the past __years. Notes on financial information:

_____

_____

_____

_____

_____

■ I've checked the financial ratios in the operation of the company (as given in Chapter 11) and here are my notes on these ratios:

_____

_____

_____

_____

_____

■ If this is a corporation, here are the principal stockholders and the percent of the shares they own:

_____   _____

_____   _____

_____   _____

_____   _____

_____   _____

- The amount of capital I will need to buy the business, make improvements, and support growth:

_____

_____

- How I'll judge the quality of the personnel I'd acquire with the company:

_____

_____

- I believe the market segment the company has been serving is appropriate for the business: Yes __; No __. If no, here's what I'd do to improve the marketing program:

_____

_____

_____

_____

_____

- A special question. What exactly would I be buying: physical plant; retail store with inventory; patents; franchise; goodwill; or . . . ?

_____

_____

_____

_____

FINAL SCREENING

- At this point we recommend that you perform a market feasibility analysis as given in Chapters 4, 5, and 6. Note your conclusions and the ways you've found to improve marketing effectiveness if you buy the company. Include your findings about the intangible assets and the physical assets of the company. Use the space below for your notes.

_____

_____

_____

_____

_____

AVOIDING LEGAL PROBLEMS

■ Note here your responses to the questions raised in this section of this chapter. Include the answers to other questions that may have occurred to you as you've worked through those given in the text.

_____

_____

_____

_____

_____

_____

_____

PICKING A LOSER

■ If you've found a loser that you believe you can turn around, state here the specific plans you've developed to make the business profitable.

_____

_____

_____

_____

_____

_____

_____

_____

_____

PERSONAL FACTORS IN THE TRANSACTION

■ I recognize that the owner will give me some open reasons for wanting to sell—and will have some hidden reasons. And I'll have my reasons for wanting to buy. It will help me to weigh these reasons side by side to balance them.

clientele 358
broker 361
franchise 366
perquisites 369
liquidation value 370

capitalization 370
amortize 374
ROI 374
goodwill 378

STUDY ASSIGNMENTS FOR REVIEW AND DISCUSSION

1. Describe at least three advantages in buying a going business.

2. Describe at least five disadvantages in buying a going business.

3. Outline the purpose and the steps that should be taken in the three stages of screening we've recommended in evaluating a going business:
Preliminary screening
Second-stage screening
Final screening

4. What specifically should you look for in analyzing the market program of a business being offered for sale?

5. Identify several typical legal issues that should be checked before buying a business.

6. Under what circumstances might it be sound practice to pick a loser?

7. Describe some personal factors buyer and seller often bring to the transaction of buying a going business.

8. Name three sources for finding a business to buy, and describe the advantages and disadvantages of each.

9. Describe three ways of evaluating a business in order to price it.

10. Define the concept of *goodwill*. What should the buyer take into account in putting a value on goodwill?

PROJECTS FOR STUDENTS

1. Several teams of two students each locate and interview persons who have bought an existing business and run into difficulty with it. The teams report to the class how these buyers went about making up their minds to buy, what they had made mistakes about in appraising the business, and any other significant information about the deal and the later history of the business.

2. A student identifies and interviews an entrepreneur who has deliberately found and bought a "loser"—and made it profitable. (Two or more students should

take on the assignment.) They report to the class why the entrepreneurs bought the particular businesses and what they did to make them profitable.

3. In this assignment for three students, each of the three asks two individual small business owners to define their concept of marketing. They then report these ideas about marketing to the class and hold an open discussion of how small businesses can use sound marketing principles.

4. Two teams of two students each locate and interview a business broker. Ask what the broker looks for in the businesses taken on to sell and how he or she "qualifies" potential buyers (what characteristics and qualifications are sought in potential buyers). Report findings to class and conduct open discussion on the information gathered.

5. Find an advertisement for a business for sale that gives little information and requires a response to a post office box number. Find another that gives enough information to present a fair picture of the business, and in which the owner or business broker is named. Bring these examples to class for discussion.

6. Describe what is meant by a doomsday evaluation of the worth of a business.

7. How would you set the worth of the goodwill of a business you were considering buying? In what kind of business might goodwill be most important?

8. Under what conditions would you consider buying a dying business?

IF YOU WANT TO READ MORE

ALBERT, Kenneth J.: *How to Pick the Right Small Business Opportunity,* McGraw-Hill Book Company, New York, 1980. This book, simply and directly written, will be found particularly useful in helping you decide on the business that fits your personal strengths. Chapter 12, "Selecting an Ongoing Business," offers comprehensive checklists of items to investigate and gives practical suggestions for pricing the business.

BURKE, Frank M., Jr.: *Valuation and Valuation Planning for Closely Held Businesses,* Prentice-Hall, Inc., Englewood Cliffs, NJ, 1981. Although the focus of this book is on valuation for federal income and transfer (gift and estate) tax purposes at the time the book was published, the principles discussed apply in other situations aimed at determining the fair market value of a closely held business.

GOLDSTEIN, Arnold S.: *The Complete Guide to Buying and Selling a Business,* John Wiley & Sons, New York, 1983. Those who intend to buy an existing company will find in this book numerous case histories that illuminate strategies for locating, investigating, and negotiating for purchase of a business. Also included are recommendations for valuing the business, treating the financial aspect of a sale, and closing the deal.

JUSTIS, Robert T.: *Managing Your Small Business,* Prentice-Hall, Inc., Englewood Cliffs, NJ, 1981. Chapter 10 of this book deals with buying an existing business. You'll find this chapter useful as a concise outline of points to consider in evaluating a business you may think of buying. Particularly interesting is the approach given for pricing a business on pp. 188–190.

LOVE, Marc J.: *Buying and Selling Small Businesses,* John Wiley & Sons, New York, 1985. This text offers a comprehensive source that deals with the state of the law and current business thought on the subject. Although somewhat technical, it presents helpful tools for assessment and decision making through examples, forms, and checklists.

MARTIN, Thomas J., and Mark R. GUSTAFSON: *Valuing Your Business,* Holt, Rinehart and Winston, New York, 1980. This book provides answers to the very sticky problem of arriving at the true value of a business. It gives the necessary information and guidelines to enable you to make an intelligent decision, whether you are buying or selling a business.

PRATT, Shannon P.: *Valuing a Business,* Dow Jones–Irwin, Homewood, IL, 1981. This book offers a primer on the theory and practice of valuing a business. Each aspect of business valuation is described in basic terms, with no prior knowledge assumed. Extensive use of examples is employed where appropriate.

TETRAULT, Wilfred F.: *Buying and Selling Business Opportunities,* Addison-Wesley, Reading, MA, 1981. This book treats with appraising, buying, and selling a business, with emphasis on handling such transactions in a legal, moral, and ethical manner.

CHAPTER 14

Is Franchising the Way to Go?[1]

TOPICS IN THIS CHAPTER

Objectives of This Chapter
Advantages and Disadvantages of the Franchised
Business
Recent History of Franchising
Types of Franchising Organizations
Nature of the Franchise Relationship
Evaluating the Franchise Relationship
Evaluating the Franchise Agreement
Trends in Franchising
Pros and Cons in Franchising—Summary
Worksheet 14: Franchising
Key Terms
Study Assignments for Review and Discussion
Projects for Students
If You Want to Read More

[1]Code numbers referring to the Outline for Developing Your Basic Business Plan (Appendix A) are not used in this chapter. The worksheet in this chapter will guide you through the planning required to assess the desirability of a franchised business. When you have finished Worksheet 14 check the items in Appendix A, point by point, to make sure you haven't omitted any important considerations.

This chapter presents another way to get into your own business—without starting with your own idea from scratch. With the selection of a franchised business that fits your background and desires, through franchising you can get into a tested business that has proved its worth. You'd also be supported by a training program that can help you avoid the difficulties often associated with starting a business of your own.

As with any human enterprise, where there are advantages there are usually disadvantages. This chapter takes a look at both to prepare you to make the decision about going the franchising route.

$$\text{You} + \text{Idea} + \begin{Bmatrix} \text{Money} \\ \text{Credit} \end{Bmatrix} + \begin{Bmatrix} \text{Facilities} \\ \text{People} \end{Bmatrix} \rightarrow \begin{matrix} \textbf{PRODUCT} \\ \textbf{OR} \\ \textbf{SERVICE} \end{matrix} + \text{Marketing} \begin{Bmatrix} \text{Money} \\ \text{Credit} \end{Bmatrix} \rightarrow \text{Profit}$$

Owning a franchised business may be a more attractive alternative than starting a business from scratch. A franchise is a prepackaged and widely known business that benefits from the national image and promotion of the franchisor. Tested operating methods and proved products lower the risk of doing business and mean that the franchise may yield profit sooner than an independent new business. But there are trade-offs in the entrepreneur's independence. Standard procedures and operating methods will have to be followed, and the franchisee will have little discretion over product and marketing strategy.

Objectives of This Chapter

This chapter presents important aspects of franchising. Learning about these can help you decide whether becoming a franchisee is the way to start your own business. Studying the material in this chapter should help you to:

- Know the general nature of the franchising method of doing business and the major types of franchising organizations

- Identify the motives a franchisor has in offering franchised outlets to entrepreneur-investors

- Assess the franchise relationship and your role as a franchisee compared with being an independent entrepreneur

- Evaluate the franchise agreement, or contract, and know what to look for in the legal commitments between you as the franchisee and the franchisor

- Recognize and avoid some of the special problems that frequently occur in the franchisee-franchisor relationship

- Ask the right questions in evaluating the franchise opportunity

- Conduct your own low-cost research to investigate the market potential for your outlet

- Understand important trends and prospects in the field of franchising

Advantages and Disadvantages of the Franchised Business

This chapter examines the advantages and disadvantages of owning and operating a franchise business instead of, for example, starting a business from scratch or buying an established business. If you have the technical know-how, owning and operating a franchised business—becoming a franchisee—is an alternative you may want to explore. For those who have already decided that a franchised venture is the way to go, many of the chapters in this text should be helpful, especially Chapters 4 through 6 on marketing.

The International Franchise Association represents franchisors in several industries, and defines franchising in these terms:

A franchise is a continuing relationship between the franchisor and the franchisee in which the sum total of the franchisor's knowledge, image, success, manufacturing and marketing techniques are supplied to the franchisee for a consideration.

Franchising is one of several systems of distribution by which a producer may bring products or services to the consumer. As such, franchising performs a major and growing distribution function in the United States. Today franchised enterprises number about a half million and account for about one-third of all retail sales.

Applied research in franchising clearly spells out the characteristics that distinguish successful franchisees:[2]

- They conduct their own independent market research and analysis in evaluating the franchised business they enter.

- Before purchasing the franchise, they use independent financial and legal counseling to assess the potential worth of the business and to prevent contractual conflicts with the franchisor.

- They develop thorough business and marketing plans, not relying completely on the franchisor to chart the future of their business.

- They have prior work experience in the business the franchisor offers.

These findings should come as no surprise, since as we've stressed, the basic requirements for starting any kind of business are the same.

Recent History of Franchising

The growth economy of the 1960s created an environment in which franchising flourished. Although many franchises were extremely profitable, franchising lured dozens of inexperienced newcomers. Many franchises, sponsored by well-known names, disappeared almost as quickly as they entered the market. Franchising attracted fewer and fewer eager investors during the economic downturn of 1974–1975. Many investors were no doubt influenced by bankruptcies that were occurring in a few franchised operations, caused by inept management.

A large majority of franchised businesses proved to be well managed and were not affected by the 1974–1975 recession. Some, however, were shaken out. The shakeout continued into the eighties, and compelled entrepreneurs and investors to become more conservative and professional.

After emerging from this depressed period franchising once more began to bloom. Excellent opportunities for entrepreneurs in franchised businesses opened up

---

[2]A study reinforcing these findings may be found in James L. Porter and William Renforth, "Franchise Agreements: Spotting the Important Legal Issues," *Journal of Small Business Management*, vol. 16, no. 4, October 1978, pp. 27–31. Summaries of several previous studies on franchising can be found in Charles L. Vaughn, *Franchising*, D.C. Heath and Company, Lexington, MA, 1974, especially pp. 37–42.

and still exist. Many such businesses are in services: inexpensive hair salons where appointments are not required, retail electronics products and computer stores, rapid electronic diagnostic auto servicing; and still many opportunities exist in new fast food chains. The latter are particularly interesting as they've developed unique ways to meet the challenge of a changing market—and to sidestep the competition of nationally known fast food chains.

An article in the November 1984 issue of *Venture* describes fast foods as a fertile field for entrepreneurs. Many of the small new franchisors and franchisees are doing well. They aim to serve primarily the baby boomers who are now in their thirties. These customers grew up with fast foods of the past but are now inclined to switch their tastes to current more healthful dietary changes that have become popular.

For example, D'Lites of America, a 60-unit Atlanta-based chain, serves gourmet hamburgers made with extra lean beef and high-fiber buns, also pita sandwiches, and various low-calorie foods. Another winner, Capt. Crab's Take-Away, headquartered in Miami, a six-unit chain, specializes in seafood, which their customers take out.

These newer small fast food chains often use unusual marketing features to attract customers. Fuddruckers, a 17-unit San Antonio–based chain, maintains a glassed-in butcher shop where customers can watch sides of beef being cut and ground.

Many of the small chains solve their problems of location in innovative ways. Marino's of Rockville, Maryland, sells franchises on a system that has as many as 10 mini-systems around a central mother unit. The mother unit in a particular territory supplies its mini-units with sauces, soups, and other staples. This system eliminates the need for a large kitchen and storage spaces in each mini-unit. Mini-units can be set up in spaces as small as 350 square feet; a mother unit takes 2500 square feet.

Papa Aldo's Take & Bake Shops, a 25-unit chain based in Portland, Oregon, developed a different approach to the pizza trade. Here customers carry away fresh ready-to-bake pizzas. The founder, John Gundle, had owned two pizza parlors before founding Papa Aldo's. Here take-out customers had often complained that their pizzas grew cold before they could get them home. To solve this problem, Gundle thought it possible to provide customers with ready-to-bake pizzas that they could slip into the oven when they got home. In this way the pizzas could be eaten at the peak of hot perfection.

Gundle had to overcome a difficult problem before the take-home pizza could be standardized. Pizza dough rises when the temperature exceeds 80°F. He and a local baker spent considerable time and money developing a 40 percent precooked dough that would withstand summer heat without rising farther than required for the pizza.

Some analysts in the field question whether these small new fast food chains can withstand competition from the large well-established chains as they swing over to up-to-date foods. For example, Wendy's now offers a "Light-Side" menu that includes whole wheat buns, tuna salad and cottage cheese platters, and hot soup. And Taco Bell features Taco Light made with whole wheat tortillas, and rice and bean platters. The entrepreneurial small chain founders say they are not worried. They say that the major chains have a slow reaction time. The entrepreneurs believe that their flexibility, speed of innovation in originating new products, and low overheads will allow them to remain competitive and profitable, and to survive.

Although franchising has seen ups and downs, excellent opportunities still exist for entrepreneurs in franchised businesses. From this point on, we'll assume that you're considering becoming a franchisee, in which case you should know the types of franchises available and be able to assess the characteristics and quality of the franchise relationship, and how to evaluate a prospective franchise venture. There are several excellent sources of information on franchising; you will find them listed at the end of the chapter.

Types of Franchising Organizations

There are several categories of franchises, ranging from those marketing products such as fast food, ice cream, and candy to those marketing services such as motels, dry cleaning, and coin-operated laundries. To simplify description, four basic types of franchises are identified, each with distinguishing economic and legal characteristics.

1. *Manufacturer-retailer franchise system.* In most cases the manufacturer franchises an entire retail outlet to stock and market its product line. Examples include manufacturers of automobiles and trucks, farm equipment, petroleum products, shoes, and paint. Midas Muffler Shops and Pappagallo shoe stores follow this pattern.

   Note that in this case the major role of the franchisee is to provide in a defined market area an outlet where the consumer may readily obtain the manufacturer's products. The franchisee has very little discretion about what products are to be marketed.

2. *Manufacturer-wholesaler franchise system.* The beverage companies, soft drink and beer primarily, dominate this form of franchising. In soft drink franchising the manufacturer supplies the syrup or concentrate to the franchised wholesaler, who adds ingredients, packages the product, and distributes to local retailers. A typical wholesaler is the Coca Cola Bottling Co. of Durango.

   Transportation and other distribution costs make it uneconomical for the manufacturer to produce the finished product centrally. In this case the franchisee performs some of the production activities and distributes the product to the retail level. As in the manufacturer-retailer franchise system, the franchisee has little control over the products to be distributed or their characteristics.

3. *Wholesaler-retailer franchise systems.* The organization of interest here is the wholesaler-sponsored retail franchise. In this case the franchisor recruits independent retailers to contract voluntarily to become franchisees. Western Auto Supply, Firestone, Goodyear, Butler Brothers, and Super Value Stores, Inc., are good examples.

4. *Trade-name franchise systems.* This is the category that has enjoyed most rapid growth in the past two decades. In this arrangement the franchisor is seldom a manufacturer or wholesaler, but rather possesses a known trade name and proved

methods for profitable operation of retail outlets. Well-known examples can be found in hotel chains (Holiday Inn, Best Western, Sheraton Inn), restaurant chains (Howard Johnson's, McDonald's, Kentucky Fried Chicken, Burger King, Baskin-Robbins), and auto rental firms (Hertz, Avis, National, Budget Rent-A-Car).In this franchise system the franchisee may manufacture or modify the product (depending on product or service) but, as in other types of franchises, must follow strict operating and marketing procedures.

In the first three franchise systems the franchisor is the producer and the franchisee the distributor. In trade-name franchising the franchisee can be either a producer or a service supplier. All types involve trademarked or nationally branded products; they usually emphasize the quality control imposed by franchisors on products made or services offered by their franchisees.

Economic and contractual obligations between franchisor and franchisee vary widely among the four types and within each type. The particular franchise relationship specifies the amount of entry capital required and degree of control held by the franchisor over the franchisee.

Growth in franchising in all four categories, especially trade-name franchising, has been influenced by trends toward national branding and increased mobility of consumers. When buying products, consumers seek the reputation of a national brand that results from mass advertising. Transportation costs are usually too high to produce in a central location and distribute nationally. As recreation and business travel have increased, so too have the consumers' preferences for consistent standards of service and known costs of accommodation. In cases like these, franchising has offered and continues to offer unique opportunities where local ownership and operation are advantageous. National reputation, image, and promotion are of overriding importance.

Nature of the Franchise Relationship

The heart of the franchise relationship is a contractual agreement governing the freedom of the grantee—you, the franchisee—to do or use something that is the property or right of the grantor—the franchisor. This binding agreement establishes your relationship and controls your distribution of products or services.

You, the entrepreneur-investor, pay an agreed-upon sum, or consideration and, in return, gain the right to sell a certain product or service, use a certain brand name, trademark, technique of operation, or technical process owned by the franchisor. But a franchise relationship is usually much more than granting a license to use certain trademarks or business techniques. Two additional features are present: first, the success of the franchise venture calls for a *continuing relationship* between the franchisor and you; second, you agree to maintain certain standards of operation specified by the franchisor.

To be sure, you give up some independence by agreeing to adhere to specified procedures and direction from the franchisor. Most forms of franchise relationships involve the sharing of decision-making and management control, issuing from brand-name affiliation, the transfer of specific management or technical expertise, and in many cases the advantage of unique products or services developed by the franchisor. In short, when purchasing a franchise you buy a prepackaged business. But you operate the venture, after purchase, under contract and in cooperation with the parent-franchisor company. Thus, crucial to your success will be careful evaluation of the particular franchise relationship.

Evaluating the Franchise Relationship

This section offers some guides to help you decide whether obtaining a franchise business would be a good way for you to start your own business. We will begin by exploring the franchise relationship and addressing these questions:

- Why do franchisors franchise? What makes franchising so attractive that they choose this method of distribution over other methods?

- What is the franchisee's role in the relationship? From a personal viewpoint, how does being a franchisee differ from being a wholly independent entrepreneur?

THE FRANCHISOR

You must understand clearly the reasons why a franchisor chooses franchising as the best method of distribution. Knowing the motives of the franchisor—"what's in it for them"—will help you in objectively evaluating your own prospects as a member of their distribution system.

Capital Acquisition In recent years the single most important reasons for adopting franchised distribution has been to acquire or conserve capital, while at the same time rapidly establishing an effective distribution network. Several well-known fast food companies use the initial fees paid by their franchisees as a major source of working capital. This is an obviously attractive funding technique, since in many cases the fees are collected long before the actual opening of an outlet. In effect the franchisor receives hundreds of thousands of dollars in interest-free loans from franchisees.

Other forms of financing are much less attractive to the franchisor. Equity financing techniques, such as sale of common stock, usually result in diluting ownership. Debt financing through borrowing weakens cash flow because of the interest and repayment obligations. Franchising offers a clever acquisition-of-funds technique, since the interest-free loans (initial joining fees) do not have to be repaid so long as the franchisor honors the contract with the franchisee.[3] It has been established that $450 million would have been required for Kentucky Fried Chicken Corp. to

---

[3]Interestingly, obtaining working capital by collecting franchise fees constitutes a self-liquidating debt obligation. The fee has to be repaid only if the franchisor does not meet all contract requirements. In the early 1970s several franchisors were reporting franchise fees as current earnings. This artificially inflated their earnings-per-share value. Practices of this nature existed in several franchising companies. Investor support declined sharply when it was found that rapid accumulation of franchise fees was being used to boost performance figures rather than records of profitability through good management.

establish its first 2700 stores. This large sum of money was available only from the method of franchisee-supplied capital.

In addition to its interest-free feature, capital financing through franchising also avoids restrictions on use of funds and procedural delays. Within very broad limits the franchisor can spend funds collected even on business activities not directly connected with the requirements of new franchisees.

The purposes for which loaned funds can be used are often restricted and delays are frequent in normal lending channels. Obtaining funds through sale of stock often takes a long time and imposes significant underwriting costs that reduce the total capital acquired by the sale.

Reduce Marketing Costs   In addition to advantages in acquiring capital, franchising can reduce marketing costs compared with what would be needed for company-owned outlets. If the company owned its stores, it would have to pay all the costs of doing business in many different locations, such as labor, overhead, insurance, personnel administration, employee training—mostly expenses that continue regardless of sales volume.

Entrepreneurship   Successful franchisors believe that the local entrepreneur-manager is a crucial factor in the performance of the franchise system. Franchisors have found that franchisees are often more likely to work hard in marketing and in controlling operating costs than are salaried employees in company-owned outlets. No doubt the large financial stake the franchisee has in the business influences this kind of commitment. But also franchisees in well-run systems tend to view themselves as entrepreneurs and important local businesspersons.

Our experience shows that success of almost any franchise system and its franchisees is linked directly to how effectively the franchisor has created and maintained favorable conditions for entrepreneurship among the franchise owner-managers. The question you must answer is: Under the franchise relationship I'm considering, will I be more of an entrepreneur, or will I be considered and treated like an employee of the parent company?

THE FRANCHISEE

Personal factors will have a lot to do with how you judge the franchise relationship and your "fit" as a franchisee. You should carefully review Chapters 1 and 2, where we presented the characteristics of successful entrepreneurs.

Many people know that they want to go into business for themselves but are hesitant to take the drastic step of starting a wholly independent business venture. As we've said, it is a risky endeavor and the failure rate is high. Lack of seasoned business experience quite appropriately makes would-be entrepreneurs uneasy about going it alone. Finally, many people know that operating a small business is what they want to do, but they lack a specific idea, product, service, or business location.

Franchising has very special appeals for such individuals, and perhaps for you. Buying a franchise means that you would not be venturing into completely uncharted waters. In buying a franchise appropriate to your capabilities, you could gain the following advantages:

■ The business itself and its methods would have been thoroughly tested and found successful.

■ You would begin with a known product or service that has already achieved customer approval and acceptance.

■ There would be a proved track record of financial and marketing success that can be transferred to the specific franchise you'll purchase.

■ Expert help would be available to aid you in actually launching and operating the business—in such areas as merchandising, inventory control, site selection, store layout, and accounting.

■ For many franchised operations, and perhaps yours, significant benefits would be found in group purchasing and national-brand advertising.

Many franchisees welcome group identity and participation in a franchise system. Observers have noted that many franchisees really don't want to be totally independent but rather seek to be both part of a large successful organization and yet maintain individual identity. Finally, the right franchise would offer you the opportunity to enter a field of business that might be prohibitively expensive to enter independently.

For many franchisors, the best type of franchisee is someone who can conform to an established way of doing business without being driven to try to improve on it. Often franchisors seek a "sergeant type," a person who can operate well between an officer who gives orders and a private who follows them.

If you want to escape taking orders by operating a franchised business, you may be frustrated by your lack of autonomy. Detailed reports will have to be prepared and submitted. Inventory levels and mix of inventory items may be set by rules, regardless of local market preferences. You may have no say in your store location and be limited in the sources from which you purchase supplies. And, although you may disagree with the franchisor's advertising program, you will probably not have any say in it.

Thus, there are important trade-offs in choosing a franchised business. Recognize that even with the best franchise operations, the franchisor tends to hold the advantage, especially in the areas of operating practices and material and supply purchasing.

To sum up, the franchising situation you should look for would combine proved expertise and marketing sophistication at the franchisor level with the requirements for some entrepreneurial drive and a manageable amount of investment capital at the franchisee level. In evaluating a specific franchising operation, you should determine whether this combination results in the exchange of mutual value and benefits. To do so, you'll need some guidelines on what to expect in the way of your obligations in securing and operating the franchise and the specific services offered by the franchisor.

Evaluating the Franchise Agreement

The franchise agreement, or contract, spells out the responsibilities of the franchisor and the franchisee. The agreement should clearly identify what the franchisor will supply in initiating your franchise and the ongoing forms of services you'll receive. The agreement will also describe, often in much detail, just how your business is to be run. Legal conflicts often arise because these kinds of commitments and responsibilities are not made sufficiently clear in the written agreement cementing the parties. All promises and agreements, oral and written, should be thoroughly checked by your attorney and spelled out in the franchise contract.

We'll examine here some of the common elements of franchise agreements.

START-UP COSTS AND CONTINUING CHARGES

The franchisor will usually require you to pay a franchise fee. This fee can run anywhere from hundreds to hundred of thousands of dollars. The purpose of the fee is, as we've said, to obtain working capital for the franchisor, but it also assures your personal involvement in running the business. Franchisors are increasingly skeptical of nonmanaging investors.

The initial fee is frequently used to compensate the franchisor for the expense of site location (sometimes charged as a separate fee), training, and other services necessary to create a prosperous franchise outlet. Franchise fees have risen rapidly in the past decade; many have tripled or quadrupled. Several successful fast food chains that charged $25,000 a few years ago now charge their franchisees $100,000 or several times more.

Some retail and service-station chains do not charge any initial fee. The franchisee pays rent for use of the franchisor's facilities and the franchisor profits most by selling products to the franchisee. In some instances, the franchisee acts as a volume purchaser and profits by this advantage. In others, like soft drink manufacturers, franchisors derive most of their revenue from sale of syrup to franchised bottlers who convert the syrup into a marketable product. In still others, the franchisor sells to the franchisee all the equipment for operating the business, plus supplies used and products offered.

In franchised service businesses, such as accounting, travel, and employment agencies, an initial fee may be the only financial charge made. Seldom are there monthly or percentage-of-sales charges. This is so because there is no continuing relationship. The franchise fee covers the use of the franchisor's name, operating methods, and business forms. In instances where continuing services are supplied, such as national promotion, the franchisee usually pays the franchisor a set percentage of sales.

In addition to initial fees, rent, and charges for supplies and products, royalty fees may be used to compensate the franchisor. The royalty fee may be charged alone or in combination with other forms of compensation. In the typical case the franchisor charges an initial fee, plus a set royalty fee, perhaps 5 percent of the franchisee's gross sales. The royalty fee is usually levied regardless of the profits earned by the franchise.

The amount you invest to obtain the franchise and any continuing charges you pay the franchisor should depend on the value you receive. The central question to address is: *What can the franchisor do for me that I cannot do for myself?*

THE BUSINESS LOCATION AND FACILITY

The success of most franchised ventures depends heavily on a convenient business location. In the past franchisors would recruit the franchisee first and then acquire the location for the outlet. This practice has changed, in fact has been reversed. Most often the franchisor identifies and purchases the site for the outlet and then recruits the franchisee. Three major factors have caused this change. First, the growth of franchising has caused the number of desirable locations to decline sharply. Second, the land price tends to escalate when it's known that a national franchisor is bidding for a particular site. And third, local zoning restrictions also contribute to the increasingly limited supply of attractive locations for franchise outlets.

Franchisors often deal through intermediaries in purchasing business property. But more important, franchisors are becoming much more thorough in researching and selecting potential sites for their outlets. Often several thousand dollars may be spent on the marketing research and feasibility studies necessary to evaluate a specific store location. As we'll point out later, you should evaluate these studies. In addition, we'll present guidelines for conducting your own low-cost assessment of market potential.

SELECTING A FRANCHISE LOCATION?

"How would you locate my shop?" asked the prospective franchisee.

"Since you want to be in the big city, rather than a smaller town, here's how we'd go about it," said the representative of the auto muffler replacement franchisor.

"We know from experience over the years that we don't want muffler shops any closer together than ten miles. In that way we don't compete.

"We also know that some of the less expensive cars need their mufflers replaced more often than the luxury cars. Our computer analysis of our muffler replacement sales over the past ten years shows two brands of cars that produce the most replacement business: Brand X and Brand Y. These cars give us about half our replacement business. We therefore search for ten-mile circles within the city where lots of these cars are registered."

"How do you find where these cars live?" asked the prospect.

"We go to the Motor Vehicle Division of the state—and for a small fee they give us a computer printout of all the Brand X and Brand Y cars in the whole metropolitan area. We then look for that particular ten-mile circle that has the most of these cars in it.

"Once we've drawn that circle on a street map of the city, we'd try to find a suitable central spot for your muffler shop. What kind of street would you expect we'd look for?"

"Why, I expect one with heavy auto traffic."

"Of course, we'd try to find a busy intersection where traffic is heavy on both cross streets. And we'd hope to find one with four filling stations, if possible—one on each corner. For some reason, often one of these will be about to close up. That's the corner we'll want for your muffler shop."

"How do you find out how much traffic on those streets?"

"Easy enough. We go to the police department or the department of street maintenance and ask. They always have records of traffic patterns and densities. From this we're able to pinpoint a location that'll prove profitable—and we negotiate a deal for you."

"Does this really work?"

"No question of it. We now have over seven hundred muffler shops franchised around the country, many located as I've explained. We've had less than two percent failures—and we've made a number of millionaires, owners with several shops. We think we can help you succeed as we've helped hundreds of our franchisees."

What general principles can you draw from this vignette for strategic location of a franchised business that depends on auto traffic for its trade?

In most cases the franchisor will define territorial boundaries for the franchised outlet, taking into account the size of the market or population. If population grows, franchisors increasingly stipulate in the franchise agreements that the franchisee's territorial boundaries may be adjusted or that additional outlets may be located in the franchisee's original territory.

Franchisors typically follow one of two location strategies. They may, for example, deliberately choose to locate their retail outlets in close proximity to other directly competitive units. These franchisors usually cater to a mass, largely undifferentiated, market. This practice is no doubt influenced by local zoning restrictions, but it follows from the belief that the increased customer traffic resulting from a cluster of competitive outlets will more than offset the impact of competition.

Other franchisors choose not to compete directly with franchise businesses like McDonald's and Burger King. Tastee-Freeze, for example, usually locates in smaller towns with 20,000 population or less. Several of the larger franchisors aim at metropolitan areas with a population of 30,000 or more.

You should examine carefully the location strategy followed by a franchisor you're interested in. In many cases the concentration of several competitors in a small geographical area has saturated the market. And in some instances franchisors in more rural areas have experienced declining population. Each franchise situation is unique. You should evaluate the location offered by the franchisor in terms of its future market potential.

TRAINING IN THE BUSINESS

Most reputable franchisors offer the franchisee thorough training in operating the business. Often they will require such training as a condition of obtaining the franchise. You'll want to check out how much background the franchisor expects you to have in the type of business you'll be running. Many actually prefer no experience so they can readily train the franchisee in their own way of doing business.

The problems in initiating and running a franchise business are no different from those encountered in any other kind of small business. Thus, franchisee training not only should cover policies, procedures, and methods but also should emphasize the entrepreneurial and management skills needed. Training should also prepare franchise managers for long working hours, stress, and frustration during the first several months of operation.

Some of the best training programs are about equally divided between classroom instruction and field experience gained through working in a franchise outlet. Programs are about 4 to 6 weeks in length, often conducted in the franchisor's special training facilities. Your initial franchise fee usually covers initial training costs and any on-the-job or follow-up training conducted by the franchisor.

One of the more common complaints of franchisees is that they still do not feel adequately prepared, despite franchisee training that features the technical, managerial, *and* emotional aspects of starting a small business. We strongly recommend that you check out the franchisor's training program thoroughly before investing, especially if you lack specific business experience. Before you start your own franchise, be sure that training includes field experience and is supplemented by training designed to update and expand your skills later on.

FRANCHISE OPERATIONS

The franchise agreement often sets rigid standards and spells out specific operating procedures the franchisee must follow. These controls on the business assure consistent practices among franchised outlets, and serve to enhance trademark awareness, community identity, and consumer image. This means that the franchisor's operating requirements can affect every aspect of your business, including store layout and design, equipment and furnishings to be used, products produced and their quality, and promotional efforts.

The amount of control the franchisor exerts crucially affects how much discretion and entrepreneurial freedom you'll have. You should check out the mechanisms used to govern business operations. The following summarizes the five different ways franchisors can control the franchise:

1. *The franchise agreement.* Typically the franchise contract will describe in painstaking detail standards, rules, and procedures to be followed. The agreement will also set the duration of the contract and the conditions under which the contract can be terminated. These controls are most effective, since the franchisee is legally bound by the contract.

2. *Franchisor policy.* Most franchisors stipulate additional rules and guidelines to be followed and spell these out in their official operating manual. Franchisors' operating manuals are usually copyrighted, and state the required day-to-day business practices. The operating manual covers such practices as hours of operation, employee hiring and firing, employee qualifications, record-keeping systems, and product storage, preparation, and handling.

3. *Franchisor approval.* In some cases, the franchisors will require franchisees to obtain approval for certain business decisions. For example, the franchisor's approval might be required before the franchisee can expand the business or add new products or services.

4. *Franchisor recommendations.* Instead of rules of prescribed procedures, in some areas franchisors may merely recommend some ways to perform certain business tasks or what kinds of business activities to undertake. Experience has shown franchisees can usually make better decisions if franchisors supply expert guidance and recommendations, rather than impose inflexible, often inappropriate, rules.

5. *Franchisee reporting.* Franchisors recognize that feedback on franchisee performance is essential to effective control. Periodic reports on unit sales, revenue, costs, and profits will be required monthly or quarterly. The franchisor's representative will probably make face-to-face visits. If results are not up to standard, the franchisor will institute corrective action.

The franchisor may use one or some combination of these franchisee governing methods. You should ascertain the particular way these control mechanisms are to be applied. It'll be important to pinpoint those areas of business operations over which:

- You have no control and where strict compliance to standards is required.

- You should have some control, but your decisions must be guided by franchisor recommendation, or your actions must have the prior approval of the franchisor.

- You have total control, and can make local decisions without consulting the franchisor.

DURATION, TERMINATION, AND TRANSFERS

Duration   The trend has been toward longer and longer franchise contract periods. Contracts that now run 10 to 20 years or more are common. In most cases the length of the franchise contract depends on the duration of the lease on the property where the outlet is located. The franchise agreement and the property lease agreement are often contained in one document, since most franchises have no value without having a specific business site.

Termination   Conditions for terminating the franchise contract should be examined closely. Franchisees are often at a disadvantage in influencing the franchisor's right to cancel or refuse to renew the contract. In the past some franchisors have threatened franchisees with cancellation to force them into accepting corporate decisions or unreasonable obligations.

The franchisor appropriately reserves the right to cancel, or refuse to renew, the contract of a franchisee who does not cooperate, mismanages, and fails in the business. However, we urge extreme caution if the franchisor requires high minimum purchases of inventory levels or unreasonably high sales quotas. The insecurity resulting from possible contract cancellation often breeds bad relations between franchisee and franchisor. Your planning and decision making should be based on careful analysis and strategy, not on fear of unreasonable demands of the franchisor.

Transfers   The franchise agreement will also stipulate the conditions under which the franchise may be bought or sold. Generally the franchisee does not have the right to sell the business or bequeath the business to heirs without formal approval of the franchisor.

The franchisor usually reserves the right to recover or buy back a franchised outlet upon termination of the franchise contract. If the franchisee has not reserved the right to renew the contract, the franchisor can deal with others in negotiating the new contract.

In the past, the "guaranteed buy-back" offer of franchisors—to buy back a franchise business that doesn't make a go of it—was the bait that lured hundreds of franchisees. However, buy-back usually didn't mean the franchisor would share in the franchisee's financial losses.

Today buy-back clauses should be examined carefully. Some major franchisors tend to repurchase franchise outlets and operate them themselves or to sell some or all outlets to larger companies. The point is that since the franchise agreement will favor the franchisor in some way, the franchisor can pressure the franchisee to sell out. When the franchisee sells a successful business back to the franchisor, there's the problem of setting a value on the business. Our recommendation here is that your contract contain a provision for independent arbitration to evaluate the business thoroughly and fairly in the event of termination. The value should include tangible assets such as equipment and fixtures and intangible assets such as goodwill.

SPECIAL PROBLEMS TO WATCH FOR IN THE FRANCHISE AGREEMENT—A SUMMARY

The franchise agreement establishes the responsibilities of each of the mutually dependent parties. Conflicts can and do arise if the agreement does not precisely spell out the rights and obligations of the franchisee and franchisor. One study identifies more than 60 well-known franchisors that have been involved in significant franchise litigation.[4] You should be aware of more frequent sources of disagreement in evaluating a potential franchise relationship.[5]

Table 14-1 shows the 10 most common legal problems reported by franchisees. Referring to the table, sharing advertising costs is the most common legal

TABLE 14-1

10 Most Common Legal Problems of Franchisees

Problem	Rank
Frequent Problems	
Sharing advertising costs	1
Inspection/evaluation by franchisor	2
Minimum performance requirements	3
Occasional Problems	
Royalty payments	4
Fees for support services	5
Territorial limits	6
Rare Problems	
Penalties for violation of contract	7
Restrictions on products or prices	8
Employee conduct/training requirements	9
Limits on competitive businesses	10

Source: James L. Porter and William Renforth, "Franchise Agreements: Spotting the Important Legal Issues," *Journal of Small Business Management*, vol. 16, no. 4, October 1978, p. 28.

---

[4]Harold Brown, *Franchising—Realities and Remedies,* Law Journal Press, New York, 1973, p. 6.
[5]The more frequent problems causing franchisee-franchisor litigation are summarized here, as reported in James L. Porter and William Renforth, "Franchise Agreements: Spotting the Important Legal Issues," *Journal of Small Business Management*, vol. 16, no. 4, October 1978, pp. 27–31.

problem. Franchisees who are required by contract to contribute money for national advertising indicated that, in some cases, they had not received their "fair share" of advertising locally. The complaint is that the franchisor, who controls the scheduling and placement of advertising, had not devoted enough to the franchisee's market. Thus, franchisees sue to reduce their assessment for advertising or to increase the amount of advertising in their locality.

The second most common problem involves the provisions for inspection or evaluation by the franchisor. Here the complaint is that franchisors are not consistent in enforcing strict adherence to standards among other members of the franchise chain. Failure of the franchisor to insist that some franchisees meet standards damages the image and reputation of those who do.

The third most prevalent source of disagreement is really the reverse of the problem just described. Disputes arise about the interpretation of minimum performance standards. As might be expected, this tends to occur among low-performing franchisees who complain that they must comply with inflexible or arbitrary minimum performance standards.

In evaluating your prospects for obtaining a franchise business, pay careful attention to whether the contract sufficiently covers the problem areas listed in Table 14-1. But give special consideration to the first three, since they occur more frequently and can be crucial to successful franchise operations.

Litigation is costly and can be avoided by adequate planning. As we've suggested, having prior business experience, consulting your own legal counsel, and conducting your own market research are the best ways to avoid potentially serious disputes.

DOING YOUR OWN MARKET RESEARCH

Conducting your own market research is the single most important ingredient in choosing the right franchise business. Franchisors wanting to expand distribution tend to feature the franchise opportunity in the best possible light. They may have elaborate location studies or consumer surveys to support their claims and fancy ways of presenting the benefits of winning one of their outlets.

Effective and profitable marketing for the franchise business is no different from that for other types of business. The marketing concepts, strategies, and tools covered in Chapters 4 through 6 are important in successfully operating the small franchise business. What is different is that some of the marketing responsibility is assumed by the franchisor, instead of you, the local entrepreneur. Prior to your investment, you should thoroughly check out the marketing expertise of the franchisor, particularly in the areas of product innovation, site location, national trademark and trade name image, advertising, and creativity in sales promotion.

These are the marketing responsibilities and benefits you buy with your investment in a particular franchise. It's up to you to determine how well these responsibilities are performed *before* you sink your money into the venture.

Product Innovation Are the products or services offered truly unique? Have the franchisor's products been tested thoroughly under market conditions? Does the franchisor seek and introduce new products and ways to improve on existing products?

What are the franchisor's plans (not promises) for new-product development and introduction?

These questions can be answered by your own observations of the franchise chain, by interviewing existing franchise owners and customers, and by reviewing critically any reports or product studies conducted by the franchisor. If you're not satisfied with the answers, it may mean that the franchisor is attempting to "sell you a franchise" rather than a business that offers proved and continually improving products.

The market concept, you'll remember, places the consumer first. Products or services offered by the franchise business must fulfill a consumer need. Huge outlays of money for advertising, site locations, and capital cannot compensate for poor or shoddy products or inadequate services.

Site Location   The success of most franchise businesses depends on a good location convenient to the customer. The amount and type of consumer traffic in close proximity to the outlet is crucial because, although the franchise may offer excellent products, the products are purchased by consumers on the basis of convenience.

As we've pointed out, franchisors usually follow one of two strategies. Either they locate outlets in areas where there is a cluster of outlets selling similar, but differentiated products, or they choose not to compete directly and locate outlets in more isolated markets. In addition, some follow the practice of having only "free-standing" outlets, whereas others locate in shopping malls or adjacent to other retail outlets in shopping centers.

The approach the franchisor uses to locate outlets depends on the market-segmentation strategy being followed. The franchisor should be able to give you hard data and professional, well-documented, market-research studies that describe the market segment reached and confirm the appropriateness of the approach to the site location.

If the outlet you're buying is new, you should review the franchisor's market studies critically.

Check the franchisor's data on consumer traffic by counting cars driving by and people walking by the store during a typical week. Check on Monday, Thursday, and Saturday; this will usually give good data during periods when you'd expect business to be good. Check the experience of other franchisees to see how traffic count translates into customers for the outlet. Compare these data with the franchisor's.

Visit the local government traffic or transportation department that controls streets and vehicle use around the potential site. Will there be changes in traffic patterns? Will parking ordinances be changed? Will streets be widened or major traffic arteries improved? In many cases accurate traffic surveys are available from local city or county governments or police departments; so you may not have to do it yourself.

Interview small business owners in the vicinity of the proposed site for your business. Seek their opinions about the appropriateness of the site for your outlet, the future of the commercial area and its potential, and any problems they foresee.

Study residential construction patterns and visit with real estate brokers to find out how population, property values, and growth in the area are changing. The local government officials who issue business permits are knowledgeable about the kinds of new businesses being attracted to the area. Editors of local newspapers may be helpful, and you should call on the local chamber of commerce.

Image and Advertising   The marketing of products and services sold by franchise outlets requires effective mass advertising. Fast food products, motels, tax services, auto mufflers, paint, hearing aids, and auto rental services need a large investment in advertising to create trade name or brand awareness on a national scale. Carefully designed advertising messages that saturate the consumer market and are repeated frequently are crucial for differentiating the franchisor's products or services from competitors'.

Most franchisors conduct national advertising campaigns to draw customers to their franchise outlets. Initial fees and often other charges paid by franchisees go to support the mass advertising effort. For a new outlet, national advertising will usually be supplemented by targeted local sales stimulation.

There are two important aspects of the franchisor-franchisee relationship to check out. First, find out what your financial commitments are in the franchisor's advertising program. How much of your initial investment goes for this purpose? What contributions will you have to make over time for the franchisor's national promotion campaign? Does the contract specifically state how the franchisor and franchisee will share in advertising expenditures?

Second, look into the nature of the advertising program itself. Will the advertising message appeal to the market for your outlet? Ask the franchisor for the year-ahead advertising plan. Comparative figures should be available to show how much advertising your market will receive versus other franchise markets. From your own experience, does it appear that the mix of mass media to be used in advertising—radio, TV, billboards, magazines, newspapers—will adequately reach the potential market for your outlet?

The franchisor should be able to show you media studies that document the effectiveness of the advertising campaign. Copy tests, for example, will demonstrate the believability and attention-getting impact of advertising messages. An analysis of the reach of the advertising program should be available to show how many consumers heard or saw the franchisor's messages, and their demographic or buying characteristics. You should also be able to learn how advertising will be programmed or scheduled in your local market—the media to be used, when ads will run, and how much will be spent.

Sales Promotion   Along with advertising efforts, sales promotion has become an important tool for stimulating consumers to patronize franchise outlets. These efforts may include special point-of-purchase display materials, in-store demonstrations, coupon-redemption deals, and premiums. Advertising is frequently used to inform consumers of the sales promotion.

As competition in franchising has increased, so too has franchisors' reliance on sales promotion as a tool to entice consumers to their outlets and to build customer loyalty. It is usually the franchisor's responsibility to design and execute creative sales-promotion programs. Concrete plans for sales promotion must be set well in advance, at least 6 months to 1 year, so that advertising and franchisee participation are properly coordinated.

Ask the franchisor for sales-effectiveness studies of past sales-promotion programs. Review the plan and approach to be used in the coming year. Will you have to pay for a share of the cost? Will particular sales-stimulation tools to be used be appropriate for your market? Will they be enough, or will you have to supplement such promotion with your own local campaign?

KEY FACTORS IN MARKETING—A SUMMARY

Be sure the investment you make will result in significantly helping you market your outlet. The franchisor's products or services must be thoroughly tested and meet an important consumer need. There should be evidence of new-product development and continual innovation. The franchisor should have a recognized trade name and a national reputation. Advertising should be geared to promoting franchise outlets and expanding the market for the franchisee's products. Creative sales promotion should supplement advertising and appeal to the potential market for your outlet.

Since the franchisor assumes some of the marketing responsibility for your outlet, nail down the specific forms and amounts of help you will get. Check past records and future plans. Verify claims by interviewing other franchisees and by doing your own local consumer analysis. Be sure all promises are put in writing, and that you'll receive your share of the franchisor's marketing resources.

Trends in Franchising

Although the franchising industry is maturing, it shows signs of continued vitality. The fast chaotic growth of the 1950s and 1960s resulted in a healthy shake-out in the early 1970s. This was caused by a combination of overexpansion, incompetent management, and poor business conditions. During the second half of the 1970s, increased legislation and surveillance by government at all levels corrected earlier abuses. Today there are far more assurances that companies offering franchise ventures are reputable and professional. The U.S. Department of Commerce reports that in the late 1980s more than 2000 business-format franchises operated in the United States, about twice as many as in the late 1970s.

Before citing some obstacles to future growth, we'll examine notable trends in franchising, including increased legislation, more power for the franchisee, and expansion in franchising services.

GOVERNMENT CONTROL

More than a dozen states have enacted legislation requiring franchising companies to register and to disclose fully their financial condition. Several other states have such legislation pending. And there are efforts to pass uniform regulations to govern franchisor-franchisee relations.

In one of the worst abuses in the past, franchisors withheld information from prospective franchisees on how well all the outlets in the chain were doing. Instead, some franchisors would present the financial data on only a few of their more profitable outlets.

Now, in addition to public disclosure, franchisors must meet tougher restrictions in the kinds of claims they can make in recruiting their franchisees and about the means by which they can terminate franchise agreements.

FRANCHISEE CONTROL

The rights of the franchisee have much better legal protection now than in the past; recent court decisions have tended to favor the franchisee. For example, court decisions have revoked the once-common practice by some franchisors of forcing franchisees to buy supplies and merchandise from them alone.

In several instances franchisees have organized into associations to negotiate more effectively with franchisors. In addition to the growing collective power of franchisees, the more profitable franchisees have substantial influence on the franchisor. There are numerous cases of franchisees, who have become successful, leaving the franchisor's chain and starting their own competitive franchise operation.

COMPANY-OWNED OUTLETS

Increased government regulation and franchisee control have heightened the interest of franchisors in buying back their franchised businesses. Moreover, to several major franchisors, the profitability of franchised outlets has made it good economic sense to manage company-owned outlets. Franchisees' profit ratios as much as four times the franchisors' have motivated franchisors to acquire their own outlets. Pizza Hut, Ponderosa Systems, and McDonald's have been active in acquiring their own outlets.

As we noted earlier, examine the termination conditions in your franchise agreement carefully. Guard against indirect methods that might be used by the franchisor to persuade you to sell out. Know what your legal rights are before you sign.

GROWTH IN FRANCHISING SERVICES

The service sector of the U.S. economy is larger than the manufacturing sector and is growing rapidly. Demand is strong and rising for consumer and industrial services. The number of franchised businesses has soared in the fields of recreation, entertainment, travel, and business services.

The financial requirements for starting the franchised service business tend to be much less than for the product business, since most are not capital-intensive. Further, as we stressed in Chapter 8, the rendering of services takes more personal involvement and interaction with consumers. Thus, small franchised businesses, owned locally and serving a limited geographical area, tend to be an ideal vehicle for expanding distribution.

OBSTACLES TO FUTURE GROWTH

We've already noted the problem of obtaining good site locations. In addition, franchisors increasingly face capital shortages in expanding operations because of rising land and construction costs. Even when good locations are available, local regulations are growing stringent in controlling building design, size of signs, building setbacks, and parking-space requirements.

Increased competition and the difficulty of finding good franchisees are also problems facing franchisors. Some key markets may be nearing a saturation point. Also, franchisors, who had numerous applications a few years ago, report that recruiting an effective franchise team is getting more difficult. This has resulted in more public appeals and advertising by franchisors to locate franchisees.

KEY TRENDS IN FRANCHISING

CHAPTER 14

409

Is Franchising
the Way
to Go?

The factors we've examined here have produced a more stable industry with tighter controls and better protection for franchisees. As the more mature phase continues, there are clear signals that responsible franchisors will pursue a more orderly, soundly based, growth pattern.

Opportunities in service-oriented franchises look promising. And as capital becomes increasingly scarce, other types of businesses, not now using the franchise method of distribution, will be drawn to franchising. Finally, franchisors may improve the benefits of obtaining and operating their franchised outlets because of the short supply of good franchisees.

Pros and Cons in Franchising

Summary

From a legal viewpoint a franchise is an agreement between a supplier and a retailer (or wholesale distributor) under which the supplier grants the right to handle its products or services to the franchisor in a mutually agreed upon way. The franchising relationship means that you operate your own business under certain defined conditions and in connection with a larger framework or chain of similar businesses. As a franchisee you are given the right to represent and market the product or service of the franchisor in a specific geographical area.

In exchange, you may pay an initial fee. Some major franchisors derive most of their revenue from this source. In other cases, either with or without an initial fee, franchisors receive continuing revenue from franchisees' payments for royalty, leasing the outlet, and supplies furnished by the franchisor.

A major benefit of franchising is the cooperative buying power and resulting lower cost of supplies, equipment, sales-promotion material, and advertising. You also receive training and other assistance to operate the business successfully.

In return for your investment, the franchisor should offer tested products, a national, presold market, proved selling methods, less business risk, and a relatively short time before your business shows a profit. Other services normally include operating manuals, management training, site selection, facility design and construction, lease negotiation, and in some cases, financing the franchising venture. Once the business is launched, continuing services often include sales promotion, merchandising, national advertising, and retraining.

The franchise contract spells out the responsibilities of the partners involved. Legal problems occur most often because of poor planning and confusion in interpreting clauses within the contract. You should get your own competent legal counsel to review the contract in detail before you sign.

Check out the reputation of the franchisor with bankers, the Better Business Bureau, and other franchisees. Extend your investigation to the product or service to be offered, the potential market in which your outlet will be located, and the advertising and sales-promotion efforts of the franchisor. Make sure you are familiar with the community's building and zoning regulations, growth pattern, highway and street plans, real estate trends and outlook, and changes in population and income. The time and effort you spend in planning for your franchise venture will reduce your risk and make your investment more secure.

Franchising

Special note: Your completed assignments for Chapters 4 through 6 will apply to some of the exercises here. If you are considering a service franchise, Chapter 8 will also apply. You may want to review them all after studying this chapter.

1. List the advantages and disadvantages to *you* for choosing the franchise route to owning and running a business compared to starting your own business from scratch. The central question to address is: What can the franchisor do for me that I cannot do for myself?

Advantages	**Disadvantages**

2. Develop an action plan for carrying out your own independent marketing research to evaluate the franchise opportunity you are considering.

   a. Product or service innovation: _____

   _____

   _____

   _____

   b. Site location: _____

   _____

   _____

   _____

c. Image and advertising: _____

_____

_____

_____

d. Sales promotion: _____

_____

_____

_____

e. Overall market trends and prospects: _____

_____

_____

_____

_____

3. Before you've made any financial commitments: How will you verify and evaluate the services the franchisor will supply you once you've made your investment? Make notes for actions you'll take to assess each category below.

a. The business location and facility: _____

_____

_____

_____

b. Training in the business: _____

_____

_____

_____

c. Franchise operations: _____

_____

_____

_____

_____

4. In evaluating a particular franchise agreement, specify below the areas of business operations over which:

a. You'll have no control: _____

_____

_____

_____

_____

_____

b. You'll have some control: _____

_____

_____

_____

c. You'll have total control: _____

_____

_____

_____

5. List below the specific features of the franchise contract you'll want evaluated by your legal counsel.

a. _____

b. _____

c. _____

d. _____

e. _____

f. _____

KEY TERMS

franchise 390

franchisee 390,395

franchisor 390

transfer 402

STUDY ASSIGNMENTS FOR REVIEW AND DISCUSSION

1. Define the essential nature of franchising and the four major types of franchising organizations.

2. What factors appear to distinguish the successful from the unsuccessful franchisees?

3. Why would a manufacturer choose franchising as a method for distributing its products over using: (1) company-owned outlets, or (2) an established channel of distribution with independently owned wholesalers and retailers?

4. What kinds of businesses, products, or services seem particularly suited to franchising? What are their characteristics?

5. In what major ways does being a franchisee differ from being an independent entrepreneur?

6. Discuss the crucial elements of the franchise contract and the several ways in which the franchisor can exert control over the franchisee.

7. What are the three most common legal problems encountered by franchisees? How can these problems be avoided?

8. Discuss ways in which a prospective franchisee can conduct market research to determine the potential of a particular outlet.

9. How can the marketing concept be used to evaluate claims made by a franchisor about market opportunities for their products?

10. Discuss important trends and prospects in the franchising field. What are the major obstacles to future growth?

PROJECTS FOR STUDENTS

1. Contact the headquarters of three franchising organizations and ask for examples of their market and site-location studies. Evaluate the information, and specify: (1) any additional data that would be desirable, and (2) ways in which a prospective franchisee could validate the information.

2. Obtain samples of franchise contracts from three different franchising organizations. Evaluate and report to the class the commitment and responsibilities of the contracting parties, including any areas that appear vague.

3. Interview franchise owners in the vicinity. Ask them about problems in dealing with their franchisor. Determine what the franchisor does that they could not

accomplish on their own. Find out how satisfied they are with their franchise relationship. Use some of the questions we suggested in this chapter for assessing the franchisor's product and marketing program. Report results to the class.

4. Choose an example of a particular type of franchise outlet. Obtain information from the franchising organization on how they select good store locations. Develop criteria for judging the potential of different site locations. Select two promising sites in your local area and conduct a field investigation, including a study of consumer traffic and the influence of local zoning and ordinance restrictions. Report back to the class on results of the feasibility study.

IF YOU WANT TO READ MORE

Books

BOND, Robert E.: *The Source Book of Franchise Opportunities,* Dow Jones–Irwin, Homewood, IL, 1985. A comprehensive directory of franchises, including up-to-date summaries of more than 1400 companies in 126 different business categories.

DIAS, Robert M., and Stanley I. GURNICK: *Franchising: The Investor's Complete Handbook,* Hastings House, New York, 1969. Although somewhat dated—the book was published just prior to the shakeout in the industry in the early 1970s—it is still one of the best nuts-and-bolts treatments of franchising from the viewpoint of the prospective franchisee.

Franchising in the Economy, 1982–1984: U.S. Department of Commerce, Government Printing Office, Washington, DC, 1984. This statistical survey is the 13th annual report on franchising in the United States during 1982–1984, prepared by the Bureau of Industrial Economics.

FRIEDLANDER, Mark P., Jr., and Gene GURNEY: *Handbook of Successful Franchising,* Van Nostrand Reinhold, New York, 1985. This book presents a simply written reference guide that describes various types of franchisors. It offers specific information to prospective franchisees aimed at helping them find the kind of business suited to their needs and purposes.

HAMMOND, Alexander: *Franchise Rights: A Self-Defense Manual,* Panel Publishers, Greenvale, NY, 1979. This guide is designed to aid franchisees to understand their legal rights in order to protect their crucial business interests.

HENWARD, DeBanks M., III, and William GINALSKI: *The Franchise Option,* The Franchise Group Publishers, Phoenix, AZ, 1979. This book is written from the franchisor's point of view. It tells what franchising is, how it works, what it takes to be successful, and how to develop a franchise system. Developed from the long-time personal experience of the authors, the book offers a practical guide for potential franchisors.

SELTZ, David D.: *How to Get Started in Your Own Franchised Business,* Farnsworth Publishing Co., Inc., Rockville Center, NY, 1980. This book gives the information needed to help franchisees to select: (1) the franchise most compatible with their qualifications, (2) a franchise with excellent potential for success, (3) a franchise within their financial resources, and (4) a reliable franchisor who will live up to contractual obligations.

SELTZ, David D.: *The Complete Handbook of Franchising,* Addison-Wesley, Reading, MA, 1982. This book provides franchising guidelines and brief information on such topics as personnel, financing, advertising, training, PERT/CPM, the break-even chart, and legal considerations.

VAUGHN, Charles L.: *Franchising,* 2d ed., Lexington Books, Lexington, MA, 1979. Gives a complete overview and history of franchising. Describes the nature, scope, and advantages in a nontechnical way. Good case histories are given covering legal and marketing problems.

Monographs

Franchising, a report published by the *Small Business Reporter,* Bank of America, San Francisco, 1975. Practical and succinct, this report covers the contractual and financial aspects of franchising.

MCGUIRE, E. Patrick: *Franchised Distribution*, The Conference Board, Inc., New York, 1971. This is a detailed report on research findings in the franchise industry. Areas covered include franchisor operations, franchisee recruitment, contracts, site selection, and training.

Directories

Directory of Franchising Organizations, Pilot Books, New York. Published annually.

Franchise Opportunities Handbook, U.S. Department of Commerce, Government Printing Office, Washington, DC, 1972.

Newsletters

Continental Franchise Review, National Research Publishing, Inc., Denver, CO. Published 26 times per year.

CHAPTER 15

Deciding on Some Key Legal Matters

TOPICS IN THIS CHAPTER

Objectives of This Chapter
Sole Proprietorship
Partnership
Corporation
Expenses of Different Forms of Business Organization
Protection of Ideas and Concepts
Finding an Attorney and an Accountant
Deciding Some Key Legal Issues—Summary
Worksheet 15: Deciding on Some Key Legal Matters
Key Terms
Study Assignments for Review and Discussion
Projects for Students
If You Want to Read More

Refer to the third segment of the flow diagram of the business process that treats MONEY and CREDIT (Figure 1-1). In Chapters 10 and 11 we dealt with financial matters, raising money for your business, and managing your financial affairs. Our aim in this chapter is to recommend ways you can preserve the financial status you've built. You'll do this by following the requirements of your local, state, and federal legislation. In addition you'll preserve the value of your unique ideas through patent, copyright, trademark, or service mark. The chapter closes with recommendations on how to find a competent attorney and accountant who can aid you in protecting your legal and financial interests.

Information in this chapter will be found pertinent to these items in the business plan:

1.A. Description of your proposed business

1.C. Summary of your financial estimates

2.A. Statement of the desirability of your product or service

3.B. Detailed explanations of your place in the state of the art

4.   Technical description of product or service

7.A. Plan of operation

9.A. Conclusions and summary

You + **IDEA** + $\begin{cases} \textbf{MONEY} \\ \textbf{CREDIT} \end{cases}$ + $\begin{cases} \textbf{FACILITIES} \\ \textbf{PEOPLE} \end{cases}$ $\begin{matrix} \textbf{PRODUCT} \\ \rightarrow \quad \textbf{OR} \\ \textbf{SERVICE} \end{matrix}$ + Marketing $\begin{cases} \text{Money} \\ \text{Credit} \end{cases}$ $\rightarrow$ Profit

Three basic forms of business structure are available to you in setting up your business. These are the sole proprietorship, the partnership, and the corporation. Each has advantages and disadvantages. You'll want to check carefully before you decide which to choose, because of two fundamental variables: cost of setting up and the tax consequences attached to each form.

You'd be wise to seek professional help in making your decision. Two professionals who can help are a lawyer and an accountant; both should be familiar with small business. They can help you decide which form will give you the best breaks on your taxes and which will protect your assets in case of financial claims against your business. They can also help you estimate the fees for setting up your business in the form you choose.

Objectives of This Chapter

This chapter describes key legal points you should know about in forming a new business. This material is not intended to make you a legal expert in these matters, nor is it designed to treat in detail the legal issues you should cover in starting a new business. It should, however, give you enough background so you can talk intelligently about your legal needs with your attorney and accountant. By studying this chapter you should be able to:

- Learn the advantages and disadvantages, and the cautions to observe, in adopting the three most common forms of legal structure for a business
  Sole proprietorship
  Partnership
  Corporation

- Understand the tax advantages and disadvantages of each form of legal structure

- Select qualified directors for the corporate form of business organization

- Estimate the approximate costs for setting up each of the three legal forms of organization

- Gain appreciation of the extent of licenses, permits, and other state and federal taxes

- Learn how to protect original ideas, concepts for patents; and what copyrights, trademarks, and service marks are

- Adopt a well-tested approach in selecting a lawyer and an accountant

Sole Proprietorship

The sole proprietorship is the easiest way to start a business. As the sole proprietor you own all the assets of the company. The legal requirements are minimum: You may need only to buy a license for doing business in your own community. If you operate under a fictitious name—that is, a name other than your own—you'll have to register that name with the appropriate authority. It's necessary that you publish your fictitious business name in an authorized newspaper and show that you're the person legally behind it. You can then open a bank account in the fictitious name. Without this formality, you might be unable to sue or collect debts due you because your business wouldn't exist under the law.

ADVANTAGES OF SOLE PROPRIETORSHIP

To start your business as a sole owner, you have merely to offer your product or service to the public and to make your first sale. You're in business when you've made that sale.

The sole proprietorship is the simplest and easiest to start. It's also the least expensive, requiring the least legal documentation of all forms of business ownership.

Another advantage of the sole proprietorship is the ease of making decisions. As the owner you can decide what to do as quickly as you make up your mind. You don't have to consult with anyone, but you'd be wise to ask for expert help in matters that are outside your own competence. In any event, one of the great advantages you have as the sole owner is the speed at which you can operate. You can see and seize an opportunity for making money quickly. And you can get under way before a larger partnership or corporation can decide to move.

The sole proprietorship uses an elementary form of organization, which may be diagramed as shown in Figure 15-1.

With the key people reporting directly to you and taking their orders directly from you, the sole proprietorship gives you the advantage of the shortest and most direct lines of communication. You'd be able to keep up with what's going on, to see how well your people are performing, and to manage proactively with minimum time lost.

DISADVANTAGES OF SOLE PROPRIETORSHIP

A major disadvantage of the sole proprietorship is that it offers no shelter from claims of creditors. If you are sued as the sole owner of the business, all your personal

FIG. 15-1

Typical organization chart for a small proprietorship.

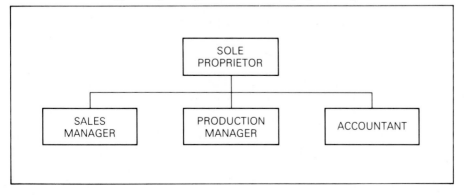

assets are subject to lien for the satisfaction of creditors' claims. That means that what you own could be taken from you to pay off the claims of a successful lawsuit against your business.

You may protect yourself against many kinds of claims by having adequate insurance. If you have proper insurance coverage, you'd be protected—for example, if a customer slips and is injured in your store or if a customer suffers injury in using your product. Here again you'd do well to get expert advice to ensure that you take the right steps.

Another disadvantage of being the sole owner is that you're alone. As the chief executive you must wear many hats. Your position demands tremendous amounts of time and energy. And you have no one to share the load.

TAX IMPLICATIONS FOR THE SOLE PROPRIETOR

Owners of sole proprietorships pay income tax as individuals. If they have income from outside investments, it is combined with the profit or loss from the business in one tax return.

Sole proprietors should prepare for continuity of the business upon their death or prolonged illness. It's difficult for self-confident, tough-minded entrepreneurs to imagine themselves falling victim to incapacitating illness or dying. Yet many a family has suffered financial disaster when either one of these has happened without the owner's having prepared for continuance of the business.

In the absence of direction given in a sound legal will or by court order, executors have no power or right to operate the business. If the incapacitated or deceased's wealth is tied up in the business or is otherwise not readily available in cash form, such as real estate, the heirs—if the sole proprietor has died—may have great difficulty in finding cash to pay the inheritance taxes. The same is true for paying debts the firm may owe. The cash shortage may require quick liquidation of the firm's assets or sale of the business, almost always at a sacrifice.

The need is clear for entrepreneurs to be proactive in preparing for continuation of the business if they are unable to work because of illness or after they have died. This they can best do by preparing directives for the business in a legally sound will *and* training capable persons to take over management of the business.

McCULLOCH INSTRUMENTS

Louis McCulloch was a dental technician with a well-developed inventive talent. He set up in business to manufacture a small line of dental instruments that he had designed and developed. His business grew as he added instruments to the line. A national medical equipment distributor took on the McCulloch line and increased the scope of the business until it was doing $2.5 million gross annually. The business was extremely profitable, producing an income before taxes of nearly 20 percent. At no time were there more than 45 employees in the shop.

McCulloch ran the business as a sole proprietor. He didn't think of himself as a businessman; he tended to be secretive and indecisive in facing crucial business decisions.

During the years, he had many offers from investors who wished to put money into the business and expand its operations. He had offers of mergers from larger firms, and recommendations from investment bankers who wanted him to take his company public. His response to these advances was inconclusive—nothing ever came of them. As a result of his do-nothing attitude, several capable managers left his employ; he became essentially a one-man operation.

In his effort to avoid paying what he thought of as exorbitant income taxes, McCulloch ignored the advice of his accountant and drew only small amounts of earnings from the business. He put the bulk of the company's earnings in government bonds and T-bills.

When the company was 10 years old, McCulloch suffered a severe heart attack that hospitalized him for many weeks. The business was left with no one qualified to run it while he was confined to his hospital bed; operation of the company continued by virtue of inertia but became shakier and shakier. After 5 months McCulloch died without having left his hospital bed. He left as heirs his wife and daughter, who had no knowledge of or interest in the business.

The Internal Revenue Service evaluated the estate on the basis of the considerable hoard of liquid assets held in the firm rather than on the miserable financial condition of the business. In order to pay the taxes and realize enough cash to more or less adequately cover her expenses, Mrs. McCulloch had to sell the sick business, which at its peak should have brought at least $2 million, for somewhat less than one-fifth of that amount.

What should McCulloch have done to secure the future of the business after his death?

Partnership

Business
Plan
Outline
1.A, 7.A, 9.A

A partnership may be thought of as an association of two or more persons who carry on a business as coowners with the intent of making a profit. A partnership may be established by oral or written agreement. It's assumed to exist when there's a clearly perceived intention to be partners, when there's coownership and community of interest in the business, and when there's sharing of profit and loss.

You may enter into a partnership simply by talking it over with an acquaintance or a friend and agreeing to go into business together. However, this way of doing it has some dangers, as the partnership is such a close relationship that it's almost like a marriage. A new business, like a new marriage, almost always goes through difficult periods. Because the partners are human beings, subject to differences of opinion and emotional responses to trying situations, it's most important that the partnership agreement be spelled out in detail before the business starts. This suggests that you carefully consider two aspects of your intended partnership: (1) Choose your partner or partners with great care. Make sure you can get along well together under difficult circumstances, and that you can work through differences and come to satisfactory agreement. (2) And get *expert legal help* in setting up the partnership. That means you should put in writing in a binding form the responsibilities of the partners and the ways in which foreseeable problems are to be solved or decisions made when these problems arise.

Your objective here should be that of proactive management. You should anticipate possible contingencies with your partner or partners. Then you should agree on how they are to be handled to produce results that all consider fair. These procedures should then be put in a legally binding document prepared with the guidance of your attorney. In this way all partners will have foreknowledge of their rights and obligations. You and your partner or partners will be able to put your energies into making the business prosper without draining energy in avoidable disputes.

RIGHTS AND OBLIGATIONS OF PARTNERS

The relationship of partners in the conduct of business has been spelled out in the Uniform Partnership Act. This model partnership law was developed by the National Commissioners on Uniform State Laws. Many states have adopted the Uniform Partnership Act in its entirety; others have enacted variations of it. You should follow the legislation in force in your state if you enter into a partnership. In any event, the Uniform Partnership Act gives useful guidelines for a partnership, in outlining both rights and obligations of partners.

Rights   Under the Uniform Partnership Act, each partner has the right to:

- Share in the management and conduct of the business

- Share in the profits of the firm

- Receive repayment of contributions

- Receive indemnification for, or return of, payments made on behalf of the partnership

- Receive interest on additional advances made to the business

- Have access to the books and records of the partnership

- Have formal accounting of partnership affairs

Obligations   Under the act each partner has the obligation to:

- Contribute toward losses sustained by the partnership

- Work for the partnership without pay in the customary sense, but rather for a share of the profits

- Submit to majority vote, or arbitration, when differences arise about the conduct of affairs of the business

- Give other partners any information known personally about partnership affairs

- Account to the partnership for all profits coming from any partnership transaction, or from the use of partnership property

As you can see from this list, the partnership relationship must rest on good faith and honest dealing. The Uniform Partnership Act was drawn up on the basic principle that each partner has a *fiduciary* obligation to other partners—that is, the relationship is founded in trust and confidence.

The importance of trust and confidence in a partnership cannot be overstated. For example, any partner may bind the partnership to a deal without the knowledge of the other partners. This means that your partner could commit your partnership business to a costly action without your agreement, and the commitment would be legally binding. Your whole fortune, all your personal assets, could be put at a risk without your knowledge or consent. For this reason, the interpersonal relations among partners must be founded on complete honesty and trust. There can be no secrets in a partnership if it's to be successful.

NEW PARTNERS

Persons entering into an existing partnership are generally held responsible for obligations of the partnership existing at the time of their entry. However, for the protection of new partners, a special provision of this rule states that incoming partners' responsibility for preexisting debts shall be limited to only the partnership property. In other words, new partners' personal assets may not be attached to satisfy preexisting debts of the old partnership. Some states still have legislation governed by common law. Here the incoming partner is not liable for debts of the firm current at the time of entry, unless there's an agreement to assume this liability.

If you consider taking in a partner after your business is established, you should carefully think through and agree on the responsibilities the new person will take on when joining the firm. Here again, you'd do well to have a written agreement prepared by an attorney.

TAX IMPLICATIONS FOR PARTNERSHIPS

If you don't yet recognize the complexities of federal and state tax laws, you will, soon after you start your business. We can't begin to deal with the intricacies of taxation for partnerships in this text. However, you should know some key points about taxation of partnerships. We'll cover them here.

The federal income tax laws give a unique status to partnerships. They aren't taxable as partnerships; partners are individually liable for their share of taxes resulting from the partnership's business.

Although partnerships don't file an income tax return, they're required to file an information return (Form 1065) signed by one of the partners. This form reports gross income, deductions, and the names and percentages of the firm's business shared by its members. Partners are individually liable for their proportionate share of taxes resulting from the business.

What this means for you as a partner in your business is that you must determine your own individual income tax, taking into account your share of the partnership income, gain, loss, deduction, or credit.

Gain and loss must be apportioned among partners in accordance with their profit and loss ratios, unless the partnership agreement specifies some other arrangement. In some partnerships, certain members will contribute capital and others only services. The usual agreement states that losses are to be borne only by those contributing capital. Partners who contribute only services usually bear losses limited to the extent of their accumulated earnings.

Tax consequences will usually follow the partnership agreement. The initial partnership agreement can, of course, be changed by mutual consent.

TERMINATION AND DISSOLUTION

Termination of a partnership is defined somewhat differently for tax purposes than for closing out the relationship and the business. The Internal Revenue Code of 1954 states that a partnership is considered terminated: (1) when partnership business activities cease, or (2) when there's a sale or exchange of an interest of 50 percent or more in capital and profits of the partnership within a 12-month period.

Termination in either case is significant for tax purposes for three reasons:

- Termination closes the taxable year of the partnership; if the partner and partnership are on different taxable years, the partners may experience a bunching of partnership income that could materially increase their income taxes.

- Termination may stop the use of a favorable fiscal year for the partnership business. If the business is succeeded by another partnership, the successor partnership will be regarded as a new partnership and will need consent from the Commissioner of Internal Revenue for the adoption of a fiscal year different from that of the principal partners.

- Termination of a partnership results in the properties of the partnership being deemed to be distributed to the partners.

Termination is defined somewhat differently for purposes other than taxation. Under the Uniform Partnership Act, termination is the final act of winding up the business; another term, *dissolution,* is defined as the change in the partnership relationship caused by any one partner ceasing to be associated with the business. Dissolution is not considered a termination of the partnership. Nor is it considered a termination of the rights and powers of the several partners. Many of these rights and powers continue during the closing-out process that follows dissolution. Termination occurs after the intent to cease operations of the partnership is expressed (dissolution) and all the affairs of the partnership are concluded.

Dissolution may be caused by any of the following:

- Expiration of a specified period of time (term certain) or the finishing of an undertaking spelled out in the partnership agreement

- Expressed wish of any partner when no definite term or particular undertaking is specified

- Expressed wish of all partners, either before or after the expiration of a term certain or specified undertaking

- Expulsion of a partner under the provisions of the partnership agreement

- Withdrawal, retirement, or death of a partner (except when a partnership agreement provides for continuation under any of these circumstances)

■ Sale or transfer of substantially all of the assets of the partnership

■ Bankruptcy of any partner or of the partnership

You can see that the partnership is a close personal relationship. When a change of partners occurs for any reason, the partnership dissolves in the eyes of the law, unless otherwise provided by agreement.

Dissolution of a partnership doesn't free the partners from the debts to creditors or from their obligation to act equitably toward one another. These duties remain until all are taken care of and the partnership is terminated. In others words, the partnership and the partners, including the estate of a partner who may have died, must fulfill all obligations of the past until these preexisting matters are taken care of. Winding up affairs for termination includes the performance of existing contracts, collection of debts or claims due the firm, and payments of debts owed by the firm.

At the time of dissolution, the partners lose their power to act for the partnership in all matters except those involved in liquidation of the partnership. They can't legally take on future obligations; potential creditors in this situation would be subject to being defrauded.

The partnership agreement should provide for the amount and method of payment of a partner's interest upon disability, withdrawal, retirement, or death. If this isn't done in the legal partnership document, bitter controversy may occur among partners when the partnership is dissolved.

LIMITED PARTNERSHIP

The limited partnership is usually used in real estate developments and some kinds of international business. It's a particular form of partnership that gives investors special tax advantages and shielding from liability.

A limited partnership is set up in the same way as a general partnership. However, in some states a special notice must be filed in the county or district where the limited partnership has its principal office.

A limited partnership is a creature of statute. Unless the legally required recording and publishing of notice are carefully followed in all details, the partnership will be considered a general partnership in the eyes of the law.

The limited partnership includes one or more general partners and one or more limited partners. The general partners manage the affairs of the partnership; the limited partners are investors only. They have the advantage of limited liability. If the business fails, the most they can lose is their original investment, any additional capital contribution, and their portion of the assets of the firm. General partners, who manage the firm, have unlimited liability as in any ordinary partnership.

Limited partners legally may have no say in the management of affairs of the firm. Those partners who violate this proscription automatically dissolve the limited status of their partnership. They then become general partners and have the same unlimited liability for the debts of the firm as the originally designated general partners.

If the assets of a limited partnership are sold or transferred, the limited partners, as major investors, usually have control of the transaction.

The duration of the limited partnership is stated in the original agreement and certificate filed with the appropriate public authority. Procedures for transfer of limited or general partner's interests should be agreed upon at the time of formation of the limited partnership.

Tax Implications   The limited partnership, as with the general partnership, is not itself a taxable entity—the partners are the taxpayers. Financial information must be reported, but taxes are levied on individual partners. The Tax Reform Act of 1986 modified the way in which limited partners can receive the benefit of noncash losses. By definition a limited partner is considered to be a passive investor. A general partner who materially participates in a real estate investment, for example, can recognize a loss up to $25,000 from that activity. This loss can be used to offset other sources of income, provided his or her adjusted gross income is under $100,000.

A passive activity is one that involves a trade or business in which the taxpayer does not materially participate. An individual materially participates only if involved in the operations of the activity on a regular, continuous, and substantial basis. Since the limited partnership requires lack of involvement in the activity for which it was established, the limited partner can only offset noncash loss in a passive activity by taxable income from another passive activity. Under these circumstances, the limited partner, usually an investor with high income, gets the tax advantages of the individual but is exposed to none of the consequences of personal liability if the project fails.

Corporation

The corporation is an "artificial being" sanctioned by law in each of the 50 states. The powers granted the corporation are those spelled out by legislation in each state. Differences in the legal requirements among the states are numerous; therefore, the discussion that follows concentrates on characteristics of corporations in general.

A typical organization chart for a modest-sized corporation is shown in Figure 15-2.

LIMITED LIABILITY

The corporate form of organization has several advantages, but high among them is that of limited liability. The liability of shareholders, who own the company, is limited to the amount of their investment in stock of the company. This means that if you set up your business as a corporation, your investment is reflected in the shares you own. Your personal liability is now limited simply to the amount of the money you used to buy the stock—provided you run the company in a way that fulfills the legal requirements for corporations in your state.

The same is true for those who may invest in your business by buying shares. Sole proprietors expose their entire net worth for the satisfaction of creditors if the business gets into difficulty. Partners have similar exposure; in addition, their responsibility is collective, and this may result in strained relations among partners in time of financial stress. Investors in the shares of a corporation, however, avoid this total exposure. Their liability to corporate creditors is limited to the purchase price of their shares.

you expect. And, what can be worse, if for several years your company has engaged in financing practices that are later shown to be improper, your tax benefits may be replaced by liabilities for back taxes plus interest. This discussion should suggest to you the desirability of consulting professional counsel—a qualified accountant or tax lawyer—before deciding in these matters.

TRANSFERABILITY OF OWNERSHIP INTEREST

The corporate form carries with it another advantage. It's easy to transfer ownership. You can add to the owners by simply allowing outsiders to buy stock in your corporation. Or if a shareholder wants to sell out, the procedure is straightforward; the shareholder's stock is sold to someone else and ownership of that portion of the company represented by the shares automatically transfers. In any circumstance, you must observe the legal formalities required in the sale of shares.

If you, or those of you who formed the corporation, want to hold the ownership to a small select group, you may readily restrict the transferability of stock. You may make provision for such restriction in the charter or articles of incorporation, in the bylaws, or in a separate agreement among the shareholders. An agreement among the original shareholders is usually the simplest way of keeping the shares among those you prefer. This agreement would provide for a first refusal or option to purchase from shareholders wishing to sell their shares.

BOARD OF DIRECTORS

The top management of a corporation rests in a board of directors by law. Too often the small businessperson overlooks the possibility of getting sound advice and counsel from a board composed of experienced and knowledgeable members. A small, closely held corporation will often have on its board the principal shareholder, spouse, or other relative, and perhaps one other person, a close friend. These may be the people most easily available to you as principal shareholder. You should, however, spend whatever energy it takes to assemble a "working" board rather than the "titular" board you may have with relatives and friends.

Your working board should have individuals who can give your company strength where it's needed. You'll recall the three basic strengths a small company can't do without (or any size company for that matter): production—ability to get out the product or service in good style; marketing—competence in identifying the right market segment and developing effective techniques for reaching it at the right price in the right quantity; and financial expertise—ability to make appropriate financial plans for the business and to control the flow and use of money to the company's best advantage. You may use these requirements as a guide in choosing people for your board of directors. If your strength is in production, you will want to make sure that you have one person on your board with a solid marketing background and one with wide experience in financial management and control. Your working board will then be a source of counsel and strength in helping you make the proper decisions needed to run your company efficiently and profitably.

A word of caution: In the past many people took on directorships in corporations for the prestige of the title or for the sake of helping a friend. Titular boards were common. This has changed today. Court decisions have recently imposed severe personal penalties on directors whose companies suffered large losses attributable to their negligence in performing their duties. In typical cases, directors have relied on financial data supplied by company management without their own independent analysis, or they have failed to use independent business judgment in assessing management recommendations. Because of this, many experienced business executives are now wary of becoming directors. You must be able to show competent people that you're willing to listen to and take sound advice if you want them to become directors of your corporation.

Inside versus Outside Boards   Boards of directors may be classified in another way as "inside" or "outside" boards. If the majority of your directors are chosen from within the company, your board is called an inside board; if the majority come from outside the company, your board is considered an outside board. You can readily see the advantages of an outside board for giving you advice based upon an objective point of view. Contrary to the case with inside board members, outside board members aren't dependent upon you for their jobs. They can use their best judgment in independent fashion to chart a course of action for your company. They're not swayed by the specter of losing their positions if they should disagree with you, the chief executive officer.

Although it's sometimes hard to accept advice from outsiders, you'd be in a much better position to form sound judgments by listening carefully to what a competent director might say. But no matter whether you choose to have an inside or an outside board, you should select only competent people to serve as your directors.

TAX TREATMENT OF CORPORATIONS

Corporations are treated like individuals for federal income tax purposes. This is different from partnerships, which are tax-reporting but not taxpaying entities. As long as the corporation observes legal requirements and behaves as a corporation should, its identity will be honored. This means that the corporation has been set up for a legitimate purpose, that there is no fraud or sham, as, for example, the intent to avoid taxes.

A taxpayer has the right, of course, to reduce taxes or to avoid them by legitimate means. One technique for reducing taxes under special circumstances is the adoption of what is known as an S corporation.

Special rules and regulations of the Internal Revenue Code of 1986, previously known as Subchapter S,[1] permit the setting aside of the corporate entity at the request of the shareholders. The effect of setting aside the corporate entity is, for tax purposes only, to have the shareholders treated as individual taxpayers. In other words, the income or loss of the corporation passes through to the individual shareholders as if they were partners.

Adopting the S form of corporation is a tricky business, as you'll see from the following discussion. Major requirements for gaining S status are given below; however, there are others that must be met in special circumstances. You'll want to consult a knowledgeable attorney in applying for this status.

---

[1]The tax laws affecting Subchapter S corporations were rewritten in 1986. Subchapter S corporations are now known simply as S corporations.

S Requirements   A corporation must meet the following requirements to qualify
for S treatment:

- It must be incorporated in the United States

- No shareholder can be an alien nonresident individual

- Shareholders must be natural persons, estates, or trusts

- No shareholder can be a partnership or a corporation

- The corporation can have only one class of common stock, and no preferred
  stock

- There cannot be more than 35 shareholders

Electing S Status   To become an S corporation, a company that meets the foregoing
requirements (plus others in special cases) must file an election of Form 2553 with
the Internal Revenue Service. All shareholders must sign the election. It must be
filed during the first 75 days of the corporation's tax year for which the election is
to go into effect, or at any time during the preceding tax year. A new corporation
wanting to start as an S corporation must file an election in the 75-day period after
it is considered to have begun its first tax year—when it issues stock to its shareholders, acquires assets, or begins to do business, whichever occurs *first*. Great care
must be taken to file the election at the right time. There can be disastrous tax
consequences if you manage the corporation as if it were an S corporation and it
isn't by law because the election is later determined to have been filed too early or
too late.

Terminating an S Election   If the shareholders decide that it is to their advantage
to terminate the S form of corporation, all they need do is have shareholders owning
over half the stock sign and file a revocation form. A revocation is effective for the
tax year it is filed, if it is filed during the first two and a half months of that tax
year. If it is filed later in that year, it does not become effective until the next year.
Once terminated, the S status cannot be reinstated for 5 years, unless the IRS gives
special consent.

Reasons for Electing S Status   The S status can offer significant advantages in
some cases; in others it can have drawbacks. If you should decide to explore the S
status, you should employ the help of a tax professional, because you will be dealing
with very complex and technical areas of the law, full of pitfalls for the amateur.
     The S status for a corporation is usually most favorable in one or more of the
following circumstances:

- The corporation expects to lose money in the first years of operation, and the
  shareholders will have income from other sources. Here the losses "passed through"
  can shelter the shareholders from income tax in greater or lesser degree. Losses
  are limited to taxpayers' basis in stock plus direct shareholders' loans.

■ Because of the tax bracket the shareholders are in, there can be tax savings if the expected profits of the S corporation are split among them.

■ The business is such that the corporation does not need to retain a significant portion of its profits. All or most of its profits can be distributed as dividends, thus avoiding the "double taxation" that the standard corporation is subject to.

■ S corporations are required to adopt the same tax year used by the principal partners, or partners owning the majority of profits and capital. It is very difficult to obtain IRS approval of a tax year other than a calendar year.

You can see from the above discussion that it is often good planning to operate a business as an S corporation in its beginning years, when losses can be passed through to the shareholders. Also shielding from personal liability as shareholders in a corporation affords advantage to individuals. Danger of failure is riskiest in the early stages of operation; therefore, many businesses start off as S corporations, gaining the advantage of limited liability for shareholders. Later, when the business has become quite profitable, the S election can be terminated and the corporation can elect standard corporate status.

Disadvantages of S Election   As in many cases, advantages are often accompanied by disadvantages. Two major disadvantages attend the election to S status:

■ The tax law governing the S corporation is *very* complex. If you decide to go this route, you'd be well advised to have superior and continuing tax advice and legal assistance. You should expect to pay well for these services—so you can avoid falling into any of the pitfalls of S. As one expert in the field put it: "In short, don't try to go through the S jungle without a trusted guide."

■ When an S corporation begins to produce very high levels of taxable income, this would be an appropriate time to terminate S status and begin accumulating profits in the corporation. These profits would then be useful to stimulate corporate growth.

Treatment of S corporations can pose some other disadvantages, such as less favorable treatment in setting up retirement programs, and in some states S corporations are taxed no differently than standard corporations. This again underlines the need for proper counsel. With counsel to help you decide, you may find it to your advantage to choose to set up an S corporation for your new business.

Expenses of Different Forms of Business Organization

Cost may be an important consideration in adopting the corporate form. You'll find relative costs for forming the sole proprietorship, the general partnership, and limited partnership, and the corporation in Table 15-1.

The sole proprietorship is the least expensive to start. The partnership involves relationships with another or others. To protect the parties in the relationship, an

TABLE 15-1

Comparison of Expenses for Organizational Setup (State of California) (Estimated for 1986)

Expense Item	Proprietorship	General Partnership	Limited Partnership	Corporation
Licenses and permits	Varies with local government imposing fees	Varies with local government imposing fees	Varies with local government imposing fees	Varies with local government imposing fees
Fictitious business name statement	$20 for each fictitious name	$20 for each fictitious name	$20 for each fictitious name	$20 for each fictitious name
Attorney's fees	Varies with amount of work done; attorney's fees ordinarily will be less than for other business formats	Varies, depending primarily on complexity of partnership agreement	Varies depending on complexity of partnership agreement and certificate and qualification of securities, if required	(See below)
Certificate of limited partnership recording fee			$4 plus $1.50 for each page after first page	
Qualification of limited partnership interests under California Corporate Securities Law, if required			Same as corporation	
Articles of incorporation filing fee				$65
Recording fee				$4
Secretary of State				$3 per copy if furnished
Certification				$3 plus $0.50 per page, if Secretary of State prepares copies
Recording fee, county clerk, county of principal place of business				$3 plus $1 per page after first page
Prepayment of minimum franchise (income) tax				$200
Attorney's fees for preparation of articles of incorporation, first minutes of first meetings, and				Varies, depending on complexity of corporate structure and work required for

TABLE 15-1

(Continued)

Expense Item	Proprietorship	General Partnership	Limited Partnership	Corporation
other initial documents				tax, securities, and other regulatory problems ($500 to $1000 for standard, new incorporations)
Qualification of securities, if not exempt				Fees of department of corporations vary depending on type of qualification and value of securities to be issued
Purchase of minute book, seal, and form stock certificates				Ordinarily $75 to $160

agreement should be drawn by a lawyer. This means that fees for this service will have to be paid.

Incorporating will take the most money in the beginning. In the long run it may prove to be the best arrangement, for many of the reasons indicated before. The primary costs of incorporation are

- Those payable at the time the charter or articles of incorporation are filed with the state agency. A state franchise tax or a minimum state income tax may be included.

- Attorney's fees.

- Miscellaneous charges and costs including stock certificates, corporate seal, and minute book.

These costs are amortizable for tax purposes over a period of usually not less than 5 years.

LICENSES AND PERMITS

You'll have to comply with several requirements for licenses and permits when you incorporate, less for other forms of ownership.

You must get a federal identification number for use on federal tax returns, statements, and other documents. This number may be obtained through the Internal Revenue Service or the Social Security Administration.

You'll have to comply with state and local requirements for business licenses. If your company plans to sell tangible goods, you must check for sales and use taxes, both state and local. You should obtain the necessary permits before you open for business.

OTHER TAXES FOR EMPLOYERS

Your company will have to withhold income tax and Social Security tax (FICA) from the taxable wages paid your employees. It must also pay a Social Security tax equal to that withheld from your employees' wages and must deposit the withheld taxes in an authorized commercial bank depository or a federal reserve bank, with an accompanying form, Federal Tax Deposit Form 501. The deposits are to be made semimonthly, monthly, or quarterly, depending upon the amount of the tax. Your company must also file an Employer's Quarterly Federal Tax Return (IRS Form 941).

Officers or other persons charged with the responsibility of withholding employee taxes must fulfill this responsibility meticulously. If they fail to do so, they may be personally liable for a 100 percent penalty for failure to collect those taxes.

As an employer, you may be subject to the Federal Unemployment Tax. If so, you'll be required to deposit taxes together with the Federal Tax Deposit Form 508. This procedure is similar to that of handling withholding tax. You'll be required also to file an Unemployment Tax Return (IRS Form 940) and pay any balance due on or before January 31 of each year.

You must find out what you need to do to comply with workers compensation laws, which are different in each state. Generally, as an employer, your company must be insured against workers' compensation liability by an authorized insurer or be self-insured with the consent of the appropriate government agency.

You'll want expert guidance in fulfilling these various federal and state legal responsibilities. You'll want to count on your attorney and your accountant in these matters, both to make sure that all bases are covered and to save your time for the important management duties your business will demand.

Table 15-2 provides a thumbnail sketch or overview of some of the major advantages and disadvantages of sole proprietorships, partnerships, and corporations. Where there are differences between a general partnership and a limited partnership, or between a "regular" corporation and an S corporation, separate comments are shown for each. Otherwise the comments regarding "partnerships" apply to both general and limited partnerships, and the comments regarding "corporations" relate to both regular and S corporations.

OTHER FORMS OF ORGANIZATION

Other forms of organization are available to you besides the three basic ones we've dealt with. They include joint ventures, real estate investment trusts, condominiums, and not-for-profit corporations. These are special adaptations of the three primary structures we've discussed.

A joint venture is really a partnership but for a special limited purpose. A condominium is a form of property ownership but not a form of business. These variations are intended for special purposes. You should seek legal advice before adopting any of them.

TABLE 15-2

Summary of the Key Characteristics of the Various
Legal Forms of Business Organization

Simplicity in Operation and Formation

Proprietorship	Simplest to establish and operate
General partnership	Relatively simple, informal, but is usually desirable to have formal written agreement between partners
Limited partnership	More complex and expensive than other unincorporated forms of business to establish. Requires written agreement, filing of certificate. Managed by general partners *only*
Regular corporation	Requires most formality in establishment and operation, generally
S corporation	Same as regular corporation, but requires oversight by a tax adviser, an additional cost

Liability for Debts, Taxes, and Other Claims

Proprietorship	Owner has unlimited personal liability
General partnership	Partners all have unlimited personal liability
Limited partnership	General partners are personally liable; limited partners liable only to the extent of their investment generally
Corporations	Stockholders not generally liable for corporate debts, but often have to guarantee loans, as a practical matter, if corporation borrows money. Also, corporate officers may be liable for failure to withhold and pay over to IRS withholding taxes on employee wages

Federal Income Taxation of Business Profits

Proprietorship	Taxed to owner at individual tax rates of 15 or 28%
Partnerships	Taxed to partners at their individual rates of 15 or 28%
Regular corporation	Small businesses with income up to $50,000 taxed at 15%; income between $50,000 and $75,000, 25%; and income over $75,000, 34%. For companies earning over $100,000, a 5% surcharge on income over that amount until the tax equals 34%
S corporation	Taxed to individual owners at their individual rates

Double Taxation If Profits Withdrawn from Business

Proprietorship	No
Partnerships	No
Regular corporation	Yes (but not on reasonable compensation paid to owners who are employees)
S corporation	No, in general

Deduction of Losses by Owners

Proprietorship	Yes
Partnerships	Yes. Limited partner's deductions generally cannot exceed the amount he or she has invested in a limited partnership interest (except for real estate)
Regular corporation	No. Corporation must "carry over" initial losses to offset future profits, if any
S corporation	Yes, in general, for federal tax purposes. But not for California tax purposes

TABLE 15-2

CHAPTER 15

437

Deciding on
Some Key
Legal Matters

(Continued)

Social Security Tax on Earnings of Owner from Business

Proprietorship	12.3% of owner's "self-employment" earnings (in 1986)
Partnerships	12.3% of each partner's share of "self-employment" earnings from the business (in 1986)
Corporations	Owner who is employee of corporation pays 7.15% of salary and the corporation also pays 7.15%. Total social security tax is 14.3% of salary

Unemployment Taxes on Earnings of Owner from Business

Proprietorship	None
Partnerships	None
Corporations	Yes. State and federal unemployment taxes apply to salaries paid to owners (some states exempt a sole stockholder)

Retirement Plans

Proprietorship	Keogh plan. Deductions, other features now generally the same as for corporate pension and profit sharing plans
Partnerships	Keogh plan. Same as for sole proprietorships
Corporation	Corporate retirement plans no longer significantly better than Keogh plans. Deduction limits same now as for Keogh. But participants can borrow from plan.
S corporation	Plans now essentially identical to regular corporate retirement plans, except that "shareholder-employee" (5% shareholder) of S corporation cannot borrow from plan

Tax Treatment of Medical, Disability, and Group-Term Life Insurance on Owners

Proprietorship	Not deductible, except part of medical expenses may be an itemized deduction on owner's tax return, including medical insurance premiums
Partnerships	See proprietorship, above
Corporation	Corporation may be able to deduct medical insurance premium or reimbursements paid under medical reimbursement plan. Generally not taxable to the employee, even if employee is an owner. Similar treatment for disability and group-term life insurance plans
S corporation	Effective as of 1983, fringe benefits for 2% shareholders not deductible by corporation (same as for partnership or proprietorship)

Source: Michael D. Jenkins, *Starting and Operating a Business in California*, 4th ed., Oasis Press, Sunnyvale, CA, 1985, pp. 2-27 to 2-31. Reproduced by permission.

Protection of Ideas and Concepts

Business
Plan
Outline
1.A, 2.A, 3.B, 4

If you have originated a new or useful concept for a product or process, you should take precautionary steps to protect it from being pirated. Ideas of various kinds, depending upon their intent, may be protected by patents, trademarks, service marks, or copyrights.

PATENTS

Patents may be obtained on a new, useful, and unobvious process (primarily industrial or technical); machine; manufacture or composition of matter (generally chemical compounds, formulas, and the like); or a new, useful, and unobvious improvement thereof. Patents may also be obtained on a new variety of plant, and on a new and unobvious original and ornamental design for an article of manufacture.[2]

You should note that ideas in themselves aren't patentable. Neither are methods of doing business, an inoperable device, or an improvement in a device that's obvious to one of ordinary skill in the field of the invention.

The Commissioner of Patents and Trademarks, U.S. Patent and Trademark Office, U.S. Department of Commerce, issues patents. A patent gives the inventor the exclusive right to make, use, or sell the patent for a period of 17 years. Design patents for ornamental devices are granted for $3\frac{1}{2}$, 7, or 14 years, as the applicant elects. A United States patent is effective in the United States, its territories and possessions, but not elsewhere. Foreign countries have their own patent systems.

Failure to file a patent application within 1 year of an offer for sale, sale, public use, or making available to the public an oral or written description of the invention bars you from obtaining a valid United States patent.

In most other countries, you are barred from obtaining a valid patent unless the patent application is filed before the invention is made available to the public by use or an oral or written description of the invention anywhere in the world.

However, if you file a patent application in a foreign country within 1 year after you file a patent application in the United States, almost all foreign countries will, under international patent treaties, allow you to claim the actual filing date of the United States patent application as the effective filing date of the foreign patent application.

Thus, if you first file a patent application in the United States, you may then make your invention publicly available, as by a sale, and still be able to obtain a valid patent in a foreign country if you file in the foreign country no later than 1 year after filing the United States patent application.

Disclosure Document Program When you conceive of an idea that you think patentable, you should take advantage of a service called the Disclosure Document Program offered by the U.S. Patent and Trademark Office. To use this service, you or your attorney or agent prepares and submits a document with the aim of establishing priority of your invention. The Patent and Trademark Office keeps this document in its files for 2 years. It is then destroyed unless it's referred to in a separate letter in a related patent application you have filed within the 2-year period.

You shouldn't think of the 2-year period as a period of grace; you can't wait until the end of the period to file application for patent. If you do, you risk losing the benefits of the procedure. You must show diligence in completing the invention or in filing application for patent after sending in the Disclosure Document.

The Disclosure Document isn't a patent application. It doesn't lessen the value of the conventional witnessed and notarized records as evidence of the conception of an invention. When you submit a Disclosure Document, you're establishing a more credible form of evidence that you've originated the concept than you would by sending yourself or someone else a disclosure letter by registered mail.

---

[2]U.S. Department of Commerce, *Patents*, p. 24, Government Printing Office, Washington, DC, 1972.

Your disclosure document should be clear, with enough explanation so someone with a reasonable knowledge in the field could make and use your invention. As in other matters having to do with legal protection, you should choose an expert to negotiate the complex procedures of securing a patent.

TRADEMARKS AND SERVICE MARKS

A trademark is a distinguishing name or symbol identifying a product used in commerce subject to regulation by Congress. The "design of a flying red horse" is one example of a trademark. A trademark can be protected by registration against use by others for a period of 20 years. It may be renewed for an additional 20 years. Registration is done by the Commissioner of Patents and Trademarks, U.S. Patent and Trademark Office. In addition to the federal government, most states offer trademark registration and service mark registration.

A service mark is similar to a trademark in that it's a distinguishing name or symbol identifying a service rather than a product.

You'll find the following descriptions of trademarks and service marks helpful in clearing up the differences between them. These are as given by the State of California Division of Business and Industry Development.

Trademark   A trademark is a word; a name, a symbol; a device; or a combination of these elements. ("Device" means generally a "design" or an "artistic figure.")

A trademark is used to identify an applicant's merchandise and to enable customers to recognize applicant's products and to distinguish them from the products of others.

A trademark should not be described ordinarily as a label. The word "label" is not included in the definition of a trademark. The trademark most usually consists of part of the matter printed on a label.

Not everything printed on a label or on a container is part of the trademark. Statements of ingredients, the name and address of a business, cautions, instructions for use: these are not part of the trademark. A trademark is the customer's recognition factor. It is intended to be something that will catch the customer's attention and enable him or her to buy again a product previously bought and liked.

Service Mark   The description must be brief but accurate. Most service marks are very simple. For example, the words "The Fog Cutters" is a service mark identifying restaurant services.

A service mark is a word or words, or a design or designs, or combinations of a word or words and design or designs. A service mark is used to advertise services. The function of a service mark is to distinguish one person's services from the services of others. Prospective customers are made familiar with the service mark by the advertising thereof. If the services are excellent, the customer in theory will deal with the person using the service mark when he or she again needs the particular service.

The following are examples of services: banking services; real estate broker's services; entertainment services by a musical group.

You should take advantage of the commercial benefits of a distinctive trademark or service mark for your business. These marks help your customers to identify and remember your product or service. And if they've once liked what you've offered, they're going to ask for more when they have need. Your special symbol will help to stimulate repeat business.

COPYRIGHTS

You may protect your *literary* or *artistic* work through a copyright. Common examples of copyrightable work are written, musical, and graphic works, sculptures, motion pictures, videotapes, and computer programs.

Copyrights are processed through the Copyright Office attached to the Library of Congress, Washington, D.C. In a fashion similar to patents, trademarks, and service marks, copyrights give a legal monopoly to the holder. Copyrights are effective for the life of the author plus 50 years.

As a small business owner, you may wish to copyright material you use in promoting your business: catalogs, catalog sheets, brochures, and instructions on how to assemble or use your product. To get copyright protection, you must first make a claim by imprinting a copyright notice in front of the item you're planning to publish. You can follow this standard form: © Copyright, followed by the year of publication and the name of the individual or company originating the piece. After publication, you must make application for copyright to the Copyright Office, Library of Congress.

Under the Semiconductor Chip Act of 1984, you may protect the design of a semiconductor chip or "mask work" from which the chip is designed for 10 years after registration under the act or first commercial exploitation of the chip product. Instead of carrying the copyright symbol, protected chip designs must be designated with the words "mask work" or the symbol M in a circle or the symbol M between two asterisks, plus the name of the owner. Unlike a copyright notice, no year is needed. The chip product or mask work must be registered with the copyright office within 2 years of the date of its first commercial exploitation.

MARKETABLE BUT UNPATENTABLE IDEAS

Once in a while you may hit upon an idea for a product or service that's not patentable but that might be good for some firm other than your own. You may want to get paid for your idea, but you may be reluctant to disclose it for fear of its being pirated. There's a way you can get the protection you would want in a situation like this. However, you can readily see that to work out a successful deal with a company capable of capitalizing on your idea presents substantial difficulties. You'd probably be approaching a company much larger than your own, with many more resources. You'll find most such companies chary of inventors or "idea persons." Nevertheless, you may be able to find the rare company that's willing to listen to you. And it may be possible to come to a mutually satisfactory arrangement based upon a binding contractual agreement.

You should know that ideas become public property under the law as soon as they're divulged. You shouldn't disclose your idea in its entirety, therefore, before you've reached agreement with the firm you're dealing with, and the agreement has been put into a binding contract signed by them and by you.

The Small Business Administration suggests use of a letter, which when signed by both parties, becomes a contract. It should be prepared in duplicate so each party may have a copy. A typical letter is shown in Figure 15-3.

This contract binds the firm to hold in confidence any features not already known to it. It may not use your idea without paying you as stipulated in the contract. By the same token, the company is protected from any unwarranted claims you may choose to make.

ADVANTAGE OF COUNSEL

To protect your creative idea, whether through patent, trademark, service mark, copyright, or in the disclosure of a unique idea to an outside firm, you should depend upon professional counsel. You'll find that's what it takes to ensure proper attention to the details of these legal procedures. And you'll surely recognize the wisdom of using such help in the beginning. It's far less expensive—and far less stressful—to avoid legal entanglements by proper procedure up front than to resolve a legal problem later by lawsuit.

Finding an Attorney and an Accountant

We've said that it's good practice, indeed it's essential, that you have the help of two kinds of professionals when you go into business: an attorney and an accountant. We're often asked, "How do you locate a competent attorney and a competent accountant?" The procedure most often used seems to be similar to that in finding a doctor or a dentist, that is, reference from others.

Friends, relatives, or neighbors may have been satisfied with a lawyer or accountant and will give you their names. You should also check with your banker. In any event, don't limit your choice. Get the names of two or three in each category. A very good way to locate competent professionals is to talk with the owners of small businesses comparable with yours but not directly competitive. Ask who handles their legal and accounting problems and find out if they've been satisfied with the service they got. Check with professors who teach entrepreneurship and small business in colleges in your community. They usually have contact with attorneys and accountants who specialize in small business clients. Compile a list of prospects among these.

Make an appointment with each. Say that you're interested in an exploratory meeting as you're starting a new business and want to locate competent professional help. Ask if there will be a charge for a preliminary meeting. Most professionals won't charge for a preliminary meeting or, if they do, will charge only a minimal fee. Be prepared to tell the attorney or accountant what your plans are for your business, and ask the questions you consider important. Ask what clients are typically served by the firm. Make sure that the firm doesn't handle direct competitors. And don't be afraid to talk openly about fees.

By following this procedure you'll be able to decide on an attorney and an accountant who would suit your business—and you personally. You should feel

FIG. 15-3

Suggested contract for submission and review of ideas.

John Doe Co.
123 Fourth Street
Anytown, U.S.A.

Gentlemen:

I have developed a new idea for the packaging of your product which I believe would greatly increase your sales and profits. The new method of packaging would not raise production costs.

If you are interested in details of the idea, I shall be glad to forward you complete information if you will kindly sign the enclosed agreement form. Promptly upon receipt of the signed form, I shall forward to you all information I have regarding the idea.

Sincerely,

Robert Roe

AGREEMENT TO REVIEW IDEA

We, the undersigned, agree to receive in confidence full details about an idea for product packaging to be submitted for our consideration by Robert Roe.

It is further understood that we assume no responsibility whatever with respect to features which can be demonstrated to be already known to us. We also agree not to divulge any details of the idea submitted without permission of Robert Roe or to make use of any feature or information of which the said Robert Roe is the originator, without payment of compensation to be fixed by negotiation with the said Robert Roe or his lawful representative.

It is specifically understood that, in receiving the idea of Robert Roe, the idea is being received and will be reviewed in confidence and that, within a period of 30 days, we will report to said Robert Roe the results of our findings and will advise whether or not we are interested in negotiating for the purchase of the right to use said idea.

Company _____

Street and Number _____

City _____ Zone _____ State _____

Official to receive disclosures (please type)

_____ Title _____

Date _____ Signature _____

Accepted: _____

Robert Roe, Inventor

comfortable with the person because you'll work together for a long time. Your attorney and your accountant will be intimately involved in your affairs. The closer the association the more likely you are to get beneficial results from their efforts, and the happier the relationship will be.

Once you decide on an attorney or an accountant, that person can very likely help you find the other.

The following article offers specific recommendations for choosing an attorney. The procedure would be the same for selecting a qualified accountant to handle your affairs. Although the legal situation described centers in a California divorce proceeding, the approach in selecting a lawyer for your small business would follow the same pattern; the questions you should ask are identical.

SELECTING A LAWYER (HOW TO FIND ONE WHO SUITS YOUR PARTICULAR NEEDS)[3]

After several years of domestic discord, Michelle Smith is going to end her marriage. She foresees a conflict over certain assets and expects a dispute with her husband over custody of their 1-year-old son. Wisely, Michelle concludes that she needs a lawyer.

Sally, a confidante of Michelle, recommends an attorney named Jackson. "After all," Sally boasts, "Jackson settled my personal-injury case for a small fortune." Fortunately, Michelle understands that a worthy personal-injury lawyer may not know the difference between matrimony and alimony.

Michelle is not sold on lawyer referral services because most do not effectively screen for competency. And she would sooner use a telephone book to find a surgeon than to find an attorney who will fight for custody of her son.

Michelle's plight is not unusual. In theory, consumers should have little trouble finding a competent lawyer at a reasonable cost. In fact, consumers have little trouble finding a lawyer, but finding a competent lawyer who will charge a reasonable fee may be considerably more difficult.

Examinations to test lawyer competency have not been overwhelmingly effective. Robert H. O'Brien, immediate past chairman of the California Committee of Bar Examiners, says: "The bar exam tests for minimum analytical ability and knowledge of the law, but it isn't designed to ensure that a person will be a competent lawyer."

Complaints Filed   O'Brien's analysis is supported by troublesome statistics on lawyer competency. For example, Travelers Insurance insures approximately one-third of the 67,000 lawyers in California. Between 1974 and 1978, more than 3200 incidents of alleged malpractice by California lawyers were reported to Travelers.

Unreasonable attorney fees are also a problem. In 1978, more than 700 client complaints alleging exorbitant attorney fees were filed with the State Bar of California.

How will Michelle Smith find a competent lawyer at a reasonable cost? Reliance on friends or the self-serving praise that an attorney heaps on himself will not guarantee

---

[3]Reproduced by courtesy of Harvey Levin, attorney and professor in the Whittier College School of Law, and the *Los Angeles Times*.

a fair return on the money she spends for legal services. Michelle needs a consumer protection plan for selecting a lawyer. The plan outlined here is basic, inexpensive, and very effective.

First, Michelle should call a local lawyer referral service and ask for the names and telephone numbers of three attorneys who say they specialize in domestic-relations law. She should not, however, assume that any of the attorneys are competent. If the service will not give Michelle three referrals, she should call other local referral services until she has the names of three attorneys. Lawyer referral services in Los Angeles County are located in Los Angeles, Beverly Hills, Hollywood, Burbank, Pasadena, Glendale, Long Beach, Montebello, Compton, Norwalk, Torrance, West Covina, and the San Fernando Valley.

Next, Michelle should call each lawyer's office and ask if he or she will speak with her about her legal problems for a nominal fee. If any of the lawyers refuse, she should call the referral service back and get the names of other lawyers. (There are more than 22,000 lawyers in Los Angeles County, many of whom would be delighted to charge a nominal consultation fee and win Michelle as a client.) Many of the referral services, such as those in Los Angeles and the San Fernando Valley, require that participating attorneys charge no more than $15 for the initial 30-minute consultation.

When Michelle meets with each attorney for a consultation, she should be politely assertive and ask questions that will reveal the attorney's competence, fee, and compatibility with her.

"How long have you practiced law?"

Analysis: When interviewing lawyers who may just recently have been admitted to practice, Michelle should evaluate their inexperience against their eagerness to handle her case effectively. Many neophyte lawyers are as bright and creative as well-established practitioners. On the other hand, because of their knowledge of the legal process, established lawyers frequently have an edge over many fledgling lawyers.

"What percentage of your practice is devoted to problems like mine?"

Analysis: Regular and dramatic changes in legal rules mark many areas of law practice. An attorney who really specializes in Michelle's legal problems may resolve the matter more quickly and effectively than an attorney who only dabbles in domestic-relations law.

"Will you be the attorney doing the work on my case?"

Analysis: Many attorneys refer their cases to associates in their law firm or to colleagues in other law offices. If another attorney will be handling her case, Michelle should request to speak with that attorney.

Various Options   "What options do I have in resolving my legal problem?"

Analysis: An attorney who says, "There is only one way to solve your problem" without discussing options may not be thoughtful enough to handle Michelle's case. The attorney's function in the interview is not to sell Michelle on one course of action; rather, the attorney should counsel her on the advantages and disadvantages of various options and allow her to choose the course of action she prefers.

"What is this going to cost me?"

Michelle should insist on a fee estimate during the consultation. An attorney who says the fee will depend on the amount of work performed should at least establish an hourly rate and estimate the number of hours to be devoted to the case. If the attorney is evasive on the fee issue, Michelle should look elsewhere.

After interviewing three attorneys, Michelle should evaluate their competence, fees, and compatibility with her. Those three factors should be central to her decision, and the attorney she selects should satisfy her on each count.

Deciding Some Key Legal Issues

Summary

In this chapter we've discussed three basic legal structures you can choose from in setting up your business: sole proprietorship, partnership, and corporation. Each has advantages and disadvantages.

The sole proprietorship is the easiest to start and has the lowest first costs. You can open your doors for business with the least amount of red tape and the least cost. However, as a sole proprietor, all your personal worth is exposed to the demands of creditors. You can protect yourself from some risks through insurance. In other cases your entire worth would be open to attachment in case of a major lawsuit.

The partnership, which involves you in an intimate relationship with one or more people, permits combining different strengths in building competent management for your company. You should take great care to prepare an agreement among the partners that would spell out actions to be taken in case of disagreement, dissolution, or termination of the partnership. Because any partner can commit the others to a business activity without their knowledge, it's of the utmost importance that you make sure you and your partners can get along well under all conditions before you work up the partnership agreement.

The partnership doesn't provide protection for the personal assets of the partners. The situation here is similar to that of the sole proprietorship. A special form of partnership does provide this protection for those partners who wish to invest money but not time in the venture; this is the limited partnership, which is used mainly for financing and managing large real estate projects.

The third major form of business structure open to you is the corporation. The corporation may be considered an artificial person sanctioned by law. If you elect the corporate form, you gain two great advantages: You and your investors are protected against exposure of your personal assets in case of suit as long as your corporation observes legal requirements; and your company has the capability of enduring beyond the active participation of its original owners.

The corporation is the most expensive form of structure to launch and requires more legal steps. Its advantages may sway you to adopt it, if not in your start-up condition, perhaps at a later point in the growth of your company.

A special form of corporate structure, known as S, permits the shareholders in a small corporation to assume the losses or profits of the company as individuals, thus bypassing the tax consequences to the corporation itself. Under some circumstances, as when the corporation is just starting and is losing money and the individual shareholders have substantial outside income, the shareholders may offset some income by assuming the losses of the corporation in proportion to their shares in the company. This, of course, could be advantageous to you if the circumstances fit.

In this chapter we've outlined some procedures you may take to secure patents, copyrights, trademarks, and service marks. We've suggested a way of selling an original concept to another company and protecting your interests while doing it. But we've also said that you'll find it a difficult process, as most companies are not inclined to listen to outsiders.

Finally, we've suggested ways of choosing an attorney and an accountant. And we've stressed the advantages of having competent counsel in legal and financial matters.

Deciding on Some Key Legal Matters

This worksheet covers some major points you'll want to consider in deciding on the legal form of business structure to adopt. Because each business is unique, it's not possible for us to suggest all the items you should think through when you begin to deal with the legal procedures. A good way to check your thinking about these matters is to review the other worksheets in the book when you work on the agreements you want and the legal requirements you'll have to meet. Studying carefully these aspects of going into business is time well spent. It's much less expensive—and much less anxiety producing—to take care of possible legal contingencies ahead of time, rather than to have to resolve them by lawsuit.

1. On the basis of the advantages and disadvantages of the three legal forms of business structure given in this chapter, decide on the form that appears best for your business.

    I have chosen the following form for my business: sole proprietorship

    _____;   partnership _____;   corporation _____;

    other _____.

    Here are my reasons for preferring this form:

    _____

    _____

    _____

    _____

    _____

    _____

    _____

    _____

    _____

    _____

2. If a sole proprietorship, I'm going to use my own name _____. If I'm going to use a fictitious name, I've recorded it with the proper agency in my community _____. If a partnership, I've chosen my partner or partners with special attention to the following:

    I've known _____ _____ for _____ years. I have a firm knowledge that we can get along well together, even in times when things go wrong _____. The following typical experience shows that we can talk things out and come to a happy solution when we hit a difficult situation:

    _____

    _____

    _____

448

_____
_____
_____
_____
_____
_____
_____
_____
_____

3. We've agreed to refer to a third-party arbitrator if we can't resolve an argument ourselves. The person or arbitrator we'll go to is _____

4. My main strength in the business is: technical _____ ; financial management_____ ; marketing_____ . In addition, I believe I can add the following competencies to the management of the business:

_____
_____
_____
_____

5. My partner or partners will add the following strengths to management:

_____
_____
_____
_____
_____
_____
_____

6. We've talked through the basis for a written agreement of partnership and have covered the following points:

- Percentage of contribution of capital and therefore of ownership and sharing of profit and loss
- Buy—sell agreement if a partner wants to get out
- Succession of ownership if one of us dies
- The fiscal year we should use
- Assigned duties and responsibilities
- Set up a formal accounting arrangement for partnership affairs
- The name of the company is to be: _____
- Have agreed on an attorney to help us prepare the partnership agreement. The attorney's name is: _____.

- Have decided on an accountant to help us with financial matters: The accountant's name is: _____.

7. If I'm going to the corporate form, there are to be a limited number of shareholders, and they are:

_____   _____

_____   _____

_____   _____

_____   _____

_____   _____

8. We've decided on the following attorney to incorporate and advise us:
_____

9. We've chosen this name for our company: _____

10. We've decided on the organization chart for starting our company. It looks like this:

11. Attached are résumés of the people on the chart.
12. We've chosen the following, and they've agreed to act as directors of our company:

_____   _____

_____   _____

They have these special strengths in giving us advice and counsel: _____

_____   _____

_____   _____

450

13. Special Notes. Note here any special items you've thought about, for example, the possibility of adopting the S form of corporation; the use of an inside or outside board of directors; patent applications; trademarks; service marks; copyrights; insurance coverage; or anything else that has legal implications for the business and the shareholders.

KEY TERMS

sole proprietorship 418

partnership 421

Uniform Partnership Act 422

termination 424

dissolution 424

term certain 424

limited partnership 425

corporation 426

board of directors 429

S corporation 430

patent 437

trademark 439

service mark 439

copyright 440

STUDY ASSIGNMENTS FOR REVIEW AND DISCUSSION

1. Describe the advantages and disadvantages of the sole proprietorship, the partnership, and the corporation.

2. What features make the limited partnership different from the customary partnership?

3. Outline the key features of the S corporation.

4. Name the rights and obligations of partners under the Uniform Partnership Act.

5. Describe what is meant by an inside board of directors and an outside board of directors.

6. How may you go about protecting an original idea for a product or process that might be patentable?

7. Define a trademark. A service mark.

8. How do you go about copyrighting an original literary or artistic work?

9. How would you find an attorney (or accountant) for your new small business? What questions would you ask to judge how competent that person might be to handle your problems?

PROJECTS FOR STUDENTS

1. List the legal requirements for establishing a corporation in your state.

2. Write a brief report on the steps you must take in your community to operate a sole proprietorship under a fictitious name.

3. Find out if your state has adopted the Uniform Partnership Act in its entirety, or some variation of it. If either, write a brief report on the rights and obligations of partners as given in the legislation in force.

4. Write a short statement of how individuals in a partnership are taxed under the federal income tax laws.

5. Two students invite the president of a small corporation to speak for the class. Have that person tell how the business came into being and when and why the

corporate form was adopted. (If possible, invite two or three corporate presidents to act as a panel in addressing these questions.)

6. Bring to class a set of six or more samples of trademarks and service marks. These may be clipped from food packages, advertisements, paper wrappers on tin cans, and the like. See if your classmates can identify the products from such marks that don't name the product or service.

7. Invite a lawyer who specializes in small business law to address your class. Have him or her talk about the legal points that small enterprises should be aware of.

IF YOU WANT TO READ MORE

The legal procedures in establishing the form of a business can become quite intricate, as you have probably noted from some portions of this chapter. It's beyond the scope of this book to get into elaborate detail on legal matters—indeed, it's a waste of time for the prospective businessperson to try to become a legal expert. The following references are therefore intended to give you additional general information and other points of view on the legal forms of business enterprise.

ADAMS, Paul: *The Complete Legal Guide for Small Business,* John Wiley & Sons, New York, 1982. This book centers on contract formulation. Although it does not attempt to replace the services of a lawyer, it does outline and explain many of the written agreements that small business owners should be familiar with.

FRANTZ, Forrest H.: *Successful Small Business Management,* Prentice-Hall, Inc., Englewood Cliffs, NJ, 1978. Chapter 10, "Law, Regulation, Risk, and Insurance," presents an overview of the major legal aspects you'll be exposed to as a small businessperson.

GOLDSTEIN, Arnold S.: *The Small Business Legal Problem Solver,* Inc./CBI Publications, Boston, MA, 1983. This reference offers comprehensive answers to most common business law problems. The presentation uses a question-and-answer format that not only states the pertinent law but also gives step-by-step instructions on how to solve the relevant problem.

HANCOCK, William A.: *The Small Business Legal Advisor,* McGraw-Hill Book Company, New York, 1982. The author recommends spending a small amount of time up front in gaining understanding of relevant laws to avoid legal difficulties. Using his experiences as a business lawyer, the author suggests how to avoid some of the more common legal problems small business owners encounter. In Chapter 1 he tells how to find and use a good lawyer.

JENKINS, Michael D.: *Starting and Operating a Business in California,* 4th ed., Oasis Press, Sunnyvale, CA, 1985. Although designed specifically for California, this book, in loose-leaf format, contains much information that will be found valuable in other states. The author, a CPA and attorney, has adopted a subtitle to the book that reads: "A Practical Guide through the Maze of Taxes, Red Tape, and Government

Regulations." The text presents in simple language not only the regulations for small business in California but also the basic regulatory requirements of a large number of federal government agencies. A valuable chapter, Chapter 9, gives sources of help and information, many universally applicable.

LASSER, J. K.: *How to Run a Small Business,* 5th ed., McGraw-Hill Book Company, New York, 1982. In Chapter Six, "Choosing a Form for Your Business," there's a description of the advantages and disadvantages of the three basic forms of ownership. The chapter is short and takes the form of a somewhat expanded outline. You'll find it useful as a quick refresher on some of the more important points about each of the three forms of business structure.

STEINGOLD, Fred S.: *Legal Master Guide for Small Business,* Prentice-Hall, Inc., Englewood Cliffs, NJ, 1983. The author, a business lawyer, explains the various legal concepts and problems a small business may encounter. The text covers a wide range of topics, including forms of business ownership, contracts, debt collection, and insurance. The book is written in a clear, straightforward manner.

VAN VOORHIS, Kenneth R.: *Entrepreneurship and Small Business Management,* Allyn and Bacon, Inc., Boston, 1980. Chapter 8, "Meeting Your Legal and Insurance Requirements," gives answers to major legal questions, including the advantages and disadvantages of the various legal forms of organizations.

SECTION VI

Some Crucial Management Functions

CHAPTER 16

MANAGING BUSINESS RISK

CHAPTER 17

MANAGING YOUR PERSONNEL FUNCTION

CHAPTER 18

SURVIVING: MANAGING FOR PRODUCTIVITY AND GROWTH

Managing Business Risk

TOPICS IN THIS CHAPTER

Objectives of This Chapter
Pure Risk Insurance
The Risk Manager's Job
Risk Transfer
Risk Reduction
Risk Absorption
Selecting an Agent, Broker, or Consultant
Types of Coverage
Desirable Coverages
Measures to Prevent Crime
How to Use the Foregoing Information—Summary
Worksheet 16: Managing Business Risk
Key Terms
Study Assignments for Review and Discussion
Projects for Students
If You Want to Read More

Managing risk is not one of the more exciting and glamorous aspects of running a small business. But it is an exceedingly important chore. Without adequate protection to cover risk in your business, a major accident or natural catastrophe could wipe out your investment and leave you seriously in debt.

---

[1]Code numbers referring to the Outline for Developing Your Basic Business Plan are not used in this chapter. This chapter aims at giving you some background in managing business risk.

This chapter is designed to prepare you for the role of risk manager. We do not purport to make you an expert in the field but will give you some understanding of the responsibilities you should accept, and some guidelines you can follow in obtaining an insurance program adequate for your business.

$$\text{YOU} + \text{Idea} + \begin{cases} \textbf{MONEY} \\ \text{Credit} \end{cases} + \begin{cases} \textbf{FACILITIES} \\ \textbf{PEOPLE} \end{cases} \begin{matrix} \textbf{PRODUCT} \\ \rightarrow \textbf{OR} \\ \textbf{SERVICE} \end{matrix} + \text{Marketing} \begin{cases} \text{Money} \\ \text{Credit} \end{cases} \rightarrow \text{Profit}$$

Objectives of This Chapter

The purpose of this chapter is to examine pure risk as it applies to the small business and show you how insurance can reduce potential losses that result from it.

Our aim is to prepare you to:

- Assume the role of risk manager—to be responsible for managing your company activities in order to avoid or lessen financial loss

- Understand the nature of risk and to identify the forms of pure risk your business is subject to

- Understand the insurance programs that have been designed to control pure risk and to know the several forms of protection that may fit your needs

- Select a qualified insurance agent, broker, or consultant and ensure that you ask the right questions about protection you need and about reasonable cost for that protection

- Use the guidelines in this chapter to set up with your agent or broker a comprehensive protection insurance program appropriate for your business

Pure Risk Insurance

When you start a business, you automatically assume risk; you intend to make money, but you also know you can lose money. Your risk has a speculative quality, but you *do* have control of how much risk you are willing to accept. Many risks have the possibility of either gain or loss: buying grain futures, gambling at the 21 tables in Las Vegas, investing in the stock market, putting capital in a limited partnership to build a condominium—these are all examples of risks with the possibility of gain or loss. Risks of this kind are all identified under the general heading of *speculative risk*.

Once you have started your enterprise, no matter how well you manage, your business can be burned down in a fire, destroyed by flood or earthquake, burglarized, or sued for damages resulting from the negligence of an employee. Accidents can happen: a pedestrian injured by your delivery van, a customer poisoned by presumably fresh food, a passerby slipping in your doorway—these can cause major lawsuits. Your business may suffer the hazard of a light-fingered clerk who spirits away valuable merchandise, or the robbery of your cash receipts by a stickup man. Risks of the foregoing kinds are classed as *pure risk*. With pure risk, the only possible outcome is loss or no loss.

Small business owners should know how to protect their business and personal assets from pure risks. Often lax in taking on this task, they should realize that the catastrophic effects of an accident could wipe out their business and their own financial resources. Every small businessperson should therefore become familiar with risk management. By working intelligently with a qualified insurance agent, broker, or consultant, the small business owner can take steps necessary to manage risks to which the business is subject.

The small business owner–CEO should of necessity take on the role of risk manager until the firm grows enough to have this job assigned to a staff member. It would be impossible for the owner to become an expert in all the ramifications of risk management, short of years of study. However, the critical function the owner should and can learn to perform well is the identification of risk in the business. This important function usually receives only lip service; yet only by becoming conversant with the risks in the business can the owner work effectively with broker, agent, or consultant to ensure adequate coverage.

The entrepreneur–chief executive should know the important things happening, or about to happen, in the company. Although risk management includes so many aspects no one can be expert in all, the key criterion for doing a good job is managerial ability. The risk manager, as in other aspects of running a business, must manage: plan, organize, and control.

THE RISK MANAGER'S DUTIES

The risk manager's job should be performed continuously. Reviews of exposure to loss, perhaps quarterly or twice a year, can support a sound program. As the owner of a small business, you'd find the following recommendations useful in guiding you to achieve a satisfactory risk management program:

- Review financial statements for clues to assets and risks that should be insured.

- Become familiar with terms of contracts, leases, bonds, and similar documents for the same reasons.

- Walk through the plant on a regular schedule and talk with key personnel and employees; observe details of operations, and note unsafe practices or conditions.

- If the firm is a corporation, read the minutes of the board of directors' meetings.

- Determine the potential causes of loss.

- Estimate dollar amounts for direct and indirect potential losses.

- Evaluate existing insurance policies in view of risks.

- Establish risk management policy: Identify those potential losses that should be covered by insurance, and those that can be avoided or reduced.

- Install loss prevention and reduction measures.

The Small Business Administration offers a checklist of items to be alert to in developing an insurance program for the small business.[2]

In conclusion, entrepreneurs should not risk more than they personally or their business can afford to lose. You should not overinsure. Through careful analysis,

---

[2]Mark R. Greene, *Insurance Checklist for Small Business*, Management Aid No. 2.018, Small Business Administration, 1984.

you can target your investment in insurance to cover those items that are financially significant, and conversely, absorb potentially trivial losses.

Three major methods are available to you to alleviate the problems of pure risk: (1) risk transfer, (2) risk reduction, and (3) risk absorption.

Risk Transfer

Insurance offers the small business the customary way to cover risk. Here the risk of an unknown number and amount of losses is transferred, or shifted, to an insurance company by paying a fixed *premium*. The insurance company accepts the risk of paying a large sum for a loss for any number of policyholders in exchange for a relatively small amount of premium from each of them. Through this procedure the small businessperson may transfer all, or part of, the financial uncertainty for many kinds of pure risk.

WHAT MAKES A RISK INSURABLE?

Specific qualifications must exist for a risk to be insurable. These are:

- The risk must be common to a large number of independent "exposure units" with similar characteristics.

- Any loss incurred must be definite in time, place, cause, and amount.

- The loss should be reasonably calculable.

- The loss must be accidental from the viewpoint of the insured.

TYPES OF INSURANCE COMPANIES

Two major types of insurance companies operate in the United States:

- *Stock companies* are profit-making corporations chartered under the laws of the states. They write about 70 percent of all property and liability insurance and about one-third of all life insurance.

- *Mutual companies* are not-for-profit organizations chartered under the laws of the various states. They account for a little less than one-quarter of all property and casualty insurance written in the country, and about two-thirds of all life insurance.

Two other types of insurers, of minor importance to the entrepreneur except in unusual circumstances, are *reciprocals* and *Lloyds Groups*. Reciprocals, known commonly as interinsurance exchanges, operate similarly to mutuals under the management of an attorney-in-fact. Very few reciprocals exist in the United States; they furnish about 5 percent of the property and casualty insurance coverage written nationally. Lloyds Groups are composed of individual insurance underwriters who each contract to accept a small percentage of an applicant firm's risks. Their premium income is less than 1 percent of all premiums dealing with property and casualty insurance in the United States.

SELECTING AN INSURANCE CARRIER

Four criteria afford a rational approach to selecting an insurance carrier for a given purpose:

▢ The financial stability of the carrier

▢ The insurer's experience in handling the type of coverage applied for

▢ The insurer's willingness to offer broad coverage

▢ The insurer's ability to offer services as claim handling and safety engineering recommendations related to the type of coverage afforded

The purchaser of insurance should compare the costs of insurance protection after being satisfied on these criteria.

Risk Reduction

Although some risks cannot be avoided, most can be sidestepped or appreciably reduced.

Risk reduction refers to the process of reducing the frequency of losses and controlling the magnitude of those that do occur. The small businessperson can reduce the frequency of loss in shop operations, for example, by training personnel in the safe use of machine tools. Properly installed guards over V-belts and safety interlocks on punch presses act to reduce the chance that an employee may be injured. Deliveries by van may be made much safer by periodic inspection and maintenance of brakes. Pretesting drivers to make sure they are not accident-prone serves the same end. And, in another area, small business owners may reduce the risk of credit losses by careful checking of customers' credit ratings.

The severity of losses that do occur can also be controlled through measures such as these:

▢ Installation of fire control sprinklers in buildings

▢ Requiring all riders and drivers in company vehicles to wear seat belts

▢ Allowing no more than one key company executive to travel on a single aircraft

In general, risk reduction results from good management practice just as it produces desirable results in other functions of the business.

Risk Absorption

In some cases it may be impractical for the small business to avoid absorbing the risk. It may be too costly to take measures to reduce certain risks. Generally, the small business owner will absorb risks in which losses that do occur will not produce significant financial consequences to the organization. Determining the amount of loss that is significant is not a precise science. Such determination depends on the financial strength of the company as well as the attitude of the owner toward accepting risk. As a general rule, a business should absorb those losses that do not exceed one-tenth of 1 percent of annual revenues for any single loss, and 1 percent of revenues for all such losses in a year.

For example, a business owning just a few vans with blue book values of just a few hundred dollars each might well decide that the cost of insuring the vehicles against collision damage is excessive. The owner might believe that the business has the financial capacity to absorb such losses. On the other hand, the risk of such vehicles causing damage to others' property or injury to others represents an exposure to loss of $500,000 or more. Liability risks of this magnitude usually demand insurance.

In some cases it is desirable for the small business to self-insure against loss. Self-insurance can be defined as the planned acceptance of the risk of loss. Here the business would build a reserve fund of adequate size to handle a given dollar amount of loss. This approach could be desirable if the business consists of a number of small units, for example, a string of hamburger stands or a chain of drive-up photo development units. Damage to one by fire would not be disastrous to the business. But in cases in which the business is concentrated in one store or one plant, it would be the exceptional entrepreneur who could, or would, put aside enough money to absorb a catastrophic accident. Small businesspersons should protect against most risks through insurance.

Selecting an Agent, Broker, or Consultant

Deciding on an insurance agent, broker, or consultant should be done in the same way as selecting a lawyer or accountant. Small businesspersons should decide what criteria are important to them and then follow procedures similar to those given in Chapter 15 for selecting an attorney. Important points in the selection process include the agent's knowledge; willingness to devote enough time to the owner's business to do a thorough job; willingness to study the possible risks and to recommend a suitable insurance program plus giving recommendations for preventing or controlling loss; finally, offering help in settling claims in time of loss.

Agents, brokers, or consultants who carry the designation of CPCU or CLU have been through rigorous examinations that testify to their professionalism. CPCU stands for Chartered Property and Casualty Underwriter; CLU stands for Chartered Life Underwriter. Each designation requires passing 10 examinations, each takes preparation of about 6 months of study.[3] These terms tend to mark the technical qualifications of the agent, broker, or consultant.

---

[3]Ibid.

TONY'S ARCADE[4]

Tony Martin's interest in pinball games motivated him to leave the accounting firm he worked for and to open an arcade. Using all his savings and some commercial financing, he was able to open Tony's Magic Flipper Arcade on the Boardwalk in Newport Beach, California. Tony purchased $100,000 worth of pinball and electronic games from several suppliers. With a former accounting client, he was able to negotiate a 5-year building lease at a rental of approximately one-half the market rate for the area. Tony also invested $10,000 in improvements to the premises and opened his doors.

The spot he chose was excellent. As people came to stroll the Boardwalk on sunny afternoons, they seemed to gravitate to the Arcade to practice their gaming wizardry. Tony knew he had to protect his investment, which represented his total personal wealth and sole source of income. He knew that it could all be wiped out by fire or some other catastrophe.

Tony called the Caring Heart Insurance Agency. After a 5-minute discussion, the proprietor, Mr. Sterling, indicated he could cover all of Tony's risks under a basic storekeeper's policy at a cost of $1000 annually. This seemed too simple a solution for Tony. He decided to call a few other insurance agents in the area. Tony found help at the Brockledge Insurance agency. Mr. Brockledge chose to visit the Arcade before offering advice. He inspected the premises, interviewed Tony, and reviewed the lease of the premises. Tony learned that Mr. Brockledge had 10 years of insurance experience, a professional designation—CPCU (Chartered Property and Casualty Underwriter), and a list of many professional references from satisfied customers in Newport Beach. Mr. Brockledge's interest in and approach to Tony's insurance needs and also his professional credentials earned him the assignment as Tony's insurance agent.

Tony learned that the basic storekeeper's policy would not have given sufficient protection. The basic policy needed to be enhanced to cover some less obvious, but important risk exposures, including:

- A leasehold interest in the premises equal to the difference between the favorable rent Tony paid and the market rate. This additional amount would have to be paid for leasing another location in the event of destruction of his premises. This insurable interest was worth $30,000 to Tony.

- Coverage for $5000 worth of currency and coin, not covered in the basic policy but subject to disappearance or destruction as it accumulates in the machines daily.

- Fire legal liability coverage to protect against Tony's legal liability for the building should Tony's negligence cause a fire that damages or destroys the structure. A special extension to the basic policy was needed to provide this coverage for limits of $300,000, the value of the structure.

For all the combined coverage Tony's agent was able to place the insurance for $1200 annual cost. Thus, for an additional $200, Tony was able to enhance his coverage significantly, better protecting his investment and himself from financial ruin.

---

[4]Prepared by Michael M. Kaddatz, CPCU.

Tony used his general awareness of pure risk to select a professional, who demonstrated technical knowledge and showed an interest in the operations, to assess the risk thoroughly and obtain the needed protection. This is a good example of managing pure risk to protect an investment in the business, which is speculative risk.

What did Mr. Brockledge do that Mr. Sterling did not do?

What important insurance coverages did Tony gain by going to a CPCU?

Types of Coverage

The following kinds of insurance are likely to be of most importance to the small business: *fire* (property), *liability, workers' compensation, automobile,* and *crime* insurance in some areas.

FIRE INSURANCE

Almost all small businesses are exposed to the peril of fire and should have coverage through insurance. Basic fire insurance policies are quite standardized in the United States; policies are nearly identical in all states. The standard fire policy contains an insuring clause; 165 lines of stipulations and conditions that govern the basic insurance contract and the additions (called extensions or endorsements) commonly attached to the basic policy; and an attachment known as *the form,* which describes the property being insured.

Perils Covered and Excluded   Excluding any endorsements, the standard fire policy covers only three perils: fire, lightning, and losses to goods temporarily removed from the business premises because of fire. *Additional perils* must be covered by adding extensions to the basic policy. Typical losses that can be insured against by extensions are loss by theft, windstorm, hail, explosion, riot, aircraft or vehicle, smoke, and smoke damage.

Most businesses find it necessary or desirable to add extended coverage endorsements to their basic fire insurance policy. Although the cost of the policy increases with such endorsements, extended coverage does not increase the face amount of the policy; it merely adds to the perils covered. The details of what perils are covered and what are excluded can be extremely intricate, which again suggests the advisability of getting technical help from a competent consultant, agent, or broker.

Other kinds of insurance coverage in which loss results as a secondary consequence of a primary loss can be covered by extensions to the basic fire insurance policy. These include, but are not limited to, the following:

Business interruption insurance

Profits and commissions insurance

Rent insurance

Demolition insurance

COINSURANCE

A *coinsurance* clause is often included in fire insurance and related policies. Most property losses are partial, although occasionally one will be total. A coinsurance clause encourages an insured to insure to value. The purchaser is ordinarily required to insure the property for 80 or 90 percent of its value at the time the policy takes effect. The owner may elect to purchase coverage to a lower percentage, say 60 percent, even though the 80 percent rate is stipulated. Should there be a loss, the insuring company will pay 60/80 of the loss and the owner will bear 20/80. To avoid becoming a coinsurer, the owner, under the above requirement, must pay for the full 80 percent coverage.

LIABILITY INSURANCE

Every business is presumed to use more than ordinary care to ensure a safe place for customers to enter and do business, for employees to work, and for others who may have reason to be on the premises. Nevertheless, negligence may occasionally occur, resulting in accident and injury to a person on the premises. The unsafe condition may have developed unintentionally. This is no defense against liability. A presumption may exist that negligence was the contributing factor in accidents arising out of business operations or on business premises.

Liability insurance is one of the most important protections the small business should have. The owner commits a most serious error in not recognizing and obtaining protection from this risk. The courts in recent years have been awarding prodigious amounts in settlements of claims, often running into hundreds of thousands, or even millions, of dollars. Not only that, the concepts of legal liability have been broadened: awards for additional types of damage such as mental anguish are not uncommon— and defenses formerly available to defendants in negligence cases have been weakened by court findings in recent years. Adequate coverage has thus become more important than ever.

LIABILITY COVERAGE

It is possible to buy liability policies that pay for these types of losses:

- Liability judgments for accidentally caused bodily injury or damage to the property of others

- Expenses incurred for immediate medical or surgical attention needed at the time of the accident

- Costs of legal defense in suits in which bodily injury or damage to property is alleged, even if such suits turn out to be specious

- Expenses of investigation, defense, or settlement of a suit in case of accident

- Cost of any court bonds or interest on judgments accumulated during an appeal of the case

A policy offering these protections ensures that the insurer will assume all the expense and trouble of settling a liability suit, to the limits of coverage spelled out in the policy. Payments under the comprehensive general liability policy spell out a limit per occurrence. Policies under today's standard are written with a single limit applying to combined bodily injury and property damage in a single accident. The small businessperson should be very careful to ensure that liability coverage meets the needs of the business insofar as foresight and common sense can estimate them. No business should have less than $1 million in liability limits; most should have at least $5 million limits; and many should buy much higher limits.

WORKERS' COMPENSATION

Federal and common law require employers to ensure that workers have a safe place to work, that workers' peers are competent to do the job required, that tools used in the work are safe; and that employees be warned of existing dangers. Small business owners need protection through appropriate *workers' compensation* insurance.

Benefits payable under workers' compensation policies are determined by the state, not by the insurer. Most governing laws provide for unlimited medical care for the injured. Benefits include lump sums for dismemberment and death; payment for disablement from occupational disease; and income for a disabled worker or dependents. Some laws require insurers to pay income for as long as the disability lasts, even for life.

Some exemptions from workers' compensation coverage exist in almost all states. Employers of a small number of employees, perhaps four or less, may be exempt. Not all kinds of employment are covered in some states; employments exempted typically include agricultural, domestic, and casual labor.

Entrepreneurs should find out what the legal requirements are for workers' compensation in the states where they do business. Most often, sole proprietors or partners will find they can reject coverage for themselves but must provide it for their employees.

AUTOMOBILE INSURANCE

This insurance encompasses both physical damage and liability coverage for company-owned vehicles or vehicles used for business purposes. This includes cars or trucks used by your employees or subcontractors' employees, whether or not your company owns these cars or trucks. The physical damage coverage includes comprehensive, essentially all-risk, protection for damage to your business vehicle from such perils as fire, wind, hail, flood, and vandalism. Collision protection is purchased separately and indemnifies for damage caused by collision of your vehicle with another object. The liability coverage protects you against negligence arising out of ownership, maintenance, or use of the business vehicle by you or one of your employees. It includes property damage and bodily injury to others for which you would be legally obligated to pay.

You can assume deductibles of almost any amount, say $250 to $500, for damage to one of your business vehicles and thereby reduce your premiums. You can generally insure a fleet of five or more vehicles operated for business purposes under a fleet policy; this policy insures against both material damage to your vehicle and liability to others for property damage or personal injury. You can buy automobile medical payments insurance that pays for medical claims, including your own, arising from automobile accidents regardless of the question of negligence. And you can purchase uninsured motorist protection to cover your own bodily injury claims from someone who has no insurance.

CRIME INSURANCE

With the exception of fidelity coverage, which is needed as your firm has one or more employees, insurance against loss by crime may not be necessary in all businesses. In some kinds of business, such as retail stores, it may be highly desirable.

Losses due to certain kinds of crime can be catastrophic. Many firms burgled, robbed, or the victims of more heinous crimes, and unprotected by insurance, have been forced to quit business. Let's look first at burglary and robbery insurance.

Burglary Insurance   The fundamental protection given by burglary insurance covers loss of inventoried merchandise and items stored in safes. The insurance policy defines burglary as "felonius abstraction of insured property" that leaves visible marks of the burglar's forced entry. It does not cover losses from abstraction of property by a sneak thief who leaves no trace of entry. The policy does, however, cover damage done in the course of burglary.

Robbery Insurance   Robbery is defined as the taking of property from a person in charge of it by force or threat of violence. Insurance in this case protects from loss of property, money, or securities, either on or off the premises. Policies typically cover property on the premises damaged by robbery. Different limits of liability can be chosen for robbery outside or inside the premises and for robbery of payroll or other money and securities.

COMPREHENSIVE CRIME POLICIES

A variety of comprehensive crime policies is available—offering cafeteria-style options. Some comprehensive contracts cover not only burglary and robbery but also other losses from theft, destruction, or disappearance of property. One broad-form policy, as an instance, insures money and securities on an all-risk basis. Thus money lost in a fire, or blown out a window during a storm, or unknowingly handed over to an imposter bill collector, is covered. Some comprehensive policies insure against loss from forgery and counterfeiting. Covered also are losses from sneak thieves who leave no evidence of forcible entry.

The storekeeper's burglary and robbery policy, a widely used contract, offers protection for the small merchant specifically. It protects up to the amount of loss the insured wants to buy for each of the following: outside robbery, inside robbery, stock burglary, safe burglary, kidnapping of the owner, burglary from the house of a custodian, and property damage by burglary or robbery. The limits of coverage may be increased—but this policy aims directly at the small business; it's not well suited to the larger firm.

Crime insurance rates vary depending upon the neighborhood, presence of guards or sentries, crime or loss prevention measures employed, type of safe, effectiveness of burglar alarm system, number of locations exposed, and characteristics of the business.

Measures to prevent or minimize crime are presented in a later section.

ALL-RISK INSURANCE

All-risk policies developed by fire insurers offer wide coverage. This insurance gives considerably improved protection to the small business owner as a purchaser of fire insurance and related lines. All-risk policies cover perils except those specifically *excluded by name*.

Advantages of All-Risk Policies   All-risk policies offer the following advantages:

1. You avoid unintentional gaps in coverage because you're insured for all perils not specifically excluded. In "named peril" policies your losses are covered only when they are caused by a peril specifically listed in the contract.

2. You're more likely not to duplicate coverage, which is always more costly than it should be. It's harder to avoid overlapping coverage when buying several named-peril policies.

3. With an all-risk policy, you can more readily avoid the conflict that can sometimes result from having a number of separate policies. Settlement of loss claims can often become complicated should you have more than one policy covering a single loss—especially if the wording of the policies treating loss settlements is not the same. For example, one policy may cover all your property, but another may cover only specific property. If loss to the specific property occurs, conflict may arise over how much each policy is to contribute. In this situation, known as *nonconcurrency,* you could well experience complicated adjustment problems and delays.

4. Your total premium on an all-risk policy would usually be smaller than on similar coverage bought separately. Larger unit sales cut down on the insurer's overhead per policy. This saving is passed on to you. Your own time spent in managing your insurance program would be reduced because you handle all coverage in one action.

It may well pay you to explore the all-risk insurance contract for the above reasons. You could obtain a policy that would cover the important needs of your business in a single form. For example, one form might contain coverage for physical damage to real and personal property, liability, theft, and medical payments. And this would be less expensive by at least 10 percent or more than if you bought several individual insurance policies to cover your needs.

Desirable Coverages

Although not absolutely essential, some types of insurance coverage will add greatly to the security of your business. These include business-interruption insurance, key-person insurance, employee health insurance, and a choice among numerous miscellaneous coverages.

BUSINESS-INTERRUPTION INSURANCE

Of the variety of insurance coverages available to the small businessperson, business-interruption insurance can be one of the most valuable. Business-interruption insurance takes the form of an endorsement to the standard fire policy, or other property insurance form. It is intended to compensate for income losses and extra expenses incurred when your business is interrupted by fire, flood, earthquake, or other covered catastrophe. Despite insurance that may compensate fully for direct losses of inventory, raw material, work in process, furniture and fixtures, equipment, and building, you will have to meet many costs during rebuilding. Your continuing cash needs would include salaries of key personnel, taxes, interest, utilities, and the like. A major shutdown lasting several months might mean closing down your business unless business-interruption insurance gave the necessary financial protection. This coverage would also pay you for loss of profits during shutdown.

KEY-PERSON INSURANCE

This form of coverage comes with the purchase of insurance on the lives of key personnel in a business. Managers in a training and succession program in a small business represent an asset of critical importance to the continuity of operations. To set the amounts of insurance for key people, you can estimate how long it would take to bring in and train replacements. Suppose it takes 4 years to hire and train a replacement for a given key position. One approach would be to multiply the mean salary received annually by 4, then add about 50 percent, to arrive at a value for an insurance policy. For example, suppose the general manager of your small firm drew an average salary of $30,000 per year. Four times that amount would be $120,000; adding 50 percent would bring the desired amount of life insurance to $180,000. This might be an adequate sum to cover the losses resulting from your general manager's death: recruiting a competent replacement, training that person, lost sales to important customers, lost profit before and during the training period, and similar kinds of losses.

Variations on this approach can readily be worked out to suit the needs of each business.

The cross-purchase plan is another form of key-person insurance. Here owners of a business buy insurance on each others' lives. If one dies, the others have the insurance funds to purchase the deceased's share of the business. A plan of this kind is best made by legal agreement at the time the company is formed.

EMPLOYEE HEALTH INSURANCE

Many varieties of group health insurance plans are available to the small business. Among these are basic medical and hospitalization, major medical, disability, and health maintenance organizations (HMOs).

Basic Medical and Hospitalization Insurance This plan pays for medical expenses, prescription medications, doctors' and hospital fees on a stated basis: a given number of dollars for each specified medical treatment, and a specified amount for each day of hospitalization. This is the customary approach taken in policies offered by commercial insurers. Another plan available is the "service" form, which offers compensation for the total costs of specified hospital care and physicians' services. Many variations exist in the details of the numerous plans on the market. You should use care in selecting a plan appropriate for your business.

Major Medical Plans   This insurance aims to meet the cost of catastrophic illness or accident to your employees. A plan of this kind is usually added to the basic plan; it often carries a substantial deductible amount for each claim but provides a large maximum benefit, as much as $1 million. Many plans now offer unlimited coverage. A major medical plan may be had in a comprehensive way, combining both a basic plan and the major medical plan.

Health Maintenance Organizations   These organizations, which have been developed in recent years, are designed to offer comprehensive health care at modest cost to your subscribing employees. Each employee and family are under the care of an eligible physician who monitors health care and coordinates any additional medical or hospitalization needs.

Standards for operation of HMOs are maintained by the U.S. Department of Health and Human Services. Membership in HMOs is available to all employees and their families where employers offer this plan.

Disability Insurance   Disability insurance compensates employees who cannot work for long periods because of non-job-related illness or accident. Employees in this circumstance are paid a given percentage (usually 60 to 70 percent) of their salary. Coverage of this kind offers a worthwhile benefit to employers. Not only does it build goodwill among your employees, but it also costs you, the employer, less than it would to continue usual salaries for incapacitated employees.

LIFE INSURANCE

Small businesspersons should carry sufficient life insurance to enable family survivors to maintain their standards of living. You can use one of two approaches to determine the amount of life insurance you should carry: the *value of human life* estimate or the *needs* method.

The value-of-human-life approach employs an estimate of your earning power for life, plus investments resulting from earnings, to support dependents in the lifestyle to which they have become accustomed.

The needs approach estimates the money that would be required to support the family in case of your death, as the head of household. Expenses considered would include household requirements, illnesses, taxes, household payments, personal loans, funeral expenses, and future needs expectancies.

Three basic forms of life insurance are available: whole life insurance, term life insurance, and endowment life insurance.

Whole life insurance affords a policy that is in force for the life of the individual. Upon death of that person, the face amount of the policy is paid to beneficiary, usually the family. The cash value of such a policy increases as the premiums are paid. The policyholder may borrow against the policy up to the cash value at any time; this can on occasion be a valuable source of funds.

Term life insurance provides coverage for a given number of years. Premiums are lower than whole life, and the policy expires after a stated number of years. For example, if the policyholder dies in the twelfth year of a 15-year policy, the face amount of the policy is paid to the beneficiary. If, however, the insured is still alive at the end of 15 years, the policy no longer has any worth—it expires.

Group life insurance is usually written on a 1-year (year-to-year) basis. No medical examinations are required. Such policies do not have cash value. Group life insurance policies generally require 10 or more participants and may include employee participation in premium payment—up to 50 percent of the total.

Endowment life insurance pays the beneficiary the face amount of the policy if the insured dies within the specified period of time known as the endowment period. If the insured lives to the end of the endowment period, the maturity value is paid to that person. The premiums for this form of policy are the highest among the three forms of life insurance described here. Larger sums of money can become available sooner under an endowment policy than under a whole life policy. However, if the equivalent sums paid out in premiums for the endowment policy were invested in a whole life policy, a larger death benefit would be written in and the policy owner would save substantially.

DOCUMENT SECURITY

Many firms have documents of special value to the business. These include such items as business records, patent disclosures, marketing plans, and trade secrets involving special fabricating techniques, processing procedures, and design criteria—know-how that ensures the success of making or doing something unique and crucial to the success of the business. You should lock away documents of these kinds, including computer record disks or tapes, in a special safe or restricted area, accessible to only one or two highly trusted personnel.

Owners should recognize that personnel who leave the company cannot be kept from making a living at their occupation. If they are suspected of carrying off company secrets, so long as they did not steal pertinent documents, it is almost impossible to restrain them legally from practicing their skills. This suggests the desirability of restricting the data on trade secrets to as few people—and trusted people—as possible.

FIDELITY BONDS

Small business owners should consider the advisability of *fidelity bonds* to protect against the risk of stealing by employees. The fidelity bond differs from the usual insurance policy in that three parties are involved, not two. These are the employee who is bonded (called the *principal*), the person or firm protected (called the *obligee*), and the licensed bonding corporation or the insurance company (called the *surety*). If the principal steals, the surety pays the obligee and has the right to try to recover its losses from the principal.

Three kinds of fidelity bonds are available:

Individual bonds naming a specific person

Schedule bonds listing all the names or positions to be covered

Blanket bonds covering all employees but not identifying them by name or position. In all circumstances blanket bonds give certain advantages. Some employees may not handle money but do have access to valuable stores of goods or inventory. Blanket bonds protect against theft of money or property by any and all employees whether acting alone or in collusion, including those who may have been hired after the bond goes into effect.

Bonds have no expiration date; they are continuous until either party cancels. A limit of liability, called the *penalty* of the bond, states the maximum amount payable for a loss.

SURETY BONDS

Surety bonds for the most part are designed to guarantee that a principal will complete work that the obligee has contracted to have done. These bonds are therefore aimed at businesspersons doing construction work under contract, involved in court actions, or applying for licenses or permits.

A surety bond aims to test that the principal is honest and has the necessary skill and resources to perform acceptably the obligation the bond covers. Sureties therefore check the reputation, credit rating, and resources of the principal in depth before issuing a bond. Should there be default in the performance of the contract, the surety has the right to recover from the principal any amounts they are required to pay to the obligee.

A major advantage of surety bonds for your small company comes from the ability it gives you to compete on equal terms with the large well-established firm. The obligee wanting the work done can depend on the small company having surety bonding; the bonding company uses the services of professional underwriters to assess the small company's competency to do the work before issuing the bond.

MISCELLANEOUS INSURANCE COVERAGES

Although the foregoing sections list a number of the more usual insurance coverages important to the small business, many special-purpose protections are available. Some are given here to show the variety of insurance forms for special circumstances:

- Contractor's equipment insurance

- Rent insurance

- Inland transit insurance

- Blanket motor cargo insurance

- Sprinkler leakage insurance

- Glass insurance

- Profits and commissions insurance

If no special coverage is available for an unusual risk, an insurer will often tailor one for the purpose.

Measures to Prevent Crime

Small business executives have at their command many measures to prevent or minimize crime. By becoming alert to tested procedures and modern instrumentation, they can not only minimize the risks and losses of crime but also reduce the premiums for insurance. Crime prevention measures should be considered for treating the following: armed robbery and burglary, shoplifting, employee theft, pilfering, white collar crime, and fraud.

Although it seems a shame that measures to deal with these kinds of crime should even have to be considered in our society, small business owners will find their business vulnerable to some kinds of crime. Owners should assess the possibilities of risk from crime in their business—and take appropriate prevention measures.

ARMED ROBBERY AND BURGLARY

Steps to reduce the incidence of armed robbery or burglary include open design of the premises, keeping interior spaces visible from the outside, sturdy closures for doors and windows, guard dogs, changing routines for banking and depositing cash, security guards, and automatic alarm systems.

- *Open design of premises.* Careful placement of trees and shrubbery to ensure a clear view of the building, coupled with well-designed night lighting, help to reduce the possibility of burglary.

- *Keeping interior visible from outside.* A clear view of the store interior from outside by proper placement of fixtures tends to discourage burglars. Effective illumination of the interior at night supports this effort.

- *Closures for doors and windows.* Inexpensive means of protection are offered by sturdy deadbolt locks on doors, making windows jimmyproof, and installing heavy-gauge screens and bars at windows.

- *Guard dogs.* Some kinds of business can use trained dogs to guard against intruders. Guard dogs have been found to be effective deterrents against armed robbers and burglars. They are trained to respond to command; a wise procedure returns these dogs to their trainers for a refresher course on a regular schedule.

- *Banking schedules.* To avoid the possibility of armed robbery, sound practice indicates the advisability of depositing cash in the bank on a daily basis. Routines varying schedules for depositing and withdrawing cash make it difficult for robbers to plan holdups.

- *Security guards.* The presence of trained armed guards on the premises, day and night, acts as a deterrent to robbery and burglary. Some firms are more able to hire guards than others; industrial companies of some size usually have more need for guards and can afford them more readily than the small firm.

- *Alarm systems.* The small business owner has the choice of a number of different automatic burglar alarm systems. Some are electric and connect directly with the police department or guard office; triggering these systems sends armed guards hurrying to the firm's location. Other versions are electronic; these when triggered activate loud sirens and may also be hooked up to the police department or guard office.

From the foregoing discussion, the small business owner can see the many measures at hand to reduce or eliminate armed robbery or burglary. Your judgment will dictate the desirability of selecting preventive measures that serve the purposes of your business at reasonable cost.

SHOPLIFTING AND PILFERAGE

Shoplifting is defined as stealing merchandise on display from a store; pilfering consists of stealing little by little from the business.

Shoplifting   Shoplifting results in a major loss to retailers in the United States. This can mean a serious loss for the small business, as it can for any business for that matter. For the national economy this means a loss of well over $20 billion annually. The small retailer should take steps to minimize shoplifting; not only does it cut materially into profit, but also it tends to increase prices to the consumer as management tries to recoup losses due to shoplifting.

A *Chicago Tribune* news release of November 14, 1982, has this to say about retail store theft:

Retail store theft is holding steady at 2 percent of sales, despite the poor economy, according to a study on retail security and shrinkage (theft) conducted by Arthur Young & Co. for the National Mass Retailing Institute.

"We had anticipated that shrinkage losses would increase in 1981, especially in view of the economy, but shrinkage has remained constant," said Gerald Smith, a partner in the Chicago office of Arthur Young & Co. and a member of its national retail committee. "We credit that to the greater attention retailers are paying to preventing theft."

The study, which included 198 retailers with 33,000 stores throughout the country, found that theft is highest—2.3 percent of sales—in traditional department stores with many separate departments, checkouts, and exits. The theft average for mass merchandisers with central checkout counters is 1.9 percent of sales, while specialty stores have a 2 percent average.

Departments with the highest theft rates include women's clothing, cosmetics, and jewelry, principally because the items are easily transported, the study found.

Electronic tags continue to be the most effective security device used on the selling floor, said 47 percent of the retailers responding to the survey. . . .

Eroll Cook, a partner in Arthur Young and chairman of its national retail group, pointed out that about 50 percent of all store theft is by store employees and 30 percent by shoplifting, while 20 percent is attributable to "poor paperwork control."

"That doesn't mean the store has actually lost the merchandise, just that it has lost the record of it," he said.

Shoplifters range all the way from juveniles who steal for kicks to professionals who steal for money through fencing the goods they lift. The category includes kleptomaniacs, drug addicts, and vagrants. The range is so wide and the techniques of shoplifters so varied as to suggest the need for the small store owner to practice the best possible preventive measures. Among approaches that have proved effective are the following:

- Comprehensive records and a carefully managed inventory control system. Records of sales, purchases, and inventory are tools that should be used to see if merchandise is disappearing without payment.

- Post signs in conspicuous places around the premises stating that shoplifters will be prosecuted. Do not make this an idle threat; the business that builds a reputation for prosecuting shoplifters finds that losses from this source diminish substantially.

- Unused checkout lanes should be kept closed.

- Small expensive items should be displayed in an enclosed locked case. The case should be visible to a clerk at all times.

- Have salespersons keep fitting rooms and restrooms under observation. Many clothing stores limit the number of items of apparel that may be tried on at one time to two.

- Place large convex mirrors around the premises so that sales areas may be seen from central points such as checkout counters and cash registers. Two-way view mirrors strategically placed can be useful in detecting shoplifting.

- Maintain a sufficient number of salespersons to ensure coverage of the sales areas.

- Use modern electronic detecting equipment; one form works by inserting a special pellet in clothing for sale. Pellets can be removed only with a special shears at the checkout location. Anyone taking an item from the store without having the pellet removed sets off an alarm that warns of attempted shoplifting.

Apprehending a shoplifter should not be attempted until that person leaves the store. The owner or store personnel must be careful not to leave themselves open to lawsuits for false arrest.

PILFERAGE

As has been stated, pilferage results from stealing little by little from the business. Many employees will make off with small items, not realizing that the loss to the firm can be large over a period of time. Pencils and erasers, postage on personal mail, small amounts of petty cash from time to time, personal phone calls on company time—these are typical of items that can cause a continuing drain on company resources. They prove very hard to stop, and perhaps the best way is to appeal to the honesty of most employees.

In an occasional case, it may be more economical to ignore a bit of pilfering than to try to stop it. This was the case in a small electronics manufacturing concern that employed a number of electronics technicians. The owner recognized, after some experience, the considerable cost of trying to maintain an ongoing inventory of components such as resistors and capacitors. He found that attrition of these small parts resulted from the technicians' lifting these items for use in their home workshops. He believed that once they had stocked up their home shops they would leave the company supplies alone. He therefore placed small common electronics items in open stock, cafeteria style. After a time, attrition diminished and the company found the open cafeteria style suitable for its purpose.

EMPLOYEE THEFT

Theft by employees can cause more loss than burglary, robbery, and shoplifting combined. It behooves the small business owner to be wary of the possibility of theft by personnel working in the business. Such thefts can be done by several different methods: pocketing cash by failing to register all sales; short-changing customers; embezzlement through manipulation of checks and accounting records; carrying out goods in lunch boxes or pockets; depositing items in trash barrels to be recovered after the barrels are removed for pickup; salespersons not charging full price to friends or not charging for all goods purchased. And other ingenious schemes are used by unscrupulous employees to steal from the business.

The following measures can help prevent employee theft:

- Keep adequate records of purchases, inventory, and sales

- Have company records and accounting books audited regularly by a competent accountant

- Assign clerks to one register only; check cash against the register tape at the end of the clerk's duty

- Make spot checks to ensure that clerks are ringing up all sales and at the correct prices

- Keep all doors locked, with the exception of doors used by customers; make one person responsible for keys

- If possible, have one door, or set of doors, for customer ingress only, and another for exit; this permits exits to be carefully watched

- Do not allow trash to accumulate on the premises; inspect trash receptacles from time to time to make sure no merchandise has been placed in them for later retrieval

- Inspect employee packages leaving the premises

- Observe loading and unloading procedures. Make sure all items ordered are received. Assign a responsible person to load outgoing shipments to ensure no more goes out than has been ordered by customers

- Let employees know that you expect honesty from them—and that theft will not be tolerated

■ Be careful in hiring to do a thorough job of checking honesty and character of applicants

■ The devices used for detecting shoplifting can be used to detect employee theft: convex mirrors, two-way mirrors, and closed-circuit TV.

It seems unfortunate that such measures often have to be taken to limit employee theft in our society. Yet the small businessperson who does not understand the potential losses possible through unscrupulous employee activity mismanages this aspect of the business.

How to Use the Foregoing Information

Summary

Each small business is different and has its own degree of risk and of loss. And most small business owners are confused (not without good reason) by the complexities of the large number of insurance policies available to them. Now that you have acquired a basic understanding of the most frequently needed types of protection, you will be able to use what you've learned not only to select a qualified agent, consultant, or broker to set up an insurance program tailored to your specific needs but also to judge the adequacy of the insurance program set up for you.

We've addressed the following key points in this chapter to guide you in arriving at appropriate coverage of the risks of your business:

■ Risks that have a possible outcome of gain or loss are called speculative risk. Risks that can have only loss as the outcome are called pure risk. You can lessen the possibility of loss in speculative risk by practicing proactive management. You can reduce the impact of loss through pure risk by proper insurance coverage.

■ In general, these broad classifications of insurance offer protection against the majority of pure risk business losses: property insurance, protection against destruction of property; business-interruption insurance, protection against loss of earnings due to damage or destruction of physical property; liability insurance, protection from loss due to negligence on the part of the business or its personnel; fidelity and surety bonds, a guarantee against loss because of employee dishonesty or failure of the business to meet legal obligations required by contract or law; and workers' compensation, which compensates employees for job-related injury.

■ We've indicated that not all pure risks can or should be covered by insurance. Four basic alternatives to insurance in such cases are the following: assumption of risk, a widely used approach in which the business owner sees the situation as one involving a reasonable chance that nothing drastic will happen; prevention of loss, which involves such things as installing a safety training program in the plant, or using a guard to patrol the premises at night; transfer of risk, such as having services performed by an outside agency rather than the firm's personnel; and self-insurance through setting up a legally qualified separate fund.

Finally, we explored the meaning and use of insurance of various common kinds to cover or lessen the impact of loss from pure risk; and we've described measures to prevent or minimize crime. The latter include armed robbery and burglary, shoplifting, employee theft, pilfering, white collar crime, and fraud.

WORKSHEET 16

Managing Business Risk

This worksheet is designed to help you identify the kinds of insurance coverage you should have for your business. You will be prepared to work intelligently with an insurance broker, consultant, or agent to get the kind of coverage you will need, at minimum premium cost. And you will be prepared to judge the competence of broker, consultant, or agent when you select one as your insurance consultant.

1. Think carefully about your business and the pure risks to which it may be subject. Make a list of those risks under the following headings:

   ■ Property insurance. _____
   _____
   _____
   _____

   ■ Business-interruption insurance. _____
   _____
   _____
   _____

   ■ Liability insurance. _____
   _____
   _____

   ■ Fidelity and surety bonds. _____
   _____
   _____

   ■ Workers' compensation. _____
   _____
   _____

2. I have considered the possibility of self-insurance in areas where I think the possibility of loss is low. These areas are: _____
   _____
   _____
   _____

   I understand that I must set up a legally acceptable procedure, a special fund, and have a qualified person to manage my self-insurance program. (You can see that most small businesses cannot take on the cost of or complexity of self-insurance. They're better off to use the services of a competent insurance agent, consultant, or broker to select the best program for their business, and to pay the required premiums.)

3. I've arrived at the conclusion that there are some risks that I don't need to cover by insurance. These are risks in which I think the potential for loss is low:

_____

_____

4. I'm prepared to transfer risk in the following, by adopting the procedures indicated:

_____

_____

_____

_____

5. Here are some measures I can take to prevent loss or reduce the size of those that do occur:

_____

_____

_____

_____

6. Here are some measures I can take to prevent or minimize crime: armed robbery and burglary, shoplifting, employee theft, pilfering, white collar crime, fraud:

_____

_____

_____

_____

_____

_____

_____

_____

_____

_____

KEY TERMS

speculative risk 459
pure risk 459
premium 461
insurance 461

crime insurance 468
burglary 468
robbery 468

STUDY ASSIGNMENTS FOR REVIEW AND DISCUSSION

1. Some risks have the possibility of gain or loss. Name two or three examples. What are these kinds of risks called?

2. Some risks have the possibility of loss only. What are these risks called?

3. Why would it be important for you to select an insurance broker, consultant, or agent to set up an insurance program for your business?

4. Describe four broad categories of business insurance.

5. Under what conditions in your business would you seek coverage of fidelity or surety bonds?

6. Several alternatives may be used instead of insurance in the management of pure risk:
   - Assumption of risk
   - Prevention of loss
   - Transfer of risk
   Tell what is meant by each of these terms.

7. Some firms choose to self-insure in some areas. What steps would this procedure require?

8. Define the characteristics of insurable losses.

PROJECTS FOR STUDENTS

1. Write a paragraph describing the difference between speculative risk and pure risk.

2. List the four broad categories of business insurance and write a sentence telling what risks each covers.

3. What is meant by assumption of risk?

4. What can a small business owner do to reduce hazards and minimize loss through proactive management? Give two examples.

5. Describe what is meant by transfer of risk. Give an example.

6. Define the requirements for self-insurance.

7. Define the characteristics of insurable risk.

8. Explain the difference between gambling and insurance.

9. Describe the difference between burglary and robbery.

IF YOU WANT TO READ MORE

These references offer wide introductory coverage of risk management for the small business. Texts, in general, are in straightforward nontechnical language.

ATHEARN, James L.: *Risk and Insurance,* West Publishing Company, St. Paul, MN, 1981. This book can help you acquire the knowledge and skill to handle risk. Because insurance and risk are so complex, the book discusses fundamental principles first and then applies them to real-world situations.

DAY, William H.: *Maximizing Small Business Profits,* Prentice-Hall, Inc., Englewood Cliffs, NJ, 1979. Chapter 9, "Risk Management," addresses the kinds of risk small businesses are exposed to, how to deal with these risks, types of insurance, and the basic rules of risk management.

GREENE, Mark R.: *Insurance and Risk Management for Small Business,* 3d ed., SBA, Washington, DC, 1981. This booklet, written specifically for the Small Business Administration, covers in simple language the major aspects of risk coverage and insurance that you, as a small business owner, are likely to be concerned with.

GREENE, Mark R., and Oscar N. SERBEIN: *Risk Management: Text and Cases,* Reston Publishing Company, Inc., Reston, VA, 1983. This book is intended for those who want an introduction to risk and risk bearing as a function of the business firm. The identification, analysis, and measurement of loss possibilities, and the principal methods of managing such contingencies constitute the core of the book.

HODGETTS, Richard M.: *Effective Small Business Management,* Academic Press, New York, 1982. The author discusses, in Chapter 20, the various types of insurance that the small business owner should be familiar with. The presentation gives particular emphasis to the need for continual evaluation of the firm's insurance needs.

JUSTIS, Robert T.: *Managing Your Small Business,* Prentice-Hall, Inc., Englewood Cliffs, NJ, 1981. Chapter 20, "Risk and Insurance," identifies some common business risks, lists the four basic types of risk management, defines different types of insurance, and discusses various options for employee group insurance and government-operated insurance programs.

KRENTZMAN, Harvey C.: *Successful Management Strategies for Small Business,* Prentice-Hall, Inc., Englewood Cliffs, NJ, 1981. Chapter 9, "Management of Insurance," details how the small businessperson can develop a risk-management program.

PICKLE, Hal B., and Royce L. ABRAHAMSON: *Small Business Management,* 4th ed., John Wiley & Sons, New York, 1986. Chapter 14, "Risk, Insurance, and Theft," deals with risk control, types of insurance for small business, shoplifting, employee theft, and burglary.

Periodicals

American Insurance Digest. Monthly, American Insurance Digest, Inc., Suite A-920, 175 West Jackson Blvd., Chicago, IL 60604.

Best's Review. Property-Liability Insurance edition and Life-Health Insurance edition. Monthly. A.M. Best Co., Inc., Morristown, NJ 07960.

Business Insurance. Weekly. Crain Communications, Inc., 740 Rush Street, Chicago, IL 60611.

Journal of Risk and Insurance. Quarterly. American Risk and Insurance Association, Illinois Wesleyan University, 112 East Washington Street, Bloomington, IL 61701.

Risk Management Monthly. 10 times a year. Risk and Insurance Management Society, Inc., 8 West 40th Street, New York, NY 10018.

CHAPTER 17

Managing Your Personnel Function

TOPICS IN THIS CHAPTER

Objectives of This Chapter
Developing Sound Personnel Policy
Typical Personnel Policies for the Small Company
Recruiting the Right People
Appraising Performance
Training for Work Improvement
Training before Performance
Management Succession
Techniques for Developing Managers
Terminating Personnel
To Unionize or Not to Unionize: That Is the Question!
Key Points in Managing Personnel—Summary
Worksheet 17: Managing Your Personnel Function
Key Terms
Study Assignments for Review and Discussion
Projects for Students
If You Want to Read More

In this chapter we come back to the fourth element, *PEOPLE*, in the flow diagram of the business process (Figure 1-1). In this extremely important function you will be concerned with *managing* people. You should work to become an effective manager of your personnel, achieving skill in developing and using desirable, workable personnel policies. You'll make sure that your employees understand these policies—and that you apply them with an even hand.

Although specific items may vary from company to company depending on the special needs of the business, four general categories of policy apply universally:

Hiring—bringing qualified people into the company

Maintenance—dealing with promotion, quality of performance, discipline, vacations, benefits, and similar matters

Firing—terminating employees

Government requirements—meeting legal requirements in hiring, maintenance, and firing

This chapter treats several of the more important elements in these subjects that you'll need to know to manage your personnel function fairly and effectively.

Information in this chapter will be found pertinent to this item in the business plan:

7.A. Description of the proposed organization

$$\text{You} + \text{Idea} + \begin{cases} \text{Money} \\ \text{Credit} \end{cases} + \begin{cases} \text{Facilities} \\ \\ \textbf{PEOPLE} \end{cases} \begin{array}{c} \text{Product} \\ \rightarrow \quad \text{or} \\ \text{Service} \end{array} + \text{Marketing} \begin{cases} \text{Money} \\ \text{Credit} \end{cases} \rightarrow \text{Profit}$$

When you first thought of starting your own business you had a gleam in your eye, a vision of the future—your company as a substantial enterprise resulting from your driving enterpreneurial spirit. By the time you've read this far, you'll have learned that you can't reach this goal alone. You'll need to surround yourself with capable people to make your vision come true.

With growth comes complexity. You reach a position in the growth of your company where you can't wear enough hats or switch them fast enough to cover the increasing variety of tasks your business will demand. You'll have to give authority to others to accomplish most of these tasks. How well they get done will depend on the competence of the people you've hired.

Objectives of This Chapter

This chapter deals with key issues the small businessperson must treat in building an effective workforce. These issues range from objective policy setting for managing personnel matters to coping with unionization efforts.

The objectives of this chapter are to:

- Stress the need for working out sound policy for managing the company's personnel function

- Recommend ways of finding and hiring qualified people

- Suggest tested procedures in interviewing candidates for jobs

- Describe a positive approach in assessing employee performance

- Point to ways of terminating personnel under different circumstances

- Outline management training methods

- Describe techniques for developing managers

- Recommend steps to be taken in facing unionization

Achievement of these objectives through the recommendations and suggestions made in this chapter will help you to manage your personnel functions proactively; you'll be seen by your employees as fair and consistent.

LEO N. HARDING COMPANY

The Leo N. Harding Company is a small, highly successful company in the research and development business. It was founded by Harding 20 years ago as a two-man precision machine shop, working for others on a job-shop basis.

After a few years, Harding shifted the emphasis of the business from mechanical work to innovative development in electromechanics, in which he had become interested. Typical projects involved the design and fabrication of prototypes of small electromechanical actuators for aircraft use. Harding was far more interested in research and development, for which he had an intuitive grasp, than in production. He therefore contracted the production of devices developed in his firm to other companies, from which he drew royalties.

Eventually Harding built up a superior technical organization comprised of 20 competent engineers and a support group of 30 technical personnel. Engineering operations were headed by his chief engineer, Ralph Morrison.

One day Harding called Morrison into his office.

"Ralph," he said, "How long have we had twenty engineers on our payroll?"

"About two years," said Morrison. "We went from fifteen to twenty then."

"O.K.," said Harding, "Now here's what I want you to do. I want you to fire five engineers by the end of the month."

Gasping with shock, Morrison said, "But, Leo, why? You remember all the trouble we went to to hire the best people we could find when we put on the last crew. We're swamped with business. . . .We'd be out of our heads to let anyone go."

"Look, Ralph, I don't want to talk about it. You fire five guys for me. That's an order! Now get out of here."

Morrison left the office, shaken and dismayed. Muttering, he said to himself, "My God, how am I going to handle this? What am I going to do?"

Developing Sound Personnel Policy

As in all other areas of management, you'll want to work from sound policy in hiring and managing personnel. Entrepreneurs in most small new businesses don't realize that they set a precedent when they hire their first employees. Owners of small new firms suffer from two deficiencies in personnel matters: lack of sufficient funds to hire the very best people and lack of appreciation that they'll be setting a style that's likely to stay with them forever after. When it needs help, the beginning firm is too likely to hire the first warm bodies that happen to walk through the door. The entrepreneur who usually does the hiring isn't ordinarily trained to do the screening necessary to assure getting competent people who can do what's needed now and who have the potential to grow with the firm.

Indiscriminate hiring in the beginning generally causes a difficult situation at a later date. The company one day finds itself burdened with more than a few incompetents; it's grown beyond the capacities of a considerable portion of its employees. The chief executive-owner then faces the disheartening problem of selecting those to eliminate from the organization. By this time friendships have developed. It's hard to terminate people who've been with the company from its beginning. We'll make some suggestions later in this chapter for doing this with the least unpleasantness. Once the disagreeable task's been done, it's necessary to replace those who've been fired with competent people who can take on positions of responsibility. The time lost in allowing incompetent people to fill positions can never be regained. How much better to have hired people with the right qualifications in the first place!

Don't fall into the trap of hiring indiscriminately. Learn the importance of setting high standards in employing people from the very beginning. Think through and set policies for both hiring and managing personnel to ensure staffing your firm with people who can do today's job and can learn to do tomorrow's job as the firm grows.

Typical Personnel Policies for the Small Company

The small company doesn't need an elaborate set of policies for guiding its management activities. However, carefully thought out policies in major areas will help you as the chief executive to be sound and consistent in making decisions. Policy manuals vary from those as simple as a few typed pages to printed booklets. For the small company the typed policy guide is usually adequate. As the company grows, the typed guide can be expanded, printed, and bound. Whatever approach you use, you will be well advised to put an end date on each policy. This will force review and updating of policies, which in most companies tend to become obsolete with changing times and conditions.

TYPICAL POLICIES FOR THE SMALL COMPANY PERSONNEL FUNCTION

- Background and image the company presents

- Standard working hours

- Pay policies
  Paydays
  Overtime pay
  Salaries

- Observed holidays

- Vacations

- Leaves of absence

- Benefits
  Retirement program
  Insurance programs

- Sick leave

- Termination of employment
  Disciplinary layoff
  Discharge
  Resignation

- Reemployment

Statements of personnel policy should be brief and clearly written. Often the reason for the policy opens the statement. The procedure for handling exceptions then may conclude the statement. An example follows:

> VACATIONS: Your company believes in the value of vacations as a way for you to relax, to enjoy your family, and to restore your energy and keenness when you come back on the job. You are entitled to 2 weeks' vacation after you have worked for a year. You must take your vacation

within 9 months after the end of each year of work. After you have worked for 5 years, your vacation increases to 3 weeks. Again, vacations must be taken within 9 months.

If you are asked to work beyond the 9 month period because of emergency requirement of the business, your supervisor will work out an acceptable vacation schedule with you.

GUIDELINES FOR HIRING POLICY

You can be guided in establishing a sound hiring policy by observing these criteria:

1. Make sure the candidate can do the job that needs doing now.

2. Make sure the candidate you hire will work well with others, because of the importance of teamwork in your business.

3. Gauge the potential of the candidate for growth, for becoming more competent with time, because growth of your employees is important to the growth of your company.

4. Make sure you feel comfortable with the people you hire. You'll work closely with them to make the company grow both technically and financially. It's important that you get along well together.

If we look closely at these statements, we see that they cover two broad subjects: technical competence in the work and interpersonal competence in relationships with others. Any business must have technical competence to survive; it must do a good job of turning out the product or service. And a high level of interpersonal competence supports the firm's technical competence because it improves the ability of the members to identify the important problems of operations that need to be solved and to solve them through teamwork of the most effective kind. Not only that, but by practicing teamwork effectively, members also learn to contribute their special knowledge in solving these important problems. The practice of interpersonal competence helps to improve the team's problem-solving ability.

Once you've thought about these foregoing guidelines and have determined your hiring policy, you're ready to adopt practices that will help you hire people who are right for your organization.

Recruiting the Right People

If you're a sole proprietor, you'll do the first hiring yourself. You can use a straightforward, well-tested procedure to make sure that you're doing a good job of getting the right kind of person for the job and for your firm. The same procedure should be adopted by anyone you delegate to do the hiring. In using a uniform approach to hiring, you'll be setting standards for sound practice in acquiring personnel; sound practice will help you build an effective workforce now and for the future.

Hiring is a three-step process: (1) defining the duties and responsibilities of the position to be filled and the skills, knowledge, and experience required to meet them,

(2) finding and attracting those people who have the qualifications for the position, and (3) screening the candidates to identify the most promising and then hiring them.

FINDING QUALIFIED APPLICANTS

Assuming that you've defined the requirements of the position you want to fill, the duties and responsibilities and the background needed to do the work, your next step is to find qualified candidates. You won't have the advantages of the large company with its specialized recruiting staff, package of fringe benefits, and high salaries. You'll have to concentrate on offering the advantages of the small company. This suggests that you'll have to use every resource at your command to find candidates who measure up to the standards given in the hiring policies you've set.

Among the many resources you can draw on to find the right people are the following:

Newspaper advertisements (see Figure 17-1). You should outline in your ad the specific duties and responsibilities of the position and the requirements the candidate must bring to it. State clearly the advantages your small company has over the behemoths: the great opportunity for innovative work, the chance to move up fast with the growth of the company, the pleasure of working closely with other competent people in a friendly environment where everyone knows everybody else, the uniqueness of your product or service, and any other features you think attractive to prospective personnel.

Business friends and acquaintances. You'll meet your counterparts at various functions, at a dinner or at a business meeting. Tell them about the position you have open and about the kind of person you're looking for to fill it. Many times your business acquaintances will be able to suggest a person who may qualify.

Suppliers and customers. Let your suppliers and major customers know about the open position. They too can often suggest likely prospects to fill it.

Technical publications. Place a carefully worded ad in the technical publication in your field. This approach may take longer than a newspaper ad because of the publication schedule of the journal. However, it can be effective because the readership will include persons acquainted with the field; some will undoubtedly have the competence you're looking for.

Trade associations. The United States boasts over 7000 trade associations. Check with the secretary of the association that represents your business to see if the association has an employment service. If so, you may find that service helpful in your search for qualified candidates.

Employment agencies. You'll find a great variety of employment agencies available to help you in your search. These range from free governmental agencies to consulting firms that specialize in finding high-level management personnel for a fee. If you choose one of the latter, be careful to check their record for integrity and success. The management search firm can often do a first-rate job of finding well-qualified, high-level managers. Employing a firm of this kind poses several problems for the new entrepreneur, not the least of which are cost

FIG. 17-1

Examples of effective recruiting ads.

and time. Good search firms charge high fees, perhaps several thousand dollars. And their searching period could run several weeks or months. You probably won't be able to absorb the cost of the management search firm when your company is new. But you may find this approach quite useful when your company grows to a size that can afford it.

Universities and technical schools. Universities and technical institutes have employment services for their graduates and alumni. You can often find qualified candidates among their young graduates or their mature and more experienced alumni.

Friends and relations. Discrete inquiry among your friends and relations may identify a candidate or two. This route can sometimes lead to difficulty. If you hire a person you've found through friends or relations and that person doesn't work out, you run the risk of losing a friendly relationship. You'd be well advised to reserve this approach for the last.

Personal file. It's good practice to keep a personal file of likely prospects for positions with your firm as you meet them in the course of business or at social affairs. Keep a notebook with you to jot down names, addresses, phone numbers of likely prospects whom you meet. Make notes about their background and your impressions of them. When you have to fill a position, you can occasionally locate a potential employee in your notebook.

Self-help clubs. Use organizations such as 40-Plus to find unemployed, mature executives who may fit nicely into your organization. More than one small company has recognized the worth of seasoned executives who've had wide experience in precisely the work of the position that's open. Many executives who've been displaced for one reason or another beyond their control are just reaching their prime after 40. They seek work eagerly and are often willing to accept positions at salaries considerably lower than they had when previously employed. You may find a powerful manager at a price your company can afford by checking with the self-help clubs in your community.

Assuming you've located two or three prospects who seem to fill your requirements for a position, your next step would be to select and hire the most promising.

THE INTERVIEWING PROCEDURE

When you tackle the interviewing job, be careful to avoid a pitfall common in most interviews. It's been found from careful study that most interviewers form an opinion about the candidate in the first 4 minutes. They then spend the rest of the interview hour seeking proof to justify that opinion. Avoid this common pitfall; when you tackle the interviewing job, try to be as objective as you can. Withhold judgment until the interview is over and you've had time to sift through what you've learned about the candidate. The people you interview will often be flustered at the start of the conversation. If you jump to a conclusion about them at that point, you can be seriously wrong. Wait and see; candidates will generally settle down after a few minutes and give you a much truer picture of themselves.

FIG. 17-2
Typical application form.

PERSONAL

Name: Social Security Number:

Address: Phone Number:

Date of Birth :
*The Employment Act of 1967 prohibits discrimination on the basis of age with respect to individuals who are at least 40 but less than 70 years of age. (Follow requirements of law that prevent discrimination on the bases of sex, race, and religion also.)

EDUCATIONAL

High School and Location: Dates: from _____ to _____

College or University: Degrees Obtained:

Other educational training, including trade, business, or military:

REFERENCES

Name three persons, preferably former supervisors or teachers familiar with your qualifications, whom we have your permission to contact:

Name   Address and Phone No.   Position

1.

2.

3.

PERSONAL COMMENTS

Use this space for comments about your special abilities, special work you have done, or special work you would like to do.

WORK EXPERIENCE

List all periods of employment since school; start with the most recent employment:

                                                    From: To:

Company:
Address:

Company:
Address:

Company:
Address:

(If more space is required for work experience, please attach additional sheet.)

I authorize _____ Company to obtain information about my employment and educational records from former employers, school officials, and persons named above as references, and I release all concerned from any liability in connection with the release of such information.

                                    _____
                                    Applicant's Signature   Date

A screening procedure that has proved itself in the practice of many companies goes through three steps. If you're the only manager in your company, you would do all three steps yourself. You might even decide to combine them into two or even one. If your company has a personnel manager, that person should handle the first interview, which serves as a preliminary screening. The second interview should be done by the supervisor for whom the candidate would work. You'd do the third step yourself to ensure that the candidate fits the guidelines you've established in your hiring policy. Whichever way is suitable for your business setup, you shouldn't omit any of the important points given in the three steps we recommend here:

1. *Preliminary screening.* This first step aims at gaining some background information about the candidate. A good way to start is to have the person fill out a simple application form listing many of the usual bits of data needed for the record. A typical form is given in Figure 17-2. The form can then be used as a guide in the interview.

    In the preliminary screening you'll seek the answers to some basic questions: What has the candidate's experience been? What has he or she done in previous jobs? What special skills have been acquired during this experience? What are the candidate's motives, drives, interests, and aspirations? From answers to questions such as these you can begin to form a judgment about the person's potential, both for doing the job you want to fill and for growth in the future.

2. *Second interview.* The purpose of the second screening is to check on the technical competence of the candidate. The aim here is to find out if the candidate brings to the job the necessary qualifications to perform well. Does the individual have the needed skills to manage a small office, design and machine a stamping die, work up a campaign for a sales promotion, or do whatever the specific job needs done?

    Your supervisor or you should try here to ensure that the person being considered has the experience and skill needed to fill the technical requirements of the job. By making a telephone call to the candidate's previous immediate boss you can verify the judgment made about the person's ability. People tend to talk more freely on the phone than they would in a letter. They'll say things that they might not want to put in writing. You'll be able to check what the candidate has told you in both interviews and can judge how truthful the candidate is likely to be. Figure 17-3 is a guide for the telephone interview.

3. *Third interview.* In the third interview you'll try to check the information you've gathered, and you'll solidify your impressions about the candidate. You'll reach answers to questions about the candidate's interpersonal competence: Would this individual fit my organization? Would he or she work well with others? Could I expect straight replies to tough questions? Does this person impress me as having potential for growth? With answers to these and similar questions that will occur to you, you'll make up your mind to reject or to hire. See Figure 17-4.

FIG. 17-3

Telephone reference.

TELEPHONE REFERENCE

(Applicant) _____ is being considered for a position as an _____ and has

given us permission to contact you (Ref., Title) _____ for a confidential reference.

We would appreciate your evaluation on the basis of the following questions:

What was his or her technical assignment? (Company, relationship, time supervised, etc.)

How was his or her performance?

Does he or she get along well with people?

Do you have any reservations about recommending him or her for hire in our proposed work
assignment?

Would you rehire him or her if the opportunity arose?

Additional Comments: (Potential, goals, interests, etc.)

_____   _____
Interviewer   Date

You understand, of course, that even though you've taken great care in putting
the candidate through a rigorous three-step screening procedure, you can't be certain
that the person *will* work out on the job. Your screening efforts will improve the
odds for success, but it's the actuality of performance on the job that will determine
whether the candidate should be kept on. You'd be well advised, therefore, to make
it clear that the new employee starts on a trial basis. If he or she doesn't work out
well in a given period, say 1 to 6 months, depending on the job, that person will be
terminated. A clean severance under those circumstances is the best answer for both
parties.

Don't overlook the point we've stressed before. With the first person you hire
you set a standard for your firm. The careful screening procedure we've outlined
here will help you develop the kind of organization you can count on for successful
and profitable growth. You fulfill this requirement by building a staff of technically
and interpersonally competent people.

Conducting the final hiring interview.

In the final hiring interview you face the fundamental question: "Is this applicant the kind of person who will fit my company—a person I can accept without reservation?" To put the candidate for the job at ease, you might start by saying, "As you've seen by now, we're a bit more cautious about hiring than many companies. We want to be sure you'll like the work and that we'll like you. We're both in this for the long haul; we don't want to hire just any warm body. We want you to have the best chance for your own future—and we'll want you to help build a future for the company. So you won't mind if I ask you a few questions that may seem a bit different. If there's anything I ask or say that bothers you, please feel free to tell me." When made in honesty, the openness of the statement tends to ease the relationship. Most candidates find such an opening acceptable.

Now you may start the interview proper by asking the following kinds of questions:

- Tell me about your schooling—and whatever you think important about your education, hobbies, jobs—and the reason you want to change jobs.

   Listen carefully to the response. Remember points that you'll want to check in more detail later. As the talk becomes more open, you can pinpoint some important data by asking more detailed questions:

- What would you describe as a project in your past work that you like to remember?

- How about some job you were asked to do that makes you unhappy to remember?

- What subject did you like best in college? Why did you like chemistry the best?

- Now, what subject did you like the least? What was there about English that you disliked?

- Finally, you might ask, "What kind of work would you like to do?"

Although it may seem late in the game to ask the candidate this question, it is very often productive of revealing information. The response may show that the candidate would prefer other work than that specified for the advertised job or would like to shift to another kind of work in the future. An interview carried out along these lines can help you answer the key question: "Is this person qualified to do the work required, with the potential for the growth I'm looking for, and the ability to fit in the organization?" When you screen the data, you'll gather impressions that will enable you to reach a decisive *yes* or *no* answer.

FEDERAL ANTIDISCRIMINATION LAWS

Federal antidiscrimination laws generally do not apply to small businesses with less than 15 employees, unless they work on government contracts or subcontracts. Regardless of size, however, employers must pay women equally to men for equal work. The various major federal laws prohibiting discrimination in employment are summarized in the following table. You should note that the individual states may have parallel or supplementary legislation. You must become familiar with them and follow them.

Name of Law	Employees Who Are Covered	What the Law Requires
Equal Pay Act of 1963	Nearly all employers with two or more employees	Equal pay for women
Title VII of the Civil Rights Act of 1964	Employers with 15 or more employees during 20 weeks of a calendar year	No discrimination in employment practices on basis of race, sex, color, religion, or national origin
Age Discrimination in Employment Act of 1967	Employers with 20 or more employees 20 or more weeks in a calendar year	No discrimination in hiring or firing on account of age for persons age 40 to 70
Executive Order 11246, as amended	Employers with federal contracts or subcontracts of $10,000 or more	No discrimination in employment practices on basis of race, sex, color, religion, or national origin

Appraising Performance

With the hiring of your first employee you've taken on the task of appraising the performance of those who work for you. This is, of course, the responsibility of the immediate manager. Therefore, as your organization grows you'll be appraising the performance of people at higher levels and increasing scope of responsibility. In this practice, as in many others, you'll set the pattern and the style for your firm. You should be aware of the pitfalls of the traditional performance appraisal so you can avoid them and so that you can take advantage of more modern thinking that has come from extensive research.

The old approach to performance appraisal has been to tell employees first what they've done well and then to tell them what they've done wrong. The idea was to take the sting out of the criticism by starting with a word of praise. The underlying concept seems to be that people can be changed by telling them to change. We've learned that this way of going about it is psychologically unsound. People don't learn much by being told.

We human beings learn better by involving ourselves in the task or process of what has to be done. We make our mistakes, and correct them—*particularly with adequate coaching*. In this way we gain skill.

Criticism, no matter how supposedly constructive, no matter how kindly intended, tends to make persons being criticized experience it as a frontal attack. They become defensive to protect their egos. When this happens, interviews with the boss miss their constructive intent.

We suggest then that as a manager your appraisal of performance should be carried on in a more modern way. Instead of being a critic, you should be a coach. This implies that you'll be working with those who report to you in an ongoing fashion. Your role will be one of coach and counselor rather than of judge and critic. You'll automatically appraise in working with your personnel, but you need not make a formal event of the process. You will want formal records of performance for purposes of promotion and, occasionally, for dismissing an employee for cause, as explained later.

Your appraisal should hinge on the question: Could this person do the work if his or her life depended on it? This is a *can-do* question. If the answer is yes but the person's performance is not up to snuff, you should look to yourself as not doing a satisfactory coaching job. So you should see that the individual gets the training or help needed to ensure improved performance, whether you do it yourself or hire someone qualified to do it. If your answer to the question is no, your problem is different. The employee should be moved to another kind of work that he or she can do. If this fails, you may have to discharge that person.

Training for Work Improvement

In a statement to the senior author of this book, Frances Torbert, formerly training director for R. H. Macy Co., said, "If there's one thing I've observed in my thirty-five years of operations as a manager and consultant to industry, it's the lack of understanding on the part of management for the desperate need of training before performance." As the entrepreneur-owner of your small business, if you take this statement to heart, you'll accept responsibility to see that your personnel get proper training in the work they must do. They must have the know-how before you can expect them to perform in superior fashion. You can become the catalyst for releasing the talents of your workforce.

Training before Performance

The enormous importance of training cannot be overemphasized. Training in skills leads immediately to better work and increased productivity. It also stimulates the desire for basic education in the area in which the skills are being used.

In backing training with basic education, the company develops a singular power for healthy growth, for it encourages an environment in which learning is valued. As people gain basic education and are trained in new skills, they improve their capacity to learn more while widening the scope of their skills. Knowledge and skill operate in this way as mutually reinforcing factors for growth. How these factors influence quality and performance may be seen in the experience of a small electro-mechanical manufacturing company of Torrance, California.

This company took on the development and production of a very small but extremely powerful electric actuator for aircraft service, on a tight schedule. The actuator consisted of a direct-current motor, guaranteed to deliver $\frac{1}{4}$ horsepower in intermittent service with an efficiency better than 65 percent. The motor was coupled to a precision gear train; both were contained within a tube 2 inches in diameter and less than 6 inches long.

The efficiency required was twice that of motors of this diameter manufactured by standard commercial practices. In any direct-current electric motor, critical factors in efficiency are the density and total quantity of magnetic flux that can be driven across the air gap between the stationary pole pieces and the rotating armature. To raise efficiency to the desired value, it was necessary to cram the limited volume with iron and copper windings, in both pole pieces and armature. The motor was therefore designed with four poles instead of the usual two. The armature was similarly designed to provide the maximum area of iron paths and volume of copper windings. These factors made the manufacturing job quite difficult, precluding the use of machine winding.

After the usual development difficulties had been overcome, 10 prototype units were built successfully in the experimental shop. The armature and field poles were wound by hand by an accomplished technician in an electric-motor specialty repair shop. The production problem of turning out 4000 actuators had now to be solved.

The production manager took the first step by hiring an experienced trainer who was himself a technician. The trainer spent sufficient time to learn how to wind the fields and armatures himself, under the tutelage of the repair-shop technician. He then worked out a step-by-step procedure for training. As an aid in training he developed, with the help of a company artist, a huge blow-apart drawing that showed each step in the sequence of assembly and winding.

The trainer then helped to hire a small group of women for the production job. Because of a tight labor market, none could be found who had had experience with this kind of exacting winding job. All, however, had had experience at delicate assembly or fabrication work of some kind.

The trainer then spent several weeks, full time, teaching and working with the women. Each motor was sent to engineering to test as it was finished. The first motors were found unacceptable, not meeting the efficiency requirement. Each was dissected after test, and the deficiency in wiring, which was the usual difficulty, was reported back to the trainer. He, in turn, worked over the problem and its solution with the woman who had done the wiring. Soon the performance of the motors began to improve. After about the eighth to tenth rejection for each woman, performance began to come up to standard.

However, the cost of the operation was excessive, as each armature and field assembly consumed approximately 4 labor hours. The trainer then held a meeting with the women and proposed that they study the winding operation step by step. Each woman was encouraged to make any suggestion that seemed to offer a possibility for speeding up the task. They were able in this way to work out improvements in technique by testing the suggestions in practice. As each woman learned the new techniques, improvement came steadily. When the first 600 units had been wired, the time had been cut to 1 hour per armature-pole assembly, an eminently acceptable figure.

It was then possible to move the total assembly job, including mechanical assembly, into this group. The first 100 completely assembled and tested actuators cost $350 apiece. At the six-hundredth actuator, the cost had flattened out at $40, a figure ensuring the profitability of the program.[1] The success of the program stemmed from the intensive training in improving skills and techniques. Without it there could have been no performance worthy of the name, in either meeting schedule or making money.

Management Succession

One area in which small business entrepreneurs often show incompetence is in training a management group and, specifically, a manager to replace themselves. The Peak Electronics case in Section VII presents a typical situation in which the boss tries to wear too many hats and finds it impossible to perform all the management tasks as his company grows.

As the top boss, you must adopt an objective point of view to observe signs of management trouble in your company:

Are you making all the basic decisions yourself? If this is so, your subordinate managers must be working at routine matters. They can't therefore get the practice required to develop key executive skills—and the skills they do have are being allowed to atrophy. A manager promoted from this background usually cannot cope with the responsibilities of the higher position.

Another sign of management trouble lies in a backlog of unsolved problems. When you prepare to step aside, or are forced to because of unexpected illness, you leave a mess of troubles for whoever must take over. These troubles may assume mountainous proportions and require heroic solutions, if indeed they can be resolved at all.

A final sign of trouble may rest in your unwillingness to call in or accept advice from qualified professional outsiders. Your reluctance to recognize the worth of objective counsel may signify trained incapacity—the shortsightedness that comes from being so wrapped up in detail that you can't see possibilities for improvement. If you are psychologically unable or unwilling to accept outside counsel, you may be jeopardizing the future of your company.[2]

Techniques for Developing Managers

You can use some specific techniques for developing managers in your small company. These include developing an heir apparent; bringing up an executive group; splitting off a separate operation, which a trainee-manager can run individually; and using day-by-day in-house training plus formal education.

The heir apparent technique requires the entrepreneur-owner to identify a younger person deemed qualified to be trained for the top position. This method permits

---

[1]Arthur H. Kuriloff, *Reality in Management,* McGraw-Hill, New York, 1966, pp. 40–41.
[2]Roland C. Christensen, *Management Succession in Small and Growing Enterprises,* Harvard Graduate School of Business Administration, Boston, 1953, p. 266.

sharp focus on the training effort, as every opportunity to learn about the company and its operations can be used to speed the growth of the individual.

It's no secret in the company that the young person is being groomed for the top executive spot. The heir, under the boss's sanction, rotates through the various management positions in the company, being given gradually increasing responsibility. Encouraged to participate in the discussions and decision making of company meetings, the young executive gains experience. The entrepreneur-owner coaches, trains, and shares experience on every possible occasion.

This technique can work well, particularly when there are no other persons in the company considered capable of being groomed for the top position. However, this technique can have its own peculiar problems.

If there exists a small group of older managers, the heir must gain their acceptance to get cooperation. The heir must show a high level of interpersonal competence to gain this acceptance. The boss may have selected the heir apparent as a kindred spirit—entrepreneurs both. The personality of the younger person may cause problems in working with the older persons. Confident, impatient with those less brash, used to winning, the young executive may fret with those who react to problems with less assuredness, may be insensitive to the needs and reactions of older persons. Unchastened in life's battles, the heir may alienate them by forthright actions and responses, destroying chances for collaboration. Behavior of this kind defeats the training and development process. Responding to insensitive treatment, the older group will very likely sabotage the heir's efforts. The young executive is sure to fail when blocked at every turn by managers who know the company's procedures so well as to be able to manipulate them carefully in a covert manner. Thus would the boss's development program be thwarted.[3]

On the other hand, should the older managers cooperate with the heir, they may themselves lose their ambition. They may view the accession of the heir apparent as a hurdle to their own desire for achieving higher status, quit trying to advance, and relax in their efforts.

The difficulties that may result from the heir apparent approach may be avoided by developing a small executive group. Here the top boss tries to train the whole management group together. The individual managers are clearly advised of the developmental character of this approach—that a top executive will be selected from the group and that each individual has a chance for selection. The boss lets the group in on company data, asks for their suggestions and recommendations, and works with them in seeking solutions to company problems. This process impels the managers in the training pool toward personal growth and, if handled properly, builds teamwork among them. They become active team members rather than passive observers of the rise of an heir apparent.

A third way of developing key executives has shown its effectiveness. That is by giving managers who show promise separate elements of the company to

---

[3]Saul W. Gellerman, *Motivation and Productivity,* American Management Association, New York, 1963, pp. 140–141.

manage as the opportunity arises. The element, perhaps a new department or section, should be self-contained so its performance can be measured. Managers of such units are forced to stand on their own feet. They should, of course, be counseled or given special help when faced with an unusually difficult situation. Here the boss should play a supportive coaching role. But the reality of running a complete operation and being accountable for its performance offers a powerful training experience. For the manager being trained it is a test by fire of managerial competence.

The behavior of the boss is the most important influence affecting management development. As Douglas McGregor put it:

When the boss gives an order, asks for a job to be done, reprimands, praises, conducts an appraisal interview, deals with a mistake, holds a staff meeting, works with his subordinates in solving a problem, gives a salary increase, discusses a possible promotion or takes any other action with subordinates, he is teaching them something. The attitudes, the habits, the expectations of the subordinate will be either reinforced or modified to some degree as a result of every encounter with the boss.[4]

Terminating Personnel[5]

Letting employees go is, at best, a distasteful procedure; it can be less so if you observe some important managerial considerations. Before you discharge someone, you should think about such things as proper timing, giving the unsatisfactory performer adequate warning, deciding on fair severance pay, and conducting the terminal interview. If these things have been given due and fair consideration, you will most probably be well within federal and state law and union contract.

Dealing with an employee's desire to quit your employ is another problem of termination that we will discuss later.

FIRING EMPLOYEES

Before you decide to let employees go because of performance deficiencies, it's only fair that they be told that their performance is not up to snuff. Then you should make the necessary training available so they have the chance to improve. Specify a date by which you expect them to reach the performance level the job requires.

You will, of course, document all the interviews concerning performance, with full knowledge of the employee and with acknowledgement implied by his or her signature on the personnel record. Documentation of this kind serves two purposes: It makes what otherwise might be considered an informal discussion into a serious procedure, not to be taken lightly. And it protects you and your company against unscrupulous or spurious legal action by the fired employee or his or her union.

---

[4]Douglas McGregor, *The Human Side of Enterprise,* McGraw-Hill, New York, 1960, p. 200.

[5]Appendix E, Hiring, Firing, and Disciplining Personnel, contains more detailed information on the legal implications of these aspects of managing personnel.

Occasions may arise where it becomes necessary to dismiss an employee for willful conduct or outright illegal acts. The following activities would be representative of unacceptable conduct, cause for dismissal:

- Refusal to carry out reasonable orders or directions—insubordination

- Unacceptable tardiness or absenteeism

- Being under the influence of drugs or alcohol on the job

- Abuse of customers

- Fighting or other disorderly conduct on the job

- Deliberate destruction of or stealing of company property

- Stealing from company personnel

- Sabotage of company processes or production

You'll use your best judgment to decide whether to discipline or to discharge. In any event, discipline or discharge should immediately follow the offensive act.

Experience of many businesspersons who've had to fire personnel for cause suggests that the following precautions be observed:

- The discharge action should be taken at the end of the workday, after the rest of the workforce has left (unless the situation is so drastic that action needs to be immediate).

- Give the employee the final paycheck at the moment of discharge; include if necessary the customary severance pay.

- Discharge the employee in the presence of a witness, preferably the person's immediate superior.

- Collect all company property in the employee's possession: keys, manuals, tools, and whatever else should be recovered.

We have become a litigious society in recent years. Some employees seem to sue for unlikely reasons. The foregoing suggestions should help you defend your action if the employee claims to be the victim of unfair labor practice and brings suit against you or your company.

EMPLOYEES FIRING YOU

If a person wants to leave your employ, on the other hand, it's good practice to arrange for an immediate severance. A statement of intent to quit shows that the employee's heart is no longer in the work. The sooner that person is gone, the less chance for disaffection and rumor to be spread among others in the organization. Your best course is to give reasonable severance pay and send the individual packing.

FIRING KEY EMPLOYEES

You may occasionally run into a situation that demands some careful thinking before you decide to fire a key employee. Your decision may require answers to questions like these: Does this employee have special knowledge that should be transferred to someone else before being severed from the company? Is there an important negotiation with a customer going on that takes a special input from this employee? Is there someone else who could take over after this person leaves? What would it cost your company to have this employee leave right now as against putting an untrained individual in the spot? Should you try to keep this person because despite some negative factors it seems clearly to the benefit of the company? These are the kinds of questions you should ask and answer when deciding whether or not to fire a key employee. If you finally decide to let the person go, you can gain much valuable information by conducting a terminal interview with the employee.

Set aside a private place and an hour or so of uninterrupted time to carry out this interview. By careful probing you can get some important and useful feedback on how employees see your ways of managing your company. As a result, you may be able to correct deficiencies that will help to improve productivity and morale in your operations. These improvements, in turn, will enable you to develop a stable and effective workforce.

During the terminal interview, the employee is likely to want to know the reasons for the severance procedure. If you've been through the warning, documentation, and trial period we've discussed, there will be little need for elaborate explanations. Speak openly and straightforwardly about the reasons for the termination. Don't permit the meeting to degenerate into a debate. If you have taken the time and trouble to tell the individual about performance deficiencies in previous meetings, there should be no need for debate. Be decisive. A clean severance is the healthiest way both for the individual and for your company.

FIRING LONG-TERM EMPLOYEES

After your company has been in business for a few years, you may have to face a somewhat different problem of termination; you may have to deal with discharging a long-term employee who has been unable to work because of a prolonged illness. You will have to face issues of conscience and equity. You may wish to treat the employee generously, but your company, like many small companies, may not have the financial resources to enable you to be as generous as you'd like. You'll have to decide how far you can go. You can guide your decision by answering these questions: How long has the employee been with the company? How long is the illness likely to keep the employee away from work? How adequate is our medical insurance coverage? Does it provide funds for convalescent care, for maintenance of family as well as for medical bills? Can the company afford to make up the difference between what the insurance pays and what is needed to sustain the family? Would a loan be a feasible solution for the employee's financial problems? What's a reasonable length of time for the company to help?

You may decide that the company can afford to help for several months. But you're more likely to be forced to compromise between doing what your moral judgment suggests and what your best business judgment indicates. If you make your decision conscientiously with the help of the foregoing guidelines, at least you'll do the best thing possible under the circumstances.

To Unionize or Not to Unionize: That Is the Question!

Most entrepreneurs believe that through hard work, carefully calculated risk taking, good management, and fair play toward their employees they can run their small company without benefit of or interference from a union. The very thought of a union operating within your company may be unsettling to you.

When your company has achieved a modest level of success, when it employs between 20 and 200 people, it may be open to unionization. And federal law says that you'll have to sit down with a union representative and bargain in good faith.

When you reach this point in the growth of your company, you should put aside any preconceived notions you may have about unionization; you should instead devote your energies to managing the negotiations in a proactive fashion—for the best interests of your company.

AVOIDING UNIONIZATION

If you wish to avoid unionization, you must understand the forces that drive employees to seek a union and through proper management prevent these forces from developing. Employees usually want unions for some quite clear reasons: to get better pay, to overcome inability to correct treatment seen as unjust, to ensure job security, to gain means for recognition, or to be protected from unpredictable behavior of the boss. If you look at these major forces for unionization, you can see what you, as a small business owner, can do to minimize their impact.

To overcome adverse effects resulting from low pay, make sure you know what the prevailing wage rates are in your community for the kinds of work done by your workforce. Check with your chamber of commerce for sources of this information. Local personnel managers associations usually gather and publish up-to-date wage rates for different kinds of labor in your area. Your state or city may have a department that does the same. With information from these sources, you can adjust your pay rates from time to time to keep them current or slightly above average. This action would remove pay as a reason for unionization.

The problem of job security is a delicate one. You must treat it carefully, with special consideration for the feelings of your personnel. Reduction in your workforce should be done on the basis of a carefully thought out policy that is made clear to your employees. Should you observe priority in letting people go—last in, first out? Should you minimize the effect on your operations by letting go first those whose skills are least important to your operations? Whichever course you choose, you should make it clear to your employees before you let anyone go. And you should use a systematic approach in reducing your workforce when it becomes necessary. You may want to review the section in Chapter 9 that treats the different ways to handle widely varying work loads to keep a stable workforce. Sound managerial practice that affords reasonable job security for your workforce will do much to allay efforts to unionize in the attempt to overcome perceptions of insecurity.

In the other matters of treating employees justly, giving recognition, and behaving in a consistent manner, you must look at your own behavior as a boss. Most entrepreneurs tend to be rugged individuals, sure of themselves and straightforward in their dealings. They are often critical of the shortcomings of others and quite directive or even abrasive in their dealings with people who work for them. Their perceptions of how things are being done may not be anywhere like those of their personnel of whom they're critical. Employees called down in a forthright manner are more than likely to resent the criticism, even though it may be warranted. They may see their safety in the job threatened by, to them, the boss's uncalled-for and often unexpected behavior. Their response may be to look toward a union as a shield against a threatening management. They believe the union will force more dignified, courteous treatment and give them a way to redress what they see as a wrong.

Patterns of behavior that might cause your employees to seek unionization can be corrected. To do this, you must be alert to your relationships with people. Building good interpersonal relationships starts with the boss. You're the one who sets the standards of behavior in your firm—the model whom your people respond to and imitate. Practice firmness coupled with respect and kindness. People respect honesty, and they also respect the boss who treats them with dignity, as responsible human beings.

If, despite your best efforts to avoid unionization, your firm should face an organizing effort, proactive management will be of inestimable value in dealing with it.

Your immediate task should be to seek competent help. This means hiring a labor lawyer to help you plan to meet the union challenge. The lawyer will also represent the interests of your company in negotiating with the union. Don't stint on fees for such counsel. The expenses for capable professional help will prove to be but a tiny part of the savings such help can secure for your company. Together with your counsel you should answer questions such as these:

- Are the wages I pay competitive in the community? What wages can I afford?

- What are the benefits my company pays? What are the maximum benefits my company can afford to pay?

- What is the best estimate of how much my company will have to concede in wages plus benefits as compared with what my competitors are paying?

- What managerial powers must I and my executive group retain at any cost? These include hiring and firing policies, overtime scheduling, administration of benefits, and similar matters.

- What are the terms of my competitors' union contracts?

If you plan proactively with counsel on the basis of the answers to these and similar questions that will suggest themselves during your deliberations, you'll be prepared to come out of negotiation with a contract that your company can live with, that costs the least, and that preserves your management rights.

The contract resulting from the negotiation should be seen as fair by the union, by your workforce, and by you; it should spell out a win-win solution for all.

Summary

When you hire your first person in your new business, you automatically set the style for the future. Before hiring that first employee, you should work out a sound policy for handling personnel matters. You'll recall that policies are guides to action. With carefully thought out guides, you'll prepare yourself to take on people who can do the work that needs doing now and have the capability of growing, of meeting more demanding tasks as your firm grows. You'll be aware of the desirability of choosing those who not only can do the work but also appear able to work well with others. You should feel comfortable with your new employees.

We've suggested sources for finding qualified personnel. By referring to these sources, you'll expand your field of choice. You should then be able to identify more than one candidate for an open position. And by following the three-step interviewing procedure we've outlined, you can improve your chances for hiring well-qualified people for your company.

We've also pointed out the negative effect of the old-fashioned way of appraising the performance of those who work for you. Criticism, no matter how well intended, usually doesn't produce the results you may intend. It's difficult to change people by telling them to change. A much better approach requires that you act as a coach. By working with your people, by showing them what and how you want things done, and by guiding their actions in the process, you can help them improve their competence. You can also judge their performance without going through a formal appraisal procedure that's more likely than not to become abrasive, to develop self-defensiveness on their part. If you find that the person can't do the job, you may want to move that individual to another kind of work. Should that prove unsatisfactory, you may find it necessary to terminate that employee.

Follow the recommendations we've made for documenting performance of your personnel. If you have to fire an employee for cause, your notations on that person's personnel record—insubordination, inferior performance, warnings given for need for improvement, counseling—will show that your action was taken in good faith. Using the steps we've suggested in firing an employee for misconduct will protect you and your company against legal suit for alleged violation of fair employment practices.

You can often learn some important things about how the employees perceive your style of management by conducting terminal interviews with personnel leaving the company. You can use the feedback from such interviews to adjust your management practices to improve the climate in your organization.

After your company is well established, you may run into the problem of what to do for a long-term faithful employee who has served the company well but who is suffering a long, disabling illness. You'll have to decide how generous you can afford to be in proffering financial support to that employee. You'll try to do what's reasonable, deciding between what your conscience says and the financial implications of your decision for your company.

You may someday face the problem of unionization. This may happen after you've achieved recognizable success— perhaps when your company has reached an employment level of 100 or so. You may not like the idea that your people want a union. But federal law says you must bargain in good faith with the union.

Employees seek unionization for well-known reasons: to increase their wages, to gain protection from what they perceive as unjust treatment, to improve their job security, to achieve ways for being recognized, or to be protected from unpredictable management behavior.

In this chapter we've given some suggestions for avoiding unionization by practicing proactive management in dealing with each of these issues. If, despite your best efforts, you must meet the challenge of unionization, be sure to hire expert counsel to head your negotiation. Find an experienced labor lawyer to work with you in planning your approach to the negotiation. Prepare to deal with the issues of pay, benefits, and management prerogatives you must retain under any circumstances. In this way you can achieve an agreement that your company can live with, that costs your company the least, and that preserves your management rights. The labor contract that results from negotiations should be seen as fair by your workforce, the union, and you—a win-win solution that will ensure a healthy relationship among all parties.

WORKSHEET 17

Managing Your Personnel Function

This worksheet is designed as a checklist to help you work out policies for managing your personnel function. Because policies afford guides to action, you will prepare yourself to handle personnel issues effectively without the difficulty of having to decide what to do on the spur of the moment. Preparation in personnel management is as important as in financial planning, marketing, or any other phase of proactive management.

1. I understand the importance of hiring people who are both technically competent and show evidence of interpersonal competence. I'll observe the following guidelines:

   a. I will make sure that those I hire can do the work that is required in the position. To support my effort to hire a technically qualified person for a position, I will write out the duties of the position, its responsibilities, and the experience needed to do the work well. This will prepare me to interview candidates competently in the first screening interview.

   b. I'll refrain from forming a too-early judgment about the candidate. I'll use an employment form to guide my preliminary screening interview, being sure that it conforms with legal requirements in not probing into prohibited personal areas.

   c. In addition to finding out about previous experience and special skills, I will try to gauge the applicant's motives, drives, interests, and aspirations. Answers to these kinds of questions will give me some insight into the likelihood of candidates performing the tasks required, their technical ability, and potential growth.

   d. In the next step I'll phone the candidate's immediate superior in the previous job to check on his or her experience. This will give me some feeling for the applicant's capability and will allow me to check on the truthfulness of what I've been told.

   e. I'll use the third step to come to a final assessment of the applicant's interpersonal competence. I want to be as sure as I can that the individual will fit well in my company, work well as a team member, and be able to grow with my company.

   f. I recognize that even the most careful screening may not guarantee that the person will work out on the job. I will therefore make sure that a new employee understands that the first period of employment is a trial period. This period shall be stated, one, two, or six months, whatever is appropriate for the kind of work to be done. If the employee doesn't work out, we will part friends.

2. I will try to avoid an authoritarian approach in appraising performance of those who work for me. My attitude will be that of coach rather than critic. By working as closely as I can with my employees I'll gain knowledge of their strengths and weaknesses. This will allow me to help them build on their strengths; I will see ways to help them overcome weaknesses.

Following this managerial style will support my efforts to build a permanent, effective organization.

3. My practice in terminating unsatisfactory performers will be to warn them about their inadequacy. I will set a time for and specify the improvement I want. I will also make training available to them so that they can overcome their deficiency. If that doesn't work, I'll move them to another job that I think they can do. If that effort fails I will let them go.

4. If employees state that they want to quit, I'll arrange for immediate severance. There's no use keeping on people who have lost their desire to stay with the company.

5. If it becomes necessary for me to discharge key people, I'll make sure that the company is not hurt for special reasons: expert knowledge that should be transferred to others who'll remain on the job, close relationship with important customers that others should take over, or other important considerations that I'll examine before I authorize severance.

6. I'll have a terminal interview with anyone who leaves the company. This will give me feedback that may help me see and correct problems in the way my company is managed.

7. If it becomes necessary to discharge a long-term faithful employee because of prolonged illness, I'll be as generous as company finances will allow me to be in granting aid to that person and family.

8. I would certainly prefer not to have a union in my company. I understand the reasons people want a union. These are to get better pay, to overcome their inability to correct treatment they see as unjust, to achieve job security, to have a way of being recognized, and to be protected from management they see as behaving unpredictably. I'll take the following steps to avoid unionization:
   a. I'll make sure that our pay rates are equal to or slightly above those prevailing in similar jobs in the community.
   b. To improve feelings of job security, I will work out policies and procedures for dealing with reduction in workforce if it becomes necessary. I will let my employees know the policies and the procedures as a matter of routine practice.
   c. I understand that my behavior must be consistent; as the boss I must respond in the same way under the same circumstances, so my people won't be confused and worry about what's likely to happen when they encounter me on the job. I will work conscientiously to establish trust with my people, because I know that good interpersonal relations make for good teamwork and company effectiveness.

9. If I cannot avoid the effort to unionize my firm, I'll hire the most competent labor lawyer I can find to help me meet the challenge. My objectives in the negotiation will be to reach a contract that my company can live with, at the least cost, and without losing any of our management rights. I accept the idea that the practice of proactive management requires the union contract to be fair to all parties—to the company, to the union, and to my workforce.

KEY TERMS

policies 488   documentation 503
candidate 491   equity 505
appraisal 498

STUDY ASSIGNMENTS FOR REVIEW AND DISCUSSION

1. Explain the importance of developing sound policy for managing personnel matters.

2. What resources are available to you in finding qualified people to hire?

3. Describe the three-step method of interviewing in hiring people.

4. What precautions should you observe in firing employees? When employees want to quit? When you think it necessary to discharge a key employee?

5. What kinds of questions should you ask and answer when you face the problem of discharging a long-term valued employee who cannot continue to work because of prolonged illness?

6. Why should the boss take responsibility for training personnel?

7. Describe three indicators of lack of adequate management in the small growing company.

8. Identify four techniques for ensuring management succession in the small growing company.

9. Why do employees sometimes seek a union? Name at least four reasons.

10. As the boss, what management measures would you take to lessen the chance for a unionization effort to develop?

11. As the boss, if you were faced with a unionization drive, what would you do to try to reach a fair agreement for both sides?

PROJECTS FOR STUDENTS

These assignments are designed to be done by students working in teams of three to five. Teams should report their results to the class. Open discussion in class should be encouraged.

1. Imagine you are preparing to go into the retail business, perhaps to sell hardware or luggage. As the owner, you are the general manager. You'll have six clerks and a secretary-bookkeeper working for you. Your assignment: Prepare a set of policies for hiring and firing personnel.

2. Collect six performance-appraisal forms from different organizations. Study them. Identify specific items that you like and that you don't like in these forms.

State your reasons. After you've done this, develop a form that you would use if you were the manager responsible for performance appraisal in your company.

3. Interview a management trainer in an organization in your area. Find out how training is done in that organization. Do they supplement training with formal education? Report your findings to the class.

4. Interview three managers in any size companies who are responsible for labor relations. Find out how they prepare to meet attempts to unionize or to deal with union negotiations if they are unionized. Report your findings to the class.

5. Check the federal antidiscrimination laws and report your findings to the class. Be sure to include at least the following: Title VII of the Civil Rights Act of 1964; Equal Pay Act of 1963; Age Discrimination in Employment Act of 1967; Executive Order 11264, as amended; Rehabilitation Act of 1973. Also check to see if your state has additional legislation in these areas. If so, report on it to the class.

6. Turn to the vignette about the Leo N. Harding Company at the front of this chapter. Read it carefully. Then answer these questions:

   How would you describe Harding?

   How would you feel in response to Harding's order if you were Ralph Morrison?

   Would you find yourself in an ethical dilemma if you were in Morrison's position? Describe it.

   What would you do to resolve the problem of releasing engineers that Harding's order has forced upon you?

IF YOU WANT TO READ MORE

We have selected the following publications as sources that you can probe as deeply as you feel the need in the several subjects covered in this chapter. You will find additional references in each of these books.

BATY, Gordon B: *Entrepreneurship: Playing to Win,* Reston Publishing, Reston, VA, 1974. In Chapter 17 the author outlines key points in acquiring and divesting people. Points covered include compensation packages, recruiting, interviewing, and reducing the workforce. The chapter gives a brief summary of various aspects of personnel administration; you'll find it a handy reference.

FEAR, Richard A.: *The Evaluation Interview,* 2d ed., McGraw-Hill Book Company, New York, 1978. This is a highly regarded how-to-do-it book that tells in step-by-step fashion how to become a good interviewer and how to interpret the facts gathered in the interview. You'll find the procedures given very much on target in helping you gain skill in the interviewing and selection process.

JONES, Seymour: *The Emerging Business,* John Wiley & Sons, New York, 1983. Chapter 10 of this book concentrates on the importance of fringe benefits to the security of the owner-manager and employees. The author describes several fringe benefit plans in detail.

McGREGOR, Douglas: *The Human Side of Enterprise,* McGraw-Hill Book Company, 1960. This is a great classic that has influenced the practice of management toward more human treatment of personnel. Chapters 6 and 7 discuss the problems of the old-fashioned or traditional performance appraisal and give suggestions of how to conduct performance appraisals and administer salaries and promotions in a psychologically sound manner. The whole book is well worth reading. It will give you insight into the modern way of viewing the people who work for you, and it will help you build a business philosophy well suited to the practice of proactive management.

RICE, Craig S.: *Your Team of Tigers: Getting Good People and Keeping Them,* AMACOM, New York, 1982. Although this book is not specifically geared to the small business, its basic premises can be readily applied to the smaller firm. The first portion of the text includes tools and techniques you can use to recruit, select, train, motivate, and supervise above average employees.

RIMLER, George W., and Neil J. HUMPHREYS: *Small Business: Developing the Winning Management Team,* AMACOM, New York, 1980. This book aims to improve the small business manager's ability to develop the human assets within the enterprise. The book focuses on human behavior and gives a motivational approach to the personnel function.

ROXE, Linda A.: *Personnel Management for the Smaller Company,* AMACOM, New York, 1979. This book affords a "hands-on" guide to establishing sound personnel practices. Among the topics discussed are hiring, paying wages, developing benefit programs, training, employee behavior and discipline, record keeping, and timekeeping. The author approaches the subject in a nontechnical, pragmatic manner to help managers use human resources effectively, while maintaining a good employer-employee relationship.

SCOTT, William H.: *How to Earn More Profits through the People Who Work for You,* Prentice-Hall, Inc., Englewood Cliffs, NJ, 1982. The text states that people must be able to satisfy a number of human needs through their jobs to perform enthusiastically. Also presented are step-by-step instructions on how to recruit and select personnel who are inclined to work hard—and how to motivate them toward high productivity.

SIEGEL, William L.: *People Management for Small Business,* John Wiley & Sons, New York, 1978. This book is a practical guide to finding the best employees. It is divided into three main parts: hiring, orientation and training, and people management.

SLIMMON, Robert J.: *Successful Pension Design for the Small to Medium Size Business,* Institute for Business Planning, Englewood Cliffs, NJ, 1984. This book unlocks the mysteries of pension design for the small business. Owners will also gain in-depth knowledge of the jargon and special rules that have previously made pension plans an excessively complicated subject.

STEINER, George A., and John B. MINER: *Management Policy and Strategy,* Macmillan, New York, 1982. In Chapters 2 and 3, the authors treat the development of business strategy and policy from the point of view of the chief executive officer. You can gain from this text an important set of ideas that will help you develop your policies for managing personnel *and* for managing the other functions of your business.

Surviving: Managing for Productivity and Growth

TOPICS IN THIS CHAPTER

Objectives of This Chapter
What Is Expected of a Good Manager?
Improving Productivity through Teamwork
Need to Change Your Entrepreneurial Qualities?
The Many Hats a Manager Must Wear
Your Basic Concern as a Manager: Productivity
A Management System for Improving Productivity
Assessing Your Productivity Performance
Surviving the Critical First Years—Summary
Worksheet 18: Managing for Survival and Growth
Key Terms
Study Assignments for Review and Discussion
Projects for Students
If You Want to Read More

CHAPTER 18

517

Surviving:
Managing
for Productivity
and Growth

If you've stayed with us this far, you've completed the worksheet assignments. You've drafted the basic plan for your business. This chapter deals with the problems, pitfalls, challenges, and opportunities that will face you almost immediately after you've opened your doors.

At no point in this book have we suggested that staying in your business will be easy once you've started it. We've tried conscientiously not to give you a pep talk on the glories of entrepreneurship. We've spelled out principles and techniques for improving your odds for survival in your small business. We now turn your attention toward solving particular problems of survival and growth of your firm.

Information in this chapter will be found pertinent to these items in the Business Plan:

2.A. Statement of the desirability of your product or service

6.A. An outline of the activities to be used in selling the product or service

7.A. Description of the proposed organization

8.A. Information required to support the major points in the business plan

YOU + IDEA + { MONEY / CREDIT } + { FACILITIES / PEOPLE } → PRODUCT OR SERVICE + MARKETING { MONEY / CREDIT } → PROFIT

You'll face predictable, and unavoidable, stages of development after you begin your business operations. Each of these stages will present a crisis of one kind or another unless you anticipate and plan for them during the first year or two. It will be necessary for you to put aside some of your entrepreneurial qualities to perform successfully as a manager of a going business. This will require a good deal of study and hard work.

We'll point out some of the common pitfalls to avoid during the growth stages of your business. We'll suggest ways to identify the strengths and to detect the weaknesses in your business. You'll then be able to build on the strengths and overcome the weaknesses. And we'll discuss ways for you to gain the special management skills you'll need to carry out your business plans during the first years you're in business. As you acquire these skills, you'll be taking steps toward becoming a professional manager.

Objectives of This Chapter

This chapter assumes that you've got your business well started. You now must face the problems of survival and growth. You'll have to deal not only with increasing the technical competence of your workforce but also with improving the interpersonal competence among your people. Improving both technical know-how and teamwork will give you the basis for a healthy, growing business.

By studying this chapter you can:

Compare your patterns of behavior as a boss against those desired by most employees—and work to improve where you'd like to change

Check to see if you should reject some bits of entrepreneurial behavior that may be blocking your effectiveness as a manager

Stimulate yourself to acquire knowledge and skill in any of the 10 basic roles of management in which you find yourself lacking

Gain background and understanding in management by objectives and learn how to introduce it in your organization

Understand the difference between efficiency and effectiveness—and the need to manage for gaining a balance between them

Use the checklists given in this chapter to judge how well you're improving in those factors that ensure increased productivity: personal growth, in relations with employees, and in relations with your suppliers, creditors, community, and government

What Is Expected of a Good Manager?

When we teach venture initiation to potential entrepreneurs, we use the following exercise to illustrate the importance of knowing and living up to the behavior people expect of a good manager. We ask participants in our classes and seminars to think about the best managers they've ever worked for and to develop a list of 10 specific attributes or characteristics the ideal manager demonstrates. (Put this book aside for a moment and do this yourself before reading further. *Note:* the term *good leader* is too general.) A composite of such lists follows:

CHAPTER 18

519

Surviving:
Managing
for Productivity
and Growth

PROFILE OF THE IDEAL MANAGER

Attributes Expected (Most Frequently Mentioned)	Typical Participant Comments
Empathetic	"Sensitive to needs of others"
Trusting, fair, honest	"Open and honest in dealing with others"
Encourages innovation	"Wants people to come forward with their ideas"
Good listener	"Reacts to what I say; listens to me actively and sincerely"
Delegates authority	"Lets others have control and freedom over some things"
Self-confident	"Acts positively and decisively with the available facts"
Loyal and supportive	"Backs up employees on controversial things"
Creative and technically competent	"Knows the business inside and out and has good ideas"
Good planner and organizer	"Looks ahead and can pull together what's needed to get there"
Gives feedback on performance	"Tells people how they're doing and is a good teacher"

In examining the foregoing list closely, you'll find there are three categories of expectations mentioned by potential entrepreneurs. First, they expect *technical competence* in the ideal manager. This needs no further elaboration, since we've stressed it throughout the book.

Second, attributes such as "good planner and organizer" can be interpreted as meaning they expect *system competence*—skills in fitting all the pieces of the business together, with the planning and organizing ability to direct them toward a desired future. Although technical competence deals with intimate knowledge of physical products, job skills, manufacturing processes, and the like, system competence has to do with ideas and concepts. The business plan you'll develop is the hard evidence of your system competence.

Third, *interpersonal competence* is a category that includes most of the role traits desired by our respondents. Being empathic, trusting, loyal and supportive, and the rest, have to do with people; these are the attributes that usually head the lists. The results of this exercise are consistent, although the terms and descriptions used vary somewhat from group to group. There is no reason to believe the results would be substantially different if the list makers were your employees. Individuals you'll employ will expect you to have and to show these same managerial qualities. They'll value above all your competence in dealing with people. As the manager-leader, the degree to which you show such competence will greatly affect the amount and quality of "followership" you achieve with them.

Your business will require the collaborative effort of individuals with different backgrounds. Cooperative effort will become ever more essential as your business expands. Your behavior should induce an environment of openness and trust. You won't needle, demean, or block others. Instead you'll encourage your people to deal forthrightly with their ideas and feelings in their relationships with you. The employee group is likely to respond in kind, reflecting your style. You show high interpersonal competence when you interact with people openly and fairly.

If you have this kind of interpersonal competence, it will also be seen in the way you isolate the important problems facing your organization. It will be seen in the supportive way you deal with employees in solving these problems, and in the universal acceptance of solutions by the group once individual differences have been resolved. Demonstrated interpersonal competence will be a major factor in facilitating the growth of your business, for it welds human resources in building a successful business venture.

Improving Productivity through Teamwork

Business
Plan
Outline
2.A, 7.A

When understanding of the importance of detailed improvement begins to filter through the organization, the manager is ready to employ value analysis. Value analysis has two important objectives: to reduce the cost of the product and, simultaneously, to improve its quality. Design, material, and methods are minutely scrutinized. Any member of the company who has anything to do with the product invariably can contribute to the program. Engineers, designers, production workers, assemblers, shipping clerks—all are involved in the operation. The background and history of a specific case illustrate the financial gains that may be accomplished by the teamwork required in value analysis.

DELTA DESIGN, INC.[1]

At one point in the history of a company in our experience, Delta Design, Inc., its catalog carried 260 separate items, presumably all standard environmental test chambers. The general manager decided on a careful value analysis of product line and product. He asked for a statement showing the revenue produced by the individual products sold during the previous year. Analysis of the statement showed that 21 of the 260 products accounted for 91 percent of the total revenue. The first step in the value analysis program was obvious—elimination of the "dogs" in the line.

At a meeting among key engineering, production, and marketing people, it was decided to concentrate on a product core of three basic designs. Each of these would be the nucleus for a small group of models incorporating a variety of features. The variety thus obtained would permit the customer wide choice, even more than in the old group of 21 best sellers. Yet limiting the basic designs to three units opened the way for use of expensive permanent production tooling. Labor costs would be reduced substantially in this way.

[1]Arthur H. Kuriloff, *Reality in Management,* McGraw-Hill, New York, 1966, pp. 63–64, reproduced by permission.

CHAPTER 18

521

Surviving:
Managing
for Productivity
and Growth

One of the three new basic designs was selected as a pilot project. The engineers were instructed to incorporate in the new chamber the improvements that they would like to see in the standard product, but only after consultation with key marketing people. They were not to proceed with the design until they and the marketing people, the production manager, the production staff, and the general manager agreed on the specifications and general concept. The engineers and the production manager agreed to work together from the moment the first lines were laid on paper. The airflow patterns, critical in performance of an environmental chamber, were to be experimentally verified in a mock-up of the chamber before any design was frozen. At each step of the development procedure, those people who could contribute from their experience were to be involved in the program.

The program was preeminently successful. Performance of the chamber exceeded that of any previously built in the company, indeed, in the industry. Better and less expensive materials were found and incorporated. Less expensive electronic components of equivalent performance were substituted in the temperature controller. Tough, durable enamel, easy to apply, displaced an expensive finish difficult to apply. Hard tooling reduced labor costs, as did improved electronic assembly techniques developed in the shop. A new method of crating cut the cost of shipping and gave better protection to the chamber.

The result of this program was salutary: The company was able to reduce the selling price from $1065 for the equivalent old model to $795 for the new, while making more profit on the new. The lower price stimulated sales, broadening the market in this class of product.

The experience proved of great value to the company in other ways. Members of the company observed the value of cooperative effort. They enjoyed contributing their bit to the program. They committed their energies and ingenuity to its successful accomplishment. In the whole program the pattern of learning and achieving set the style for future company operations.

From this example, what results could be expected from an effective value analysis on: A product? A service? Profit? Teamwork in a business organization?

Much of the discussion that follows relates both to personnel management in a broad sense and to the varied management skills so crucial to surviving the first year or two of operation.

Need to Change Your Entrepreneurial Qualities?

As we stated early in this book, some of the very qualities that impel entrepreneurs to start a business can cause problems once it's under way. Descriptions of the entrepreneurial personality in the literature of management use words like promoter, operator, developer, doer, independent, and shrewd. These may be considered to describe positive attributes that support achieving behavior in entrepreneurial activity. However, along with these another kind of terms occur: self-centered, smug, arrogant, biased toward expediency, stubborn, bull-headed, anxious, impatient, and argumentative. These terms describe less desirable modes of behavior that work against the attainment of professional management—that kind of management needed to support the growth of the firm. Entrepreneurs who want to build a substantial business must therefore rid themselves of less desirable behaviors, which means changing some values and some personality characteristics. In short, if you are an entrepreneur who suffers from some of the less desirable modes of behavior you will find it necessary to change to become a professional manager.

TOWARD BENEFICIAL CHANGE

Truly professional managers command the respect of their people. They exhibit leadership that induces commitment to the task and followership from those who work for them. Perhaps in assessing the quality of your leadership you may decide some personal change would be beneficial.

Change, when it occurs at all, usually follows long and arduous trying. We human beings are subject to human frailty. When we work at changing we tend to move two steps forward, then slide one step back. But if we persist, we can change, although the process may be long and hard. Entrepreneurs who seize the opportunity to change engage in a truly entrepreneurial act. They can apply their entrepreneurial drive for achievement in the campaign for professional management competence. So, as the chief executive of your growing company, if you really wish for this kind of achievement, you can do it.

NEED FOR CHANGED VALUES

As the boss who wants to move toward professionalism in managing your growing firm, you should look inside yourself to understand the values upon which your past behaviors have been based. The insights you gain will undoubtedly prove painful; yet they are fundamental, for behavior rests on values—what you consider important. And the values of prime importance in the search for excellence in management stem in large part from the entrepreneur's perceptions of people in the workforce.

Have you considered your personnel as objects, or tools, for the performance of specific tasks? Have you seen them as somewhat lazy, incapable of thinking for themselves—as having to be coerced to get the job done? This kind of managerial behavior flows from traditional concepts about people who work, concepts that Douglas McGregor called Theory X.[2]

Although the professional manager automatically has one method of influencing employees through the *authority of position,* other methods are far more potent psychologically—and much more acceptable in today's democratic society. These are the *authority of knowledge* and the *authority of charisma.* The authority of knowledge means simply that the chief knows the business thoroughly and demonstrates technical competence, not only in product or service, but also in managing the business.

The boss who is blessed with charisma, personal magnetism, charms people into doing what is appropriate for the business. Not many bosses are favored in this way; yet it is possible for those who will to approximate this characteristic through consultation and discussion.[3] Through demonstration of knowledge and the special

---

[2]Douglas McGregor, *The Human Side of Enterprise,* McGraw-Hill, New York, 1960, chap. 5.
[3]McGregor, op.cit., pp. 18–19.

form of salesmanship by consultation and discussion, the professional manager builds respect and healthy followership from employees. What steps can the entrepreneur take to change existing behaviors from the old-fashioned authoritarian to the newer humanitarian kind? A respected psychiatrist, Allen Wheelis, suggests techniques that entrepreneurs can use to make the necessary behavior changes.

CHAPTER 18

523

Surviving:
Managing
for Productivity
and Growth

HOW PEOPLE CHANGE

Wheelis states a basic concept for achieving change in behavior: "We are what we do . . . and may do what we choose. What we do, our actions, describes our characters and the kinds of persons we are."[4] As the old adage has it: What you *do* speaks so loud I cannot hear what you say.

So long as we live change is possible. We are free to choose new ways of behaving in emerging situations, ways that are more effective than those to which we were accustomed in the past. Freedom implies awareness of alternatives—and the ability to choose. Entrepreneurs striving for professionalism in management of their growing firms, conscious of the need to improve their behavior, have great opportunity to change by *changing what they do*. What is needed to move toward more productive behavior is to cast out the outmoded concepts; they should be replaced with concepts about people (values) in keeping with modern research in the behavioral sciences. In terms of McGregor's Theory Y, human beings are fundamentally energetic, will work hard toward goals they see as important, have the capacity for innovative thought and action, and will learn and grow in the right environment.

To become a powerful and respected professional manager you must accept this challenge of changing old ways of viewing your people. You should accept the difficulty of making the transition from values of Theory X to Theory Y, accepting Wheelis's admonition that change comes only after long and hard trying—taking two steps forward and sliding one step back, falling down and picking oneself up again, and moving doggedly forward until the new values and the new behaviors become habituated. When you reach this point you will have become a truly professional manager. You will now be capable of modeling the behavior you'll want in your organization—setting the norms of behavior—for developing an effective and efficient organization.

The Many Hats a Manager Must Wear

Business
Plan
Outline
7.A.

Entrepreneurs are doers; they are independent and action-oriented and rely on their own ingenuity and energy to plan and accomplish desired results. To get the business going, the entrepreneur must use his or her own financial, intellectual, and emotional resources. Once underway the picture changes subtly but substantially. Now you'll need to develop and maintain effective, ongoing relationships with employees, customers, lenders, investors, and suppliers. You could rely primarily on yourself before you opened your doors for business. But once underway you'll have to depend on

---

[4]Allen Wheelis, "How People Change," *Commentary*, May 1969.

others to help you get the results you want. This will require you to make the transition from being a loner-doer to being a professional manager.

Of the many highly successful entrepreneurs we've known, those who've built eight- and nine-figure businesses, the special quality that sets the very successful apart from the less successful has been their ability to make this transition—usually during the first years of operating their business. As we've pointed out, most businesses don't survive the first two years. The principal reason emerges as the entrepreneur's inability to *manage*. Again, this doesn't imply that you'll have to change your basic character. It just means that you must acquire and use new skills in addition to the positive entrepreneurial skills that drove you to create the business.

TEN BASIC ROLES OF MANAGEMENT

As a manager you'll have to fill 10 basic roles. It would be absurd to suggest that you must be expert in all these roles; nevertheless, you should have background and general knowledge in these areas and expertise in a number of them. Here, then, are the 10 major roles in which you should develop skill, and a brief summary of the competence pertinent to each role:

1. The manager as *communicator*. Understanding of, and competence in, developing effective communications in your organization; including understanding of business-performance data and keeping your employees informed about these.

2. The manager as *integrator*. Ability to coordinate activities of individuals and groups; competence in dealing with outside community groups.

3. The manager as *planner* and *decision maker*. Knowledge of planning techniques; knowledge of techniques for identifying and assessing alternatives in decision making; knowledge about budgeting and control; understanding of the management of financial resources.

4. The manager as *organizational designer*. Knowledge of methods for determining organizational needs to meet market changes and ability to design organization structure to accommodate these needs.

5. The manager as *innovator*. Understanding of creative ways for using organizational resources, human and physical; competence in implementing organizational change; understanding of the impact of market forces on the organization; competence in the continual revitalization of the organization.

6. The manager as *problem solver*. Competence in the techniques of problem analysis and solution; ability to diagnose conflict and resolve it.

7. The manager as *coach* and *counselor*. Ability to encourage and assist in the personal growth of individuals. Ability to help subordinates overcome blocks interfering with their performance.

8. The manager as *teacher* and *learner*. Understanding of the proper use of human resources; understanding of the development of leadership qualities; knowledge of alternate ways of functioning in the management role.

9. The manager as *advocate*. Knowledge of the processes through which negotiation, acceptance, and action take place in decision making; understanding the nature of interdependence in the organization; competence in diagnosing and improving intergroup relations.

10. The manager as a *model of style*. Understanding of how management style influences organizational effectiveness; knowledge of the concepts of motivation in work.

These roles suggest areas in which the acquisition of knowledge and skill will prove desirable for your personal growth as your company grows. They are presented as a guide to the kinds of competencies you'll need to make the transition from entrepreneur to professional manager.

Your Basic Concern as a Manager: Productivity

Business Plan Outline 2.A, 6.A

The foregoing discussion focused on the roles you'll need to assume once your venture is launched. Performance of these management roles has this unifying purpose: **achievement and maintenance over time of the highest level of productivity possible for your enterprise.**

DEFINITION OF PRODUCTIVITY AND RELATIONSHIP TO PROFIT

Productivity is the relationship between inputs and outputs. The term productivity encompasses both the resources (inputs) used in producing and marketing your product or supplying your service and the market results you achieve with them (outputs). Productivity refers to the amount and cost of labor, supplies, equipment, fuel, and capital required to produce and distribute your product or service in order to develop consumer acceptance and achieve sales.

The ultimate aim of any business is profit. Profit is the measure of financial performance that reflects the difference between inputs and outputs. In this sense productivity and profit are parallel terms. Profit is expressed as a dollar figure on the income statement at the end of the year. But the concept of productivity is broader: it focuses on a manager's conscious actions taken during the year to adjust the proper relationship between inputs and outputs needed to reach a desired *level* of profit.

EFFICIENCY VERSUS EFFECTIVENESS

The proper balance between inputs and outputs is not easy to manage. Inputs represent time and expenditures you make to obtain revenue from consumers. On the input side your management concern is with *efficiency: "Are we doing things right;* are we keeping expenditures low?" And on the output side the concern is with *effectiveness: "Are we doing the right things?* Are we achieving maximum exposure in (or impact on) the market?"

Efficiency and effectiveness conflict with one another to some extent. If efficiency were carried to the extreme, the most efficient operation would have zero costs. Your concern for efficiency will be seen in day-to-day business operations,

CHAPTER 18

525

Surviving:
Managing
for Productivity
and Growth

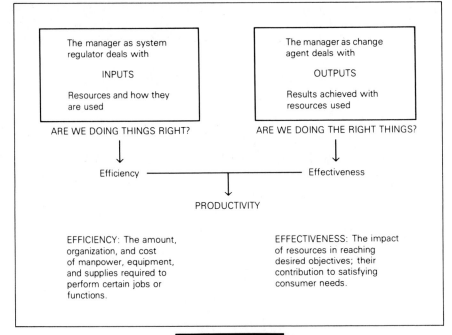

FIG. 18-1

The concept of productivity.

such as making sure material waste is kept to a minimum, keeping operating costs as low as possible, taking advantage of discounts on supply orders, and controlling personnel costs. Effectiveness, on the other hand, deals with the future and change. Here, your concern will focus on issues such as whether the business is positioning itself properly in the market, whether promotion is reaching potential customers, whether new products are needed, and in general, whether the market segments you want are responding to your marketing program.

In managing, efficiency matters deal with the here and now and require attention to details and cost control. Effectiveness looks to the future and requires innovation and creativity. Efficiency means that you must be proficient at being a *system regulator;* effectiveness requires you to be a *change agent* for your business. Figure 18-1 summarizes this discussion.

When you are in the process of regulating your business system, you may overemphasize efficiency at the expense of effectiveness. For example, if you overstress efficiency with your employees, they may be fearful of experimenting with new ways of performing tasks or may become reluctant to suggest new ideas for improving customer satisfaction. On the other hand, stressing effectiveness too much may lead to chaos—too much experimentation on the job to get the work out, lack of consistency in work methods, and overspending on marketing to get customers.

Your organization will reflect your management style; good managers blend change agentry with system regulation. As we've said, striking the proper balance between efficiency and effectiveness is difficult. But recognition of the nature of productivity will help you to achieve the necessary balance as you deal with the issues of efficiency and effectiveness that arise as you begin operations.

A Management System for Improving Productivity

Productivity improvement comes from:

1. Keeping resources used constant while improving results achieved

2. Keeping results constant while reducing resources used

3. Increasing resources used by improving results at an even higher rate

But how is productivity to be achieved? Surviving the first year or two depends on your ability to adapt to change. This early period will be filled with uncertainty as you attempt to get a toehold in the market. You'll be stretched to the limit. You'll be squeezing every ounce of production out of equipment and people who work for you; you'll be spending every waking minute in building consumer awareness and patronage; you'll be dealing with brush fires that flare up—in cash flow and marketing, for example.

You'll be working harder during the first year than you've ever worked in your life. What you'll need is a system of managing that allows you to work *smarter*. The management system you employ must therefore have the necessary flexibility to adjust quickly to change and bring order out of chaos.

The system of *management by objectives* (MBO) is a tested and proved way to increase the productivity of your enterprise during the first critical period of operation—and ever after.

MANAGEMENT BY OBJECTIVES

The concept of management by objectives was first stated by Peter Drucker in 1954.[5] He said that after he had observed how good managers achieve and maintain high productivity in successful companies he found that they followed a similar pattern. Instead of being directive bosses, they tended to act as teachers, coaches, and counselors with their subordinates. They helped their people set goals for work in keeping with their own goals. They let people have a great deal to say about their jobs and how they did them. Drucker called the basic strategy *management by objectives and self-control*.

In 1960, Douglas McGregor expanded on Drucker's approach.[6] He called the management strategy *management by integration and self-control*. He suggested that to increase productivity and build teamwork and commitment throughout the company, all members should be working toward the same end. As your company grows and you add managers, you'll be able to introduce them into the MBO system from the day they go to work. The way to do this is to have all members of the company

---

[5]Peter Drucker, *The Practice of Management,* Harper & Row, New York, 1954, chap. 11.
[6]McGregor, op.cit., chap. 5.

set their own objectives in collaboration with their boss. Starting with you, all personnel would set their key objectives in keeping with yours.

When the process is properly done, your company operates from an integrated network of plans. All who work for you have had a great deal to say about their contribution to the mainstream effort of the company. And all see how their effort fits with that of others in achieving the overall productivity objectives of the company.

People tend to support the plans they have themselves developed. They are committed psychologically to making them work. After all, you don't throw your own baby out the window: you nurture it and see that it grows healthy and survives.

Putting Management by Objectives to Work for You   As the chief executive officer of your company, you can make management by objectives (MBO) work for you. You'll find its strategy and tactics follow the behavior recommendations made in Chapter 17 for managing the people who work for you.

You gain a great advantage when you use MBO for managing your new company right from the very start. That's because you won't have to undo less effective, more traditional ways of management that have become ingrown, as happens in so many companies that have operated in the old ways.

The new way is to sit down with those who report directly to you and work out with them the major objectives for your company. When you start your company, there may be only one or two people who work for you; as your company grows and adds managers, you'll want to go through the same procedure with a larger group.

Then you'll work with each of your subordinates in helping them set their personal objectives. Since they now know what the major objectives of the company are, they can fit their plans in with yours. You may assign the authority for carrying out one or two of the company objectives to each of the people who report to you. They will then develop the plans for the activities they will engage in to accomplish these major objectives. The result will be a network of plans aimed at achieving the overall objectives of the company.

All personnel will know how their efforts fit in with the total effort of the company. The network of plans composes a productivity improvement program for your business, and each member will have had something to say about his or her contribution to the total.

All plans will be written down informally in memos from subordinate to boss. In essence these memos will be a record of agreement between the two. They become a confirmation of a psychological contract of work. The subordinate says in essence; "We've agreed to what I'm supposed to accomplish during the next six months or year, and I understand how my efforts will contribute to the productivity of the business. You've done your part by coaching me in the discussion we've had. In one or two instances you've shown me that I'm reaching too high; in others I set too low a target. But now we're agreed, and I'm willing to be judged by how well I do in reaching those targets. Of course we both understand that if I fail to achieve an objective because of circumstances beyond my control, you'll take that into consideration in assessing my performance."

When you put MBO to work for you, the process should result in plans and objectives that contribute to the input and output aspects of productivity improvement.

Be sure that plans contain an appropriate *balance* between efficiency-type objectives and effectiveness-type objectives.

CHAPTER 18

529

Surviving:
Managing
for Productivity
and Growth

Kinds of Plans   It's wise to limit the number of terms used in planning to a tested few. Here are our suggestions:

- *Objectives* are overall purposes or positions to be reached. They are relatively long-range, perhaps a year or so for practical managerial purposes. Larger companies in the United States often consider objectives as 5-year plans. The requirements of the business will set the length of an objective. Small companies usually find a period of 1 year most practical in planning objectives.

- *Subobjectives* are end results desired by a specific time. Subobjectives tend to be more concrete, more limited in scope and time, than objectives. Generally, several subobjectives will have to be achieved and put together, or integrated, to reach an objective.

- *Action plans* are steps, activities, tasks, projects, or programs, which when put together accomplish subobjectives. Action plans are the ultimate step that makes MBO work. Action plans imply activities—people doing things, working and interacting with others inside and outside the company.

Guides to Writing Plans   Here are some well-tested guides that will help you and your managers write the plans used in MBO:

- No company, division, department, or individual management position should have more than six or seven major objectives in work at any time. Management by objectives avoids spelling out in step-by-step detail how people should do their jobs. Planning in MBO affords guides that are specified as *results,* which may be thought of as standards of performance. Therefore, managers are free to do their jobs in ways they feel comfortable with. The ultimate criteria of performance are: Do they do a good job—that meets the specifications, on time, and within the budget of money and resources allocated?

- Plans should be written informally, not on standard forms developed for the purpose. Use of standard forms tends to move the system toward bureaucracy, in which filling out the forms becomes the important part of the MBO process. Means become ends and the whole purpose of gaining enthusiastic commitment to achievement is thwarted.

- Each plan should contain only one idea. The point is to keep the procedure simple. If you want to deal with two ideas, write two plans.

- Plans should be stated in simple, clear language. A clear, crisply stated plan says what is intended without being hard to interpret or causing confusion.

- Each plan should start with an active verb, which says *do something;* don't just sit there. Verbs show action. Here are typical active verbs that might start a plan: *Reduce* scrap, *increase* net *profit* from . . . , *hire* two people for . . . , *buy* a new site for. . . .

Each plan should have an end date by the calendar. This means a specific date such as June 15, 1989, or November 10, 1990. A specific date sharpens the focus of timeliness of achievement. Take advantage of it.

Each plan should specify a way of measuring achievement toward its accomplishment. Wherever possible numbers should be used, for example, dollars of profit, pounds of scrap, or percentage of turnover. Some plans aim at goals that can't be put in numbers. If so, use a scale of some kind, for example, ranging from poor through fair, good, and excellent.

The final suggestion: In addition to a means for measuring progress toward a goal, there should be a statement of how often feedback on progress should be checked. Looking at performance too often tends to be disruptive. Looking at performance at too long an interval may cause trouble by allowing performance that's too much at variance from that desired; it may be impossible to correct in the time left. The appropriate interval for checking progress must be set by sound managerial judgment.

Planning Should Be Practicable   Planning in MBO should be practicable. It should be within the capacity of the company and the individual. It should not be blue-sky. But planning should stimulate growth of the company and the people who make up the company. Plans should be set at high enough levels to stimulate growth but not so high as to be clearly out of reach. By encouraging growth, individuals become more competent and the company becomes more effective.

An Example of Plans in MBO   Figure 18-2 shows typical plans in MBO for a small company. Plans should be set in areas of major importance to the company or position, such as innovation, marketing, profit, growth, and management succession.

Advantages of MBO   The system of managing by objectives carries certain distinct advantages over more traditional ways of managing. Most important, MBO will assure that efforts are directed toward specified results in achieving high productivity. When introduced into your company, it promotes individual commitment to work. Once the ideas for planning in the fundamental business requirements have taken hold, the system of MBO can later include features such as appraising individual performance, gaining insight into individual strengths and weaknesses, adjusting salaries and other compensation, and developing a management succession program.

Cautions in Introducing MBO   We should point out that these various uses of MBO should never be introduced all at once. They should follow one another gradually over a long period, perhaps 2 or 3 years, as the company grows and management gains experience in the use of MBO. If all these features were introduced as a package, the learning needed to make the MBO system operate well would be too complicated, confusing, and self-defeating.

MBO, a Human Strategy   Management by objectives offers the means for fusing individual and company effort. Its strategy supports individual differences. Members of the firm can do things in their own way. Individual style or method are not of

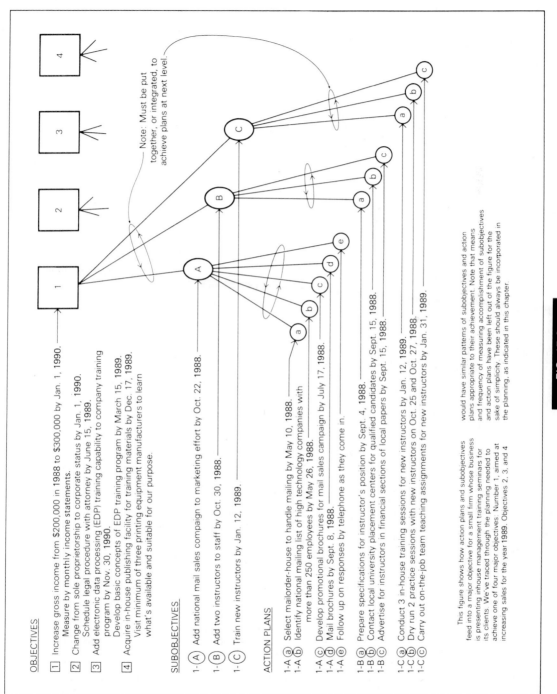

OBJECTIVES

1. Increase gross income from $200,000 in 1988 to $300,000 by Jan. 1, 1990.
   Measure by monthly income statements.
2. Change from sole proprietorship to corporate status by Jan. 1, 1990.
   Schedule legal procedure with attorney by June 15, 1989.
3. Add electronic data processing (EDP) training capability to company training program by Nov. 30, 1990.
   Develop basic concepts of EDP training program by March 15, 1989.
4. Acquire in-house publishing facility for training materials by Dec. 17, 1989.
   Visit minimum of three printing equipment manufacturers to learn what's available and suitable for our purpose.

SUBOBJECTIVES

1-Ⓐ Add national mail sales campaign to marketing effort by Oct. 22, 1988.

1-Ⓑ Add two instructors to staff by Oct. 30, 1988.

1-Ⓒ Train new instructors by Jan. 12, 1989.

ACTION PLANS

1-Ⓐ(a) Select mailorder-house to handle mailing by May 10, 1988.
1-Ⓐ(b) Identify national mailing list of high technology companies with more than 250 employees by May 26, 1988.
1-Ⓐ(c) Develop promotional brochures for mail sales campaign by July 17, 1988.
1-Ⓐ(d) Mail brochures by Sept. 8, 1988.
1-Ⓐ(e) Follow up on responses by telephone as they come in.

1-Ⓑ(a) Prepare specifications for instructor's position by Sept. 4, 1988.
1-Ⓑ(b) Contact local university placement centers for qualified candidates by Sept. 15, 1988.
1-Ⓑ(c) Advertise for instructors in financial sections of local papers by Sept. 15, 1988.

1-Ⓒ(a) Conduct 3 in-house training sessions for new instructors by Jan. 12, 1989.
1-Ⓒ(b) Dry run 2 practice sessions with new instructors on Oct. 25 and Oct. 27, 1988.
1-Ⓒ(c) Carry out on-the-job team teaching assignments for new instructors by Jan. 31, 1989.

Note: Must be put together, or integrated, to achieve plans at next level.

This figure shows how action plans and subobjectives feed into a major objective for a small firm whose business is presenting in-house management training seminars for its clients. We've traced through the planning needed to achieve one of four major objectives: Number 1, aimed at increasing sales for the year 1989. Objectives 2, 3, and 4 would have similar patterns of subobjectives and action plans appropriate to their achievement. Note that means and frequency of measuring accomplishment of subobjectives and action plans have been left out of the figure for the sake of simplicity. These should always be incorporated in the planning, as indicated in this chapter.

FIG. 17-2

How objectives, subobjectives, and action plans tie together.

concern; what is important is the achievement of the results needed to contribute to the accomplishment of the company's overall productivity objectives. The only constraint on members of the firm is that they behave in a legal and ethical way. In a word, the strategy of MBO permits individual freedom in a disciplined approach to organizational achievement.

Although focusing on individual needs and performance, MBO ensures the development of teamwork through the need to consult with others and to arrive at mutually acceptable planning in the process. The consultative procedures inherent in MBO support the emergence of an open climate of management. This in turn supports the teaching, learning environment from which innovative and powerful proactive management develops.

Assessing Your Productivity Performance

Business
Plan
Outline
2.A, 7.A, 8.A

After the business gets going, how can you determine its performance in achieving a high level of productivity? The crucial, key test is, of course, profit, but changes occur so rapidly, you can't wait until the end of the year or even until the end of the quarter to find out about the health of your business. You must continually ask the key productivity questions we raised earlier: Are we doing things right? Are we doing the right things? In using MBO as your system of management, you employ a powerful tool for guiding your efforts and those of people who work for you toward the highest possible level of productivity performance.

You've solved half of the productivity-assessment problem if you're asking the right questions. We'll cover here the crucial areas in which to assess productivity performance and supply you with some probing questions you'll need to answer.

THE INTERNAL COMPONENT

The health of your business will depend on how well you're managing. The discussion in this chapter should help you to assess yourself in this role.

You   You must learn and grow as a manager if your business is to grow and prosper. Your own personal growth will be reflected in the continually increasing productivity of your venture. Here are some questions to test the quality of your personal growth:

- Do you know more about managing your business well now than you did a month ago?

- Are you able to see more relationships in knowledge than you did before? Are you developing wisdom by being able to correlate and apply different kinds of knowledge purposefully for achievement?

- Are you more creative, more innovative than you were, through combining what you know in newer, better, more effective ways?

- Do you tolerate and deal with ambiguity and uncertainty more effectively than in the past?

- Are you able to work cooperatively with others while preserving your unique qualities?

Are you showing real growth through the acquisition of increasingly higher levels of competence?

The first five criteria center in assessing specific skills, the sixth, in judging overall personal growth.

CHAPTER 18

533

Surviving:
Managing
for Productivity
and Growth

Your Employees   Productivity increases with satisfying working conditions, as does morale. Your employees' morale may be judged by their attitudes toward work and their cooperation in trying to achieve the objectives of your business; high morale is a key test of a well-managed organization. You'll have satisfied workers and high morale if you possess and demonstrate the characteristics of the ideal manager we have described. As your business expands, you might ask yourself these kinds of questions about factors that influence morale:

- Do I let my employees know what's expected of them?

- Am I sensitive to their needs?

- Am I open and honest in dealing with them?

- Do I encourage them to come forward with their ideas?

- Do I communicate clearly with them and listen actively to what they have to say?

- Do I let them have some control and let them alone to do it their way?

- Are they paid adequately compared with other businesses?

- Do they feel a sense of participation and pride in the business, and believe they're doing something worthwhile?

High morale doesn't necessarily guarantee high productivity. Employee attitudes toward the job and your business will also be affected by outside conditions beyond your control. But high morale indicates a strong predisposition toward increased productivity and presents clear evidence of sound management of people.

THE EXTERNAL COMPONENT

Your business will have important relationships with the community, suppliers, government, and creditors as well as with customers. These relationships affect both the input and output sides of productivity.

Your Customers   Developing and maintaining a customer orientation has been a persistent theme of this book. Your business will thrive or fail depending on how consumers cast or withhold their dollar votes. That is why we've devoted so much attention to marketing. Favorable consumer response to your marketing strategies is, of course, the principal output or result you want. Some questions to guide you in assessing productivity of your marketing efforts are:

- Am I maintaining or improving the quality of my products or services?

- Is the right quantity of my products or services available at the right place, at the right time?

Am I maintaining expertise and improving my technical knowledge of my product or service?

Am I constantly gathering new information about the market my business serves? Am I alert for changes in consumers' needs?

Am I keeping track of competition and staying ahead of it?

Do I have new products or services in development to satisfy present customers better or to tap new market segments?

Are my marketing expenditures related to specific marketing objectives?

These questions and others like them will have to be raised to guide your business toward its ultimate goal—consumer satisfaction that produces profit. Remember, the consumer is now your boss in the market you serve.

Your Community   Your business must pay its civic rent. This requires your active participation in local affairs and local clubs or organizations to gain community goodwill. Your business should become part of the social as well as the commercial fabric of the community. In addition to the personal satisfaction of making social contributions, civic involvement benefits both the input and the output sides of productivity. From informal relationships with community business leaders, you'll learn about changes in the local market, new business techniques, and new sources of supplies or business services. You may even pick up hints for new products or services your business might offer or economical ways you haven't tried before to reach potential customers.

The questions here are straightforward:

Am I an active member in appropriate civic organizations?

Have I assumed or can I attain leadership in any local clubs, committees, or civic groups?

Have I contributed to or has my business sponsored any local drives, charities, or fund-raising activities?

Your Suppliers   Suppliers are a major input, but they can also affect the output side of productivity. The businesses that supply your firm with operating materials, equipment, or inventory can become an extension of your business. Establish and nurture good working relationships and they will become assets that supply much more than physical goods. Industrial salespeople are usually much more than order takers. They are professionals who keep abreast of trends and state-of-the-art techniques in their field. They'll be able to give you advice on technical matters and keep you informed of what other companies in your industry are doing. Your business will reap dividends far beyond acquisition of needed supplies if you treat them right. Some questions to test your responsiveness follow:

Am I prompt in paying my accounts?

Am I fair in negotiating transactions?

Do I take full but fair advantage of purchase discounts offered?

Am I receptive to suggestions made?

Do I display and promote the suppliers' inventory as I assured them I would?

Do I allow enough lead time for the supplier with my reorders?

Do I thoroughly and fairly analyze cost and service before switching to a new supplier?

CHAPTER 18

535

Surviving:
Managing
for Productivity
and Growth

Your Government   Your relations with the federal, state, and local governments affect productivity too—both positively and negatively. Taxes reduce the financial results or outputs of your business. But the services of government available for small business, as we've described previously, can be major inputs in the form of capital or technical and management assistance. You should take full advantage of these services, since you'll be helping to pay for them with the taxes your business pays. Ask yourself:

Do I fill out forms properly and am I paying taxes on time to avoid reprimands, censures, or penalties?

Am I exploiting the governmental resources available, both financial and human, to help make my business successful?

Your Creditors   Commercial banks or other institutions will be lending you working capital as inputs to enable you to purchase tangible resources. Like suppliers and some government agencies, creditors can also give sound business advice that helps achieve greater outputs. For example, the loan officer you deal with at the bank will know your financial condition and may be able to suggest ways to economize on purchases or minimize loan-carrying charges. Having financial dealings with other small businesses, the banker will know firsthand some of the pitfalls to avoid. In addition, the loan officer may be able to steer you to advisers to help you resolve unique problems, to individuals with ready cash to invest, or to suppliers of special business services you may need. Some questions to help you assess your relations with creditors are:

Am I meeting my loan repayment commitments on time?

Am I planning far enough ahead to get working capital when I need it?

Am I keeping my banker informed of the progress of my venture?

Have I let my banker know enough about my business and my problems to be able to help me?

You should establish the same confidential and professional relationship with your banker as you would with your accountant and attorney. All three of them will want you to be successful and can help you along the way.

Summary

Your success in getting your business off the ground will depend on your ability to get things done through and with other people. Your entrepreneurial talents and the detailed planning you've accomplished with the help of this book will serve you well in getting your business started. However, shortly after you launch your business, you'll need additional managerial skills. You will need to make the transition from entrepreneur to manager.

We've outlined the three kinds of competence you'll seek to achieve to make this transition: technical competence, system competence, and interpersonal competence. Technical and system competence concern your skills in manipulating and integrating things in an innovative way. Interpersonal competence measures your ability to work effectively with people: your employees, customers, business associates, creditors, and suppliers.

Your success in surviving the first years in your business will depend on how well you fill the basic roles of the professional manager as we've described them in this chapter. Your performance in these roles will, in turn, depend upon the levels of your technical, system, and interpersonal competencies.

You will aim for the highest possible productivity in every aspect of your business. To do this you'll use the best managerial judgment you're capable of to strike a proper balance between efficiency and effectiveness. You'll reach this balance by answering the two key questions: Are we doing things right? Are we doing the right things? These questions will challenge you continually in your position of chief executive officer of your company.

Management by objectives is a tested and accepted management system for improving productivity in your business. During your first year or two in business, with the need to take care of myriad tasks, you should be wary of being caught in the "activity trap." If you are trapped, you can readily find yourself swamped in detail, ignoring the forward-looking planning and doing mandatory to the survival of your business.

Management by objectives gives you the way to avoid the activity trap. Its systematic approach to management makes it easy for you to set objectives for increasing productivity in every aspect of your business, for assigning accountabilities for results, and for gaining commitment for achievement from all members of your company. MBO offers a methodology for attaining unified organizational effort. By using it, you will build teamwork and high morale in your workforce. You'll build an achieving firm.

You'll want to keep an eye on the internal and external elements of your business and the internal and external forces that develop pressure for change. By asking and answering the right questions you'll be able to plan appropriately for improving productivity—for doing things right and for doing the right things. We've suggested a number of questions that should help you get started in deciding where the payoff is in your planning. By continually adjusting your plans to take care of anticipated change, you'll practice proactive management—and you'll control the destiny of your company.

Managing for Survival and Growth

1. Study the list of attributes expected of an ideal manager. Comments associated with each of these attributes are given in this chapter. Evaluate yourself: Rank your attributes on the lines below, from the strongest, in which you feel most proficient, to the weakest, in which you feel the least proficient.

a. _____

b. _____

c. _____

d. _____

e. _____

f. _____

2. Review your list. In the space below make notes to yourself about the implications of your strong and weak points. Answer the question: How can I use my strong points to advantage and how can I overcome my weak points? Add notes about your strengths and weaknesses as shown in exercise 1 above.

_____

_____

_____

_____

_____

_____

_____

_____

_____

_____

3. Develop major objectives for your first year of business operation. Key your objectives to levels of productivity, including consideration of both efficiency and effectiveness. Before you begin, review the section on MBO in this chapter. Pay special attention to the definition of *objective* and to the guidelines for writing plans.

a. _____

_____

_____

_____

_____

b. _____

_____

_____

c. _____

_____

_____

d. _____

_____

_____

e. _____

_____

_____

f. _____

_____

_____

4. In what ways will you evaluate productivity performance in your business? Using the questions we presented in this chapter as guides, under each section below list at least three of the most important questions you should ask and answer about productivity in your business.

a. Internal—activities or operations inside the company:

(1) _____

_____

_____

(2) _____

_____

_____

(3) _____

_____

_____

b. External—activities or operations outside the company:

(1) _____

_____

_____

_____

_____

_____

(2) _____

(3) _____

KEY TERMS

efficiency 525
effectiveness 525

empathic, empathetic 519
integrator 524

STUDY ASSIGNMENTS FOR REVIEW AND DISCUSSION

1. Check three elementary textbooks on management. See how they define management. Then write your own definition.

2. Review the 10 basic roles of management given in this chapter. Discuss with a classmate or two how skill in these roles might be applied in the management job.

3. Define productivity. Describe the difference between efficiency and effectiveness.

4. Describe the system of management by objectives. How can MBO stimulate productivity?

5. Tell how plans in MBO should be written, giving recommendations and cautions.

6. Describe desirable relationships with various people you must work with inside and outside your organization—and how to achieve these relationships.

PROJECTS FOR STUDENTS

These projects will probably prove most effective if students work together in teams of two or three:

1. Talk with a number of individuals who work for a living. Ask them to describe the qualities they'd look for in a good boss. Record the answers. Check to see how well your list corresponds to the profile of the ideal manager as given in this chapter.

2. Gather in class a panel of six or eight successful entrepreneurs, small businesspersons who've made it. Ask them to respond to these questions:

    What personal problems did you have to fight to overcome in managing your business?

    What did you consider your superior strengths in running your business?

    How about weaknesses? Did you make special efforts to plug the gaps resulting from your lacks? How?

    What did you do about developing backup management to support you?

    Did you do any formal planning in your business? If so, tell us about it. (Do not be afraid to ask direct questions of this kind. Successful entrepreneurs enjoy talking about their business and will almost always give frank answers to politely asked direct questions.)

3. Invite to class two or three key managers who have had experience with MBO in their companies. Ask them to describe their experiences with it, bad and good.

IF YOU WANT TO READ MORE

Not too many references are yet available on the subjects taken up in this chapter, with the exception of management by objectives. You will find some material in the following books:

BAUMBACK, Clifford M.: *Basic Small Business Management,* Prentice-Hall, Inc., Englewood Cliffs, NJ, 1983. This textbook was written primarily from the managerial rather than the entrepreneurial perspective. The author uses case histories in explaining management styles for the small business.

BRANDT, Steven C.: *Strategic Planning in Emerging Companies,* Addison-Wesley, Reading, MA, 1981. This text examines long-range planning and strategy for small business. It traces the stages of growth and typical management styles of small companies and then attempts to demystify the strategic planning process.

DELANEY, William A.: *Micromanagement: How to Solve the Problems of Growing Companies,* AMACOM, New York, 1981. The information presented in this book was gathered during the author's 15 years of experience in operating a small business. It is oriented toward microeconomics and micromanagement, focusing on the small, specific, individual, and everyday level.

DRUCKER, Peter: *The Practice of Management,* Harper & Row, New York, 1954. You'll find the original description of management by objectives in Chapter 11 of this book; the chapter is titled "Management by Objectives and Self-Control." Drucker here laid down the fundamental concepts of MBO as a strategy and practice of management. These basic ideas have been developed and elaborated by many others since.

EDMUNDS, Stahil W.: *Performance Measures for Growing Businesses,* Van Nostrand Reinhold, New York, 1982. This book presents performance measures designed to help small business executives improve their feedback control loop, so that they know early what corrective actions to take for successful operations.

HOGSETT, Robert N.: *Profit Planning for Small Business,* Van Nostrand Reinhold, New York, 1981. This book is intended as an aid to the person already operating a small business. It offers a series of explanations of management methods that the author has found useful in operating his own business and in advising others.

KURILOFF, Arthur H.: *Organizational Development for Survival,* American Management Association, New York, 1972. Chapters 9 and 10 of this reference give the behavioral research background and the practical management methodology for using

MBO. If you want to delve a bit more deeply into both theory and practice than we do in Chapter 18, you will find the material in this book suitable.

MALI, Paul: *Improving Total Productivity,* Wiley-InterScience, Somerset, NJ, 1978. Showing specifically how to deal with productivity problems, the author explores what productivity is, how it operates in an organization, and how it can be improved. Step-by-step operating procedures are included to guide the organization toward higher productivity. Although the book isn't designed specifically for the small business, the concepts and guidelines can be easily adapted by entrepreneurs for their own organizations.

SECTION VII

Cases

MULTILUBE SUPPLY COMPANY
A PROSPECTUS FOR CARLA FASHIONS
BUYING A GOING BUSINESS
PEAK ELECTRONICS
A CASE OF SUMMARY TERMINATION
NAUTILUS ENGINEERING CO., INC.

This section presents six cases, each drawn from a different kind of business. They address the key subjects presented in the text of this book. The cases are intended, through individual study and class discussion, to highlight major ideas, principles, and practices in starting and managing the small business.

Each case represents reality; all come from experiences that occur in small businesses. Names and places have been changed where necessary to preserve the anonymity of the firms that furnished the information.

MULTILUBE SUPPLY COMPANY

The Multilube Supply Company of Southern California was started 12 years ago by Arthur Newman, 55, a petrochemical engineering salesman. He had always wanted to be his own boss and was eventually able to start his own business as an outcome of calling on the aerospace industry. There he uncovered a profitable niche in the market for specialized lubricants and petrochemical products. He set up in business with the aid of a brilliant young organic chemist. Together they were able to compound strategic products that met the demanding needs of their customers.

Newman was a tough-minded entrepreneur with a tendency toward paternalism in dealing with those who worked for him. He had no patience with paperwork and managed by making spur-of-the-moment intuitive decisions as the need arose. The company grew slowly but steadily over the years. Growth was spurred when Newman increased the size, capabilities, and personnel of the company laboratory. This improved facility enabled rapid expansion of the company's product line.

In the late eighties the company reached 200 employees and $10 million in annual sales. As his company prospered, Newman added six salespeople to his 18-person staff, which now covered the state and many industries. Without company compensation policies for sales personnel, Newman followed his usual tactic of negotiating a deal with each new salesperson. Newman now found his business growing so fast that he could scarcely keep up with his proliferating management duties. He was advised by his friends in the small business presidents club to which he belonged that his company had now grown to the point at which he should be hiring professional managers.

His first reaction was negative. He disliked the idea of moving from his free-wheeling, seat-of-the-pants way of running his company. And yet, the more he thought about it, the more he realized that he must now delegate authority to others— or see the business get into trouble as control of affairs slipped from his grasp. He couldn't wear several hats at once, or change them fast enough to keep up with his multiplying management requirements.

Besides, he was now faced with a situation that forced him to take a decisive step. A salesperson himself, he tried to keep in touch with his expanded sales operation as he had in earlier days. But he soon found this a losing game in view of the growing demands on his time. To worsen a deteriorating situation, he learned from the grapevine that a number of his salespeople were griping about conditions under which they were working. That, he thought, might be just the tough issue to test the quality of a professional manager.

He thereupon hired away from a successful larger petrochemical firm an experienced and likeable marketing and sales manager, Peter Lindsey. Lindsey was 20 years younger than he. In talking of this move with an older member of his presidents club, he was cautioned, "When this man takes on his duties for you, let him have some time to find out how things are done in your company. Don't tell him what to do. Give him full authority to do things his way. He's one of the new breed of younger managers; he's undoubtedly learned a lot of newer ways of doing things since we've been in business. You can always check him if you aren't getting the results you want—but I'd say let him have his head for a good while."

Newman responded, after thinking for a moment, "I guess you're right. As long as I'm letting go, I'll go whole hog. We'll see what happens. As you say, I can always call the game if I don't like the score."

Peter Lindsey, the new sales manager, spent the first three months on the job traveling throughout the state, meeting the salespeople and customers. He learned all he could about the business. By this time, he was on a first name basis with the staff. He had been able, through his charismatic personality, to get them to open up and tell him about the things that were bothering them. It was time to try improving the effectiveness of the sales effort by improving the morale of the sales crew.

Lindsey arranged a meeting with his boss.: "Art," he said, "we have some tough problems with the men in the field."

"Tell me," said Newman, "what kinds of problems?"

"I've heard the same things all over the state," said Lindsey. "The boys are unhappy about the way they're being paid."

"What do you mean?" said Newman. "They're all getting what they want . . . I hired every one of those men. I gave them what they wanted. I don't see why anyone should be griping. What's going on, anyway?"

"What's bothering the men might be called perceptions of inequity—they see unfair things going on, and they don't like it," said Lindsey. "Art, I've been studying the way our men get paid. And I've talked with them at length. The upshot is that we seem to have a crazy quilt of a compensation program—or I should say a catch-as-catch-can program, *if* you can call it a program.

"Theoretically everyone is supposed to be paid on commission. Yet I find different arrangements with the men. The oldtimers have a generous draw—might even be called a salary—that's subtracted from their commission. The newer men have a minimum draw and this disturbs them when they find out how much the oldtimers can draw. There are several other points the men have raised."

"O.K. Shoot," said Newman. "Let's hear."

"Let me tick them off," said Lindsey: "Several of the older men drive company cars; the others drive their own. Some men use company credit cards; others pay for gas themselves and turn in mileage.

"They don't like the ceiling on earnings. Although you've raised it from time to time, the men feel it places an arbitrary limit on what they can earn each month. And when things began to roll about four years ago, and sales began to boom as the company's products got known, the commission rate was pared down. They say that's not fair.

"Art, I remember that you told me you had worked on commission in your early days in sales. You didn't work on a salary because you didn't want your ability to make money limited. And yet you suffered ceilings put on your earnings once in a while. Didn't you dislike that—and maybe some of the other restrictions you had to work under? Don't you think that a lot of the things that bothered you then are bothering our men?"

"Sure, when I was on commission a lot of things bothered me," said Art. "But that was the way it was. We had to be tough, and us salesmen had to live with it. Do you think you can do any better in managing the men—in handling the issues you've told me about? . . . Have you covered all the points you wanted to tell me?"

"No, Art, there are a couple more," said Lindsey. "The men are somewhat confused about commission calculations. Over the years the oldtimers were permitted to work out their own discount arrangements with their customers. We just don't seem to have a standard policy. All the variations in billing make it time-consuming to get the commissions figured out and paid. Not only that, some of the men are complaining about the wide differences in the potentials of the sales areas they've been allotted. They think something ought to be done about that."

At this point, suddenly remembering the advice of his sage old executive friend, Newman, said, "Now these are the kinds of situations I expect you to manage. I think you've got a tiger by the tail, but go ahead and do what you think you should. You have full authority to do the job; I don't want any part of it.

"Let's set a goal—a trial period of, say, 12 months. If you can increase the company's net profit by 10 percent in a year, I'll consider you successful. Does that seem fair?"

"Yes, it's fair, and I believe I can do it," said Lindsey.

"You've got it," said Newman. "And don't forget, it's your baby. I'll want a very brief report each month, not more than one page, just to let me know how things are going. Don't come to me unless you get into a jam and need special help. I'm staying out of it."

When Lindsey left the office he mused: "One basic I've learned about management in the years I've been practicing is that when there's a serious problem in your group, it's wise to get the members to help solve the problem. That way you can usually come up with a solution that the people and the boss can be happy with. I must involve the men in finding answers to the problems that are bugging them.

"Yes, I think I can make it work out so even the boss'll go along. I'll get the men together and run a self-directed meeting. That way I'm sure we'll get satisfactory answers."

Lindsey arranged to have all the sales force attend a two-day meeting in San Luis Obispo, midway between Los Angeles and San Francisco. Here they wouldn't be disturbed by telephone calls or interruptions for messages.

Lindsey explained the purpose of the meeting to the men: "I've asked that we all get together here to see if we can straighten out some of the problems I've been hearing about in the field. I'm sure that these have been interfering with our ability to concentrate on our marketing and sales jobs. I'd like to see if we can come up with an acceptable and uniform way of paying everybody—and get rid of some of the older ways that seem to be bugging us.

"Here's how we'll do it. First of all, let's break up into four groups of six each. Let's have oldtimers mix with the newer men, and let's have a mixture of north sales and south sales in each group. Let's select a spokesman in each group. Now get your heads together and list all the things that have been bothering you about your jobs. We can take an hour or so to do that."

Lindsey sat quietly as the men discussed and listed their concerns. He then had each spokesman call out the items in his group's list. Lindsey wrote them on a blackboard, coming up with a single list after eliminating duplications.

The final list of major items represented consensus among the salespeople, and were written in priority sequence, like this:

- Reduction of commission rates when the salespeople's earnings rose above what the boss considered excessive

- Ceilings placed on earnings for the same reason

■ Variances in compensation resulting from intricate and devious discount procedures the individual salespeople had been allowed to negotiate with their customers over the years

■ Nonuniform compensation practices: some men were on straight commission, some were on a small salary plus commission, and some were on a draw against commission

■ Annoying delays before commissions were paid

■ Wide differences in sales potential of territories assigned to individuals

■ No policy on use of automobiles: some men used company cars and company credit cards; some used their own cars and reported mileage

Lindsey led the whole group through a discussion of each issue. He encouraged the men to talk openly about their feelings and desires in reaching consensus on each issue. After two long days of working through pros and cons, the following agreements were reached:

■ No ceiling was to be placed on earnings once the level of sales for each salesperson passed the allotted break-even point for the month.

■ A simplified and standardized approach to customer discounts, based on quantities of product sold, was to be installed. This would do away with variations in compensation resulting from previous nonstandard discount procedures.

■ All sales personnel were to be put on the same compensation schedule, with a modest monthly salary as the men wanted. Their desire was to be able to smooth out irregularities in monthly income during times of lower than normal commission.

■ Clarification of procedure and improved delivery of compensation from commissions were to be adopted.

■ Wide differences in sales potential of territories assigned to individuals were to be eliminated.

■ A standard policy on use of automobiles for company business would be established.

Lindsey guided the group through to solutions for these problems. He listened carefully to what the men had to say, issuing no commands and offering no unilateral solutions himself. He acted as coordinator and tried to help the group reach consensus on the solution to each problem. Only when a proposed solution seemed to him impractical or in violation of good management practice did he state his reasons for objecting—and then steered the discussion into a more acceptable channel.

He agreed that the company would place no ceiling on earnings, unless economic conditions changed substantially. Such reduction would be installed only after the sales force was informed in a joint meeting with management. The company would adopt a standardized procedure for discounts, based on quantities of various products sold. A modest monthly salary would be paid to all salespeople; this would enable them to weather short periods of smaller than usual commission. Individual territories were to be realigned to ensure essential equality of sales potential. This would be done on the basis of computer analysis of 10 years of sales records, including addition of newer industrial companies, potential customers whose impact on sales could be estimated. A uniform standard was to be installed governing the use of automobiles. This would follow the wishes expressed by the men. They would use their own cars and report mileage at a rate sufficient to permit them to replace their cars every two years.

Through the help of the company's computerized management information office it was found possible to realign territories in the desired manner. Each man could now see his commission for the month on a monthly printout, available within the first week of the new month. As final steps in procedure, Lindsey agreed to review basic sales and demographic data monthly and to bring the sales force together for consultation twice a year.

Lindsey then met with Newman and reviewed the results of the meeting. After some muttered grumbling to himself, Newman said, "I have a reservation or two . . . but I've promised you a clear field, and I'll stick to my promise. So you go to it. I look forward to your first report next month."

At the end of the 12-month trial period, Lindsey was able to show his boss an increase in profit of 11.7 percent over the previous 12-month period. Complaints from the salespeople had dropped sharply and had changed from bitter grumblings about inequities formerly perceived to the more normal kind of ebullient bickering expected from a group of extroverted and lively salespeople.

A PROSPECTUS FOR CARLA FASHIONS[1]

Charisma Apparel, Inc., aimed to develop a chain of women's specialty stores in southern California. It opened its first store, Carla Fashions, in Miami in April 1977. It proposed to open a second store, first of a chain, in California in the spring of 1978. This prospectus is designed to outline the steps to be taken in development of the second store and to estimate the funding needed for this venture.

Background of the Owners

Charisma Apparel, Inc., is a family-owned corporation; it has four shareholders: Rudolph Jaffe (31), vice president and treasurer of Charisma, is a graduate of Notre Dame University and holds a master's degree in business administration from the University of Utah. He is a management consultant with a national public accounting firm.

Charles Jaffe (28), president and general manager of Charisma, graduated in hotel management from Michigan State University. He has had extensive experience in retailing with Austins, Inc. in Mississippi and the May Co. in California.

David Jaffe (25), vice president and secretary of Charisma, has a Master of Business Administration degree from the University of California, Los Angeles.

---

[1]This case was prepared from data furnished by Dennis Moritz.

Shirley Jaffe (20) is enrolled in the University of Florida and intends to join the Charisma organization when she graduates.

Background of Charisma Apparel, Inc.

The first store opened by Charisma Apparel, Inc., Carla Fashions of Miami, offers diversified apparel appealing to contemporary women's tastes and life-style. Casual sportswear, dresses, and coordinates are carried at moderate to somewhat higher price points. Promotional merchandise (20 percent of inventory) is brought in for special sales to offer value to consumers and to maintain a competitive position in the market.

Carla offers its customers more coordinate lines than its competitors, who tend to emphasize separates. Carla also carries accessories such as belts, hosiery, purses, and costume jewelry.

Marketing Strategy

In women's apparel, the traditional division of stores has been along age and income groups. Ages 16 to 25 have been considered a "junior" market and specialty stores have catered to this group with "trendy" merchandise. Ages 30 to 60 have been considered a "missy" market with more traditional apparel offered and a stronger emphasis on division by price and quality of product or service.

Charisma rejects this market segmentation by age and income groups. The company believes women consumers are more concerned with life-style attitudes and individual recognition than with traditional market segmentation by age and income groups.

Financial and Background Information

Charisma's studies show that starting capital should not exceed $75,000 for leasehold improvements, furniture and fixtures, opening inventory, and organization costs. Planned sales in the first year of operation should reach $350,000; the second year should see a 15 percent increase to $525,000. Net income before taxes in the first year of business should reach 5.5 percent of sales, or $19,500, for a 25 percent return on investment (ROI).

Normal industry profits on sales for specialty stores range from 8 to 15 percent for a mature store—one that has been in business for 3 to 5 years. Inventory turnover should be in the 5.5 to 6.5 range in the first year of operation. The gross profit before expenses should average about 40 percent, which reflects a similar markup on merchandise. Details of financial planning will be found in the appendix; projections include Income Statement, Break-Even Analysis, Monthly Sales Plan, and Cash Flow Analysis.

As women have entered the labor force in increasing numbers, as the population has matured in average age, as the size of the American family has decreased, buying patterns of American households and American women have changed dramatically.

The customer is more demanding, expects quality products and services at a reasonable price, and is less willing to be categorized.

Today, middle-aged women are more likely to wear trendy, youthful, and colorful apparel than they did two decades ago. Young women shoppers are more willing to wear sophisticated, "classic" looks with expensive price tags than they did 5 or 10 years ago.

Charisma recognizes these changes. Carla will become a *contemporary* women's apparel business with products appealing to many income groups, ages, and individual backgrounds. Carla will not label the woman shopper a "junior" or "missy" market. The old distinctions are breaking down, and retailers who change with changing market forces will be successful. Carla presents a significant formula for success in this competitive market.

Pricing Policy

Shopping malls in southern California's Orange County are centered in a strategic retail trading area. Income groups are drawn primarily from middle-class families. Wage earners are by and large skilled workers and managers: incomes range from $15,000 to $50,000 per year.

Most malls house major retailers such as Bullock's, Robinsons, I. Magnin, and Saks Fifth Avenue.

Carla has tried to position itself in the price point area. Dresses range from $40 to $100, coordinate sportswear blazers from $50 to $125, pants $35 to $80, blouses $30 to $60.

Promotional merchandise has been very effective. Charisma has purchased merchandise for this purpose at close-out and off-price values at major markets in New York and Los Angeles. Therefore, even with promotional goods, appropriate markups were maintained.

Charisma uses the services of two national buying offices, one in New York and one in Los Angeles. The president and general manager of Charisma participating in the organized markets makes the major buying decisions on a seasonal basis.

Promotion

The concepts proposed for the California Carla's opening include sale items, shopping sprees, free scarves, 10 percent discounts to direct-mail customers, newspaper advertising, and participation in special events held in the mall. Displays have been designed to advertise and promote life-style apparel. All these promotion schemes will be highlighted by the appearance of a glistening sports car in the main show window. This theme will be continued by showing mo-peds along with active Tropical Life Style sportswear.

Site Selection

Charisma Apparel, Inc. searched intensively to find a location in a new shopping mall in an upper-middle-class trading area. After scouring the country, they finally decided to look at a site in a fast-growing area of southern California.

Orange County in southern California is one of the fastest-growing communities in the United States. A predominantly suburban community with middle-income and high-income sections, Orange County has become an attractive area for the development of regional shopping malls and neighborhood centers. South Coast Plaza, Orion Mall, Cerritos, Bullock's Fashion Square, and the City are prominent shopping attractions. All feature major department stores: Sears, Macy's, K-Mart, J. C. Penney's, May Co., Bullock's, Robinsons, Orbachs, The Broadway—and national, regional, and local specialty shops.

The regional mall has become increasingly important to consumers in southern California as gasoline prices and car expenses have soared in recent years. Mall traffic has increased significantly and continues to increase as consumers learn the advantages of one-stop shopping convenience.

Retailers, such as Carla Fashions, rely on the large chain stores, the "majors," to draw consumers to the mall. Major department stores can afford expensive advertising campaigns using radio, TV, newspapers, and direct mail, which the small retailer cannot afford. The retailer must draw the mall traffic into the specialty shop through attractive store design, eye-catching displays, acceptable pricing policies, superior customer service, and product differentiation or specialization.

Charisma, as an independent retailer faced by high rent in any attractive location, looked for a site that would enable it to use a cubic-space concept that could absorb an inventory large enough to make the operation profitable with limited floor space.

The optimum size for a Carla Fashions store is between 1600 and 2000 square feet of retail space in regional shopping malls and neighborhood centers in suburban locations. A location with 1600 to 2000 square feet can absorb an average inventory of $70,000 at retail price, with five to six stock turns per year by using vertical, double and triple rods, and flexible fixtures. At these numbers satisfactory sales volume can be achieved.

Rents vary from mall to mall and with the specific location within the mall: ground floor, second floor, central court, or at primary or secondary entrances. Today's rate for a prime location in a "strong" mall ranges from $8 to $10 a square foot. At these rates, plus environmental fees, mall association fees, and other fees, it is essential for the retailer to obtain an attractive location. Charisma was fortunate in securing for Carla a central court location within the Orion mall; the store contains 2600 square feet of floor space.

OTHER CRITICAL ITEMS

Other critical items Charisma took care of in site selection included leasehold allowance (amount of capital the developer was willing to spend to finish construction to meet Carla's needs), length of the lease, lease protection in the event of business reversal or natural disaster, percentage of overage dependent on business volume, and ownership of leasehold improvements such as carpeting, attached fixtures, and wall fixtures.

STORE DESIGN

Store design is also of critical importance. Some stores have incorporated the "antique" look into the decor to build a particular image. Carla has adopted the most modern concepts in store design. Within the cubic-space principle, a dynamic entrance; a strong and appealing window configuration; effective use of lighting; oval image synthetic glass ceilinged rotunda; and mirrored tree create a unified aesthetic design. Wall displays throughout the store suggest careful merchandise selection to the customer. The store colors have been chosen to be attractive and appealing, using earth tones—rust, brown, yellow, blue, and gray for a year-round, all-seasons look.

Organization

The retail store can be adequately staffed with a manager, assistant manager, and three to five salespeople. Wage and salary expense should not exceed 15 percent of the planned sales volume. All sales personnel are paid on a commission basis to encourage high productivity. Job descriptions have been included in the appendix for manager and sales positions.

Appendix I: Carla Fashions Retail Business Background

Retailing generally is divided into four classifications: department stores, mass merchandisers, discounters, and specialty stores. Department stores operate on a regional or national basis with services and diversified product lines in general merchandise: hardgoods, softgoods, casegoods, and apparel. Successful department stores tend to be regional, as are Dayton Hudson in the Midwest and Rich's in the South. The very successful Federated Stores are national. Department stores have come under increasing competition from discounters and specialty stores in recent years. A number of these stores are moving out of traditional product lines (hardgoods, appliances, furniture) with low profit margins and low rates of inventory turnover and concentrating on higher-profit-margin products such as apparel, cosmetics, softgoods, and life-style products.

J. C. Penney's, Sears, and Montgomery Ward are three leaders in mass merchandising. With stores nationwide, strong consumer identification, product price appeal, product quality and dependability, and strong marketing and promotional campaigns, the mass merchandisers offer products and services of many kinds to lower- and middle-income groups. High-income groups have also turned to mass merchandisers for appliances, casegoods, and hardgoods.

S.S. Kresge's K-Mart stores and J. C. Penney's Treasury stores are perhaps the best examples of the discounters, who have become increasingly significant in total retail trade in the last two decades. They offer little in the way of customer service, are unconcerned about the aesthetics of store design, rely on high rates of inventory turnover, and buy in large quantities from worldwide manufacturers.

Specialty stores offer products and services in general merchandise: women's and men's apparel, children's wear, sportsgoods, hardware, furniture, appliances. They seek to establish consumer identification by promoting a wide selection of products backed by courteous customer service. Typical examples are Radio Shack, a national organization of specialty stores in the electronics products field, and Casual Corner, a national organization specializing in women's apparel. Specialty stores tend to be most successful when they concentrate in a particular geographic region.

Appendix II: Financial Planning Details for Carla Fashions

CONTENTS

Break-Even Analysis

Pro Forma Income Statement

Monthly Sales Plan

Cash Flow (2-Month Sample)

Daily Sales Plan

Daily Sales Report

Merchandise Report—Average Unit Price

Vendor Structure

Grand Opening Advertising Proposal

Advertising Budget Summary

Employment Application

Job Descriptions—Store Manager and Sales

Break-Even Analysis, Orion Mall

Fixed Expenses	
Rent, environmental, utilities	$ 36,000
Wages, salaries, payroll taxes	42,000
Advertising	10,000
Insurance	1,700
Legal and accounting	1,500
Auto expense	1,500
Travel expense	1,500
Repairs and maintenance	750
Bank service charge	480
Credit card expense	3,600
Supplies	3,000
Interest (6% of $75,000)	4,500
Depreciation	7,000
Taxes	3,000
Total Fixed Expense	$116,530

Assumptions:
1. Assume gross margin of 40% of sales, cost of goods sold should not exceed 60% of sales volume.
2. Wages and salaries will vary with sales volume; for this exercise assume a sales volume of $350,000. Wages and salaries should not exceed 15% of sales; for the first full month payroll expenses including taxes total $3150. The assumption here is an expense of $3600 a month.

Break-Even Point: $116,530/0.40 $291.325

Carla Fashions
Pro Forma Income Statement

Sales per square foot	$ 113	$ 122	$ 132	$ 141
Sales	$300,000	$325,000	$350,000	$375,000
Cost of goods sold	$180,000	$195,000	$210,000	$225,000
Gross margin	$120,000	$130,000	$140,000	$150,000
Operating expenses				
Rent, environmental, utilities	$ 36,000	$ 36,000	$ 36,000	$ 37,500
Wages and salaries	42,000	44,000	46,000	48,000
Advertising	10,000	10,000	10,000	10,000
Insurance	1,700	1,700	1,700	1,700
Legal and accounting	1,500	1,500	1,500	1,500
Auto expense	1,500	1,500	1,500	1,500
Travel expense	1,500	1,500	1,500	1,500
Repairs and maintenance	750	750	750	750
Bank service charge	480	480	480	480
Credit card expense	3,600	3,600	3,600	3,600
Supplies	3,000	3,000	3,000	3,000
Depreciation	7,000	7,000	7,000	7,000
Interest	4,500	4,500	4,500	4,500
Total operating expenses	$116,530	$118,530	$120,530	$122,530
Earnings before tax	$ 3,470	$ 11,470	$ 19,470	$ 27,470
Taxes	(1,735)	(5,735)	(9,735)	(13,735)
Net income	$ 1,735	$ 5,735	$ 9,735	$ 13,735
Income as a percentage of sales	0.5%	1.8%	2.8%	3.7%

Monthly Sales Plan 1977–1978

Month	Volume (in $)	Percentage	
January	24,000	6.7	
February	24,000	6.7	
March	24,000	6.7	1st Quarter $72,000
April	24,000	6.7	
May	24,000	6.7	
June	24,000	6.7	2nd Quarter $72,000
July	30,000	8.4	
August	30,000	8.4	
September	35,000	9.7	3rd Quarter $95,000
October	30,000	8.4	
November	40,000	11.1	
December	50,000	13.8	4th Quarter $120,000
Total:	360,000		

Cash Flow Projections (in $), 2-Month Intervals, June 1–July 31

	6/1–6/4	6/5–6/12	6/12–6/17	6/19–6/26	6/26–7/3	7/3–7/10	7/10–7/17	7/17–7/24	7/24–7/31	8/1
Bank balance	13,800.00	9,600.00	8,150.00	8,850.00	5,200.00	6,400.00	350.00	5,050.00	6,640.00	6,240.00
Receipts	3,400.00	5,000.00	5,000.00	5,000.00	5,000.00	6,000.00	6,000.00	6,000.00	6,000.00	
Funds available	17,200.00	14,600.00	13,150.00	13,850.00	10,200.00	12,400.00	6,350.00	11,050.00	12,640.00	
Expenses										
Rent	5,250.00									
Payroll	1,550.00			2,000.00	3,000.00	1,500.00		2,000.00		
Taxes				1,100.00				1,360.00		
Construction			3,400.00							
Display			100.00						100.00	
Advertising	250.00	2,400.00	250.00		250.00		250.00		250.00	
Auto	50.00	50.00	50.00	50.00	50.00	50.00	50.00	50.00	50.00	
Purchases		13,000.00				10,000.00				
Other	500.00	1,000.00	500.00	500.00	500.00	500.00	1,000.00	1,000.00	1,000.00	
Total expense	7,600.00	16,450.00	4,300.00	3,650.00	3,800.00	12,050.00	1,300.00	4,410.00	1,400.00	
Balance	9,600.00	(1,850.00)	8,850.00	10,200.00	6,400.00	350.00	5,050.00	6,640.00	11,240.00	
Loan		10,000.00								
Loan repayment				5,000.00					5,000.00	
Balance forward	9,600.00	8,150.00	8,850.00	5,200.00	6,400.00	350.00	5,050.00	6,640.00	6,240.00	

Daily Sales Plan

Months	January–June	July, August, October	September	November	December
Monday	$ 300	$ 375	$ 450	$ 525	$ 650
Tuesday	500	600	700	820	1,025
Wednesday	575	700	820	950	1,200
Thursday	650	850	1,000	1,160	1,450
Friday	1,150	1,400	1,650	1,900	2,375
Saturday	1,750	2,200	2,600	3,000	3,750
Sunday	575	700	800	930	1,160
Weekly total	$5,500	$6,825	$8,020	$9,285	$11,610

These daily sales figures, if attained, translate into the anticipated volume in the monthly sales plan.

Daily Sales Report

Date _____
Day _____
NOZA# _____

Per Register Tape:
1. Cash (CaQ) _____(1)
2. Adjustments _____(2)
3. Net cash sales _____(3)
4. Layaway payments (RcQ) _____(4)
5. Adjustments _____(5)
6. Net layaway payments _____(6)
7. Charge sales (ChQ) _____(7)
8. Adjustments _____(8)
9. Layaway sales (Add tickets) _____(9)
10. Net charge sales _____(10)
11. Layaway paid outs (PdQ) _____(11)
12. Adjustments _____(12)
13. Net layaway paid out _____(13)
14. Refunds (RfQ) _____(14)
15. Deposit per register tape
(line 3 + 6 + 10 − 13) _____(15)

Actual Count:
16. Currency and coin _____(16)
17. Checks _____(17)
18. Total currency, coin and
checks (lines 16 and 17) _____(18)
19. Total B/A and M/C slips _____(19)
20. Actual deposit (18 and 19) _____(20)
21. Cash over or (short)
20-15 _____(21)

Number of refund transactions (RfQ) _____
List refund ticket number _____ and place refund tickets in daily detail envelope.
Refund tickets must be signed by customer and attached to original purchase receipt.

Layaway control:
Previous balance _____(1)
Layaway sales _____(2)
Layaway payments _____(3)
Layaway return to stock _____(4)

Daily Sales Report (*Continued*)

Current balance
(transfer to next report,
previous balance line 1)

_____

(Line 1 + 2 − 3 − 4)

Merchant copies of B/A and M/C slips and all void tickets should be placed in daily detail envelope.

Merchandise Report

Average Unit Price—Depts. 1–5

Date _____
Day _____

Departments	1	2	3	4	5
Sales					
Units sold					
Average unit price					

Total sales _____
Units sold _____
Average unit price _____

Vendor Structure

Dresses	Coordinates	Separates	
Act I	Panther	JPT	Disco Jeans
Gunne Sax	College Town	JWP	Laura International
Barbara Barbara	Ellen Tracy	Jackson Square	Peppermill
Phase II	J.H. Collectibles	Ellanee	Spare Parts
Nu Phase	Modern Juniors	Rose Hips	Smart Parts
On the Rocks	Patty Woodard	Mickey	
Jackson Square	Rose Hips	Unzarra	
Young Edwardian	Campus Casuals	Tucci	
	Latch-On	Jonathan Martin	
	Mushrooms	Gotcha Covered	
	Darling Debs	Coed Sportswear	
	Put ons	Crazy Horse	
		Barbara Barbara	

Concept

Lighthearted copy will be used for customer appeal. We are considering a

"What's Carla?"

theme, which could be directed to convey (1) store image, (2) in-store promotion, (3) selectivity of merchandise, (4) "what a Carla Girl is made of . . ." which would lead to the human elements involved.

Method

A combination of newspaper and direct mail requiring direct response with an incentive program will be used in order to ensure the greatest exposure into the primary trade area.

Newspaper

Grand opening ad:
Full-page ad (black and one color)
96 column inches at 7.99 per inch (discount extended to merchants reserving   ($767.00)
one full page or more)
Cost: $613.00
Ad to run in the *Orion Tabloid*
Date to run: April 28th Camera-ready art deadline: 4/22/77
Circulation:
50,000 inserted into the *Los Angeles Times* (to cover 8- to 9-mile radius of shopping center)
50,000 inserted into the *Santa Ana Register* (2-zone coverage)
Penetration factor: 70% of trade area

Direct Mail

$8^1/_2 \times 11$ personalized letter with tear-away coupon in certificate form at top of letter. (Letter will issue an invitation to customers personally to visit the store during the grand opening period and receive a 10 percent discount on any purchase made by tearing away the coupon and bringing it in.)

Enclosed with the letter will be a separate coupon to receive a *FREE SCARF* simply by bringing the coupon in and taking a look at the new store. No purchase necessary.

Another coupon will be used as an entry form to enter the drawing for $20 to $50 shopping sprees. The drawing would be held at the end of the grand opening period.

Another coupon will be used as an entry form to enter the drawing for the FIAT GIVE-A-WAY. This drawing would also be held at the end of the grand opening period.

COST:
10,000 mailing (2 miles radius of shopping center)
Residents list including apartments

Letter four-color printing, 65-pound high-bulk mustang paper. Three coupons, two-color
   printing, 60-pound mustang paper.

Printing, folding, and mailing	$ 275.00
Press setup	75.00
Postage, $7^1/_2$ cents each	750.00
Bulk mailing fee	40.00
Tax	23.70
Envelopes and inserting	220.00
	$1383.70

20,000 mailing (3- to 5-mile radius of shopping center)	
Printing, folding, and mailing	$ 500.00
Press setup	75.00
Postage, $7^1/_2$ cents each	1500.00

Grand Opening Advertising Proposal (*Continued*)

Bulk mailing fee	40.00
Tax	44.40
Envelopes and inserting	390.00
	$2559.40

Radio

At this time radio is not affordable for the opening as average 30-second commercial costs range between $70 and $90 per announcement.

To run a minimum flight of radio commercials at 18 spots per week on one station, the cost would be somewhere in the range of $1500 to $1800 per station. Also there would be the cost of producing the commercials, which can be quite costly.

Advertising Budget Summary

Media	
Direct mail	$2559.40
Newspaper	613.00
Layout, design, concept, and copy (Kittie Allen & Associates)	500.00
Production (typesetting, etc.)	60.00
Promotion	
Shopping sprees	1000.00
Scarf GIVE-A-WAYS	2000.00
Markdown (for 10% discount)	?
Flyers with entry form for shopping sprees to be on hand in store	50.00
	$6782.40

Anticipated return:
    Direct mail: 7 to 10% from a 20,000 mailing (1400 to 2000)
    Newspaper: 1% from a circulation of 100,000 (1000)

The entry form for the DRAWINGS will be used to create a mailing list for future promotions.

Employment Application

(Print)
Last Name   First Name   Middle Name   Today's Date

Home Address (Street and No.):   City   Zip Code   Home Telephone

Social Security No.:

Indicate desired
work schedule: Full time _____ Part time _____ Temporary _____
specify hours and
days available, if   Sunday   Monday   Tuesday   Wednesday   Thursday
part time   Friday   Saturday

What types of merchandise have you sold?

Education	Name of School	City	Circle Year Completed	Date Last Attended
High School:			9 10 11 12	
Tech or Trade School:			1 2 3 4	
College:			1 2 3 4	

Employment Record—List Current or Last Position First

(1)
Company name:

Address:

Your position and duties:

Reason for leaving:

Employed from _____ to _____

Start salary _____ Final salary _____

(2)
Company name:

Address:

Your position and duties:

Reason for leaving:

Employed from _____ to _____

Start salary _____ Final salary _____

(3)
Company name:

Address:

Your position and duties:

Reason for leaving:

Employment Application (*Continued*)

Employed from _____ to _____

Start salary _____ Final salary _____

<u>Applicant's Statement of Health</u>
Do you now or have you ever had any of the following (please check)

	yes	no		yes	no
Allergies			Hearing problem		
Arthritis			Hernia		
Asthma			High blood pressure		
Back trouble			Knee injury		
Broken bones			Nervous disorder		
Cancer			Skin disease		
Diabetes			Severe/frequent colds		
Fainting spells			Tuberculosis		
Epilepsy					
Eye trouble					

<u>Agreement</u>
I hereby affirm that my answers to the foregoing statements and questions on this application are true and correct. I agree, during employment with the company, to observe all rules and regulations adopted by Carla Fashions.

Applicant's Signature: _____ Date: _____

Job Descriptions

(G)

Position:
Store manager

Department:
Operations/Individual stores

Basic Function:
To supervise and coordinate the selling activities of the individual store. To assume authority and responsibility for store maintenance, customer service, operating activities, sales personnel, and workroom maintenance.

Reports to:
General manager

Duties and Responsibilities:
To supervise and coordinate the selling activities of the specific store. To determine appropriate work schedules for the store's employees. To evaluate the sales personnel on a periodic basis and make recommendations to the general manager in regard to retention, salary adjustments, and promotions. To determine the needs of part-time sales and support personnel during heavy-sales-volume periods, and to make recommendations to the general manager for final approval or disapproval on hiring or releasing such personnel. The store manager will also be responsible for training such sales personnel.

To be responsible for the maintenance and appearance of the sales area and workrooms of the store. To make recommendations to the general manager on the needs for major repairs and renovations. Maintenance of normal recurring items (heat, light, power, ventilation, air conditioning, use of janitorial service, etc.) will be the responsibility of the store manager. To make sure that the various workrooms are maintained and that merchandise is properly handled and distributed to the floor.

To be responsible for customer service. The sales manager will promote business enthusiastically, greet customers, determine appropriate customer needs and wants, and support the sales force during especially busy sales periods. The store manager should determine in conjunction with company policy the appropriateness of credit applications (to persuade or dissuade their use).

To have responsibility for receiving, checking, and marking merchandise. To determine with the assistance of the merchandise manager the appropriate store layout or display and stocking of merchandise in the sales periods, promotional activities, and timeliness of advertising. Merchandise for appropriate window and in-store displays should be selected by the store manager with assistance from the general manager and merchandise manager.

To be responsible for generating the various daily reports necessary for operation of the business. Daily business reports, deposits, sales analysis reports, inventory counts, merchandise movement reports, and the like should be either prepared, organized, or reviewed by the store manager daily before being routed to another department (accounting or merchandising). In addition to these duties, the store manager should determine the need for supplies, equipment, and other store property. Purchases of a material amount should be approved by the general manager.

To provide input into the buying process by participating in company meetings to discuss merchandise trends, meeting with vendors and manufacturers on a periodic basis, shopping competitors in the region, and working closely with merchandise manager to determine appropriate inventory levels, merchandise mix, product line and price determination, and the like, for the store. All merchandise purchases of a material amount should be approved by the general manager and/or the president.

(H)

Position:
Salesperson

Department:
Store operations

Basic Function:
To perform the daily, recurring sales activity.

Reports to:
Store manager

Duties and Responsibilities:
To greet customers, to determine customer needs, to locate merchandise for customer in the store, and to attend to the sales transactions (filling out the various sales forms and checking for correct information recording).

In addition to these duties salespeople will mark, stock, display, move merchandise, and perform other specific duties as directed by the store manager.

BUYING A GOING BUSINESS

Leo's Pharmacy, a sole proprietorship begun in 1920, is now over 65 years old. During its existence it has gone through several changes of ownership, but always as a sole proprietorship. Kurt Ziegler, a pharmacist, bought the store in 1972. He ran the business himself, aided by two women clerks.

After a decade of 6 days a week labor, Ziegler, 60 in 1982, got psychologically tired—burned out—and decided to sell the store and retire. He put the business on the market at a price of $95,000 in 1983.

By this time the midwest town in which Leo's Pharmacy was located had grown to 35,000 in population with another 15,000 in the agricultural area that surrounded the town. In 1978, Ziegler began to experience serious competition from a major chain drugstore, a supermarket, and two discount houses that had opened in the town. Each had installed a pharmacy section and both were selling many drugs at greatly reduced prices.

Ziegler's was the last individually owned pharmacy in town. He had carried forward customers from the previous owner, and in order to meet the new chain competition he had expanded his credit business somewhat hastily until it represented about 60 percent of his total volume. Major income was primarily from prescriptions; the balance came from nonprescription drugs, medical supplies, and miscellaneous knickknacks.

By 1980, Ziegler experienced a serious falling off in sales of high-volume proprietary drugs such as Motrin® and Premarin®. He discovered that his competitors were selling these kinds of drugs below their cost. These items were being used as loss leaders. Ziegler now worked hard to offer his customers generic equivalents of the popular proprietaries, generics that often he could buy for about 10 to 85 percent of the cost of the proprietaries. He added $4 to the cost of each prescription of a proprietary or generic as a service fee; this was his gross profit on each transaction.

Background of the Purchaser

Frank Kelleher was 34 years old when Leo's Pharmacy came on the market in 1983. His education included a B.S. in Pharmacy, an Associate in Nursing, and a Doctorate in Pharmacy from the University of Minnesota. His practical experience included 4 years as a physician's assistant, 1 year and 2 months as a medical corpsman in Vietnam, and 8 years as a pharmacist administrator in a large metropolitan hospital. In the latter position he supervised 10 pharmacists and 14 support personnel.

Tiring of big city life, he then moved to the smaller town much like that in which he had grown up. Here he worked as a pharmacist in the drug department of the chain store for 2 years, starting in 1983.

Kelleher had long wished to be his own boss. This desire was intensified by the constraints of working under formal conditions in the chain drugstore. His favorite professional work was compounding prescriptions for drugs not generally available, which could not be done in a chain drug department.

When Leo's Pharmacy came on the market, Kelleher approached Ziegler and explained his interest in acquiring the pharmacy. The asking price of $95,000 was far beyond Kelleher's reach. Reluctantly he put aside the idea of buying but kept in touch with Ziegler.

During the next two years, working in the chain drug department, Kelleher kept alert to the policies and practices under which he worked. He learned that the chain pharmacies are interested in high-volume sales on high-demand items. Regional managers dictate what high-demand items to carry. Hard to find items or those with a relatively small demand are ruled out, as they are considered lost shelf space. Chains buy high-demand items in large quantities at greatly reduced prices; these are then marked up to produce substantial profit—even though the selling prices are below standard retail prices.

Kelleher discovered that a common practice in the chain drug department was to charge at least half the price of the equivalent proprietary drug for the generic, even though often the cost may have been only 10 to 20 percent of that of the proprietary item. For example, Motrin®, a proprietary that cost $16.00 for 100 tablets, was sold for $14.50 per 100, thus becoming a loss leader. The generic equivalent, Rufed, cost $8.50 per 100 tablets and was sold for $12.00 per 100, ensuring a handsome profit. Another proprietary in high demand, Premarin®, cost $11.50 per 100 tablets and was sold for $9.95 per 100, producing a small loss. The generic equivalent, conjugated estrogen, cost $4.99 per 100 tablets and was sold for $7.49 per 100. Obviously, the generics were recommended whenever possible. Ziegler, not knowing of this practice in the chains, sold generics at his cost plus $4 a prescription. This scarcely covered his overhead at worst, and limited his profit at best. He sold proprietary drugs in the same way, adding $4 to his cost per prescription; this lost him many customers who believed he was overcharging when they compared his prices with those of the chain drugstores.

Background of the Business in 1983

After several visits to Leo's Pharmacy, drawn by the hope of acquiring it some day, Kelleher collected his observations and impressions of the business. The store was located at one end of a small in-line shopping center. Next door was a medical equipment supply store, and next to that a medical office. Access was readily available from the street, with adequate parking directly in front of the pharmacy. The store was located in the center of a middle-class neighborhood, old and well kept. The majority of customers came from within a 3-mile distance.

The interior of the store was clean and well arranged. A prescription counter ran alongside a recessed drug department at the left. A waiting area in front of the counter offered two comfortable chairs, a couch, and magazines for customers waiting for prescriptions. The balance of the store carried shelves around the walls and display counters in the center of the floor. Aisles were wide and made for ease of customer circulation.

Kelleher was satisfied with the physical arrangement of the premises. What concerned him at the beginning of 1984 was how he could possibly manage to work out a deal for acquiring the pharmacy. Ziegler had had no legitimate potential buyers during 1983. Those few inquirers had lost their interest when they learned of the intense competition they could expect from the chain pharmacies in the town. With the passage of time, Ziegler became less enthusiastic about holding on and reached a mood where a deal with Kelleher seemed possible. Ziegler had seen his gross revenue slip from over $300,000 in 1980 to $200,000 by the end of 1983—a disheartening situation. Kelleher believed the time was ripe to press for a deal that he could manage.

How the Financial Deal Was Packaged

Kelleher worked with Ziegler over a period of several meetings, gradually thrashing out the details that he could manage and that would be acceptable to Ziegler. Here are the elements of the final deal and how they were put together:

They arrived at a selling price of $50,000 for the business, provided certain conditions were met. The inventory of drugs on hand at the beginning of 1983 was worth $65,000. Ziegler would allow this to fall to about $35,000 through sales and attrition during 1983. Kelleher believed he could start the business successfully with limited drug supplies; if he needed a pharmaceutical that was out of stock, he could get overnight delivery from a metropolitan center 100 miles away. He planned to build up the stock as cash flow improved under his management.

Ziegler would reduce the value of inventory of merchandise from $31,000 to $15,000 by not replacing merchandise sold during the year.

Kelleher would take over the business on January 2, 1985.

Ziegler agreed to accept 10 percent down, or $5000 cash, which was all Kelleher could afford. Kelleher gave Ziegler a note for $45,000 at 12 percent interest for the balance of the payment.

Kelleher paid nothing for goodwill.

The next problem Kelleher faced was that of raising working capital to operate the business. He owned two automobiles and a pickup truck. Using these vehicles as collateral, plus a lien on the fixtures and inventory in the store, he borrowed $15,000 at $15\frac{1}{2}$ percent from the bank. This money allowed him to start in business.

Kelleher's Marketing Approach

Kelleher thought long and hard about the competitive position he would face as the sole proprietor of Leo's Pharmacy. He drew up a schedule of plans he would follow to build a clientele of satisfied customers. He determined to do the following:

Give intensely personalized service to each customer. Never treat the individual customer as just "a face in the crowd" or "take a number and wait until it's called."

Give customers a comfortable place to wait for prescriptions; keep waiting time to less than 10 minutes.

Know regular customers by name.

Give "senior citizen" discounts to anyone over 60.

Give professional discounts of 10 percent to medical professionals: doctors, dentists, nurses, and assistants.

Build rapport with the local doctors, encouraging them to call for information about new drugs or rarely specified ones—about such data as availability, usage, side effects, and compatibility with other drugs. Advise the doctors about the expertise available in compounding special prescriptions (which are profitable, and the chains are unable to do).

- Eliminate delinquent charge accounts; reduce the volume of credit business from 60 to 30 percent.

- Offer credit to creditworthy customers; recommend the use of Visa or MasterCard credit cards.

- Price shop competitive pharmacies to keep in step with them on popular proprietaries pricing.

- Undercut prices on frequently bought items such as aspirin, antacids, and laxatives; these will become loss leaders that will bring in customers who may buy more expensive and more profitable items.

- Compete with the chains by taking a leaf out of their book: If a customer insists on a proprietary drug, meet the chain's price even at a loss.

- Try to get customers to accept the generic drug; charge half the price of the proprietary in most cases, as the chains do.

- Set up a file of patient profiles to cross reference for possible drug incompatibility.

- Provide customers with statements for tax and insurance purposes.

- Furnish customers educational handouts about health problems.

- Offer free weekly blood pressure tests.

- Deliver prescriptions to handicapped or customers too ill to come to the pharmacy.

- Have available a private cubicle for counseling or offering advice on health problems.

- Build a reputation for carrying "one of a kind" or hard to find items—or being able to obtain them quickly.

- Use care about collections through Medicaid. (Medicaid will pay only the state allowed maximum price, which is based upon the lowest price listed for a given generic drug. If billing is submitted on a name brand drug, payment will be made according to the generic price, and a loss will result.)

- Do some advertising in the local and neighborhood papers. But build clientele primarily through word-of-mouth references from satisfied customers.

Financial Prospect

During the months that Kelleher worked in negotiating to buy Leo's Pharmacy, he developed financial projections to guide his management of the business. He was careful to repeat his projections on the basis of different assumptions. And he was cautiously conservative in his estimates. He projected sales, balance sheets, income statements, and cash flow for 4 years ahead. A small sampling of his projections is shown here:

Leo's Pharmacy
Projected Sales for First 4 Years

	1985	1986	1987	1988
January	$ 29,250	$ 37,513	$ 48,767	$ 56,082
February	28,500	36,551	47,517	54,644
March	27,750	35,589	46,266	53,205
April	25,500	32,704	42,515	48,892
May	23,250	29,818	38,764	44,579
June	19,500	25,009	32,511	37,388
July	18,750	24,047	31,261	35,950
August	19,500	25,009	32,511	37,388
September	22,500	28,856	37,513	43,140
October	25,500	32,704	42,515	48,892
November	28,500	36,551	47,517	54,644
December	31,500	40,399	52,518	60,396
Total:	$300,000	$384,750	$500,175	$575,200

There will be seasonal highs in colder months of the year due to increased respiratory ailments. Revenues are also expected to increase in December because of the holiday season.

Leo's Pharmacy
Balance Sheet
January 2, 1986

Assets	
Cash (beginning cash balance)	$ 5,000
Inventory	
Drugs	40,000
Front end merchandise	20,000
Fixtures	
Prepaid expenses	25,000
Rent (2 months)	1,500
Other advance payments	2,000
Cushion for unexpected costs	2,500
Total assets	96,000
Liabilities	
Bank loan	42,000
Proprietor's capital	54,000
Total liabilities	$96,000

Leo's Pharmacy
Balance Sheet Projections 1986

	July	Aug	Sept	Oct	Nov	Dec
Assets						
Cash	$ 21,244	$ 14,074	$ 280	($ 13,489)	($ 24,509)	($ 31,664)
Inventory	55,670	62,475	75,982	89,714	100,917	108,475
Fixtures	22,088	21,672	21,256	20,840	20,424	20,008
Prepaid expenses						
Rent (2 months)	1,500	1,500	1,500	1,500	1,500	1,500
Other advance payments	2,000	2,000	2,000	2,000	2,000	
Cushion for unexpected costs	2,500	2,500	2,500	2,500	2,500	2,500
Total assets	105,002	104,221	103,518	103,065	102,832	102,819
Liabilities						
Bank loan	15,463	11,672	7,881	4,090	299	0
Proprietor's capital	89,539	92,549	95,637	98,975	102,533	102,819
Total liabilities	$105,002	$104,221	$103,518	$103,065	$102,832	$102,819

Leo's Pharmacy
Projected Cash Flow Analysis 1986

	July	Aug	Sept	Oct	Nov	Dec
1. Projected sales	$18,750	$19,500	$22,500	$25,500	$28,500	$31,500
2. Cash sales (75%)	14,063	14,625	16,875	19,125	21,375	23,625
3. + Credit sales (25%)	4,875	4,688	4,875	5,625	6,375	7,125
4. Total cash receipts (2 + 3)	18,938	19,313	21,750	24,750	27,750	30,750
5. Costs of goods sold (70%)	13,256	13,519	15,225	17,325	19,425	21,525
6. + Ending inventory required	65,494	73,500	89,390	105,546	118,726	127,618
@ 85% of these values	55,670	62,475	75,982	89,714	100,917	108,475
7. Total required (5 + 6)	68,926	75,994	91,207	107,039	120,342	130,000
8. − Beginning inventory	50,426	55,670	62,475	75,982	89,714	100,917
9. Purchases required (7 − 8)	18,500	20,324	28,732	31,057	30,628	29,083
10. Cash payment (75%)	13,875	15,243	21,549	23,293	22,971	21,812
11. Credit payment (25%)	4,625	5,081	7,183	7,764	7,657	7,271
12. Total payment (10 + 11)	18,500	20,324	28,732	31,057	30,628	29,083
13. Salary—proprietor	1,689	1,723	1,757	1,793	1,828	1,865
14. Salary—other	1,125	1,170	1,350	1,530	1,710	1,890
15. Total salaries (13 + 14)	2,814	2,893	3,107	3,323	3,538	3,755
16. Rent	800	800	800	800	800	800

Projected Cash Flow Analysis 1986 (*Continued*)

17. Advertising & promotion	165	165	250	330	440	550
18. Delivery charges (0.6%)	113	117	135	153	171	189
19. Supplies & postage (1.2%)	225	234	270	306	342	378
20. Taxes (payroll, state, etc.)	281	293	338	383	428	473
21. Insurance (0.8%)	150	156	180	204	228	252
22. Travel & entertainment (0.4%)	75	78	90	102	114	126
23. Bad debt (4%)	750	780	900	1,020	1,140	1,260
24. Professional fees (0.3%)	56	59	68	77	86	95
25. Telephone (1%)	188	195	225	255	285	315
26. Other operating expenses (2%)	375	390	450	510	570	630
27. Total payments (15 to 26)	5,992	6,159	6,812	7,462	8,141	8,822
28. Beginning cash balance	26,798	21,244	14,074	280	(13,489)	(24,509)
29. + Cash receipts	18,938	19,313	21,750	24,750	27,750	30,750
30. Total cash available	45,736	40,557	35,824	25,030	14,261	6,241
31. − Cash outlays (12 + 27)	24,491	26,483	35,544	38,519	38,770	37,905
32. − Interest expense						
33. Cash balance before borrowing	21,244	14,074	280	(13,489)	(24,509)	(31,664)
34. Additional borrowing						
35. Cumulative borrowing						
36. Cash balance after borrowing (33 + 34)	$21,244	$14,074	$ 280	($13,489)	($24,509)	($31,664)

Leo's Pharmacy
Projected Income Statement 1987

Projected sales	$24,047	$25,009	$28,856	$32,704	$36,551	$40,399
Cost of goods sold	16,833	17,506	20,199	22,893	25,586	28,279
Gross margin	7,214	7,503	8,657	9,811	10,965	12,120
Salary—proprietor	1,689	1,723	1,757	1,793	1,828	1,865
Salary—other	1,443	1,501	1,731	1,962	2,193	2,424
Total salaries:	3,132	3,224	3,489	3,755	4,022	4,289
Rent	800	800	800	800	800	800
Advertising & promotion	165	165	250	330	440	550
Delivery charges	144	150	173	196	219	242
Supplies & postage	289	300	346	392	439	485
Taxes	361	375	433	491	548	606
Insurance	192	200	231	262	292	323
Travel & entertainment	96	100	115	131	146	162
Bad debt	962	1,000	1,154	1,308	1,462	1,616
Professional fees	72	75	87	98	110	121

Projected Income Statement 1987 (*Continued*)

Telephone	240	250	289	327	366	404
Other operating expenses	481	500	577	654	731	808
Depreciation	416	416	416	416	416	416
Total payments:	4,219	4,332	4,871	5,405	5,969	6,533
Net profit (loss)	(137)	(53)	297	651	975	1,298
YTD profit (loss)	6,062	6,009	6,306	6,957	7,932	9,229

Since acquiring the pharmacy, Kelleher has made it standard practice to revise his projections every month. These are estimated on the basis of actual figures from the monthly business activity. He plans to continue doing this as a matter of good management.

In 1984, the last year Ziegler operated the pharmacy, his gross volume was approximately $200,000, with an income after taxes of $14,000. Under Kelleher's management, through the marketing planning outlined, the pharmacy produced a gross income of a little over $400,000 in 1985 with a small profit. The bank loan was paid off and the store's inventory increased to $93,000.

As 1985 drew to a close, Kelleher was pleased with the steadily improving volume of sales and increasing income. Gross income by the end of 1985 topped $400,000. These results Kelleher attributed specifically to the marketing planning that he had brought to reality. He could now draw money from the business without straining its finances. He started doing this in 1986 after taking bare living expenses in 1985.

He met his objective of $500,000 gross income in 1986 and planned to reach $575,000 in 1987. At that point he believed the business possible in the existing facility would top out. He would be at a time of decision: If he wished to grow, he would have to relocate to larger quarters and add more employees—at least a third clerk and an assistant pharmacist. He planned to be prepared to make that decision when the time seemed ripe.

PEAK ELECTRONICS[2]

Donald Peak had been a manufacturer's representative selling electronic components, primarily miniature insulators, in the greater southwestern United States during the early 1960s. He had observed in this experience that no manufacturer of insulators was adequately satisfying the experimental and pilot-run needs of either small or large users. Although Mr. Peak had no formal training as an engineer, he was technically competent and had a flair for design. After he conducted extensive market surveys, he decided to abandon his job as manufacturer's representative and start his

---

[2]From Hans Schollhammer and Arthur H. Kuriloff, *Entrepreneurship and Small Business Management*. Copyright 1977 by Arthur H. Kuriloff and John Hemphill, pp. 590–595. Reprinted by permission of John Wiley & Sons, Inc.

own business. He formed a sole proprietorship to manufacture miniature insulators by a unique technical process that he originated.

He developed a basic marketing strategy for providing full prototype and pilot-run service to all customers. His company now offered both an off-the-shelf product line of high-quality insulators and the special capability of satisfying the short-run needs of small and large manufacturers quickly and at low cost.

Company Background

The company started with three employees in Mr. Peak's garage. Within 4 years the company experienced such growth that it moved to a 12,000-square-foot facility and employed 45 persons. It was incorporated as Peak Electronics in 1968. With an expanding market and Mr. Peak's ingenuity and drive, the company added capacitors and precision delay lines to its products. Sales reached $300,000 in 1970 and doubled during the next 2 years. Mr. Peak projected the 1975 volume to be at least $2,000,000.

Donald Peak attributed the success of the company to four major factors. First, the sound technical design of products was reflected in the acceptance given the products by the company's many customers and the repeat business the company enjoys. Second, the company's technical strategy, and marketing strategy and segmentation give it the ability to provide short-run or pilot production quantities quickly and economically. (The minimum order is 275 pieces.) The company builds and controls its own tooling; therefore, it can meet special design requirements in short order. Third, the company maintains a strong financial position through sound fiscal practice: Peak employs a stringent credit and collection policy. Fourth, an important factor in the success of the company is the loyalty of key personnel, who have worked hard and long to ensure productive output. Many key people in the company view their loyalty as being to the president, Donald Peak, personally.

Organization Structure

Personnel in 1973 comprised 70 operators and assemblers, and 12 persons serving in supervisory or staff positions. Although positions and reporting relationships were loosely defined, the organization appeared to be as shown in the accompanying organization chart (Figure 1).

Most employees in supervisory or staff positions had started with the company as soon as they had completed high school. A few, including Dennis Thompson, Tom Wacker, and Stan Sanders, were taking evening courses toward a college degree. Howard Warner had worked with the company since it had operated in Mr. Peak's garage. He was appointed vice president in 1969. Close family ties were ubiquitous in the organization. For example, John Peak was the son of Donald Peak, Jim Hill was the son-in-law of Donald Peak, Dennis Fritz was the son of Sylvia Fritz, and Bob Carnes was married to the daughter of Bonnie Parks. Several family relationships existed at the operator and assembler level.

The clerical group took care of phone-in order-taking activities and secretarial duties. The production section, the largest operating unit, manufactured miniature insulators and was headed by Jim Hill. Dennis Fritz and Tom Wacker shared su-

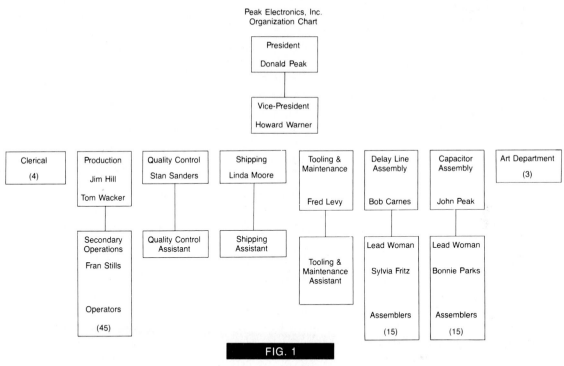

Peak Electronics, Inc.
Organization Chart

FIG. 1

Peak Electronics Inc. organization chart.

pervision and training duties with Jim Hill, while Fran Stills assisted in supervising and working in the secondary operations activities: primarily filing, drilling, and deburring the insulators.

As indicated on the organization chart, all supervisors and staff persons reported to Donald Peak and Howard Warner. Linda Moore in shipping, however, reported only to Mr. Warner.

Stan Sanders had the responsibility for "100 percent testing" of all products. Linda Moore, like Hill, Fritz, Sanders, Levy, and several others, had been with the company over 5 years. She received raw material shipments and prepared Peak Electronics' products for delivery. Fred Levy prepared precision tools and molds for production.

The delay line and capacitor assembly sections were relatively new, having been formed in 1970. Donald Peak hired Bob Carnes away from a competitor because his technical expertise would help the company get into the manufacturing of delay lines and capacitors. Mr. Carnes trained John Peak, the president's son, to supervise the capacitor unit. The lead women trained new workers for their unit and provided coordination assistance in addition to their assembly tasks.

Outside Advice Is Enlisted

In September 1973, Donald Peak asked two management consultants to analyze the company and help him to redesign the organization. It was learned that the company would move to a new location in the northern part of the state and begin operations there in January 1974. Mr. Peak gave as reasons for the move the need for a larger and more stable pool of labor, an expanded and more modern facility, and easier access to customers. In redesigning the organization, Mr. Peak emphasized his desire to devote more of his attention to the marketing aspects of the business and to spend more time pursuing other business interests and leisure activities.

He stated that he was considering the implementation of the 4-day work-week in the company. He asked the consultants to determine the feasibility of such action and to provide their conclusions in the final report. He summarized by saying to the consultants, "I want to clean up all the problems before we move into our new plant."

Interviews Provide Raw Data

After the consultants became familiar with the operational aspects of Peak Electronics, they conducted several depth interviews. Data were obtained from all supervisory and staff personnel and from a sample of operators and assemblers. The interviewees seemed to welcome the opportunity to discuss internal aspects of the company with the consultants. Although the interviews were anticipated to last 30 to 40 minutes, many continued for more than an hour, and some lasted twice that long. Several interviews were conducted to obtain additional data and to check for reliability.

The data were grouped into six categories, and a content analysis was conducted. Responses from the interviewees are reproduced below for each category. The comments were selected on the basis of frequency of mention. The last category, morale, includes data that either overlap or tend to clarify data in other categories.

INTERPERSONAL RELATIONS

"Talking among ourselves while working used to be outlawed, but now it's tolerated."

"There is a mismatch of personnel and positions, especially at the supervisory level."

"Bob Carnes is after Howard Warner's job and everybody knows it."

"Mr. Peak is moody, unfair, and unpredictable; you can't get his undivided attention."

"We need more direct communication in this company, and less gossip."

"People don't view Howard Warner as a vice president; he's just one of the boys."

"Family squabbles tend to interfere with the work sometimes."

COMPENSATION POLICY

"It pays to lay low and keep quiet in the company. If you don't make waves, you get the same raise as everyone else regardless of how hard you work."

"Superior work isn't rewarded."

"We need a sick leave and overtime policy for salaried people."

"It's a complete mystery to most people around here as to how they are evaluated."

"Mr. Peak has always insisted on hiring people at the minimum wage and only grants raises after a one-month trial period."

WORKING CONDITIONS

"The place needs a janitor; it's dirty all the time."

"I wish we could have music. It would help pass the time."

"Our work is dull, hot, and dirty."

"Even the hourly people are sick and tired of working six days every week. We know orders need to be filled, but nine months of this is long enough."

TURNOVER AND ABSENTEEISM

"John Peak's capacitor group supposedly has 8 to 10 jobs, but only 5 or 6 people usually show up."

"Absenteeism sometimes runs as high as 50 percent. I think most people think up some excuse to get two days off each week."

"Turnover in assemblers has caused a 'rat-race' for the past couple of years."

"I'll bet 60 percent of the assemblers and operators quit each year."

MANAGEMENT SUCCESSION

"Mr. Peak can't handle the tremendous work load—he should delegate more."

"Howard Warner is just a high-priced delivery boy and messenger."

"I don't see any evidence of planning or thinking ahead."

"Dennis Fritz is viewed as the most likely replacement for Howard Warner."

MORALE

"During Mr. Peak's month-long vacation, the company had an extraordinary volume. When he returned, you couldn't tell whether he was pleased or not."

"It would help if Mr. Peak were interested in you as a person—he used to be!"

"We need clarification of jobs around here."

"It will be difficult to get respect for supervisors who have been drones."

"Mr. Peak should stop touring the departments. He disregards supervisors and mostly criticizes as he goes—it disrupts people unnecessarily."

"I think Mr. Peak likes to see people capitulate."

"The Peak family causes problems. John gets paid more than any employee and he doesn't do anything—people don't know what he does."

"Mr. Peak leads people by fear and intimidation."

"Mr. Peak doesn't compliment anyone, and his demands are excessive."

"I didn't know I was a supervisor until I was informed of this interview."

"Nobody has defined authority and responsibility in the company."

"People go to Dennis Fritz with problems; Jim Hill and Tom Wacker yell at them too much."

"There's some clannishness, and confrontation between families causes problems."

"Turnover is extremely high, and the operators are unhappy across the board."

"The company runs smoother and people feel more relaxed when Mr. Peak is gone."

"I'm tired of being yelled at every day; supervisors show no respect for their people."

"Too many people overlap in their work."

Peak Reacts to the Data

The consultants summarized the data so as to assure anonymity of the speakers. They then reviewed their findings with Mr. Peak. After hearing some of the comments related to compensation, he said, "I just informed people of their raises a month ago and told them why they got what they did. I think they're just bickering." One of the consultants replied that "perceptions tend to form an individual's view of reality." As the review continued, Peak asked a few questions for clarification and listened quietly.

The consultants then proceeded to prepare their final report.

A CASE OF SUMMARY TERMINATION

Gene Wildcroft became national sales manager for Pleiades Motor Homes, Inc., a midwestern motor home manufacturer that was one of five such companies scattered across the country. All were owned by a holding company, Arcturus, Inc., located in Texas, and each was set up to operate nationally as a profit center. Coordinating the operations of the five plants was Luke Moynihan, executive vice president of the holding company.

Being well acquainted with the volatile characteristics of the recreational vehicle (RV) market and the unfavorable reputation of many companies for turning out jerry-built products, Wildcroft had been wary of this opportunity when it was offered and was hesitant to accept the deal. He insisted on an employment contract. This was a requirement not normally asked for or habitually given by the Pleiades company. The president of Pleiades, Terry Ranford, was an old and respected associate of Wildcroft's. Ranford had been production supervisor of a motor home manufacturing plant that Wildcroft had managed some years before. Because Ranford had recruited him for the sales manager's position, Wildcroft believed it safe to make the deal. Ranford simply copied his own one-page letter contract and filled in Gene Wildcroft's name; both signed the document. The contract is reproduced here:

PLEIADES MOTOR HOMES, INC.
Elkhart, Indiana

April 20, 1984

Mr. Gene Wildcroft
11006 Bluewater Ave.
San Francisco, CA 94034

Dear Gene:

The purpose of this letter is to confirm your appointment as Vice President—Sales and Marketing of Pleiades Motor Homes, Incorporated.

1. Effective Date: On or before May 4, 1984.
2. Base Salary: $60,000 per annum.

3. Bonus: One percent (1%) of the pre-tax operating earnings of Pleiades Motor Homes, Incorporated.
4. Company Car: You will be assigned a company car (1984 Oldsmobile 88) including applicable operating expense.
5. Relocation: All reasonable relocation expense such as interim living expense and movement of furniture shall be reimbursed.
6. Other: In the event your employment is terminated for any reason other than for "cause" during your first year of employment, Pleiades Motor Homes, Incorporated, shall reimburse you in an amount representing one year's then current base salary which shall be no less than $60,000.
7. Insurance and Other Benefits: You shall participate in the normal executive benefit program offered by Pleiades Motor Homes, Incorporated.

On behalf of everyone at Pleiades Motor Homes, Incorporated and its parent, Arcturus, Inc., we are proud to welcome you to our organization and we look forward to a long and mutually rewarding relationship.

Accepted By:

Gene Wildcroft
Gene Wildcroft

Date: __4/20/84__

Terry Ranford
Terry Ranford, President
Pleiades Motor Homes, Inc.

A week later, Wildcroft assumed the position, having moved his furniture and household possessions to Elkhart, Indiana, where Pleiades was located.

Gene Wildcroft's Background

Gene Wildcroft was 43 years old at the time he assumed the post of national sales manager for Pleiades Motor Homes. His work history almost always centered in selling and marketing. Often the work involved developing a new business or turning around a business whose profits were flagging; these efforts involved innovative marketing.

Of major importance in his work history was his 11-year experience with the largest swimming pool contractor in the west, Sierra Industries. Here he began by soliciting buyer's insurance for swimming pools. He worked into finance and credit management with the corporation, and then into general management. Subsequently, as manager of Sierra's northern California operations he gained experience in swimming pool construction. He rose to vice president in charge of Sierra's western gunite pool division, where sales reached $20 million annually.

Sierra Industries bought Friendship Motor Homes, a manufacturer with a new plant in a small town in southern California. Wildcroft was appointed president of Friendship, which was set up as a subsidiary of Sierra. Here he was given the mission of building a viable business. In the 4 years he held this position he accomplished the objective of building the business to the satisfaction of the parent company. However, the motor home industry went into a steep decline during the fuel crisis of 1973–1974. Sierra was forced to close out the Friendship subsidiary.

Wildcroft's experience during this crisis period gave him insights into every phase of motor home manufacture, marketing, and finance. He faced and had to overcome personnel problems that included a threatened strike and high turnover of middle management engineers and supervisors. During this troubled time he worked closely with Terry Ranford, who was plant production supervisor, and they became friends.

This experience, among others like it, tended to modify Wildcroft's managerial behavior. In his earlier roles his success resulted from his hard-driving, energetic, imperious style of management—typical of superior sales personalities. However, as often happens when the needs of specific jobs moderate behavior, Wildcroft's increasing career responsibilities developed in him at least a patina of compassion for the human needs of his personnel.

Wildcroft next started a small solar energy business with a partner. This business focused on contracting the installation of solar hot water systems for the home. It grew steadily until the recession of 1982. Wildcroft sold out to his partner, who took over the business in 1983.

Wildcroft then bought a travel agency and turned his energies to building its future. He directed the business toward medium-sized accounts with recurring travel patterns, exploiting his wide contacts from his previous business experiences, particularly with key executives, marketing managers, and purchasing agents. Because the travel agency did not at that time provide enough cash flow to meet Wildcroft's living needs, he was receptive to Terry Ranford's offer to become national sales manager of the Pleiades firm of which his old friend was president.

What Happened

Luke Moynihan, the executive vice president of Arcturus, Inc., the holding company that owned Pleiades Motor Homes, visited Pleiades about once a month. From the first meeting there was friction between Moynihan and Wildcroft. Although Moynihan was not responsible for the operation of the facility or its profitability, he arrogated to himself active participation in its affairs. He ran management meetings during which he issued arbitrary orders, cutting across the established authorities and responsibilities of the management staff.

Moynihan had come up in his background through the automobile manufacturing route. He had been for several years a middle manager for General Motors and later held a management position in the ill-fated DeLorean adventure in Ireland. After that he moved to an executive position in a Dublin manufacturing plant that made "caravans" such as the gypsies use in traveling about Ireland. He later returned to the United States, where he wound up as executive vice president of Arcturus, Inc., the holding company that owned Pleiades Motor Homes.

Moynihan had risen through the ranks in the harsh ambience of the automotive industry where the order of the day was to be completely directive in management. His behavior was grounded in the bull-of-the-woods approach—or what might be more elegantly called authoritarian.

From their first meeting friction erupted between Moynihan and Wildcroft. Wildcroft took exception to sales policies and promotional material that Moynihan had prepared; this difference in opinion opened a gap between them. Wildcroft believed that Moynihan did not understand recreational vehicle marketing strategies. For example, Moynihan's brochures were comparable with those used in the automobile industry, concentrating on specifications and performance data. Wildcroft's approach, based on wide experience in marketing in the RV field, emphasized interior features, color coordination, floor plans, ingenious appliances—promotion aimed at emphasizing the glitz of the vehicle, not its mechanical design. This practice was that used by the more successful RV producers.

Other issues arose between Wildcroft and Moynihan. Moynihan's handling of salespeople was opposed to Wildcroft's. Moynihan laid out a specific schedule of number of sales pitches to be made each day, insisted that the salespeople follow a canned sales presentation, and was generally dictatorial. In a couple of petty instances, Moynihan took exception to Wildcroft's beard and told him to shave it off. Wildcroft refused. Informality and profanity were the norm in offices and on the factory floor. Moynihan in puritanical fashion was openly critical of Wildcroft's and Ranford's standards of deportment. They considered him a hypocrite. Wildcroft, on the other hand, tailored his approach to the salespeople on the basis of feedback about their current experiences in the market. Wildcroft in this way tried to remain flexible, and through adjusting sales techniques to the requirements of the market, to stimulate the salespeople's initiative.

Thus there was a large psychological gap between Wildcroft's and Moynihan's behavior; the behavior of each was evidenced by a difference in managerial style. Although in many instances he did not understand the problem, Moynihan made snap decisions and insisted that they be carried out. Wildcroft, on the other hand, with his wide experience in selling and marketing, was more careful in assessing business problems and applying relevant knowledge to their solution.

Wildcroft Is Terminated

The motor home market tends to be extremely volatile. Sales are linked to fuel prices, fluctuations of the interest rate, and the ups and downs of the costs of financing. The market segment for the relatively midrange motor homes fabricated by the Pleiades company numbered a majority of typically retired blue collar workers. Such customers were particularly sensitive to these varying expenses, and these factors exaggerated the fluctuation in RV sales versus those of automobiles.

During the spring of 1984 when Wildcroft went to work for the Pleiades company, the motor home market was soft and sales were off from previous periods. Moreover, there were major quality problems with the product, and coaches were being rejected by the dealers. Some of these units had been delivered in previous accounting periods and returns were recorded in the sales journal as negative sales. All this resulted in record-breaking losses for the quarter ending June 30, Wildcroft's first accounting period on the job. The total sales dollars amount was a negative figure. Wildcroft had been on the job 10 weeks at this point.

On orders from Moynihan to Ranford, as the president of Pleiades, Wildcroft was terminated for "cause" the first week in July. Ranford strongly opposed this decision but was told to fire Wildcroft or lose his job. Wildcroft demanded reimbursement under the terms of his contract. Moynihan refused. Wildcroft advised the company that he would start legal action to obtain compensation due him.

The lawsuit that eventually ensued centers around a definition of the word "cause." At the time Wildcroft and Ranford entered into the contract agreement, Wildcroft had asked Ranford what was meant in the contract by the wording that "he could be terminated for cause."

Ranford told him that it was for the usual reasons—"stealing, lying, cheating, or insubordination." It immediately became clear that in Moynihan's lexicon "cause" included falling sales and a number of petty side issues.

After Wildcroft left the company, depositions were taken from other members of the staff about Wildcroft's performance. One specific was the question of authorization for the return of a defective coach from a distributor, which Wildcroft was said to have approved without higher authority. Another centered on the question of how daily contact with district salespeople was to be accomplished. A third was the allegation that Wildcroft could not write a proper letter. In the comptroller's deposition was the remark that "no one but Moynihan could write a proper letter."

The Lawsuit

Legal action was filed in the Federal District Court in San Francisco because the corporation had nationwide operations: the Pleiades plant was in Indiana, the parent corporation was in Texas, and the plaintiff, Wildcroft, lived in San Francisco. The parent company employed a prominent Los Angeles law firm and Wildcroft used a San Francisco attorney with whom he had a long relationship. Depositions were taken at the Pleiades plant in Indiana, and at other plants in Florida, Tennessee, and Ohio where key personnel were located.

Delays and postponements ensued and the action did not reach the courtroom for 26 months. Needless to day, expenses to both the plaintiff and defendant were substantial. Aside from attorneys' fees, travel expenses, transcriptions and long-distance telephone calls, charges accumulated and required out-of-pocket payment. This held true for both plaintiff and defendant, with one exception. Wildcroft's case seemed solid, so his attorney took it on a contingency basis.

Although the original suit did not name Arcturus, Inc., the parent holding company, as a defendant, after proceedings started it became evident that they must be named in the complaint as the initiative for Wildcroft's termination had been made by Moynihan, the executive vice president of Arcturus. This development necessitated the intervention of the parent corporation's legal staff, thus adding significant costs to the defendant's legal efforts.

From its first contact, the Federal District Court advised that the case be settled out of court. The court opined that there was a narrow point of dispute where the facts were essentially agreed upon—and that a compromise on payment under the contract should be worked out. However, there was intransigence on both sides. Even though the attorney for the defense recommended settlement for a substantial payment, the president of the parent company, now involved, was adamant and refused to settle, believing that Wildcroft had no case. (Moynihan too had been terminated 12 months before the trial.)

The case went on the docket. A jury was impaneled. The trial went through attorneys' opening statements and 3 hours of Wildcroft's initial testimony. The court recessed until the following morning. Before the trial continued on the second day a settlement was hammered out among the attorneys and the trial was discontinued. The settlement agreed upon stipulated payment of 91.6 percent of the yearly salary of $60,000 stated in the contract. This was clearly a vindication of Wildcroft's position. Although he was reimbursed for most of the services he had contracted for, his expenses were great and the disruptions to his life were not compensated for. After paying his out-of-pocket expenses and attorney's fee, Wildcroft emerged from the legal experience with about $1/2$ year's salary.

The settlement was far from favorable for Wildcroft's employer. Legal expenses for the defense approximated the amount of the settlement. And the defendants' notion that the case would never come to trial proved wrong. Had the company simply paid off Wildcroft at the time he was terminated, the whole costly fracas would have been avoided.

As the depositions revealed, the Pleiades plant had gone through five sales managers in one year. Wildcroft was the only one who had had an employment contract.

NAUTILUS ENGINEERING CO., INC.[3]

Nautilus Engineering Co., Inc., of Portsmouth, New Hampshire, manufactures and distributes equipment used principally in the deep-sea-diving industry. Its main product is an environmental control unit, which is augmented by a line of other equipment for the industry. The company has a strong research and development commitment that supports its superior technical quality and marketing leadership in this growing field. Widely known for sophisticated technology, the company's products command the highest respect from divers whose lives depend upon their efficient operation. By achieving leadership in its field, Nautilus has had a 30 to 40 percent growth rate since its startup as a tiny three-man operation.

Background to the Consulting Assignment

The company has experienced a rapid surge in growth during the past year and now has more than 50 employees. With this growth the company has found it more and more difficult to meet production schedules. The chief executive officer, William Swanson, asked for a student team to help identify the problems that were affecting the firm's ability to meet schedules—and to suggest some solutions.

A team of three students started the consulting assignment by interviewing Mr. Swanson. The interview showed that the company had reached a stage in its growth that required more than the old one-to-one communications that had been adequate to keep production up when the company was smaller. The company now needed

---

[3]This case was prepared by Irwin Berger, Theodore Kreiver, and Joseph Montes.

an efficient control and communication system if it was to continue to be successful. Mr. Swanson could no longer get around often enough, or change hats fast enough, to take care of all the company functions that needed managing.

In a second interview, Mr. Swanson agreed that the students should interview his management team and workforce as necessary to find out what people believed was slowing down production. Interviews were thereupon scheduled with middle management and production personnel. The following report of the consulting assignment is in the students' own words.

SURVEY THROUGH INTERVIEWS

During four half-day visits to Nautilus, we asked all the managers to explain their jobs and to talk about the problems they faced. Our investigation focused at first on production employee absenteeism and tardiness. Through our discussions we learned that even though Nautilus has developed an industry-leading worker-benefit plan, the production schedule was still not being met.

We then directed our questions to the larger problem of production delays. After talking with a majority of the production employees and the operations, accounting, manufacturing, and marketing managers, we found that the cause seemed to center on the delay in arrival of component parts in the assembly area. This delay was causing workers, who were scheduled to work a 4-day week, to work 5 and sometimes even 6 days. The drive to do the job was high. Inability to complete units on schedule caused frustration.

During the course of the second interview, personnel spoke of problems in the inventory system, purchased parts ordering lead time, in-house fabricated parts, receiving inspection orders, back-order follow-ups, and the order and control documents.

THE CONSULTING APPROACH

It was evident that a large factor in employee frustration, and resulting absenteeism and lateness, was disruption of work caused by late arrival of assembly parts. A review of employee time records over the previous 2 months showed a 1.5 percent combined absenteeism and tardiness person-hour loss. This appeared to be a symptom of a more serious problem. Production delays were caused by lack of component parts, both purchased and fabricated in-house. The system of ordering and inventory control was still in the developmental stage. Each department was doing its best to make the system work, but effectiveness was far short of being adequate for the need.

At this point we had two options as a consulting team. We could analyze the parts problem and prepare a report recording our solutions. Or we could use an organizational development (OD) intervention method and have the Nautilus people identify the problems and find their own solutions. We believed that this participative approach had a higher probability of generating solutions that would be implemented than if we proposed solutions. When people directly involved define the problems and generate potential solutions, they commit themselves to make the changes work.

In the OD approach participants receive training in a method of effective group problem solving. With this group-problem-solving method, more time is spent in problem definition and study of alternatives. Individuals tend to spend much less time on applying Band-Aids, which in the end come unglued and leave them with missed opportunities and problems not much altered.

The suggestion was well received by the chief executive officer (CEO) William Swanson. The people at Nautilus have the skills, motivation, and energy to solve their problems and are currently in the process of doing so. We decided to propose the organizational development approach.

The Organizational Development Process

STAGE 1: ORIENTATION

1. The managers with the power, authority, and influence to manage the problems were gathered in a room and seated in a semicircle. The OD facilitator (one of us) was at the head of the table. People present were:

Name	Title	Reports to
William Swanson	Chief Executive Officer	
Elmer Rousseau	Controller	CEO
Oscar Bowles	Vice President	CEO
Harold Traynor	Manager of Manufacturing	Vice President

A number of people who would have given the group a total problem definition and solving capability were not present. They were:

Name	Title	Reports to
Sam Carruthers	Manager, Engineering	Vice President
Boyd Johnson	Purchasing Agent	Operations Manager
Tom Tripett	Stockroom Supervisor	Operations Manager

2. Two large chart pads and 3 × 5 cards were available.
3. A brief lecture was given explaining the process and stressing that:
   a. Spending efficient time on the definition of the problem would help them to arrive at an appropriate solution.
   b. They would "own" the problems they would define.
   c. No single person has the total ability to produce a workable system, but together they do.
   d. The group's areas of concern were frustration of employees and delays in production.
   e. There was no restriction on expression of any other problems.
4. Participants were asked in turn how they felt about being in the group. This loosening activity helps to lower psychological barriers and get ideas flowing.

STAGE 2: GENERATION OF POTENTIAL IMPROVEMENT POINTS

Potential improvement points are items that participants think need to be improved. They were instructed to make the points short and factual, and not personal. Points were to be stated, not proposals for solution or change. Example: "Lack of component parts," rather than "Increase size of inventory." Solutions were to be considered premature at this point.

1. Participants were requested to write their points without conferring with their neighbors.

2. They were asked, in turn, to state one point, which was then written on a large chart paper and a 3 × 5 card.

3. If persons did not want to give a point or did not have any more points to give, they said "pass."

4. The process was ended after three clear passes around the group with no additional points given. It was important that members express every point that was bothering them. (Unspoken points would continue to distract participants and interfere with the rest of the process.)

5. A short break was called.

STAGE 3: GROUPING OF THE POINTS INTO PROBLEMS

1. All points not accepted by the total group were discarded.
2. After much discussion, the *points* were grouped into the following *problems.*
   - T. Management Development
     1. Lack of utilization of subordinates.
     2. More realistic schedules and forecasts.
     3. Improved understanding of personnel handling by managers and supervisors.
     4. More freedom of communication among managers.
   - E. Engineering
     1. Lack of timely updating of bills of materials.
     2. Engineering changes made directly to vendors after parts placed on order.
     3. Method of better handling special projects.
     4. More timely bill of materials for new products.
   - I. Inventory
     1. Need for min/max system RE: spares, fabricated parts, hardware, expendables.
     2. Lack of fabricated parts in inventory.
     3. System and utilization of the inventory control system.
     4. Inappropriate inventory buildup.
     5. Less time on road by driver.
     6. Better inventory control for commercial and fabricated parts.
   - X. Follow-Up
     1. Better follow-up on purchased parts.

C. Commitments
    1. Improvement in the sense of commitment by personnel.
P. Paper Flow
    1. Lack of time for stockroom to accomplish daily reports.
    2. Lack of notification of stock being transferred to R&D.
    3. Daily P.O. location sheets. A possibility?—To accounting department.
    4. Speed with which paper flow must occur.
    5. Lack of communication (feedback) of order information to original requisitioner.
A. Production Efficiency
    1. Improve production efficiency.
    2. Lack of effective use of open stock.

STAGE 4: ESTABLISHING PRIORITIES

A priority value was established for each problem according to the following system:

1. Starting to the right of William Swanson, the senior group member, each member of the group made a judgment of when the problem had to be solved. They called out the S number from 0 to 10 (see table below). When the round arrived at Mr. Swanson, he called out his S number. If all numbers were within a range of 3, Mr. Swanson's number was posted. If the spread was greater than 3, a discussion ensued until the range narrowed to 3.

2. Using the same process, a B number value was determined for the time it would take for the problem to be solved by business as usual. This assumed no additional effort made by this group to solve this problem.

3. The priority was calculated by dividing S by B.

When does the problem have to be solved?		When will the problem be solved with no special effort applied?	
Time	S (shorter)	Time	B (business as usual)
0–3 months	8	0–3 months	10
3–6 months	6	3–6 months	8
6–12 months	4	6–12 months	6
1–2 years	2	1–2 years	4
2–3 years	1	2–3 years	2
3 years +	0	3 years +	0

Values used to establish priority: The following ranking resulted:

X	Follow-Up	2.5
I	Inventory	2.2
P	Paper Flow	2.0
C	Commitment	1.6
T	Management Development	1.33
E	Engineering	1.33
A	Production Efficiency	1.25

After group discussion of each problem, the top three were chosen on the basis of being solvable with the resources that the group had available to them. This meant these three problems would be worked on first: follow-up, inventory, and paper flow. Improvements sought were to speed up follow-up 2.5 times, flow of inventory 2.2 times, and paper flow 2.0 times.

STAGE 5: SETTING UP ACTION TEAMS

The following action teams were set up and the meeting was adjourned:

Action Team 1 Inventory	Action Team 2 Follow-Up	Action Team 3 Paper Flow
Sally Meadows	Sally Meadows	Elmer Rousseau
Elmer Rousseau	Boyd Johnson	Boyd Johnson
Harold Traynor	Martha Sinkwich	Sally Meadows
Penny Gerais		Penny Gerais
Tom Tripett		Tom Tripett
		Sam Carruthers

A fourth team will be required to determine the quality and rapidity of paper flow that top management needs and to give this information to task team 3.

**Action Team 4
Reporting Needs**

William Swanson
Elmer Rousseau
Anthony Gonzales
Oscar Bowles

HOW TO MAKE THIS OD PROCESS PAY OFF

1. Initiate the action teams and formalize their charter.

2. Organize the main team of William Swanson, Sally Meadows, Elmer Rousseau, and Harold Traynor to coordinate and support the action teams.

3. Conduct an OD process for each action team, similar to this reported main team exercise. This would bring out the specific improvement points for each team's narrower area of concern. Have one of the people who went through the original exercise be facilitator—but not be a member of that specific action team.

4. Provide time and priority for each action team to solve its chosen tasks within the schedule mutually agreed upon by the main team and action team.

5. If the action team does not have the technical expertise for a specific task, use an inside or outside consultant.

In our consulting experience with Nautilus we saw a group of people capable of working well together in an environment that promoted cooperative behavior. We helped them focus on a process that they can use to solve their inventory and paper flow problems. We believe that this OD process will be an effective tool for them if properly developed and used.

Appendixes

APPENDIX A
OUTLINE FOR DEVELOPING YOUR BASIC BUSINESS
PLAN (PROSPECTUS)

APPENDIX B
EXAMPLES OF BASIC PLANNING FOR THE SMALL
BUSINESS

APPENDIX C
HOW A TYPICAL MESBIC OPERATES

APPENDIX D
A SUCCESSFUL PROSPECTUS

APPENDIX E
HIRING, FIRING, AND DISCIPLINING EMPLOYEES

Outline for Developing Your Basic Business Plan (Prospectus)

In this appendix the Business Plan is shown in condensed reference form. As explained in Chapter 1, major headings throughout the text carry reference numbers that correspond to particular parts of the outline shown here. For example, the reference 1.A, 2.A says that the information given under the heading "You Must Know the Business" fits in the outline at point 1.A (description of proposed business) and at point 2.A (statement of the desirability of your product or service).

1. Executive summary
    A. Description of your proposed business
        (1) Describe your product or service
        (2) Support with diagrams, illustrations, or pictures (if available)
    B. Summary of your proposed marketing method
        (1) Describe the market segment (or submarket) you're aiming to reach
        (2) Outline the channel you plan to use to reach this market segment (retail, wholesale, distributors, mail order, or other)
    C. Summary of your financial estimates
        (1) State the dollars in sales you aim for in each of the first 3 years
        (2) State the estimated profit for each of the first 3 years
        (3) State the estimated starting capital you'll need
2. Statement of objectives
    A. Statement of the desirability of your product or service
        (1) Describe the advantages your product or service has, its improvements over existing products or services
        (2) State the long-range objectives and the short-range sub-objectives of your proposed business
        (3) Describe your qualifications to run the business
        (4) Describe the "character" you want for your business, the image you'd like your customers to see
3. Background of proposed business
    A. Brief summary of existing conditions in the business you're intending to enter (the "state of the art")
        (1) *Where* the product or service is now being used
        (2) *How* the product or service is now being used
    B. Detailed explanations of your place in the state of the art
        (1) Describe the projections and trends for the industry or business field
        (2) Describe competition you face (place competitors' advertisements and brochures in the appendix at the end of your prospectus)
        (3) State your intended strategy for meeting competition
        (4) Describe the special qualities of your product or service that make it unique
4. Technical description of product or service
    A. A complete technical description of product or service
        (1) Describe in a technically accurate way how the product works or how the service is used
        (2) Outline the tests that have been made and give the test data and results
        (3) Outline the tests that are to be made and describe the test objectives
        (4) State briefly your concepts for follow-on (next generation) products or services
5. Marketing strategy
    A. A comprehensive description of marketing strategy
        (1) Describe the segment of the market you plan to reach
        (2) Describe in full detail the distribution channel you plan to use to reach your market segment: retailers, jobbers, wholesalers, brokers, door to door, mail order, party plan, other
        (3) Describe the share of the market you expect to capture versus time

6. Selling tactics
   A. An outline of the activities to be used in selling the product or service
      (1) State the methods you expect to use to promote your product or service: direct calling, telephone, advertising, mail, radio, television, or other
      (2) Include a sample brochure or dummy advertisements, announcements, or other promotional literature
      (3) Present data supporting your ability to meet your sales goals: actual orders, personally known prospective key accounts, and potential customers
      (4) Explain the margins of safety you've allowed in your sales forecasts
7. Plan of operation
   A. Description of the proposed organization
      (1) Show an organization chart describing the needed business functions and relationships
      (2) Describe the key positions and identify the persons to fill them
      (3) Give résumés of the key persons
      (4) List equipment or facilities and the space and location required
      (5) Describe the research and development facilities you'll need
      (6) If manufacturing, outline the kind of production you'll do in-house and that to be subcontracted
8. Supporting data
   A. Information required to support the major points in the business plan
      (1) Include a set of drawings of the product to be manufactured or a detailed description of the service to be offered
      (2) Show a list of the tooling you'll require for production and estimated costs of the tooling
      (3) List the capital equipment you'll need and its estimated cost
      (4) Provide a layout of your proposed plan, supported by a manufacturing flowchart (include the estimated cost of manufacturing your product)
      (5) Give a packaging and shipping analysis
      (6) List a price schedule for your product or service
      (7) Include your detailed market-survey data
      (8) Supply the following financial data:
      (a) Projected income statement and balance sheet for the first 2 years by the month and for the third year by the quarter
      (b) Cash flow projection for 2 years by the month
      (c) Break-even chart for 2 years, by the year
      (d) Fixed asset acquisition schedule by the month, showing each item you expect to buy and its cost
9. Conclusions and summary
   A. A statement of proposed approach in starting the new organization
      (1) State the total capital you'll need, the safety factor you've used, and how the capital is to be made up:
      (a) Your share of the starting investment
      (b) How much more you'll need from others and when you'll need the money
      (c) What share of the business you'll give to the investors or lenders for this additional capital

APPENDIX A

593

Outline for
Developing Your
Basic Business Plan
(Prospectus)

(2) State how much profit you expect and when you expect to show it
(3) Tell what percentage of ownership you want for yourself and your partners
(4) Indicate the total capital you need and how it's to be made up
(5) State your planned schedule for starting your business

Examples of Basic Planning for the Small Business

In this appendix we include examples of planning for a retail bookstore and a small manufacturing concern, and also of planning assumptions and important parts of a business plan for a service firm. You can use these examples as guides for your projections and planning in developing a prospectus for your own business.

FINANCIAL PROJECTIONS FOR A BOOKSTORE

The following financial projections were prepared for a mythical bookstore. They are presented as a sample of the package of financial plans that should be made on an ongoing basis by all entrepreneurs. Although the bookstore, Tobias Booksellers, is fictional, the assumptions upon which these financial projections are based were drawn from real data graciously furnished us by the American Booksellers Association. In addition, we took some fundamental concepts and financial ratios from *A Manual on Book-Selling,* published by the American Booksellers Association, New York.

We've included here complete financial projections for the first year of operation of Tobias Booksellers, 1988. You'll also find a projection of planned sales for the years 1989 and 1990. These estimated sales are keyed to the business growth desired by the proprietor in those years.

These data will give you the opportunity to practice making financial projections. We suggest that, on the basis of the planned sales, you work up balance sheets, cash flow projections, monthly income statements, and yearly income statements for 1989 and 1990. If you do this before you start the financial projections for your business, you'll be well prepared to accomplish your planning readily and efficiently.

Two suggestions may help you in this learning process: (1) We've drawn some direction arrows on the cash flow analysis to show how key numbers are derived and how they are moved from column to column. (2) When you have a question about where a number comes from, go back to the assumptions. The assumptions will tell you the procedure for arriving at a specific quantity.

ASSUMPTIONS

The financial projections given here for a new bookstore were derived from the following assumptions:

1. The store opens for business on January 2, 1988.

2. The owner, an experienced bookseller, aims for a $30,000 gross income (before-tax income) from sales in the third year.

3. Sales volume is expected to increase 20 percent in each of the second and third years; thereafter the growth of the business will slow down gradually over a period of 3 years to 5 percent.

4. The business will generate $150,000 in sales the first year; with sound management this volume can be achieved in a store of 1500 square feet area. Rent costs 6 percent of this gross volume, or $9000 per year.

5. The inventory of stock will turn three times during the first year. Books for inventory are bought at 40 percent discount from the retail price. The *average* inventory at cost for the first year of business is therefore: 60 percent of $150,000 divided by 3, which equals $30,000.

6. Fixtures for the store cost $4000 and are to be depreciated at 1 percent a month.

7. Deposits and advance payments will require $3000.

8. A cushion for unexpected costs or setbacks will be included, in addition, at about $1000.

9. Estimated cash required to open the store:

Inventory (average per month)	$30,000
Three months' rent, at $750	2,250
Fixtures	4,000
Advance payments	3,000
Cushion for unexpected costs, at least	1,000
Total	$40,250

EXHIBIT 1

Balance Sheet
2 January 1988

Assets		Liabilities	
Cash (beginning cash balance)	$ 3,000	Bank loan	$10,000
Inventory	10,575	Proprietor's capital	15,000
Fixtures	4,000	TOTAL	$25,000
Two months' rent	1,500		
Other advance payments	3,000		
Cushion for unexpected costs	2,925		
TOTAL	$25,000		

EXHIBIT 2

Planned Sales

	1988	1989	1990
Jan	$ 6,000	$ 7,200	$ 8,640
Feb	8,500	10,200	12,240
Mar	9,000	10,800	12,960
Apr	11,000	13,200	15,840
May	13,000	15,600	18,720
Jun	10,500	12,600	15,120
Jul	6,500	7,800	9,360
Aug	6,500	7,800	9,360
Sep	10,000	12,000	14,400
Oct	13,500	16,200	19,440
Nov	16,500	19,800	23,760
Dec	39,000	46,800	56,160
	$150,000	$180,000	$216,000

Note: The book business tends to be highly seasonal, with much of the sales volume for the year occurring in the year-end holiday season. The planned, or forecasted, sales figures are therefore shown as building up heavily toward the end of the year.

EXHIBIT 3

Cash Flow Analysis for Tobias Booksellers—1988

	Jan	Feb	Mar	Apr
1. Planned sales (retail)	$ 6,000	$ 8,500	$ 9,000	$11,000
2. Cash sales (75%)	4,500	6,375	6,750	8,250
3. + Credit sales (25%)	0	1,500	2,125	2,250
4. Total cash receipts (2 + 3)	4,500	7,875	8,875	10,500
5. Cost of goods sold (60%)	3,600	5,100	5,400	6,600
6. + Ending inventory required	17,100	19,800	20,700	18,000
@ 75% of these values	12,825	14,850	15,525	13,500
7. Total required (5 + 6)	16,425	19,950	20,925	20,100
8. − Beginning inventory	10,575	12,825	14,850	15,525
9. Purchases required (7 − 8)	5,850	7,125	6,075	4,575
10. Cash payment (75%)	4,387	5,344	4,556	3,431
11. Credit payment (25%)	0	1,463	1,781	1,519
12. Total payment (10 + 11)	4,387	6,807	6,337	4,950
13. Salary—proprietor	0	0	0	0
14. Salaries—other (W-2)	378	378	546	546
15. Total salaries (13 + 14)	378	378	546	546
16. Rent	750	750	750	750
17. Advertising & promotion	500	150	100	100
18. Delivery charges (0.6%)	36	51	54	66
19. Supplies & postage (1.2%)	200	80	100	130
20. Taxes (payroll, state, etc., 1.4%)	84	119	126	154
21. Insurance (0.8%)	100	100	100	100
22. Travel & entertainment (0.4%)	50	50	50	50
23. Bad debts (0.1%)	0	8	9	11
24. Professional fees (0.3%)	150	0	0	100
25. Telephone (0.6%)	36	51	54	66
26. Other operating expenses (1.8%)	108	153	162	198
27. Total payments (15 to 26)	2,392	1,884	2,045	2,265
28. Beginning cash balance	3,000	5,846	6,110	7,074
29. + Cash receipts (4)	4,500	7,875	8,875	10,500
30. Total cash available	7,500	13,721	14,985	17,574
31. − Cash outlays (12 + 27)	6,779	8,691	8,382	7,215
32. − Interest expenses	75	114	123	127
33. Cash balance before borrowing	646	4,910	6,474	10,226
34. Additional borrowing	5,200	1,200	600	0
35. Cumulative borrowing	15,200	16,400	17,000	17,000
36. Cash balance after borrowing (33 + 34)	5,846	6,110	7,074	10,226

10. The proprietor plans to start with $25,000 cash investment with an inventory smaller than the average required for the year. The inventory will be built up rapidly as sales grow and the holiday season at the end of the year approaches. The proprietor invests $15,000 from personal savings and borrows $10,000 at the bank against a collateral of blue chip stocks worth $35,000 on the current market. Money will be borrowed against this collateral as the business shows the need for cash. Interest will be paid monthly on borrowings at the rate of 3/4 percent per month.

May	Jun	Jul	Aug	Sep	Oct	Nov	Dec
$13,000	$10,500	$ 6,500	$ 6,500	$10,000	$13,500	$16,500	$39,000
9,750	7,875	4,875	4,875	7,500	10,125	12,375	29,250
2,750	3,250	2,625	1,625	1,625	2,500	3,375	4,125
12,500	11,125	7,500	6,500	9,125	12,625	15,750	33,375
7,800	6,300	3,900	3,900	6,000	8,100	9,900	23,400
14,100	13,800	18,000	24,000	41,000	37,620	33,840	16,920
10,575	10,350	13,500	18,000	31,050	28,215	25,380	12,690
18,375	16,650	17,400	21,900	37,050	36,315	35,280	36,090
13,500	10,575	10,350	13,500	18,000	31,050	28,215	25,380
4,875	6,075	7,050	8,400	19,050	5,265	7,065	10,710
3,656	4,556	5,287	6,300	14,287	3,949	5,299	8,032
1,144	1,219	1,519	1,762	2,100	4,762	1,316	1,766
4,800	5,775	6,806	8,062	16,387	8,711	6,615	9,798
0	0	200	200	400	400	600	800
546	546	378	378	546	1,050	1,400	1,600
546	546	578	578	946	1,450	2,000	2,400
750	750	750	750	750	750	750	750
100	100	100	300	200	250	400	500
78	63	39	39	60	81	99	234
150	100	70	70	100	150	200	450
182	147	91	91	140	189	231	546
100	100	100	100	100	100	100	100
50	50	50	50	50	50	50	50
13	10	7	7	10	13	16	39
0	0	100	0	0	100	0	0
78	63	39	39	60	81	99	234
234	189	117	117	180	243	297	702
2,275	2,112	2,035	2,135	2,590	3,451	4,252	5,999
10,226	15,518	11,623	10,201	6,423	8,480	9,772	21,077
12,500	11,125	7,500	6,500	9,125	12,625	15,750	33,375
22,726	26,643	19,123	16,701	15,538	21,105	25,522	54,452
7,075	7,887	8,841	10,197	18,976	12,162	10,867	15,797
127	127	75	75	75	165	172	222
15,518	18,623	10,201	6,423	(3,520)	8,772	14,477	38,426
0	(7,000)	0	0	12,000	1,000	6,600	(29,600)
17,000	10,000	10,000	10,000	22,000	23,000	29,600	0
15,518	11,623	10,201	6,423	8,480	9,772	21,077	8,826

11. The stock of inventory on hand at the beginning of any month will not exceed the total of planned sales for the next 3 months. Inventory level is therefore set at 75 percent of cost of books sold for the next 3 months. This working rule gives a reasonable way, on the basis of experience, for estimating the dollars' worth of books to be bought each month.

12. Exhibit 2 shows the sales forecasted for 3 years ahead. These figures are based on the proprietor's experience plus analysis of the marketing data for the segment of the market expected to be reached.

13. Three-fourths of sales are for cash. One-fourth of sales are for credit, with collection in 30 days.

14. Three-fourths of purchases are for cash. One-fourth are to be paid in 30 days.

15. Beginning cash balance for any month should be at least one-half of sales for that month. The beginning cash on hand at the start of the business, January 2, 1988, is $3000.

16. On the basis of a reasonably profitable first year, income taxes are projected at 28 percent of gross profit.

Break-even Chart for Tobias Booksellers, 1990

The break-even chart for Tobias Booksellers (Exhibit 7) for the year 1990 was prepared on the basis of data representative of average practice in the trade.

The assumptions upon which the various figures for the chart were developed are as follows:

1. Planned sales for the year = $216,000

2. Cost of books sold = 60% of 216,000 = $129,000 (V)
   Direct labor @ 11.9% =   25,074 (V)

EXHIBIT 4

Income Statement by Month

	Jan	Feb	Mar	Apr	May	Jun
Sales	$ 6,000	$ 8,500	$ 9,000	$11,000	$13,000	$10,500
—Cost of sales	3,600	5,100	5,400	6,600	7,800	6,300
Gross margin	2,400	3,400	3,600	4,400	5,200	4,200
—Cash payments	2,392	1,884	2,045	2,265	2,275	2,112
—Interest	75	114	123	127	127	127
—Depreciation	40	40	40	40	40	40
Total	2,507	2,038	2,208	2,432	2,442	2,279
Before-tax profit	(107)	1,362	1,392	1,968	2,758	1,921

	Jul	Aug	Sep	Oct	Nov	Dec
Sales	$ 6,500	$ 6,500	$10,000	$13,500	$16,500	$39,000
—Cost of sales	3,900	3,900	6,000	8,100	9,900	23,400
Gross margin	2,600	2,600	4,000	5,400	6,600	15,600
—Cash payments	2,035	2,135	2,590	3,451	4,252	5,999
—Interest	75	75	75	165	172	222
—Depreciation	40	40	40	40	40	40
Total	2,110	2,250	2,705	3,656	4,464	6,273
Before-tax profit	490	350	1,295	1,744	2,136	9,339

Rent @ 4.2% =   9,000 (F)
Advertising and promotion @ 1.9% =   4,104 (F)
Delivery charges @ 0.6% =   1,296 (V)
Supplies @ 1.2% =   2,592 (V)
Taxes, payroll, state and local @ 1.4% =   3,024 (V)
Insurance @ 0.8% =   1,728 (F)
Travel @ 0.4% =   864 (F)
Bad debts @ 0.1% =   216 (V)
Professional fees @ 0.3% =   648 (F)
Telephone @ 0.6% =   1,296 (F)
Other operating expenses @ 1.8% =   3,888 (F)
Owner's salary @ $800 per month =   9,600 (F)

Items that increase with sales (variable items) are identified by the symbol (V); items that stay essentially the same regardless of sales volume (fixed items) are identified by the symbol (F). Judgment must often be applied in deciding whether an item should be classified as variable or fixed. Since the items that might be questioned tend to be small, classifying them one way or the other has little effect on the significance of the break-even chart.

EXHIBIT 5

Yearly Income Statement—1988

Sales		$150,000
Cost of sales		90,000
Gross margin		60,000
Salaries	$10,892	
Rent	9,000	
Advertising & promotion	2,800	
Delivery charges	900	
Supplies & postage	1,800	
Taxes (payroll, state, etc.)	2,100	
Insurance	1,200	
Travel & entertainment	600	
Bad debts	143	
Professional fees	450	
Telephone	900	
Other operating expenses	2,700	
Interest	1,477	
Depreciation	480	
	35,442	
Total expenses		35,442
Before-tax profit		24,546
Taxes (28% per IRS table for sole proprietorship)		6,873
After-tax profit		17,673
Proprietor's capital (2 Jan 1988)		15,000
Proprietor's capital (31 Dec 1988)		$ 32,673

28% income tax rate assumes that this profit figure represents clear profit above deductible personal expenses.

You will recall from Chapter 11 that the break-even chart is a tool of proactive management. It need not be minutely accurate to serve the purposes of management choice and decision making.

3. The owner draws a salary of $800 a month. Gross income will therefore be figured as salary plus gross profit for income tax purposes, as the owner will be taxed on both combined. The owner estimates combined gross income will be about $30,000 for 1990. Therefore, income taxes will be at the 28 percent level or about $4400 on the assumption that allowable personal deductions are not here considered.

4. The break-even chart, as shown in Exhibit 7, is made by combining the fixed and variable numbers as shown below and plotting them in the way described in Chapter 11.

ASSUMPTIONS

1. Planned sales for 1990 = $216,000

2. Fixed costs:
    a. Owner's salary, $800 per month = 9,600
    b. Rent, $750 per month = 9,000
        $ 18,600

    c. {
        Advertising and Promotion, 1.9% — 4,104
        Insurance, 0.8% = 1,728
        Travel, 0.4% = 864
        Professional fees, 0.3% = 648
        Telephone, 0.6% = 1,296
        Misc. operating expenses, 1.8% = 3,888
        $ 12,528

3. Variable costs:
    a. Cost of goods sold, 60% = $129,600
    b. Direct labor, 11.9% = 25,704

    c. {
        Delivery charges, 0.6% = 1,296
        Supplies, 1.2% = 2,592
        Taxes, payroll, state, local, 1.4% = 3,024
        Bad debts, 0.1% = 216
        $ 7,128

USES OF THE BREAK-EVEN CHART

The break-even chart may be used for many purposes of proactive management. Some typical data that can drawn from the chart are:

1. What is the break-even point in gross sales? The chart shows this figure to be $125,000. At this value of sales, Tobias Booksellers neither makes nor loses money for the year.

2. What is the break-even point to provide for the estimated income taxes of $8790? This value shows as $145,000 on the chart.

EXHIBIT 6

Balance Sheet—December 1988

Assets			Liabilities & Equity		
Cash		$ 8,826	Accounts payable		$ 2,678
Accounts receivable		9,750	Taxes payable		6,873
Inventory, ending		12,690	Bank loan		0
Fixtures	$4,000		Proprietor's capital		32,673
—Depreciation	480		TOTAL		$42,200
	3,520	3,520			
Two months' rent deposit		1,500			
Other advance payments		3,000			
Cushion for unexpected costs		2,925			
TOTAL		$42,200			

Note: Totals rounded to 3 figures

EXHIBIT 7

Break-Even Chart for Tobias Booksellers—1990

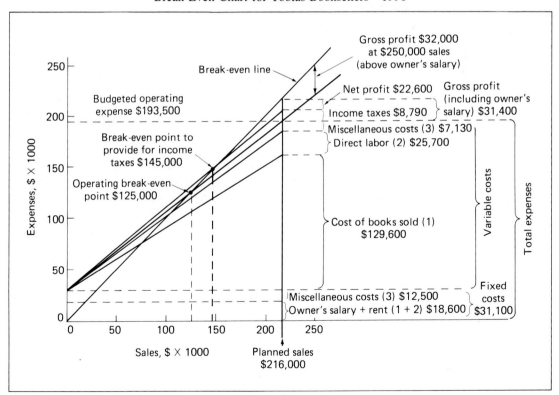

3. What would the gross profit be if sales could be increased by $34,000 for the year without increasing fixed costs? The new gross sales would be $250,000. At this value, gross profit would rise to $41,600 for the year ($32,000 + $9,600 salary).

4. What is the effect of decreasing or increasing the cost of direct labor for the year? Direct labor is the largest single variable cost. Decreasing this cost a small amount may be seen to move the break-even point down significantly. The amount of change may be found by redrawing the variable cost lines after lowering the direct labor point at the planned sales vertical. The effect of increased direct labor cost may be found in the same way.

5. The break-even chart offers a graphic way of showing the possibilities for making money in the business. It's easier to see the effect of changing costs in fixed and variable items than it is to analyze columns of figures. Therefore, the break-even chart makes an effective communication and sales tool.

FINANCIAL PROJECTIONS FOR A SMALL MANUFACTURING PLANT

Prepared by Keith V. Smith.

Background and Assumptions

1. The product to be produced is a bench-size laboratory temperature test chamber. It is used to test the performance of electronic and electromechanical components under programmable temperature conditions from -300 to $+800°F$.

2. Units (chambers) are produced on assembly lines. Each line has a capacity of forty units per month. Each line requires production equipment costing $20,000.

3. Two partners set up a corporation and invest a total of $50,000 to launch the business. They purchase equipment for one line for $20,000 cash. They buy raw stock and components for eighty units for $24,000; they pay out for this material $12,000 in cash; the remainder of $12,000 is due in thirty days.

4. The business begins at the end of December 1986.

5. The beginning Balance Sheet is shown in Exhibit 1.

EXHIBIT 1

Balance Sheet
December 31, 1986

Cash	$18,000	Accounts Payable	$12,000
Inventory	24,000		
Equipment	20,000	Common Stock	50,000
	$62,000		$62,000

6. Each unit is sold for $1000. Collections for sales are expected to be 50 percent in thirty days, and 50 percent in sixty days.

7. For each unit produced:

Materials cost	$300	Purchases to be paid for in thirty days
Direct labor	180	Paid in cash
Manufacturing expense	80	Paid in cash
Cost of goods sold	$560	

EXHIBIT 2

Income Statements for 1987 and 1988

	1987	1988
Sales	483,000	1,460,000
− CGS	270,480	817,600
Gross profit	212,520	642,400
− Operating expenses	221,800	465,700
EBIT	(9,280)	176,700
− Interest	17,840	35,680
Earnings before taxes	(27,120)	141,020
− Taxes, 25%	0	35,255
Earnings after taxes	(27,120)	105,765
+ Beginning retained earnings	0	(27,120)
Ending retained earnings	(27,120)	78,645

EXHIBIT 3

Balance Sheets
at End of Years 1987 and 1988

		1987		1988
Assets				
Cash		74,160		139,580
A/R		115,000		230,000
Inventory				
Raw material		48,000		96,000
Finished goods		87,920		76,720
Equipment	40,000		80,000	
− Accumulated				
Depreciation	3,200	36,800	10,400	69,600
		361,880		611,900
Liabilities & Equity				
A/P		24,000		48,000
Needed financing		315,000		400,000
Taxes payable		0		35,255
Common stock		50,000		50,000
Retained earnings		(27,120)		78,645
	TOTAL	361,880		611,900

EXHIBIT 4

Month & year	Number of Units of Final Product — Beginning Inventory (2)	Production Schedule (3)	Sales Forecast (4)	Ending Inventory (5)	Cash Receipts — $ Sales (6)	Cash Collection (7)	Accounts Receivable (8)	Capital Expenditures (9)	Number of Units of Raw Material — Beginning Inventory (10)	Purchases (11)	Ending Inventory (12)	Purchase Payments (13)	Direct Labor & Mfg. Exp (14)
Dec 86	0		0	0	0	0	0	20,000		80	80	12,000	10,400
Jan 87	0	40	0	40	0	0	0		80	40	80	12,000	10,400
Feb	40	40	1	79	1,000	0	1,000		80	40	80	12,000	10,400
Mar	79	40	5	114	5,000	500	5,500		80	40	80	12,000	10,400
Apr	114	40	12	142	12,000	3,000	14,500		80	40	80	12,000	10,400
May	142	40	20	162	20,000	8,500	26,000		80	40	80	12,000	10,400
Jun	162	40	35	167	35,000	16,000	45,000		80	40	80	12,000	10,400
Jul	167	40	55	152	55,000	27,500	72,500		80	80	120	12,000	10,400
Aug	152	40	60	132	60,000	45,000	87,500	20,000	120	80	160	24,000	10,400
Sep	132	80	65	147	65,000	57,500	95,000		160	80	160	24,000	20,800
Oct	147	80	75	152	75,000	62,500	107,500		160	80	160	24,000	20,800
Nov	152	80	80	152	80,000	70,000	117,500		160	80	160	24,000	20,800
Dec	152	80	75	157	75,000	77,500	115,000		160	80	160	24,000	20,800
—	0	640	483	157	483,000	368,000	115,000		80	720	160	204,000	166,400
Jan 88	157	80	85	152	85,000	77,500	122,500		160	80	160	24,000	20,800
Feb	152	80	90	142	90,000	80,000	132,500		160	120	200	24,000	20,800
Mar	142	80	90	132	90,000	87,500	135,000	20,000	200	120	240	36,000	20,800
Apr	132	120	100	152	100,000	90,000	145,000		240	120	240	36,000	31,200
May	152	120	115	157	115,000	95,000	165,000		240	120	240	36,000	31,200
Jun	157	120	120	157	120,000	107,500	177,500		240	120	240	36,000	31,200
Jul	157	120	130	147	130,000	117,500	190,000		240	120	240	36,000	31,200
Aug	147	120	135	132	135,000	125,000	200,000		240	160	280	36,000	31,200
Sep	132	120	140	112	140,000	132,500	207,500	20,000	280	160	320	48,000	31,200
Oct	112	160	145	127	145,000	137,500	215,000		320	160	320	48,000	41,600
Nov	127	160	160	127	160,000	142,500	232,500		320	160	320	48,000	41,600
Dec	127	160	150	137	150,000	152,500	230,000	40,000	320	160	320	48,000	41,600
—	157	1,440	1,460	137	1,460,000	1,345,000	230,000		160	1,600	320	456,000	374,400
Jan 89	137	160	150	147	150,000	155,000	225,000		320	160	320	48,000	41,600
Feb	147	160	160	147	160,000	150,000	235,000		320	160	320	48,000	41,600
Mar	147	160	160	147	160,000	155,000	240,000		320	160	320	48,000	41,600
Apr	147	160	170	137	170,000	160,000	250,000		320	160	320	48,000	41,600
May*													
Jun													
Jul													
Aug													
Sep													
Oct													
Nov													
Dec													

Calculating equations: 24 = 13 + 14 + 19 − 18 + 9   26 = 23 + 7 − 24 − 25   28 = 26 + D 27

*Figures for May–Dec. 1989 have been omitted to give you the opportunity to practice financial planning by developing these figures yourself.

15 Rent & Utilities	16 Marketing Expense	17 Admin. Expense	18 Depreciation	19 Operating Expense	20 C.G.S.	21 Gross Profit	22 Debit	23 Beginning Cash Balance	24 Cash Disbursements	25 Interest	26 Bal. before Borrowing	27 Cumulative Borrowing	28 Ending Cash Balance	29 Month & Year
1,500	2,000	6,000	200	9,700	0	0	(9,700)	18,000	31,900	0	(13,900)	45,000	31,100	Dec 86
1,500	2,000	6,000	200	9,900	0	440	(9,460)	31,100	32,100	360	(1,360)	80,000	33,640	Jan 87
1,500	3,000	6,000	200	10,700	560	2,200	(8,500)	33,640	32,900	640	600	110,000	30,600	Feb
1,500	4,400	6,000	200	12,100	2,800	5,280	(6,820)	30,600	34,300	880	(1,580)	150,000	38,420	Mar
1,500	6,000	6,000	200	13,700	6,720	8,800	(4,900)	38,420	35,900	1,200	9,820	180,000	39,820	Apr
1,500	9,000	6,000	200	16,700	11,200	15,400	(1,300)	39,820	38,900	1,440	15,480	210,000	45,480	May
1,500	13,000	6,000	200	20,700	19,600	24,200	3,500	45,480	42,900	1,680	28,400	240,000	58,400	Jun
1,500	14,000	6,000	200	21,700	30,800	26,400	4,700	58,400	75,900	1,920	25,580	285,000	70,580	Jul
1,500	15,000	8,000	400	24,900	33,600	28,600	3,700	70,580	69,300	2,280	56,500	300,000	71,500	Aug
1,500	17,000	8,000	400	26,900	36,400	33,000	6,100	71,500	71,300	2,400	60,300	315,000	75,300	Sep
1,500	18,000	8,000	400	27,900	42,000	35,200	7,300	75,300	72,300	2,520	70,480	315,000	70,480	Oct
1,500	17,000	8,000	400	26,900	44,800	33,000	6,100	70,480	71,300	2,520	74,160	315,000	74,160	Nov
18,000	120,600	80,000	3,200	221,800	270,480	212,520	(9,280)	18,000	609,000	17,840		315,000	74,160	Dec
1,500	19,000	8,000	400	28,900	42,000	37,400	8,500	74,160	73,300	2,520	75,840	315,000	75,840	Jan 88
1,500	20,000	8,000	400	29,900	47,600	39,600	9,700	75,840	74,300	2,520	79,020	340,000	104,020	Feb
1,500	20,000	8,000	400	29,900	50,400	39,600	9,700	104,020	106,300	2,720	82,500	360,000	102,500	Mar
2,000	22,000	10,000	600	34,600	50,400	44,000	9,400	102,500	101,200	2,880	88,420	375,000	103,420	Apr
2,000	25,000	10,000	600	37,600	56,000	50,600	13,000	103,420	104,200	3,000	91,220	385,000	101,220	May
2,000	26,000	10,000	600	38,600	64,400	52,800	14,200	101,220	105,220	3,080	100,440	385,000	100,440	Jun
2,000	28,000	10,000	600	40,600	67,200	57,200	16,600	100,440	107,200	3,080	107,660	385,000	107,660	Jul
2,000	29,000	10,000	600	41,600	72,800	59,400	17,800	107,660	108,200	3,080	121,380	400,000	136,380	Aug
2,000	30,000	10,000	600	42,600	75,600	61,600	19,000	136,380	141,200	3,200	124,480	400,000	124,480	Sep
2,000	31,000	12,000	800	45,800	78,400	63,800	18,000	124,480	134,600	3,200	124,180	400,000	124,180	Oct
2,000	34,000	12,000	800	48,800	81,200	70,400	21,600	124,180	137,600	3,200	125,880	400,000	125,880	Nov
2,000	32,000	12,000	800	46,800	89,600	66,000	19,200	125,880	135,600	3,200	139,580	400,000	139,580	Dec
22,500	316,000	120,000	7,200	465,700	817,600	642,400	176,700	74,160	1,328,900	35,680		400,000	139,580	Jan 89
2,000	32,000	12,000	800	46,800	84,000	66,000	19,200	139,580	135,600	3,200	155,780	380,000	135,780	Feb
2,000	34,000	12,000	800	48,800	89,600	70,400	21,600	135,780	137,600	3,040	145,140	370,000	135,140	Mar
2,000	34,000	12,000	800	48,800	89,600	70,400	21,600	135,140	137,600	2,960	149,580	360,000	139,580	Apr
2,000	36,000	12,000	800	50,800	95,200	74,800	24,000	139,580	139,600	2,880	157,100	340,000	137,100	May
														Jun
														Jul
														Aug
														Sep
														Oct
														Nov
														Dec

8. Equipment to be depreciated at the rate of 1 percent per month.

9. Rent, utilities, marketing expense, and maintenance expense as shown in Monthly Cash Projections (Exhibit 4).

10. As additional financing is needed, it is to be borrowed by the corporation in $5000 increments. Interest on this financing is to be paid monthly at the rate of 0.8 percent.

11. Taxes are estimated at the rate of 45 percent, due at the end of the calendar year.

12. No dividends are to be paid to the shareholder partners; all earnings are to be retained.

PACIFIC CLEAR WRITING CLINICS: A PROSPECTUS

This prospectus outlines a plan for a venture aimed at teaching adults in business, government, and not-for-profit organizations how to write clear, concise memos, letters, and reports. The venture stems from the founder's experience in teaching professionals and managers the craft of clear writing.

Pacific Clear Writing Clinics recognizes the need for clear writing that exists at all management, administration, and supervisory levels in most organizations today. Pacific offers a training service designed to fill this need.

We conduct in-house clear writing clinics for adults whose jobs require writing of a professional quality: executives, managers, administrators, engineers, scientists, technical writers, supervisors, secretaries—all persons who need or wish to improve their writing skills.

Planned Market Segments

Pacific addresses three market segments; each of our clinics is designed for a special market:

1. *Overcoming Fear of Writing* keys its contents to individuals who must write or want to write and who experience difficulty in getting started. This clinic is psychologically oriented and teaches techniques for unblocking, for liberating creativity.

2. *The Craft of Clear Writing* is skills-oriented. It is designed for people in industrial, business, government, and not-for-profit organizations who must write clear reports, letters, and memos. This clinic presents techniques for writing clear, concise, expository prose.

3. *The Technique of Proposal Writing* fits a market segment consisting of organizations that get some or much of their business through bidding by proposal. Bidding is usually highly competitive. Proposals must be prepared skillfully to

win business. This clinic offers methods and techniques for acquiring the skills to prepare successful proposals.

Reaching Our Markets

Our programs for *Overcoming Fear of Writing* and *The Craft of Clear Writing* have been tested, modified, and strengthened over the past seven years in many university-sponsored continuing education seminars for adults. During this time we gathered information about our participants.

The audience for *Overcoming Fear of Writing* consists mainly of mature professionals, administrators, and writers of all kinds who write but who have many difficulties associated with their writing.

The Craft of Clear Writing attracts mainly people in business, managers, technical professionals, secretaries, and supervisors whose jobs require them to write for themselves and for their bosses.

The Technique of Proposal Writing attracts as clients technically oriented companies for the most part.

Our experience to date shows that the most effective way to reach our audience for *Overcoming Fear of Writing* is through limited local advertising and direct mail advertising, and through word-of-mouth referral from previous clients.

Promotion for *The Craft of Clear Writing* and *The Technique of Proposal Writing* gets the best results with least expense through telephone contacts and referrals from one satisfied client organization to another. Successful contacts result in clinics conducted on the client's premises. *The Craft of Clear Writing* may well respond to a mail order and limited advertising campaign; we plan to experiment with this approach this year.

Financial Estimates

We estimate gross sales for the next three years as follows:

1984	$ 68,750
1985	$157,000
1986	$206,000

On the basis of these annual gross sales, we expect to produce a gross profit before taxes of:

1984	0
1985	$27,000
1986	$33,000

We estimate the starting capital we will need to found Pacific at $7000.

Pacific's Objectives

We have tested our market in the past two years by conducting clear writing clinics for the general public under university sponsorship and in-house for several companies. We have seen substantial and rapid improvement in the writing of participants in our seminars. This has been evidenced by feedback from both individuals and the companies for which they work. As a result of these experiences we are able to state that our clinics promote clear, concise writing. They serve the purposes of the organization in achieving clarity in internal and external written communications, and they therefore help individuals achieve their career goals.

The teaching approach Pacific uses in its clinics offers unique advantages. It is designed for adults. The instructors present principles of clear writing in short talks. The participants engage in exercises tailored to reinforce the learning of the basic principles of clear writing to which they have been exposed. Exercises are practiced individually and in small groups.

This method of teaching has been developed by the founder of Pacific over a twenty-three-year period. Pacific's director and instructors have been consistently gratified to see quick, positive, and permanent results from our seminars. Our participants experience immediate and substantial improvement in their writing.

Qualifications of the Managing Director

The managing director of Pacific, Anthony Herald, B.S.M.E., M.B.A., brings to his position as chief executive an extensive background in both business and management and in teaching clear writing. Mr. Herald has had over twenty-five years of line management experience in small and large business organizations.

Herald experienced the need for clear writing in the reports submitted to him for his signature by senior engineers who worked for him in the research and development division of a large corporation in 1974. At that time he asked the management training group to teach his engineers how to write clear, well-organized, concise reports. The training group countered with the suggestion that he do this himself. Herald agreed to take on the teaching chore with management training assisting in the preparation of a course syllabus.

At the end of the first training sessions, which took fifteen instruction hours, Herald saw a clear improvement in the writing that came from his group. At the request of the chief engineer of the company, Herald took on the task of training 5000 other technical people in the company in the craft of clear writing.

Anthony Herald has taught this subject ever since, both for educational institutions and for private organizations.

Character of the Business

Pacific wishes to project a professional image as a highly qualified company capable of fulfilling its promise to help its clients gain significant improvements in the subject areas of our clinics. Our selling approach will be low key, without fanfare and hoopla. We aim for a careful presentation of professional competence in all aspects and details.

All promotional materials, including logo, letterheads, memos, reports, telephone manners, and advertising will be tailored to support the image of professional competence we wish to portray.

Dealing with Competition

A limited number of individuals and companies now offer the kind of service we have described. In this county not more than a dozen individual consultants present seminars in writing. Half of these concentrate on writing from a literary point of view. The others gear their work primarily to business writing. As far as our research shows, no firm in the county offers the specific programs we offer. Nor do they use the advanced pedagogical techniques we have adopted and continue to perfect. Most of our competition comes from university professors or ex-English teachers.

Our strategy for meeting competition centers in our unique approach to instruction and on reference to satisfied clients. We use three avenues for substantiating our claims: letters from satisfied clients, phone checks to former clients by prospective clients, and written appraisal of our clinics by the participants.

Features of our teaching methods include using modern applied psychology to help clients unblock; presentations carefully prepared in the language of the organization; specific tools for achieving clear, concrete, concise writing; exercises in writing developed from the client organization's own examples of bad writing; and a carefully developed, lively, and supportive climate that makes learning a joyful occasion.

Description of Our Service

Overcoming Fear of Writing presents a workshop-clinic designed especially for those who want or need to write but who have trouble getting words on paper. This clinic helps participants gain self-confidence and unlearn the psychological obstacles to writing easily and well. Techniques derived from current research in brain hemisphere function and from holistic learning theory are used in an innovative approach to writing with minimum anxiety and maximum competence.

Overcoming Fear of Writing, conducted in a supportive environment, is an introduction to the process and psychology of writing and to practical strategies for unblocking, for discovering one's personal voice, and for becoming one's own teacher.

Participants are given the opportunity to explore the process of composition, to share their experience and insights, to discover meaning in resistance, and to practice specific techniques and strategies that reduce anxiety and enhance the writer's natural fluency and skill.

The Craft of Clear Writing offers a workshop-clinic in written communication skills for executives and professionals. The goal of this clinic is to enable each participant to write clear, simple, direct, and persuasive expository prose and to do so with a minimum of anxiety and a maximum of competence. Most business writing is bad writing. It fails to communicate. It is often unclear, badly organized, and dull. It is hard to read (and harder to write). Most people have been taught to fear and hate writing. This clinic is conducted in a lively and supportive environment; it is designed to help participants improve the ease and competence with which they write.

Topics include:

- Analysis of individual writing problems

- Writing for the boss, associates, customers

- How to get started when you can't

- Writing for readers

- Testing for your obscurity quotient

- Building a blacklist of words you won't use

- Beginning and organizing

- Being persuasive but honest

- Language as power

Individual and small group exercises in the special language of the organization allow opportunities for practice and feedback. Our instructors welcome discussion. Participants are encouraged to share their experience and insights.

The Technique of Proposal Writing is for those who have to prepare proposals for government procurements, internal company or agency purposes, grants, or commercial purposes. It is designed as a workshop-clinic in which the participants are given the opportunity to practice the kind of writing that makes for a good proposal.

Major topics covered in this clinic are:

- What makes a good proposal?

- What make a bad proposal?

- Fixing a faulty proposal

- Why are so many proposals bad?

- Avoiding pitfalls

- Proposal format and structure

- Exercise in proposal writing

- Controlling the cost of the proposal

- Organizing to write the proposal

- Techniques and procedures for proposal writing

- Elements of clear writing

This clinic was designed on the basis of eighteen years' experience in writing proposals in industry. The principles and procedures offered have been used by the instructors in actuality to produce proposals that resulted in many millions of dollars worth of business.

Cost of Pacific Clear Writing Clinics

We usually recommend a series of three five-hour workshop-clinics for in-house programs. Groups are limited to twenty-five people for best teaching results. Our fee for this program is $2750, plus out-of-pocket expenses, as is customary, at cost. A reference book and complete course outline are given to each participant at the onset.

Marketing Strategy and Selling Tactics

In the beginning, the marketing strategy for *Overcoming Fear of Writing* requires a somewhat different approach from *The Craft of Clear Writing* and *The Technique of Proposal Writing*.

Data collected about the attendees in university-sponsored *Overcoming Fear of Writing* seminars show that the typical audience is composed of women and men predominantly in the twenty-five to thirty-five-year-old bracket. Women make up about two-thirds of any seminar group. The typical participant is well-educated, articulate, and has an annual income in the range of $25,000 to $50,000. A specialized mail campaign appears the most logical method for developing business for this clinic.

As clinics are put on through mail campaigns, data will be gathered from the participants. This information will be converted into a mailing list that will be expanded with time and used for future promotional purposes.

The other two clinics, *The Craft of Clear Writing* and *The Technique of Proposal Writing*, will be promoted through personal selling. First contacts will be made by telephone. These will be followed by personal meetings with executives who have the power to authorize the clinics. As an aid to campaigning for business, satisfied clients will be asked to give the names of friends in other organizations that might be developed into clients. Referrals of this kind make calling easier and more productive than cold calling.

CLIENTS SERVED RECENTLY

Anthony Herald has tested the market and the material presented at the clinics by conducting actual workshop-seminars for a number of different organizations. In the past several years he has conducted clear writing clinics for adults in the Industrial Relations Center at Caltech, for continuing education programs through the University of California, for Michigan State University, and for many business, industrial, and government clients. Among his clients have been the key executive groups of:

- Forest Lawn
- Southern California Gas Company
- Automobile Club of Southern California

- Pertec

- Logicon Corporation

- Perkin-Elmer

- City of Inglewood

- City of Garden Grove

- Orange County Transit District

- Pioneer Hospital of Norwalk

On the basis of this experience, the programs we offer have a tested foundation upon which to build the Pacific Clear Writing Clinics's future.

PLAN OF OPERATION

The Pacific organization consists of a small central staff employing external consultants who have been specially trained to conduct our seminars. The central staff includes:

Anthony Herald, Managing Director

Lucille Romand, Associate Director

Marie Enciso, Secretary

Consultants trained and available to instruct in the workshop-clinics are:

Alathena Kennert, M.A., M.L.S.

Robert J. Langloise, D.B.A.

Karen H. Johnson, Ph.D.

Anne I. Grayson, Ph.D.

RÉSUMÉS OF KEY PERSONNEL

Anthony Herald, managing director, brings to Pacific over twenty years in line management and much experience in writing successful proposals for both private industry and government contracts. He has started and run three successful small businesses and keeps his hand in now by running his own consulting firm.

Herald has conducted educational seminars for executives at many universities and colleges. His academic experience includes a stint as visiting fellow in the Industrial Administration Department at Yale University, two years as lecturer in the Graduate School of Administration at the University of California, Irvine, and ten years as lecturer in the Graduate School of Management, UCLA. He is the author of five books on management subjects as well as numerous articles on management principles and practice.

Herald has taught the craft of clear writing in university-sponsored programs and in in-house clinics for business organizations for the past twenty-three years.

Anne I. Grayson, Ph.D., consultant-instructor, has taught writing at UCLA, Berkeley, and other campuses of the University of California as well as at Golden Gate University and the Industrial Relations Center of the California Institute of Technology. Her doctoral studies at the University of California, Berkeley, were in higher education, with a concentration in learning psychology and creativity.

Grayson's special clinic, *Overcoming Fear of Writing,* is the direct result of her dissatisfaction with traditional approaches to teaching composition, of her concern about the epidemic among adults of the "battered writer" syndrome, and of her research in therapeutic learning.

Herself a writer, Anne Grayson's poetry has appeared in the *Atlantic, Chicago Review, Yankee,* and *Ploughshares,* among others.

Grayson serves as consultant to business and government and works extensively with private clients.

Alathena Kennert, M.A., M.L.S., consultant-instructor, has worked for the past ten years as an independent consultant to technologically based firms, helping them to improve their report writing. Her background includes eight years of teaching English composition at the college level. Kennert then spent seven years at a large aerospace company, first as a technical writer, then as a trainer in report writing for engineers and scientists in that company. She brings a solid background of principle and practice to her teaching in our clinic-workshops.

Karen H. Johnson, Ph.D., taught creative writing at the university level for six years. She then devoted two years to writing articles and short stories for various journals and magazines. More recently she consults with television and movie script writers, helping them to solve their writing problems. Johnson brings her special competence in this area to our staff of Pacific's consultant-instructors.

Robert J. Langloise, D.B.A., worked as a specialist in organization development for Mille International Corporation for seven years before setting up his own management consulting office in Chicago. During his assignments, he became aware of the difficulty his client firms had with written communications. He noticed particularly the need for training in technical and business proposal writing and decided to develop a specialty in this area. His work came to the attention of many technically oriented firms including Orion Research & Development Corporation. This company and other West Coast companies have used his consulting help in the preparation of various kinds of reports for the past eighteen years.

Langloise's affiliation with our firm adds great strength in teaching the techniques of proposal writing.

Location and Facilities

Pacific's operations require only a modest office. A central location is not important because business is conducted by telephone, mail, and in person at the client's office. Therefore, an office of about two hundred square feet is adequate for our purpose; it can be located in a low-rent area.

Facilities required are also modest and include the following: desk, conference and work table, six chairs, three three-drawer file cabinets, one typewriter, microcomputer and printer, copying machine, and miscellaneous small office equipment.

Starting Capital, Expenses, and Profit

The starting capital for Pacific is estimated to be $7000 and the estimated expenses for the first year of operation are $18,000. Breakdowns of these figures are given in the tables that follow.

On the basis of the forecasted sales for the first three years, the estimates of fees to be paid to consultant-instructors, and the estimated expenses for each year, the funds available for salaries to staff and draw to the proprietor are shown at the end of these tables. Profit that may be reinvested is also shown.

The fundamental characteristic of the business permits a high contributed value once the first stages of investment, development of the programs, training of consultants in the instructional techniques, and growth have taken place. Simply stated, Pacific has a high potential for producing profit.

EXHIBIT 1

Estimated Starting Capital Required and Expenses

1. Rent, three months advance @ $250/month:		$ 750
2. Office equipment and supplies:		

2 desks	$ 500	
3 3-drawer file cabinets	150	
1 executive typewriter	900	
Microcomputer + printer	2,400	
Secretary's chair	90	
6 office chairs	390	
Conference table	400	
Miscellaneous small equipment	100	
Stationery and supplies, including graphic art work	600	
Miscellaneous advance payments	750	
Cushion for unexpected costs	2,000	
Total		8,280
		9,030
Estimated starting capital, say,		$9,000

3. Estimated expenses per month, first year:		
Rent	$	250
Telephone		150
Utilities		100
Promotion		150
Supplies		100
Postage		75
Insurance		75
Fees		50
Miscellaneous		250
Taxes		300
		1,500

Total for the year = $18,000

4. Forecasted sales

	1987	1988	1989
Jan	$ 2,750	$ 11,000	$ 16,500
Feb	2,750	11,000	16,500
Mar	2,750	11,000	16,500
Apr	5,500	13,750	16,500
May	8,250	13,750	19,250
Jun	5,500	13,750	19,250
Jul	2,750	11,000	16,500
Aug	2,750	11,000	13,750
Sep	5,500	13,750	16,500
Oct	8,250	13,750	16,500
Nov	11,000	16,500	19,250
Dec	11,000	16,500	19,250
	$68,750	$156,750	$206,250
	25	57	75	client assignments

5. Estimated fees to consultants:

Year	Fees
1987	25 × $750 per 15-hour work-shop = $18,750
1988	57 × 825 per 15-hour work-shop = 47,025
1989	75 × 900 per 15-hour work-shop = 67,500

6. Estimated funds available for salaries, draw for proprietor, reinvestment in the business, and taxes:

1987

Gross income		$ 68,750
Expenses	$18,000	
Fees	18,750	
		36,750
Available funds		$ 32,000

1988

Gross income		$156,750
Expenses (increased 15%)	$20,700	
Fees	47,025	
		67,725
Available funds		$ 89,025

1989

Gross income		$206,250
Expenses (increased 25%)	$25,875	
Fees	67,500	
		93,375
Available funds		$112,875

7. *Note:* If the owner draws the amounts shown each year, the amounts available for profit and reinvestment in the business would be as follows:

	1987	1988	1989
Available funds	$32,000	$89,000	$113,000
Owner's draw	16,000	32,000	45,000
For profit and reinvestment	$16,000	$57,000	$ 68,000
Assume reinvestment of	16,000	30,000	35,000
Gross profit before taxes	0	$27,000	$ 33,000

EXHIBIT 2

Typical Announcement for Promotional Brochure

PACIFIC CLEAR WRITING CLINICS
The Craft of Clear Writing

The goal of this program is to enable each participant to write clear, simple, direct, and persuasive expository prose and to do so with a minimum of anxiety.

Most business writing is bad writing. It fails to communicate. It is often unclear, badly organized—and dull. It is hard to read (and hell to write). THIS IS NOT YOUR FAULT. Most people have been TAUGHT to fear and hate writing. This program is a clinic for adults, specifically tailored to the requirements of executives, managers, administrators, administrative and staff assistants, and engineers and other professionals whose work requires them to write well.

Writing without Tears

The format of the program includes:

Specific principles of effective writing—we will NOT concern ourselves with the traditional emphasis on mechanics of "grammar" and "composition" to which you may have been subjected as a student.

Class and small group exercises in the techniques and skills relating to these principles.

Minimum of lecturing by the instructor.

Two texts and a notebook containing detailed outlines and notes will be given to each registrant.

Specific Topics to Be Covered

- What you should know about your readers; improving readability.
- Using outlines and file cards.
- Methods for organizing a logical structure.
- Writing like you talk—approximately.
- How to judge when your writing is clear and effective, and what to do about it when it isn't.
- How to write when you can't: techniques for overcoming blocks to writing.
- Formats for memos, letters, and short and long reports.
- How to influence your boss—and make him or her like it.

How a Typical MESBIC Operates

Associated Southwest Investors, Inc., is a minority enterprise small business investment company (MESBIC) founded by the National Council of La Raza in 1971, and licensed by the Small Business Administration. ASI raises private capital from its stockholders and borrows money from the Small Business Administration in order to form a pool of finance available for minority enterprises.

ASI is a for-profit company which must pay interest and principal on all money it borrows and make a fair return on investment for its private shareholders. ASI makes its own profits by serving as a lender collecting interest on loans or as a coinvestor with the minority entrepreneurs earning income on equity.

All the profits from ASI's investments are targeted for reinvestment in minority business concerns and communities.

WHAT SERVICES DOES ASI OFFER?

ASI works with minority entrepreneurs to finance and structure businesses. ASI also offers expertise in financial structuring, management technique, crisis management, and business development.

WHO IS ELIGIBLE FOR ASI FINANCING?

Minority business people trying to start up, purchase, or refinance a business are eligible for financing from ASI.

HOW MUCH MONEY DOES ASI INVEST?

ASI's loans and investments range from $50,000 to $250,000 per transaction. Participation of banks and other investors is normal.

WHAT KINDS OF FINANCING DOES ASI DO?

ASI endeavors to structure financings according to what makes the best sense for each company. Thus, ASI's investments range from secured bank-type loans to debt securities to equity.

IS ASI FINANCING CHEAPER THAN THE GENERAL MARKET?

Generally not. Since ASI is a private for-profit corporation, the same factors which govern general market rates also control the costs of ASI's funds. Sometimes, ASI appears less expensive to minority entrepreneurs because minority entrepreneurs often must pay premium prices in the general market. Because ASI is able to be very flexible in structuring financings, the burden placed on businesses by the cost of ASI's money is frequently less than that by the general market's finance.

WHAT IS THE PROCESS FOR RECEIVING FINANCING FROM ASI?

1. Preliminary screening takes place between the entrepreneur and ASI management.

2. The entrepreneur prepares a first-draft business plan.

3. The entrepreneur and ASI management work together to structure a financing and finalize the business plan.

4. The package is presented to ASI's board of directors.

The successful application averages from 1 to 4 months depending upon the complexity of the entreprise and its proposed financing.

WHAT GEOGRAPHIC AREA DOES ASI SERVE?

The whole Southwest.

HOW DOES ONE GET IN TOUCH WITH ASI?

Write or call the company at Associated Southwest Investors, Inc., 2425 Alamo SE, Albuquerque, NM 87106, (505) 842-5955. Ask for John Rice, president.

November 29, 1985

Mr. Arthur H. Kuriloff
PO Box 916
Taos, NM 87571

Dear Mr. Kuriloff:

In response to your query, ASI is a MESBIC, an SBIC which finances only minority businesses. Our business criteria are generally as follows:

1. ASI recruits only communication ventures. We hold 30 to 40 percent of the portfolio in such ventures. To date these have included magazines, radio, and television.
2. ASI reviews *all* proposals which we receive. Nine out of ten do not survive the first reading/hearing. The primary reasons for this massive "first cut" are:
   - The business is a veiled rescue not an upbeat growth opportunity.
   - The proposal shows a glaring weakness or absurdity which an able businessperson would never permit to be presented.
   - The proposed investment is simply too small to provide venture capital rewards even if highly successful by its own plan.
3. The 10 percent of deal flow which we take a second look at usually leads to 3 to 5 percent hard candidates of which we will close financings on most, but not all.
4. The criteria for successful investments for ASI have proven out to be companies:
   - Whose success does *not* require them to significantly better the performance of the prior owners within two years if the deal is a buyout.
   - Whose success does not require the capture of a major market share within two years.
   - Whose managements impress us with their flexibility during the process of putting together a business plan.
   - Whose managements are aggressive about having financial controls.
   - Whose managements have experience with cash flow shortages.
5. The investments' financial requirements are that reward balance risk, and that, in general, a 40 percent compounded annual rate of return after 5 years be the market value of our interest in the company.

Every deal has provisions for exit: puts/calls, key man insurance, partnership buyout insurance, and piggy back rights on public offerings.
6. The most up-to-date text on venture capital is, I believe, just released by Arthur Lipper of Venture Magazine.
I remain,

Sincerely,

John R. Rice
President

APPENDIX D

A Successful Prospectus[1]

June 16, 1975

Mr. John R. Rice, President
Associated Southwest Investors, Inc.
2425 Alamo SE
Albuquerque, New Mexico

Re: Funding for proposed motion picture theater business in Espanola, New Mexico

Following up on our recent discussions, I am pleased to submit this proposal and request for funding for a new motion picture theater and business that I wish to locate in Espanola, New Mexico.

I propose to start construction as a sole proprietor and to convert to a corporation, to be known as Gallegos and Associates, as speedily as possible.

The funding I request from Associated Southwest Investors would be part of a package as follows:

From Leonel Gallegos personally	$ 25,000
From ASI MESBIC	25,000
From a direct loan from ASI	50,000
Total	$100,000

The direct loan from ASI would be secured by a mortgage on the theater and property. The corporation would pay 10 percent interest, with monthly payments of principal and interest over a 15-year period. The ASI MESBIC loan could be converted into shares of the corporation and would produce dividends quarterly. Sale of shares at an appropriate time would permit repayment of the MESBIC loan.

---

[1]Reproduced by courtesy of Leonel Gallegos. This proposal, developed in the mid-seventies, would be equally effective today if the prices and labor costs were updated. It presents an unusually persuasive business plan that immediately captured the attention of the investor MESBIC. It successfully raised the money requested for starting a new business. This business plan's features can well serve as a model for entrepreneurs seeking funding for starting a new business or expanding an existing one. *Authors' Note:* We have eliminated most of the appendixes as requiring many pages of text. However, a sampling of some appendixes is included to capture the thoroughness of coverage that rounded out this proposal.

This proposal addresses the following points:

- Description of the proposed business
- Objectives of the business and its background
- Location of the theater
- Plan of operation
- Marketing and promotion
- Financial projections
- Operating the business
- Future objectives

I offer this proposal as a prospectus that will justify the funding I request from ASI. You will find in this prospectus a detailed presentation of the proposed business from its background to its development and plans for the future. If you desire further details, I will prepare them for your consideration.

Sincerely yours,

Leonel Gallegos

Prospectus for a Motion Picture Theater and Business
in Espanola, N.M.

CONTENTS

ABSTRACT

THE BUSINESS

MARKETING

FINANCIAL REQUIREMENTS

STATEMENT OF OBJECTIVES

    Long-range objectives

    Short-range objectives

    My qualifications

BACKGROUND OF PROPOSED BUSINESS

MARKETING STRATEGY

LOCATION

PROMOTION

PLAN OF OPERATION

PROJECT PLAN

COSTS AND FINANCING

FINANCIAL PACKAGE

FORECASTED FINANCIAL DATA

    Forecasts

SUMMARY AND CONCLUSION

APPENDIXES

ABSTRACT. This prospectus solicits funding for the construction of a motion picture theater and subsequent entertainment business in Espanola, New Mexico. My proposal includes building a 300-seat, 4400-square-feet theater and operation of the theater as an entertainment business.

THE BUSINESS

Espanola is the only city of its size in New Mexico that does not have an indoor motion picture theater. The theater I propose would offer family entertainment all year round, in good weather and bad. I project four sources of income:

- Films for the family trade, rated G or GP

- Matinees for children on Saturday and Sunday, from 1:00 to 3:00 p.m., featuring cartoon-type films

- Concession sales of candy, popcorn, hot dogs, and soda

- Ads for local merchants, shown before and between films

MARKETING

The marketing area I visualize covers a radius of 40 miles, with Espanola at its center. This area would include a small percentage of the population of Santa Fe and Taos, which lie within the market area I've described. New Mexicans are accustomed to driving long distances on open highways, and driving 40 miles to see a movie would be no novelty to residents of these two towns.

The population within this marketing area includes 33,480 people, two-thirds Hispanic versed in both English and Spanish. I would concentrate on showing English-version films, with an occasional film in Spanish.

I will promote and advertise film showings through three media:

- Signboards posted along the major highway, Route I-25, on which the theater would front. An average of 24,000 cars a day pass by the proposed theater site. Passengers would see what's playing as they drive by.

- Ads in two newspapers, the weekly *Rio Grande Sun* published in Espanola, and the *New Mexican,* published daily in Santa Fe.

- Radio programs through KDCE in Espanola and KVSF in Santa Fe.

FINANCIAL REQUIREMENTS

As in our preliminary discussions, I estimate the capital investment required to bring this project to fruition would total $100,000. This sum would be comprised of three parts: $25,000 contributed by me, Leonel Gallegos; $25,000 as a loan from the Minority Enterprise Small Business Investment Company (MESBIC), Associated Southwest Investors, Inc.; and $50,000 as a direct loan from ASI. The latter would be a 15-year loan at 10 percent interest, secured by a mortgage on the theater and its equipment.

STATEMENT OF OBJECTIVES

As a major objective, I will work to have my theater project an image of a wholesome, clean, comfortable place of entertainment for the whole family. The theater will be easy to reach, with adequate close-up parking contributing to its convenience.

OBJECTIVES

I have both short-range and long-range objectives for the proposed theater business:

Short-Range Objectives My short-range objectives for the business:

To offer family entertainment through showing wholesome first-run films throughout the year.

To provide suitable entertainment for children in Saturday and Sunday matinees.

To sell suitable snack food at a concession stand.

To show local merchants' advertising on the screen between and before features.

Long-Range Objectives   My long-range objectives for the business:

To increase the scope of the business by adding a second unit to the first theater to make it a twin. The first unit will be designed to accept a second at minimum cost.

To add two more profit-making structures on the property, a small department store and a market; the property has sufficient room for these.

My Qualifications   I believe I am qualified to bring this project into successful actuality because of my background and experience:

I hold a B.A. degree in Marketing and an M.B.A. in Management.

I have taught Introduction to Business, Retailing, and Accounting at the junior college and university levels.

I have had a variety of experience in retail businesses, having served from clerk to manager.

I have done marketing analyses for a number of clients, including Presbyterian Hospital, Technical Vocational Schools in Santa Fe, the New Mexico Technical Vocational School, and the Luna Technical School.

I have personally done the marketing analysis for this proposal.

BACKGROUND OF PROPOSED BUSINESS

Espanola at one time had an indoor theater. It was forced to close in 1970 as a fire hazard. No attempt was ever made to build and open another.

The only direct competition my proposed theater would have is a local drive-in theater, which can operate only in warm weather. The drive-in attracts mostly teenagers. Because of the quality of most of the films it shows, it does not bring in the family trade that I see as a major part of the audience I'd want.

Indirect competition consists primarily of television, a bowling alley, a few local night clubs, and high school athletic events. I believe that the family trade will find my theater programs of first-run films attractive enough to ensure adequate attendance for profitability of the venture. As will be seen later, viewers need attend only once every six weeks to make the business profitable.

In addition, motion pictures are becoming more lavish, interesting, and exciting with the recent resurgence in film making. First-run movies are not available on TV, the most intensive form of competition to movie going for my intended audience. Therefore, I believe my theater would become more attractive as time goes along.

MARKETING STRATEGY

Espanola is located in a valley on the Rio Grande 25 miles north of Santa Fe and 40 miles south of Taos. The market area that would be served by the theater I propose includes both Santa Fe and Taos. But because they are somewhat distant from Espanola, I have included only 10 percent of the population of each in my population summary.

The total population in the market area I've described is 33,840, according to U.S. Census figures. These data show there are 2966 single persons, 1791 couples, and 4839 families averaging 4.6 members within the marketing area. Of the age distributions given in the population statistics, 43 percent make up the bulk of movie goers according to U.S. Department of Commerce data. These comprise 16 percent in the age group up to 19, and 27 percent in the 20- to 44-year age group. The percentage of consistent movie goers in the market area I've identified would therefore be 43 percent of the total population, or 14,550. To be a bit conservative, I've reduced this by 10 percent to 13,000.

The proposed theater would have 300 seats. Although it would be possible to project three shows a day, from 5:00 p.m. to 11:30 p.m., I've based my income projections on two shows a day. This means, at 52 weeks a year and 5 days per week, again to be conservative, the number of seatings available would be $52 \times 5 \times 2 \times 300 = 156,000$ seat-days available. Assuming 13,000 theater goers, each would have to attend 156,000 divided by 13,000 or 12 times a year, once a month on the average. However, in accordance with information from government statistics for 3335 theaters reporting income taxes for 1970, average theater attendance was at 30 percent seating. My break-even estimate shows that value at 20 percent seating. Using the 30 percent figure means that the number of times viewers would have to attend showings would be 30 percent of 12, or 3.6 times per year. This appears a reasonable figure. My cash flow projections, on the average, are based on this approach.

The distribution of income within the market area shows that the families, which represent about half the population, have incomes ranging from $4900 to $14,900 annually. This suggests that admission fees of $2 for adults and $1 for children would be quite feasible.

LOCATION

The centralized location of the theater will make it easy to reach. The 4-acre plot on which the theater would be located has a 300-foot frontage on highway I-25 and is two blocks north of Fairview Lane. The theater would be situated toward the rear central portion of the property. Parking would be available for 186 cars, with additional space adjacent if required. The north and south forward portions of the plot would be left vacant until such time as income-producing structures could be built on them.

A traffic count has shown that 24,000 autos a day pass on the highway in front of the site. This is expected to increase to about 27,000, some 15 percent, as the new bridge across the Rio Grande, just south of the theater site, is opened shortly. Another factor that should increase the movie trade comes with the existing trend of the business center's moving north toward the theater location.

PROMOTION

I propose to promote the feature films to be shown through four media: billboards facing the highway; newspapers distributed locally; radio stations in the local area; and fliers to be distributed around Espanola.

I would install two large billboards at the front of the property. One would be angled to face north and the other south. Passengers on the highway could see them clearly from each direction. Lettering would be large enough to be read from 75 to 100 yards away. If the average car passing by carries $1\frac{1}{2}$ passengers, the film billings would be read by 36,000 people a day.

Two newspapers offer local advertising. The first is the *Rio Grande Sun,* published weekly in Espanola. I would advertise each week, primarily in English, but occasionally in Spanish when a Spanish film would be shown. Size of the ads would depend on recommendation of the distributor of the particular film. The other paper, the *New Mexican,* is published daily in Santa Fe. It is delivered daily in Espanola in the early edition. A late edition is aimed at Santa Fe. I'd place ads in the early edition, and only toward the end of the week and on Sunday. Three ads per week seem at this time to be appropriate to pick up trade from Santa Fe, which would occur mostly on weekends. I would propose to gain data on the effectiveness of ads by questionnaire sampling of audiences.

I'd propose to use two radio stations to tell what is and will be playing in the theater. Radio KDCE is the Espanola station. It broadcasts mainly in Spanish, but since the majority of the Hispanic population are bilingual, it will serve to advertise both English *and* Spanish movies. The adult listeners tend to tune in this station at various times of day. Therefore, I would scatter my advertising throughout the day. KVSF, the Santa Fe station, plays pop tunes and attracts teenagers. I'd plan to advertise on this station during after-school hours and on Saturdays. Again the hours would be staggered to ensure reaching a wide teenage audience.

The final medium would be advertising circulars posted in public places—markets, drugstores, post office, and other spots where the proprietors would permit. I would put these out monthly and have them distributed on a regular basis.

PLAN OF OPERATION

The operation of the theater would require the services of a general manager and a staff of four:

General manager, a position I would fill, will select the films to be shown, manage the operation of the theater, instruct the staff in their duties, and make sure all work is performed in satisfactory fashion.

Cashier, to sell tickets. Tickets would be disbursed in standard issue technique. The cashier will be responsible for the cash register. Tickets will be taken at the door by a security guard as part of his functions. Theater goers will pass through turnstiles when entering the house. The cash register should agree with the number of customers counted automatically at the turnstiles.

- Two attendants at the concession stand in the lobby. They will sell popcorn, soft drinks, candy, and hot dogs. They will also be trained to take care of the projection machines, which are highly automated and need virtually no attention. (If need arises I will be available most of the time to do this myself.)

- Security guard. He will collect tickets at the door before shows, but his main function will be to patrol the parking lot to assure that cars are not broken into and a peaceful atmosphere is maintained.

To hire employees I would seek students who want part-time work from the New Mexico Technical Vocational School in Espanola and the University of New Mexico Branch College.

Although I would manage the operation of the theater in all respects, I would hire professional checkers from time to time. These professionals would attend the theater and observe operations. They would make sure that money is handled honestly at cash registers, that personnel are courteous, and that the total operation of the theater is at high standard.

PROJECT PLAN

My plan for performing and completing the total project focuses on three basic parts: acquiring the plot of land on which to build, constructing the theater, and financing the project.

The Land   The plot of land on which I propose to build the theater would be composed of two adjacent parts. One part of $3\frac{1}{3}$ acres I own outright; the adjoining plot of $^2/_3$ acre I have arranged to lease from the owners, Mr. and Mrs. Alvaro Gallegos. The lease would be for 20 years with an option to extend it for 5 more years. Under terms of the lease, rental would start at $200 per month for the first year, increasing $100 per month for each succeeding year.

The combined property has a frontage of 300 feet along highway I-25. I would locate the theater at the rear center of the property. This siting would permit the building of income structures, as I've mentioned, at the front of the property without impairing access to the theater or obstructing sight of the theater from the highway.

Construction   As a licensed contractor, I would manage the construction of the theater in all its aspects. I would subcontract items such as foundations, electrical installation, rough plumbing, and roofing. I plan to do some of the finish work myself, having had personal experience in remodeling houses, plastering and tile work, and finish plumbing. I have no objection to getting my hands dirty to save construction costs where I can in building the theater.

The schedule for constructing the theater would be as shown on the following Gantt chart.

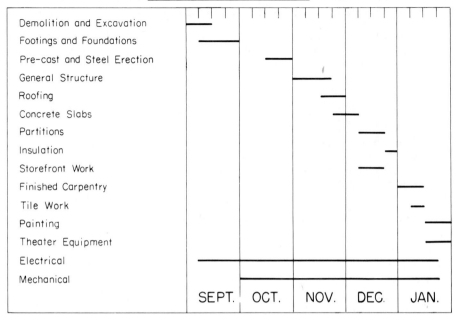

COSTS AND FINANCING

Arden D. Wetterau of Golden, Colorado, an architect who specializes in theater design, estimates the construction cost of the theater would be $126,437 if it were built in Denver. Because it would be built in New Mexico where costs are considerably less, I estimate a saving of about 20 percent on the overall construction. This would bring the cost of construction down to $100,000.

Major elements of this cost reduction would be:

I would save the usual 20 percent fee of a general contractor by doing the contracting myself. This would reduce costs by $20,000.

I would buy the materials for construction at the contractor's discount. I estimate this would save about $15,000.

I estimate a saving in the cost of skilled labor of about $10,000. The architect's estimate was based on the costs of union labor in Denver, from $7.00 to $9.00 per hour. In the Espanola area there are no labor unions; the equivalent rates for skilled labor run from $3.50 to $5.00 per hour.

In addition to the foregoing savings, I would do some of the rough framing, plastering, tile work, and finish plumbing myself with the help of unskilled labor. This should produce a saving of about $5000.

These savings all together would bring the cost of construction of the theater down to $50,000.

The cost of equipping the theater with projection equipment, seating, interior acoustical wall treatment and auxiliary items is estimated by Western Service and Supply, Inc., at $40,934. The total projected cost of the theater, ready to show films, would thus be about $91,000. This would leave a safety margin of 10 percent, or $9000.

FINANCIAL PACKAGE

The total financial package would be made up as follows:

To be invested by Leonel Gallegos . . . . $ 25,000

To be borrowed from MESBIC, ASI   25,000

To be borrowed from ASI directly, ...   50,000
secured by a mortgage on theater and its equipment, at 10 percent interest
Total . . . . $ 100,000

FORECASTED FINANCIAL DATA

I have prepared the following financial pro forma statements on a conservative basis. The national average for seat occupany in small theaters is about 30 percent of seat capacity; I have used this figure as a baseline, with the exception of the first few months, as will be explained. My forecast in general is based on 14 shows per week at $2.00 per admission. This income does not include Saturday and Sunday matinees or possible revenue from advertising sold to the local merchants. If these prove out, the added income will improve profitability of the theater.

Forecasts Following are breakdowns of the line items in both income statements and cash flow projections for the years 1976 and 1977.

  Line 1, Total Sales, includes box office income plus net income from concessions. Concessions gross is based upon the national average of 20 percent of the box office dollar; concession net is based upon 65 percent of the concession gross. I have assumed that during the first 4 months the occupancy rate will be 50 percent because the novelty of the new theater will attract that occupancy at least. Thereafter the rate declines to 30 percent for the next 6 months, then to 25 percent, then moves up to 30 percent. I assumed it would stay at 30 percent after that. (I have estimated that my break-even point would be at about 18 percent occupancy.)

  Line 2, Cost of Sales, on film rental is set at 50 percent of box office sales. Film rental varies from 30 to 50 percent of box office sales depending on the type of picture and whether or not it is a first-run feature. I propose to run nothing but first-run features; therefore, the cost is shown at 50 percent.

  Line 3 shows gross profit.

  Line 4 is left blank.

Line 5 shows salaries on the basis of three persons at $1.75 per hour and 40 hours per week, and one guard at $2.50 per hour for 35 hours per week. Personnel will clean the theater, prepare film for showing, and perform minor chores as required; the guard will patrol the parking area and keep an eye on the interior of the theater.

Line 6, Payroll Taxes, recorded at 8 percent of payroll.

Line 7, Rent, as required by ground lease of $^2/_3$ acre not owned by me, at $200 per month for the first 5 years.

Line 8, Utilities, presents an estimate of these costs.

Line 9, Insurance, fire and liability coverage up to $300,000 at an estimated cost of a maximum of $75 per month.

Line 10, Professional Services, including accounting and legal fees, estimated at $60 per month.

Line 11, Taxes and Licenses, estimated as a contingency item, since these figures do not include federal and state income taxes or local taxes.

Line 12, Advertising, a major expenditure including radio, newspaper, and monthly fliers. Although this figure will vary from month to month, I have used an average of $300 per month.

Lines 13 and 14, Supplies for Business, includes office and janitorial supplies for cleanup and maintenance.

Line 15, Monthly interest on the $50,000 loan from ASI, at 10 percent ($259.63 per month for 15 years).

Line 16, Depreciation, estimated on a straight-line basis for building and equipment for 20 years. This figure may vary, depending on accounting procedures that may be found advantageous when tax considerations are studied.

Lines 17 to 21. These items are not pertinent to the business.

Line 22, Total expenses by the month are $2938, the sum of lines 5 through 21.

Line 23, Profit before taxes varies from $6862 per month at 50 percent occupancy to $2001 at 26 percent occupancy. For the second year of business these numbers are more modest, ranging from $2751 to $1810 per month.

Line 24, Income, the same figure that occurs on line 1 of the Forecast for Profit. This line is left blank.

Line 25, Cash Sales repeats the same data as line 1 of Forecast for Profit.

Lines 26 and 27 are not applicable.

Line 28, Total Income, shows $7420 at 50 percent occupancy and $3739 at 25 percent occupancy.

Line 29, Disbursements, is left blank. These data will appear in line 37.

Line 30, Owner's Draw, records the owner's monthly take-home.

Line 31, Loan Repayments, principal only.

Line 32, Cost of Sales, from line 2.

Line 33, Total Expenses, from line 16 less depreciation.

Line 34, Capital Expenditures; none are foreseen in the first 2 years.

Line 35, Reserve for Taxes, estimated at $1000 per month.

Line 36, Other Reserve, not required for the present.

Line 37, Total Disbursements, $12,133 at 50 percent occupancy to $8661 at 25 percent occupancy.

Line 38, Cash Flow Monthly, varies from plus $4667 to negative $194 at 25 percent occupancy. This does not take into consideration the possibility of Saturday and Sunday matinees or sale of advertising to be shown on the screen. The estimated gross for the matinees is $58,000 for the year.

Line 39, Cumulative Cash Flow, shows net cash by the month. The total is $22,762 for the first year and $24,729 for the second.

Because of expected increase in expenses due to inflation, those for the second year have been increased by 10 percent, but the admission charge has been held at $2.00. Occupancy in the second year is expected to remain between 25 and 30 percent.

SUMMARY AND CONCLUSION

As the theater is being built, I propose to convert the sole proprietorship to a corporation to be called Gallegos & Associates. This would allow additional financing to be obtained relatively readily when the time becomes ripe to convert the single theater into a twin, and to build the income structures of a department store and market in front of the property.

The corporation would pay off the loan of $50,000 to ASI on a monthly basis, including interest and principal. In addition, the corporation would pay reasonable dividends quarterly, based on profit performance of the theater. ASI's investment of $25,000 as a MESBIC could be converted into shares of the corporation, giving not only return on investment, but also the opportunity to liquidate its loan through sale of shares at any time in the future it wishes.

With the growth of Espanola and the growing desire of people to attend better movies, the theater business and the future development of income properties I propose should prove eminently successful.

[*Authors' Note:* Leonel Gallegos' business was successful. He carried out the proposed program completely, with the exception of building the two income properties at the front of the site. The company was able to build another unit to make the theater a twin. The company paid off all debts and eventually sold the theater at a handsome profit.]

1976 Forecast of Profit (Loss)

	Start-up or Prior to Loan	Jan	Feb	Mar	Apr	May	Jun	Jul	Aug	Sept	Oct	Nov	Dec
1. Total Sales (Net)		16,800	16,800	16,800	16,800	10,080	10,080	10,080	10,080	8,467	10,080	8,467	10,080
2. Cost of Sales*		7,000	7,000	7,000	7,000	4,200	4,200	4,200	4,200	3,528	4,200	3,528	4,200
3. Gross Profit (line 1 minus 2)		9,800	9,800	9,800	9,800	5,880	5,880	5,880	5,880	4,939	5,880	4,939	5,880
4. Expenses (operating)													
5. Salaries (other than owner)		1,190	1,190	1,190	1,190	1,190	1,190	1,190	1,190	1,190	1,190	1,190	1,190
6. Payroll Taxes		95	95	95	95	95	95	95	95	95	95	95	95
7. Rent		200	200	200	200	200	200	200	200	200	200	200	200
8. Utilities (incl. phone)		50	50	50	50	50	50	50	50	50	50	50	50
9. Insurance		75	75	75	75	75	75	75	75	75	75	75	75
10. Professional Services (i.e., Acct.)		60	60	60	60	60	60	60	60	60	60	60	60
11. Taxes and Licenses		50	50	50	50	50	50	50	50	50	50	50	50
12. Advertising		300	300	300	300	300	300	300	300	300	300	300	300
13. Supplies (for business)		50	50	50	50	50	50	50	50	50	50	50	50
14. Office Supplies (forms, postage, etc.)		25	25	25	25	25	25	25	25	25	25	25	25
15. Interest (loans, contracts, etc.)		260	260	260	260	260	260	260	260	260	260	260	260
16. Depreciation		583	583	583	583	583	583	583	583	583	583	583	583
17. Travel (incl. operating vehicles)		—	—	—	—	—	—	—	—	—	—	—	—
18. Entertainment		—	—	—	—	—	—	—	—	—	—	—	—
19. Dues and Subscriptions		—	—	—	—	—	—	—	—	—	—	—	—
20. Other		—	—	—	—	—	—	—	—	—	—	—	—
21.													
22. TOTAL EXPENSES (add lines 5–21)		2,938	2,938	2,938	2,938	2,938	2,938	2,938	2,938	2,938	2,938	2,938	2,938
23. PROFIT BEFORE TAXES (line 3 minus 22)		6,862	6,862	6,862	6,862	2,942	2,942	2,942	2,942	2,001	2,942	2,001	2,942

Total 49,102 for the year

1976 Forecast of Cash Flow

24. Income (cash received)												
25. Cash Sales	16,800	16,800	16,800	16,800	10,080	10,080	10,080	10,080	8,467	10,080	8,467	10,080
26. Collection of Accts. Receivable	—	—	—	—	—	—	—	—	—	—	—	—
27. Other	—	—	—	—	—	—	—	—	—	—	—	—
28. Total Income (add lines 25–27)	16,800	16,800	16,800	16,800	10,080	10,080	10,080	10,080	8,467	10,080	8,467	10,080
29. Disbursements (cash paid out)												
30. Owner's Draw	1,500	1,500	1,500	1,500	1,500	1,500	1,500	1,500	1,500	1,500	1,500	1,500
31. Loan Repayments (principal only)	278	278	278	278	278	278	278	278	278	278	278	278
32. Cost of Sales (line 2)	7,000	7,000	7,000	7,000	4,200	4,200	4,200	4,200	3,528	4,200	3,528	4,200
33. Total Expenses (minus line 16)	2,355	2,355	2,355	2,355	2,355	2,355	2,355	2,355	2,355	2,355	2,355	2,355
34. Capital Expenditures (equip., bldg., veh., leasehold improvements)												
35. Reserve for Taxes	1,000	1,000	1,000	1,000	1,000	1,000	1,000	1,000	1,000	1,000	1,000	1,000
36. Other												
37. TOTAL DISBURSEMENTS (add lines 30 through 36)	12,133	12,133	12,133	12,133	9,333	9,333	9,333	9,333	8,661	9,333	8,661	9,333
38. CASH FLOW MONTHLY (line 28 minus line 37)	4,667	4,667	4,667	4,667	747	747	747	747	(194)	747	(194)	747
39. CASH FLOW CUMULATIVE (line 38 plus line 39 of previous month)	4,667	9,334	14,001	18,668	19,415	20,162	20,909	21,656	21,462	22,209	22,015	22,762

*Line 2—Cost of Sales: *Retail*—beginning inventory plus purchase, minus ending inventory. *Manufacturing*—cost of material, labor manufacturing.

635

1977 Forecast of Profit (Loss)

	Start-up or Prior to Loan	Jan	Feb	Mar	Apr	May	Jun	Jul	Aug	Sept	Oct	Nov	Dec
1. Total Sales (Net)		8,467	8,467	10,080	10,080	10,080	10,080	10,080	10,080	8,467	10,080	8,467	8,467
2. Cost of Sales*		3,528	3,528	4,200	4,200	4,200	4,200	4,200	4,200	3,528	4,200	3,528	3,528
3. Gross Profit (line 1 minus 2)		4,939	4,939	5,880	5,880	5,880	5,880	5,880	5,880	4,939	5,880	4,939	4,939
4. Expenses (operating)													
5. Salaries (other than owner)		1,309	1,309	1,309	1,309	1,309	1,309	1,309	1,309	1,309	1,309	1,309	1,309
6. Payroll Taxes		105	105	105	105	105	105	105	105	105	105	105	105
7. Rent		200	200	200	200	200	200	200	200	200	200	200	200
8. Utilities (incl. phone)		55	55	55	55	55	55	55	55	55	55	55	55
9. Insurance		83	83	83	83	83	83	83	83	83	83	83	83
10. Professional Services (i.e., Acct.)		66	66	66	66	66	66	66	66	66	66	66	66
11. Taxes and Licenses		55	55	55	55	55	55	55	55	55	55	55	55
12. Advertising		330	330	330	330	330	330	330	330	330	330	330	330
13. Supplies (for business)		55	55	55	55	55	55	55	55	55	55	55	55
14. Office Supplies (forms, postage, etc.)		28	28	28	28	28	28	28	28	28	28	28	28
15. Interest (loans, contracts, etc.)		260	260	260	260	260	260	260	260	260	260	260	260
16. Depreciation		583	583	583	583	583	583	583	583	583	583	583	583
17. Travel (incl. operating vehicles)													
18. Entertainment													
19. Dues and Subscriptions													
20. Other													
21.													
22. TOTAL EXPENSES (add lines 5–21)		3,129	3,129	3,129	3,129	3,129	3,129	3,129	3,129	3,129	3,129	3,129	3,129
23. PROFIT BEFORE TAXES (line 3 minus 22)		1,810	1,810	2,751	2,751	2,751	2,751	2,751	2,751	1,810	2,751	1,810	1,810

Total = 28,307

1977 Forecast of Cash Flow

24. Income (cash received)												
25. Cash Sales	8,467	8,467	10,080	10,080	10,080	10,080	10,080	8,467	10,080	8,467	8,467	
26. Collection of Accts. Receivable												
27. Other												
28. Total Income (add lines 25–27)	8,467	8,467	10,080	10,080	10,080	10,080	10,080	8,467	10,080	8,467	8,467	
29. Disbursements (cash paid out)												
30. Owner's Draw	1,500	1,500	1,500	1,500	1,500	1,500	1,500	1,500	1,500	1,500	1,500	
31. Loan Repayments (principal only)	278	278	278	278	278	278	278	278	278	278	278	
32. Cost of Sales (line 2)	3,528	3,528	4,200	4,200	4,200	4,200	4,200	3,528	4,200	3,528	3,528	
33. Total Expenses (minus line 16)	2,546	2,546	2,546	2,546	2,546	2,546	2,546	2,546	2,546	2,546	2,546	
34. Capital Expenditures (equip., bldg., veh., leasehold improvements)												
35. Reserve for Taxes	1,000	1,000	1,000	1,000	1,000	1,000	1,000	1,000	1,000	1,000	1,000	
36. Other												
37. TOTAL DISBURSEMENTS (add lines 30 through 36)	8,852	8,852	9,524	9,524	9,524	9,524	9,524	8,852	9,524	8,852	9,852	
38. CASH FLOW MONTHLY (line 28 minus line 37)	(385)	(385)	556	556	556	556	556	(385)	556	(385)	(385)	
39. CASH FLOW CUMULATIVE (line 38 plus line 39 of previous month)	22,762	22,377	21,992	22,548	23,104	23,660	24,216	24,772	25,328	24,943	25,499	25,114	24,729

*Line 2—Cost of Sales: *Retail*—beginning inventory plus purchase, minus ending inventory. *Manufacturing*—cost of material, labor manufacturing.

637

Excerpts from Prospectus Appendixes

TABLE 1

Age Distribution of Service Area

County	Total Population	Age 0–19 (years)	% Area	Age 20–44 (years)	% Area	Age 45–64 (years)	% Area	Age 65+ (years)	% Area	Age 20–64 (years)	% Area
Rio Arriba	25,170	12,243	16	7,065	14	3,993	13	1,869	14	11,058	14
Taos	17,516	8,014	11	4,860	10	3,018	10	1,624	12	7,878	10
Los Alamos	15,198	6,716	9	5,060	10	3,108	11	314	2	8,168	11
Santa Fe	53,756	22,974	31	16,997	35	9,574	33	4,211	32	26,571	34

Source: 1970 U.S. Census.

TABLE 2

Family Unit Distribution of Service Area

County	Total Population	Family Unit Distribution (a) Single Persons	(b) Couples	(c) Families	Total	Avg 2+ Family Size	% In Categories (a)-(b)-(c)	% Total in Area Single	Couple	2+ Family
Rio Arriba	25,170	2,409	1,433	4,134	7,976	4.81	30-18-52	13	13	16
Taos	17,516	1,809	1,196	2,785	5,790	4.75	31-21-48	10	11	11
Los Alamos	15,198	663	1,104	2,783	4,550	4.42−	15-24-61	3	10	11
Santa Fe	53,756	6,188	3,830	8,418	18,436	4.49−	34-21-46	33	35	32

Source: 1970 U.S. Census.

TABLE 3

Income Distribution of Service Area

County	Families	$ 0–4.9*	%	$ 5–7.9	%	$ 8–9.9	%	$ 10–14.9	%	$ 15+	%	$ 5–14.9	%	% In Each Category by County 4.9 < 14.9 < 15+
Rio Arriba	5,620	2,579	18	1,292	17	650	16	787	12	312	6	2,729	15	46-49- 5
Taos	4,099	1,965	14	747	10	581	14	513	8	293	5	1,841	10	48-45- 7
Los Alamos	3,877	152	1	261	3	336	8	1,145	18	1,983	37	1,742	10	4-45-51
Santa Fe	12,228	3,251	23	2,849	37	1,480	36	2,621	42	2,027	37	6,950	38	27-57-16

Source: 1970 U.S. Census.
*Thousands of dollars annual income.

TABLE 4

APPENDIX D

639

A Successful
Prospectus

Population of Service Area by County Subdivision*

Rio Arriba†			
Alcalde Div.	4,215		
Chimayo	2,723		
Coyote	1,585		
Dixon	1,153		
Espanola	7,673		
Rio Chama	2,641		
Tierra Amarilla (Chama not included)	2,000		
Vallecitos	562		
		22,552	
Taos†			
Penasco Div.	1,263		
Picuris	1,497		
Taos (Taos Village not included)	4,325		
Tres Piedras	356		
		7,441	
Santa Fe‡			
Pojouque Div.	1,583		
Santa Cruz	2,264		
		3,847	
			33,840

*Los Alamos and White Rock are not included in the total, although they can be considered in the service area (total for Los Alamos County is 15,198).
†Note total population of counties in Table 2.
‡Santa Fe area is not considered; the only areas are the two subdivisions of Santa Cruz which is part of the city of Espanola and Pojouque, which is closer to Espanola than Santa Fe.

APPENDIX E

Hiring, Firing, and Disciplining Employees

With the advent of the industrial revolution in this country, employers could hire and fire employees at will. A typical statement of the law governing the employer-employee relationship was, as in California: "Any employment having no specified term may be terminated at the will of either party on notice to the other."[1] This basis of the "at-will" employment relationship existed unmodified until recent years. In 1964, a California Court of Appeals[2] ruled that under an at-will contract, the right to discharge, with or without cause, is absolute, even if ill-will or improper motive is involved. The usual at-will employment relationship, as distinguished from that of a written contract specifying a term of employment, was the most common before that time.

The Labor Code of California[3] also stated: "An employment for a specific term may be terminated at any time by the employer in case of any wilfull breach of duty by the employee in the course of his employment, or in the case of his habitual neglect of his duty or continued incapacity to perform it."

Thus some years ago California law was protective of the rights of employers to hire and fire at will, presumably in recognition of the right of business to manage its affairs. But now, following the lead of California, Michigan, and other states,

---

[1] California Labor Code §2911.
[2] Citation.
[3] Citation.

massive limitations are imposed on employers through state and federal laws and regulations, and more recently, by the courts.

The attitude of the Supreme Court and other courts has changed greatly in recent years. These changes now focus upon sympathy for the rights of employees as contrasted with the rights formerly guaranteed to employers. As a small businessperson, you should recognize that severe restrictions now exist on your employer's rights to discharge employees. The courts are flooded with lawsuits by ex-employees alleging wrongful discharge. Many employers, now reluctant to fire because of inadequate understanding of how to protect their prerogatives, are experiencing lowered productivity as a result. You must evaluate the impact of your selection and personnel procedures to avoid the potential difficulties in the unintended consequences of casual approaches.

Hiring Procedures   You should set up standards of performance in hiring. Your recruitment and hiring procedure should follow carefully thought out policy, observing the restrictions imposed by law and the courts, which are briefly outlined below. You should view your recruitment interview and your employee manual, no matter how simply prepared, as a unilateral contract that induces a candidate to come to work. Or better still, see these as a bilateral contract in which the candidate has read the manual and signs off as having read and understood your employee policies.

The Manual or Handbook   The employee's manual or handbook should distinguish between a *regular* job and a *permanent* job. This has often been a cause for contention in recent court cases—whether the employee was employed as a permanent employee subject to tenure, or a regular employee subject to discharge for legitimate cause at any time. If you're hiring a permanent employee, perhaps a manager, then you'd be wise to use a separate written contract spelling out pertinent terms, requirements, compensation, termination, and any other important conditions of employment. If you're hiring a blue-collar worker, be sure that your manual specifies a regular job.

The manual should contain a list of rules and penalties for violations of them. Penalties should be exacted in a progressively more severe manner for more serious infractions. The list on page 489 of this text recommends specific items that you might consider placing in such a table. Having taken care of the foregoing matters, you'll minimize the chances for troublesome repercussions on discharging employees.

Employees' Legal Protections   Knowledge of protections afforded employees under the law will help you, the chief executive officer of your firm, avoid expensive pitfalls. In general, two types of protection are given to employees under law enacted by legislatures: *status* protection and *conduct* protection.

- Status protection offers immunity from discrimination because of intrinsic and immutable characteristics, such as race, color, religion, national origin, medical condition, physical handicap, sex, and though not necessarily immutable, marital status.

- Conduct protection prohibits retaliation against employees who assert status rights.

Public Policy   A discharge that violates *public policy* is an unlawful discharge. An employee discharged for this reason can sue the employer. How can you know when you're violating public policy? It's a matter of common sense. Anyone brought up in the social climate and mores of our society should know intuitively what violates the standards of behavior of our culture. The following are examples of public policy issues that have been before the courts and denied as reasons for discharge.

- Engaging in union activity, or attempting to join a union

- Being absent for jury duty

- Refusing to commit perjury on the employer's behalf

- Refusing to work under unsafe conditions

- Having wages garnisheed

- Filing a worker's compensation claim

- Refusing to submit to a lie detector test

- Refusing to engage in a price-fixing scheme or other violation of antitrust laws

- Refusing to date the foreman

The federal Fair Labor Standards Act (Wage and Hour Law) also offers protection to employees against discharge based on certain forms of conduct. Essentially, an employee who seeks to assert a right pertaining to his or her statutorily guaranteed minimum wage, overtime pay, or equal pay for equal work is entitled to protection from any retaliation for having asserted those rights or participated in protest over those claims.

Disciplining Employees If you have developed an established system of rules to follow in reviewing and rewarding exceptional performance and disciplining unsatisfactory performance, you are likely to have little or no trouble from litigious ex-employees. Establishment and maintenance of sound disciplinary policies and procedures can work for you as a positive management tool. Such procedures ensure consistent managerial behavior, and consistency in managerial behavior is a value highly regarded by all who work for you.

With sound disciplinary policies you'll show procedural fairness in discharging personnel. On the other hand, if an employer has an established system of rules to follow—and fails to follow them—this may be an evidence of bad faith. If an employee is not given the chance to tell his or her side of the story, this too may show bad faith by the employer. In circumstances such as these, in a suit brought by the employee, the court may find the reasons for firing arbitrary and capricious.

This was the case in a recent landmark lawsuit in California, Cleary vs. American Airlines. Mr. Cleary was discharged from American Airlines after more than 18 years of service. He claimed that he was fired because of union activities and, further, that American Airlines did not follow the established rules and regulations it should have followed in the discharge process. Initially, the court ruled that Mr. Cleary's discharge for union activities violated public policy and that he therefore had a cause of action against the company for wrongful discharge.

The court then went further and held that Mr. Cleary also had a cause of action for wrongful discharge based on two factors of "paramount importance." The first was the employee's longevity of service—over 18 years of apparently satisfactory service. In the court's mind, termination without legal cause after such a period of time violated the covenant of good faith and fair dealing implied in every contract, including contracts of employment. The second factor of significance was the company's establishment in writing of specific procedures to adjudicate disputes with employees including disputes over discharges. This established policy was an indication to the court that the employer recognized its responsibility to engage in good faith and fair dealing with its employees and had, in effect, promised them that they would not be discharged except for good cause. Having so promised, the employer, the court held, was stopped from asserting a right to fire at will an employee for any reason or no reason at any time, despite California Labor Code §2922. The court said these two factors together precluded the discharge of Mr. Cleary by American Airlines without good cause.

In sum, the Cleary case and others like it have created something approximating a limited just cause requirement to discharge all employees. At least, a requirement to exercise good faith will be read into all employment relationships whether or not a formal written contract stating this requirement exists. This case and many others like it firmly establish the right of a discharged employee to sue a former employer for wrongful discharge. Moreover, this wrongful discharge action exists not only in contract law but also in tort law, which means that the employer's exposure is increased by adding the possibility of punitive damages, as well as compensatory damages for lost pay and other benefits.

Safeguarding Small Employers' Rights In view of the erosion of the at-will doctrine of earlier years, it now behooves small employers to take clear-cut steps to avoid being sued by litigious ex-employees. In taking these steps, small employers not only protect themselves against potential trouble but also automatically induce a disciplined improvement within their firms. This shows itself in improved morale and productivity. As the small business chief executive of your company, you can achieve these results by following these recommendations:

- Prepare a detailed employees' manual following the suggestions and cautions listed previously in this appendix.

- Follow a consistent procedure in hiring; have the job candidate read the manual and sign a statement showing that he or she has read and understands it.

- Learn the legal protections employees have under the law.

- Follow the rules incorporated in your employees' manual for reviewing, rewarding, and disciplining employees. Have them sign statements that they have read and understood each review.

- Document unacceptable performance carefully and have employees acknowledge understanding by signature.

Refer to page 489 of the text for guidance in this procedure.

In conclusion, good documentation not only lets an employee know about his or her performance, or deficiencies in performance or conduct, and corrective action expected, but also serves as a record of actual corrective action taken and achieved. In today's legal climate, the importance of accurate and objective documentation cannot be overemphasized. The law in many states requires that all documentation maintained on an employee that can affect his or her employment status must be shown to that person on demand. These provisions refer also to any files a supervisor at any level may maintain on an employee.

Glossary

Access To retrieve information from or store data in a computer memory

Amortize To write off expenditures for capital equipment by prorating the costs over a fixed time period

Appraisal Evaluation of individual performance on the job; estimate of the worth of assets

Assets Items of worth owned by the company and shown on the balance sheet, including cash, accounts receivable, inventory, machinery, equipment, and the like

Balance sheet A statement of the assets of a business and the claims against them, including the claims of its owners (owners' equity)

Board of directors A minimum or more, as required by state law, of directors, persons appointed by the shareholders of a corporation to provide top management to the business

Break-even The dollar value of sales that must be made in a given period for the company neither to make nor to lose money

Broker An agent who receives a fee for selling a business or real estate

Budget A plan for use, or allocation, of resources, such as money, personnel, or time for the accomplishment of a defined management purpose

Budget, affordable method Spending as much as seems reasonable for advertising

Budget, fixed-dollar-per-unit Spending an absolute dollar amount for each unit of product produced or sold

Budget, matching competition Spending as much on advertising as the competition spends

Budget, percentage-of-sales A percentage of projected sales revenue to be devoted to advertising

Burglary Felonious taking of property from inside the premises leaving visible marks of forced entry

Candidate An applicant for a job or position

Capitalization The total invested by the owners in a business plus its long-term debt

Cash flow A measure of the money taken in versus the money paid out on a periodic basis, as monthly

Channel of distribution A series of steps through which the product passes from producer to ultimate consumer

Classification control A system for keeping track of how general classifications of merchandise have been selling

Clientele An established group of repeat customers

Copyright Legal protection of literary or artistic work through federal legislation; copyrights give protection against pirating for the life of the author plus 50 years

Corporation A business (a so-called artificial person) set up under state law, owned by shareholders who buy stock, and under top management of a board of directors

Creativity, external Innovative effort achieved by finding useful ideas from observation or reading

Creativity, internal Innovative effort resulting from searching the ideas in the memory; combining these ideas in newer and useful ways

Decline stage The fourth stage in the product life cycle in which demand falls off at an increasing rate

Demographic variables Those characteristics of a given population such as average age, sex, family makeup, income, and ethnic background that should be considered in selecting market segments

Depreciation Decrease in the value of assets over their expected life by an accepted accounting method

Discretionary income Money available for spending after basic living costs have been met

Diskette Often called a floppy disk; a thin, flexible, plastic disk upon which computer data are stored magnetically

Dissolution A change in the partnership relationship caused by any one partner ceasing to be associated with the business

Documentation A formal written record of performance appraisal, discussions of problems, training needs, or the like, with individuals in the company

Economic opportunity Ability to earn profit by marketing a product or service in a given market segment

Effectiveness The quality of the managerial act of doing the right things—those in which the payoff is the greatest for the time, money, and effort put in

Efficiency A measure of the value of output divided by input in a given process

Empathic, empathetic The quality of being able to put oneself in other persons' shoes—to see the world as they see it

Entrepreneur One who starts, manages, and assumes the risk of a business enterprise

Equity Owners' claim to capital they have invested in the business plus earnings retained in the business; perceived fairness in settling disputes, rendering decisions, granting or withholding raises, and the like

Equity capital The owners' claims to funds invested in the business plus retained earnings in the business

Experiential products or services Products or services that give the consumer firsthand experience (as playing tennis rather than watching a tennis match)

Extensively Working manufacturing machinery on a one-shift basis

Feedback Data or information that signals the level of performance of managerial effort, such as profitability, productivity, or reduction in absenteeism

Finder An agent who for a fee brings together the businessperson seeking funding and a wealthy investor searching for a promising business to invest in

Focus-group interview A selected group who are asked about their responses to such aspects of a new product or service as the advantages, disadvantages, and acceptable price range

Franchise An agreement between producer of a product or service and a retailer that permits the retailer to sell the product or service; the seller's know-how, image, success, and manufacturing and marketing techniques are supplied to the retailer for a fee

Franchisee The retailer who enters into an agreement with a supplier to sell that supplier's goods or services for a fee

Franchisor The supplier of product or service who enters into an agreement with a retailer to sell that product or service for a fee

Functional discounts See trade discounts

Goodwill The value of a business in patronage and reputation over and beyond its tangible net worth

Growth stage The second stage of business development, in which the firm has overcome its initial hurdles and is now making profit and growing

Inequities Perceptions of unfairness

Insurance Transfer of risk from an individual or a business to a group and the sharing of losses on a fairly distributed basis among members of the group

Insurance, crime Coverage protection against criminal activities committed by persons not connected with the business

Intangibles Services that cannot be perceived by the senses before the service activity has been performed

Integrator A manager who shows the ability to coordinate the activities of individuals and groups, to build teamwork among subordinates

Intensively Working manufacturing equipment on a three-shift basis

Introduction/growth stage The first period in the entry of a product or service in the market

Keystone Used by apparel retailers, this term means to set the sales price by doubling the wholesale cost

Liabilities Debts the business owes, including accounts payable, taxes, bank loans, and the like

Life cycle, product or service The four-stage cycle through which a product or service goes in its history: introduction/growth, maturity, saturation, decline

Liquidation value The bankrupt (or doomsday) value of the assets of a company

Markdown A reduction in the sales price of a specific item to stimulate lagging sales

Markdown, cancellation of Action to cancel the gross markdown and restore the original price

Markdown, gross The first reduction in retail price of an item, often called the gross markdown

Markdown, net The final amount of markdown expressed as a percentage of net sales, which is officially recorded as a price reduction

Market access The ability to reach customers in a market segment

Market aggregation The strategy of offering a single product to all consumers through a single marketing program

Market measurement The process of identifying and assessing the characteristics and size of a market segment

Market-penetration price An introductory low price for a new product or service, intended to achieve a high volume of sales quickly

Market segmentation The process of selecting from a population of mixed characteristics a group, or groups, having similar characteristics representative of a desired market

Marketing A system of getting goods or services to the customer, involving research, product or service development, promotion, advertising, distribution, pricing, and selling

Markup The difference between the cost of an item of merchandise and the original selling price

Markup, maintained After price has been reduced through markdowns to a point where the merchandise moves well, the final, or stabilized, price is called the maintained markup

Marketing myopia Shortsightedness in not recognizing that a given product or service should meet the needs of the consumer

Maturity stage The second stage of product or service sales in which rate of volume declines, competition increases, and profitability declines. The third stage of business development in which the company is experiencing rapid growth and needs a substantial infusion of capital to support further growth

Median The middle in an ordered set of quantities—there are as many numbers above as below

Me-too pricing A price strategy similar to that set by competition

Memory The part of a computer where information is stored; it contains both data and programs

Multifunctionality The ability to do many tasks rapidly and easily

Need for achievement (n Ach) A psychological trait that impels people to take on challenging tasks within their perceived capability and that appear to offer reasonable reward for the effort

Need for affiliation (n Affil) A psychological trait that impels people to work closely with others, to be friendly, and to seek jobs that require helping relationships

Need for power (n Pow) A psychological trait that impels people to want to manipulate the behavior of others and to control the means for doing so

Objective A major achievement to be reached, usually long-term, ordinarily about 1 year in the small business

Open-to-buy The budgeted dollars to rebuild inventory to the level needed to meet forecasted sales for the next selling period

Ordinance A statute enacted by a city government that states what may or may not be permitted in setting up a business in that community

Partnership An association of two or more people running a business for the purpose of making money

Partnership, limited A form of partnership that gives investors special tax advantages and shielding from liability; one or more general partners manage affairs; limited partners invest money only and legally can have no say in management

Patent An exclusive right, granted by the federal government, "to make, use, or sell a new, useful, and unobvious process; machine; manufacture or composition of matter; or any, new, useful, and unobvious improvement thereof"

Peripheral Any auxiliary input-output device of a computer system, such as a printer, terminal, or modem that remains under control of the central processing unit

Perquisite A privilege, gain, or profit in addition to regular salary or wages, for example, stock options, access to the executive dining room, a company-sponsored membership in a country club

Personal selling Selling the customer directly on a one-to-one basis

Point-of-purchase display A fixture showing, promoting, and offering goods for sale at the cash register or checkout counter

Policies Guides for management planning and action

Premium A fee paid for insurance coverage. A reward or prize used to encourage customers to buy

Price lining Offering a limited range of prices for items within a given class of products

Proactive The quality of planning for a desired result and developing the strategy and activities to make it happen

Product differentiation See market aggregation

Program A set of instructions for a computer, written in a language that humans can understand, and converted to a language the computer understands

Promotion A planned and continuing program of communicating with consumers in the effort to influence them toward accepting and buying your product or service

Promotional discounts Price reductions given intermediaries in the distribution channel for carrying out activities designed to promote the product or service

Publicity Free advertising gained from communicating newsworthy items about the business through newspapers, radio, or TV

Quartile Designates any of the values in a series dividing the distribution of the individuals in the series into four groups of equal frequency

Ratio analysis A measure of business performance that comes from comparison of one variable with another, for example, current assets divided by current liabilities gives the current ratio

Return on investment (ROI) Earnings divided by funds invested equals percent return on investment

Reverse technology Adapting an obsolete method, process, mechanism, or device for modern use

Risk, pure Risk in which the only outcome can be loss

Risk, speculative Risk with the possibility of gain *or* loss

Robbery Taking property from a person in charge of it by force or threat of violence

Sales promotion Stimulating sales through tools such as free samples, contests, and discount offerings

Saturation stage Segment of the product-service life cycle during which the rate of profit declines under increasing competition and sales volume gradually falls off

Seasonal discounts Price reductions offered to encourage sales during off seasons

Seed money Initial funding needed to start a business

Service mark A word or words, or a design or designs, or combinations of these used to advertise a specific service

Site analysis Finding the most acceptable location for a business through study of the various factors that determine the suitability of the location

Skimming-the-cream price A high price well above the cost of the product or service, intended to recover the cost of development quickly

Software Collectively, any of the wide variety of application programs, languages, operating systems, or utilities used in a computer; includes the documentation to explain the software

Sole proprietorship A form of business organization in which ownership is vested in one person

Spreadsheet A display presenting a rectangular grid of horizontal rows and vertical columns for showing data

Stagflation Economic conditions in which inflation and recession exist at the same time

Start-up stage That part in the early history of a company when it organizes so it can function and make its first sale

Stockout Running out of an item of supply needed for manufacturing

Stock-to-sales ratio Another term for stock turnover

Stock turnover The number of times average inventory has been replaced within a given period, often a year, measured by retail dollar value of merchandise

S corporation A special form of corporation set up under the Internal Revenue Code of 1954 that permits shareholders to be treated as individual taxpayers—the income or loss from the corporation passes through to the individual shareholders as if they were partners

System A group of parts functioning together to serve a central purpose

Tangibles Those products that can be seen, touched, tasted, smelled, or heard—that have substance

Template Software that controls the formation of a spreadsheet

Terminal A term applied to an input-output device used by humans for communicating with a computer; usually contains a keyboard and cathode ray tube (CRT) display

Term certain A legally specified period of time

Termination The final act of winding up the business of a partnership, which ends the partnership

Trade discounts Price reductions given to intermediaries in the distribution channel as payment for services rendered

Trademark A word, name, symbol, device, or a combination of these used to identify specific products and to help customers identify them

Trading area The geographical area from which a store draws the majority of its customers: neighborhood, community, town, network of towns, or metropolitan district

Transfer The act of buying or selling an existing franchise, usually under terms stipulated by the franchisor in the franchise agreement

Undifferentiated marketing See market aggregation

Uniform Partnership Act A model partnership law outlining the rights and obligations of partners, giving guidelines for the relationship

Unit control A system of control in which the broad classifications of merchandise are divided into parts that identify the quantity of each item in stock by size, color, style, combinations of these, or other characteristic features. This control also records the specific items sold

Unrecognized need A need not previously observed, but capable of being converted into a business opportunity when recognized

Vendor A supplier of goods, raw materials, components, and the like

Warranty A manufacturer's written promise that the product will perform its intended purpose

Word Processor A computerized writing and editing system, generally consisting of a computer, video terminal, keyboard, printer, and application software for performing the writing and editing functions; may include spelling and grammar checkers

Index

Abbott-Lane Company, 43
ABC method of inventory control, 247–248
Accountants, locating, 442–443
Accounts receivable and computers, 185–186
Achievers, 19–23
  behavior of, 23
  language of, 22
  planning by, 22–23
  reinforcing motivation, 22
  thinking like, 22
Acid-test ratio, 320
Administrative system, 335
Advertising, 138–147
  budget strategy for, 139–140
  of businesses for sale, 360–361
  characteristics of persuasive, 190
  copy strategy for, 144, 147
  employment, 491, 492
  for franchises, 406
  media, 190–195
    strategies for, 140–144
  publicity, 149–150
  for retail businesses, 189–196
  for service businesses, 220–222
  (*See also* Promotion)
Advertising agencies, 147
Advocate role of managers, 525
Aesthetic needs of buyers, 86
Affordable method for budgeting, 140
All-risk insurance, 469
Alverez, Antonio, 102
Amortizing costs, 373
Anticipated consequences of buying decisions, 86, 89
Antidiscrimination laws, 498
Apollo Solar Corporation, 275–276
Appraisal of performance, 498–499
  productivity and, 532–535
Arcturus, Inc., 576, 578, 580
Arm & Hammer Baking Soda, 126
Armed robbery, prevention of, 474–475

Assets, 293, 298–300
Associated Southwest Investors, Inc. (ASI),
    619–621
  prospectus for, 622–639
Attorneys, locating, 442–445
  (*See also* Legal issues)
Auburn, Nancy, 43–44
Auburn Associates, Inc., 43–44
Automobile insurance, 467–468
Avis, 394

Bad-debt losses, estimating, 373–374
Balance sheet, 293, 298–300
Balzano, Joe, 46
Banks:
  during growth stage of businesses, 277–278
  as sources of financial or marketing
      information, 108–109
Bascom, Ralph, 42
Bascom Products, Inc., 42
Baskin, Burton, 148, 149
Baskin-Robbins, 47–48, 81–82, 148–149, 394
Best Western, 394
Blackstone, Ruth, 216–217
Board of directors, 429–430
  inside versus outside, 430
Bookstore, financial projections for a, 596–604
Break-even analysis, 293, 314–319
Brunelle, Sam, 18–19
Budget Rent-A-Car, 394
Budgets, 139–140, 291, 292
Burger King, 394, 400
Burglary, prevention of, 474–475
Burglary insurance, 468
Business, nature of, 64–71
Business brokers, 361–362
Business development corporations (BDCs), 280
Business development stages and raising money,
    273–282

Business-interruption insurance, 470
Business organization (*see* Corporations;
    Partnerships; Sole proprietorships)
Business plans:
    developing, 7–8
        outline for, 9–14, 591–594
    examples of basic, 595–618
    financial requirements and, 292–319
    purposes of, 8
    role of managers, 524
    successful, 622–639
Business risk (*see* Risk)
Butler Brothers, 393
Buyers:
    behavior of, 82–99
    credit sales to, 94–96
    role of, 81–82
    sales outlets and, 96–98
    (*See also* Consumers; Customers)
Buying, 176
    guidelines for, 178–179
    plans for, 177–178
        sample, 179–180
Buying decisions, 78–99
    carrying out, 94–96
    demographics and, 82–83
    nature of products bought and, 90–94
    reasons for, 83–90
    for retail operations, 176–180
    role-playing and, 81–82
    time and place utility and, 96–98
    timing of, 98–99
Buying a going business, 355–387
    advantages of, 358–359
    avoiding legal problems, 367–368
    case study, 563–571
    closing the deal, 378–379
    disadvantages of, 359–360
    finding the business, 360–363
    goodwill and, 378
    liquidation value and, 370
    market price and, 370–371
    personal factors in, 368–369
    picking a loser, 368
    profit potential and, 371–378
    screening the offerings (*see* Screening
        business offerings)
    steps in, 360–367

Cancellation of markdown, 186
Candidate, 490
Capital acquisition:
    franchising and, 395–396
    venture capital firms and, 280–281
    (*See also* Financial requirements; Raising
        money)

Capital budgets, 292
Capital investment, initial, 296–297
Capitalization, 371
    external factors in setting rate of, 377–378
Capt. Crab's Take-Away, 392
Carla Fashions, 549–563
Cash discounts, 133
Cash-flow analysis, 293, 304–308
Census tract data, typical, 103–105
Chambers of commerce as sources of financial
        or marketing information, 109
Change:
    in environmental forces, 44–45
    forces of, 65–71
    and managerial behavior, 521–523
Change agent, 526
Channels of distribution, 134–137
Charisma Apparel, Inc., 549–563
Chartered Life Underwriter (CLU), 463
Chartered Property and Casualty Underwriter
        (CPCU), 463
Cities, retail operations in, 170–172
    downtown, 170–171
    neighborhoods, 171–172
    secondary business district, 171
Classification control, 184
Clientele, 358
Coach role of managers, 524
Coca Cola, 393
Coinsurance, 466
Collecting your money, 322–324
Collection-period ratio, 321–324
Commercial banks, 277–278
Commissioner of Patents and Trademarks, 438,
        439
Commitment, 20
Communicator role of managers, 524
Community and productivity performance, 534
Company-owned outlets, 408
Competition:
    changes in, and service businesses, 215–216
    effects of, on markets, 71
Computers, 336–346
    costs of, 338, 339
    data storage, 341–342
    described, 336–337
    hardware, 339–340
    leasing or buying, 345–346
    mainframe, 340
    microcomputers, 337–338
    minicomputers, 338–339
    peripherals, 339–340
    programs, 337, 341
    in retail businesses, 185–189
    software, 337, 341
    spreadsheets, 342–344
    system components, 340–341

Computers (*Cont.*):
  word processing, 344–345
Condominiums, 435
Consumer products, 91–94
Consumers:
  reasons for buying and not buying services,
      211–214
  role of, 81
  (*See also* Buyers; Customers)
Convenience items, 91–92
Convenience services, 223–224
Cook, Eroll, 475
Copy strategy, 144, 147
Copyright Office, 440
Copyrights, 440
Corporations, 426–437
  board of directors of, 429–430
  comparison of expenses of, 432–434
  key characteristics of, 436–437
  legal requirements of, 427–428
  licenses and permits, 434–435
  limited liability of, 426–427
  S, 430–432
  tax treatment of, 428–432, 435
  transferability of ownership interest, 429
Costs:
  production, 250–251
  of service business sites, 224
Counsel, professional, 442–445
Counselor role of managers, 524
Creativity, 40–41
Credit management, 189
Credit sales, 94–96
Creditors and productivity performance, 535
Crime, measures to prevent, 474–478
  armed robbery and burglary, 474–475
  employee theft, 477–478
  pilferage, 476–477
  shoplifting, 475–476
Crime insurance, 468
  comprehensive, 468–469
Critical Path Method (CPM), 244
Crom, 337
Cross-purchase plan, 470
Cumulative quantity discounts, 133
Current ratio, 320
Customers:
  identifying retail, 174–176
  orientation toward, 62–63
  productivity performance and, 533–534
  reaching, 118–163
  (*See also* Buyers; Consumers)

Date of starting business, 297–298
Debt capital, 277–278
  equity versus, 281

Decider, role of, 81
Decision maker role of managers, 524
Decline stage of life cycle, 125
Delta Design, Inc., 520–521
Demographic factors, 82–83
Department of Commerce, U.S., 108
Depreciation, 310
Direct-mail advertising, 194
Directory advertising, 194
Disability insurance, 471
Disciplining employees, 643–644
Disclosure Document Program, 438–439
Discounts, 132–134
Discretionary income, 215
Disk drives, 341
Dissolution of a partnership, 424–425
Distribution strategy, 134–137
  for service businesses, 223–225
D'Lites of America, 392
Document security, 472
Documentation, 503
Dollar control, 184
Doomsday value, 370
Door-to-door advertising, 194
Dot matrix printer, 345
Drexel, Stan, 45–46
Drexel Irrigation Products Co., 45–46
Drucker, Peter, 4, 527
Dun & Bradstreet, 61, 95, 303

Earnings, estimation of business, 373
Ecomar Inc., 5
Economic forces, effects of:
  on markets, 66–67
  on service businesses, 215
Economic opportunity, 101
Effectiveness, 525–527
Efficiency, 525–527
Elk Horn Resort, 25
Emergency items, 91–92
Empathy, 519
Employee health insurance, 470–471
Employees:
  dealing ineffectively with, 26
  inequities involving, 240
  prevention of theft by, 477–478
  productivity performance and, 533
  (*See also* Personnel policies)
Employment agencies, 491, 493
Endowment life insurance, 472
Entrepreneurial characteristics, 20–23
  changing, 521–523
  as potential liabilities, 24–26
Entrepreneurship and franchises, 396
Environmental forces, changes in, 44–45
Equity, 298

Equity (fairness) to fired long-term employees, 505

Equity capital, 275
  debt versus, 281
  from venture capital firms, 280–281

Established businesses:
  buying (see Buying a going business)
  innovation in, 48–50
  new approaches for, 47–48

Esteem needs of buyers, 86

Evaluators, role of, 81

Experiential products or services, 69–70

Extensive equipment use, 239

External creativity, 40

Extraordinary uses for ordinary things, 43

Failure of businesses, 61

Family influence, 82

Family life cycle, 99, 100

Feedback, need for, 21

Fidelity bonds, 472–473

Financial projections, 596–605

Financial requirements:
  managing, 289–331
  planning for, 292–319
  raising money, 271–288

Financial statements, 188–189

Finders, 275

Fire insurance, 465–466

Firelight Chimney Sweep, 44–45

Firestone, 393

Firing employees, 503–506
  employees firing you, 504
  key employees, 505
  long-term employees, 505–506

Fixed-dollar-per-unit budget method, 140

Flexible pricing, 131

Floppy disk, 341

Focus-group interview, 87–90

Forces of change, 65–71

Forecasted monthly sales, 293, 300–304

Formal information, 334

Franchisees, 390
  characteristics of successful, 391
  control by, 408
  franchise relationship and, 396–397
  reporting by, 401

Franchises, 370, 388–415
  advantages and disadvantages of, 390–391
  agreements involved in, 397–407
  buy-backs, 402–403
  company-owned outlets, 408
  continuing charges, 398
  duration and, 402
  evaluating the relationship, 395–397

Franchises (Cont.):
  fast food, 392
  government control and, 407
  growth in services, 408
  location and facility, 398–400
  market research for (see Market research for franchises)
  nature of the relationship, 394–395
  obstacles to future growth, 408
  operations of, 401–402
  recent history of, 391–393
  start-up costs, 398
  termination and, 402
  training in the business, 400–401
  transfers and, 402–403
  trends in, 407–409
  types of, 393–394

Franchisors, 395–396
  approval of, 401
  capital acquisition and, 395–396
  entrepreneurship and, 396
  policy of, 401
  recommendations of, 401
  reducing marketing costs and, 396

Freedman, Jeffrey, 343–344

Friends and relatives:
  during the start-up stage of businesses, 275
  job applicants and, 491, 493

Fuddruckers, 392

Functional discounts, 133

Gallegos, Leonel, 622–639

Galley, John, 63

Gauss, Adolph, 374–375

Gauss ElectroMechanical, Inc., 374–375

Goodwill, 378

Goodyear, 393

Government:
  franchise control and, 407
  productivity performance and relations with, 535
  as source of marketing information, 107–108
  [See also Small Business Administration (SBA)]

Grayson, Anne I., 105, 615

Gross markdown, 186

Group assembly methods, 254–255

Group life insurance, 472

Growth stage of businesses, raising money in, 277–281

Gundle, John, 392

Hansen, Tolly, 135–136

Hard disk, 342

Harding, Leo N., 487–488
Hardware, computer, 339–340
Head sensor, 341
Health maintenance organizations (HMOs), 471
Herald, Anthony, 610, 614
Hertz, 394
Hiring and recruitment procedures, 490–498, 642
Hobbies and ideas for businesses, 41–42
Holiday Inn, 394
Horchak, Joe, 218
Horizon Air Industries, 4, 24–25
Howard, Jack, 237
Howard Johnson's, 394
Howard Products Company, 236–237

Ideas for businesses, 36–55
    guidelines for generating, 41–47
    innovation and, 40–41, 48–50
    new approaches for an established business, 47–48
    sources of, 40–41
Ideas and concepts, protection of, 437–442
    advantage of counsel, 442
    copyrights, 440
    marketable but unpatentable ideas, 440–442
    patents, 437–439
    service marks, 439–440
    trademarks, 439
Impact printer, 345
Impulse items, 91
In-store advertising, 194–195
Income statements:
    monthly, 293, 308–310
    yearly, 293, 310–314
Industrial products, 94
Inequities, employee, 240
Influencer, role of, 81
Informal information, 334
Information sources:
    for financial planning, 302–304
    for management, 334–336
    for market segmentation, 107–110
Initial markup, 186
Initiator, role of, 81
Innovative ideas:
    in an existing business, 48–50
    need for continuing, 48
    sources of, 40–41
Innovator role of managers, 524
Inside boards of directors, 430
Insurance:
    all-risk, 469
    automobile, 467–468
    business-interruption, 470

Insurance (Cont.):
    coinsurance, 466
    crime, 468–469
    document security, 472
    employee health, 470–471
    fidelity bonds, 472–473
    fire, 465–466
    key-person, 470
    liability, 466–467
    life, 471–472
    miscellaneous coverages, 473
    premium, 461
    pure risk, 459
    selecting an agent, broker, or consultant, 463
    selecting a carrier, 462
    surety bonds, 473
    types of companies, 461
    workers' compensation, 467
Intangibles:
    evaluating, 366–367
    services as, 209
Integrator role of managers, 524
Intelligent terminals, 337
Intensive equipment use, 239
Internal creativity, 40–41
Internal Revenue Code, 424, 430
Interpersonal competence, 519–520
Interviewing procedures:
    to analyze customer behavior, 87–90
    for hiring new employees, 493–497
Introduction-growth stage of life cycle, 125
Inventory, 176
    managing, 247
    valuation of, 184–185, 374
Inventory control, 180–185
    ABC method of, 247–248
    computers and, 185–187
    graphing and, 248–249
    manufacturing operations and, 247–249
    markdowns, 184
    overstocks, 183–184
    pricing and, 186–187
    sales analysis and, 185
    small parts and components, 247
    stock turnover, 181–183
    tools for, 184

Jaffe, Charles, 549
Jaffe, David, 549
Jaffe, Rudolph, 549
Jaffe, Shirley, 500
Joan's Apparel, 41
Job applicants, locating, 491–493
Johnson, Karen H., 615
Joint ventures, 435

Kelleher, Frank, 546–571
Kennert, Alathena, 615
Kentucky Fried Chicken, 64, 394
Key-person insurance, 470
Keystone, 187
Knowledge of business, 6–7
Kuchak, Stanley, 275–276
Kuolt, Milton J., II, 4, 24–25

Labor supply and plant sites, 236
Land, Edwin, 41
Land and buildings for service businesses, 224
Langloise, Robert J., 615
Laser printer, 345
Leader, 337
Learner role of managers, 524
Learning curve, 241
Leasing retail space, 174
Legal issues, 416–453
    in buying a business, 367–368
    of corporations, 426–437
    finding an attorney, 442–445
    other forms of organization, 435
    of partnerships, 421–426
    protection of ideas and concepts, 437–442
    of sole proprietorship, 418–421
Leo N. Harding Company, 487–488
Leo's Pharmacy, 563–571
Liabilities, 298, 300
Liability insurance, 466–467
Libraries as sources of financial information,
    303–304
Licenses for corporations, 434–435
Life cycle of products or services, 124–126
    extending, 126
    as a proactive management tool, 127–128
Life insurance, 471–472
Limited liability of corporations, 426–427
Limited partnership, 425–426
    tax implications of, 426
Lindsey, Peter, 546–549
Liquidation value of businesses, 370
Lloyds Groups, 461
Location:
    of franchises, 398–400
        market research on, 405–406
    of plants, 236–237
    of retail operations, 169–173
    of service businesses, 233–235
Long-term financing, 292
Loss leaders, 132
Low-tech enterprises, 5

McClelland, David C., 19–23
McCulloch, Louis, 420–421

McCulloch Instruments, 420–421
McDonald's, 394, 400, 408
McGregor, Douglas, 503, 527
Mail advertising, 194
Mainframe, 340
Maintained markup, 186
Major medical plans, 471
Management:
    of business risk, 457–484
    of financial requirements, 289–331
    of personnel function, 485–515
    proactive (see Proactive management)
    for productivity and growth, 516–542
    skills, 7
    succession, 501
    ten basic roles of, 524–525
    (See also Managers)
Management by objectives (MBO), 527–532
Management consultants, 186
Management information, 334–336
    formal, 334
    guides to generating, 334–336
    informal, 334
Managers, 518–525
    change and, 521–523
    developing, 501–503
    entrepreneurial qualities and, 521–523
    many hats of, 523–525
    productivity and (see Productivity)
    profile of ideal, 519–520
    teamwork and, 520–521
Manufacturer-retailer franchise system, 393
Manufacturer-wholesaler franchise system, 393
Manufacturing operations, 233–267
    financial projections for, 604–605
    inventory, 247–249
    purchasing, 246–249
    research and development, 242–246
    (See also Plants; Production of goods)
Marino's, 392
Markdowns, 184
Market access, 101
Market aggregation, 122
Market differentiation, 122
Market measurements, 101
Market penetration pricing, 130
Market price of businesses, 370–371
Market research for franchises, 404–407
    image and advertising, 406
    product innovation, 404–405
    sales promotion, 406–407
    site location, 405–406
Market segmentation, 65, 99–110, 123
    requirements for effective, 101–102
    sources of information for, 107–110
    of your market, 103–106
Marketable but unpatentable ideas, 440–442

Marketing:
    avoiding marketing myopia, 62–64
    customer orientation, 62
    defined, 61
    franchises and, 396
    of service businesses, 206–232
    small businesses as a system of, 59–77
    strategies of, 122–123
        carrying out, 124–128
    (*See also specific aspects of marketing*)
Marketing objectives, 121
Markup, 185
Martin, Jim and Roger, 128
Martin, Tony, 464–465
Martineau, Pierre, 83
Maslow, Abraham, 39
    hierarchy of needs of, 83, 85–86, 92–94
Matching competition advertising budget
        method, 140
Maturity stage of businesses, 125
    raising money in, 281–282
Me-too pricing, 130
Media advertising strategy, 140–144
    availability of, 144
    comparison chart for, 141–143
    cost of, 144
    selection of, 144
    target market and, 140, 144
    typical, 145–146
Median, 303
Medical and hospitalization insurance, 470–471
Meek, Robert P., 5
Memory, 341
Menda Scientific Products, 49
Microcomputers, 337–338
Midas Muffler Shops, 393
Minicomputers, 338–339
Minority Enterprise Small Businesses Investment
        Companies (MESBICs), 280, 619–621
    prospectus for, 662–639
Model shop, 242–243
Model of style role of managers, 525
Modem, 337
Money:
    attitude toward, 21–22
    collecting, 322–324
    raising, 271–288
    (*See also* Capital acquisition; Financial
        requirements)
Monthly income statements, 293, 308–310
Morgan, John, 101
Moynihan, Luke, 576–580
Multifunctionality, 336
Multilube Supply Company, 545–549
Murphy, Thomas P., 370
Mutual insurance companies, 461
Myers, Tom, 44–45

n Ach (need for achievement), 19
    entrepreneurial characteristics and, 20–23
Naisbitt, John, 69
National car rentals, 394
National Cash Register Company, 303
Nautilus Engineering Co., Inc., 581–587
Necessity and ideas for a business, 45–46
Net markdown figure, 186–187
Net profit to net sales, ratio of, 321
Newman, Arthur, 545–549
Newspapers:
    advertising in, 193
        for job applicants, 491, 492
    as sources of financial or marketing
            information, 107, 302
Nonconcurrency, 469
Noncumulative quantity discounts, 133
Nonintelligent terminals, 337
Not-for-profit corporations, 435

Objectives:
    management by (MBO), 527–532
    marketing, 121
O'Brien, Robert H., 443
Ochman, B. L., 213
Odd-even pricing, 131
Open-to-buy estimate, 177–178
Opportunities, seizing, 20–21
Optimism, 21
Ordinances, zoning, 224, 236
Organizational designer role of managers, 524
Organizational development, 582–583
    process of, 583–587
Outside boards of directors, 430
Overstocks, 183–184
Ownership interest, transferability of corporate,
        429

Pacific Clear Writing Clinics, 105–106, 605–618
Pacific Coast Faultfinders, Inc., 46
Packaging, 123
Papa Aldo's Take & Bake Shops, 392
Pappagallo shoe stores, 393
Partnerships, 421–426
    comparison of expenses of, 432–434
    dissolution of, 424–425
    key characteristics of, 436–437
    limited, 425–426
    new partners, 423
    rights and obligations of, 422
    tax implications of, 423–424, 426
    termination of, 424
Patents, 437–439
    Disclosure Document Program, 438–439
Peak, Donald, 571–576

Peak Electronics, 501, 571–576
Penalties of business ownership, 27–28
Percentage-of-sales budget method, 140
Performance appraisal, 498–499
    productivity and, 532–535
Peripherals, 339–340
Permits for corporations, 434–435
Perquisites, 369
Personal factors:
    in buying a business, 368–369
    in starting a business, 16–35
Personal file for job applicants, 493
Personal interests and ideas for businesses, 41–42
Personal resources during the start-up stage of businesses, 274–275
Personal selling, 149
    for service businesses, 222–223
Personnel policies, 485–515, 640–644
    appraising performance, 498–499
    developing, 488
    developing managers, 501–503
    disciplining employees, 643–644
    hiring procedures, 642
    legal protections of employees, 642
    management succession, 501
    manual or handbook, 642
    public policy, 642–643
    recruitment, 490–498
    safeguarding small employers' rights, 644
    terminating personnel, 503–506
    training, 499–501
    typical, 489–490
    unions, 506–507
Physical assets, evaluating, 367
Physiological needs of buyers, 85
Pilferage, prevention of, 476–477
Pixel, 337
Pizza Hut, 408
Place utility, 96, 97
Planning:
    of financial requirements, 292–319
    as role of managers, 524
    (See also Business plans)
Plants:
    design of, 236–238
        features, 237–238
        flexibility of, 239
    labor supply and, 236
    layout of, 238–239
    location of, 236–237
    machine capacity and, 239
    maintenance of, 239
    number of shifts worked in, 239–240
    seasonal changes in, 241–242
    taxes and, 237

Plants (Cont.):
    utilities and, 237
    working hours in, 240
    zoning and, 236
Pleiades Motor Homes, Inc., 576–581
Point-of-purchase display, 195–196
Policies, 235
Political-legal forces, effects of, on markets, 67–68
Ponderosa Systems, 408
Positive behavior, 23
Premium, insurance, 461
Price lining, 131–132
Pricing:
    a business, 370–378
    common mistakes in, 129
    image and, 128–129
    inventory control and, 186–187
    marketing approaches to, 129–130
    for service businesses, 216–219
    strategies for, 128, 131–134
Proactive management, 22, 67
    planning for, 293–319
    product-service life cycle and, 127–128
Problem solver role of managers, 524
Problems, overreaction to, 25–26
Product(s):
    buying decision and nature of, 90–94
    ideas for (see Ideas for businesses)
Product differentiation, 122
Product innovation and franchises, 404–405
Product-service life cycles, 124–126
    extending, 126
    as proactive management tool, 127–128
Product/service market matrix, 48–50
Production of goods, 249–255
    cost control, 250–251
    designing for, 245–246
    group assembly methods, 254–255
    managing variables, 249–250
    quality control, 254
    scheduling, 250
    scrap and waste control, 251–252
    value engineering, 252–253
Productivity, 525–535
    assessing your performance, 532–535
    defined, 525
    efficiency versus effectiveness, 525–527
    management by objectives (MBO) and, 527–532
    profit and, 525
    teamwork and, 520–521
Professional consulting help, 186
Profit:
    potential for, when buying a business, 371–378
    productivity and, 525

Program Evaluation and Review Technique (PERT), 244
Programs, 337
Promotion:
  personal selling and, 149, 222–223
  publicity and, 149–150, 223
  sales, 150, 223
  service businesses and, 212, 220–223
  strategies for, 137–138
  (*See also* Advertising)
Promotional discounts, 133–134
Promotional pricing, 132
Proprietorship ratio, 321
Prospectus (*see* Business plans)
Protection of ideas and concepts, 437–442
Psychological pricing, 131
Public policy, 642–643
Publicity, 149–150
  for service businesses, 223
Purchasing:
  for manufacturing operations, 246–249
  for retail operations, 176–180
  (*See also* Buying decisions)
Pure risk, 459

Quality control, 254
Quantity discounts, 133
Quartiles, 303

R&D Wall Paneling Company, 135–136
Radio advertising, 193–194
Raising money, 271–288
  during growth stage, 277–281
  during maturity stage, 281–282
  during start-up stage, 274–277
  preparations for, 274
  (*See also* Capital acquisition; Financial requirements)
Ranford, Terry, 576–580
Ratio analysis, 319–325
  acid-test ratio, 320
  collection-period ratio, 321–324
  current ratio, 320
  net profit to net sales, 321
  proprietorship ratio, 321
  stock to sales ratio, 324
  use of, 324–325
Real estate investment trusts, 435
Reciprocals, 461
Records:
  financial statements and, 188–189
  keeping, 188

Recruiting employees, 490–498
  antidiscrimination laws, 498
  finding qualified applicants, 491–493
  interviewing procedure, 493–497
Reference-group influence, 82–83
Reinventing the wheel, 25
Relatives:
  during the start-up stage of businesses, 275
  job applicants and, 491, 493
Renquist, Fred, 218–219
Rent A Kvetch, 212–213
Renting retail space, 173–174
Repayment terms during start-up stage of businesses, 275
Research and development (R&D), 242–246
Resignations, 504
Retail operations, 167–205
  advertising and promotion for, 189–196
  computers for, 185–189
  identifying customers, 174–176
  inventory control for, 180–185
  purchasing for, 176–180
  renting or leasing, 173–174
  selecting a location for, 169–173
  theft from, 475–476
Return on investment (ROI), 374
Reverse technology, 68
Rewards of business ownership, 26–27
Rhodes, John, 4
Rhodes, Lou, 43
Risk, 457–485
  absorption of, 462–463
  choosing moderate, 20
  pure, 459
  reduction of, 462
  risk manager's job, 460–461
  speculative, 459
  transfer of, 461–462
  (*See also* Insurance)
Risk insurance, 459
Robbery insurance, 468
Robbins, Irvine, 48, 148
Romney, Dave, 357–358
Ross, Jim, 135–136

S corporations, 430–432
Safety needs of buyers, 85
Sales, credit, 94–96
Sales analysis and inventory control, 185
Sales forecasts, 293, 300–304
Sales promotion, 150
  for franchises, 406–407
  for service businesses, 223

Sales ratios:
  net profit to net sales, 321
  stock to sales, 324
Saturation stage of life cycle, 125
Scheduling production, 250
Schools, job applicants and, 493
Schumpeter, Joseph A., 38, 48
Scrap control, 251–252
Screening business offerings, 362–367
  final, 366
  intangible assets and liabilities, 366–367
  physical assets, 367
  preliminary, 363–365
  second-stage, 365–366
  stages of, 362–363
Searches for businesses to buy, 362
Seasonal changes in manufacturing plants, 241–242
Seasonal discounts, 134
Seed money, 274, 275
Self-actualization needs of buyers, 86
Self-help clubs, job applicants and, 493
Selling-price formulas, 378
Selling relationships, 175–176
Selling transaction, 123–124
Semiconductor Chip Act of 1984, 440
Service businesses, 5
  buyer behavior and, 211–214
  capacity problems and, 210, 214
  distribution strategy for, 223–225
  inseparability of service and seller, 210
  intangibles and, 209
  interdependence of buyers and sellers, 209
  marketing of, 206–232
  perishability and, 210
  pricing of, 216–219
  promotion of, 212, 220–223
  site analysis for, 224–225
  social, economic, and competitive change and, 215–216
  standardizing quality and, 210
  uniqueness of, 209
  unrecognized needs and, 212–214
Service marks, 439–440
Service-product life cycles, 124–126
Service/product market matrix, 48–50
Services, 124
Sheraton Inn, 394
Shoplifting, prevention of, 475–476
Shopping centers, retail operations in, 172–173
  community centers, 172–173
  neighborhood centers, 172
  regional centers, 173
Shopping products, 92
Shopping services, 224
Short-term financing, 292

Shortcomings in existing products or services, 42–43
Site (see Location)
Site analysis, 224–225
  for franchises, 405–406
Skimming-the-cream pricing, 130
Small, Jonathan (Joe), 322–324
Small Business Administration (SBA), 68, 302, 619
  during growth stage of businesses, 278–280
  as source of financial or marketing information, 107–108, 302
Small Business Investment Companies (SBIC), 280, 619–621
Small communities, locating retail operations in, 170
Smith, Michelle, 443–445
Snelling, Joan, 41
Social and cultural change, effects of, on markets, 68–71
Social-class influence, 83–85
Social custom, changes in, 43–44
  service businesses and, 215
Social needs of buyers, 85
Social system, 335
Software, 337, 341
Sole proprietorship, 418–421
  advantages of, 419
  comparison of expenses of, 432–434
  disadvantages of, 419–420
  key characteristics of, 436–437
  tax implications of, 420
Specialty products, 92
Specialty services, 224
Speculative risk, 459
Spinoffs from your present occupation, 46–47
Spreadsheets, 342–344
Stagflation, 66
Stanhope, Joe, 273–274
Staple items, 91
Start-up stage of businesses, raising money in, 274–277
Stevenson, Robert, 46–47
Stevenson Associates, 46–47
Stock insurance companies, 461
Stock-to-sales ratio, 181–182, 324
Stock turnover, 181–183
Stockout, 247
Store layout, 195–196
Strategic objectives, 124
Subchapter S corporations, 430
Super Value Stores, Inc., 393
Suppliers:
  job applicants and, 491
  productivity performance and, 534–535
  role of, during growth stage of businesses, 277

Supporting services for service business sites, 224
Surety bonds, 473
Swanson, William, 581–583
System competence, 519
System regulator, 526

Taco Bell, 392
Tangibles, 209
Target market, 138, 140, 144
Tastee-Freeze, 401
Tax Reform Act of 1986, 426, 428
Taxes:
    for corporations, 428–429
        S, 430–432
        withholding, 435
    for limited partnerships, 426
    for partnerships, 423–424
    plant sites and, 237
    for sole proprietorship, 420
Teacher role of managers, 524
Teamwork and improved productivity, 520–521
Technical competence, 519
Technical publications, job applicants and, 491
Technical system, 335
Technological advance and ideas for a business, 46
Technological change, effects of, on markets, 68
Television advertising, 193–194
Term certain, 424
Term life insurance, 472
Terminating personnel, 503–506
Termination of a partnership, 424
Thornley, John, 42–43
Thornley Molded Products, 42–43
Thousand Trails, 24
Time of purchases, 98–99
Time utility, 96, 97
Tobias Booksellers, 596–604
Toffler, Alvin, 69
Tony's Arcade, 464–465
Torbert, Frances, 499
Trade associations:
    job applicants and, 491
    as sources of financial or marketing information, 109, 303
Trade credit, 277
Trade discounts, 133
Trade-name franchise systems, 393–394
Trademarks, 439
Trading area, 169–172
Training, 499–501
Transactional matrix, 335
    example of, 336

Transit advertising, 194
Treese, Jacqueline, 343–344
Turnover ratios, 181–182

Undifferentiated marketing, 122
Uniform Partnership Act, 422–424
Unions, 506–507
Unit control, 184
Universities:
    job applicants and, 493
    as sources of financial or marketing information, 109, 302–303
Unrecognized needs and, 212–214
Unsought products, 92
User-friendly computers and software, 337, 341
Utilities and plant sites, 237

Vacations, 489–490
Value, 66–67, 128
Value analysis, 520
Value engineering, 252–253
Venture capital, 5
Venture capital firms, 280–281

Warner, W. Lloyd, 83
Warranties, 124
Waste control, 251–252
Waterbeds East, 293–296
Wealthy investors in the start-up stage of businesses, 275
Wendy's, 392
Western Auto Supply, 393
Whole life insurance, 471–472
Wholesaler-retailer franchise systems, 393
Wildcroft, Gene, 576–581
Woodworth, Elaine, 87–90
Word processing, 344–345
Workers' compensation, 467
Working capital, 320
Working hours at plants, 240

Yearly income statements, 293, 310–314

Ziegler, Kurt, 563–566, 571
Zoning restrictions:
    for plants, 236
    for service businesses, 224